E A

PAPHLAGONIA

PONTUS

BITHYNIA

Sangartos R.

• Nyssa   • Caesarea

CAPPADOCIA

• Nazianzus

ISIDIA   • Iconium
           (Konia)

ISAURIA

ARMENIA
MINOR

PAMPHYLIA

CILICIA

Seleucia •   •Antioch

Orontes R.

CYPRUS

A   N   S   E   A

• Damascus

Jordan R.

•   Jerusalem
      (Aelia Capitolina)

kandria

Nile R.

| 0 | 50 | 100 | MILES | 200 | | 300 |

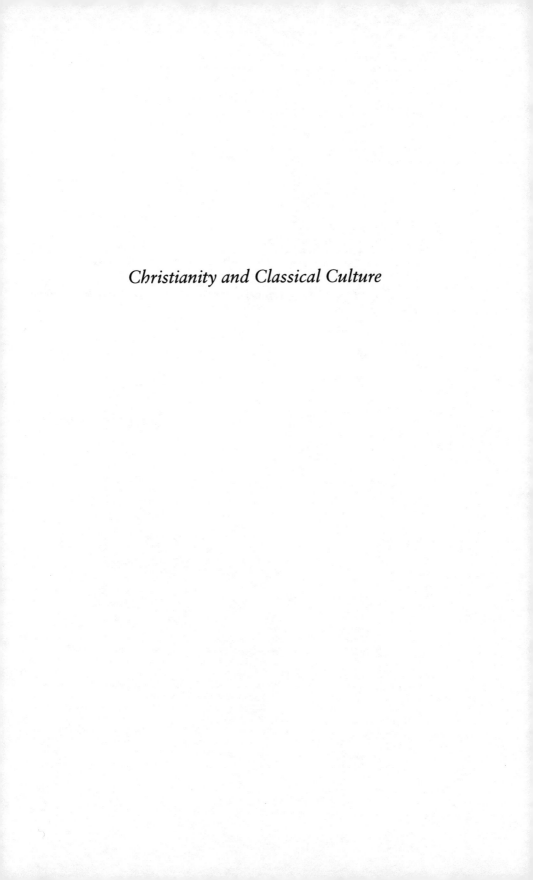

Christianity and Classical Culture

CHRISTIANITY AND CLASSICAL

The Metamorphosis of Natural Theology in

Jaroslav Pelikan

CULTURE

the Christian Encounter with Hellenism

Gifford Lectures at Aberdeen, 1992–1993

Yale University Press
New Haven & London

Designed by Deborah Dutton.
Set in Sabon type by The Composing Room of Michigan, Inc.,
Grand Rapids, Michigan.
Printed in the United States of America by Vail-Ballou Press,
Binghamton, New York.

Library of Congress Cataloging-in-Publication Data

Pelikan, Jaroslav Jan, 1923–
    Christianity and classical culture : the metamorphosis of natural
theology in the Christian encounter with Hellenism / by Jaroslav
Pelikan.
        p.   cm. — (Gifford lectures at Aberdeen ; 1992–1993)
    Includes bibliographical references and index.
    ISBN 0-300-05554-4
    1. Natural theology—History of doctrines—Early church, ca.
30–600.   2. Cappadocian Fathers.   3. Macrina, the Younger, Saint,
ca. 330–379 or 80.   4. Christianity and culture—History—Early
church, ca. 30–600.   5. Civilization, Classical.   I. Title.
II. Series: Gifford lectures ; 1992–1993.
BL245.P45   1993
210'.939'34—dc20   92-42407
                                                                           CIP

A catalogue record for this book is available from the British Library.

10 9 8 7 6 5 4 3 2 1

To my daughter, Miriam,
who has deepened and enriched my
own encounter with Hellenism

CONTENTS

PART TWO

Natural Theology as Presupposition

Eleventh-century mosaic, Church of Saint Sophia, Kiev; *left to right*, Basil of Caesarea, Gregory of Nazianzus, and Gregory of Nyssa. Photograph courtesy of St. Vladimir's Seminary Press.

PREFACE

When I received the invitation of the Principal and Senatus Academicus of the University of Aberdeen to deliver the Gifford Lectures on Natural Theology in 1992–1993, I knew immediately that I would use the lectureship as an opportunity to address, head-on and at length, the perennial issue of the Christian encounter with Hellenism, because that has been the historical matrix for the very idea of "natural theology." It is an issue with which I had been preoccupied throughout the four decades of preparing and writing my history of Christian doctrine, not least because the greatest of my predecessors in the field, Adolf von Harnack, had made "the Hellenization of Christianity" central to his own interpretation. I have discussed it here by looking at the encounter in the fourth century, which Gilbert Highet has called "*the* vital period for the synthesis of Greco-Roman philosophy and Christian thought," as both the encounter and the synthesis were embodied in the thought of the so-called Three Cappadocians, Gregory of Nazianzus, Basil of Caesarea, and Gregory of Nyssa, and of "the Fourth Cappadocian," Macrina, sister of the last two.

By the title of this book I pay tribute to two scholarly works that have employed it before (Cochrane 1944; Nock 1972, 2:676–81). But I should perhaps make clear from the outset in what sense these Gifford Lectures deal with the "Classical culture" that forms part of this title—and, perhaps even more important, in what sense they do not. During their preparation it has been a constant temptation to trace the lines of development back from the Cappadocians through Plotinus to Aristotle, Plato, and the Presocratics, and thus to write, fifty years later, my own drastically different version of Werner Jaeger's controversial three-volume opus, *Paideia* (and in more than three volumes). It is a temptation I have resisted, not alone because it would far exceed my scholarly competence but because I am considering Classical culture here only in the light of what the subtitle calls "the Christian encounter with Hellenism," rather than in its own right, which is of course how it deserves above all to be considered.

For that matter, I am also resisting a temptation from which I cannot excuse myself on similar grounds of scholarly competence, namely, the temptation to trace the career of the "encounters" and ideas of the Cappadocians back to their Greek Christian predecessors, especially Justin, Clement of Alexandria, Origen, and Athanasius, for I have dealt with at least some of this in the first volume of *The Christian Tradition,* as well as in other works, and I did not want this to expand into another five-volume work. But for the Christian Greeks as for the Classical Greeks, I am, by and large, introducing questions of intellectual genealogy here only when and insofar as they have come up explicitly in the writings and thought of the Cappadocians themselves. They tend to identify Aristotle and especially Plato far more frequently and explicitly than they do Plotinus or Porphyry, who are closer to them in time and often in thought, and I follow their lead in this regard. The Bibliography, in which I have included a number of previous Gifford Lectures, does, however, suggest some of the works of other scholars on whom I have relied for these questions and to whom a reader may also turn for guidance on the course of Greek intellectual development from Homer, Hesiod, and the earliest Presocratics to the Cappadocians—a development, it must be remembered, that took a millennium.

Although for a few passages (notably, Rom 12:1, 1 Cor 13:12, and Phil 4:8) other English versions have seemed to be preferable, I have, in the case of the Christian Scriptures, usually followed the Revised English Bible of 1989 as closely as possible. An exception to this practice are those passages that my authors have read quite differently, sometimes because of textual variants in the New Testament (e.g., Jn 1:18 and 1 Tm 3:16) and more often because of the renderings of the Septuagint (LXX), which was their Old Testament. Therefore, I have consistently observed the Septuagint's peculiar numbering of chapters and verses, also in the

Book of Psalms, following, for all uses of the Septuagint, the most recent edition by Alfred Rahlfs (Athens and Stuttgart, 1979).

As has been my wont in previous books, I have adopted or adapted earlier English translations (including my own) at will, or have provided entirely new ones, without pedantically making changes for their own sake and without indicating when I was following which of these courses. This book employs the scheme of documentation developed for the five volumes of *The Christian Tradition,* which enables the reader to follow the exposition without interruption but to pick up a reference to a primary source with a minimum of effort. Therefore, I have followed the standard system of citing the Greek church fathers by title of work (employing the usual Latinized sigla, as listed under Abbreviations) and by book, chapter, and paragraph, with a reference to the best edition of the Greek text available to me; from this it should usually be possible to locate the passage in other editions of the Greek, as well as in most English, French, or German translations.

In quoting primary sources—and in preparing the Bibliography of secondary sources—I have not assumed that my readers necessarily have a knowledge of any of the languages of the Eastern Christian tradition, and therefore I have, with some reluctance, felt obliged to confine the Bibliography to works in Western languages. But in hopes that it may be helpful also to such readers, I have at places inserted the original words of the Greek primary sources, in transliterated form. I have also appended a Glossary of some two dozen Greek technical terms in Anglicized spelling, which will, I hope, permit me to use such terms without stopping to define or translate them each time; to indicate a reference to the Glossary, these terms appear in italics throughout, and no other terms do.

It is a scholarly duty, but it is also a personal pleasure, to record my thanks to the many who have contributed to this book: my audiences at Aberdeen, which included some who have been listening to Gifford Lectures for several decades; librarians in various places, and especially at Dumbarton Oaks; critical readers, among them my late friend, Father John Meyendorff; and my editors, above all Laura Jones Dooley.

ABBREVIATIONS

Sources

(After Liddell-Scott-Jones, *Greek-English Lexicon*, and Lampe, *Patristic Greek Lexicon*)

Arist.*Cat.*	Aristotle *Categoriae*
Arist.*Cael.*	Aristotle *De Caelo* [On the Heavens]
Arist.*An.*	Aristotle *De Anima* [On the Soul]
Arist.*EN.*	Aristotle *Ethica Nicomachea*
Arist.*Met.*	Aristotle *Metaphysica*
Arist.*Pol.*	Aristotle *Politica*
Ath.*Ar.*	Athanasius *Orationes adversus Arianos*
Ath.*Ep.Afr.*	Athanasius *Epistola ad Afros episcopos*
Aug.*Conf.*	Augustine *Confessiones*
Aug.*Enchir.*	Augustine *Enchiridion*
Aug.*Trin.*	Augustine *De Trinitate*
Bas.*Ep.*	Basil *Epistolae*
Bas.*Eun.*	Basil *Adversus Eunomium*
Bas.*Hex.*	Basil *In Hexaemeron*
Bas.*Hom.*	Basil *Homiliae*
Bas.*Leg.lib.gent.*	Basil *Ad adolescentes de legendis libris gentilium* [Letter to young men on reading the books of the Gentiles]
Bas.*Mor.*	Basil *Moralia*
Bas.*Spir.*	Basil *De Spiritu sancto*
C Chalc.*Def.*	Council of Chalcedon *Definition*
CCP (381)	First Council of Constantinople

CFlor.(1438–45) *Def.*	Council of Florence *Definition*
Cyr.*Juln.*	Cyrillus Alexandrinus *Contra Julianum*
Eun.	Eunomius
Gr.Naz.*Carm.*	Gregorius Nazianzenus *Carmina* [Poems]
Gr.Naz.*Ep.*	Gregorius Nazianzenus *Epistolae*
Gr.Naz.*Or.*	Gregorius Nazianzenus *Orationes*
Gr.Nyss.*Anim.res.*	Gregorius Nyssenus *De anima et resurrectione* [On the soul and the resurrection]
Gr.Nyss.*Apoll.*	Gregorius Nyssenus *Adversus Apollinarem*
Gr.Nyss.*Beat.*	Gregorius Nyssenus *Orationes de beatitudinibus*
Gr.Nyss.*Cant.*	Gregorius Nyssenus *Homiliae in Cantica Canticorum* [Commentary on the Song of Songs]
Gr.Nyss.*Comm.not.*	Gregorius Nyssenus *Adversus Graecos ex communibus notionibus*
Gr.Nyss.*Deit.*	Gregorius Nyssenus *De deitate Filii et Spiritus Sancti* [On the deity of the Son and the Holy Spirit]
Gr.Nyss.*Diff.ess.*	Gregorius Nyssenus *De differentia essentiae et hypostaseos*
Gr.Nyss.*Ep.*	Gregorius Nyssenus *Epistolae*
Gr.Nyss.*Eun.*	Gregorius Nyssenus *Contra Eunomium*
Gr.Nyss.*Fat.*	Gregorius Nyssenus *Contra fatum*
Gr.Nyss.*Fid.*	Gregorius Nyssenus *De fide ad Simplicium* [On the faith]
Gr.Nyss.*Hex.*	Gregorius Nyssenus *Apologia in Hexaëmeron*
Gr.Nyss.*Hom.opif.*	Gregorius Nyssenus *De hominis opificio* [On the making of man]
Gr.Nyss.*Infant.*	Gregorius Nyssenus *De infantibus qui praemature abripiuntur* [On infants who are taken away prematurely]
Gr.Nyss.*Maced.*	Gregorius Nyssenus *De Spiritu sancto contra Macedonianos*
Gr.Nyss.*Or.catech.*	Gregorius Nyssenus *Oratio catechetica*
Gr.Nyss.*Or.dom.*	Gregorius Nyssenus *Homiliae in orationem dominicam* [On the Lord's Prayer]
Gr.Nyss.*Ref.*	Gregorius Nyssenus *Refutatio confessionis Eunomii*
Gr.Nyss.*Res.*	Gregorius Nyssenus *In Christi resurrectionem*
Gr.Nyss.*Tres dii*	Gregorius Nyssenus *Quod non sint tres dii* [That there are not three gods]
Gr.Nyss.*Trin.*	Gregorius Nyssenus *Ad Eustathium de Trinitate*
Gr.Nyss.*V.Macr.*	Gregorius Nyssenus *De vita Macrinae*
Gr.Nyss.*V.Mos.*	Gregorius Nyssenus *De vita Mosis*
Gr.Nyss.*Virg.*	Gregorius Nyssenus *De virginitate*
Gr.Presb.*V.Gr.Naz.*	Gregorius Presbyter *Vita Gregorii Nazianzeni*
Hdt.	Herodotus Historicus
Hom.*Il.*	Homer *Ilias*
Hom.*Od.*	Homer *Odyssea*
Iren.*Haer.*	Irenaeus *Adversus haereses*
Jo.D.*F.o.*	Joannes Damascenus *De fide orthodoxa*
Jo.D.*Trans.*	Joannes Damascenus *Homilia in transfigurationem Domini*

Juln.Imp.	Julianus Imperator
Lib.	Libanius Sophista
Lit.Bas.	*Liturgy of Saint Basil*
Macr.	Macrina (the Younger)
Or.*Cels.*	Origenes *Contra Celsum*
Pi.O.	Pindar *Olympian Odes*
Pl.*Ap.*	Plato *Apologia*
Pl.*Cri.*	Plato *Crito*
Pl.*Lg.*	Plato *Leges* [Laws]
Pl.*Men.*	Plato *Meno*
Pl.*Phd.*	Plato *Phaedo*
Pl.*Phdr.*	Plato *Phaedrus*
Pl.*Prt.*	Plato *Protagoras*
Pl.*R.*	Plato *Respublica*
Pl.*Smp.*	Plato *Symposium*
Pl.*Tht.*	Plato *Theaetetus*
Pl.*Tim.*	Plato *Timaeus*
Ptol.Alm.	Ptolemaeus Almagest
Socr.*H.e.*	Socrates Scholasticus *Historia ecclesiastica*
Soz.*H.e.*	Sozomen *Historia ecclesiastica*
Symb.Nic.	*Symbolum Nicaenum*
Symb.Nic.-CP	*Symbolum Nicaeno-Constantinopolitanum*
Tert.*Praescrip.*	Tertullian *De praescriptione haereticorum*
Th.	Thucydides *Historicus*
Thos.Aq.*S.T.*	Thomas Aquinas *Summa Theologica*

Editions and Reference Works

Alberigo-Jedin	Alberigo, Giuseppe, and Jedin, Hubert, eds. *Conciliorum oecumenicorum decreta.* 3d ed. Bologna: Istituto per le scienze religiose, 1973.
Bauer	Bauer, Walter. *A Greek-English Lexicon of the New Testament and Other Early Christian Literature.* Translated and adapted by William F. Arndt, F. Wilbur Gingrich, and Frederick W. Danker. 2d ed. Chicago: University of Chicago Press, 1979.
Brightman	Brightman, Frank Edward, ed. *Liturgies Eastern and Western.* Oxford: Clarendon Press, 1896.
Courtonne	Courtonne, Yves, ed. *Saint Basile: Lettres.* 3 vols. Paris: Société d'édition "Les Belles Lettres," 1957–66.
CCSL	*Corpus Christianorum: Series Latina.* Turnhout: Brepols, 1953 ff.
DTC	*Dictionnaire de théologie catholique.* 15 vols. Paris: Letouzey et Ané, 1903–50.
Florovsky	Florovsky, Georges. *Collected Works.* 14 vols. to date. Belmont, Mass.: Nordland, 1972–.

Gallay   Gallay, Paul, ed. *Saint Grégoire de Nazianze: Lettres*. Paris: Société d'édition "Les Belles Lettres," 1964–.

GCS   *Die griechischen christlichen Schriftsteller der ersten drei Jahrhunderte*. Berlin: Akademie-Verlag, 1897–.

Harvey   Harvey, W. Wigan, ed. *Sancti Irenaei episcopi Lugdunensis Libros quinque adversus Haereses*. 2 vols. Cambridge: Cambridge University Press, 1857.

Hussey   Hussey, Robert, ed. *Socratis Scholastici Ecclesiastica Historia*. 3 vols. Oxford: Oxford University Press, 1853.

Jaeger   Jaeger, Werner, ed. *Gregorii Nysseni Opera*. Berlin and Leiden: E. J. Brill, 1921–.

Lampe   Lampe, Geoffrey W. H., ed. *A Patristic Greek Lexicon*. Oxford: Clarendon Press, 1961.

LTK   *Lexikon für Theologie und Kirche*. 10 vols. and index. 2d ed. Freiburg: Herder, 1957–67.

Méridier   Méridier, Louis, ed. Grégoire de Nysse. *Discours catéchétique: Texte grec, traduction française*. Paris: Libraire Alphonse Picard et fils, 1908.

Meyendorff   Meyendorff, John. *Byzantine Theology: Historical Trends and Doctrinal Themes*. New York: Fordham University Press, 1974.

Müller   Müller, Guido, ed. *Lexicon Athanasianum*. Berlin: Walter de Gruyter, 1952.

OCD   *The Oxford Classical Dictionary*. Edited by N. G. L. Hammond and H. H. Scullard. 2d ed. Oxford: Clarendon Press, 1970.

ODCC   *The Oxford Dictionary of the Christian Church*. 2d ed. Edited by F. L. Cross and E. A. Livingstone. Oxford: Oxford University Press, 1983.

OED   *The Oxford English Dictionary*. Edited by James Augustus Henry Murray et al. 12 vols. Oxford: Oxford University Press, 1933.

PG   *Patrologiae cursus completus: Series Graeca*. 162 vols. Paris: Jacques Paul Migne, 1857–66.

Quasten   Quasten, Johannes. *Patrology*. 4 vols. Westminster, Md.: Newman Press and Christian Classics, 1951–86.

SC   *Sources chrétiennes*. Paris: Cerf, 1940–.

Sophocles   Sophocles, Evangelinus Apostolides, ed. *Greek Lexicon of the Roman and Byzantine Periods*. Boston: Little, Brown, 1870.

Van Heck   Van Heck, Arie, ed. *Gregorii Nysseni de pauperibus amandis orationes duo*. Leiden: E. J. Brill, 1964.

Wilson   Wilson, Nigel Guy, ed. *Saint Basil on the Value of Greek Literature*. London: Duckworth, 1975.

PART ONE

Natural Theology as Apologetics

What born fools were all who lived in ignorance of God! From the good things before their eyes they could not learn to know him who is, and failed to recognize the artificer though they observed his handiwork! Fire, wind, swift air, the circle of the starry signs, rushing water, or the great lights in heaven that rule the world—these they accounted gods. If it was through delight in the beauty of these things that people supposed them gods, they ought to have understood how much better is the Lord and master of them all; for it was by the prime author of all beauty they were created. If it was through astonishment at their power and influence, people should have learnt from these how much more powerful is he who made them. For the greatness and beauty of created things give us a corresponding idea of their Creator.

Wisdom of Solomon 13:1–5

CHAPTER 1

Classical Culture and Christian Theology

It remains one of the most momentous linguistic convergences in the entire history of the human mind and spirit that the New Testament happens to have been written in Greek—not in the Hebrew of Moses and the prophets, nor in the Aramaic of Jesus and his disciples, nor yet in the Latin of the imperium Romanum, but in the Greek of Socrates and Plato, or at any rate in a reasonably accurate facsimile thereof, disguised and even disfigured though this was in the Koine by the intervening centuries of Hellenistic usage. As a result of this convergence, every attempt to translate the New Testament into any of almost two thousand languages—including a Semitic language such as Syriac, despite all its affinities with Hebrew and Aramaic—has, on encountering any term, been obliged to consider above all its previous career in the history of the Greek language; and that was a problem of natural theology no less than a problem of philology. It has long seemed unavoidable to invoke this method, for example, when dealing with such a term as *logos* in the first chapter of the Gospel according to John, or *hypostasis* in the first chapter of the Epistle to the Hebrews. There was ample precedent for both of these Greek words and for many others like them in the Septuagint translation of the Hebrew Bible, but they had come to the Septuagint and then to the Christian vocabulary from the language of Classical and Hellenistic philosophy and science. And when the last book of the New Testament opened with the salutation, "Grace to you and peace, from 'he-who-is,' and 'he-who-was,' and 'he-who-is-to-come' [charis hymin kai eirēnē apo ho ōn kai

Vööbus 1987,9–11

Jn 1:1
Heb 1:3
Gr.Nyss.Or.catech.1
(Méridier 8–16)

Rv 1:4

3

Hahn 1963

ho ēn kai ho erchomenos]," leaving those "christological titles of majesty" and of transcendent being in the nominative even though the Greek preposition "apo" was supposed to govern the genitive, that solecism and "intentional tour de force," as J. H.

Moulton 1908,9n

Ex 3:14
Ath.*Ar.*1.11
(*PG* 26:33)

Gottwald 1906,22–23
Gr.Nyss.*Eun.*1.637
(Jaeger 1:209)

Moulton once characterized it, has been used to justify the identification of that eternal "ho ōn," the one who is, with the eternal "egō eimi ho ōn" of the theophany to Moses at the burning bush, but also with the metaphysical "ho ōn" of Classical Greek ontology. For the word "ōn" was taken to refer to "continuity and eternity and transcendence over all marks of time." Historically, the problem of "promoting, advancing, teaching, and diffusing the study of natural theology," to which the will of Adam Lord Gifford in 1885 dedicated the lectureship that bears his name,

ap.Jaki 1986,72

may in a sense be said to be one of determining the right answer to such lexicographical questions of continuity; and the present lectures, in keeping with what an earlier Gifford Lecturer called "Lord Gifford's further stipulation that the lectures may also deal

Jaeger 1947,1

with the history of these problems," examine one of the most ambitious of all the efforts to find such an answer.

Perhaps the best way to define the topic and venue of this set of Gifford Lectures at Aberdeen is by triangulation from two predecessors. In 1931 and 1932 the Gifford Lectures at the University of Aberdeen were delivered by Etienne Gilson of the Collège de France; they were published as *The Spirit of Medieval Philoso-*

Gilson 1944

phy. In his lectures Gilson summarized the central themes of natural theology as these had been interpreted by the major thinkers of the Latin West during the Middle Ages. Indeed, as his biographer has noted, "Gilson would be the first Gifford lecturer

Shook 1984,183

to focus his attention on the thought of the Middle Ages." A few years later (after the intervening Gifford Lectures of William David Ross in 1935 and 1936 on *Foundations of Ethics*), Karl Barth—almost as if he were responding specifically to Gilson, although he was in fact reacting against an entire intellectual and theological tradition—delivered his own Gifford Lectures at Aberdeen under the title *The Knowledge of God and the Service of*

Barth 1938

Jaki 1978

God according to the Teaching of the Reformation. Stanley L. Jaki, Gifford Lecturer at Edinburgh in 1974 and 1976 and historian of the Gifford Lectures, has observed that "Barth was certainly alone among Christian Gifford Lecturers in inveighing

Jaki 1986,39

against natural theology." Those two series of Gifford Lectures, Gilson's on the Middle Ages and Barth's on the Reformation, have, however, still left a significant lacuna in the examination of the theme of "natural theology" in the history of Christian

Gilson 1944,50n

Newman 1852,3.10
(Ker 1971,71)

Cross 1945,10

thought; for both Gilson and Barth dealt almost exclusively with the Latin West, whether Catholic or Protestant, and neither addressed, except in passing, the place of "natural theology" in the Greek Christian East.

When the Gifford Lectures were inaugurated in 1881, the most eminent religious thinker in the British Isles—who was, by almost universal consensus, John Henry Newman, eighty years old but destined to live on for almost another decade—was not named as the first incumbent. (This slight to Newman was paralleled by the failure a few years later to confer the first Nobel prize in literature on Leo Tolstoy.) The reason could not have been an assumption that Newman was not interested in "natural theology," for he had made this the foundation for the most influential of his books, *The Idea of a University*. If Newman's previous scholarship is any indication, he would, as Gifford Lecturer, have addressed the issue of natural theology from the perspective of the Greek church fathers of the fourth century; for, as F. L. Cross has suggested, "There was perhaps no one in any country who, in the first half of the nineteenth century, had a greater knowledge of Athanasius than Newman." But as it stands, the record of the Gifford Lectures does contain Werner Jaeger's series of 1936 and 1937, *The Theology of the Early Greek Philosophers*, Arthur Darby Nock's series at Aberdeen in 1939 and 1940 (unfortunately, left unpublished at his death in 1963) on "Hellenistic Religion—The Two Phases," and William Inge's Gifford Lectures of 1917 and 1919, *The Philosophy of Plotinus*. But there have been no Gifford Lectures that continued Jaeger's, Nock's, and Inge's analyses of natural theology in the Greek tradition beyond the Ancient and Hellenistic periods into the Patristic and Byzantine periods, despite Jaeger's brief but distinguished contribution to that theme in his final book, published just six days before he died in 1961, *Early Christianity and Greek Paideia*, as well as in his monumental edition of the writings of Gregory of Nyssa.

It has become a truism of the comparative intellectual history of the Middle Ages to observe that Byzantium never had an Augustine and that this constituted a fundamental difference between East and West. Whether that represents a disadvantage or an advantage for the East is a matter of considerable dispute in both East and West. Although no one figure among later Greek Christian thinkers occupied the same heights that Augustine of Hippo did among the later Latins, the truism needs qualification in several important ways. For if it means that there has never been in the Christian East a theological-philosophical genius worthy of being placed alongside Augustine for sheer creativity and power as an individual intellectual virtuoso (whether heretical or orthodox), it is mistaken, because Origen of Alexandria, who was born circa 185 and died circa 254, does deserve to be counted as his peer. But if the chief emphasis lies, as it probably should, on Augustine's position in the century after the "peace of the church" under Constantine and after the codification, at the Council of Nicaea in 325, of the faith that Augustine transmitted to the Latin Middle Ages with his own special stamp upon it, then his place in Western Christian history has its counterpart in the joint achievement of three Eastern Christian thinkers belonging to the generation immediately following that of Nicaea and preceding that of Augustine: Basil of Caesarea, who died in 379; his brother Gregory of Nyssa ("Nyssen"), who died circa 395; and Gregory of Nazianzus ("Nazianzen"), who died in 389—often

Holl 1904

grouped as the Three Cappadocians. Together the Cappadocians did occupy a place in what Endre von Ivánka has called "early

Ivánka 1948

Byzantine intellectual life"—after Constantine, Nicaea, and Athanasius but before Justinian, Pseudo-Dionysius the Areopagite, and the Iconoclastic controversy—that suggests intriguing analogues to the place of Augustine in the Western Middle Ages.

Careful study, including the study leading up to this book, has repeatedly confirmed the impression of "a striking similarity

Norris 1991,185

among the Cappadocians" in thought and even in language, a similarity that reflects but goes beyond their having shared a common background and social class (whether this be the "country aristocracy," the "Roman senatorial class," or the "Cappado-

Kopecek 1973,453

cian curial class"). Therefore, the examination of their natural theology here is intended to address the need once defined by Brooks Otis: "Though everyone recognizes the agreement of thought among the great Cappadocians, not enough explicit attention has as yet been given to the real coherence of their doctri-

Otis 1958,97

nal system." Borrowing a remark I once heard Henrich Bornkamm make about the theology of Martin Luther, I shall seek to treat their thought systematically without imposing a system upon it, "systematisch, aber nicht systematisierend." Wherever possible, their concurring statements on various issues will be brought together. This book does not, therefore, address them as discrete individuals and thinkers, important though such an approach has been in the scholarly literature, which is reflected in the Bibliography and which underlies much of the discussion.

This is also not the place to recount the fascinating biographies of each of the Cappadocians in any great detail nor to analyze "the nature of friendship in late antique, Christian Cappadocia" as this is reflected in their lives and letters, nor to attempt to unravel the still unresolved chronological and codicological problems, nor to settle the undetermined questions of the authorship of various writings. Even the philosophical and theological differences among them cannot claim primary attention here, although the differences on such questions as the creation of the angels and above all on eschatology, as well as their contrasting relations to the thought of Origen, will receive some attention. Yet it may be useful to say at least something about each of them as persons and about the relations among them. Their careers collided at many points, and the personal relations among the three men were complicated and intriguing. As John Meyendorff has said in introducing the fascinating collection of their letters and other personal documents edited by Georges Barrois, here "these three men appear to us as real human beings, reveal the substance of their Christian vocation, uncover the program of their spiritual life, unveil the intellectual background of their use of Greek philosophy at the service of Christian theology, and explain the meaning of their ministry as monastic leaders and bishops of the Church." Those letters and other writings reveal repeated conflicts of opinion and clashes of personality, for example between Gregory of Nazianzus and Basil, and again between the two brothers, Basil and Gregory of Nyssa. Yet in these same letters they could also repeatedly speak of one another with cordial affection and fraternal admiration, an admiration expressed, for example, by Gregory of Nazianzus for Basil: "Whenever I handle his *Hexaemeron* and take its words on my lips, I am brought into the presence of the Creator, and understand the works of creation, and admire the Creator more than before, using my teacher as my only means of sight."

In his standard manual on ancient Christian writers, Johannes Quasten characterized Basil as "the man of action," Gregory of Nazianzus as "the master of oratory," and Gregory of Nyssa as "the thinker." Basil, he explained, was the "only one among the three Cappadocian Fathers to whom the cognomen *Great* has been attributed." Gregory of Nazianzus, he continued, "might be called the humanist among the theologians of the fourth century in so far as he preferred quiet contemplation and the union of ascetic piety and literary culture to the splendor of an active life and ecclesiastical position"; he also earned the epithet "the

Vam Dam 1986,68–73

Giet 1941b,67–82;
Gribomont 1953,323–32;
Pasquali 1923,96–102;
Cavallin 1944,71–98

See pp.259–62,324–26,
225–27, below

Giet 1941b

ap.Barrois 1986,9

Gr.Naz.Or.43.59
(PG 36:572–73)
Bas.Ep.58
(Courtonne 1:145–47)

Gr.Naz.Or.43.67
(PG 36:585)

See p.265 below

Theologian" for his defense of the doctrine of the Trinity. And Gregory of Nyssa was "neither an outstanding administrator and monastic legislator like Basil, nor an attractive preacher and poet like Gregory of Nazianzus"; nevertheless, "as a speculative theologian and mystic" he was "by far the most versatile and successful author" among "the three great Cappadocians," so that "if we compare Gregory of Nyssa as a theologian with the other two Cappadocians, Basil and Gregory of Nazianzus, we recognize his superiority immediately." For that matter, his prominence over the other two also in this book—where statistical analysis would probably reveal that well over half the references are citations from his works—will indicate that "superiority," as would almost certainly be the case with Augustine in any book encompassing the theological and philosophical thought of Ambrose, Jerome, and Augustine, the younger Western contemporaries of the Cappadocians, even though it remains the case, as Joseph Lebon has said, that Basil was "incontestably the master and the head of the group." In his own way, Georges Florovsky has also drawn some of the comparisons that Quasten has, but he has sharpened the point in relation to the present theme. Basil, Florovsky said, "did not so much adapt Neoplatonism as overcome it"; as for Gregory of Nazianzus, "the idea which he expresses in Platonic language is not itself Platonic"; and of Gregory of Nyssa, Florovsky wrote, also somewhat paradoxically, that "Gregory's enthusiasm for secular learning was only temporary. . . . However, he always remained a Hellenist."

Quasten 3:204,236,254, 255,283

Lebon 1953,632

Florovsky 7:107,119,147

To the three Cappadocians should be added, as "the Fourth Cappadocian," Macrina (the Younger), the oldest sister of Basil and of Gregory of Nyssa, named for their grandmother, Macrina the Elder. Not only was she, according to Gregory's accounts, a Christian role model for both of them by her profound and ascetic spirituality, but at the death of their parents she became the educator of the entire family, and that in both Christianity and Classical culture. Through her philosophy and theology, Macrina was even the teacher of both of her brothers, who were bishops and theologians, "sister and teacher at the same time [hē adelphē kai didaskalos]," as Gregory called her in the opening sentence of the dialogue On the Soul and the Resurrection (as he elsewhere referred to Basil, his brother, as "our common father and teacher"). Adolf von Harnack once characterized the Life of Macrina by Gregory of Nyssa as "perhaps the clearest and purest expression of the spirituality of the Greek Church," which anyone looking for an epitome of Greek Orthodoxy should consult

Gr.Nyss.V.Macr. (Jaeger 8–I:383)

Gr.Nyss.Anim.res. (PG 46:12)

Gr.Nyss.Hom.opif.pr. (PG 44:125)

Harnack 1931,2:60

at the outset. Its author did intend it to be an authentic portrait of this saint who was his sister, of whom he said elsewhere that she was the only one on whom, in her final hours, he could rely to answer the objections of unbelievers to the resurrection. Al-

Gr.Nyss.*Anim.res.*
(PG 46:129)

though various scholars have pointed out the parallels between this statement by Gregory of Nyssa about Macrina and Plato's description of the disciples of Socrates in the *Phaedo*, that literary device does not necessarily take away from its historical veri-

Pl.*Phd.*84c-d

similitude, any more than it does from that of Plato's accounts of the public defense and the final hours of Socrates. But without reopening here the entire quest for the historical Socrates, it does seem to be at least permissible, if perhaps not obligatory, to take Gregory of Nyssa at his word about Macrina's philosophical

Cherniss 1930,3;
Apostolopoulos
1986,109–10

learning and about her doctrinal orthodoxy, and therefore to link her name with those of her two brothers and Gregory of Nazianzus as the Fourth Cappadocian.

As Arnaldo Momigliano has observed, Gregory of Nyssa was "not simply a great thinker, but specifically the most versatile and creative Christian biographer of the fourth century. Furthermore, the life of Macrina is the most accomplished and least conventional biography he ever wrote, the most closely related to his philosophic meditations." Momigliano concluded: "The relation between Macrina, Gregory of Nyssa, and Basil of Caesarea is evidently exceptional. It presupposes a combination of high birth, high intellectual power, and, what is rarest even among aristocrats, extraordinary discretion. Gregory knows how to de-

Momigliano 1987,
208,219–20

scribe a life which is to him both exemplary and indicative of disturbing realities without ever falling into the wrong word." It can be argued, moreover, that if Macrina as a historical personage had not been in fact as she was portrayed in the biography, it would have been extremely difficult for a fourth-century Greek Christian writer, even if he was her brother and a bishop of the church, to make up such a portrait and to claim that a real woman had been not only as pious but as learned and as articulate as this if she had not been. All of this, in turn, makes it all the more curious, as Peter Brown has noted, that "it is possible to read all the works of Basil of Caesarea without being able to guess, for a moment, that he had a sister, much less that that sister

Brown 1988,342

was none other than the great Macrina."

Each of the three (or four) Cappadocians stood squarely in the tradition of Classical Greek culture, and each was at the same time intensely critical of that tradition. Each was in constant intellectual interchange, and in no less constant controversy, with the monuments of that culture and with contemporary expositors of the monuments. Gregory of Nazianzus claimed that there was nothing inconsistent with the Christian gospel in the Classical learning of such Christian scholars as his brother, Caesarius. After all, even the sainted Athanasius of Alexandria had studied Classical literature and philosophy. Gregory of Nyssa was conscious of the cultural differences between more cultivated and "more barbarian peoples," a term that does seem to have referred to the differences between the Greek-speaking peoples and those who did not speak Greek; he also added the warning, however, that sin and vice were universal, regardless of language or level of culture. For him, the supreme example of how the believer could properly benefit from pagan learning was Moses, who had, according to the Book of Acts, " 'received a *paideia* in all the *sophia* of the Egyptians,' a powerful speaker and a man of action." Therefore "the *paideia* of the outsiders" was not to be shunned, but cultivated. What it imparted, moreover, as the text of Acts conceded, was not nonsense, despite its pagan origins, but an authentic *sophia* of some kind. According to Basil, "even Moses, that illustrious man, with the greatest name for *sophia* among all mankind, first trained his mind in the learning of the Egyptians [tois Aigyptiōn mathēmasin angynasamenos tēn dianoian], and then proceeded to the contemplation of the one who is [tēi theōriai tou ontos]." Macrina, too, drew on the ideas of "various writers," chiefly pagan philosophical writers, in her disquisition on the soul, and she quoted "wise men"—whom she did not identify by name in this context, although from other statements attributed to her it would appear to have been Greek philosophers whom she had in mind—about man as "microcosm."

Among the Cappadocians, Basil has been in some respects the most influential exponent of such Christian Hellenism, at any rate in its purely literary aspects, as well as of the Christian critique of Hellenism. It was true of him, as it was of the other Cappadocians, that, as Werner Jaeger once observed specifically with them in mind, "the love of simplicity in the Church Fathers is often only a traditional Christian attitude, and the sophisticated style in which they actually write proves that it is a concession which they have to make, just as nowadays even the most fastidious aesthete starts with a bow to the 'common man.' " In describing the virtues of "the gentleman" as the product of a liberal education that included generous doses of Classical culture, John Henry Newman commented: "Basil and Julian were fellow-

Coulie 1983,42–46

Gr.Naz.*Or.*7.7–8
(*PG* 35:761–64)

Gr.Naz.*Or.*21.6
(*SC* 270:120)

Gr.Nyss.*Or.dom.*5
(*PG* 44:1188)

Acts 7:22

Gr.Nyss.*V.Mos.*1
(Jaeger 7–I:7–8)

Gr.Nyss.*V.Mos.*2
(Jaeger 7–I:139)

Bas.*Leg.lib.gent.*3
(Wilson 21–22)

Macr.ap.Gr.Nyss.
Anim.res. (*PG* 46:28)

Cazeaux 1980

ap.Highet 1957,560

Newman 1852,8.10
(Ker 1976,181)

Wright 1923,3:xli–xliii

Kertsch 1978

Seeck 1906,30–34,
468–71

Schucan 1973

Bas.*Leg.lib.gent.*
(Wilson 19–36)

Goemans 1945

Armstrong 1984,8
Büttner 1908,59–60

Whittaker 1979,213

Asmus 1910,325–67

students at the schools of Athens; and one became the Saint and Doctor of the Church, the other her scoffing and relentless foe." The supposed correspondence between Basil and Julian to which Newman may have been alluding is assuredly not authentic, although it remains historically true that Gregory of Nazianzus was Julian's fellow student at Athens in the summer of the year 355 and that they shared a rhetorical tradition and rhetorical teachers. Yet, most scholars today are prepared to accept the authenticity of most if not all of the letters exchanged between Basil and the pagan rhetor Libanius of Antioch. Above all, it was Basil's educational treatise on the reading of pagan books by Christians, generally cited by the Latin form of its title as *Ad adolescentes de legendis libris gentilium,* that decisively articulated in a succinct but comprehensive summary his positive assessment of the Classical tradition, an assessment that for the most part he shared with the other three Cappadocians. Although there was, according to Basil, much in the Classical tradition that was morally repugnant and doctrinally erroneous, there was also much to be gained from an exposure to it; and his nephews, to whom he addressed the treatise in the form of a letter, were to take advantage of the opportunity to study it. Hence it would be, he insisted, a mistake for anyone to spurn Classical learning in the name of Christian piety and orthodoxy. Basil believed, as A. Hilary Armstrong has put it, "that by judicious selection and Christian teaching the classics could be, so to speak, 'decaffeinated,' their pernicious pagan content neutralized, and what was useful in them turned to wholly Christian purposes." In Basil's treatise, according to one study, the purely Christian sources played a relatively minor role; and another study has used it to document the "widespread willingness to admit unhesitatingly the identity of the highest pagan and Christian ideals of morality."

At least some of these positive assessments of the Classical tradition and recommendations that it be studied by Christians came from the Cappadocians in response to the conscious revival of that tradition in the name of a recrudescent paganism by the emperor Julian ("the Apostate"), which took place during the less than two years of his brief reign as sole emperor between November 361 and June 363. In a rescript forbidding Christian professors to teach the pagan Classics, Julian sought to break up the alliance between Christianity and Classical culture and to reclaim that culture for paganism by wresting it from the hands of

Downey 1957,97–103

ap.Cochrane 1944,
286–88

Albertz 1909,228
Gr.Naz.Or.4.23
(SC 309:116–18)

Gr.Naz.Or.4.43
(SC 309:142–44)

Kurmann 1988,339–42

Jul.ap.Gr.Naz.Or.4.102
(SC 309:250)

Gr.Naz.Or.4.5;103
(SC 309:92;252–54)

Bas.Hex.3.8
(SC 26:232–34)

Bas.Hex.1.10
(SC 26:130)
2 Cor 6:15
Bas.Eun.1.9
(SC 299:200)
Unterstein 1903,74–76
Acts 8:22

Bas.Eun.1.6
(SC 299:184)

the church and its educators. It was, he declared, "absurd that persons expounding the work [of the Classical authors] should pour contempt on the religion in which [those authors] believed," and he insisted: "They ought to refrain from teaching what they themselves do not believe to be true." Gregory of Nazianzus, in a lengthy tractate on the vendetta of the emperor against the church, saw it as attacking the doctrines of Christian orthodoxy, as well as the practices of Christian ethics, and as infiltrating the ranks of the Christian clergy. He also portrayed Julian as being engaged in a conscious effort to displace the authority of Christian orthodoxy by reinstating the authority of various Classical philosophies, including Platonism and Stoicism, and by enlisting the services of various teachers, legislators, and other colleagues in this campaign. "The [Greek] language," according to Julian as Gregory quoted or paraphrased him, "belongs [exclusively] to us, as does the right to speak, write, and think in Greek [hēmeteroi hoi logoi kai to Hellēnizein], because it is we who worship the [true] gods." As for the Christians, "What belongs to you is irrationality and peasant ways, and that so-called wisdom of yours consists in nothing except blind faith [ouden hyper to 'pisteuson' tēs hēmeteras esti sophias]." This was a direct attack on the effort of such thinkers as the Cappadocians "to speak, write, and think in Greek" as Christian theologians—that is, to claim to be Greek in their language and even in their way of thought without having to be Greek in their religion.

But the obverse side of that effort of the Cappadocians was their critique of Greek thought in the name of the Christian gospel. Basil of Caesarea, author of *Ad adolescentes de legendis libris gentilium* though he was, extolled the "simple and inartificial character of the utterances of the Spirit" in the Scriptures of the Hebrews as infinitely superior to "the inquisitive discussions of philosophers" among the Greeks. On the basis of such a superiority, he admonished his hearers to "prefer the simplicity of faith to the demonstrations of reason." Quoting the stern words of the New Testament, "Can Christ agree with Belial?" he applied them to the *Categories* of Aristotle. Although the New Testament employed the philosophical word for "concept [epinoia]" only once, and there in a rather nontechnical sense, Basil demanded that his opponent Eunomius square his usage of that word with that of Scripture (rather than with that of the Greek philosophical tradition). For such "accommodation of his language to the simple believers in his audience" and for his rejection

Gr.Nyss.*Hex.*
(PG 44:65)
Gr.Nyss.*V.Mos.*1
(Jaeger 7–I:7–8)

Gr.Nyss.*V.Mos.*2
(Jaeger 7–I:37)
Gr.Naz.*Or.*7.8
(PG 35:764)
Hauser-Meury 1960,
134–35

Gr.Naz.*Or.*18.10
(PG 35:996)

Jul.ap.Gr.Naz.*Or.*4.102
(SC 309:250)

Gr.Naz.*Or.*4.107
(SC 309:258)
Gr.Naz.*Or.*5.30
(SC 309:354)

Gr.Naz.*Or.*23.12
(SC 270:304–6)
Ernst 1896,626–64;
Scazzoso 1975,249–59
Bas.*Ep.*90.2
(Courtonne 1:195–96)

1 Cor 3:19

Gr.Naz.*Or.*36.12
(SC 318:266)

Gr.Naz.*Or.*4.73
(SC 309:188–90)

Fabricius 1962,118–32

Way 1927; Gallay 1933

Hdt 1.57–58

Norris 1991

of "various doctrines of alien philosophy," he was celebrated by his brother Gregory of Nyssa. Gregory himself, paralleling his tribute to the "pagan learning" of Moses," issued, in the same treatise on the life of Moses, a criticism of those who, regarding such learning as "more powerful [ischyroteros]," neglected the faith of the fathers and the Christian tradition in favor of Classical Greek sophistication. Gregory of Nazianzus praised his brother, Caesarius, as a scholar, but he praised his mother, Nonna, as one who had refused "to have her ears or tongue, which had received and uttered divine things, defiled by Grecian tales or theatrical songs." When the emperor Julian in the name of a pagan revival laid exclusive claim to the Greek language and to the right to speak, write, and think in Greek, part of the Christian answer was to affirm the chronological priority—and thus, because what was ancient was thought to possess special authority, the cultural superiority—of the Phoenicians, Egyptians, and above all Hebrews over all the Greeks. Against all the "royal and sophistic words, the syllogisms and enthymemes" of the emperor, there stood the testimony of the disciples of Christ, simple and unsophisticated "fishermen and peasants." Yet Basil could complain, in one of his many letters to the bishops of the West, that "the despisers of the doctrines of the fathers and the belittlers of the apostolic traditions" were reserving their highest praises for "the wisdom of this world." And Gregory of Nazianzus could insist that so-called "philosophers [philosophoi]" were not "wise men [sophoi]" at all. Indeed, he claimed that the common people among the Christians were superior in wisdom to the philosophers among the Greeks.

It is evident, however, both from their attitude and from their "imitation of classical expressions, phrases, and passages" that among the several legacies that the Cappadocians had received from Classical culture they manifested the least ambivalence toward the Greek language itself, thus perpetuating a Hellenic prejudice that went back at least as far as Herodotus, according to whom "the Pelasgian people, so long as it spoke a non-Greek [barbaros] tongue, never grew great anywhere." Even the most elegant versions of the writings of the Cappadocians in a modern language, such as the translations of Gregory of Nyssa into French by Jean Daniélou, or the most precise and careful versions, such as the translations of Gregory of Nazianzus into English by Lionel Wickham and Frederick Williams, cannot do justice to the pliant and musical qualities of their Greek, as those translators have been the first to acknowledge. Conversely, any student who is so unfortunate as to learn New Testament Greek without first having studied Classical Greek will be unprepared to cope with the subtleties and difficulties of the language of the Cappadocians and their Byzantine successors (or, for that matter, with many of the lexicographical and syntactical nuances of the New Testament Koine itself). As E. A. Sophocles put it, after a lifetime of studying Patristic and Byzantine Greek, "the language, notwithstanding the changes it had undergone, retained its original character as late as the sixth century; that is, it was ancient

Sophocles 9

Greek in the strictest sense of the expression," in a way and to a degree that definitely could not be applied to the Koine of the New Testament. That "fidelity . . . to the rules of classical Greek

Hoey 1930,124

prose" accounts for the indignation with which Gregory of Nazianzus could treat the effort of the emperor Julian to exclude Christian scholars, thinkers, and rhetors from the practice and teaching of the Greek language. Gregory rejected as high-handed and arbitrary the emperor's identification of the Classical lan-

Jul.ap.Gr.Naz.Or.4.102
(SC 309:250)

guage with Classical worship, as though it were necessary to be Greek by religious practice to be legitimately Greek by language

Gr.Naz.Or.4.5;103
(SC 309:92,252–54)

and culture. When Gregory of Nyssa attacked an opponent with a sarcastic tribute to "these flowers of the old Attic dialect [anthē

Gr.Nyss.Eun.1.482
(Jaeger 1:166)

tēs archaias Atthidos], the polished brilliance of diction playing over his composition," that was both a criticism of fancy language in someone else and a demonstration of his own ability to use it effectively whenever it appeared to be called for. All of this was, however, tempered by their consciousness of the historical

Gr.Nyss.Eun.2.246
(Jaeger 1:298)

relativity of all language, "according to the differences of country." It was tempered even more fundamentally by their profound recognition of the limitations imposed on all language about transcendent reality, as a consequence of which the proper way to speak about God and things divine, in Greek or in a barbarian

See pp.40–56,200–214

tongue, was through negation rather than through affirmation.

The correspondence, at least some of it genuine, between Basil of Caesarea, as a spokesman for the new and now triumphant tradition of Christian culture, and Libanius of Antioch, as one of the last spokesmen for the old tradition of pagan Classical cul-

OCD 605–6

ture, was replete with explicit statements as well as implicit examples that illustrated the fondness of both for the beauties of Greek. Thus when Libanius, in one of the letters usually regarded

Quasten 3:222–23

as genuine, responded to a letter from Basil with the words, "I am vanquished. I am beaten in beautiful letter-writing. Basil has

Lib.ap.Bas.Ep.338
(Courtonne 3:205)

won. But I love him, and so I am delighted," this must be read with an awareness of the conventions of flattery in Classical epistolography and rhetoric; but it was also a tribute, though with more than a slight edge, to the shared linguistic and stylistic tastes of the two men despite their metaphysical and theological differences. Sometimes Basil could exhibit his Classical learning and stylistic sensitivity to good advantage, as when he commented on two treatises by a Christian colleague, Diodorus, presbyter of Antioch, one of the treatises being pithy in language but the other quite elaborately wrought: "I know that your intelligence is perfectly aware that the heathen philosophers who wrote dialogues, Aristotle and Theophrastus, went straight to the point, because they were aware of their not being gifted with the graces of Plato. Plato, on the other hand, with his great power of writing, at the same time attacks opinions and incidentally makes fun of his characters. . . . When, however, he introduces unidentified characters into his dialogues, he uses the interlocutors for making the point clear, but does not admit anything more belonging to the characters into his argument. An instance of this is in the *Laws*." That disquisition made it seem almost comic when he continued in the same letter with the disclaimer that Christians (himself included) were indifferent to elegance of style and language, merely "writing . . . from the design of bequeathing counsels of sound doctrine to the brethren."

Bas.*Ep.*135.1–2
(Courtonne 2:49–50)

What Basil and Libanius had in common, moreover, was not only a dedication to the Greek language but a devotion to "the specific object of Greek education and the highest Greek culture," namely, to Greek rhetoric, which Basil had in common as well with the other Cappadocians (even though they all claimed to be putting their *logoi* as language into the service of Christ as the *Logos* of God). As George Kennedy has put it, "The most important figure in the synthesis of classical rhetoric and Christianity is Gregory of Nazianzus, whose speeches became the preeminent model for Christian eloquence throughout the Byzantine period." Macrina, too, was said to be well acquainted with rhetoric. Therefore, when, in the dialogue about the soul and the resurrection, her brother Gregory resorted to rhetorical techniques (or tricks), she was in a position immediately to identify them as such and to call him down for them. He himself, in his polemic against Eunomius, disclaimed possession of any "weapon of argument shaped by rhetoric to bring forward to aid us in the fight with those arrayed against us." He also accused Eunomius of "playing the rhetorician" and of employing a "rhetorical stroke of phrases framed according to some artificial theory." For he knew that it was characteristic of a rhetorician to

Marrou 1956,268
Campbell 1922

Camelot 1966,23–30

Kennedy 1983,215
Gr.Nyss.*V.Macr.*
(Jaeger 8–I:375)

Macr.ap.Gr.Nyss.
Anim.res. (PG 46:145)

Gr.Nyss.*Eun.*3.1.2
(Jaeger 2:3–4)

Gr.Nyss.*Eun.*3.3.27
(Jaeger 2:117)

Gr.Nyss.*Or.dom.*1
(*PG* 44:1121)

"prefer study to prayer" when he was composing a speech and to "pursue his own and his pupils' studies as if he had brought himself into this existence."

Gr.Naz.*Ep.*11.4
(Gallay 1:17)

In this Nyssen was speaking from the personal and professional experience of having at one time "preferred to be called a professor of rhetoric rather than of Christianity," as Gregory of Nazianzus said of him. Thus also, according to Gregory of Nyssa, the young Basil had been "puffed up beyond measure with the pride of oratory," and it was none other than Macrina who even-

Gr.Nyss.*V.Macr.*
(Jaeger 8–1:377)

tually led him "toward the mark of 'philosophia,'" which was in this context a term not for technical Classical philosophy but for

See pp.181–82 below

Christian asceticism. Although by ability and training "an orator among orators, even before the chair of the rhetoricians," one for whom "eloquence was his bywork [parergon]," Basil was praised for putting rhetoric and eloquence into the service of "Christian philosophy"; for "his purpose was philosophy, and breaking

Gr.Naz.*Or.*43.13
(*PG* 36:512)

from the world, and fellowship with God." Nor did Gregory of Nazianzus, in criticizing both Basil and Gregory of Nyssa for their past addiction to rhetoric, spare himself in this criticism, but

Gr.Naz.*Or.*7.1
(*PG* 35:756)

he admitted that he also had once been "ambitious above all for oratorical renown." This was in keeping with the spirit prevalent among those with whom he and Basil had studied in Athens,

Gr.Naz.*Or.*43.15
(*PG* 36:513–16)

where "most of the young men were mad after rhetorical skill." In this way the Cappadocians continually served as examples to one another, both of the temptations of Classical rhetoric and of its serviceability to the Christian cause, because it was the common property of Classical and of Christian culture. This eloquence, according to Gregory of Nazianzus, originally "was the product of a training in the doctrines on the outside," in the culture of the Classical tradition; but, he added, it had now been

Gr.Naz.*Or.*36.4
(*SC* 318:248)

"ennobled by the divine doctrines" of the Christian tradition. Therefore, it was unwarranted for champions of Classicism like

Gr.Naz.*Or.*4.5;4.103
(*SC* 309:92;250–52)
Young 1989,182–99
Gr.Naz.*Ep.*51
(Gallay 1:66–68)
Pellegrino 1932;
Ackermann 1903,82–87;
Sykes 1985,433–37;
Dubedout 1901,97–110;
Sajdak 1917,14

the emperor Julian to deny the Christians a right to the Greek language and to Greek rhetoric. Rhetoric helped to shape biblical exegesis; and also as a mature Christian, indeed as a bishop, Gregory of Nazianzus continued to pay careful attention to the rules of literary composition, as the Classical skill and technical correctness of his poetry, even of his didactic and dogmatic poetry, amply demonstrated.

Bas.*Leg.lib.gent.*
(Wilson 19–36)

In addition to rhetoric as a vehicle for the Greek language, Classical literature also held a place of honor, though often of rather ambiguous honor, in the writings of the Cappadocians. They were critical of the "poets and moulders of mythology" for

Gr.Nyss.*Eun.*2.619
(Jaeger 1:407)

Gr.Naz.*Or.*4.115
(SC 309:272–74)

Gr.Naz.*Or.*39.7
(PG 36:341)
Gr.Nyss.*Virg.*3
(Jaeger 8–1:265–66)

Gr.Naz.*Or.*4.71
(SC 309:182)

Gr.Naz.*Or.*4.116
(SC 309:276)

Browning 1975,15–33
Gr.Naz.*Or.*43.3
(PG 36:497)
Hom.*Od.*9.27
Gr.Naz.*Or.*43.17
(PG 36:520)
Hom.*Il.*11.496
Hom.*Od.*8.492
Gr.Naz.*Ep.*5.1
(Gallay 1:5–6)
Pi.*O.*6.1
Gr.Naz.*Or.*43.20
(PG 36:521)

Bas.*Ep.*147
(Courtonne 2:68)

Pl.*R.*488

Bas.*Ep.*3.1
(Courtonne 1:14)

Bas.*Ep.*204.5
(Courtonne 2:177)

their practice of inventing a "combination of the superhuman with human bodies." They knew and despised the theogonies of Hesiod as unworthy depictions of the sublimity of the divine nature. They recited the various myths from Classical literature only in order to ridicule them as "the amusement of the children of the Greeks" and to blame the myths on the influence of demons. The "myths" of Classical literature contained "shocking extravagances." Addressing himself to the emperor Julian, Gregory of Nazianzus could speak contemptuously about "that Homer of yours," with all of his demonic myths and legends. Homer, he told Julian, had become "the great satirist of your gods—or, perhaps more precisely, their tragedian." Among themselves, however, or in communications with other Christians, the Cappadocians could treat Homer much more gently, as the major figure in the history of Greek literature. The same Gregory of Nazianzus in one of his orations, in order to "describe [someone] fully in Homer's language," could allude to the *Odyssey* without a specific citation. Later in the same oration he made similar use of the *Iliad* of Homer. When addressing Basil of Caesarea rather than Julian, he selected a line from the eighth book of the *Odyssey* as the epigraph for his epistle. In Nazianzen's Christian panegyric for Basil, the language of Pindar in the *Olympian Odes* came quite naturally to his pen. Basil in turn invoked "Homer, in the second part of his poem, narrating the adventures of Odysseus" (seemingly taking the *Iliad* as the first part and the *Odyssey* as the second part of a single poem). He praised Candidianus, a governor of Cappadocia: "You do not give up the study of literature, but, as Plato has it, in the midst of the storm and tempest of affairs, you stand aloof, as it were, under some strong wall, and keep your mind clear of all disturbance." And he identified himself with the Classical literary establishment, whether pagan or Christian, when he lamented the contemporary cultural scene, in which people were "setting themselves up for a position as literary critics [logōn kritēs], without being able to tell where they went to school or how much time was spent on their education, and without knowing anything at all about literature."

If the attitude of the Cappadocians toward Classical literature is best characterized as one of ambivalent identification with it, such a term would apply preeminently to their use of Classical philosophy, which for the examination of our theme in this opening chapter was at the same time the most pertinent to their natural theology. That ambivalence made itself strikingly evident in the place of Classical philosophy in their discussions of Chris-

Bas.*Ep.*8.2
(Courtonne 1:23)

Bas.*Spir.*3.5
(SC 17:264)

Gr.Nyss.*Eun.*3.6.56
(Jaeger 2:206)

Gr.Nyss.*Eun.*2.405
(Jaeger 1:344)

Gr.Nyss.*Eun.*1.186
(Jaeger 1:81)

1 Cor 1:20

Gr.Nyss.*Eun.*3.8.43
(Jaeger 2:255)

Gr.Nyss.*Eun.*3.2.35
(Jaeger 2:63)

Arist.*Cat.*1a
Gr.Naz.*Or.*29.15
(SC 250:208)

Gr.Naz.*Ep.*101
(PG 37:188)

tian heresy. In keeping with their criticisms of Greek thought, the Cappadocians repeatedly put the blame for heresy on those whose object it was "not to teach simple souls lessons drawn from Holy Scripture, but to mar the harmony of [Christian] truth by heathen philosophy." For example, those Christian theologians who mistakenly subordinated the *hypostasis* of the Holy Spirit to the *hypostasis* of the Father in the Trinity had been "led into this error by their close study of heathen writers," with their philosophical doctrine of causes. Gregory of Nyssa found the source for the heresies of Eunomius in the influence that came "from the alien *sophia*" of pagan philosophy. A Neoplatonist himself, he could nevertheless charge Eunomius with trying "to make Plato's theory a doctrine of the church." And yet, while accusing Eunomius of making excessive concessions to philosophy, he could at the same time accuse him of neglecting philosophy. When Eunomius distinguished the "being" of the Father from the "being" of the Son and the "being" of the Spirit, Gregory of Nyssa charged Eunomius with "unphilosophically [amathōs] piling up being over being, one above the other, one proper, one not such, for no discoverable reason." He rejected the Eunomian distinction not only on the grounds of Nicene trinitarianism but on the grounds that "this folly" had not appeared in "any of the infidel philosophers, nor in the inspired writings, nor in the common apprehension of humanity." After the rhetorical question, "What fellowship is there between the creed of Christians and the *sophia* [of the philosophers], which 'has been made to look foolish'?" he concluded, with apparent ambivalence toward ratiocination: "Let us bid farewell to such philosophy, and proceed to discuss this point according to the measure of our intelligence."

To refute a Christian heresy that had, in his judgment, been corrupted by "the foolish belief of the Greeks," Gregory of Nyssa made use of a disjunctive [diazeuktikos] syllogism, a device taken directly out of Classical logic and rhetoric. Also contending against the heretical trinitarianism of Eunomius, Gregory of Nazianzus found in it the fallacy "called by the logicians 'arguing from the particular to the general.'" And arguing against the Apollinarists that the divine *Logos* had not taken the place of the human soul in the incarnation but that Christ had to have had an authentically human mind, he claimed to have demonstrated his point, "like it or not, by—to use their own expression— geometrical and necessary proofs." In opposition to the same adversaries, however, Gregory of Nyssa identified "the teacher of

Gr.Nyss.*Apoll.*45
(Jaeger 3–I:206)

Bas.*Eun.*1.5
(SC 299:172–74)

Macr.ap.Gr.Nyss.
Anim.res. (PG 46:52)

Ghellinck 1930,5–42

I Cor 1:17

Gr.Naz.*Or.*29.21
(SC 250:224)

Gr.Naz.*Or.*25.6
(SC 284:168)

Gr.Nyss.*Eun.*1.46
(Jaeger 1:37–41 [var.])

Bas.*Spir.*17.42
(SC 17:396)

Acts 17:18
Macr.ap.Gr.Nyss.
Anim.res. (PG 46:21)

Apollinaris," namely, the sophist Epiphanius, as the source for his distorted way of treating syllogisms. Basil, too, arguing against Eunomius, challenged the assumption that "the syllogisms of Aristotle and Chrysippus" were needed by the orthodox to establish their doctrine. One of the most perceptive analyses of the ambivalent position of logic and dialectic came from the Fourth Cappadocian. "Subtle dialectic," according to Macrina, "possesses a force that may be turned both ways, as well for the overthrow of truth as for the detection of falsehood." Because it was such a two-edged sword, she continued, "We begin to suspect even truth itself when it is advanced in company with such a kind of artifice, and to think that the very ingenuity of it is trying to bias our judgment and to upset the truth." Elaborating on that insight into the ambivalence of logical argument, Gregory of Nazianzus warned: "When we leave off believing, and protect ourselves by mere strength of argument, and destroy the claim that the Spirit has upon our faith by questionings, and then our argument is not strong enough for the importance of the subject (and this must necessarily be the case, since it is put in motion by an organ of so little power as our mind), what is the result? The weakness of the argument appears to belong to the mystery, as Paul also thought. For faith is that which completes our argument." Or, as those closing words have also been translated, "reason is fulfilled in faith."

The treatment of the metaphysics of Classical philosophers and philosophical schools in the works of the Cappadocians manifested even more of this ambivalence toward Classical culture evident in their handling of logic and dialectic. It was a favorite rhetorical device of the Cappadocians to recite a catalog of the Greek philosophical schools, with an epithet or two for each; but they also frequently singled out one of the philosophers or philosophical schools for critical attention. Thus Gregory of Nyssa, in connection with his polemic against the heretic Eunomius and his teacher Aetius, attacked Aristotle's "evil skill" for having "supplied Aetius with his impiety" by enabling him to "lay a train of syllogisms from what he remembered of Aristotle." Basil rejected heretics on the doctrine of the Holy Spirit as worthy of being "classed for the future with Stoics and Epicureans." Macrina reminded herself and her hearers that the apostle Paul, when he came to Athens, was obliged to deal with "Epicurean and Stoic philosophers." She was especially critical of Epicurus for denying divine providence and, as a consequence, the immortality of the soul. And Gregory of Nazianzus, despite his "Chris-

See pp.58–59 below
Harnack 1906,27–48

Gr.Naz.Or.4.72
(SC 309:184–86)

Jaki 1978,47

Apostolopoulos 1986
O'Meara 1982

Courcelle 1967,402–6

See pp.95–97

Giet 1968,57–59
Gr.Nyss.Maced.
(Jaeger 3–I:99)
Pl.Tim.29e

Pl.Tim.27d

Gr.Nyss.Cant.6
(Jaeger 6:173)

Gr.Naz.Or.28.4
(SC 250:106–8)

Pépin 1982,251–60
Pl.Tim.28c
Pl.Tim.19b
Gr.Naz.Or.4.113
(SC 309:270)

tian Socratism," which he shared with many ancient Christian writers and which became especially evident in his treatment of the subjective and objective elements of epistemology, reminded his hearers, including the neo-Hellenic philosophical moralist on the imperial throne, of the immorality of Socrates.

Throughout this book we shall turn to what Stanley L. Jaki in his Gifford Lectures has called "the enormous difference which there is between Platonism and Christian Platonism," and to specific instances of the use of Plato and Platonism by the Cappadocians, which was constitutive, for example, of their doctrine of the soul, whether philosophical or theological. But Platonism (including, of course, Neoplatonism) deserves special notice even here at the outset as perhaps the most important instance of the attitude of these Christian theologians toward Classical culture. As became especially evident in the cosmology of the Cappadocians, moreover, there was probably no writing within the Platonic corpus that stood above *Timaeus* for sheer importance in Cappadocian thought, and not only because both Basil and Gregory of Nyssa were authors of Christian cosmogonies bearing the title *Hexaemeron,* in which *Timaeus* and Genesis were played off against each other in continuing dialogue. It is illustrative of that importance that Gregory of Nyssa could quote *Timaeus* almost offhand, without bothering to cite or identify it. Similarly, he drew from it one of his most fundamental distinctions, that between a nature that was "material and perceptible by the senses," shared by humanity with the physical world, and a nature that was "rationally intelligible and nonmaterial [noēton te kai aÿlon]," shared by humanity with God and the angels. For the indispensable principle of the undefinability of God, which pervaded the negative theology of the Cappadocians, it was once again to this source that they were obliged to turn. When Gregory of Nazianzus asserted that it was "difficult to conceive God, but impossible to define God in words," he quoted as his authority not the testimony of the Christian Scriptures or of the writers of the Greek Christian tradition, as he might have done and as he and the other Cappadocians did elsewhere and at length, but "what one of the [pagan] Greek teachers of divinity taught, not unskillfully." He did not name this source; although some scholars have identified it as a Hermetic fragment, it may also have been Plato's *Timaeus.* Elsewhere, too, Gregory of Nazianzus found it possible to weave a quotation from this Platonic work into an oration directed against Julian's glorification of the Classical over the Christian tradition.

The natural theology of the Cappadocians, and of the Greek Christian tradition as a total entity from the Patristic through the Byzantine period, was the product of these encounters with Hellenism. The outcome of that encounter and the interactions between Greek and Christian thought within it have been persistent themes of debate throughout the following centuries, a debate that reached its "qualitative high point" in the first half of the eighteenth century. As Edward Caird said in the conclusion to his Gifford Lectures, "There are many writers, and not only sceptical writers, but Christian theologians—including, indeed, the most important school of German theology in recent times—who hold that the great controversies of the early Church about the Trinity and the Incarnation were . . . about subtleties introduced by Greek philosophy into the Christian religion." Especially since the Protestant Reformation, charges and countercharges of "Hellenization," together with the question of whether Hellenization represented "apostasy" or "progress," have shaped theological controversy, philosophical speculation, and historical interpretation. For those like the Cambridge Platonists, who affirmed the validity of attempts at a synthesis of Hellenism and the gospel, the kind of natural theology epitomized by the Cappadocians was a foundation for even bolder attempts. In contrast, those like Albrecht Ritschl and Adolf von Harnack, who strove to purify the gospel of alien elements, saw in such natural theology the channel for a distortion that was all the more insidious because it was invoked in support of orthodox dogma. Frequently overlooked in the polemics of these debates have been the specifics of this "natural theology" and of its place not only in the speculative system of the Cappadocians but in the Greek-speaking Orthodox Christianity for which they were such influential interpreters. Those specifics constitute the subject matter of this investigation.

Glawe 1912,150–76

Caird 1904,2:359

Florovsky 12:23–30
Grillmeier 1958,332–43

Cragg 1968,3–31

Meijering 1985,11–48

Unterstein 1903

CHAPTER 2

Natural Theology as Apologetics

Bas.*Leg.lib.gent.*5
(Wilson 23)
Owen 1925,64–71
Gr.Naz.*Or.*4.103
(*SC* 309:252–54)

See pp.74–89

Gr.Naz.*Or.*2.95
(*SC* 247:212–14)

Gr.Naz.*Or.*43.13
(*PG* 36:512)
Gr.Nyss.*V.Macr.*
(Jaeger 8–I:403)

Gr.Nyss.*Or.catech.*18.3
(Méridier 94)

Hom.*Il.*1.39

Ps 10:4; Rv 3:12

It is clear that the thought of the Cappadocians was by no means uniform in its treatment of the various aspects of Classical Greek culture. For although it is probably fair to say that some ambivalence characterized their attitude toward the whole of Classical culture, the ambivalence ranged across a wide spectrum, as they themselves acknowledged, from their positive view of the Greek tongue to their condemnation of other aspects of the Hellenic tradition. The opposite end of the spectrum from the Greek tongue was occupied by Greek religion, toward which their language was consistently harsh and their assessment uniformly negative. They identified themselves as priests, and they knew themselves to be standing in the succession of the Old Testament priesthood. Indeed, Gregory of Nazianzus prized this as chief among the accomplishments of Basil: "an orator among orators, even before the chair of the rhetoricians; a philosopher among philosophers, even before the doctrines of the philosophers; highest of all, a priest among Christians, even before the priesthood." Macrina was likewise remembered as always having held the priesthood in great honor. They also celebrated the "rise, in the name of Christ, of temples and altars [naous te kai thysiastēria] and of a holy and unbloody priesthood"—a word like "naos" being borrowed from the vocabulary of Classical Greek religion, as well as from that of the Septuagint and the New Testament. Nevertheless, in their interpretations of the religious beliefs and practices that they encountered among non-Christian Greeks they did not align themseles with the Greek priests at all,

Gr.Naz.Or.5.23
(SC 309:336)

1 Cor 4:1

Gr.Naz.Or.2.26
(SC 247:124)

See pp.298–301

Antoniadis 1939,
149–52,346–57

1 Cor 5:8

Gr.Naz.Or.11.6
(PG 35:840)

Gr.Naz.Or.45.10
(PG 36:636)

ap.Cochrane 1944,
286–88

Gr.Naz.Or.39.1
(PG 36:356)
Gr.Naz.Or.39.7
(PG 36:341)
Gr.Nyss.Eun.2.618–19
(Jaeger 1:407)

Gr.Naz.Or.30.6
(SC 250:236)

1 Pt 4:13
Gr.Naz.Or.25.13
(SC 284:186)

Gr.Nyss.Beat.2
(PG 44:1209)

but with the anticlerical, rationalistic exponents of a philosophical natural theology among pagan Greek thinkers; for they were conscious of the distinction between traditional Greek religion and critical Greek thought. They knew themselves to be as well, in the New Testament title, "stewards of the mysteries of God," a title that they understood to refer also to the sacramental "mysteries" of the church, not only to the mystery of revelation through the *economy* of Christ as such. Yet they found no positive connection between the sacramental mysteries over which they were presiding and the pagan "mysteries," even though these did bear some similarities to the Christian ritual, especially in the forms which that ritual had acquired by the fourth century (regardless of whether the liturgy traditionally attributed to Basil came directly from him, in whole or in part). Much of the vocabulary that was used in Christian Greek to speak about the observance of these Christian mysteries was, moreover, dependent on such liturgical terminology as the Classical Greek verbs "panēgyrizein [to celebrate]," which did not appear in the New Testament at all, and "heortazein [to keep a festival]," which occurred in the New Testament only once. Somewhat to their embarrassment, the expositors of Christian liturgical theology seem to have found such terminology almost indispensable, in spite of the parallel use of these terms in the language of pagan religion, although they were also aware at the same time that some of the vocabulary of the Christian liturgy had come from Hebrew rather than from Greek.

With their cultivation of Greek language and literature, they fundamentally rejected the emperor Julian's linkage between the writings of the Classical authors and "the religion in which they believed." For them, therefore, "Greek error" seems in the first instance to have been a term for the "solemnities [semna]" of Greek religious observance. Greek religious practice and the Greek myth underlying it were both dismissed as the invention of demons. The Cappadocians were consistently critical of the "poets and moulders of mythology" in the Greek tradition. They did speak of the Gospel accounts of the crucifixion of Christ as "a marvelously constructed drama"; and because the persecution endured by Christians in the Roman Empire east and west was a "sharing" in the crucifixion, they could likewise describe this as a "drama." The illustrations that Christ employed in his preaching were likened to the costumes and stage props in the performance of the Greek tragedies, which symbolized the truth being conveyed but were not identical with it. But such usage, reflecting as

Gr.Nyss.*Virg.*3
(Jaeger 8–I:265–66)

it did the language and allusions that would have come naturally to the lips of highly educated students of Classical Greek in any age, should not be permitted to obscure their attacks on the dramatic poets of Classical literature for retelling the shocking stories of ancient Greek mythology, which did not teach people about divine truth, as they purported to do, but about the "network of evils that human life is." In spite of its appeal for students of Greek literature in every era, including Racine and Goethe in the modern era, a dramatic legend like that of Iphigenia was simply "too disgraceful" to serve as the basis for "emulation"

Gr.Naz.*Or.*43.8
(*PG* 36:504)

and edification. For all their knowledge of Classical Greek literature and their readiness to cite it with familiarity and affection, therefore, they followed the widespread practice of early Christians in using the word "theater" primarily as a term of contempt. They also distinguished, as Gregory of Nazianzus did

Eriau 1914
Gr.Naz.*Or.*4.114
(*SC* 309:272)

when writing against the emperor Julian, between the "myths" of Greek religion and literature, be they true or false, and the "natural theologians" among the Greek thinkers. The Christian encounter with Hellenism had to do primarily with these "natural theologians." Therefore, it was the consistent assumption of Cappadocian apologetics that, in the words of Werner Jaeger,

Gr.Naz.*Or.*4.117
(*SC* 309:280)

"the Greek spirit reached its highest religious development, not in the cults of the gods . . . but chiefly in philosophy, assisted by the Greek gift for constructing systematic theories of the universe." It

Jaeger 1939–44,2:43

was chiefly in critical and constructive relation to these Classical philosophical and scientific theories rather than to Classical myths or rituals that they formulated their own natural theology.

For Gregory of Nyssa was, in effect, articulating the foundation for a natural theology when he defended Christian orthodoxy against heresy by invoking three authorities, whose relative force he did not specify here, although he did make it somewhat clearer elsewhere: the Greek thinkers whom he identified as "those who philosophized outside the faith"; "the inspired writings" of the Old and the New Testament; and what he called "the

Gr.Nyss.*Eun.*1.186
(Jaeger 1:81)

Gr.Nyss.*V.Mos.*2
(Jaeger 7–I:43)

common apprehension" of humanity. Elsewhere, too, he spoke of a "moral and natural philosophy [hē ēthikē te kai physikē philosophia]," in which each of these three authorities had some part. As reported by him, Macrina's formulation of this juxtaposition between "the common apprehension of humanity" and "the inspired writings" spoke about "believing on the basis both of the prevailing opinion and of the tradition of the Scriptures

Macr.ap.Gr.Nyss.
Anim.res. (*PG* 46:72)

[pepisteuetai ek te tēs koinēs hypolēpseōs, kai ek tēs tōn graphōn paradoseōs]." Their brother Basil, in discussing the Christian doctrine of the Holy Spirit, seems to have been operating with a tripartite taxonomy of authorities that was similar though not identical: "our common conceptions"; "those conceptions that have been gathered by us from Holy Scripture"; and "those which we have received from the unwritten tradition of the fathers." Although the third of these has evoked the most spirited discussion because of Christian theological debates about the relation between Scripture and tradition, it is not clear whether by the first of them he meant conceptions that were truly "common" and universal and therefore "natural," or only conceptions "common" to all Christians, because what he was talking about was, as the complete phrase indicated, "common conceptions concerning the [Holy] Spirit" or perhaps "common conceptions concerning the spirit" as such, whether divine or human. But it would appear to be at least permissible, in the light of their common use of the word "common [koinos]," to see in these "common conceptions" of Basil's some equivalent of Gregory's "common apprehension of humanity" and of Macrina's "prevailing opinion." And Gregory of Nazianzus, though writing chiefly for a Christian audience rather than a pagan one, could declare: "That God, the creative and sustaining cause of all, exists, both our sight and the law of nature inform us."

See pp.227–29

Because the Christian audience whom Gregory of Nazianzus was addressing with these words about an agreement on this point between "the law of nature" and personal experience included those whom he regarded as heretics on the doctrine of the relation between the Father and the Son in the Trinity, the position of those Arian heretics on natural theology is of more than incidental interest. "The most important man in the neo-Arian church" and the most able as a "technologue" of dialectic was Eunomius. At any rate as he was quoted in the fragments of his works that have been preserved in the writings of the Cappadocians against him, Eunomius does seem to have set forth an interpretation of the relation between (using the formulas of Gregory of Nyssa) "the common apprehension of humanity" and "the inspired writings" that implied a coordination bordering on identity. For example, he supported his insistence on a strict monotheism—and hence his opposition to Cappadocian trinitarianism, which he regarded as a betrayal of monotheism—by an appeal, as reported by Basil, "both to natural knowledge and to the teaching of the fathers [kata te physikēn ennoian kai kata tēn tōn paterōn didaskalian]." When Basil sought to square Nicene orthodoxy with the troubling language of the New Testa-

Bas.*Spir*.9.22
(SC 17:322)

Gr.Naz.*Or*.28.6
(SC 250:110)

Albertz 1908,5
Vandenbussche 1944–45, 57

Eun.ap.Bas.*Eun*.1.5
(SC 299:170)

Acts 2:36
See pp.264–66
Bas.*Eun*.2.2–3
(*SC* 305:12–18)

Eun.ap.Gr.Nyss.*Eun*.
3.3.19 (Jaeger 2:114)

Eun.ap.Gr.Nyss.*Eun*.
3.10.26 (Jaeger 2:299)

Eun.ap.Gr.Nyss.*Eun*.
3.7.26 (Jaeger 2:224)

Gr.Nyss.*Eun*.3.1.6
(Jaeger 2:5)

Gr.Nyss.*Eun*.3.7.34
(Jaeger 2:227)

Gr.Nyss.*Eun*.1.186
(Jaeger 1:81)

Gr.Nyss.*Hom.opif*.pr.
(*PG* 44:128)

Gr.Nyss.*Or.dom*.2
(*PG* 44:1140)

ment about the history of Jesus by invoking the traditional distinction between the *theology* of the Godhead in and of itself and the *economy* of the Godhead in its relation to history, Eunomius attacked Basil's effort on the grounds that "the very nature of things" was repugnant to this harmonization, as was also the teaching of the Scriptures. Elsewhere, too, it was on the basis simultaneously of the way "things themselves [auta ta pragmata]" were and of "the sayings accepted on faith [ta pepisteumena logia]" that Eunomius argued. Articulating the first principles of his theology, he appealed "at once to nature itself and to the divine laws" to prove that his position could not be refuted. Gregory of Nyssa summarized Eunomius's doctrine of the relation between the natural and the revealed this way: "If . . . this is a standard of truth that admits of no deception [horos tēs alētheias aparalogistos], that these two concur—the 'natural order,' as he says, and the testimony of the knowledge given from above concerning the natural interpretation—it is clear that to assert anything contrary to these is nothing else than to fight manifestly against the truth itself." That paraphrase of Eunomius's presuppositions appears to have been fair, and in itself it was not overtly condemnatory of them. Later in the same treatise, however, Gregory did take exception to these presuppositions when he objected that nature was "not trustworthy for instruction as to the divine process of generation [within the Trinity], not even taking the universe itself as an illustration of the argument." Yet, he could, near the beginning of the treatise, attack Eunomius for a method of theological argumentation that proceeded "unphilosophically."

Inconsistent though it might seem for the Cappadocians to have invoked these devices in their argumentation against the heretics, charging them first with not understanding philosophy and then with overestimating it, both ways were part of an integrated theological and apologetic method. It was a method that was precisely formulated by Gregory of Nyssa in an essay on Christian doctrine: "To fit together, according to the explanation of Scripture and according to that derived from reasoning, statements that seem, by a kind of necessary sequence, to be opposed, so that our whole subject may be consistent in train of thought and in order." Human thought, in its effort to "understand God as far as possible" on the basis of the divine names, could "learn about the divine nature, whether from Sacred Scripture or from its own reasonings [dia te tēs theias graphēs kai tōn eikeiōn logismōn katanoēsas]." For there were two ways of "joining

Gr.Nyss.Cant.13
(Jaeger 6:376)

LTK 7:830–35
Gr.Nyss.Cant.7
(Jaeger 6:209–10);
Bas.Eun.2.24
(SC 305:98)

Gr.Nyss.Infant.
(Jaeger 3–II:86)

Bas.Ep.160.2
(Courtonne 2:88–89)

Bas.Leg.lib.gent.2
(Wilson 21)

Gr.Nyss.Anim.res.
(PG 46:64)
Gr.Naz.Or.29.21
(SC 250:204)

See pp.215–30

[prosoikeiounta]" divine knowledge and human knowledge, namely, true doctrine and "clear reasoning [katharos logismos]." Occasionally—though much more rarely than in Western Augustinianism, and with quite different assumptions—these two ways and other such distinctions were even spoken of in the terminology of the dichotomy between "nature [physis]" and "grace [charis]." When Gregory of Nyssa, after enumerating "the appropriate studies for sharpening the mind towards moral excellence," including astronomy and various branches of mathematics, placed "before all these, the philosophy contained in the inspired writings [pro toutōn tēn tēs theopnestou graphēs philosophian]," he did not make it immediately clear whether this preposition "before [pro]" referred only to logical and epistemological priority or also to chronological priority in the method of framing the argument. For sometimes this duality did seem to require an order of presentation (as Basil defined it) of first "urging, as of most importance in such matters, our own custom, with the force of law," whose authority was derived from its "being based upon the rules laid down by holy men," whether in Scripture or in the unwritten tradition of the church, and only then of invoking "the aid of reasoning."

At other times, however, Basil could reverse this sequence of argumentation, prescribing: "We . . . must first, if the glory of the good is to abide with us indelible for all time, be instructed by these outside means, and then [tēnikauta] we shall understand the sacred and mystical teachings." Gregory of Nyssa agreed with that sequence when he said, in reaction to Macrina's method of theologizing, that it was proper first to propound a doctrine "for those trained only in the technical methods of proof," by means of a "mere demonstration, sufficient to convince" within the limits of reason alone, and only then, because "the teachings of the Holy Scripture" were "more trustworthy than any of these artificial conclusions," to inquire whether everything that had been proved by reason could also be harmonized with those scriptural teachings. That sequence rested on the axiom of Gregory of Nazianzus: "Faith is what gives fullness to our reasoning [hē gar pistis tou kath' hēmas logou plērōsis]." In a way that went beyond the antithesis between the formulas familiar to students of the history of Western philosophy and theology, both "faith in search of understanding [fides quaerens intellectum]" and "understanding in search of faith [intellectus quaerens fidem]" had a part in such a method. For even in the case of a doctrine that was "true already at first sight, as well as credible on

Gr.Nyss.*Anim.res.*
(PG 46:108)

the basis of Scripture," it was not desirable "to leave this part of the subject without philosophical examination," because "the weakness of the human understanding" could be "strengthened still more by any intelligible rational arguments [logismois]." As the polemic against Eunomius illustrated, this coordinate use of revelation and reason was also intended, within the circle of orthodox Christian theological discourse, as a weapon against heretical doctrine. Here it acted as "our reason, under the guidance of Scripture." This instrumental use of reason in the service of theology helped to clarify, for example, the status of metaphysical distinctions within the divine nature, which superficially seemed to be able to claim authority "either from the teaching of the Scriptures or from our common conceptions [ek tōn koinōn ennoiōn]," but which in fact conflicted with the fundamental teaching, on which Scripture and those common conceptions agreed, of "the utter simplicity of the divine and transcendent nature." But at least as important was the distinct, though not always separate, role that this method of coordinating reason and revelation played in the Christian encounter with Hellenism. The two tasks of polemics against heresy and apologetics against Hellenism were often seen as connected, as when the twofold method of true doctrine and clear reasoning was said to be directed "against both the heathen and the heretical systems of belief about God [eis ethnikas te kai hairetikas peri tou theou doxas]." But the function of continuing the Christian apologetic enterprise, an enterprise that had begun when the apostle Paul encountered "the Stoics and Epicureans collected at Athens," received new prominence as the Cappadocians encountered both the political and the intellectual reassertions of the case in support of Hellenism during the second half of the fourth century.

Gr.Nyss.*Eun.*1.315
(Jaeger 1:120)

Gr.Nyss.*Maced.*
(Jaeger 3–I:90–91)

Gr.Nyss.*Cant.*13
(Jaeger 6:376)
Acts 17:18
Macr.ap.Gr.Nyss.
Anim.res. (PG 46:21)

Asmus 1910,325–67

The polemical aspect of this twofold apologetic method, therefore, was to seek to show that, for example, the Greek doctrine of *tyche,* which was condemned by "true religion" in the name of the doctrines of divine providence and of human free will, was also an error that was "inconsistent with common sense." On the positive side, this method of apologetics proceeded by attempting to tease out true doctrines that were, howsoever indistinctly, implicit in the natural theology of the Greeks. The relation of polytheism to monotheism provided the Cappadocians with an opportunity to do just that, for the implicit assumption behind the philosophical critique of the passion-ridden gods of Mount Olympus by the "natural theologians" among the Greeks seemed to be a shadowy monotheism. More

Bas.*Ep.*236.7
(Courtonne 3:54)

See pp.82–84

Gr.Nyss.*Eun.*3.9.59
(Jaeger 2:286)

Gr.Naz.Or.31.16
(SC 250:306)
Dt 6:4
Gr.Nyss.Tres dii
(Jaeger 3–I:55)

shadowy still, yet perhaps not altogether indiscernible, were some possibilities of a Greek anticipation of the Christian doctrine of the Trinity. All of this still fell far short of the authentic monotheism of the Shema, "Hear, Israel: the Lord is our God, the Lord our one God," which the Cappadocians defended as the bulwark of the Nicene dogma of the Trinity. Nevertheless, the natural theology of the Greeks had come at least part of the distance toward a doctrine of one God.

The display of Classical learning that figured so often in the apologetics of the Cappadocians was of a piece with their high estimate of scholarship in general, as in its own way an instrument of apologetics. So was their extensive use of Classical and Hellenistic science, both their rhetorical use of it for purposes of illustration and their logical use of it for purposes of demonstra-

See pp.99–105

Gr.Nyss.V.Mos.2
(Jaeger 7–I:37);
Bas.Leg.lib.gent.3
(Wilson 21–22)

tion. As mentioned earlier, they treated Moses as the case study for such scholarship and science: because he was educated simultaneously by his believing Israelite parents and by the learned but unbelieving Egyptian scholars at the court of Pharaoh, Moses imbibed profane as well as sacred learning, both of which stood him in good stead in his encounter with paganism, including the

Ex 7:8–13

pagan sorcerers with whom he and his brother, Aaron, competed in performing feats of magic. A prominent feature of this use of scholarship for apologetics was the ability to invoke the example of Christian scholars past and present, over the three centuries since the apostolic era, whose deep learning had been matched

Gr.Naz.Or.21.6
(SC 270:120)

only by their deep spirituality. Many of the compliments that the Cappadocians exchanged in their expressions of mutual admiration were based on scholarly eminence, as when Gregory of

Gr.Nyss.
Hom.opif.ep.ded.
(PG 44:125)
Gr.Naz.Or.7.7–8
(PG 35:761–64)

Nyssa honored the scientific and philosophical learning of his brother Basil, just as Gregory of Nazianzus had a brother, Caesarius, whom he celebrated as "first among scholars."

Yet by any standard, the "first" among all Christian scholars in these first four centuries, first both in eminence and in the ability to evoke controversy, had been the third-century theologian Origen of Alexandria. Therefore, even apart from the

See pp.324–26

troublesome question of his influence on their eschatology, Origen remained, more than a century after his death, a major force

Diekamp 1899,129–38;
Holl 1928,310–50;
Richardson 1937,50–64;
Ivánka 1951,291–303

to the Cappadocians for his sheer brilliance and learning; in fact, he was to go on being such a force long after the era of the Cappadocians. Gregory of Nyssa was fully aware of Origen's problematical position. Without identifying the author by name, Gregory raised objections to the doctrine of the preexistence of

Rebecchi 1943,322–25

souls set forth in the book On First Principles, which, he said, was

Gr.Nyss.*Hom.opif.*
(*PG* 44:229–32)

not "clear of the influence of the theories of the Greeks [tōn Hellēnikōn dogmatōn], which they held on the subject of successive incorporations" of the soul. Yet, when he undertook his own massive *Accurate Commentary on the Song of Songs,* he was obliged to pay tribute to the learning and allegorical skill of his great predecessor, "Origen, who expended great industry in working through this book [philoponōs peri to biblion touto

Gr.Nyss.*Cant.*pr.
(Jaeger 6:13)

spoudasantos]." Basil, by contrast, having earlier been an enthusiast for Origen, spoke out severely in his *Commentary on the Hexaemeron* against Origen's penchant for allegorical exegesis,

Bas.*Hex.*3.9
(*SC* 26:236)

dismissing such interpretations as "dreams and idle tales." Later in the commentary, without naming Origen, he attacked those who did not accept "the common sense of Scripture" when it

Gen 1:24
Bas.*Hex.*9.1
(*SC* 26:478–80)

spoke, for example, about "water." He added: "I myself take it all in the literal sense." Yet it was on the basis of this kind of biblical exegesis in the *Commentary on the Hexaemeron* of Basil, anti-Origenistic and literalistic though it may have been, that his brother Gregory, who differed from Basil in being as much of an Origenist as his orthodoxy would permit him to be, praised Basil

Gr.Nyss.*Hom.opif.*pr.
(*PG* 44:125)

for "having made the sublime working of the universe as cosmos generally intelligible"—an achievement that had far-reaching consequences for the apologetic defense of Christian cosmology

See pp.101–6

against Classical physics and metaphysics.

As apologetics, the natural theology of the Cappadocians was, in the formula of Gregory of Nyssa quoted earlier, a "moral and natural philosophy [hē ēthikē te kai physikē philosophia], which was to be wedded to a more sublime life [tōi hypsēloterōi biōi

Gr.Nyss.*V.Mos.*2
(Jaeger 7–I:43)

syzygos]." Therefore, the parallels between this "natural philosophy" and this "more sublime life"—that is, between Classical ethical theory and Christian ethical theory—as well as the contrasts between Christian moral behavior and Classical immoral behavior, could be mined for their apologetic value. "Does not nature say the same?" asked Basil, after having drawn one such

Bas.*Hex.*9.4
(*SC* 26:498)

parallel. Elsewhere he went further in making the concession: "Although we Christians shall, I suppose [pou], learn all these things more thoroughly in our own literature, yet for the present at least, let us trace out a kind of rough sketch, as it were, of what

Bas.*Leg.lib.gent.*10
(Wilson 35)

arete is according to the teaching of the pagans." Commenting on this passage, the editor of the Greek text of the treatise *Ad adolescentes de legendis libris gentilium,* N. G. Wilson, has found that Basil's use of " 'pou' makes the assertion that we shall learn the same lessons more completely from the Bible surprisingly diffi-

Wilson 1975,69

dent. Did Basil really appreciate the nuance of the particle?" For

Gr.Nyss.*Apoll.*
(Jaeger 3–I:164)

Arist.*EN.*1128a.25
Gr.Nyss.*V.Macr.*
(Jaeger 8–I:401)

Scholl 1881,97–100

Bas.*Hex.*9.4
(SC 26:496–98)

Bas.*Hex.*7.5
(SC 26:414–16)

Gr.Naz.*Or.*30.19
(SC 250:264–66)
Gr.Naz.*Or.*18.38
(PG 35:1036)

Ps 89:9

ap.Hdt.1.32

Gr.Naz.*Or.*4.121 (SC
309:286)

Eph 6:4
Bas.*Hex.*9.4
(SC 26:498)
Gr.Naz.*Or.*42.22
(PG 36:485)

Bas.*Leg.lib.gent.*7
(Wilson 27)

Mt 5:40–44

Gr.Naz.*Or.*37.6
(SC 318:282–84)
Bas.*Ep.*217.73
(Courtonne 2:213)

Gr.Nyss.*Or.catech.*40.8
(Méridier 196)

Gr.Nyss.*Or.catech.*pr.1
(Méridier 2)

Christian morality and Classical morality agreed in defining virtue as "praiseworthy" and vice as "altogether devoid of praise."
What Greek moralists had said about "good order and decency"
could be applied by Christian theologians to exemplary Christian morality, too. According to Basil's view of "the possibility of
morally good behavior without grace," it was "by nature herself,
not by education," which would seem to include even Christian
catechetical education, that the human soul had affinity with
arete. Without education and by nature alone, then, there existed
"a natural rationality implanted in us, telling us to identify ourselves with the good and to avoid everything harmful." This it did
by appealing to motivations that were also naturally implanted in
the human heart, including "fear of punishment, hope for salvation and glory too, and the practice of the *aretai,* which results in
these." What Gregory of Nazianzus, on the basis of the Psalms,
referred to as "David's limit of our age" to seventy was precisely
corroborated by the Greek lawgiver and wise man Solon of
Athens. The Cappadocians gave no indication of having found
such parallels with the Classical tradition threatening to their
Christian faith. They recognized the universal character of the
moral imperatives for children to honor their parents and for
parents to respect their children. The parallels between the Classical and Christian doctrines simply meant: "Paul teaches us
nothing new, but only tightens the links of nature." The Classical
arete of "moderation" was one to which a Christian might also
aspire. Classical examples of restraint, according to Basil, tended
"to nearly the same end as our own precepts [schedon eis tauton
tois hēmeterois]," as these were set forth by Christ in the Sermon
on the Mount. For all the parallelism in ethical theory, however,
Cappadocian apologetics was always ready to point out the glar-
ing inconsistency between Classical theory and Greco-Roman
practice, notably in the area of sexual morality, while acknowledging also that Christian practice often fell short of the ideal.

But in apologetics no less than in dogmatics, the admonition
of the moral imperative to "be weaned away from all experience
of evil," with which the *Catechetical Oration* of Gregory of
Nyssa concluded, was based on the affirmation of doctrine, with
which the *Catechetical Oration* began, "the need of a system of
instruction [ho tēs katēcheseōs logos]." The apologetic method
of pointing out parallels but also contrasts between Christianity
and Classical culture, and then of teasing out the truth in the
parallels, suited the doctrinal realm at least as well as it did the
ethical. Gregory of Nyssa, in a succinct passage of his *Life of*

Gr.Nyss.V.Mos.2
(Jaeger 7–I:44)

Gr.Nyss.V.Mos.2
(Jaeger 7–I:37)

Bas.Hex.3.9
(SC 26:236)

Moses, itemized several major doctrines to which he applied this method. It should not be surprising that he chose this venue, in the light of the place of Moses as an epitome of this very method of relating the profane and the sacred. But it is perhaps somewhat suprising that he should have done so by means of the allegorical method of exegesis, which his brother Basil denounced as "dreams and idle tales." He applied his allegory to the practice of circumcision, interpreting the "foreskin" as a symbol of the false notions that were attached to philosophy and must be cut away. Gregory enumerated four specific doctrines of Classical philosophy, sound in and of themselves, from each of which such a false notion needed to be removed. The Classical doctrine of the immortality of the soul was the first of these, which by this time was

See pp.131–34

as integral to Christian as it had been to Classical anthropology; but in Classical thought this doctrine had been intertwined with the mistaken idea of metempsychosis, which, as Macrina pointed out, recognized correctly that the immortal soul needed to be united to a body but incorrectly connected it to bodies other than

Macr.ap.Gr.Nyss.
Anim.res. (PG 46:108–9)

its own. The second doctrine in Gregory's catalog was the doctrine of God, which, however, as Gregory of Nazianzus also charged, was corrupted by the habit of "looking at visible things

Gr.Naz.Or.28.13
(SC 250:128)

and out of some of them making a god" who was material. Related to this was the doctrine of creation in Classical thought. Gregory of Nyssa apparently interpreted creation with Plato's *Timaeus* in view. For he gave the Classical philosophers credit for

See pp.95–97

affirming the doctrine of creation but faulted them for failing to remove from this doctrine the mistaken notion of the coexistence of matter with God, and therefore for ending up with what he

Gr.Nyss.Hom.opif.23
(PG 44:212)

called elsewhere a theory of "two eternal and unbegotten existences, having their being concurrently with each other." The fourth and final doctrine in Gregory's list was the doctrine of a good and powerful divine providence, which Classical thought at its best shared with Christian theology, at least in some measure, but which was vitiated when equated with "the *ananke* of

See pp.155–58

heimarmene."

Bas.Eun.2.22
(SC 305:88)

Because it was, as Basil called it, "the chief dogma" of the Christian faith, the Nicene dogma of the Trinity occupied a special position in Christian theology, and particularly in the positive doctrinal theology of the Cappadocians. Therefore, it is to be expected that it should have had such a position also in their natural theology as apologetics. Gregory of Nyssa seemed almost to be going out of his way to interpret it that way when he declared that the orthodox doctrine of the Trinity passed "in the

Gr.Nyss.Or.catech.3.2
(Méridier 18–20)

See pp.244–47

Gr.Naz.Or.31.10
(SC 250:294)

Gr.Nyss.Tres dii
(Jaeger 3–I:38)

Bas.Ep.38.5
(Courtonne 1:89)

Gr.Naz.Or.31.5
(SC 250:282–84)

Gr.Naz.Or.31.11
(SC 250:294–96)
Hom.Il.15.189

Gr.Naz.Or.31.16
(SC 250:306)

Bernardi 1968

Bas.Eun.1.2
(SC 299:148)

See pp.17–19

middle between the two conceptions [of polytheism and of un-differentiated unity], destroying each heresy and yet accepting everything useful from each." The natural theology at work in this statement of trinitarian doctrine will claim our close attention later, but already here it suggests how dogmatics and apologetics interacted in the Cappadocian system. A sensitivity to the limitations of the argument from analogy prompted each Cappadocian to be cautious about "taking from things below a guess at things above," but it certainly did not paralyze them in their speculative and apologetic enterprise. A reading of the doctrine of the Trinity that would end up preserving the Three by asserting that there were "three gods" would be, according to Gregory of Nyssa, "blasphemous [athemiton]," whereas a reading that preserved the One by denying divinity to the Son and the Holy Spirit would be at one and the same time "irreligious and absurd [a-sebes te kai atopon]," which it would seem to be acceptable to paraphrase as: contrary both to revealed theology and to natural theology. There were natural phenomena, such as the rainbow, which showed that "speaking of the same thing as being both conjoined and parted," as the orthodox dogma of the Trinity did in speaking about God, was not altogether unheard-of even apart from revelation. Similarly, there were some schools of thought among the Greeks, "those more inclined to speak of God and to approach nearest to us," where there was some anticipation of the orthodox doctrine of the Holy Spirit, which they had "addressed as the mind of the world, the external mind, and the like." Even for the Nicene homoousion there were some natural analogies, such as the consubstantiality of Adam, Eve, and Seth, which showed, howsoever imperfectly, that those with a different individual being could nevertheless be homoousios. When Homer spoke of "all things being divided thrice," this, too, could perhaps be seen as an anticipation, albeit dim, of the Christian doctrine of the Trinity.

These various themes indicate that the Cappadocians had in mind several overlapping but distinct audiences to whom they were addressing their apologetics, and therefore several distinct uses to which they intended to put their apologetics. For it was not only truth but also heresy that could set forth an "apologia." Therefore, when the Cappadocians referred in a single phrase to "the heathen and the heretical systems of belief about God," they were expressing not only their oft-expressed opinion that the false teachings of the heretics were the result also of the corrosive influence of alien philosophy and belief, but a sense of strategy

Gr.Nyss.*Cant.*13
(Jaeger 6:376)

corresponding to that belief, that the same apologetic argument could apply to such false teachings, whether they appeared in their original "heathen [ethnikos]" form or in their borrowed "heretical [hairetikos]" form. In that polemical-apologetic lumping together of "the heathen and the heretical systems of belief about God," they were at the same time quite aware of the differences between the two. It was, no doubt, sarcasm when Gregory of Nyssa credited Eunomius with "an extraordinary amount of research into the oracles of God" and an "extreme devotion to the inspired Scriptures," as he made clear when he also denounced him for "openly impugning the words of the inspired testimony." Such language was nevertheless a recognition that with a "heretic," but not with a "heathen," the orthodox Cappadocians did share the acceptance of the formal authority of the Bible, regardless of what might have happened to that authority in the concrete exegetical practice of the heretic. They shared a Holy Scripture as well with Judaism, which they credited with having preserved it through the centuries leading up to Christ. The saying of Jesus to the Jews, "It is the Father who glorifies me, he of whom you say, 'He is our God,'" was proof that "Jews believe in God, who is our God, too." But the Cappadocians identified Judaism with certain heresies, as they identified Hellenism with others. Gregory of Nazianzus could even find parallels between various Christian heresies and "the three infirmities with regard to the doctrine of God—namely, atheism, Judaism, and polytheism—one of which was patronized by Sabellius the Libyan, another by Arius of Alexandria, and the third by some of the ultra-orthodox among us." He also described Judaism as a halfway house between Classical paganism and Christianity. At the same time, the Cappadocians represented the Christian message as an acceptance of what was correct in both Judaism and Classicism, coupled with an avoidance of the errors in each. Thus, they also bracketed "the Jew" and "the Greek," in order to draw a contrast between both of them and Christian worship of the true God. In addition to being the reiteration of arguments against Jewish teaching going back to the New Testament, this apologetic expressed the reluctant recognition by the Cappadocians of the continuing vitality of Judaism as still a serious religious and intellectual option alongside both Classicism and Christianity in the fourth-century Greek-speaking world of the Mediterranean.

Gr.Nyss.*Ref.*43
(Jaeger 2:329)

Gr.Nyss.*Eun.*2.444
(Jaeger 1:356)

Gr.Nyss.*Or.catech.*18.4–5
(Méridier 94–96)

Jn 8:54

Gr.Nyss.*Maced.*
(Jaeger 3–I:101)

Bas.*Spir.*30.77
(SC 17:524)

Gr.Naz.*Or.*2.37
(SC 247:136)
Gr.Naz.*Or.*31.25
(SC 250:324)

Gr.Nyss.*Or.catech.*3.2
(Méridier 20)
Gr.Naz.*Or.*11.6
(PG 35:840);
Bas.*Eun.*1.27;2.22
(SC 29:569;620)
Rom 2:17–3:31;
Gal 3:6–29

Wilken 1983,66–94

As it has often been, the task of the apologist in the theology of the Cappadocians was closely related to the tasks of the evangel-

Florovsky 3:163–70

ist and of the pastor. Reciting the standard objection to the doctrine of the incarnation, "Could [the *Logos*] not have remained in his transcendent and divine glory and saved humanity by a command, instead of taking such a tedious and circuitous route, submitting to a bodily nature, entering life through birth, passing through the various stages of development, finally tasting death, and so attaining his goal by the resurrection of his own body?" Gregory of Nyssa responded: "To such objections we must oppose the truth, so that those who are seriously searching for the rational basis of the mystery may find no obstacle in the way of the faith." A little later in the same treatise, Gregory suggested that "every objection of unbelievers [to para tōn apistōn hēmin prospheromenon]" would be removed if the Christian hope had already been transformed into sight. But "the fullness of the riches of God" was hidden, and therefore, the only way to meet those objections of the unbelievers was to "search out, as far as possible, some reasonable solution of the question posed"—namely, why salvation could not have been accomplished by a simple divine fiat. For it was not only from the mind of the unbelievers that these and similar "objections" proceeded but from the mind and heart of believers, and therefore the apologetic task addressed itself also to them. Writing a letter of consolation to a friend upon the "unendurable loss" of the death of a son, Basil invoked the standard example of the sufferings of Job, and he quoted the words of Job that have always been the recourse of believers in such grief, "The Lord gives and the Lord takes away." But he appealed as well to "the gift stored by God in our hearts, namely, sober reason [ton logismon sōphrona], to draw lines of limitation around our souls in our happy days, and, in the time of troubles, to recall the limitations of our humanity to our minds." And he reminded his friend of "God's supreme command," that because of their hope in the resurrection, believers in Christ were not to grieve over those who fell asleep in death. It was an echo of the methodology being employed here by Basil when Gregory of Nazianzus described "the commission to guide and govern souls" as the "one branch of philosophy" that he found to be "too high."

So comfortable a correlation between revelation and reason in pastoral counsel about how to ponder the hope of the resurrection indicated what the Cappadocians thought a sound and complete understanding ought to be able to do, were it not impeded simultaneously by the divine "mystery" of which the Scripture spoke and the human "objections" to which the unbelievers

Gr.Nyss.*Or.catech.*15.4
(Méridier 80)

Gr.Nyss.*Or.catech.*17.3
(Méridier 92)

Gr.Nyss.*V.Macr.*
(Jaeger 8–I:390)

Gregg 1975,219–64

Jb 1:21

Aug.*Civ.*1.10
(CCSL 47:11)

1 Thes 4:13

Bas.*Ep.*5.1–2
(Courtonne 1:16–18)

See p.181
Gr.Naz.*Or.*2.78
(SC 247:192)

Macr.ap.Gr.Nyss.
Anim.res. (PG 46:145–
48)

Bas.Hex.3.7
(SC 26:224)

Bas.Hex.3.5
(SC 26:212)

pointed. It was in response to an entire battery of such objections specifically against the hope of the resurrection, enumerated in the course of the dialogue, that Macrina on her deathbed, in *On the Soul and the Resurrection,* formulated it as "our duty not to leave the arguments brought against us in any way unexamined," and then proceeded to examine them. But in taking on such arguments and objections, the interpreters of the faith sought to relate themselves not to those "masters of omniscience" among the unbelieving who had nothing to learn, but rather to "those with the most cultivated minds, and with piercing eyes to penetrate this perishable and fleeting nature." For those were the ones truly prepared for the most authentic kind of natural theology as apologetics, a natural theology that did not, as the "masters of omniscience" did, claim to understand the mystery of the divine nature and to make affirmative statements about it by "comparing the eternal things with the perishing things of time," but one that had learned instead "to proceed on the principle of opposites [ek tōn enantiōn]," saying: "Since thus and so is the mortal, not thus and so is the One who is immortal," invoking the *apophatic* language of negation, which was the proper language of transcendence. At that level and by that method, faith and reason were mutually complementary, and faith was confirmed by reason.

Bas.Ep.52.3
(Courtonne 1:136)

Gr.Nyss.Cant.15
(Jaeger 6:460)

Diekamp 1896,18–26
Gr.Nyss.Or.catech.15.4
(Méridier 80)

Gr.Nyss.Eun.1.315
(Jaeger 1:120)

Gr.Nyss.Paup.1
(Van Heck 13)

Sometimes reason spoke in such a way as to state "the rational basis of our religion" for the sake of those who were "seriously searching for the rational basis of the mystery": this was what we are calling here "natural theology as apologetics." At other times it was "our reason, under the guidance of the Scripture" or "reason, the interpreter and instructor in divine matters [ton noun tōn theiōn hermenea kai paideutēn]" that spoke: this was what we are calling here "natural theology as presupposition." Although it was possible to contrast the two kinds of theology, as Basil sometimes did, by dismissing the first as "the vanity of outsiders for those on the outside" and then going on to describe the second as "the theme proper to the church [ton ekklēsiastikon logon]," such a contrast was ultimately unfair to both; and Basil knew that it was, for in other places he was quite willing to go a long way in drawing parallels between the natural and supernatural realms. Macrina appeared to be speaking in a similarly disparaging tone when she attributed to the adherents of pagan philosophical thought "the license of affirming" whatever they pleased, a license to which Christians were not entitled,

Malingrey 1961,212–13

Bas.Hex.3.3
(SC 26:202)

Bas.Ep.38.3
(Courtonne 1:82–84)

because for them "the Holy Scriptures" stood as "the rule and the measure of every tenet." Yet in the actual presentation of her argument, as her brother and interlocutor told her, her "exposition, advancing in this consecutive manner, though plain and unvarnished," had, without any explicit reference to revelation, borne "the stamp of correctness" and had "hit the truth, by employing the technical methods of proof and demonstration." Gregory of Nazianzus drew the contrast in a manner that was both fair and balanced when he distinguished between "truths given to faith alone and truths given also to reasonings [tina men tēi pistei doteon monēi, tina de kai tois logismois]." As has been observed, "He does use a type of natural theology, but only on an ad hoc basis. He does not employ it as an overarching apologetic that operates without faith."

Yet of the four Cappadocians, it was, as might have been expected, Gregory of Nyssa who—more than Basil, Gregory of Nazianzus, or Macrina—repeatedly made explicit the congruence between natural theology as apologetics and natural theology as presupposition, arguing that in a proper statement of orthodox doctrine—in this case the doctrine of the Trinity—there would be a harmony with the presupposed truths to which a rational theology could also attain: "If someone keeps steadfast to the sound doctrine, and believes that the Son is of the nature that is divine without admixture, everything will be seen to be in harmony with the rest of the truths of religion, namely, that the Lord is the Maker of all things, and is king of the universe, not set above it by an arbitrary act of capricious power, but ruling by virtue of a superior nature," all of these latter "truths of religion" being truths of Christian revelation, but also in some sense first principles of rational, natural theology. Athanasius of Alexandria, whom Gregory of Nazianzus celebrated in one of his most eloquent panegyrics, composed, apparently while in his twenties, the treatises *Against the Heathen* and *On the Incarnation of the Logos*. As Johannes Quasten has pointed out, these two brief treatises were "in reality two parts of a single work," the first an exercise in apologetic theology and the second an exercise in systematic theology. In fact, the points that Athanasius had set forth as conclusions in the apologetics of the first went on to become presuppositions to help shape the systematics of the second. Almost a century earlier, a similar complementarity between apologetic theology and systematic theology had manifested itself, though on a far grander scale, in Origen's two spec-

Macr.ap.Gr.Nyss.
Anim.res. (PG 46:64)

Gr.Nyss.*Anim.res.*
(PG 46:64)

Gr.Naz.*Or.*22.11
(SC 270:242)

Norris 1991,127–28

Gr.Nyss.*Eun.*1.530
(Jaeger 1:179)

Gr.Naz.*Or.*21
(SC 270:110–92)

Quasten 3:24–26

Camelot 1947,7–106;
Bernard 1952,71–83

ulative masterpieces, *Contra Celsum* and *On First Principles*. Much the same was true of the natural theology of the Cappadocians.

Part I of this book, therefore, examines the chief components of "Natural Theology as Apologetics," and Part II then reviews the same themes under the rubric of "Natural Theology as Presupposition." As a consequence of this parallelism, each chapter bears a relation not only to what immediately precedes and follows it within Part I or Part II but to the corresponding chapter in the other part of the exposition, and the two chapters may profitably be considered together. The distinction between Parts I and II is in keeping with Nazianzen's distinction between "establishing one's own position [to oikeion kataskeuazein]" and "refuting the opposing case [to antipalon anatrepein]." Nazianzen followed the sequence of "expounding our own, before refuting our opponents' arguments"; but the exposition of the Cappadocian system in this book, like that of Nyssen against Eunomius, begins with the Cappadocians' "refutation [anatropē]" of opposing views and then follows this with, in his words, "a dogmatic exposition of our own teaching [ekthesis tōn hēmeterōn dogmatōn]." What the subtitle of the entire book is calling "the *metamorphosis* of natural theology" is to be seen in the subtle and complex interactions of this natural theology as apologetics with this natural theology as presupposition. For in the Classical systems, natural theology tended to present itself primarily as an alternative—or even as an antidote—to the cultic practices and sacred narratives of traditional religious observance. Its principal expositors were not the official spokesmen for traditional observance, nor the priests of the cult, but lay philosophers and apologists, and sometimes opponents and critics who were skeptics or agnostics or even atheists.

But at the hands of such thinkers as the Cappadocians—who were philosophers and apologists and yet at the same time priests and prelates, but neither opponents nor critics of the orthodox cult—natural theology underwent a fundamental *metamorphosis*. It became not only an apologetic but a presupposition for systematic, dogmatic theology. How well natural theology fared in such a *metamorphosis* is a serious historical and theological-philosophical question. At least as serious, at any rate for Christian theology, is the question of how the gospel and the dogma fared in the process. For it can be—and has repeatedly been—argued that the concessions and adjustments to the natural theology of Greek culture made in the name of apologetics came back

Gr.Naz.*Or*.29.1
(*SC* 250:178)

Gr.Nyss.*Ep*.29.9
(Jaeger 8–II:89)

Hatch 1957

to haunt the church's doctrines in their positive formulations. To put the crucial question in the Cappadocians' own language: How was divine *apatheia* as impassibility, which was known also to natural theology, related to the divine "begetting [gennēsis]" of the Son by the Father, which was known only to revealed theology—and which did sound very much like an instance of divine passibility? In the apologetics against the gods of Olympus, the central point of the argument was that the divine nature, as rational analysis could also discover, was passionless and incapable of suffering (*apathes*), so that the human, all too human, passions of these so-called gods were a blasphemy. But what happened to that doctrine of the *apatheia* of the divine nature when the apologetics became in turn the presupposition for the interpretation of a message whose central figure—as was affirmed in the creed adopted at the Council of Nicaea in 325 and then in the creed adopted in 381 by the Council of Constantinople (during which Gregory of Nazianzus was chosen to be bishop of Constantinople)—was "God out of God, light out of light, true God out of true God, begotten not made [gennēthenta ou poiēthenta], who was crucified also for us under Pontius Pilate and who suffered," so that it was, in Basil's words, through the suffering of the one who was *apathes* that the gift of *apatheia* was conferred on passible mortals?

Bas.*Eun.*2.22
(*SC* 305:92)

Symb.Nic.-CP
(Alberigo-Jedin 24)

Bas.*Spir.*8.18
(*SC* 17:308)

CHAPTER 3

The Language of Negation

Owen 1925,64–71

Gottwald 1906,45–47

One of the most important measures both of the continuity and of the change that took place in the transition from Classical culture to the dominance of Christian theology is to be found in the history of the Greek language itself, especially of its vocabulary for rational and natural theology. Thus, of the 1,568 pages in the Lampe *Lexicon of Patristic Greek,* 281 pages, or 18 percent, are given over to the letter alpha, while in the Liddell-Scott-Jones *Greek-English Lexicon,* the ratio, though still remarkably high considering the number of letters in the Greek alphabet, is significantly lower, 300 of 2,042, or 15 percent. Such statistical comparisons are, of course, always crude and often misleading. Nevertheless, this one may be taken as an index not only to the preponderance in all Greek, whether Classical or Patristic, of prefixes derived from such prepositions as "anti" and "apo" but to the function of the letter alpha, the so-called alpha privative, as a prefix of negation; and without wishing to draw too fine a point on it, one may take it as an indication of a reliance on the negative prefix in Patristic Greek that was perhaps even greater than it had been in Classical Greek, as it was greater in Greek Christian

Armstrong 1985,78

thought than in Latin Christian thought. The Cappadocians were acutely conscious of the alpha privative also as a grammatical and lexicographical phenomenon. It was, Gregory of Nyssa declared, "plain to everyone at all acquainted with the use of words" that words formed on the alpha privative denoted "the absence of noninherent qualities rather than the presence of inherent qualities." As examples of such adjectives, he cited:

40

"harmless, painless, guileless, undisturbed, passionless, sleepless, undiseased, impassible, blameless, and others like these [to akakon kai alypon kai aponēron kai atacharon kai aorgēton aypnon anoson apathes anepilēpton kai hosa toiauta]." When they pertained to the divine nature, he continued, such terms taught "under what conditions [it was permissible to] conceive of God as existing." But they did not inform mortals about "the being of God essentially." Or, in the formula of Gregory of Nazianzus, drawing on a concept with a long tradition in Greek philosophy, the only thing that could be comprehended about the incomprehensible divine nature was its "boundlessness [apeiria]," what it was not rather than what it was.

Such an abdication of the desire to know, which Aristotle in the opening sentence of the *Metaphysics* had called a universal trait common to all humanity, seemed to fly in the face of the entire tradition of Greek intellectualism, in which the Cappadocians, too, were so thoroughly steeped. According to Eunomius, their principal opponent, it seemed to be evidence of sheer ignorance to maintain that "definitions of the terms expressive of things spiritual" were an impossibility for human beings. In response to that criticism, the Cappadocians sometimes spoke as though definition by negation, or *apophasis,* and definition by affirmation, or *cataphasis,* were somehow two interchangeable ways of saying the same thing, so that there would be no intrinsic difference between speaking about "goodness" and speaking about "the absence of evil." But when they came down to specifying their position more strictly, such interchangeability proved illusory. The question, "The soul is not material, but what is it positively?" gave the impression that there could be a positive definition by inclusion, corresponding to the negative definition by exclusion. But in fact the nature of the soul was an apt illustration of the general rule: "We learn much about many things by this same method, for by the sheer act of saying that a thing is 'not so and so,' we by implication interpret the very nature of the thing in question." As that method was applicable to the soul, and in some sense even to the material world, so, when "the thing in question" was not this thing or that thing—in fact, not any "thing" at all—but ultimate reality and pure being itself, it behooved anyone who wanted to think and speak clearly to resort to the language of negation, heaping up negative terms like "not ['ou' or 'mē']" and alpha privatives to eliminate from consideration everything that being was not. Against any and all "fabulous imaginations," then, natural theology was in the first in-

Gr.Nyss.*Eun.*2.142–44 (Jaeger 1:266–67)

Tumarkin 1943,55–71

Gr.Naz.*Or.*38.7 (*PG* 36:317)

Arist.*Met.*980a

Stritzky 1973,79–83

Eun.ap.Gr.Nyss. *Eun.* 3.7.15 (Jaeger 2:220)

Gr.Nyss.*Eun.*2.133–34 (Jaeger 1:264)

Macr.ap.Gr.Nyss. *Anim.res.* (*PG* 46:40)

Gr.Nyss.*Cant.*12 (Jaeger 6:357); Gr.Nyss.*Eun.*1.365–69 (Jaeger 1:135–36)

Bas.*Hex.*2.2
(SC 26:148)

Gr.Nyss.*Cant.*12
(Jaeger 6:358)

Gr.Nyss.*Eun.*2.79
(Jaeger 1:250)

Bas.*Hex.*2.2
(SC 26:148)

Bas.*Eun.*2.9
(SC 305:36)
Gr.Nyss.*V.Mos.*2
(Jaeger 7–1:92)

Bas.*Ep.*7
(Courtonne 1:22)

Bas.*Hex.*2.1
(SC 26:138)

Gn 1:3

Gr.Nyss.*Eun.*2.246
(Jaeger 1:298)

Bas.*Eun.*2.4
(SC 305:22)

Ps 18:4

Gr.Nyss.*Eun.*2.220–21
(Jaeger 1:289)

Mt 3:17;17:5

Gr.Nyss.*Eun.*2.247–48
(Jaeger 1:298)

stance negative theology: its subject matter was, as Basil of Caesarea put it in a lapidary formula, "inexpressible by the human voice," and it was "incomprehensible to human reason"; it was outside every linguistic system of meaning, and it was outside the analytic and reflective powers of the rational soul. Negative theology was indispensable, because resorting to either language or thought in hopes of comprehending the Incomprehensible was like playing a children's game and deluding oneself into imagining that the fantasy was for real.

Because the subject matter of theology was, in Basil's phrase, "inexpressible by the human voice," *apophatic* theology was a theory of language. It was possible to apply to it the distinction formulated by the Classical grammarians, according to which some words were "absolute [apolelymena] and apart from relation," while others were "expressive of some relationship [pros hetera legomena]," and the Cappadocians did invoke this distinction. But the distinction appeared to promise a greater measure of "precise meaning" than it could actually deliver. For this was a universal axiom, which the Cappadocians could take for granted in their discussions with one another: "Our thought is weak, but our tongue is still weaker than our thought." Even in coping with created realities, human language was "powerless to express the conceptions formed by the mind." It was fatuous, indeed blasphemous, to suppose that because, according to the opening verses of the Bible, "God said, 'Let there be light,'" there had to be a divine language, Greek or even Hebrew, which human hearing could understand and, in understanding it, could use as a means to understand God. Languages, including Greek and even Hebrew, were a product of historical development and of national character, not of direct divine invention. Things came first, and these were created by God; but the names for things had developed afterward, through human history. The words of the psalm, "without speech or language or sound of any voice," implied, according to Gregory of Nyssa, "words without sound [aphthongon], and declaration without language [alalon], and announcement without voice." In those historical situations, such as the baptism of Christ or his *metamorphosis*-transfiguration, where God had been heard to speak and had been understood by human ears, the speaking, whatever its language, had been "accommodated to the language of the day," but this language was not to be regarded as the native tongue of the Almighty. Not even for the language of Holy Scripture, unques-

See p.220
Gr.Nyss.*Eun*.2.265
(Jaeger 1:303–4)

Bas.*Spir*.4.6
(SC 17:268)

Bas.*Eun*.2.7
(SC 305:30)

Bas.*Spir*.6.13
(SC 17:288)

1 Cor 1:20;
Bas.*Spir*.17.41
(SC 17:392)

Bas.*Ep*.125
(Courtonne 2:30–34)

DTC 14:1786–90

Gr.Naz.*Or*.21.22
(SC 270:156)

Bas.*Spir*.1.2
(SC 17:252)

tionable though its divine inspiration was for all the Cappadocians, was it legitimate to make any such claim, but this language, too, had been recorded and written "after human fashion." It was evident from the sacred text itself, moreover, that in its vocabulary for making these declarations that went beyond language, inspired Scripture had "varied its expressions as required by the occasion, according to the circumstances of the case."

The sensitivity of the Cappadocians to the historical relativity and semantic ambiguity inherent in all language was responsible for a certain amount of apparent equivocation on their part about whether the orthodox Christian theology of the church had the right to make use of phraseology that had been derived from such historical development, for example—to cite the example that was the most crucial one for the purposes of the present inquiry—from the development of Greek philosophical terminology. Sometimes they could seem to urge that theology had to stick to the terminology of Scripture, and they could, for example, laud the translators of the Septuagint for not having rendered into Greek words, but only having transliterated into Greek letters, such Hebrew terms as "Sabaoth." When they took that biblicist position, they could speak disparagingly of a "technical terminology" that heretics had foisted on unsuspecting believers to "subvert the simplicity and artlessness of the faith," and they rejected it as an element "from 'the wisdom of this world' smuggled into our language." Yet at the same time they could defend the Council of Nicaea for having introduced the *homoousion* into its very creed from outside Scripture—and, as they themselves had to acknowledge, from a heretical source at that, which made it in some sense even more highly suspect than a merely philosophical and pagan source would have. In this instance they were quite willing to construe such "technical terminology" as not merely licit but orthodox. Accordingly, they denounced the formula substituted for the *homoousion* by the Synod of Seleucia in 359, "similar, according to the Scriptures [homoion kata tas graphas]," as, despite its biblicist tone, an evasion intended to deceive the naive. But it was through their reliance on the language of negation that they were able to overcome this apparent inconsistency in their attitude toward language. On the one hand, they deemed it essential for anyone who professed theology "to count the terms used in theology as of primary importance, and to endeavor to trace out the hidden meaning in every phrase and in every syllable." Yet in the very

Gr.Nyss.*Eun.*1.539–40
(Jaeger 1:182–83)

Gr.Nyss.*Eun.*2.61
(Jaeger 1:243–44)

Bas.*Spir.*4.6
(SC 17:270)

Gr.Naz.*Or.*37.4
(SC 318:278)

Jn 1:1–14

See pp.103–4
Gr.Nyss.*Eun.*3.2.17
(Jaeger 2:57);
Bas.*Spir.*6.14
(SC 17:290)

Gr.Nyss.*Eun.*3.2.17
(Jaeger 2:57)

Bjerge-Aspergen 1977

Gr.Nyss.*Eun.*3.1.23
(Jaeger 2:11)

process of doing this, negative theology served as a protection against any pettifoggery about theological terminology that would have equated orthodoxy with the right language rather than with the correct belief and thought, lying within and beneath the language and expressed as well as possible—which was in fact never very well at all, even at best, because the thought was no match for the reality and the language in turn was no match for the thought. All language about the divine was inadequate, not only the language that followed "heathen example" but also the language of "apostolic usage," not only pagan language but scriptural language, not only heretical language but orthodox language. "But having no other words to employ, we employ what we have," they said resignedly, protecting such words against blasphemous distortion by means of negation (expressed here by introducing the Classical rhetorical figure of chiasmus): "Thou art called *Logos,* and thou art above *logos;* thou art above light, yet art named light."

These two, *Logos* and light, were, along with the trinitarian metaphor of Father and Son as invoked in the language of the baptismal formula, central metaphors employed by the church in its language about the relation between the first and the second *hypostasis* of the Trinity: *Logos* was the key title in the prologue of the Gospel of John, "light out of light" a key title in the Nicene Creed. In fact, both terms did appear in the prologue of John, which, for reasons about which the Cappadocians sometimes speculated, did not, however, include the metaphor "Son of God"; on the other hand, *Logos* did not appear in the Nicene Creed, whereas "Son of God" did. Both *Logos* and light illustrated very effectively how indispensable metaphorical and analogical language could be and yet how fraught with danger it was, and therefore how indispensable the methodological function of negation was in controlling metaphor and analogy. An analogy or a metaphor was in this respect like a proverb: "A form of speech which, by means of one set of ideas immediately presented, points to something else, which is hidden, or a form of speech that does not point out the aim of the thought directly, but gives its instruction by an indirect signification [kata to loxon tēn didaskalian poioumenon dia plagias emphaseōs]." Thus, Cappadocian orthodoxy could press the analogy of *logos* as word to argue that if even a human word was generated from the mind without incurring a division between mind and word, this had to be true in a preeminent manner and degree of the mysterious

Gr.Nyss.*Ref.*58
(Jaeger 2:335)

Bas.*Spir.*6.15
(*SC* 17:290)

Gr.Nyss.*Eun.*1.300–301
(Jaeger 1:115)

Bas.*Spir.*9.22
(*SC* 17:322)

Gr.Nyss.*Eun.*1.645
(Jaeger 1:211–12)
Arist.*Cat.*1b;
Arist.*Met.*1007a
Bas.*Spir.*17.41
(*SC* 17:394)

Gr.Nyss.*V.Mos.*1
(Jaeger 7–1:22)

Gr.Nyss.*Eun.*3.6.15
(Jaeger 2:191)

Scheve 1943

process by which the Son as the divine Word was generated from the Father as the divine Mind in the undivided Trinity. The root metaphor of Father and Son, in turn, was not to be used to imply "a kind of degradation of the Son in relation to the Father, as though the Son were in a lower place" and on a lower throne than the Father. "What could the 'throne' of the immaterial, incomprehensible, and formless Deity be anyway?" the language of negation could ask, answering that clearly these were "metaphors [ainigmata], containing a meaning deeper than the obvious one."

There were also some terms which, although they were *cataphatic* in etymology and in their grammatical form, nevertheless conveyed unmistakably *apophatic* connotations. Without itself being cast in the form of an alpha privative, for example, the sublime name of the Holy Spirit immediately called to mind an entire chain of them: "incorporeal, purely immaterial, and indivisible . . . infinite in power, unlimited, unmeasured by times or *aeons* [pantos tou asōmatou kai katharōs aylou te kai amerous . . . apeiron kata dynamin, megethei aperioriston, chronois ē aiōsin ametrēton]." Regardless of whether they were *cataphatic* or *apophatic* grammatically, the names used for God, also in the language of Scripture and of the church, referred to qualities and attributes that it would be blasphemous to predicate of the eternal one in a positive or literal sense. The doctrine of predication, familiar from the textbooks of Greek logic to everyone with a Classical education, simply did not apply to "the God of the universe." To protect themselves against distortion, whether accidental or deliberate, any "proper conceptions about the divine nature," therefore, needed to begin from the fundamental premise that the divine nature was "unlike anything known" that might be used in speaking about it.

On the basis of this *apophatic* theory of language, it was clear that there was not, and could not be, a perfectly adequate analogy for God. It was, according to Gregory of Nyssa writing against Eunomius, impossible to "find among existing things a likeness of the object of our inquiry, sufficient in all respects for the presentation of the matter in hand by way of some kind of analogy and resemblance." Earlier in the same polemical work, however, he had accorded a more favorable treatment to analogy, as part of a discussion of the problem of theological method. In that discussion he not only warned, "Even if it were possible to draw an analogy for this from created things, such conjecturing about the transcendent from lower existences would not be altogether sound"; but then he immediately conceded, "The error of arguing from natural phenomena to the incomprehensible might be pardonable" if one observed the proper *apophatic* limitations. It was legitimate to employ "understandable examples, in order to form some sort of proper conception," provided that such an illustration was not pressed beyond an appropriate point. For, in the formula already quoted from Gregory of Nazianzus, having no other words to employ, they employed what they had, always remembering that even while it was being employed, all language continued to be inadequate and that therefore there was an obligation to hedge it in by the appropriate *apophatic* specifiers.

Basil's insistence that the truth about the divine nature was and remained "inexpressible by the human voice" applied no less strictly also to the language of morality and of religion. It was self-evident that it would be altogether illegitimate to construct a theory about "the immutability of the divine nature" that would be based, after the manner of pagan myth, on "the human propensity to vice"; for there was no "common ground to the peculiar nature of human life and the peculiar nature of divine life, their distinctive properties standing entirely apart from each other." Such a word as "divergence [parallagē]," when proposed as a technical term in trinitarian dogmatics, carried already in Classical Greek too many of the connotations of "divergence from *arete*" to be admissible into the vocabulary of theological discourse concerning the distinction between the Father and the Son within the divine nature. When the relation between master and slave was under consideration as an analogical device to preserve the sovereignty of God the Father by describing the Holy Spirit as "doulos [servant or slave]," that provided the occasion for repudiating any effort "to apply to the ineffable nature of God that common custom in human life of establishing differences of degree in society," but also for proving at considerable length that no one was a slave by nature within human society, and that this was infinitely less so within the Godhead.

But the restriction also struck down other analogies from structures of human society and morality that truly were natural— indeed, divinely ordained—and that were not a direct consequence of sin, as was slavery. Two such structures were government and marriage. Christ himself had spoken repeatedly about "the kingdom of God" and "the kingdom of heaven." But when he did so, he was pointing beyond all political and social structures to "ineffable" reality, "in order not to put it altogether

Gr.Nyss.*Eun.*1.213
(Jaeger 1:88)

Gr.Nyss.*Or.catech.*10.4
(Méridier 68)

Gr.Naz.*Or.*37.4
(SC 318:278)

Bas.*Hex.*2.2
(SC 26:148)

See pp.16–17,75–76

Gr.Nyss.*Eun.*3.2.10
(Jaeger 2:55)

Gr.Nyss.*Eun.*3.2.139
(Jaeger 2:97–98)

Bas.*Spir.*20.51
(SC 17:426–30)

Gr.Nyss.*Or.dom.*3
(PG 44:1156–61)

beyond the grasp of our imagination," even though its "proper name" was not available within human speech. A similar qualification attached also to "other names expressive of mutual relationship." Within human life and human society there were hierarchies of power and different gradations of honor, but those could not be used as analogies for the divine life. Again, not only was marriage a social structure, but it was also called a divine "mystery [mystērion]" (or "sacrament") in the New Testament—"mystērion" being the technical term in Patristic Greek for "sacrament"—and was in fact the only of the traditional "sacraments" of the church to have been so designated in the New Testament. It was divinely instituted, and the mutual love between bride and bridegroom was invoked as an analogy for the love between God and the soul or between Christ and the church in many parts of the Bible, preeminently in the Song of Songs, ascribed to King Solomon. Showing himself to be, here as elsewhere, the orthodox disciple of the learned and saintly but sometimes recklessly audacious Origen of Alexandria, Gregory of Nyssa devoted his longest biblical commentary to the Song, elaborating on its colorful nuptial imagery at length. Even more than other such analogies, however, this one needed to be explained carefully, in such a way as to protect the image of the divine nature and of its love for humanity from any connotations of the human sexual passions, just as the language of faith about the divine nature had to distance itself from the other connotations of gender. For it was an a priori principle of natural theology, which had to be acknowledged even by the most narrow-minded, that the divine and blessed nature was to be regarded as utterly free of passion: the principle of *apatheia*.

Still more than the language of morality, the language of religion, by its very subject matter and form, could and often did beguile the speaker into supposing that it was somehow exempt from any *apophatic* qualifiers and limitations and that it did not have to confess to being ignorant. Yet it was not only here on earth among the humble and material objects of sense experience but also, as the Psalm had said, "in the clouds," in the very objects of religious devotion and theological speculation, that there was none "to be compared unto the Lord"; for as Solomon admonished, "God is in heaven and you are on earth, so let your words be few." Thus, Solomon was a paradigm for a consecrated ignorance about God. When David had been "lifted by the power of the Spirit out of himself, to see in a blessed state of ecstasy the boundless and incomprehensible beauty," he had to exclaim, as

Gr.Nyss.*Beat*.2
(*PG* 44:1209)

Gr.Nyss.*Eun*.1.554
(Jaeger 1:186)

Gr.Nyss.*Eun*.1.334
(Jaeger 1:126)

Lampe 892–93

Eph 5:32

Matter 1990

Riedel 1898,66–74
Horn 1925,378–79

Gr.Nyss.*Hom.opif*.17
(*PG* 44:188)

See pp.87–89
Gr.Nyss.*Or.dom*.1
(*PG* 44:1132);
Gr.Nyss.*Eun*.1.418
(Jaeger 1:148)

Bas.*Eun*.3.6
(*SC* 305:166)

Ps 88:7

Eccl 5:1
Gr.Nyss.*Eun*.2.93–94
(Jaeger 1:254)
Gr.Naz.*Or*.20.5
(*SC* 270:266)

the Psalm put it (or at any rate as the Psalm put it in the Greek of the Septuagint), "I said in my ecstasy [en tēi ekstasei mou], 'All men are liars!'" This was taken to mean that those who entrusted to language the task of presenting the ineffable light were "liars, not because of any hatred on their part for the truth, but because of the feebleness of this instrument for expressing the very thing being thought of." Before David, Abraham had likewise been raised to the summit of sublime knowledge, so that God had even taken the name "'the God of Abraham,' as though God were a discovery of the patriarch." Yet concerning this "acme of human perfection" it was said in Scripture that at the divine command he "went away without knowing where he was to go."

After both Abraham and David, Paul in his own ecstasy put behind him the air and the stars and whatever else was perceptible to the senses. Nevertheless, even there, in "the third heaven," Basil's rule that ultimate reality was "inexpressible by the human voice" prevailed. For that "school above the heavens" was a place "of silence for every voice conveying meaning by verbal utterance, and of unspoken meditation as the word of instruction, teaching the purified heart, by means of the silent illumination of the thoughts, the truths transcending speech." Having been transported in rapture just as far as any human mind could go, and much further than any except a select few like Abraham, Moses, and David had ever been permitted to go, Paul still had to confess the limits both of knowledge and of speech in the comprehensive disclaimer: "Our knowledge and our prophecy alike are imperfect [ek merous]." In short, as Gregory of Nazianzus summarized the *apophatic* interpretation of Paul and of all other visionaries, using some of these same proof texts from the New Testament being cited by Gregory of Nyssa: "If it had been permitted to Paul to utter what the third heaven contained, and his own advance, or ascension, or assumption thither, perhaps we should know something more about God's nature, if this was the mystery of the rapture. But since it was ineffable, we will honor it by silence. This much we will hear Paul say about it, that 'our knowledge and our prophecy alike are imperfect.'" Even Paul, he had said in another oration, had to confess to seeing "only puzzling reflections in a mirror."

In yet another oration, Gregory of Nazianzus pressed this *apophatic* critique of the language of religion further still, to include the very term "God." He was inclined to follow some schools of Greek thought, both Classical and Christian, in deriv-

Ps 115:2

Gr.Nyss.*Virg.*10
(Jaeger 8–I:290)

Ex 3:6

Heb 11:8
Gr.Nyss.*Eun.*2.86–87
(Jaeger 1:252)

2 Cor 12:2–4

Bas.*Hex.*2.2
(SC 26:148)

Gr.Nyss.*Eun.*3.1.16
(Jaeger 2:9)

2 Cor 12:2–4;1 Cor 8:2;
Phil 3:13

1 Cor 13:9
Gr.Nyss.*Cant.*11
(Jaeger 6:326)

1 Cor 13:9
Gr.Naz.*Or.*28.20
(SC 250:140)
Gr.Naz.*Or.*20.12
(SC 270:82)

1 Cor 13:12

Gr.Naz.*Or*.30.18
(*SC* 250:262–64)

Gr.Nyss.*Tres dii*
(Jaeger 3–I:44)

Gr.Naz.*Or*.30.18
(*SC* 250:262–64)

See p.42

Gr.Nyss.*Eun*.1.568–71
(Jaeger 1:190–91)

Mt 28:19

See pp.211–12

Gr.Nyss.*Ref*.14–15
(Jaeger 2:318)
Bas.*Spir*.6.14
(*SC* 17:290)

Gr.Nyss.*Eun*.1.314
(Jaeger 1:120)

Eun.ap.Socr.*H.e*.4.7
(Hussey 2:482)

Gr.Naz.*Or*.29.11
(*SC* 250:200)

Gr.Nyss.*V.Mos*.2
(Jaeger 7–I:87)
Gr.Nyss.*Eun*.3.8.8
(Jaeger 2:241)
Jn 1:18;1 Tm 6:16;
Ex 33:20

Gr.Nyss.*Eun*.2.89
(Jaeger 1:252–53)

ing the Greek name for "god [theos]" from "theein [to run]" or from "aithein [to burn]." Gregory of Nyssa, in contrast, suggested: "Godhead [theotēs] is so called from 'thea [beholding],' and the one who is our 'theatēs [beholder],' by customary use and by the instruction of the Scriptures is called 'theos.' " But whatever its correct etymology might be, Gregory of Nazianzus insisted, even the word "God" was "still a relative name," not an "absolute" one. The category of "relative nouns" in Greek grammar, Gregory explained, included not only such obvious nouns of relationship for God as "Father" or "King," which necessarily implied the corollary "child" or "subject," but also the noun "God" itself and all other names for God. Even when commanding baptism "in the name of the Father and the Son and the Holy Spirit," Christ was not specifying "the actual term of signification indicated by the noun 'the name,' " but was referring to "the unnameable name." Thereby he "gave authority to apply alike to Father, Son, and Spirit whatever name could be discovered by human intelligence through the pious effort to indicate the transcendent nature." Behind or beyond this "name" that was not really a name at all, it was not possible to go.

By contrast, it was characteristic of "foes of the truth" to "rush in upon the ineffable." Such was, according to the fifth-century ecclesiastical historian Socrates Scholasticus, the presumptuous assertion of Eunomius, the principal opponent of the Cappadocians: "God does not know any more about his own essence than we do. None of it is known better to him than to us. But whatever we know about the divine *ousia*, that precisely is known to God; and on the other hand, whatever God knows, the same you will find without any difference in us." An "infatuation" like that presumed to define the divine *ousia*, in an enterprise that according to the Cappadocians might become possible, if indeed it ever would, only in the life everlasting. Therefore, when the language of religion, not only in natural theology but also in Christian revealed theology, spoke about "seeing God," what it really meant was the very opposite, that God could not be seen. That was evident not only from paganism but also from the Scriptures, which repeatedly denied the possibility of seeing God. It was evident as well from the lives of the greatest saints and seers, who, "beyond every conjecture regarding the divine nature suggested by any name among all our conceptions of God," found only one "sure and manifest token of the knowledge of God, namely, the belief in a God greater and more sublime than any token of divine knowledge."

When it set forth this theory of language, *apophatic* theology could be read as though it were nothing more than an elaboration of the semiotic doctrine that all language was, in the words of Basil of Caesarea, "by natural necessity too weak to act in the service of objects of thought," which could in turn be taken to imply that although human language could not encompass ultimate reality, human thought could do so. Elsewhere, however, Basil made clear his position not only that ultimate reality was "inexpressible by the human voice" but that it was at the same time "incomprehensible to human reason." *Apophasis* represented a critique not only of all language, including religious, mystical, and theological language, but also of all thought, including philosophical, metaphysical, and theological thought. Gregory of Nyssa described how, "when from the sublime words of the Lord resembling the summit of a mountain [he had] looked down into the ineffable depths of the Lord's thoughts," his mind had experienced the vertigo of "someone gazing from a high ridge into the immense sea below." It was "impossible for words to mount along with thought"; but even apart from words, "upon having reached the highest limit of the human faculties, the utmost height and magnificence of idea ever attainable by the mind," it was necessary for the seer or visionary to believe that this, too, was far below the glory belonging to God. And therefore, when Gregory of Nazianzus asked, "On what subjects and to what extent may we philosophize?" his answer was: "Only on matters within our grasp," which obviously did not include the divine *ousia*. Accepting those limitations of human reason, functioning within them, and not allowing the reach of reason to exceed its grasp was not a sacrifice of the intellect, nor an abdication of the rational philosophical enterprise. Rather, "quietly remaining within our proper limits" was not only "more reverent" religiously; it was also "safer" and ultimately more productive philosophically, because "believing the majesty of God to be greater than any understanding of it" protected the philosophical reason from "supposing that after having circumscribed the divine glory by misconceptions," there was nothing beyond those misconceptions. By its use of alpha privatives for the Deity, terms such as "boundless and limitless and formless and impalpable and invisible [apeiron kai aoriston kai aschēmatiston kai anaphes kai aoraton]," *apophatic* theology challenged anyone who was tempted to boast of being "the greatest of human philosophers and the best of theologians" to accept the boundaries within which alone reason could be relied upon to speculate.

Bas.*Ep.*7
(Courtonne 1:21–22)

Bas.*Hex.*2.2
(SC 26:148)

Gr.Nyss.*Beat.*6
(PG 44:1264)

Gr.Nyss.*Maced.*
(Jaeger 3–I:107)

Gr.Naz.*Or.*27.3
(SC 250:78)

Gr.Nyss.*Eun.*2.96
(Jaeger 1:254)

Kannengiesser 1967,
55–65

Gr.Naz.*Or.*28.7
(SC 250:112–14)

Meyendorff 11–12

See pp.115–16
See pp.92–95

Underlying these differences of both doctrine and method in the treatment of negative theology was a fundamental difference about why it was necessary at all to resort to the language of negation. Was it because of the fall into sin that human language about the holy God now had to be negative, or was it because of the metaphysical chasm between the infinite one and all things finite, the Creator and the creature, that human language about the transcendent God would have been obliged to resort to negation even had sin not come along to corrupt the human soul? The position of Eunomius against which the Cappadocians were contending attributed the necessity for negative theology—if indeed negative theology was necessary—primarily to sin. "It by no means follows," they quoted him as declaring, "that if someone's mind, blinded by intellectual malignity and for that reason unable to see anything in front of or above its head, is but moderately competent for the apprehension of truth, we ought on that

Eun.ap.Gr.Nyss. *Eun.*
3.8.1 (Jaeger 2:238)

ground to think that the discovery of reality is unattainable by the rest of humanity." According to this diagnosis, the limitation under which the human mind labored, or under which at any rate the minds of some human beings labored, was the consequence of "intellectual malignity [kakonoia]." Yet even those who suffered from this, although they were "blinded," were to be described as "but moderately competent for the apprehension of truth," less competent than they should have been by nature but somewhat competent nevertheless. Still, the main point of the argument was that this "moderate competence" and "blindness," being the result of their "intellectual malignity" and sin rather than of their creaturehood and finiteness, was not to be ascribed to others who were not afflicted similarly, or any rate not afflicted to the same degree. Therefore, it was utterly unwarranted to conclude from this unfortunate state that the discovery of reality, including above all the reality of God, was unattainable by the rest of humanity.

See pp.259–62

As the Cappadocians made clear at considerable length also in their doctrine of angels, they believed that it was metaphysically naive and theologically shallow to interpret the transcendence of God in this way. The holy angels, as distinguished from the devil

Bas.*Spir.*16.38
(SC 17:376)

and the other fallen angels, had not been blinded by intellectual malignity or by any other evil. In vision and intellectual acuity, as well as in sheer power, they far exceeded any creatures of flesh and blood. But by confessing in its opening sentence that God was "Maker of all things, both of those that are visible and of those that are invisible [pantōn horatōn te kai aoratōn poiētēn],"

Symb.Nic.
(Alberigo-Jedin 5)
Symb.Nic.-CP
(Alberigo-Jedin 24)

the Nicene Creed—both in the form originally adopted at the Council of Nicaea in 325, and then in the form adopted at the Council of Constantinople in 381—drew the ontological line of the ultimate division here: between the one transcendent Creator God on one side and, on the other side, all creatures, whether visible (as human bodies, insects, and stones were) or invisible (as angels, human souls, and Platonic forms were).

This was, according to Cappadocian thought, the only way to confess the total transcendence of God the Creator over all creatures, whether visible or invisible, rational or irrational, holy or sinful. In this the Nicene Creed was following the precedent of the apostle Paul, who had put all spiritual beings, including angels, into the category of creatures, as distinguished from God in Christ: "I am convinced that there is nothing in death or life, in the realm of spirits or superhuman powers, in the world as it is or the world as it shall be, in the forces of the universe, in heights or depths—nothing in all creation that can separate us from the love of God in Christ Jesus our Lord." And when Paul spoke elsewhere about "the peace of God, which is beyond all understanding," as the Revised English Bible translates "panta noun hyperechousa," this did not mean merely "beyond our understanding," as the Jerusalem Bible renders it, nor even "beyond our utmost understanding," as the New English Bible has it, but beyond "all understanding," whether human or angelic or satanic. That was how Gregory of Nyssa interpreted the verse: "beyond the reach not only of the human but of the angelic and of all supracosmic intelligence." Thus he connected "all understanding [panta noun]" to "all beings [panta ta onta]." For it was the divine *ousia* itself to which the attribute of "surpassing all understanding" was most properly applied. Gregory of Nazianzus, with a quotation of this passage, also asserted that the comprehension of the transcendent reality of God was "quite impossible and impracticable, not merely to the utterly careless and ignorant, but even to the highly exalted," adding: "and in like manner to every created nature." Having said that, however, he did go on to qualify his statement by suggesting that the angels, as "higher natures and purer intelligences, because of their nearness to God and because of their illumination with the light of God," might be able to see, "if not the whole, at any rate more perfectly and distinctly than human beings," and he suggested that this ability might vary among the angels "in proportion to their rank." Yet even this variation among angels, as well as between angels and human beings, was ultimately a difference

Rom 8:38–39

Phil 4:7

Gr.Nyss.Eun.1.683
(Jaeger 1:222)
Gr.Nyss.Cant.5
(Jaeger 6:157)

Gr.Nyss.Eun.2.154
(Jaeger 1:270)

Gr.Naz.*Or*.28.4–5
(*SC* 250:108–10)

Bas.*Eun*.1.14
(*SC* 299:220)

See pp.99–105

Bas.*Hex*.1.11
(*SC* 26:134–36)

Gr.Nyss.*Eun*.2.71
(Jaeger 1:247–48)

Bas.*Hex*.1.8
(*SC* 26:118–20)

Gr.Nyss.*Eun*.1.330
(Jaeger 1:124)

Gr.Naz.*Or*.28.5
(*SC* 250:110)

Macr.ap.Gr.Nyss.
Anim.res. (*PG* 46:121)

Söll 1951,298
Gr.Nyss.*Or.catech*.11.2
(Méridier 70)

Gr.Nyss.*Eun*.1.376
(Jaeger 1:137)

of degree, not of kind, between higher and lower rational creatures. Basil, writing against Eunomius, explicitly identified not
only human understanding but that of "every rational nature" as
being transcended; and to confirm the distinction, he explained,
"When I say 'rational,' I mean by that 'belonging to creation.'"

Although the apologetic intent of the Cappadocians in this
apophatic analysis was primarily metaphysical and ultimately
theological, one foundation for it was an examination of the
general limitations placed on all natural knowledge even as it
concerned created realities, a direct implication of which could
then be an argumentation a fortiori to the limitations of reason if
it sought to deal with the uncreated God. As was especially evident from Basil's commentary on the creation narrative in the
first chapter of Genesis, a frequent theme in their works was their
reflection upon created realities, on the basis of the available
scientific information. These created realities, even when considered on their own, were "so marvelous as to make the knowledge
of the least of the phenomena of the world unattainable to the
most penetrating mind." Sense-experience of such phenomena as
empirical data left one in no doubt as to their existence, but this
unequivocal repudiation of any empirical skepticism had as its
corollary a profound metaphysical skepticism about the possibility of "comprehending their nature" or of "seeking out
the underlying substance [hypokeimenon]" concealed beneath
them. Nor was it possible or necessary for the theologian, as
someone whose subject matter was the dogmas of the faith, "to
be able to philosophize about the sequence of the realities created
in the cosmogony," as though his theology based on revelation
had made him a scientist or a natural philosopher. Less possible
still was a comprehension of "that [divine] nature above them,
out of which they have sprung"; in dealing with this, speculation
had to fall back once more on such negatives as "nonprehensible
and incomprehensible [alēptos te kai aperilēptos]." For such a
comprehension would have required reasoning beyond "the fact
that [hoti]" created realities had come into existence, in order
somehow to grasp "the process how [pōs]" that had happened.
That limitation on knowing "the process how" and the conse-
quent restriction to accepting "the fact that" applied in a special
way to the mystery of the incarnation, though not only to it. Even
were it possible for an "ambitious investigator" by some means
to grasp the created world "in its own beginning, whatever that
may be," this would not grant access to that which was "above
it," behind it, and beyond it. It was possible to believe "that God

Gr.Nyss.*Eun*.2.98
(Jaeger 1:255)

is," but it was false to claim that this provided insight into "what God is."

The negatives proliferated still further when the issue became speculation in the opposite direction—namely, "settling questions about the creatures of God on the basis of the nature of the Creator," and laying claim to a knowledge acceptable to "those in the natural sciences [physiologountes]," a knowledge that had been extrapolated by a professed theologian from the nature of a God who was "immaterial, invisible, formless, ungenerate, everlasting, incapable of decay and change and alteration, and all such things." For, Gregory of Nyssa continued, "How will anyone get an idea about a thing that is visible on the basis of the invisible, about the perishable on the basis of the imperishable, about that which has a date for its existence on the basis of that

Gr.Nyss.*Eun*.1.435–36
(Jaeger 1:153)

which has never been generated, about that which has duration only for a time on the basis of the everlasting?" A similar metaphysical skepticism applied to another methodology that also claimed to be reasoning in the opposite direction, this time from the nature of the Father to the nature of the Son within the Trinity. Even the attempt to reason from the nature of the Son to the nature of the Father was attended by great peril, both metaphysi-

See pp.232–34

cal and religious. Yet it at least had some sort of explicit biblical warrant in such statements of the Gospel as the saying of Jesus, "No one knows the Father but the Son and those to whom the

Mt 11:27

Son chooses to reveal him." But to the Cappadocians the supreme act of theological hybris seemed to be for any theologian to "presuppose, as more comprehensible, the being of the Father,

Gr.Nyss.*Eun*.1.459–60
(Jaeger 1:159–60)
Bas.*Eun*.1.7
(SC 299:192)

and then to attempt to trace and syllogize about the nature of the Son on the basis of that." At the same time, as was pointed out by Basil, and then by Gregory of Nyssa quoting the words of Basil in defense of Basil, this proliferation of negatives was not merely some kind of rhetorical pleonasm implying that their meanings (or rather nonmeanings) were identical: each negative, by its exclusion, proceeded by its own "specific application of

Gr.Nyss.*Eun*.2.506–7
(Jaeger 1:374)

thought" and represented a slightly different nuance of "conception [epinoia]" about the *apophatic* mystery of the divine nature.

Apophatic metaphysics, then, was inseparable from *apophatic* epistemology, whose fundamental axiom was: "The divine being is to be known of only in the impossibility of perceiving it." The divine being—to whom, at Athens in the very first confrontation between Christianity and Classical culture, the apostle

Acts 17:28
Gr.Nyss.*Paup*.2
(Van Heck 22)

Paul had applied a quotation from a pagan Greek poet, "In him we live and move, in him we exist"—could not be compared with

Gr.Nyss.*Eun*.1.373–75
(Jaeger 1:137)

Gr.Nyss.*V.Mos*.2
(Jaeger 7–I:86–87)

Bas.*Ep*.234.1
(Courtonne 3:41–42)

Gr.Nyss.*Eun*.2.501
(Jaeger 1:372)

See pp.259–60

Gr.Nyss.*Beat*.1
(*PG* 44:1197)

Arist.*Met*.1028b2–4
Gr.Nyss.*Beat*.6
(*PG* 44:1268);
Bas.*Eun*.1.12
(*SC* 299:214)

Rom 11:33

1 Tm 2:4

See pp.325–26

Gr.Nyss.*Ref*.16–17
(Jaeger 2:318–19)

any of the other beings to which the terms "being" and "knowing" had ever been applied. In the case of these other beings, a growth in human knowledge meant an increase in understanding and comprehending the subject, but here it meant the opposite, an ever-deepening awareness of the incomprehensibility of the subject. There were, as the Cappadocians well recognized, implications potential in this epistemology that could unmistakably lead to nihilism. Basil formulated the first half of a reply to that potential implication in a letter: "[People ask], 'Do you worship what you know or what you do not know?' If I answer, 'I worship what I know,' they immediately reply, 'What is the essence of the object of worship?' Then, if I confess that I am ignorant of the essence, they turn on me again and say, 'So you worship you know not what!' I answer that the word 'to know' has many meanings. We say that we know the greatness of God, the power of God, the wisdom of God, the goodness of God, the providence of God over us, and the justness of the judgment of God—but not the very *ousia* of God." Nor did this mean, as it might seem, that while no one of these constituted the nature of God, the Deity could be thought of as "composed of these various elements or attributes" somehow put together. The human mind—and, for that matter, even the angelic mind—could not, by the exercise of its reasoning and knowing faculties, attain to the knowledge of "being itself [to on]," which was, in Aristotle's celebrated formula, "the ancient and persistent and perpetual question, the eternal conundrum [to palai te kai nyn kai aei zētoumenon kai aei aporoumenon, ti to on]." In fact, no human faculty was "capable of perceiving the incomprehensible" ways of God, which ever remained, according to another Pauline *apophatic* formula with an alpha privative, "unsearchable [anexichniastoi]."

The second half of the response to the accusation of nihilistic skepticism was somewhat more subtle, and more dependent on the particularity of Christian revelation. If the God whose will it was that all should find salvation and come to know the truth had deemed it necessary for salvation that they should know the divine essence, that would have been revealed; but it had not been revealed, which proved that such knowledge was not necessary. What was necessary, however, was that the human memory learn and retain all the various names under which knowledge of the divine had come to it; and because it would have been impossible to keep memory unconfused without the notation of words to distinguish from one another the things stored in the mind, the

Gr.Nyss.*Eun*.2.281–83
(Jaeger 1:309)

human mind needed such names and words even though the divine mind did not. The incomprehensibility of divine being and the unattainability of the transcendent *kalon* did not imply at all "a need to despair of winning this object of our love." The imperative was just the opposite: "The more reason shows the greatness of this thing that we are seeking, the higher we have to lift our thoughts and excite them with the greatness of that object; and

Gr.Nyss.*Virg*.10
(Jaeger 8–I:291)

we have to be afraid of losing our participation in the good." If negation was not to end in nihilism, its corollary had to be a careful and continuous review of the ways of knowing. "Our grasping of God," Gregory of Nyssa declared, "would indeed be easy, if there lay before us one single assigned way to the knowledge of God." Instead, there were many ways to it, not because the attributes of God were separate or even separable entities, but because the human mind had to "grope after the ineffable being

Gr.Nyss.*Eun*.2.475–78
(Jaeger 1:364–65)

in diverse and many-sided ways and never pursue the mystery in the light of one idea alone." This consideration of *apophasis* led Cappadocian thought, therefore, to an examination of the relation between God and the ways of knowing.

CHAPTER 4

God and the Ways of Knowing

Bas.*Hex.*2.2
(SC 26:148)

1 Cor 13:13
ap.Bas.*Eun.*2.24
(SC 305:100)
Mühlenberg 1966,
142–47

See pp.127–29,216–30
Gr.Nyss.*Beat.*6
(PG 44:1269–72)

Horn 1927,113–31

Unterstein 1903,21
ap.Gr.Naz.*Or.*27.8
(SC 250:90)

When the language of negation was being directed against the presumption by some schools of Classical thought—and even by some of Christian thought—of being able to perceive the divine nature in its essence, it could be devastating in its refutation of all ways of knowing as they were supposed to lead to any knowledge of natural theology. "Knowledge" of this kind was not only "inexpressible by the human voice," it was also "incomprehensible to human reason." From such polemics of Cappadocian *apophaticism* it would be easy to conclude that in their judgment the epistemological enterprise—indeed, the very enterprise of faith and hope, and by implication the enterprise also of love—was doomed to failure and therefore not worth attempting. Such a conclusion would be easy, but it would be mistaken. For negative theology could be construed not only as a limitation on the mind but at the same time as a liberation of the mind, setting the human reason, as the image of God, free to pursue its speculations within the boundaries that had been set for it. And in fact the Cappadocian system of epistemology was an ambitious and daring exploration of the ways of knowing, pushing these ways of knowing to their limits (and occasionally, perhaps, beyond their limits) and relating them, though not without the correctives of the language of *apophasis,* to the enterprise of natural theology as a whole. This they did not only in their apologetic works but in their other writings as well. Gregory of Nazianzus quoted with approval the words of his opponent about "different patterns of life and avocations," which led "to different places according to

Rom 12:6
Daniélou 1957
the proportion of faith," and therefore were called "ways," ways of knowing.

Thus, having warned any overly audacious inquirer against laying claim, in word or even in thought, to a knowledge of "that divine and ineffable world," which it was presumptuous to claim to be able to understand, Gregory of Nyssa went on to itemize in Weisswurm 1952 precise detail four ways of knowing, which, taken together, embraced "every individual thing actually coming within our comprehension." They were: "Contemplation of an object as existing in an extension of distance; an object suggesting the idea of a capacity in space, within which to detect its details; an object coming within the field of vision through being circumscribed by an *arche* or a *telos* and being bounded by the nonexistent in each direction; a phenomenon grasped by means of an association of qualities, combining dying, and sufferance, and change, and Gr.Nyss.*Eun.*2.578
(Jaeger 1:395) alteration [phthora kai pathos kai tropē kai alloiōsis]." From such a catalog, however, was it valid to proceed to speak, with Eunomius, about "preserving natural order [physikēn taxin]" Eun.ap.Gr.Nyss. *Eun.*
3.1.4 (Jaeger 2:4)
Eun.ap.Socr.*H.e.*4.7
(Hussey 2:482) also in the consideration of "those things known to us from above," and therefore was it valid to be able to claim to know as much about the *ousia* of God as God himself did? At one level, there did seem to be a "natural order" and some discernible symmetry between these ways of knowing everything else and the ways of knowing God, and therefore it was useful to catalog the general ways of knowing about creatures as a kind of prolegomenon to the discussion of the somewhat parallel ways of knowing about the Creator. But at a deeper level, thanks to *apophatic* theology, such symmetry and parallelism were seen to promise more than they could ever deliver as a key to ultimate reality. Nyssen's catalog was in fact intended as little more than a convenient way of classifying knowledge, but he did not mean it as a way of arriving at knowledge, and especially not as a way of arriving at knowledge about God.

In keeping with their particular version of what Etienne Gilson 1944,214–34 Gilson in his Gifford Lectures called "Christian Socratism," the general epistemology of the Cappadocians, as well as their con- Galtier 1946,175–79;
Jaeger 1966,101–21;
Girardi 1978,187 sideration of the epistemology of natural theology, found one starting point in subjectivity and self-knowledge. As Florovsky has put it, on the basis of a quotation from Gregory of Nazianzus, "the main distinctive mark of Patristic theology was its 'existen- Florovsky 4:17 tial' character." There was a distinction to be drawn between "knowledge [gnōsis]" defined as "skill [epistēmē] and acquaintance with something," hence as in that sense objective or scien-

Gr.Nyss.*Hom.opif.*20
(PG 44:197)

tific knowledge, and "knowledge" understood as "the disposition towards the agreeable [hē pros to kecharismenon diathesis]," hence as a way of knowing that also encompassed desiring the object of the knowledge. Certainly for an understanding of this latter, "subjective" brand of knowledge, but ultimately also for an accurate and honest accounting of what was involved in "objective" knowledge, a study that concentrated exclusively on the world external to the self was insufficient. The safest first step in the evaluation of every claim to knowledge was to overcome the ignorance of oneself and to replace it with an accurate knowl-

Gr.Nyss.*Cant.*2
(Jaeger 6:64)

Pl.*Prt.*343b; see p.121

edge of oneself, which also involved a precise judgment upon oneself. This self-knowledge, enjoined in the Classical tradition by the formula of the Delphic oracle, "Know thyself," was the way of knowing likewise suggested in the Christian tradition by the words of the Song of Songs, "If you do not know yourself

Sg 1:8

[Ean mē gnōis seautēn]." Another of the writings attributed to Solomon, in this case the Book of Proverbs, actually defined "the wise" as "those who have an accurate knowledge of themselves

Prv 13:10

[hoi heautōn epignōmones sophoi]," which in the context of his citation of this passage Gregory of Nyssa seemed to be taking as a reference to "the wise" wherever they might appear, whether among the people of Israel or even among the Greeks, as well as of

Gr.Nyss.*Beat.*5
(PG 44:1260)

course within the church.

On the basis of such a knowledge of the self and therefore on the basis of such an analysis of the knowing mind, it was possible to proceed to a consideration of the several human senses, for example of the sense of hearing, and of the relation of each to the

Ivánka 1936,179–80;
Weiswurm 1952,83–118
Gr.Nyss.*Hom.opif.*10
(PG 44:152–53)

mind. Without such preparatory analysis, the danger was, according to Macrina, that one would follow the example of Epicurus and "make our senses [aisthēsis] the only means of our apprehension of things," with the result that the "eyes of the soul" would be closed to the possibility of "seeing anything in the

Macr.ap.Gr.Nyss.
Anim.res. (PG 46:21)

world of intelligible and noncorporeal realities [tōn noētōn te kai asōmatōn kosmon]." Yet none of this attention to the intelligible and noncorporeal world was intended to belittle the indispensable contribution that sense experience did make to authentic knowledge, which was, at any rate initially, a knowledge "of the

Gr.Nyss.*Hom.opif.*27
(PG 44:228)

facts known to us through sense experience [tōn tēi peirai gnōrizomenōn]." There was, therefore, nothing about addressing an appeal to such "sense experience [peira]" that was inconsistent with this method. It needed to be added immediately, however, that arbitrarily restricting the judgment about the world and about the human condition to the knowledge available through

Gr.Nyss.*Or.catech*.5.8
(Méridier 28–30)

empirical observation was unfair even to sense experience itself, for it was an unjustifiable limitation both on knowledge and on self-knowledge. A sound epistemology, and underlying it a sound human psychology, recognized in the ways of knowing, "as foundations, the instincts of a twofold organization," which was attuned simultaneously to the divine and nonmaterial world of mind and to the human and material world of the senses, with

Gr.Nyss.*Hom.opif*.2
(*PG* 44:133)

their affinities for "the good things of the earth."

But "the direction, as far as possible, of every operation and movement of sound thinking to the knowledge and the contemplation of some reality" made it necessary to recognize that "the whole world of realities" included, in addition to that known through the senses, which was valid in its own right, "the contem-

Gr.Nyss.*Eun*.2.572–74
(Jaeger 1:393–94)

Gr.Nyss.*Cant*.14
(Jaeger 6:411)

plation of the intelligible world, transcending the grasp of the senses." The mind, also apart from divine revelation, had to begin to learn the art of clearing away the encumbrances created by the senses, in order to rise "to the invisible." That process could never be complete in this world of sense and matter, because it was impossible "for those living in the body to be conversant with objects of pure thought, altogether apart from bodily objects." Even the names used for God as the first nature—such as spirit, fire, light, love, wisdom, righteousness, mind, reason—

Gr.Naz.*Or*.28.13
(*SC* 250:126)

all still tended to carry some physical connotations, and the human mind could not conceive of them utterly apart from such connotations. Within those inescapable limitations, it was nevertheless possible even for the natural human mind, for example through such an intellectual exercise as "the methods of geometry," to be led "step by step through visible delineations to truths beyond sight." That gift of "transcendent reflection," which

Macr.ap.Gr.Nyss.
Anim.res. (*PG* 46:33)

Unterstein 1903,74–76

Greek called "epinoia," was the foundation of all the human sciences and skills, and it was "more precious than any other" quality of the human mind. Gregory of Nyssa defined it, in a careful and comprehensive formula, as "the method by which we discover things that are unknown, going on to further discoveries by means of what adjoins to and follows from our first perception with regard to the thing studied." He explained the formula to mean: "When we have formed some idea of what we seek to know, by adapting what follows to the first result of our discov-

Gr.Nyss.*Eun*.2.182
(Jaeger 1:277)

eries we gradually conduct our inquiry to the end of our proposed research."

This precise analysis of the anatomy of scientific hypothesis deserves to be parsed carefully, for it was proposing a general theory of epistemology, together with a methodology for extending the borders of the known. The methodology began with a "first perception," obtainable through the five senses. Yet it was characteristic of the human mind that it could not be content with such perceptions but had to press on toward "further discoveries." This it did by prosecuting its inquiry in the direction of something that it sought to know, though this was still unknown on purely empirical grounds. Step by logical step, the mind could construct, by transcendent reflection, a theoretical knowledge also of "unknown things." This theoretical knowledge, too, had to be squared with "the first result of our discoveries" in order to be valid. Thus, by a method of proceeding that was empirical and yet more than empirical, the inquiry could be gradually conducted "to the end of our proposed research." The "twofold organization" of the ways of knowing required, therefore, a corresponding twofold recognition. It was a recognition that implied, on the one hand, that there could be a knowledge that was present in the mind but "not in the eyes," and that therefore the reasoning mind could sometimes be preferable to the senses as a guide to truth. For after all, it was reason, not the sense perception shared with other creatures in which those other creatures sometimes excelled, that was "the distinctive quality" of human nature. Yet, it also meant that even in the expression of such a truth obtained by reason, human thought and language were still compelled to speak "on the basis of metaphor," rather than being able to claim a knowledge that had been obtained "without the mediation of the senses [amesōs]."

Although a critical analysis of the theory of knowledge and of the ways of knowing did not yield a perfect parallelism or "natural order" for the treatment of "those things known to us from above," it was not a waste of time to study them together. For as there were several ways of knowing "all things actually coming within our comprehension," the ways of knowing God, too, were multiple: "Many are the modes [tropoi] of such perception," according to the axiom of Gregory of Nyssa. The apologetic enterprise of Capppadocian thought rested on the presupposition that through these various modes or "tropes" of perception, reason could "supply us with some comprehension of the divine nature," albeit "dim and imperfect." For what it was "necessary to know about God" was not in a direct continuity with "the things known on the basis of human comprehension." As "the *ousia* of God" was unknowable, it was possible, "while holding

Gr.Nyss.*Hom.opif.*2
(*PG* 44:133)

Gr.Nyss.*V.Mos.*2
(Jaeger 7–I:97)

Bas.*Hex.*6.11
(*SC* 26:384)

Bas.*Hex.*4.5
(*SC* 26:264–66)

Gr.Nyss.*Comm.not.*
(Jaeger 3–I:27)

Eun.ap.Gr.Nyss. *Eun.*
3.1.4 (Jaeger 2:4)
Gr.Nyss.*Eun.*2.578
(Jaeger 1:395)
Gr.Nyss.*Beat.*6
(*PG* 44:1268)
Unterstein 1903,25–27

Gr.Nyss.*Eun.*2.130
(Jaeger 1:263)

Gr.Nyss.*V.Mos.*2
(Jaeger 7–I:88)

in our mind wisdom itself and power itself [tēn autosophian kai tēn autodynamin]," to achieve some knowledge of God neverthe-less. Because that God was also "truth itself [autoalētheia]," it was "the primary function of our mind to know one God," but such knowing was possible only in the sense and to the extent that the infinitely great could be known by the very small. In sum: "The judgment of the mind is good and has been given to us for a good end, namely, the perception of God; but it operates only as far as it can."

Therefore, it was incumbent on the human mind to "grope for the ineffable being 'in many and varied ways,' and never to pursue the mystery in the light of one idea alone; for our grasping of God would indeed be easy if there lay before us one single assigned path to the knowledge of God," rather than the many paths made obligatory by the fragmentary glimpses granted to the limited human mind. Yet this did not imply a "splitting up" of the divine nature itself on the basis of these diverse ways of knowing about God. From the beauty of the sunlight "the beauty of the real sunlight" of God could be known, from the solidity of the firma-ment "the unchangeableness of its Creator," from the immensity of the heavens "the vast infinity of the power encompassing the universe"—all of these being one and the same divine nature, simple and uncomposite. In developing an apologetic case "with an adherent of Greek ideas," whether an atheist or a polytheist, on the basis of these various ways of knowing, the place to start was with the logic of theism itself: with the atheist it was desirable to argue "from the consideration of the skillful and wise *econ-omy* of the universe" to the acknowledgment of "a certain over-mastering power manifested through these channels"; with the polytheist, the case could be based on the presupposition of the perfectness of deity, which was patently incompatible with "these scattered notions of a plurality of gods." God was and remained the ineffable truth. But by paying attention to these several ways of knowing it was possible to begin the process, in one sense subjective and in another sense objective, of following the one of whom the prophet Habakkuk said, "He sets my feet on the heights [epi ta hypsēla]," toward what was knowable about the sublime in its transcendence. It was in this sense that Macrina could come up with the bold proposal, as something correctly "surmised by our reason," of an analogy between "the specula-tive, critical, and world-surveying faculty of the soul" as the im-age of God and "the universal supervision and critical discern-

Gr.Nyss.*Hex.*
(PG 44:72)

Bas.*Ep.*233.2
(Courtonne 3:40–41)

Heb 1:1

Gr.Nyss.*Eun.*2.475–78
(Jaeger 1:364–65)

Gr.Nyss.*Infant.*
(Jaeger 3–II:85)

Gr.Nyss.*Or.catech.*pr.6
(Méridier 6)
Gr.Nyss.*V.Mos.*2
(Jaeger 7–I:39)

Hb 3:19
Gr.Nyss.*Beat.*3
(PG 44:1224)

Macr.ap.Gr.Nyss.
Anim.res. (PG 46:57)

Daniélou 1944; Viller-
Rahner 1990,140–45
Heine 1975,103–14
Gr.Nyss.*Cant*.4
(Jaeger 6:115)
Gr.Nyss.*Cant*.4;6
(Jaeger 6:115;175–76)

Gr.Nyss.*Virg*.6
(Jaeger 8–I:278)

Gr.Nyss.*Hom.opif*.20
(PG 44:197)

Gr.Naz.*Or*.40.44
(PG 36:421)

Bas.*Ep*.223.3
(Courtonne 3:12–13)

Gr.Nyss.*Maced.*
(Jaeger 3–I:93–94)

Dölger 1932,82–83

Nock 1972,1:368–74

Gn 28:12; Mt 1:20
Gr.Nyss.*Hom.opif*.13
(PG 44:165–76)
Gr.Nyss.*V.Macr.*
(Jaeger 8–I:372–73;387)

ment between good and evil," which was "a manifestation of divinity itself."

The technical term for this subjective-objective process in Cappadocian spirituality—and in other systems as well, whether or not it is appropriate to call them "mystical," a question about which there has been extensive scholarly debate—was "the ascent [anodos] of the soul." The process could be charted as passing through several stages or degrees. Also before Christ, such mystagogues as Elijah and John the Baptist had followed this path, with their "thoughts fixed upon the invisible" and their "judgments as to the true good not confused or led astray." Therefore, the subjectivist definition of "knowledge" quoted earlier, as "the disposition towards the agreeable," a way of knowing and at the same time a way of desiring the object of knowledge, did have a special relevance to the knowledge of God. In inviting to Christian baptism those citizens of Constantinople who were still lingering outside the fellowship of the church a half-century or more after the conversion of Constantine, Gregory of Nazianzus addressed an appeal from his own subjectivity to theirs, with deep calling unto deep: "If your heart has been written upon in some other way than as my teaching demands, come and have the writing changed. I am not an unskilled calligrapher of these truths. I write that which is written upon my own heart, and I teach that which I have been taught, and which I have kept from the beginning until these gray hairs." Basil, too, could draw upon the continuity of his own personal knowledge of divine truth as a standard. Subjective knowledge, when enlightened, could also be relied upon to provide discernment, so that "a just idea and devout intuitions [tas eusebeis ennoias] concerning the divine and transcendent nature" could even constitute a norm for evaluating which of "the conceptions appropriately applied to deity [tōn theoprepōn noēmatōn]" were valid and which were not. This interest in an epistemology that could be characterized as the objectivity of subjective knowledge was also reflected in the detailed attention—for which there were parallels both in pagan sources and in the Christian Scriptures of both the Old and the New Testament—given by Gregory of Nyssa to the problem of dreams, their causes and their interpretation. For his sister, Macrina, and their parents also, some dreams could clearly be a reliable medium of divine knowledge.

Macrina was also the origin of another apologetic proof that was both subjective and objective. It was a version of the moral

Unterstein 1903,52–57

argument for the existence of God when she cited the desire for
arete as "clear evidence against the chronological priority of vice,
before the act of beginning to live," as well as against the related
notion that human nature had derived its source from evil, rather

Macr.ap.Gr.Nyss.
Anim.res. (PG 46:120)

than "from the *sophia* of God, in the governance of its *economy*
over all things." Several times in his *Catechetical Oration*, Gregory of Nyssa invoked yet another such combination of subjective
and objective arguments when he based his apologetic case on
the testimony of history. "To anyone except a vehement antago-
nist of the truth," he contended, there was "no slight proof of the
Deity's having sojourned here" within the realm of time and
space. That proof, "exhibited now in this present life before the
beginning of the life to come," consisted of "the testimony borne

Gr.Nyss.Or.catech.18.1
(Méridier 92)

Lenz 1925,51–55

by actual facts [dia tōn pragmatōn autōn]." This emphasis of
Gregory of Nyssa on the concrete evidence of "actual facts" was
congruent with his interpretation of how God generally dealt
with the human race, "less by instruction than by what the one

Gr.Nyss.Or.catech.35.1
(Méridier 160)

who entered into fellowship with mankind actually did"; for in
the life of Christ "life became a reality." This was a proper apologetic method for the doctrine of creation, which was knowable by
reason, and even for the doctrine of the incarnation, which was
not: "Someone who is looking for proofs of God's self-
manifestation in the flesh must look at the divine actions [ener-

Isaye 1937,422–39

geiai], for one can discover no other demonstration at all of the
existence of the Deity than that which the testimony of those

Gr.Nyss.Or.catech.12.1
(Méridier 70)

actions supplies." The same was true also of the divine self-
manifestation in the flesh through the coming of Jesus Christ.

Gr.Nyss.Or.catech.18.4
(Méridier 94–96)

Such evidence came not only from the events actually recorded in
Scripture but from subsequent history as well. For, as he summa-

Gr.Nyss.Beat.6
(PG 44:1269)

rized the case elsewhere, "The one who is by nature invisible
becomes visible in the actions of history."

These "subjective-objective" methods of Christian apologetic
argumentation were an important component of what we are
calling in this book the *metamorphosis* of natural theology, for
they reflected the perspectives, not entirely brand new perhaps
but nevertheless novel in their emphases, that the Christian
worldview brought to the traditional concerns of natural theology. Without radical distortion, these perspectives on natural
theology could even be construed as natural counterparts to the
revealed trinitarian theology so central in the system of the

See pp.231–47
Gr.Naz.Or.40.44
(PG 36:421)
Gr.Nyss.Maced.
(Jaeger 3–1:93–94)

Cappadocian theologians. Thus the readiness of Gregory of
Nazianzus to argue on the basis of that which was written upon
his own heart, or of Gregory of Nyssa to invoke devout intuitions

Macr.ap.Gr.Nyss.
Anim.res. (PG 46:120)

Gr.Nyss.*Beat.*6
(PG 44:1269)

Gr.Nyss.*Or.catech.*35.1
(Méridier 160)

See pp.263–79

Gr.Nyss.*Eun.*2.232
(Jaeger 1:293)

Gr.Nyss.*Or.catech.*pr.4
(Méridier 4)

Rom 1:20

Bas.*Hex.*1.6
(SC 26:110)

Bas.*Hex.*3.10
(SC 26:242)

concerning the divine and transcendent nature as a norm, or of Macrina to cite conscience as clear evidence for the derivation of human nature from the *sophia* and *economy* of God may all be seen as an expression of the existential dimension that the experience of the Holy Spirit and the doctrine of the third *hypostasis* of the Trinity as the giver of holiness brought to their theological methodology, even to its "natural" expressions. Similarly, when seen in context, an apologetic "proof" based on the assertion that the one who was invisible had become visible in the actions of historical events was clearly a reflection of the attention to history that was derived above all from the doctrine of the incarnation of the second *hypostasis* of the Trinity in the *economy* and history of Christ. Here it became evident in a special way that "instruction" was less decisive than what had "actually happened" in "a living reality" and that the communication of the knowledge of God, both through revelation and even through natural means, did not consist so much in the transmission of certain truths as in the historical *economy* of certain events. "To those who can understand it," the principle ran, "the cosmos speaks through the things that are being done, without regard or care for verbal explanation." But that statement suggested that because the starting point in the encounter with Hellenism, be it atheistic or polytheistic, had to be the existence of the one true God, the relation of the cosmos to its Creator and thus, in a special sense, to the first *hypostasis* of the Christian Trinity, and with it the special Cappadocian version (or versions) of the various cosmological proofs for the existence of God, necessarily became the first item on the apologetic agenda.

Yet consideration of the logical status of these proofs of natural theology shows them to have been quite ambiguous in the eyes of the Cappadocians. The key text in the New Testament for the cosmological argument was a verse from the first chapter of the Epistle to the Romans: "Ever since the world began [or, following the Cappadocians and taking 'apo ktiseōs kosmou' logically rather than chronologically: on the basis of the creation of the world], his invisible attributes, that is to say his everlasting power and deity, have been visible to the eye of reason in the things he has made." This verse meant to Basil that "by the sight of visible and empirical realities" the human mind was "led, as by a hand, to the contemplation of invisible realities." Later in the same treatise Basil read the verse as an admonition "to be raised from visible things to the invisible being," and from "the grandeur and beauty of creatures" to derive "a just idea of the Creator." Still

Bas.*Hex*.6.11
(*SC* 26:386)

Pease 1941,163–200

Ps 18:2

Gr.Nyss.*Eun*.2.224
(Jaeger 1:290–91)
Ps 8:2

Gr.Nyss.*Maced.*
(Jaeger 3–I:96–97)

Gr.Nyss.*V.Mos*.2
(Jaeger 7–I:89)

Gr.Nyss.*Eun*.1.435–36
(Jaeger 1:153)

1 Cor 2:18

Gr.Nyss.*Beat*.6
(*PG* 44:1269)

Gr.Nyss.*Eun*.2.224
(Jaeger 1:290–91)

Arist.*Ph*.241b
Norris 1991,113–14

later, however, Basil added the warning that it was impossible for "the whole universe to give us a right idea of the greatness of God." Paraphrasing this passage from the New Testament in combination with its Old Testament counterpart, the words of the psalmist David, "The heavens tell out the glory of God, the firmament makes known his handiwork," Gregory of Nyssa could assert what seemed to be the standard cosmological argument in the strongest of possible terms: "The very heavens . . . all but shout aloud . . . : 'O humanity, when you gaze upon us and behold our beauty and magnitude, and this ceaseless revolution, with its well-ordered and harmonious motion, working in the same direction and in the same manner, turn your thought to the one who presides over our system, and, by the aid of the beauty that you see, imagine to yourselves the *kalon* of the invisible prototype.'" Nevertheless, as another psalm made clear, the words of this psalm really meant something else: "Although 'the heavens tell out the glory of God,' they are counted poor heralds of the worth of God, because the majesty of God is exalted, not as far as the heavens, but 'high above those heavens [hyperanō tōn ouranōn].'" And so what the heavens were telling, according to David, was the unknowability of God, that God was "the unknown and the uncontemplated [to agnōston te kai atheōrē-ton]." The subtlety and the ambiguity of the witness of the works to the Maker also implied that it was presumptuous in the extreme to claim to be able to "settle questions about the works of God by means of the nature of the worker." In spite of that, there did remain the possibility of a natural theology, if it was possible "perhaps for the 'wise by the standards of this age,' too, to gain some knowledge of the transcendent wisdom and power from the beautiful harmony of the cosmos."

As was evident from the reference to "this ceaseless revolution, with its well-ordered and harmonious motion, working in the same direction and in the same manner," this cosmological argument put special emphasis on the argument from motion. Throughout most of its history, the argument from motion has been based on Aristotle's classic axiom in the seventh book of the *Physics:* "Everything that is in motion must be moved by something." Gregory of Nazianzus, responding to Aristotle's identification of God as a "fifth element" alongside the traditional four *stoicheia,* asked: "What is the force that moves your 'fifth element,' and what is it that moves all things, and what moves that, and what is the force that moves that?" And if an infinite regress

Gr.Naz.*Or.*28.8
(*SC* 250:116)

Bas.*Hex.*1.8–9
(*SC* 26:120–22)

Gr.Nyss.*Beat.*8
(*PG* 44:1292)

Gr.Nyss.*Eun.*2.224
(Jaeger 1:290–91)

Gr.Naz.*Or.*6.15
(*PG* 35:741)

Thos.Aq.*S.T.*1.2.3

Dörrie et al. 1976,253

Gr.Nyss.*Infant.*
(Jaeger 3–II:76–77)

Gr.Nyss.*Eun.*1.548
(Jaeger 1:184–85)

of movers and of motions was inconceivable, then there had to be a prime unmoved mover. Basil, too, invoked the impossibility of conceiving an infinite regress of motion, at which "the mind would reel," as an argument for the existence of God. Gregory of Nyssa refined the argument by introducing a distinction among the kinds of motion. Earth, he said, was "the place of variation and flux." But the case was different with the things that appeared moving in heaven, because they did not behave in such a way. Instead, it was characteristic of the motion of "all heavenly things" to "move in their own courses in series of orderly sequence [eirmōi kai taxei kai akolouthiai pros ton idion dromon]." Despite the contrast between the flux on earth and the orderly sequence in the heavens, it remained the case that also in heaven there was "nothing moving of its own proper motion"; what was evident in the motion of the heavens no less than in motion on earth was "the dependence of everything visible, or even conceivable, on inscrutable and sublime power." The movement of the seasons, and of day and night, all bore witness to that power, transcendent beyond all motion or change.

Although Thomas Aquinas made "the argument from motion the first and more manifest way" of demonstrating the existence of God, his second way was "from the notion of efficient cause." Both in the argument from motion and in the argument from cause, moreover, it was the impossibility of positing an infinite regress that was seen as clinching the case, so that then God could be identified as the prime unmoved mover or as the first uncaused cause. Gregory of Nyssa took this conception of the first cause to be "a proposition superfluous to prove," because he was confident that it was undeniable by "anyone with even a little insight into the truth of things," whether Greek or Jew or Christian. This was therefore a first principle of natural theology: "Everyone agrees that the universe is linked to one first cause [homologeitai para pantōn mias aitias exēphthai to pan]; that nothing in it owes its existence to itself, so as to be its own origin and cause; but that there is on the other hand a single uncreated eternal nature, the same forever, which transcends all our ideas of distance." In discussing the first cause, Gregory probed the metaphysical meaning of the term "Father" as applied to God, in the sense of "the causality [ton aition] of all beings"; "for if," he argued, "there had been some further cause transcending the Father, it would not have been proper to use the name 'Father,' because that title would have to be transferred higher, to this presupposed cause." Causation was a natural and rational category under which to consider any object of experience, for whose existence it would be "logical to presuppose 'the operation of the Maker.'" Hence it was "allowable to describe deity as the first cause of all." Conversely, it was not permissible, even in the language of ortho-

dox trinitarianism about the relation between the Father as Creator and the Creator-*Logos,* to predicate two "first causes." As Gilson has described "the notion of 'negative theology'" as "es-

sential to Thomism and expressive of its very spirit," so it was even more for the Cappadocians. Any such language about "causality" had to be based on *apophasis:* it was more precise to say that deity had no cause beyond itself, and therefore to define the meaning of "first cause" as "not having its subsistence from any

cause superior to itself." Only in that *apophatic* sense was it legitimate to apply to God the notion of the inconceivability of an infinite regress, whether of cause or of motion.

A closely related variant of these cosmological proofs for the existence of God from motion and from cause was the argument from design. What Basil called "the good order reigning in visible things" was, he said as he opened his exposition of the biblical account of creation, "the right way to begin for anyone undertak-

ing to narrate the formation of the world." Reflection on the design in the universe produced "a consideration of the harmony of the whole" and of "the concert resulting even from opposite

movements in the circular revolutions" in the sky. That concept of universal harmony, "good order," and design stood in the

sharpest possible contrast to various theories of cosmic randomness or of an "arbitrary distribution" as if by lot. The interrelated searches for ultimate causation, for cosmic design, for meta-

physical continuity, and for an ordered teleology, as Nyssen described and analyzed them, thus were based upon the empirical observation and intuitive awareness of "good order." Even in observing the smallest of objects it was possible to discern "the divine order [tēn theian diataxin]," to which the irrational creatures often seemed more willing to conform than were the rational creatures, with their "resistance to the disposition of the Creator"; irrational creatures lacked "the gift of reason," Basil

explained, but they did have "the law of nature [tēs physeōs nomon] firmly seated within them, to show them their duty."

Such "resistance to the disposition of the Creator" was responsible for the inability of "narrower souls," when confronted by the evident design in the world, to recognize "the one made manifest by all of this around us." As Macrina put it, "While the sight of a garment suggests to anyone the weaver of it, and the thought of the shipwright comes to mind upon seeing the ship, and the hand of the builder is suggested to anyone who sees the building, these little souls gaze upon the world, but their eyes are blind." Sometimes this formulation of the argument from order and design could also include the theory from the Platonic doctrine of ideas, that even before this world there had existed "an order of things imaginable to the human mind." But that statement of the theory was accompanied by the warning that this was "too lofty a subject" for any but the more advanced thinkers, at least some of whom were Classical pagans, such as the Platonists. The combination of the argument from design with a warning about transcendence achieved definitive formulation in one of the orations of Gregory of Nazianzus. "Sight and instinctive law," he argued, showed "the existence of God, the creative and sustaining cause of all." That was the teaching of sight, when it would "light upon things seen as nobly fixed in their courses, borne along in, so to say, motionless movement." It was as well the teaching of "instinctive law," which had the power to "infer their author through seeing things in their orderliness." Yet the presentation of this argument led Gregory to a paradox that epitomized Cappadocian apologetics: "Anyone who refuses to progress this far in following instinctive proofs must be very wanting in judgment. But still, whatever we have imagined or figured to ourselves or whatever reason has delineated is not the reality of God." For God transcended all thought and language. All apologetic argumentation for the existence of God, like the optimistic view of the image of God as reason that underlay such argumentation, was sharply qualified by the severe stipulations of Cappadocian *apophatic* theology. Awareness of the paradox was responsible in Cappadocian apologetics for a dialectic between an *apophatic* doctrine of divine transcendence that emphasized, far more radically than Thomism did, what Thomas Aquinas called the "via eminentiae," and a doctrine of analogy that also was, in many respects, more radical than the Thomistic one.

The "via eminentiae" was fundamental to the Cappadocian version of natural theology. As Auguste-Joseph Gaudel has summarized it, "To the doctrine of Eunomius, according to which the notion and the term 'agennētos [unoriginated]' are the only proper representations of the divine essence, the Cappadocian fathers reply with a doctrine of the divine names that is completely the opposite. As a consequence of divine incomprehensibility, which is based on the fullness of the first cause and on our own mode of knowing, we are not able to conceive of God by

Macr.ap.Gr.Nyss.
Anim.res. (PG 46:24)

See pp.96–99

Bas.*Hex.*1.5
(SC 26:104–6)

Gr.Naz.*Or.*28.6
(SC 250:112)

See pp.127–29

See pp.40–56

DTC 4:2428

Geyer 1960,437

means of one single notion, but we are able to consider and construct [a doctrine of God] with the aid of multiple conceptions and various names derived from created things." The argument on the basis of "grades of perfection" was the fourth of the "five ways" of proving the existence of God in the *Summa Theologica*. Significantly, as commentators have observed, Aquinas drew not on Aristotle for this proof, as he did for the other four, but, by way of Augustine, on the tradition coming from Plato, who had described the process this way: "He who has been instructed thus far in the things of love, and who has learned to see the *kala* in due order and succession [ephexēs te kai orthōs], will suddenly perceive a nature of wondrous beauty . . . beauty absolute, separate, simple, and everlasting, which is imparted to the ever growing and perishing beauties of all other beautiful things." That "order and succession" was the principle at work in the suggestion of Gregory of Nyssa that the knowledge of the *Logos* came "from applying, by raising them to an infinitely higher degree [anagōgikōs], our own attributes to the transcendent nature," not only the attribute of *logos* itself as rationality, but all the noble attributes of human nature and of nature generally. Elsewhere he elaborated on these "many modes of perception." For example, it was possible, "by way of inference [stochastikōs] through the *sophia* appearing in the universe, to see the one who 'made all things by *sophia*.'" A similar process of inference could be applied to "all other things elevating the mind to transcendent goodness," which thus became "apprehensions of God," because each of these sublime meditations placed God, in some sense, within human sight. Among these apprehensions of God available through the "via eminentiae" were: "power, purity, constancy, freedom from contariety," all of which could "engrave on the soul the impress of a divine and transcendent mind."

Pl.*Smp.*210e-211b

Gr.Nyss.*Or.catech.*2.1
(Méridier 16)

Ps 103:24

Gr.Nyss.*Beat.*6
(*PG* 44:1268–69)

The reason for the relative prominence of this argument in the apologetics of the Cappadocians, by comparison with its place in Thomistic apologetics, was to be found in their total reliance on the principles and methods of *apophatic* theology. As Burrell has observed concerning Aquinas, "The main line of his exposition leaves 'perfection' undeveloped." In Cappadocian thought, by contrast, the concept of "perfection" was not only highly developed but situated at the center of their system. It was characteristic of the creation to "attain excellence by participation in something better than itself" and to "be constantly in a state of beginning to be in excellence, by its continual advance in im-

Burrell 1973,142

Gr.Nyss.*Eun*.3.6.74–75
(Jaeger 2:212)

provement"; but because of its perfection, the Godhead was different from the creation, not only quantitatively but qualitatively. Each stage of created good pointed beyond itself to a higher stage, more nearly approximating the perfect good; but God, as that perfect good, was "a nature surpassing every conceivable idea of the good and transcending all other power, being in no need of anything outside itself definable as good, and thus in itself the

Macr.ap.Gr.Nyss.
Anim.res. (PG 46:92)

plenitude of every good [tōn agathōn ousa to plērōma]." Therefore, although it was, in the fullest sense of the word, correct to regard "every good as by its very nature unlimited," it was an obvious characteristic of the so-called perfection of the empirical, natural world that it was bounded by limits; the true good, there-

Gr.Nyss.*V.Mos*.1
(Jaeger 7–I:3)

fore, was the negation of any of the goods known here and now. All the goodness and beauty of the cosmos were nothing more

Gr.Nyss.*Virg*.11
(Jaeger 8–I:293–94)

than "a hand to lead us to the preeminent beauty." Socrates had taught: "We ought to fly away from earth to heaven as quickly as we can; and to fly away means to become like God, as far as this is possible; and to become like him means to become holy, just, and

ap.Pl.*Tht*.176b

wise." So it had to be, according to the Cappadocians, not only with holiness, justice, and wisdom, but with every created and therefore imperfect quality of human nature, whose perfection

Gr.Nyss.*Cant*.15
(Jaeger 6:439)

was to be found in God alone. Every human power, Gregory of Nyssa warned as he opened his exposition of the creation narra-

Gr.Nyss.*Hex*.pr.
(PG 44:61)

tive, was to be transcended by the appeal to its perfection. All that moved and changed in the world, and beyond it in the stars with their "orderly array [diakosmēsis]," found its perfection only in

Gr.Nyss.*Or.dom*.2
(PG 44:1140)

the eminence of "the stable nature, the immovable power, existing in its own right."

Nevertheless, this emphasis on the preeminence and transcendence of all the qualities of the divine mind over the human mind,

Gr.Nyss.*Beat*.6
(PG 44:1269–72)

far from producing "despair of ever beholding the desired object," did make possible an exploitation of the possibilities of thinking about God by means of analogy. That enterprise received a license, indeed an imperative, from the statement of the Wisdom of Solomon: "The greatness and beauty of created

Wis 13:5

things gives us an idea of their Creator through analogy"—the only passage in the Greek Bible, whether Old or New Testament, where this adverbial form "through analogy [analogōs]" ap-

Gr.Nyss.*Eun*.2.13
(Jaeger 1:230)

peared. The willingness of the Cappadocians to resort to analogies was in part a response to the contemptuous way in which Eunomius treated the practice of "ascribing homonyms, drawn from analogy, to human thought and conception," which he dismissed as "the work of a mind bereft of all judicial sense,

Eun.ap.Gr.Nyss. *Eun.*
2.306 (Jaeger 1:316)
Gr.Nyss.*Comm.not.*
(Jaeger 3–I:27)

studying the words of the Lord with an enfeebled understanding and a dishonest habit of thought." As "metaphor" was necessary though limited in the ways of knowing generally, so analogy was necessary though limited in the ways of knowing God. In the use of such analogies for the divine essence, it was essential to keep one general principle in mind: "We do not seek to glory in it by the names we employ, but to guide our own selves by the aid of such terms toward the comprehension of the things that are

Gr.Nyss.*Eun.*2.154
(Jaeger 1:270)

Gr.Naz.*Or.*31.31–32
(SC 250:338–40)

Gr.Naz.*Or.*31.10
(SC 250:294)

Bas.*Spir.*26.61
(SC 17:466)

hidden." Those things remained hidden also when they had been "comprehended." Every analogy for the Holy Trinity was flawed, Gregory of Nazianzus warned, including those to which Scripture and dogma had given their approval. "All the same," he asserted earlier in the same oration, "to oblige you, I shall try to get a picture even from this source to give my argument some support." Such analogies, even for the Trinity, could be drawn not only from Scripture, dogma, and empirical observation but also from philosophical speculation itself. Yet there was no "precise set of technical terms [onomatikē sēmasia di' akribeias]" with which to describe "the invisible nature," which was instead to be "hinted at by some sort of analogy [katastochazetai . . . ek

Gr.Nyss.*Cant.*1
(Jaeger 6:36–37)

Gr.Nyss.*Cant.*13
(Jaeger 6:385–86)

tinos analogias]." Thus "the empirical cosmos" could serve as an "analogy" of the cosmos to come, and could be a way of knowing God. For "by observing the beauty of this material sunlight" one could "grasp by analogy the beauty of the real sunlight," which was God: it was not that God somehow resembled the material sunlight but that the sunlight resembled, howsoever dimly, the God who was the true light.

Gr.Nyss.*Infant.*
(Jaeger 3–II:85)

As this discussion of applying the problem of God and the ways of knowing to the doctrine of the Trinity made clear, Cappadocian apologetics strove simultaneously to give natural theology its full due and yet to urge the absolute necessity of revelation, without abridging either of these for the sake of the other. But the ultimate purpose and function of natural theology as apologetics was to prepare for the message of "the Christian faith," whose source, as Gregory of Nyssa declared, was "neither of human origin nor of human authority, but our Lord Jesus Christ himself, the *Logos,* the life, the light, the truth, and God, and *Sophia.*" In asserting their apologetics, they could criticize "these little souls" whose eyes were blind to the evidences for natural theology in the world; and they could confidently associate themselves with the view on which everyone agreed: "That the universe is linked to one first cause; that nothing in it owes its existence to itself, so as to be its own origin and cause; but that there is on the other hand

Gr.Nyss.*Ref.*1
(Jaeger 2:312)

Macr.ap.Gr.Nyss.
Anim.res. (PG 46:21–24)

Gr.Nyss.*Infant.*
(Jaeger 3–II:76–77)

Gr.Nyss.*Eun.*1.435–36
(Jaeger 1:153)

Gr.Nyss.*Eun.*1.459–60
(Jaeger 1:159–60)

a single uncreated eternal essence, the same forever, which transcends all our ideas of distance." Yet they reserved their sharpest polemics for those who claimed to know the secret being of God well enough to use it as a basis for the knowledge of the creation, or who, starting from natural theology about that secret being, presumed to judge and to distort revealed theology in the light of it. This methodology had far-reaching implications for the Cappadocians' own views of revelation, reason, and faith.

CHAPTER 5

The Many and the One

Gr.Nyss.*Eun.*2.578
(Jaeger 1:395)

Gr.Nyss.*Beat.*6
(PG 44:1268–69)

Gr.Nyss.*Ref.*24
(Jaeger 2:321–22 [var.])

Gr.Nyss.*Eun.*2.475–78
(Jaeger 1:364–65)

The Cappadocians recognized that in any speaking about knowledge it was necessary to acknowledge a multiplicity of ways of knowing in general, and that in speaking specifically about the knowledge of God it was necessary to acknowledge a plurality of "modes of perception" of a "nature above every nature, a nature invisible and incomprehensible." But this recognition carried with it the potential danger that such multiplicity and plurality could be interpreted as being applicable also to the object of knowing, not only to the process of knowing. Therefore, they emphasized "the contrast between the One and the many, between the true and the false, between so-called gods and the one true God." Gregory of Nyssa admitted that because there was not only "one single assigned path to the knowledge of God" but a variety of paths, depending on which of the divine attributes was being pursued, someone might conclude that "the splitting up of such attributes" implied the "splitting up of the subject of the attributes"; he accompanied this admission with strong disavowals that he and his orthodox colleagues could be charged with doing anything of the kind by their trinitarian distinctions among the three divine *hypostases* within the single divine *ousia*. It was, however, he surmised, some such process of pluralistic reasoning about immanent realities that had been at work in the history of religions:

"Seeing that [the pagans], with their untrained and narrow intelligence, were disposed to look with wonder on the beauties

74

of nature, not employing the things they beheld as a leader and guide to the beauty of the [divine] nature that transcends these things, they rather made their intelligence come to a stop on arriving at the objects of its apprehension, and they marveled at each part of the creation separately. For this reason they did not bring their conception of the Deity to a halt at any single one of the things they beheld, but deemed each thing they looked on in creation to be divine." Once they had made the assumption that the nature they worshiped was not one, there was nothing to prevent them, in their "progress through creation," from attributing divinity distributively to each of the multiple objects of their wonder. Thus the Classical poets of Greece described "the gods as being many [hōs peri pollōn], and these, too, not even in accord with one another."

And so polytheism was born—or, as Gregory of Nyssa called it, "the superstition of polytheism [tēs polytheïas deisidaimonia]." This designation was an apt summation of the Cappadocian apologetic critique, which found it essential, in dealing with this aspect of Classical culture, to face both the "superstition" of its practices and the "polytheism" of its doctrines. The belief system of polytheism was as vital to Cappadocian apologetics as the belief system of Christian orthodoxy to Cappadocian dogmatics. But just as the latter was "made effectual not so much by [Christ's] precepts in the way of teaching as by the deeds of the one who accomplished an actual fellowship [of God] with humanity," so it was, too, with the pagan antithesis to the gospel, where actions also spoke louder than words. For although it was "a distinguishing peculiarity of the Greeks to think that piety should consist in doctrines only," Christian apologetics, like Christian dogmatics, held "doctrines" and "piety" together. Toward the "piety" of pagan worship, with its "ceremony and mystery," which they sometimes recounted in gruesome detail, the Cappadocians were fundamentally unsympathetic. "The deceit of demons" had filled every corner of the world, producing an "idol mania." It was also from the demons that superstitious practices had taken their origin. Greek festivals in honor of their "gods and demons" were a celebration of the illicit "passions" that were characteristic both of the gods and of their worshipers. Even Greek theater—despite its powerful language and dramatic force, or perhaps precisely because of these very qualities—was not spared in such apologetic attacks. The masterpieces of Greek literature, too, were "regarded as myths on account of their

Gr.Nyss.*Eun*.3.3.5
(Jaeger 2:108–9)

Bas.*Leg.lib.gent*.4
(Wilson 22)

Gr.Nyss.*Eun*.3.2.94
(Jaeger 2:83)

Gr.Nyss.*Or.catech*.35.1
(Méridier 160)

Gr.Nyss.*Eun*.3.9.59
(Jaeger 2:286)
See pp.300–305

Gr.Naz.*Or*.39.3–6
(PG 36:336–41)

Gr.Nyss.*Or.catech*.18.2
(Méridier 92)
Gr.Naz.*Or*.4.53
(SC 309:156)

Gr.Naz.*Or*.41.1
(PG 36:429)

Gr.Naz.*Or*.36.3
(SC 318:246)

Gr.Nyss.*Virg.*3
(Jaeger 8–I:265–66)

shocking extravagance, such as murders and the eating of children, murders of husbands, murders of mothers and brothers,
and incestuous unions."

Gr.Naz.*Or.*28.15
(*SC* 250:132)

Gr.Nyss.*Cant.*7
(Jaeger 6:205)

Gr.Naz.*Or.*28.14
(*SC* 250:130)

Idolatry was, therefore, the perversion of the desire for God.
That desire was in itself natural, noble, and divinely created, but
idolatry abused "the *kalon* to an evil purpose [to kakon]." In this
sense it was correct to interpret idolatry as a symptom of "ignorance of the knowledge of the true God." It was "ignorance of the
first nature" that prompted idolaters to "follow the traditional
honor [to images] as lawful and necessary." For when the human
mind, instead of "assenting to its diviner part" as by nature it was
intended to do, remained "alone and unaided," it began to substitute "monstrous fancies" for "its proper judgment" and therefore to conclude that so useful a product as wood was "no longer
wood but a god," and that gold was no longer a medium of

Bas.*Ep.*233.1
(Courtonne 3:39)

Gr.Naz.*Or.*39.7
(*PG* 36:341)

Lefherz 1958,33–59

Gr.Naz.*Or.*40.17
(*PG* 36:381)
Gr.Nyss.*V.Macr.*
(Jaeger 8–I:404)

Rom 12:1

Dölger 1932,81–116

commercial exchange but "an object of worship." Such practices
were best left to "the amusement of the children of the Greeks
and of the demonic authors of their folly, with their diversion of
the honor of God to themselves." That sense of abhorrence at the
practices and myths of paganism was intensified if Christians
themselves were still being observed resorting to "amulets or
incantations, those instruments for the devil to come in and steal
worship from God." Yet, it was seen not as superstition but as
authentic Christian piety and an authentic component of "the
worship offered by rational creatures" for Macrina to preserve
fragments of the true cross and to wear a pendant and a ring
containing them. Therefore, the charge that Cyprian, one of the
orthodox fathers of the church, had been a sorcerer—a charge
stemming from the mistaken identification of the Christian mar-

Delehaye 1921,314–32
Gr.Naz.*Or.*24.12
(*SC* 284:64–66)

Gr.Nyss.*Eun.*3.10.40–41
(Jaeger 2:305)

tyr Cyprian of Carthage with the pagan sorcerer Cyprian of
Antioch—had to be taken with great seriousness. Conversely, it
was a grave charge against a heretic to attribute to him an affinity
for paganism and superstition. And in the systematic articulation
of Christian orthodoxy, above all in the formulation of the
church's dogma of the One and the Three in the Holy Trinity, it
was obligatory at all costs for the interpreters of the orthodox

Gr.Nyss.*Tres dii*
(Jaeger 3–I:39)

doctrine, despite the superficial resemblances, "to avoid the appearance of any similarity with Greek polytheism." The apostle
Paul disavowed any such similarity in his declaration: "Even
though there be so-called gods, whether in heaven or on earth—
and indeed there are many such gods and many such lords—yet
for us there is one God, the Father, from whom are all things, and
we exist for him; there is one Lord, Jesus Christ, through whom

1 Cor 8:5–6   are all things, and we exist through him." Alluding to these
                    words, Basil saw it as vital to specify that biblical language about
                    God as "one" and "only" was directed against "the unreal gods
Bas.*Ep*.8.3   falsely so called," not against the deity of the Son and the Holy
(Courtonne 1:25)   Spirit. When the Bible used the term "the gods of the nations" to
Ps 95:5   refer to these false deities, calling them "demons," it was doing so
                    "in an equivocal sense [kath' homōnymian]," since in reality
Gr.Nyss.*Ref*.24   these "gods" were not gods at all.
(Jaeger 2:321–22)   In this attack on "the superstition of polytheism," Cappado-
Gr.Nyss.*Eun*.3.2.94 cian thought felt justified, while distancing itself in every possible
(Jaeger 2:83)   way from Greek religion, in attaching itself to the pagan philo-
                    sophical critique of polytheism, as Gregory of Nazianzus summa-
                    rized that critique: "Nor do those whom the Greeks worship as
                    gods and (to use their own expression) 'demons' need us in any
Jaeger 1947,4–9;   respect to be their accusers. For they are convicted upon the
Jaeger 1961,31n   testimony of their own natural theologians, some as subject to
                    passions, some as given to faction, and full of innumerable evils
                    and changes, and in a state of opposition, not only to one an-
                    other, but even to their first causes. . . . And if these are but
                    myths and fables, as they say in order to escape the shamefulness
                    of the story, what will they say in reference to the dictum that all
Hom.*Il*.15.189   things are divided into three parts, and that each god presides
                    over a different part of the universe, having a distinct province as
Gr.Naz.*Or*.31.16   well as a distinct rank? But our faith is not like this." It was,
(*SC* 250:306)   therefore, not only the adherent of Christian revelation but "ev-
                    eryone possessing a spark of practical sagacity" who had to see
                    what was at work in the writings of the "poets and moulders of
                    mythology" and of those who were "stringing together the myths
                    in their poems, fabricating a Dionysus, or a Hercules, or a Minos,
                    and the like, out of the combination of the superhuman with
Gr.Nyss.*Eun*.2.618–19 human bodies." But as should have been evident to the pagans,
(Jaeger 1:407)   too, "polyarchy," the theory that there was more than one su-
                    preme *arche*, led to "disorder" and eventually to "dissolution"
Gr.Naz.*Or*.29.2   and to the twilight of the gods.
(*SC* 250:178)   Other elements from the pagan critiques of polytheism were
                    also included in the Cappadocian critique. One was the sugges-
                    tion of the philosophers that perhaps polytheism itself, by pre-
                    supposing the existence of a supreme deity who stood above all
                    the gods of the myths and rituals, was somehow implicitly mono-
Gr.Naz.*Or*.4.117   theistic. As Werner Jaeger has said, "When we stop to consider
(*SC* 309:280)   for a moment with what a Greek could compare the phenome-
                    non of Jewish-Christian monotheism we find nothing but philos-
Jaeger 1961,29   ophy in Greek thought that corresponds to it." Alluding to that

Pl.*Tim.*39e-41a

Gr.Nyss.*Ref.*48
(Jaeger 2:332)

Cooke 1927,400–401
Schippers 1952,46–48

OCD 414–15;
ODCC 480

Gr.Naz.*Or.*28.14
(SC 250:130)

Gr.Naz.*Or.*21.36
(SC 270:188)

Gr.Nyss.*Apoll.*
(Jaeger 3–I:228–29)

Gr.Naz.*Or.*14.29
(PG 35:896)
Gr.Naz.*Or.*38.6
(PG 36:316–17)

Gr.Naz.*Or.*39.7
(PG 36:341)

Gr.Nyss.*Cant.*5
(Jaeger 6:147)

Gr.Nyss.*Cant.*7
(Jaeger 6:205)

Gr.Nyss.*Eun.*1.231
(Jaeger 1:94)

Gr.Nyss.*Or.catech.*pr.4
(Méridier 4)

suggestion, Gregory of Nyssa attributed to Plato the teaching of "the existence on high of a Maker and Creator of certain subordinate gods." Another explanation of the origins of polytheism that was very popular among some Christian apologists, especially the Latin theologian Lactantius, who had died just before the Cappadocians were born, as well as the earlier Greek apologist Clement of Alexandria, has acquired the name "euhemerism," from the theory of Euhemerus of Messene, a contemporary of Epicurus. Euhemerism explained the gods of pagan religion as human heroes who had been promoted to divine status. Adopting the euhemerist theory, Gregory of Nazianzus suggested "that some who were courtiers of arbitrary power, who extolled bodily strength and admired the *kalon,* made a god in time out of the one whom they honored, perhaps getting hold of some fable to help them with their imposture." Elsewhere, in his panegyric on Athanasius, he echoed this explanation while ridiculing it, when he extolled the Christian patriarch of Alexandria for having "really combined in himself alone the whole of all the attributes that have been parceled out by the sons of Greece among their various deities." Appropriating some of the Classical criticisms of Olympian theology, Cappadocian apologetics repeatedly disqualified any "degraded and abject thinking about God [chamairiphē kai chamaizēla peri ton theon ennoein]," whether it appeared in heretical Christianity or in paganism. Examples of such thinking were the portrayals of the gods in Greek polytheism as beings afflicted with the same passions to which human beings were subject. In their intemperance and debauchery, these "gods" exceeded human beings not in virtue but only in endurance. Such polytheism was not only "degraded and abject" as a portrayal of the divine, but disgraceful and demeaning as well to the human beings who professed and practiced it. And gradually the idolaters, having created the divine in their own image, had begun to resemble their immoral idols.

If, then, even within the confines of natural theology idolatry was to be rejected as the consequence of ignorance, and if, also within natural theology, the rational absurdity and religious unacceptability of polytheism was something that was "undeniable by the most boorish and simple-minded," what were, for a rational natural theology, the alternatives to polytheism? To the Cappadocians it was important, philosophically as well as rhetorically, "in a discussion held with one of those favoring Greek ideas," to be clear about that person's presuppositions, whether these included "the existence of a god or the atheistic view."

There were, Basil urged, "of necessity" only three alternative
answers to the problem of God: the "multiplying of godheads,"
that is, polytheism; the "denial of the Godhead altogether," that
is, atheism; and the refusal "ever to use in the plural any one of
the nouns relating to the Divinity, the insistence upon always
speaking in the singular number about one goodness . . . about

Bas.*Ep.*189.3–4
(Courtonne 2:134–35)

one power, about one Godhead"—that is, strict monotheism. In
the judgment of the Cappadocians, however, there was not as
much difference as might initially appear between the first and
the second of these, polytheism and atheism. For it was equally
impious, and equally unreasonable, to adhere to atheism or to

Gr.Nyss.*Virg.*7
(Jaeger 8–I:283)

superstition, "to deny the existence of any god at all or to believe
in many gods." Therefore Gregory of Nazianzus could speak in

Gr.Naz.*Or.*25.15
(SC 284:192)

the same sentence about "the superstition of the Greeks" and
about what he called "that polytheistic atheism of theirs." Yet
within Basil's set of alternative categories—polytheism, atheism,
and monotheism—some additional variations remained. During
the reign of the emperor Julian ("the Apostate"), from 361 to
363, the Cappadocians, who were also engaged in literary and

See pp.10–13,170–71

philosophical controversy with him, confronted one such variation. They sometimes attacked him for having "bartered the sa-

Gr.Naz.*Or.*42.3
(PG 36:461)

cred books for sacrifices to the nongods" by forsaking the Christianity of his youth and embracing polytheistic paganism. But
they pointed out that although the religion espoused and promoted by Julian was, in one sense, the reinstatement of polytheism, its conscious and systematic borrowing of elements of both
belief and practice from other religious traditions, including
above all Christianity and Judaism, marked it as, strictly speak-

Gr.Naz.*Or.*5.32
(SC 309:356–60)

OCD 999

ing, syncretistic rather than simply polytheistic. They also
pointed out that in Julian's theology the worship of the sun was

Bas.*Hex.*5.1
(SC 26:280)

being assigned the primary place, in a way that set it apart from

Cochrane 1944,285

conventional polytheism. Although Julian's theology has sometimes been called "Platonic solar monotheism," in the judgment
of the Cappadocians that was finally of a piece with the tendency
of the polytheists to "make a god of the sun, or of the moon, or of
the host of stars, or of heaven itself with all its hosts, as the power

Gr.Naz.*Or.*28.14
(SC 250:128)

guiding the universe."

As that attack on the identification of God with the forces of
the universe suggested, there were, in addition to such syncretism, two other major alternative doctrines of the divine that did
not fit neatly into the tripartite taxonomy of polytheism, atheism,
and monotheism—namely, dualism and pantheism. Dualism
was a special problem (and a special temptation) for Christian

thought because it gave metaphysical and theological status to an intuition that was, existentially but by no means ontologically, central to the gospel: that "the reign of darkness," as Christ called it in the Garden of Gethsemane, did have its "hour"; that the devil was, as the apostle Paul called him, "the god of this passing *aeon*," and, as Christ called him more than once in the Gospel of John, "the prince of this world"; and therefore that evil was a force in the world that needed to be taken with utmost seriousness. From the Gospel of John to Milton's *Paradise Lost,* this need repeatedly threatened to make Satan into a second god and to tilt the Christian doctrine of God in the direction of a thoroughgoing dualism, which Christian thought has resisted. The problem went back much farther than that, to the primal struggle between light and darkness, when, as Gregory of Nyssa put it, "at the entrance of light, by the will of God the darkness that prevailed over the earliest creation was scattered." Yet "it was necessary, when light traveled over one side and the earth obstructed it on the opposite by its own bulk, that a side of darkness should be left by the obscuration." As Basil admitted, the second verse of the Bible, "Darkness was over the face of the abyss," had become "a new source for fables and most impious imaginations" for the dualistic Manicheans, who used these words to posit an interpretation of darkness as "the very personification of evil." But Basil insisted in reply that evil was "not a living animated essence" with a reality of its own and that there was not "an original nature of wickedness" but a negation of reality through a "falling away from the good."

A certain kind of "superficial plausibility" had to be granted to these dualistic Manichean theories. For they argued that "if the operating force in accordance with the good" were entirely that of a divine nature that was good, then it would not do to "refer this painful and perishing life to the workmanship of the good, but rather to suppose for such a life as this another author, as the origin of the tendency to misery in our nature"; this implied that it was necessary to protect the integrity of God against the implications of the problem of evil by positing a second god. Whatever its motivation, any such theory of "two opposite principles" that were different "both in nature and in will" but equal in power, and any such picture of "a drawn battle because of the inexhaustibleness of their powers," posed a basic threat to the doctrine of creation, and still more fundamentally to the very doctrine of the oneness of God. Paradoxical though it seemed to say so, natural theology was sounder when it reasoned from evil

Lk 22:53

2 Cor 4:4
Jn 14:30;16:11

Portmann 1954,104–8;
Philippou 1966,251–56

Bring 1929

Gr.Nyss.*Eun.*2.277
(Jaeger 1:307–8)

Gn 1:2

Bas.*Hex.*2.4–5
(SC 26:152–60)

ap.Gr.Nyss.*Or.catech.*7.1
(Méridier 44)

Gr.Nyss.*Eun.*1.503–7
(Jaeger 1:171–73)

to transcendent monotheism, from "the execrable character of evil" to "the unalterable pureness of God"; for "a consideration of death's dissolution as the worst of ills" led to "giving the name of 'immortal' and 'indissoluble' at once to the one removed from every conception of that kind." Ultimately (in the literal sense of the word "ultimately"), the true meaning of evil could be understood only in the light of the eventual victory of God over evil, which was a central component of the eschatology of the Cappadocians, especially in the form this took in Nyssen's doctrine of *apocatastasis*. As an alternative to polytheism, therefore, Manichean or Marcionite dualism was unacceptable, even on the grounds of natural theology.

Yet the apologetic case of the Cappadocians was no less vigorously concerned that this rejection both of polytheism and of dualism not be turned into a pantheistic blurring of the ontological difference between the creation and the Creator. To speak of God as having a "nature" meant to say, despite the terminology, that God did not resemble the nature of the universe but transcended it. It seemed self-evident, therefore, that the term "nature [physis]" was an equivocal one here, not referring to "God" and to "the cosmos" as though these were alternate ways of speaking about the same reality. Gregory of Nyssa made the point clear in drawing, as a first principle to be comprehended by "the mind," the sharpest possible distinction between the term "begetting [gennēsis]" as applied to humanity in common usage and the same term as applied to deity in orthodox trinitarian usage, that is, between its applicability to any creature whatever and its applicability to the Creator: "[In human begetting] beneath it all is nature, by God's will, with her wonder-working. . . . In a word, nature, advancing through all these processes by which human life is built up, brings the non-existent to birth. . . . But when it comes to the divine begetting, the mind rejects this ministration of nature. . . . Anyone who enters on divine topics without any carnal conceptions will not . . . count the Creator of all nature as in need of help from nature, or admit any extension of time into the life of the eternal." That kind of pantheism was definitely not what was meant by the teaching that the cosmos was a "complete whole."

The rational rejection of all these philosophical-theological isms—polytheism, atheism, syncretism, dualism, and pantheism— left, as a reasonable and acceptable view of the divine, only monotheism, which was the one and only system that drew with the greatest possible precision "the contrast between the

Gr.Nyss.*Eun*.2.477
(Jaeger 1:365)

Vollert 1897,36–55
See pp.324–26

Bas.*Eun*.2.34
(*SC* 305:140)

Gr.Naz.*Or*.28.14
(*SC* 250:128–30)

Gr.Nyss.*V.Mos*.1
(Jaeger 7–I:22)

Gr.Nyss.*Eun*.1.626–28
(Jaeger 1:206–7)
See pp.92–93
Gr.Nyss.*Eun*.3.4.34
(Jaeger 2:147)

One and the many, between the true and the false, between so-called gods and the one true God." For the Cappadocians as Christian believers and as theologians of the orthodox church, monotheism was guaranteed by a testimony whose authority they regarded as far more reliable than the "dim and imperfect comprehension of the divine nature" provided by reason. That testimony was contained in countless affirmations both of Sacred Scripture and of Christian tradition. Speaking through the prophet Isaiah, God had declared: "I am the first, and hereafter am I, and no god was before me, and no god shall be after me." With such authority behind it, monotheism was beyond all question. It was from "this inspired utterance spoken by the mouth of the prophet," Gregory of Nyssa affirmed on the basis of this passage, that there came "the doctrine of the divine nature as one, continuous with itself." For these words of Isaiah meant: "That which is after God is the creation, and that which is anterior to God is nothingness, and nothingness is not God; or one should rather say, that which is anterior to God is God in his eternal blessedness, defined in contradistinction to nothingness [pros ouden orizomenos]." For God transcended all notions of "before" and "after," and therefore time itself. Writing against the same opponent, Nyssen went on to clarify what the oneness of God meant in the orthodox tradition. The saying of Christ, "The Father and I are one," proved that despite "the signification of not being coupled with anything else" that the word "one" carried in the ordinary system of counting, even that could not be used to "separate the Father from the Son." The one single "Godhead [theotēs]" was common to Father, Son, and Holy Spirit. Nothing, and certainly not the church's orthodox dogma of the Trinity, could be permitted to compromise the absoluteness of monotheism, although it did eventually compel the Cappadocians to posit a basic redefinition of divine oneness.

Nevertheless, it would be a misreading of Cappadocian thought to conclude from this strong emphasis on the authority of revelation through Scripture and tradition that in their view monotheism lacked support also from rational thought and natural theology. Gregory of Nyssa opened the argument of his *Catechetical Oration* with a claim of such support for his doctrines of "the Deity" and even of "the *Logos*" from "the outsiders to our dogma." According to Basil, when "the judgment of the mind, such a good thing and one given to us for a good end, namely, the perception of God," was used properly for that end, the human mind was carrying out, albeit within the limitations of its capacity

Gr.Nyss.*Ref.*24
(Jaeger 2:321–22 [var.])

Gr.Nyss.*Eun.*2.130
(Jaeger 1:263)

Is 44:6

Gr.Nyss.*Eun.*3.3.10
(Jaeger 2:110)

See pp.115–18

Koperski 1936,45–65

Jn 10:30

Gr.Nyss.*Eun.*3.9.20–21
(Jaeger 2:271)
Gr.Naz.*Or.*25.16
(SC 284:194–96)

See pp.245–47

Gr.Nyss.*Or.catech.*1.2
(Méridier 8)

The Many and the One

83

Bas.*Ep.*233.2
(Courtonne 3:40–41)

Eun.ap.Bas.*Eun.*1.5
(SC 299:170)

Gr.Naz.*Or.*31.15
(SC 250:304)

Gr.Nyss.*Eun.*3.9.59
(Jaeger 2:286)
Pl.*Tim.*39e-41a
Gr.Nyss.*Ref.*48
(Jaeger 2:332)

DTC 7:620
OED 5–I:223

See pp.259–62

Col 1:16

and under the constraints of *apophatic* theology, its "primary function, namely, to know our God" as one. He did not seem to object, moreover, when Eunomius set forth the "confession of God as one, both in accordance with natural knowledge [kata physikēn ennoian] and in accordance with the teaching of the fathers [kata tēn tōn paterōn didaskalian]," thus coordinating "natural" and "traditional" authority in support of the monotheistic position. From their study of the Classical tradition, these Christian theologians were aware that "the more advanced philosophers among the Greeks" had believed in "one Godhead [theotēta]," despite their having had "many gods, not one." Although not strict monotheists in the biblical and Christian sense, therefore, these Classical Greek thinkers did postulate "one great god of some sort, pre-eminent above the rest," in relation to whom there were "some subject powers, differing among themselves in the way of superiority or inferiority, in some regular order and sequence, but all alike subject to the supreme [power]." Plato, for example, was read as having, in the *Timaeus,* asserted the existence of "a Maker and Creator of certain subordinate gods."

Such language about "subject powers" and "subordinate gods" in relation to a "Maker and Creator" who was "supreme" suggested that not "monotheism" but "henotheism" (a term that appears to have been a nineteenth-century coinage) might be the best designation for the doctrine of God, and of the gods, that the Cappadocians claimed to have found in the Greek philosophical tradition. Yet this problem of the metaphysical relation between the supreme Deity and subordinate powers was not confined to polytheistic pagans. It appeared within the Cappadocian system of natural and revealed theology itself, in connection with their doctrine of angels. There were evident—and troubling— parallels between Judeo-Christian angelology and pagan polytheism. The conventional division by the Cappadocians of all reality between the world perceived by the senses and the world perceived by the mind did line up, on one side of the boundary marked by that distinction, the entire physical cosmos including the human body, and on the other side of the boundary marked by that distinction, not only God but other spiritual beings, as belonging to the realm of timeless spirit. The apostle Paul himself drew such a distinction between "things visible" and "things invisible." On the basis of that Pauline distinction, Gregory of Nyssa proposed a grand schematization of "the things cognizable by the senses" as one category, and "the intelligible [noētos] world" as the other category. But then within this latter category he asserted a distinction that was ontologically even more basic: "the things that have been made in the way of creation" versus "the existence that is above creation." It was into the class of intelligible but created existence that Paul in that same passage had put "thrones or dominions or rulers or powers—all things have been created"; they had been "created," Gregory explained, by one who stood above all of creation, whether visible or invisible. Therefore he went on to argue that "the interval dividing and fencing off uncreated from created nature" was metaphysically "wide and insurmountable," so much so that only the language of *apophasis* was appropriate in speaking about that which was "transcendent over all notion of degree," admitting neither *arche* nor *telos* and experiencing "neither addition nor diminution." Thus, while it was legitimate to employ such terms as "uncreated intelligible nature" (God) and "created intelligible nature" (angels and the human soul) in contradistinction to "visible and empirical nature" (the physical universe and the human body), the more important distinction by far for "our conception of existences" was that between "the creation [whether visible or invisible] and the uncreated nature" of the one true God. Ultimately only that distinction was consistent with authentic monotheism.

In some passages that appeared in their writings the Cappadocians did give the impression that in speaking about this oneness of God, especially in connection with the trinitarian doctrine, they were applying to the doctrine of God a generalized Platonic system of universals, and that the universal "deity [theotēs]" was that shared by Father, Son, and Holy Spirit. This came in response to the argument of certain heretics, who reasoned: "Peter, James, and John, being in one human nature, are nevertheless called three men, and there is no absurdity in describing those who are united in nature, if they are more than one, by the plural number of the name derived from their nature." Therefore, so the argument of the heretics continued, it would, by a similar reasoning, be acceptable to refer to Father, Son, and Holy Spirit as "three gods." But it was in fact, Gregory of Nyssa replied, a catachresis even to use the plural "three men [treis anthrōpoi]" in speaking about Peter, James, and John; for although there were "many sharing in the nature," what they shared—namely, "humanity [anthrōpos]"—was still one. In arguing that way, he could be construed as maintaining that it was nothing more grave than a similar "imprecision of language" to speak of Father, Son,

Gr.Nyss.*Eun.*1.306–7 (Jaeger 1:117)

Gr.Nyss.*Eun.*2.69–70 (Jaeger 1:246–47)

Gr.Nyss.*Eun.*1.275–77 (Jaeger 1:106–7)

Gr.Nyss.*Eun.*3.3.2 (Jaeger 2:107–8)

Mateo-Seco–Bastero 1988,269–84

Gr.Nyss.*Tres dii*
(Jaeger 3–I:40)

Bethune-Baker 1901

Gr.Nyss.*Eun.*1.231–32
(Jaeger 1:94–95)

Quasten 2:57–62
Gr.Nyss.*Eun.*3.2.17
(Jaeger 2:57)
Gn 1:1
Jn 1:1

Gr.Nyss.*Eun.*3.6.33
(Jaeger 2:226)

See pp.66–68

and Holy Spirit as "three gods," because, like Peter, James, and John, the three divine *hypostases* shared in one nature, "deity [theotēs]." Thus, they could be accused of having salvaged monotheism by resort to the abstractions of the Platonic doctrine of ideas and of having equated the oneness of God, the most fundamental confession of biblical faith, with a philosophical theory borrowed from Hellenism. Although that would be a drastically reductionist way of reading the trinitarian monotheism of the Cappadocians and therefore a radical oversimplification of their profound and complex position, it is nevertheless correct to say that monotheism was, in their judgment, a valid philosophical theory based on reason, not only a valid biblical tenet based on revelation. Monotheism was a necessary rational inference from the rational principles of *apophasis.* "The impossibility of conceiving of the viewless, formless, and sizeless as multiform and composite" was a corollary of *apophatic* theology to which even the unlettered and naive would have to assent.

It was indispensable to this monotheism that there be only one single *arche* for all reality. As applied to God, the term *arche* was familiar not only from the works of centuries of Classical philosophers but also from the writings of Greek Christian theologians, above all of Origen in the title of his most brilliant speculative work, *On First Principles,* called *Peri Archōn* in Greek. It was sanctioned through its appearance in the first sentence of the Septuagint version of the Old Testament, and then in the first sentence of the Gospel of John in the New Testament. Nevertheless, the Cappadocians found it imperative to interpret even this venerable biblical, philosophical, and theological term by means of *apophasis;* for both *arche* and *telos* were "terms for limits of extension," so that because, in the case of God, there was no extension, there could be no limit either. Only on that basis could even a Greek term with such impressive credentials, both Classical and Christian, as *arche* be said to apply to a "divine nature without extension and with no limit." Commenting on the first verse of the Bible, Basil cataloged the several meanings of the word *arche* in both biblical and Classical usage: "The first movement was called *arche.* . . . Again, we call *arche* the essential and first part from which a thing proceeds, such as the foundation of a house. . . . Often even the good that is the final cause is the *arche* of actions." In any of these senses, it was "ridiculous to imagine a beginning of a beginning." And, in keeping with the rejection of the notion of an infinite regress, it followed: "If we divide the *arche* into two, we make two instead of one, or rather

Bas.*Hex*.1.5–6
(SC 26:108–10)

we make several; in fact, we really make an infinity, for all that which is divided is divisible to the infinite." Even in the formulation of the Christian doctrine of the Trinity, therefore, it was "Greek or polytheistic," but neither rational nor orthodox, to posit "three *archai*," whereas it was necessary at the same time, in affirming a single *arche*, not to make it "constricted and en-

Gr.Naz.*Or*.25.16
(SC 284:194)

vious and powerless," but to see it as eternally sharing and being shared. Nor did the acceptance of the orthodox doctrine of the Son as "*homoousios* with the Father," which meant "acknowledging one nature with the difference of *hypostasis*," lead in any

See pp.238–41
Gr.Nyss.*Eun*.1.483–86
(Jaeger 1:166–67)

way to the opinion that there were two first causes. On the contrary, there was one first cause, one *arche*, one transcendent.

Any other conception of the divine would have been, in the judgment of the Cappadocians, a violation of fundamental metaphysical principle (as well as, more obviously, a violation of biblical teaching and of orthodox dogma). It was an implication of the natural knowledge of God, available to anyone who was not completely "narrow-minded," to affirm "a divine and blessed

Gr.Nyss.*Eun*.1.418
(Jaeger 1:148)
Ps 78:5–6
Gr.Naz.*Or*.31.22
(SC 250:316–18)

nature free from the passion of envy," as well as from every other passion. The Bible spoke of God's "indignation [zēlos]" and "wrath [orgē]"; but this was spoken from the human standpoint, because "we have made his punishing us his 'being angered.'" Once again, it was mandatory not to permit even the orthodox doctrine that the Father had "begotten [gegennēken]" the Son to compromise in any way the fundamental metaphysical principle:

Gr.Naz.*Or*.25.17
(SC 284:198)

"The divine is characterized by *apatheia*." For because that divine and blessed nature was "simple, uniform, and incomposite," it was devoid of any "complicity or composition of dissimilars." As a result, the acceptance of "the idea of a divine nature" carried with it, "by the implication of that very name, the perfection in it

Gr.Nyss.*Maced.*
(Jaeger 3–1:91)

of every conceivable thing befitting the Deity." But "stability [stasis]" did not have a proper place among those conceivable forms of perfection, even though it might seem to be an attribute of deity; for it was axiomatic, in the light of negative theology, that neither "conflict [lysis]" nor "stability [stasis]," which were in fact corollaries of each other, could be predicated of the divine

Gr.Naz.*Or*.6.12
(PG 35:737)

nature. A sound conception of the divine nature, which had to be an *apophatic* one, could act as a restraint on such unworthy images, to which either learned speculation or naive spirituality might lead: any "degraded and abject thinking about God [chamairiphē kai chamaizēla peri ton theon ennoein]," whatever

Gr.Nyss.*Apoll.*
(Jaeger 3–I:228–29)

its origin might be, was ruled out. But that methodological limitation had its constructive side as well. The identification of "the conceptions appropriate to attribute to deity [tōn theoprepōn noēmatōn]" implied that a proper awareness of divinity brought with it "devout intuitions of that divine and transcendent nature." These "intuitions," in turn, could perform a normative function in the task of discriminating between "the conceptions appropriate to attribute to deity," above all, monotheism, and all "degraded and abject thinking about God," above all, polytheism, superstition, and idolatry.

There was one category of such "degraded and abject thinking about God" to which the Cappadocians were especially sensitive: the ascription of gender to deity. That sensitivity was related to the ascetic element in their anthropology and moral theology, of which the most far-reaching institutional expression was the monastic *Rule of Basil* in its various recensions (whatever the relation of the *Rule of Basil* to Basil's ascetic works may have been). The most trenchant summary of ascetic theory in the works of the Cappadocians was probably the treatise *On Virginity,* which is regarded as the earliest of the writings of Gregory of Nyssa, being assigned to the year 371. It was as much an exposition of the doctrine of God as it was an exhortation to virginity. It was also rooted at least partly in a revulsion against the language of polytheistic mythology, in which a flagrant sexuality was all too often the most evident characteristic of so-called divine beings that were regarded as superior to human beings. And it was one of the most obvious implications of *apophasis;* for if it was illegitimate to attribute to the Deity, as literally and affirmatively true, even such predicates as *Logos* and light, with all their biblical authorization and orthodox validation, how much less justification was there for entertaining about the divine nature any connotations coming from the metaphors of gender, including the metaphors of gender that Scripture itself employed! At this point the excellent training of the Cappadocians in Greek grammar likewise stood them in good stead. They were able, for example, to take advantage of a singular circumstance in the very nouns that the trinitarian orthodoxy of the church used in Greek to speak about God: the grammatical gender of the title "God [theos]" and of the title "Father [patēr]" was masculine; the grammatical gender of the term "Deity [theotēs]" (and of the name "Trinity [trias]") was feminine; and the grammatical gender of the word "Spirit [pneuma]" was neuter. No one would have had a right on the basis of these grammatical idiosyncracies to describe "our God as a male" or to think of the Deity as a female or to suppose that the Holy Spirit as the third *hypostasis*

Gr.Nyss.*Maced.*
(Jaeger 3–1:93–94)

Viller-Rahner 1990, 122–46; Blond 1944, 157–210; Keenan 1950, 167–207

Florovsky 10:139–48

Morison 1912,15–21; Clarke 1913,63–106

Quasten 3:269–72
Gr.Nyss.*Virg.*
(Jaeger 8–1:247–343)

Gr.Naz.*Or.*38.6
(*PG* 36:316)

Gr.Naz.*Or.*37.4
(*SC* 318:278)

Gr.Naz.Or.31.7
(SC 250:288)

See pp.291–93
Gr.Nyss.Cant.7
(Jaeger 6:213)
Gr.Nyss.Hom.opif.22
(PG 44:205)
Gr.Nyss.Cant.7
(Jaeger 6:213)

Eph 3:14–15

Gr.Naz.Or.25.16
(SC 284:196)
Jn 15:26
Gr.Naz.Or.29.2
(SC 250:180)

Gr.Nyss.Eun.1.548
(Jaeger 1:184–85)

Gr.Nyss.Eun.2.419
(Jaeger 1:348)

See pp.218–19
1 Chr 24:31;27:22;
2 Chr 19:8;23:20;26:12;
4 Mc 7:19;16:25
Acts 2:29;7:8;7:9;
Heb 7:4

(also a feminine noun) in the Trinity was devoid of the sexuality of the first and the second *hypostases*.

Indeed, according to Gregory of Nyssa, sexuality would not continue to be characteristic even of human nature when this had been glorified; nor had gender originally belonged to the lofty character of human nature, but to its irrational element. Infinitely less permissible was it to apply gender to God. When the language of the Bible and of the church employed for God titles and metaphors such as "Father," which to human ears connoted gender, that was in fact a reminder of the biblical truth that it was the God beyond gender, as the New Testament affirmed, "from whom every fatherhood [patria] in heaven and on earth takes its name." Every other father was also a son, every other "begetter" had first been "begotten"; such words, therefore, were being used here in a unique sense. Therefore, the real metaphor was not at all in the use of the name "Father" for God but in the application of such a term to human procreation and to human fatherhood, which was always one in a series of fatherhoods and of sonships. Yet, that metaphor did not in the least inhibit, but in fact facilitated, ascribing to a genderless Deity the qualities not only of a transcendent fatherhood but of a transcendent motherhood: "The divine power . . . , though exalted far above our nature and inaccessible to all approach, like a tender mother who joins in the inarticulate utterances of her babe, gives to our human nature what it is capable of receiving; and thus in the various manifestations of God to humanity, God both adapts to humanity and speaks in human language." Both this free use of the maternal metaphor and this severe limitation on the paternal metaphor came from Gregory of Nyssa, and from the same treatise; they were paralleled, in his writings and in those of the other Cappadocians, by the ease in moving back and forth between the masculine title *Logos* and the feminine title *Sophia* for Jesus Christ as the second *hypostasis* of the Trinity. Despite the use of the post-Classical title "patriarch [patriarchēs]," which appeared in some seven passages in the Septuagint and then was employed four times in the New Testament, it would be a draconian misreading of their thought to attribute to the Cappadocians what is sometimes labeled a "patriarchal" vision of deity, as though God were the projection of maleness writ large. For their theological understanding of both of the components of that word—"patēr" and "arche"—was the affirmation of a divine nature that transcended gender, together with all other anthropomorphic and anthropopathic images. Thus gender, too, was

Gr.Nyss.*Ref*.24
(Jaeger 2:321–22 [var.])

See pp.231–47

an index of "the contrast between the One and the many, between the true and the false, between so-called gods and the one true God." But this apologetic monotheism was challenged and therefore deepened when it became a presupposition in the Cappadocian defense of the orthodox dogma of the Trinity.

CHAPTER 6

The Universe as Cosmos

The doctrine of God rendered the apologetic rejection of polytheism of supreme importance in the Cappadocian system of thought. Even apart from its destructive implications for prayer and spirituality, through which, in the words of Gregory of Nazianzus, worshipers were "disgraced by the objects of their worship" rather than ennobled as they should have been, polytheism was to be repudiated because it presented a distorted picture of divine reality. Its corrupting effect on human morality was likewise inseparable from its deadly combination of irrationality and blasphemy. In a grotesque counterpart to the sublime process of *theosis,* through which those who worshiped the true God came to "share in the very being of God," idolaters became copies of the idols they worshiped. The immorality of the gods on Mount Olympus was mirrored in the immorality of the human feasts and festivals in their honor. Both corollaries of polytheism, the devotional and the ethical, were essential components of the apologetic case of the Cappadocians. So, too, was the cosmological corollary of polytheism. Already under the rubric of natural theology as apologetics, therefore, polytheism also represented an unacceptable subversion of the idea of the world as cosmos as the all-inclusive universe.

Closely paralleling Basil's method of sorting out theories of deity, Gregory of Nazianzus, in a taxonomy of systems of natural theology that was in both form and terminology reminiscent of Aristotle's classification of forms of government in Book III of the *Politics,* identified "the three most ancient opinions concerning

Gr.Naz.Or.39.7
(PG 36:341)

Gr.Naz.Or.14.29
(PG 35:896)
See pp.285–86,295
2 Pt 1:4
Gr.Nyss.Cant.5
(Jaeger 6:147)

Gr.Naz.Or.38.6
(PG 36:316–17)

Pease 1941,163–200
Bas.Ep.189.3–4
(Courtonne 2:134–35)

Arist.Pol.1279

God" as: "anarchia," "polyarchia," and "monarchia." "The first two," he went on, were "the sport of the children of Hellas," adding: "And may they continue to be so!" Despite the distinction between these, moreover, both led to the same cosmological conclusion. For anarchy, the absence of any *arche,* defined itself as "a thing without order," either within itself or in the world. Polyarchy, in contrast, the existence of many *archai,* was "factious"; and therefore in its cosmological implications it was in fact no less "anarchical, and thus disorderly." In sum, both anarchy and polyarchy tended "to the same thing, namely, disorder; and this to dissolution, disorder being the first step to dissolution." Only a divine "monarchia," therefore, could salvage order in the world. This divine monarchy pertained, according to Macrina, both to the creation of humanity and to the creation of the rest of the universe. Basil of Caesarea, too, opened his exhaustive treatise on cosmology with the assertion that "the good order reigning in visible things" was the proper starting point for "anyone undertaking to narrate the formation of the world." And Gregory of Nyssa rejected as "usurpation" any theory that declined to ascribe authority in the world on the basis of "an ontological superiority"; such a theory of "arbitrary distribution" assigned authority as though it "had been piled at random on [God], who after that distribution obtained preference over his equals," without having such preference based on "ontological superiority," indeed on metaphysical transcendence.

All four Cappadocians, then, posited a fundamental philosophical connection between the correct doctrine about divine being and the quest for the world order. It was the task of speculative thought to render "the sublime ordering of the universe as cosmos generally intelligible." For it was axiomatic that order was preferable to disorder and anarchy. As polytheism led by inexorable logic to chaos and cosmic disorder, so conversely the existence of the world as a cosmos, as "a vast nature and an elaborate system," was a correlative of monotheism and was inconsistent with any of the alternatives to monotheism. What made the search for some kind of order within or beyond the welter of natural phenomena necessary, but also difficult, was the sheer quantity of "nature's inevitable changes." Natural theology, no less than revealed theology, was impelled, when faced with these changes, to look for a comprehensive worldview. "A cause of the system and government of the universe, on which all nature depends, to which it owes its origin and cause, toward which it inclines and moves, and in which it abides" was the

Gr.Naz.Or.29.2
(SC 250:178)

Macr.ap.Gr.Nyss.
Anim.res. (PG 46:57)
Cesaro 1929,77–89

Bas.Hex.1.1
(SC 26:86)

Gr.Nyss.Eun.1.526
(Jaeger 1:178)

Gr.Nyss.Hom.opif.pr.
(PG 44:125)
Gr.Naz.Or.2.4
(SC 247:90)

Bas.Hex.5.10
(SC 26:320–22)

Gr.Nyss.Virg.4
(Jaeger 8–I:276)

Gr.Nyss.*Eun*.2.222
(Jaeger 1:290)

Gr.Nyss.*Eun*.3.4.34
(Jaeger 2:147)

Gr.Nyss.*Eun*.3.2.124
(Jaeger 2:92–93)

Gr.Nyss.*Eun*.1.402
(Jaeger 1:143–44)
Gr.Nyss.*Hex*.
(PG 44:92)
Courtonne 1934,131–36

Bas.*Hex*.2.2
(SC 26:148)

Gr.Nyss.*Infant*.
(Jaeger 3–II:71)

See pp.74–81

Gr.Nyss.*Eun*.3.4.34
(Jaeger 2:147)

comprehensive formula of Gregory of Nyssa for this comprehensive worldview. Such a worldview was equally necessary whether one looked "at the cosmos as a whole, or at the parts of the cosmos making up that complete whole." Each of those many parts of the cosmos was an individual unto itself, incapable of comparison with the universe as a whole or with the other individual natures within the universe. Empirical observation would confirm such a "dissimilarity among the elements of the world," by which there was "in each thing making up the framework of the whole, an adherence to its natural opposite." Nevertheless, each individual creature was beautiful in its own way. But most beautiful of all was the world order as cosmos, binding "all the diverse parts of the universe by such links of indissoluble attachment and by so perfect a fellowship and harmony as to make the most distant, in spite of their distance, appear united in one universal sympathy." Therefore, someone who started "from a philosophical perspective" and came to the study of science would "possess the soul-insight" that made possible "a consideration of the harmony of the whole." Such an observer would "inspect the beautiful harmony that resulted even from opposite movements in the circular revolutions" of the heavens, according to the Ptolemaic solar system, and would note "the inner circles of these turning in the opposite direction from that of the fixed stars."

As part of its rejection, on grounds of natural theology, of all alternatives to monotheism, Cappadocian apologetics on the doctrine of God repudiated any pantheistic interpretation of this doctrine that the cosmos was a "complete whole," as though the cosmos possessed such wholeness because of the metaphysical identity of the creation with the Creator. The repudiation of pantheism was important also for their cosmology. For a necessary corollary of the doctrine of God, within natural theology as well as within revealed theology, was the principle that the concept of a "complete whole" was not to be permitted to lead to the theory that the stuff of which the cosmos was made had from eternity coexisted with God but separately from God. That theory was opposite to pantheism in the sense that it did not identify God and the world, and yet in certain ways it was akin to it, because it attributed to the world an eternity that was to be attributed to God alone. By applying also to this issue the *apophatic* method of affirmation-through-negation, which was worked out above all in their doctrine of God and their doctrine of the knowledge of God, the Cappadocians made use of their cosmology as a means of reaffirming in yet another form their doctrine of divine transcendence. Therefore, Gregory of Nyssa was obliged to assent when Eunomius's confession of faith declared: "In the act of creation, God does not stand in need of matter or parts or natural instruments"; this meant, Gregory agreed, that there was "in the power and the *sophia* of God no need of any external assistance."

1 Cor 1:24
Gr.Nyss.*Ref*.68–69
(Jaeger 2:340–41)

The phrase of Eunomius, "matter or parts or natural instruments," by putting "matter" first, suggested that a principal threat to the concept of divine transcendence, and therefore to the definition of the world as cosmos, came from the various Classical theories of matter as preexistent and therefore as coexistent with God, as well as from the effort of certain heretical systems within Christian thought to accommodate the church's doctrine of creation to such theories. The starting point of those heretical systems—about which later generations have, as usual, been informed almost exclusively on the basis of the critical reports coming from their orthodox opponents, including the Cappadocians, the original writings of the heretics having meanwhile been destroyed—was the orthodox teaching about divine transcendence. These systems professed to see in a doctrine of the eternity of matter the only means of safeguarding the transcendence of God from the dangers that appeared to lie in the orthodox doctrine of creation, which, they judged, involved the transcendent nature of God too intimately and directly in the stuff of the material world, and therefore also in evil. The transcendence of God meant that God was (in a series of alpha privatives) "by nature simple and immaterial, without quantity, or size, or combination [aÿlos, apoios te kai amegethēs, kai asynthetos], and removed from the idea of circumscription by way of figure." Matter, on the other hand, was "apprehended in extension measured by intervals" and was perceptible to the human senses through "color, and figure, and bulk, and size, and resistance, and the other attributes belonging to it." If God was truly transcendent, "the impossibility of conceiving of any of these [attributes] in the divine nature" necessarily followed. That posed the dilemma, formulated in the name of his opponents by Gregory of Nyssa: "What method is there for the production of matter from the immaterial, or of the nature that has dimensions from that which is without extension?" To resolve the dilemma, this compromise position put forth a theory of "double origin," attributing "the form of the world to the supreme Artificer" and "matter to a source external to the Creator."

ap.Gr.Nyss.*Hom.opif*.23
(*PG* 44:209–12)

ap.Bas.*Hex*.2.2
(*SC* 26:146)

The Cappadocians countered these speculations with several of the apologetic arguments formulated in their consideration of the natural theologies of their opponents, both pagan and Christian. Therefore they rejected, as not only heretical but logically untenable, this theory of "two eternal and unbegotten existences [duo anarcha kai agennēta], having their being concurrently with each other." All the rational arguments for monotheism and against polytheism applied with equal force to this "lie following from the first fable." That fundamental difference set the doctrine of the oneness of God apart from all doctrines that fell short of strict monotheism by hypothesizing more than one center of divine being, whether they posited a plurality of such centers, as polytheism did, or only two such centers, as this species of cosmological dualism did. It was frivolous, both mathematically and metaphysically, to argue that "two" was closer to "one" than "many" was; for the oneness of God, as laid down once and for all time in the Shema of the Fifth Book of Moses, "Hear, Israel: the Lord is our God, the Lord our one God," was absolute and beyond all compromise, no less so in the face of the orthodox dogma of the Trinity, which the Cappadocians interpreted as the only way to vindicate the Shema, in the face of the Christian worship of Christ as divine. Similarly, all the apologetic arguments in support of *apophasis* were employed to refute the theory of the eternity of matter. For while representing themselves as a means of safeguarding the doctrine of divine transcendence, such theories constituted an unwarranted effort "to measure a power both incomprehensible to the human reason and unutterable by the human voice." This put them into the same class with all the other presumptuous attempts to encompass the ineffable mystery of divine being within the limitations of "the human reason" and "the human voice." The sovereign and overruling power of God was not comprehended in words, not even in divine words, but it was witnessed to by the works of God, "the boundless *aeons* and the beauties of the cosmos."

All of these cosmological and metaphysical theories being refuted by the Cappadocians could be traced to Classical sources as well. Each in his own way, both Plato and Aristotle had posited a preexistent (and therefore, in some sense, eternal) matter, which the Creator (who was therefore, in some sense, coexistent with it) had shaped into a cosmos. Basil appears to have had both the Platonic and the Aristotelian versions of the doctrine of the eternity of matter in view when he summarized such speculation:

ap.Gr.Nyss.*Hom.opif.*23
(*PG* 44:212)

Bas.*Hex.*3.3
(*SC* 26:198)

Dt 6:4

Gr.Nyss *Tres dii*
(Jaeger : –I:155)

Bas.*Hex.*2.2
(*SC* 26:148)

Gr.Nyss.*Eun.*2.291
(Jaeger 1:312)

"Such is the idea that they make for themselves of the divine work of creation [dēmiourgia]. The form of the world is due to the wisdom of the supreme artificer, matter came to the creator from without, and thus the world results from a double origin." Elsewhere, however, Basil found the distinction between "matter" and "form" sufficiently attractive to see in it a fitting analogy for the doctrine of the Holy Spirit. It was the Aristotelian version of these questions that was to leave its mark permanently on what the Gifford Lectures of Etienne Gilson called "the spirit of medieval philosophy," for it proved to be eminently useful to medieval Western scholastic philosophy, specifically also in its interpretation of the universe as cosmos. But as was evident from Basil's brief summary, Aristotle combined this "hylomorphism" with the view that creation consisted in bringing preexistent matter together with form to produce reality, and therefore that matter itself was not created out of nothing. The regard of Thomas Aquinas for Aristotle's natural wisdom was sorely tested by a doctrine that was so overtly contradictory to the Christian doctrine of creatio ex nihilo. Having affirmed that both the existence of God itself and the concept of creation could be demonstrated by natural reason without the aid of divine revelation, Thomas was then obliged to acknowledge that creation out of nothing could not be demonstrated by reason but only by revelation.

Although the Cappadocians were repeatedly obliged to address this and other challenges from Aristotelian cosmology, it was clear even on the basis of the language quoted from Basil that the principal Classical foil for their cosmological thought, as for their metaphysical thought generally, was not Aristotle but Plato. Especially was this so if, whatever their reading of the writings of the Neoplatonists may have been, "Plato" was lumped with the systems of later Middle Platonic and Neoplatonic thinkers (the sharp distinction between Plato and Neoplatonism, and then the interposition of the additional category of "Middle Platonism," being largely a phenomenon of modern scholarship). Often they reached back over Neoplatonism to Plato himself. Although the term "dēmiourgos" did appear once in the Septuagint and once in the New Testament, while the cognate verb "dēmiourgein" appeared three times in the Septuagint but not in the New Testament, Basil's use of "dēmiourgia" for the creation carried unmistakable echoes of the most important Platonic dialogue to deal with the doctrine of creation, the Timaeus. It is noteworthy that all the Cappadocians repeatedly turned to this dialogue in

Bas.Hex.2.2
(SC 26:146)

Bas.Spir.26.61
(SC 17:466)

Gilson 1944

McKeon 1939,206–31

Jacks 1922,82–105;
Ghellinck 1930,35–38

Dehnhard 1964;
Courcelle 1967,402–6;
Pépin 1982,251–60

Merlan 1960

Cherniss 1930,12–25

2 Mc 4:1; Heb 11:10
Wis 15:13;2 Mc 10:2;
4 Mc 7:8

Cornford 1957,33–39

their explanations of creation, including their exegesis of what Gregory of Nyssa called "the cosmogonic narrative [ho tēs ko-smogeneias logos]" in the Book of Genesis. As James Adam said of the *Timaeus* in one of the earliest series of Gifford Lectures, delivered at Aberdeen in 1904 and 1906, "It is difficult to over-estimate the influence which the dialogue exercised on religious thought and speculation during the last century and a half before the birth of Christ, and also in the early centuries of the Christian era. The *Timaeus* did more than any other literary masterpiece to facilitate and promote that fusion of Hellenism and Hebraism out of which so much of Christian theology has sprung." Or, in the words of George Grote, which Adam also quoted, "It was thus that the Platonic *Timaeus* became the medium of transition, from the Polytheistic theology which served as philosophy among the early ages of Greece, to the omnipotent Monotheism to which philosophy became subordinated after the Christian era." The interaction throughout Christian theological, philo-sophical, and exegetical history between these two accounts of creation in Genesis and in *Timaeus*—going back, as so many such historical problems did, to Philo of Alexandria and Helle-nistic Judaism—is an issue deserving of more attention from scholars than it has received. But even now it is possible to see that (employing the terms in the title of Jean Daniélou's pioneering study of Gregory of Nyssa, which helped to set off fifty years of debate) the Christian "mystical theology" of Nyssen and the other Cappadocians owed much of its vocabulary and concep-tual framework to "Platonism," but that in many fundamental respects it also transcended the Platonic or Neoplatonic frame-work.

In the articulation of their cosmology, it was above all the Platonic doctrine of ideas that came naturally to the minds of the Cappadocians as they addressed the problem of the incongruity in attributing the founding of this immanent and material world to a transcendent and spiritual Creator. Their underlying as-sumption was that creation had proceeded "by a sort of gradu-ated and ordered advance to the creation of humanity" from that of the earlier and lower creatures, an advance that was described in the successive days of the creation narrative of the Book of Genesis but that was likewise evident from the very nature of things. There was, moreover, an even more all-inclusive "gradu-ated and ordered advance" in the creation, which was evident in the development of each creature, such as the *stoicheia* of heaven, earth, and fire: from the ideas to the particular phenomena, and

Gr.Nyss.*Eun.*1.330
(Jaeger 1:124–25)

Adam 1908,373–74

Grote 1865,3:285

Wolfson 1947,2:483–84

Daniélou 1944

Gr.Nyss.*Hom.opif.*24
(PG 44:212–13)

Macr.ap.Gr.Nyss.
Anim.res. (PG 46:57)

from the particular phenomena to the cosmic harmony of them all. First came "the form that God wished to give" to each creature; then God "created matter in harmony with" that form; and "finally, God welded all the diverse parts of the universe by links of indissoluble attachment and established between them so perfect a fellowship and harmony that the most distant, in spite of their distance, appeared united in one universal sympathy." Thus when, according to Genesis, God placed man into Paradise "to be a tiller [ergazesthai]," this could be allegorized to refer to "a tiller of the divine conceptions [theiōn ennoiōn], both the simpler and the more perfect." This, too, was a kind of "preexistence," which such Classical cosmogonic theories as Aristotle's doctrine of the eternity of the world or Plato's doctrine of the demiurge strove to articulate; but it was a "preexistence in the power of God's foreknowledge" rather than in independence from the Creator. The Bible spoke of this in the exclamation of Susanna: "Eternal God, you know all secrets and foresee all things [ho eidōs ta panta]!" As the "Maker of heaven and earth," God was "the Creator even of the essence of beings," not merely "an inventor of figures" but the Creator of "the *ousia* with the form [eideis]." Although the number of individual human souls was countless, therefore, there was "nevertheless one *ousia* underlying them all." Indeed, God was, in this sense, the essence of essences, "a single uncreated eternal *ousia*," which produced "time and space with all their consequences," but also (in apparent reference to the Platonic ideas) "anything previous to [time and space] comprehensible to thought in the intelligible, supramundane world." Beyond the visible *kalon*, therefore, was "the idea of the *kalon*," identifiable as "that intellectual *kalon*" from which all other *kala* derived their existence and name.

As an *apophatic* truth about the transcendent Creator, this doctrine, too, was "conceivable to our mind, but beyond all words, being too lofty a subject for mere beginners and babes in knowledge"—which really meant everyone, regardless of how learned or pious. Yet even within those severe limitations it was possible to speak about a divine creative process in which, "even before the existence of all those things now attracting our notice, God, after casting about and determining to bring into being that which had no being, had imagined the world such as it ought to be." And by this process matter was created in harmony with the form that God wished to give it. The systematic arrangement of the cosmos was, then, even before "the birth of the world," predetermined by the free and sovereign will of the Creator to be "a

Bas.*Hex*.2.2
(*SC* 26:148)

Gn 2:15

Gr.Naz.*Or*.38.12
(*PG* 36:324)

Sus 42

Gr.Nyss.*Hom.opif*.29
(*PG* 44:233)
Bas.*Hex*.2.3
(*SC* 26:148)

Gr.Nyss.*Eun*.3.5.62
(Jaeger 2:183)

Gr.Nyss.*Infant*.
(Jaeger 3–II:77)

Gr.Nyss.*Virg*.11
(Jaeger 8–I:292)

Bas.*Hex*.1.5
(*SC* 26:104–6)

Bas.*Hex*.2.2
(*SC* 26:146–48)

Bas.*Hex*.1.5
(*SC* 26:104–6)

Bas.*Hex*.2.2
(*SC* 26:144–46)

See pp.268–79

Gr.Nyss.*Hom.opif*.24
(*PG* 44:212–13)

Bas.*Hex*.2.2
(*SC* 26:146–48)

Gr.Naz.*Or*.38.12
(*PG* 36:324)

1 Cor 13:12

Bas.*Ep*.8.12
(Courtonne 1:36)

Gr.Nyss.*Hom.opif*.24
(*PG* 44:212–13)

condition suitable for the exercise of supernatural powers, out-stripping the limits of time, eternal and infinite." It was deceiving to draw analogies from human crafts, in which *techne* took pre-existent "matter [hylē]" and imposed "form [morphē]" upon it. This Christian adaptation of the various Classical doctrines of "form" was nevertheless an analogy sufficiently apt to supply several distinct advantages to the apologetic enterprise. On the one hand, it provided a structure within which it was possible to address the always vexing problem of the metaphysical relation of an intellectual-spiritual Deity to the physical reality of a body. To resolve that problem, it was necessary to posit a definition of *logos* as "an intellectual and not a corporeal method of examina-tion." Color, quantity, and the other properties of a body, which were necessary "to keep the whole idea of the body from being dissolved," were themselves "intelligible," that is, perceived by the intellect; and a "Divinity also intellectual in nature" could be seen as having endowed these "intellectual potentialities" with being, enabling them, by their "mutual concurrence," to bring the material world of the body into being. On the other hand, the Christianization of the doctrine of ideas made it possible to argue that although here below *technai* were subsequent to matter, it was a "debasement of reasonings" to make such a transfer to the action of God the Creator; for God created the ideas before the particulars of matter, thus bringing being out of nonbeing. In a way it could be said, then, that here the Platonic doctrine of ideas in the *Republic* and other dialogues served to refute or at least to modify the Platonic doctrine of creation in the *Timaeus*. Just as the doctrine of ideas made possible an explanation of the primi-tive state of human nature before the fall, according to which the "divine conceptions" preexisted along with the created inno-cence of man, so, at the other end of human history, the supreme activity of human nature—contemplation—could be seen es-chatologically as the definition of the kingdom of heaven. Basil summarized that definition in the formula: "Now we behold their shadows 'in a mirror,' but hereafter, set free from this earthly body and clad in the incorruptible and the immortal, we shall behold their archetypes."

Yet the Platonic doctrine of ideas could not be taken to imply—certainly not in dogmatics, but not even in apologetics—that because a Divinity that was intellectual in nature had created "intellectual potentialities," from which in turn the material world had come, God was, strictly speaking, the Creator only of the former and not of the latter, or only of the cosmos as a whole but not of its particular components. The knowledge of God embraced the universe, "not only comprehending the total of the aggregate quantity, but having an exact knowledge also of the individual units comprising it." While insisting, against the heretic Eunomius, on the vast difference—a difference that was qualitative and not merely quantitative—between a transcendent divine knowledge of these units of the created world and that partial and limited knowledge of which the human mind was capable, Gregory of Nyssa could declare that the transcendent power of God was attested, also to natural human knowledge, by all the particulars and universals of the creation: "the infinite *aeons,* and the beauties of the cosmos, and the beams of the heavenly luminaries, and all the wonders of land and sea, and the angelic hosts and supracosmic powers, and everything else." With full confidence in the outcome, therefore, he felt able to meet that philosophical challenge to trinitarian orthodoxy with the response: "Investigate the work of nature!" With this scientific empiricism, as Karl Unterstein has put it, the Cappadocians "forsake Plato and his doctrine of ideas and make a connection with Aristotelian philosophy."

Such scientific investigation of nature could, then, be invoked as a component part of the methodology for the apologetic interpretation of natural theology. As was the case elsewhere in the systems of the Cappadocians, they did not always make it easy for their readers—and it seems sometimes to have been difficult also for them—to recognize when this appeal to what was regarded as scientific fact was intended for illustration as a rhetorical technique and when it was intended for proof as a logical argument; for in their thought, and not only in theirs, the line between the two was easier to cross than it was to draw. Basil's use of the relation between unity and plurality in the rainbow as an analogy for the Trinity, for example, would seem to fall on the side of illustration. So perhaps would the use by his sister, Macrina, of detailed scientific information, derived from the teaching of the Greek astronomers that "the moon always receives its light from the sun," as proof that not all knowledge was empirical. The same would seem, at least initially, to apply to the references by their brother Gregory of Nyssa to mercury and to botany in support of the doctrine of the resurrection, until he made it clear that the purpose of his illustrations had been to prove that there was no contradiction between "the preaching of the resurrection" and "the facts known to us experientially." Gregory of Nazianzus, in referring to the order in the universe and to the

Gr.Nyss.*Eun.*2.435
(Jaeger 1:353–54)

Gr.Nyss.*Eun.*2.291
(Jaeger 1:312)

Gr.Nyss.*Eun.*1.388
(Jaeger 1:140)

Unterstein 1903,58

Levie 1920,135–44

Joosen 1941,116–33

Bas.*Ep.*38.5
(Courtonne 1:87)

Ptol.*Alm.*4.1
Macr.ap.Gr.Nyss.
Anim.res. (PG 46:32–33)

Gr.Nyss.*Hom.opif.*27
(PG 44:228)

Gr.Naz.Or.6.15
(PG 35:741)

Gr.Nyss.Beat.8
(PG 44:1292)

Gr.Nyss.Eun.2.71
(Jaeger 1:247–48)
Sg 4:16
Gr.Nyss.Cant.10
(Jaeger 6:294–95)

See pp.152–61

Gr.Naz.Or.7.7
(PG 35:761)

Bas.Hex.6.5
(SC 26:348)

Bas.Ep.16
(Courtonne 1:47)

Gr.Nyss.Eun.2.77–78
(Jaeger 1:249–50)

Bas.Hex.6.11
(SC 26:386)

sequence of summer and winter, and of day and night, did seem to be invoking some version of the familiar cosmological argument for the existence of God. Expanding on this same theme in greater detail, Gregory of Nyssa drew a contrast between the earth as "the place of variation and flux" and "heavenly things, moving in their own courses in a series of orderly sequence." Elsewhere he displayed his knowledge of astronomy to good advantage in arguments against heretics; it also stood him in good stead in explaining the invocations of the "north wind [borras]" and "south wind [notos]" in the Song of Songs. Nevertheless, as the Cappadocians maintained in their polemics against Classical doctrines of *tyche* and *ananke,* all of this attention to astronomy and other "dangerous sciences" was not to be permitted to lead to the error of eliminating contingency and of "attributing all existing things and all events to the influence of the stars." What was "dangerous" about astronomy or any other science, then, was not at all its science or its understanding of the cosmos and of the natural working of the cosmos, all of which were affirmed, but its very supernaturalism and its pseudoscience, which were rejected in the name of science and of natural theology (as well as of revealed theology).

Scientific observation could sometimes illustrate, and sometimes even confirm, the conclusions at which reason or even revelation arrived by other means. It could, for example, provide a telling refutation of the claim that it was possible for the human mind to acquire absolute and objective knowledge concerning the nature of God. For careful scientific investigation of "the least of visible beings," such as the ant, had to conclude that their deepest essential "nature" was beyond human understanding. If "the comprehension of actual existences" here below among creatures exceeded human capacity, then it followed a fortiori that no one could claim to be able to "bring the human apprehensive faculty to bear on [a divine reality] transcending all intelligence." Higher levels of scientific knowledge documented even more irrefutably how "presumptuous" it was "to promise an explanation" even of natural phenomena, and much less of ultimate reality. Yet all such usage of terms like "lower" and "higher" orders of natural phenomena was fundamentally relativized by the overwhelming ontological difference between the Creator and all creatures, whether higher or lower. In short, as Gregory of Nazianzus showed in great scientific detail, the wonders of the natural world already surpassed human understanding; consequently, whatever infinitely surpassed the natural world had to surpass human understanding infinitely.

But the contemplation of these scientific realities had as well a positive contribution to make to natural theology. "A single plant, a blade of grass," Basil declared, "is sufficient to occupy all your intelligence in the contemplation of the *techne* that produced it." If properly directed, such contemplation of the *techne* of the Creator as it was evident in individual creatures could not "fail to be taught, by means of such a spectacle, about the existence of a divine power, working with *techne* and method, and manifesting itself in the actual world." From such contemplation it was evident, moreover, that this divine power was "penetrating each portion, combining those portions with the whole, and completing the whole by the portions." Thus, the divine power made them into a "universe [to pan], encompassed with a single all-controlling force, self-possessed and self-contained, never ceasing from its motion, yet never altering its position." Purely empirical observation did not suffice for arriving at such conclusions of natural theology, but empiricism was not adequate even for valid scientific study, as Basil argued: "We must not measure the moon with the eye [alone], but with reasoning. Reasoning, for the discovery of truth, is much surer than the eye." For this insight, too, it was appropriate for the Cappadocians to acknowledge their indebtedness to Classical thought: "It is most true," Macrina conceded, "what one of alien *paideia* is recorded to have said, that it is the mind that sees and the mind that hears."

Among the several disciplines of human thought, mathematics stood as the supreme instance of this epistemological principle of the superiority of reason to empirical perception, as it had for many other Greek and Latin thinkers, Classical and then Christian. Therefore, the Cappadocians acknowledged that in their application of mathematics to natural theology they had as predecessors the ancient Pythagoreans. The apologetic value of geometry, according to Macrina, lay in its capacity to "lead us step by step through visible delineations to truths lying out of sight." Such acts of "apprehension" were proof of "the work of an intellectual essence deeply seated in our nature," which in some sense preceded the empirical perceptions of the physical senses and functioned through them. Whether a circle was without beginning or end was a question that had to be answered on other than empirical grounds. Withal, it was to be kept in mind, as a "necessary consequence" of the nature of things, that number, too, was a constituent part of the created order. Although it had been

Gr.Naz.Or.28.22–30
(SC 250:144–70)

Bas.Hex.5.3
(SC 26:290)

Macr.ap.Gr.Nyss.
Anim.res. (PG 46:25–28)

Bas.Hex.6.11
(SC 26:384)

Macr.ap.Gr.Nyss.
Anim.res. (PG 46:32)

Ladner 1959,212–
22,227–29,454–59

Gr.Naz.Or.41.2
(PG 36:329)

Macr.ap.Gr.Nyss.
Anim.res. (PG 46:33)

Bas.Hex.1.3
(SC 26:96–98)
Wis 11:20
Gr.Nyss.Hex.
(PG 44:85)

"devised as a symbol indicative of the quantity of objects," this element of rational knowledge and natural theology was being abused by those Christian heretics who, not knowing that "the addition of number" did not change a thing, tried to cite it in refutation of the orthodox concept of the three equal *hypostases* in the Trinity. Yet, a well-informed grasp of numbers, as a part of natural theology, made it possible for the orthodox biblical exegete, as an exponent of revealed theology, to apply this knowledge to the explanation of mystical numbers in Scripture.

Within the sciences, it was from medicine and physiology, alongside these applications of mathematics, that these thinkers, as Christians but especially as Greek-speaking Christians, derived some of their insights into natural theology. The mystery of human digestion was to Gregory of Nyssa a part of the total mystery of creation, and in that sense part of natural theology. But sometimes it became a matter of considerably greater importance than that also for his dogmatics, when the everyday transformation of bread into body provided him with a means for speaking about the far more profound and complex mystery of the presence of the body and blood of Christ in the Eucharist, as well as about the question of its "assimilation." Although Macrina refused medical help for her tumor and was nevertheless healed by employing the sign of the cross, that did not alter the belief she shared that "the medical art was sent from God for the saving of human life." The teaching of the church, Gregory argued elsewhere, not only permitted but commanded research into medicine and physiology, including the use of dissection; therefore he felt free to quote "experts in the practice of medicine" (whom he never identified by name anywhere in his works) in drawing an analogy for the healing of the soul, as well as in exhorting his hearers to practice temperance and abstinence. What a physician, skilled in the *techne* of healing and well-informed about "physiology," had once said about physical health could be applied to the health of the soul, for it was true of both that "the principal cause of a state of illness" could be said to be "the deviation from the right proportion by one of the *stoicheia* in us." Therefore, as his brother Basil put it, human beings should be ashamed of rejecting the "precepts of 'sōtēria,'" a Greek word that meant both "healing" and "salvation." Although other creatures did not have the gift of reason, they did had "the law of nature implanted in them" and they obeyed it, whereas by contrast rational human beings, in their "resistance

Bas.*Spir.*18.44
(SC 17:402–4)

Gr.Nyss.*Cant.*6
(Jaeger 6:193)

Keenan 1941,8–30;
Keenan 1944,150–61;
Janini Cuesta 1947,
337–62
Janini Cuesta 1946,
118–20
Gr.Nyss.*Hex.*
(PG 44:104–5)

See p.299
Gr.Nyss.*Or.catech.*37
(Méridier 172–82)

Gr.Nyss.*V.Macr.*
(Jaeger 8–1:405)

Gr.Nyss.*Hom.opif.*30
(PG 44:240)

Janini Cuesta 1946,29
Gr.Nyss.*Beat.*4
(PG 44:1232)
Gr.Nyss.*Paup.*1
(Van Heck 7)

Goggin 1947,137–44

ap.Gr.Nyss.*Or.dom.*4
(PG 44:1161)

Lampe 1369

Bas.*Hex*.7.4
(*SC* 26:408–12)
to the disposition of the Creator," refused to accept the limitations that creation had imposed on them for their own good.

Significant though the contributions of insights from mathematics and medicine were for the natural theology and apologetics of the Cappadocians, it would seem that the metaphysics of

Bultmann 1948,1–36

Pelikan 1962
light was for them, as it had been for other Greek Christian thinkers before them and especially for Athanasius, the most far-reaching contribution of natural science to natural theology, as well as to revealed theology. Here again, the distinction between rhetorical illustration and logical proof was not always precise. Thus Gregory of Nyssa recognized that even the metaphor "light

Symb.Nic.(325)
(Alberigo-Jedin 5)
out of light," which the creed of the Council of Nicaea had applied to the relation between the Father and the Son in the Trinity, was at one and the same time both useful and limited, and he

Gr.Nyss.*Eun*.1.533
(Jaeger 1:180–81)

Dt 4:24; Heb 12:29
warned against any application of it that would ignore the limitations. In the portrayal of God as a fire, he warned elsewhere, alluding to passages from both the Old and the New Testament, it

Gr.Nyss.*Hex.*
(*PG* 44:81)
Zec 6:12
Gr.Nyss.*Cant.*10
(Jaeger 6:299)
was necessary to think of "something other than ordinary fire" and light. The prophet Zechariah in the Old Testament had promised that the very name of Christ would be "the East [anatolē]," from which the eternal sun would rise. And just as in the use of astronomy for natural theology it was necessary to warn

See pp.155–57
against the danger of astrology, so in the application of light as a

Gr.Naz.*Or*.28.14
(*SC* 250:128–30)
metaphor for the divine the corresponding danger was the worship of the sun. Living in the fourth century, the Cappadocians

Bas.*Hex*.5.1
(*SC* 26:280)

Usener 1911,348–78
were especially sensitive to this, because of the revival of such worship by the emperor Julian, which stood in the tradition of the cult of "the unconquered sun [sol invictus]." Even the majesty

Bas.*Hex*.6.10
(*SC* 26:376)
of the sun, therefore, pointed not to itself but beyond itself to "the *sophia* of the Creator with the *techne.*" At the same time it was necessary to be reminded that "light" was a key term for God and

Bas.*Eun*.1.7
(*SC* 299:188)
1 Jn 1:5
Gr.Naz.*Or*.32.15
(*SC* 318:116)
for Christ, especially in the Gospel and the Epistles bearing the name of the apostle John. And John was also the evangelist who, by divine inspiration, had made the equation, which went well beyond a simple metaphor: "God is light."

The Cappadocians found that in dealing with the metaphysics of light in a dogmatic context, it was essential, for the sake of intellectual integrity as well as of apologetic credibility and theological accuracy, to speak about it in a way that was informed by

Gr.Nyss.*Cant.*4
(Jaeger 6:105)
the best of what came from "the scientific experts on the physics of the question [hoi ta toiauta physiologein epistēmones]." That duty to be well informed scientifically applied with equal force to

Gn 1:4
Gr.Nyss.*Eun.*2.278
(Jaeger 1:308)

Gr.Naz.*Or.*40.37
(*PG* 36:412)
Gr.Nyss.*Eun.*1.388
(Jaeger 1:140)

Bas.*Hex.*6.1
(*SC* 26:326)

Gr.Naz.*Or.*40.5
(*PG* 36:364)

Kertsch 1978,150–216

Gr.Nyss.*Infant.*
(Jaeger 3–II:85)

Lampe 1260–61

Pl.*Tht.*201e
Pl.*Tim.*48b

2 Pt 3:10;3:12

Gal 4:3; Col 2:8;2:20

See p.12

the exegesis of such biblical passages as the words of the creation narrative in the first chapter of Genesis: "And he separated light from darkness." For the contrast between light and darkness was, in natural theology as well as in revealed theology, an indispensable way of speaking both about moral and about metaphysical teachings. In this scientific field, the imperative to "investigate the work of nature" paid great dividends. For someone who "studied the marvels of light" could have the experience of being "raised by visible things to the invisible being." Such elevation of the mind beyond the limits of the world of sense could lead to the contemplation, in suitably *apophatic* terms, of God as transcendent light, "the highest, the unapproachable, the ineffable light, neither conceivable by the mind nor describable with the lips, but granting life to every reasoning creature." God as light, therefore, was "in the realm of thought like the sun in the world of sense," the sun "pouring itself out upon everything external to it"; so it was with God as everlasting light. Or, to be utterly precise, the relation between the light of the sun and God as everlasting light was the reverse of what a shallow symbolism or theory of analogy would suppose; for to "observe the beauty of the material sunlight" was to "grasp by analogy the beauty of the real sunlight," namely, God.

One of the most intriguing terms from Greek science to find its way into the theological vocabulary of the Cappadocians was the word *stoicheia*. Originally the name for the letters of the alphabet, *stoicheia* was a technical term from Classical physics and metaphysics, apparently beginning (at any rate in literary sources that have been preserved) with Plato's *Theaetetus* and then in the Cappadocians' favorite Platonic dialogue, the *Timaeus*, for fire, water, air, and earth as the four elements. In the New Testament, where the term appeared seven times and always in the plural, it seems to have had this meaning at least in the two apocalyptic passages that spoke about "the elements" being "dissolved in flames" and "melting in flames" at the end of time; and it has often, though by no means always, been taken to mean that as well in the three Pauline references to "the *stoicheia* of the cosmos," variously (and controversially) translated as "the elemental spirits of the universe" or "the elements of the natural world" or "elementary ideas belonging to this world." But whatever it may have meant in those seven passages of the New Testament, the word *stoicheia*, like "epinoia," does seem to have undergone a transition from New Testament usage to Patristic

Bas.*Ep.*8.2
(Courtonne 1:24);
Gr.Naz.*Or.*28.14
(*SC* 250:128)
Gr.Nyss.*Hex.*
(*PG* 44:104)

Gr.Nyss.*Eun.*2.222
(Jaeger 1:290)

Gr.Nyss.*Maced.*
(Jaeger 3–I:91)

Macr.ap.Gr.Nyss.
Anim.res. (*PG* 46:33)

Macr.ap.Gr.Nyss.
Anim.res. (*PG* 46:108–9)

Gr.Nyss.*Or.dom.*4
(*PG* 44:1161)
See p.299
Gr.Nyss.*Or.catech.*37.12
(Méridier 182)

usage, as a result of which it recovered some of its earlier and Classical scientific meaning. Basil and Gregory of Nazianzus spoke in the scientific sense about "the *stoicheia:* earth, water, air, fire." Gregory of Nyssa employed the word in that sense, too. He cited it as a commonly accepted truth in his polemics against the doctrine of *tyche.* He also took it for granted in enumerating the *stoicheia* of fire, water, air, and earth as a way of providing "material instances" for his doctrine of the Holy Spirit. The word appeared as a scientific term in Macrina's dialogue, in which she spoke of "a substantial diminution of the *stoicheion*" of the moon and then formulated her own distinctive doctrine of the resurrection of the body on the basis of the *stoicheia* of which the body was composed. Gregory of Nyssa also identified the presence of the *stoicheia* in the human body, defining disease as an imbalance between them. All of this made it understandable when he used the concept of *stoicheia* for his discussion of the nature of the eucharistic presence.

The use of science, whether only as rhetorical illumination or also as logical proof, had a legitimate place in the structure of Cappadocian natural theology because the Cappadocians viewed the world as a cosmos, "a vast nature and an elaborate system." Yet it was absolutely essential to insist that the world was a cosmos not of its own initiative or by some *ananke,* but contingently, because of the free and sovereign will of God: in an evident echo of the key passage about the incarnation of the *Logos* from the prologue to the Gospel of John, Gregory of Nyssa could write: "The divine will became nature." He also spoke about it in the same treatise not as an independent nature but as "nature by God's will," because in the case of God there was "no difference between will and action." For, as Basil said in a parallel formulation, "It is the voice of God that makes the nature [of a thing]." But he had already explained this earlier: "It has to be well understood that when we speak of the voice, of the word, of the command of God, this divine language does not mean to us a sound that escapes from the organs of speech, [but] . . . a simple sign of the will of God." The "word" of God, then, was equal to the "will" of God, which was in turn equal to the action of God— all of these, of course, understood in a transcendent and *apophatic* sense, fundamentally different from the sense that each of these concepts and terms conveyed when applied to human words or wills or actions. It was because of this will and power of God that there could be, within one cosmic system, the great

Bas.*Hex.*5.10
(*SC* 26:320–22)

See pp.256–59

Jn 1:14
Gr.Nyss.*Eun.*2.232
(Jaeger 1:293)

Gr.Nyss.*Eun.*1.626
(Jaeger 1:206)
Gr.Nyss.*Eun.*2.228
(Jaeger 1:292)

Bas.*Hex.*4.2
(*SC* 26:250)

Bas.*Hex.*2.7
(*SC* 26:172–74)

Bas.*Hex.*3.2
(*SC* 26:192–94);
Gr.Nyss.*Eun.*3.6.17
(Jaeger 2:191–92)

variety evident both to everyday experience and to scientific study. Yet it was also because of this will and power of God that all this variety could be brought together "into the cosmos as a whole." In this sense it was possible to move "from the part to the whole," but also from the whole to the part. For the same reason, it was the fact of their having all been brought out from nonbeing to being, through a creation defined as creation out of nothing, that gave to all created things their affinity with one another within this single cosmic system. Once again, therefore, Cappadocian natural theology was simultaneously addressed to the apologetic task of finding within Classical thought the anticipations of revealed truth and of pointing beyond all this to the revealed truth itself, in whose formulation at least some Classical presuppositions of natural theology also found their place. For this, however, it was necessary to see that God was not only "the Creator of the universe" but its "just Judge, rewarding all the actions of life according to their merit," and therefore to move also from cosmology as such "to the idea of the *apocatastasis* of all things."

Gr.Nyss.*Eun.*1.402
(Jaeger 1:143–44)

Gr.Nyss.*Eun.*3.4.34
(Jaeger 2:147)
Gr.Nyss.*Eun.*2.430
(Jaeger 1:352)

Gr.Nyss.*Or.catech.*39.6
(Méridier 188)

Bas.*Hex.*1.4
(SC 26:102)

CHAPTER 7

Space, Time, and Deity

Rom 1:20

Bas.*Hex*.1.6
(SC 26:10)

When Basil of Caesarea, rehearsing the traditional cosmological argument for the existence of God on the basis of the standard proof text from the Epistle to the Romans, declared that "the sight of visible and empirical realities" was able to "lead the mind, as by a hand, to the contemplation of invisible realities," he was, by the use of that plural, "invisible realities [aorata]," referring not only to the reality of the one invisible God but to the reality of the entire invisible realm of the spirit, with its countless inhabitants. When his brother Gregory of Nyssa, having established "the knowledge and the contemplation of some reality" as "the goal, as far as possible, for every operation and movement of sound thinking," went on to divide "the whole world of realities" for such knowledge and contemplation into the two parts of "the intelligible [noēton]," which was a "world transcending the grasp of the senses," and "the empirical [aisthēton]," which was

Gr.Nyss.*Eun*.2.572–74
(Jaeger 1:393–94)

knowable through the senses, he was presenting not only an epistemology for natural theology but an entire ontology. In doing so, he felt able to cite the authority of "the divine apostle"

2 Cor 4:18

Paul, who wrote (also employing a plural for the invisible realm as well as the language of *apophasis*): "Our eyes are fixed, not on the things that are seen [ta blepomena], but on the things that are unseen [ta mē blepomena]; for what is seen is transient, what is

Gr.Nyss.*Cant*.14
(Jaeger 6:411)

Pl.*Phd*.75b;115d-e

Bas.*Leg.lib.gent*.9
(Wilson 31)

unseen is eternal." Echoing this Pauline passage together with some similar-sounding passages from Plato, Basil quoted as a "wise precept" the principle, "That which is seen is not the man." In another passage employing such plurals, the apostle

Col 1:16

Gr.Nyss.Eun.1.270–71
(Jaeger 1:105–6)

Paul had also distinguished between "things visible" and "invisible," both of which were created in Christ. That Pauline passage, too, gave Gregory of Nyssa an opportunity to contrast the "empirical" world and the "intelligible" world. Comparing the materialism in which most people lived with "the mentality of the disciples of the *Logos* [hē dianoia tōn mathēteuomenōn tōi Logōi]," he once again employed a plural to contrast a life groveling in the dust with one that had been elevated "to the yearning for the transcendent realities [pros tēn epithymian tōn hyperkeimenōn]." And their sister, Macrina, in a polemic against Epicureanism, rejected the idea of "the visible as the limit of existence" and (employing plurals for the invisible realm yet once more) accused Epicureanism of being "incapable of seeing any of the intelligible and noncorporeal realities [tōn noētōn te kai asōmatōn]."

Gr.Nyss.Cant.11
(Jaeger 6:315)

Macr.ap.Gr.Nyss.
Anim.res. (PG 46:21)

This emphasis of all four Cappadocians on "the intelligible and noncorporeal realities" could sometimes be formulated in such a way as to appear to be denying reality to anything else, and therefore also as denying validity to the ordinary perceptions of reality by which people had to function in everyday life. For at times they could speak of God as "that which alone 'is,' in the real sense of 'being,'" even though this was "not knowable," and could characterize "being in the true sense of the word" as "the special distinction of the Godhead." When the verb "to be" was predicated of any reality other than God, therefore, it was being employed improperly. They resorted to such extreme formulations when they were intent on drawing, usually by means of the language of *apophasis,* the most radical possible distinction between the divine being and all created beings. But when they were propounding their entire worldview in a balanced and systematized form, they spoke more precisely, and more comprehensively, of God as "the causality of being for all [ton aition tou einai tois pasin]," that is, for "beings" that therefore could legitimately be characterized as such. Then they were prepared to attribute being and essence to other realities than God, though always of course with the proviso that God was "the Creator even of the essence of beings." For the same reason, as they sometimes made clear, they did not intend their critique of a philosophy that "made our senses the only means of our apprehension of things" to be taken as in any way a repudiation of the legitimacy of "the facts known to us through experience." It was the unique ability of the human mind, as having been made in the image of God but also as having been deposited in a physical body, that it could

Gr.Naz.Or.31.23
(SC 250:318–20)

Gr.Nyss.V.Mos.2
(Jaeger 7–I:115)

Gr.Nyss.Eun.3.8.32
(Jaeger 2:251)

Gr.Naz.Or.30.18
(SC 250:262–64)

Gr.Nyss.Eun.2.515
(Jaeger 1:377)

Gr.Nyss.Eun.1.548
(Jaeger 1:184–85)

Bas.Hex.2.3
(SC 26:148)

Macr.ap.Gr.Nyss.
Anim.res. (PG 46:21)

Gr.Nyss.Hom.opif.27
(PG 44:228)

work "through both [di' amphoterōn]," through the physical senses in relation to the physical realities of this world and through the intellectual nature in relation to the intelligible and nonvisible realities of that other world. The empirical "world of sense" contained "everything comprehended by our organs of bodily sense." From this duality it followed that although, as Classical thought had also recognized, the ability of speech set humanity apart from the unreasoning animals, it was, nevertheless, the necessity of resorting to the physical organs of speech instead of employing a direct, nonverbal communication from one rational intellect to another that set it apart from the angels.

The Cappadocian worldview, therefore, should not be characterized as some sort of doctrine of absolute idealism that rejected the testimony of the senses in the name of the supremacy of spirit. They were critical of a philosophical theology that claimed to be able to "overleap" the data provided by the senses. For the testimony of the senses was, within its appropriate sphere, both trustworthy and necessary, and it was proper for the human mind to rely on sense experience. It was by the senses, and by the experience of "the actual world" through the senses, that valid if limited knowledge of that actual world could be acquired. Gregory of Nyssa devoted an entire chapter of his treatise *On the Making of Man* to an examination and defense of sense experience. Through "the operation of sight," he noted, drawing on Greek theories of optics, the mind could "apprehend the things external to the body, and draw to itself the images of phenomena, marking in itself the impressions of the things seen." This functioning of the sense of sight was not invalidated by the recognition that reason could sometimes see more clearly than the eyes themselves could, so that, as Socrates had argued, the mind could see and hear "through [dia] the eyes and through the ears," rather than "by means of the eyes and ears." Alongside the knowing that was "not in the eyes," nor in the tongue or nostrils or ears or fingers, was the "knowing given to us by taste, smell, hearing, touch, and sight." Gregory of Nyssa, in a passage that has been quoted earlier, invoked the trustworthiness of the experience of the senses as the basis for a scientific method by which to discover the unknown, going on to further discoveries step by step.

Yet contrary to any theory that would ignore human uniqueness and that would suppose, on the basis of the physical nature, including the physical senses, of dogs, camels, and elephants, that the fundamental and defining characteristic of human life was the mutual resemblance between human beings and other animals, it

Gr.Nyss.*Hom.opif*.2
(PG 44:133)

Gr.Nyss.*Eun*.2.271
(Jaeger 1:305–6)

Pl.*Prt*.322a

Gr.Nyss.*Eun*.2.391
(Jaeger 1:340)

Eun.ap.Gr.Nyss.*Eun*.
3.8.14 (Jaeger 2:243)

Gr.Nyss.*Hom.opif*.27
(PG 44:228)

Macr.ap.Gr.Nyss.
Anim.res. (PG 46:25–28)

Arist.*An*.418a27–419b3

Gr.Nyss.*Hom.opif*.10
(PG 44:152–53)

Bas.*Hex*.6.11
(SC 26:384)

ap.Pl.*Tht*.184c
Gr.Nyss.*V.Mos*.2
(Jaeger 7–I:97)

Gr.Nyss.*Hom.opif*.10
(PG 44:153)
See pp.60–61

Gr.Nyss.*Eun*.2.182
(Jaeger 1:277)

Gr.Nyss.*Eun*.1.448
(Jaeger 1:156–57)

Apostolopoulos 1986,
277–320

Macr.ap.Gr.Nyss.
Anim.res. (PG 46:32)

Gr.Nyss.Virg.6
(Jaeger 8–I:278)
Gr.Nyss.V.Mos.2
(Jaeger 7–I:84)

Gr.Nyss.Infant.
(Jaeger 3–II:85)

Bas.Hex.6.1
(SC 26:326)

Gr.Nyss.Hex.
(PG 44:69)

Gr.Nyss.Cant.15
(Jaeger 6:439)

Rom 1:20

Bas.Hex.1.6
(SC 26:110)

Alexander 1920

Gr.Nyss.Eun.1.361
(Jaeger 1:134)

was essential to remember that it was the distinctive quality of human nature to be endowed with "a seeing mind and a hearing mind." This human quality was, moreover, knowable also through a "metaphysical theory of immortality" and not only through a Christian "faith in the resurrection," thus without the aid of revelation and through natural theology, from which indeed it came into Christian theology, as Macrina appeared to acknowledge. Although the testimony of sense experience was valid, therefore, it could be valid only when its limits were clearly observed. Anyone who recognized the reality of the invisible realm of spirit was "necessarily separated from all the ordinary events of life," and could no longer "be confused and led astray by the deceits arising from the senses"—not because the senses were deceitful in and of themselves, but because they could deceive the uncritical observer into supposing that their data were the total content of the world. This was what it meant to be purified "of sense experience and irrationality." To know the limits of the world of sense meant to know that the material and created world of the senses was derived from, dependent upon, and subordinate to the "real" world of the spiritual Creator. It meant to acquire the ability "to rise by means of visible things to the invisible being." This upward path went "by means of the senses [tēi aisthēsei]" and "through the phenomena [dia tōn phainomenōn]," not around the senses and the phenomena, until it attained "to the transcendent realities [pros ta hyperkeimena]" of the spiritual realm, though always *apophatically.* Thus, it put behind itself "every material deed and thought" for the sake of "the intelligible and nonmaterial."

The most visible characteristic of this spiritual realm was its invisibility. That oxymoron was no more than a paraphrase of the familiar New Testament formula, quoted by the Cappadocians, that "the invisible attributes [ta aorata]" of God were "visible [nooumena kathoratai]." That, in turn, raised inevitably the entire cluster of philosophical and theological issues summarized in the formula that served as the title of Samuel Alexander's Gifford Lectures of 1916 and 1918, "space, time, and deity." Gregory of Nyssa set it forth as an axiom that creation was "to be viewed in an extension of distances," therefore that it was spatial. It was, he said elsewhere, characteristic of material reality that it was "apprehended in an extension measured by intervals," being knowable to the senses "in color, and figure, and bulk, and size, and resistance." The spiritual reality, by contrast, was by definition "nonmaterial," and consequently "without quantity, or size, or combination, removed from the idea of circumscription by way of figure," and hence "unextended" in space. The terms "boundless and limitless [aoristos kai apeiros]" pertained specifically to this transcendence over space, although they could also be used about transcendence over time. "Nontransient [aphthartos]" was the more specific and precise term when transcendence over time rather than transcendence over space was the issue; the term "eternal [aiōnios]" had a special place in the vocabulary of Gregory of Nyssa. In language that almost seemed to anticipate what Alfred North Whitehead in his Gifford Lectures of 1927 and 1928 called "the 'receptacle' theory of space-time" in "the Newtonian cosmology," the Cappadocians asserted that it was not necessary to have recourse to divine revelation, but only to "have an insight, however moderate it might be, into the nature of things," to recognize that space, together with time, represented "a sort of receptacle [ti chōrēma]" for all the visible and material realities of the universe. It followed from this status of space as the "receptacle" that space was also the presupposition and the determinant of motion, and that space was, "for things subject to motion, the limit of a nature that is dimensional [diastēmatikē]." Therefore, it was evidence of "ignorance" and "absurdity" when someone made the error of "predicating place of incorporeal things [topon epi tōn asōmatōn]."

Yet could not natural theology and even revealed religion be justly accused of doing just that? For in response to the disjunctive syllogism, "God is either nowhere or somewhere," the answer "nowhere" seemed to suggest the logical inversion, "Since the nonexistent is nowhere, then perhaps that which is nowhere is also nonexistent." Therefore, the necessary alternative appeared to be to say, "God is somewhere, either in the universe or above the universe"; for it was unthinkable that God should be nonexistent, and therefore God could not be "nowhere." Such language did seem to come dangerously close to "predicating place of incorporeal things." So did the language of the New Testament when, in speaking about the inhabitants of the spiritual and intelligible realm, it prophesied "that at the name of Jesus every knee should bow—in heaven, on earth, and in the depths," a text that served Nyssen as the ground for a dissertation on the "unnameable name" of God and of the Son of God, as well as providing him with one of the grounds for his special version of the Christian eschatological hope. These words sounded, Macrina had to admit, as though "the divine apostle were dividing the intellectual world into localities." But then she explained that

Gr.Nyss.*Hom.opif.*23
(*PG* 44:209–12)

Bas.*Eun.*1.7
(*SC* 299:192);
Gr.Nyss.*Eun.*2.506–7
(Jaeger 1:374)

Bas.*Eun.*1.7
(*SC* 299:192)

Florovsky 7:209–10

Whitehead 1929,97

Gr.Nyss.*Eun.*1.370
(Jaeger 1:136)
Gr.Nyss.*Hex.*
(*PG* 44:84)
Dörrie et al. 1976,
243–60

Bas.*Spir.*6.15
(*SC* 17:290–92)

Gr.Naz.*Or.*28.10
(*SC* 250:120)

Bas.*Spir.*6.15
(*SC* 17:290–92)

Phil 2:10

See pp.212–13

See pp.324–25

what it actually meant to posit was "three possible states [katastaseis] for a rational nature." The term "in heaven" applied to "the one with a noncorporeal life from the very first, called the angelic." "On earth" identified the one "in union with the flesh, called the human." And "in the depths" referred to "the third, released by death from fleshly entanglements, and found in souls pure and simple," after death but before the resurrection of the

Macr.ap.Gr.Nyss.
Anim.res. (PG 46:69–72)
Gr.Nyss.V.Macr.
(Jaeger 8–I:396)

body. It could as well be interpreted as a spatializing of the spiritual that she herself, as she was dying, had her couch turned toward the East, thus following the Classical pagan practice of "orientation." Her brother Gregory of Nyssa, who reported this incident in his biography of her, justified the practice elsewhere, in his commentary on the Lord's Prayer. "We turn towards the

Gr.Nyss.Or.dom.5
(PG 44:1184)

East," he explained, "not as if God were present only there for our contemplation, for the one who is everywhere is not particularly apprehended in any part, embracing the entire universe equally," but because God planted the garden of Eden "in the

Gn 2:8
Zec 6:12
Gr.Nyss.Cant.10
(Jaeger 6:299)
Bas.Spir.27.66
(SC 17:484)

See p.229

East." Such prayer was an acknowledgment of the prophecy that Christ, as the true sun, "rose from the East." The universal Christian practice of orientation also served Basil as evidence that not all of apostolic tradition was contained in Scripture.

That sort of spatial metaphor was implied when religious language spoke as though the transcendent nature of the divine were

Gr.Nyss.Cant.15
(Jaeger 6:438)

"located" in those who were pure of heart. For the meaning of true transcendence could be formulated this way: "That which is altogether infinite cannot be limited in one respect while it is left unlimited in another, but infinity is free from limitation alto-

Gr.Nyss.Tres dii
(Jaeger 3–I:52)
Mt 5:9
Mt 5:10

gether." Although the Lord's Prayer spoke of God as a Father "in heaven" and of the kingdom of God as "coming," such language was not to be taken to prove "a spatial [topikē] distance between the divine and the human, so as to need some mechanical device for this heavily weighted flesh to be able to migrate into the bodiless and intelligible life [pros tēn asōmaton te kai noeran diagōgēn]," or for the bodiless life to descend to this earth. On the contrary, because of "*arete* really being separated from evil," the movement toward being with God was a matter of human free

Gr.Nyss.Or.dom.2
(PG 44:1145)

will and decision rather than of locomotion. The Samaritan woman in the Gospel account mistakenly supposed that God was "in one particular circumscribed place," the Samaritan temple on Mount Gerizim; but Christ—although it was valid to use

Col 1:19
Gr.Nyss.Ref.192
(Jaeger 2:393)

spatial language in declaring of him, as the New Testament did, "In him God in all his fullness chose to dwell"—taught her the

Jn 4:16–26
Gr.Nyss.*Apoll.*
(Jaeger 3–I:212)

rule, "God is spirit," and therefore to be worshiped "neither on this mountain nor in Jerusalem" but in the infinity of spirit. This *apophatic* interpretation of the relation of "infinity" to "space" provided the basis for an especially fascinating case study of the Christian encounter with Hellenism, when Gregory of Nyssa invoked it in his examination of the Christian imitation of the

Kötting 1950,421–24

Classical pagan custom of pilgrimage. The Christian practice of pilgrimage was closely associated with the piety of the empress Helena, mother of Constantine, who in 326 had gone to Palestine and had, according to tradition, found the holy sepulcher as well

Socr.*H.e.*1.17
(Hussey 1:104–8)

as the true cross. No one could honestly imagine, Nyssen argued, that Jesus Christ was "living, in the body, there [in the Holy Land] at the present day," or that the Holy Spirit was present in abundance at Jerusalem but was unable to travel elsewhere. He himself confessed, after having made his own pilgrimage to Jerusalem, perhaps in the autumn of 379, that his "faith was not increased any more than it was diminished." For, as he summa-

Gr.Nyss.*Ep.*2.7–15
(Jaeger 8–II:15–18)

rized the apophatic case, "Change of place does not effect any drawing near to God." Being "without quantity and without extension" and hence infinite, the transcendent divine nature was beyond any limit, beyond any space, and beyond "the measure expressed by time," because *arche* and *telos* were "terms for

Gr.Nyss.*Eun.*3.6.32–33
(Jaeger 2:226)

things with an extension." The divine nature was "neither in

Gr.Nyss.*Beat.*3
(PG 44:1225)

place nor in time, eluding all limitation and every form of definition."

As that coordination of the two indicates, both "time and space" were seen as the foundation on which God had built the universe, and therefore it was "not possible for anything now in

Gr.Nyss.*Eun.*1.370–71
(Jaeger 1:136)

being or now coming into being by way of creation to be independent of space or of time." For that reason, "time and space, with all their consequences," were taken together as "the productions" of the divine essence, although they were not characteristics of the divine essence itself (nor, so it would seem, of "anything previous to them comprehended by thought in the

Gr.Nyss.*Infant.*
(Jaeger 3–II:77)
Gr.Naz.*Or.*20.9
(SC 270:74)
Gr.Nyss.*Eun.*1.624
(Jaeger 1:206)

intelligible, supramundane world," such as the Platonic forms). When space was presupposed in metaphysics, time was usually being presupposed also. A human life began "at a stated time, with a particular place as its receptacle." But whereas space in its contrast with infinity was the more visible of the two, it was the

Callahan 1958b,36–39
Dörrie et al. 1976,
128–55

Cappadocians' reflection on "the nature of time" and simultaneously on the relation between "eternity and time" that permitted them to articulate more profoundly both the affinities and the

Ladner 1959,227–29

Otis 1976,327

Cushman 1981,23
Pl.*Tim.*36e–39e

See pp.20,95–97

See pp.266–70

Bas.*Spir.*6.14
(SC 17:290)

Gr.Nyss.*Eun.*3.7.23
(Jaeger 2:223)

Gr.Nyss.*Eun.*1.365
(Jaeger 1:134–35)

Bas.*Hex.*1.5
(SC 26:104–6)

Gr.Nyss.*Cant.*13
(Jaeger 6:381)

differences between the way they understood reality and the way Hellenism did, or at any rate the way they thought Hellenism did. Regarding their articulation of these issues, Brooks Otis has even proposed the thesis: "The Christian doctrine of creation is virtually identical with the Christian doctrine of time and both doctrines were first made intelligible by Gregory of Nyssa." By contrast with these Christian Platonists, as Robert Cushman has suggested, "Plato's treatment of time is meager and, apart from three pages of the *Timaeus* . . . entirely casual." But it was, as has been noted at several earlier junctures, with the *Timaeus* that the Cappadocians were occupied, more than with any other of the Platonic dialogues.

Because of the centrality of the doctrine of the incarnation of the *Logos* in time and history, much of that reflection pertained specifically to their exegetical, liturgical, and dogmatic systems rather than to their natural theology, and thus to their doctrine of the divine *economy*. Nevertheless, their thought about time, like all the other themes of Cappadocian speculation being discussed here, was simultaneously apologetics and presupposition, belonging to their exposition of natural theology, as well as to their interpretation of revealed theology. A confusion of the ontological distinction between time and eternity was, Basil insisted, not only "a breach of true religion" in relation to revealed theology but also "really the extremest of folly" in relation to natural theology. Such a confusion, according to Gregory of Nyssa, led to the literal interpretation of such terms as "before" and "after" in speaking about "a Lord 'before' times and 'before' *aeons*," to whom therefore "terms expressing temporal interval" were not to be applied properly and literally, because they were "devoid of all meaning"; this was, or should have been, evident not only to orthodox believers, but to "anyone endowed with reason." Therefore, as he said in the same treatise: "It is clear, even with a moderate insight into the nature of things, that there is nothing by which we can measure the divine and blessed life. It is not in time, but time flows from it." The "supernatural powers" of God, being "eternal and infinite," transcended and outstripped "the limits of time." Conversely, it was not only those who were obliged to operate within the limits of reason alone who had to accept these limits of time; but orthodox believers as well, with all of their access to divine revelation, had to recognize that eternal reality, in its transcendence, remained incomprehensible even after it had made itself known in Christ.

As was evident in most of the passages just quoted from their works, the Cappadocians were especially intent on adhering to the strict requirements of *apophasis* when speaking about eternity in relation to time. In thinking about God, the language of "time and creatureliness" was to be avoided. While in this created world "all order and sequence of time in events" could be perceived "only in the *aeons*" and in their succession, that did not apply to human thought about "the nature preexistent to those *aeons*"; it was impossible for "reason to see in that divine and blessed life the things observed, and that exclusively, in creation." As a consequence, Gregory of Nyssa warned, "Every discursive effort of thought to go back beyond the *aeons* will ascend only so far as to see that what it seeks can never be penetrated." The reason for this was the *apophatic* affirmation-by-negation: "No form, no place, no size, no reckoning of time, nor anything else knowable is there; and so it is inevitable that our apprehensive faculty, seeking as it always does some object to grasp, must fall back from any side of this incomprehensible existence." Sometimes what came first seemed to be an affirmation of eternity rather than a negation of time. "The eternity of God's life" meant that God was "to be apprehended as always in being." But thereupon such an affirmation almost immediately took the more precise form of negation, on the basis of the principle, "The idea of eternity is completed only by the negation both of an *arche* and of a *telos*." Although eternity was neither time nor part of time, because it could not be measured, it was permissible to speak in the language of analogy and to say: "What time, measured by the course of the sun, is to us, that eternity is to the everlasting one, namely, a sort of timelike movement and interval coextensive with their existence." Eternity meant a God "transcending the limit of any *telos,* the idea of any *arche,*" and a God, as "the possessor of the beyond [hou to epeikena], presupposed before all existence."

That *apophatic* recognition, which was axiomatic also according to natural theology if it could think straight, served to define and to interpret the language of all theology and religion. From the human perspective, time was "measured by a threefold division, past, present, and future." But when the spontaneous formula of religious faith applied that measure of time to God by saying, "God always was, and always is, and always will be," this was, on deeper reflection, seen to be naive and imprecise: "God always 'is'; 'was' and 'will be' are fragments of our time, and of

Gr.Naz.Or.25.17
(SC 284:198)

Gr.Nyss.Eun.1.361
(Jaeger 1:134)

Gr.Nyss.Eun.1.365–69
(Jaeger 1:135–36)

Gr.Nyss.Eun.1.666
(Jaeger 1:217)

Gr.Nyss.Eun.1.676
(Jaeger 1:220)
Gr.Naz.Or.38.8
(PG 36:320)

Gr.Naz.Or.45.4
(PG 36:628)

Gr.Nyss.Eun.1.574
(Jaeger 1:192)

Gr.Nyss.Or.dom.1
(PG 44:1124–25)

Gr.Naz.Or.38.7
(PG 36:317)

changeable nature, but God is eternal being," without a beginning in the past or an end in the future—indeed, without any past
or any future as such. Both in natural theology and in revealed
theology, God was spoken of as *arche*, but even such a term was
intended to mark the boundaries beyond which human thought
could not go, rather than to give precise information about an
existence that transcended time. God was also spoken of as "the
first [ho prōtos]" and as "hereafter [meta tauta],]" but that was
only a way of declaring "by this means the doctrine of a single
divine nature, continuous with itself, and without interruption,
not admitting in itself priority and posteriority." When such a term
of temporal designation as "this day [sēmeron]" was used in
connection with God, also in the language of Scripture, that
referred to an eternal now, in which there was neither today nor
yesterday nor tomorrow. Or when the creation narrative presented its cosmogony as having taken place over a series of six
"days," that was to be interpreted in the light of the axiomatic
apophatic principle that such a sequence was not to be attributed
to "the prime nature, transcending all idea of time and surpassing
all reach of thought." The "day" and the "week" of the Genesis
narrative were to be understood in the context of the relation of
time to eternity. Applying ontological language to the divine and
speaking of the divine as "being [ōn]" anything did not imply
encompassing it within time; on the contrary, it meant attributing to it "continuity and eternity and superiority to all marks of
time." Gregory of Nazianzus frankly admitted the problem:
"Such expressions as 'when' and 'before' and 'after' and 'from
the beginning' are not timeless, however much we may force
them—unless indeed we were to take the *aeon,* that interval
which is coextensive with the eternal things, and is not divided or
measured by any motion, or by the revolution of the sun, as time
is measured." But even with regard to this term Gregory of Nyssa
pointed out, though probably not explicitly in response to
Gregory of Nazianzus but to Eunomius or to the Macedonian
heretics, that when the psalm described the kingdom of God as "a
kingdom of all the *aeons,*" the word *aeons,* too, referred to "every
substance in them created in infinite space, whether visible or
invisible." Thus it was vain to "inquire with curiosity into the
'priority' of the *aeons.*"

By introducing into the discussion of eternity and time such
questions as the "days" of the creation narrative in Genesis, or
such phrases of their own as "created in infinite space," the Cappadocians were likewise making a point of relating the concept of

Gr.Naz.Or.45.3
(PG 36:625–28)

Bas.*Spir.*6.14
(SC 17:290)

Is 44:6

Gr.Nyss.*Eun.*3.3.10
(Jaeger 2:110)

Ps 2:7

Gr.Nyss.*Apoll.*
(Jaeger 3–I:225)

Gn 1:5–31

Gr.Nyss.*Eun.*1.341
(Jaeger 1:128)

Bas.*Hex.*2.8
(SC 26:178–80)

Heb 1:3

Gr.Nyss.*Eun.*1.637
(Jaeger 1:209)

Gr.Naz.Or.29.3
(SC 250:182)

Ps 145:13

Gr.Nyss.*Maced.*
(Jaeger 3–I:103)
Gr.Nyss.*Eun.*1.364
(Jaeger 1:134)

Gr.Nyss.*Eun.*1.341
(Jaeger 1:128)
Gr.Nyss.*Maced.*
(Jaeger 3–I:103)

See pp.92–97
Gr.Nyss.*Hom.opif.*23
(*PG* 44:212)

Gr.Nyss.*Eun.*1.625
(Jaeger 1:206)
Callahan 1958a,437
Aug.*Conf.*11.1
(*CCSL* 27:194)

Gr.Naz.*Or.*29.9
(*SC* 250:194)

Gr.Nyss.*Eun.*1.381
(Jaeger 1:138)

Gr.Nyss.*Eun.*1.341
(Jaeger 1:128)

Gr.Nyss.*Or.dom.*1
(*PG* 44:1124–25)

Gr.Nyss.*Eun.*1.625
(Jaeger 1:206)

Gr.Nyss.*Infant.*
(Jaeger 3–II:77)

Bas.*Spir.*16.38
(*SC* 17:376)

Gn 1:5

Bas.*Hex.*2.8
(*SC* 26:180)

time to the concept of creation. As they formulated it, this position was also aimed at several opposing views. In part it was the polemic against the Classical theory of the eternity of matter that occasioned their reflection on the principle that not only matter, but time itself, was a creation of the one eternal God. But this emphasis also came from the polemic against the various forms of the heresy according to which the Son was inferior to the Father in the Godhead because he had come "after" the Father, as though "these ideas of time" could "enter into the eternal world." In language that seemed, in conjunction with that of the other Cappadocians, to anticipate Augustine's opening words in Book XI of the *Confessions,* Gregory of Nazianzus was prompted, in reply to heretical speculations about the relation of the Son of God to time, to ask: "Is time in time, or is it not in time? If it is contained in time, then in what time, and what is it except that time, and how does it contain it? But if it is not contained in time, what is that surpassing wisdom that can conceive of a time that is timeless?" Therefore, "the generation of the only-begotten one," as Nyssen responded to the heresy with which Nazianzen was also dealing, did "not fall within the *aeons,* any more than the creation was before the *aeons.*" For it was "only in the case of a creation known empirically" that it was true "to speak about 'priority [to presbyteron],'" but not in the divine nature. It was true to say about those who were born into this world, with its threefold division into past, present, and future, that there had been a time when they were not, that they existed now, and that there would be a time when they would cease to exist. There was no room, however, for "these ideas of time in the eternal 'begetting,'" and they had "nothing akin to that world"; for that world it was necessary to "get beyond the 'sometime,' the 'before,' and the 'after,' and every mark whatever of this extension in time." Therefore, that "single, uncreated, eternal essence," which was God, while transcending time, was also the Creator of "time and space, with all their consequences."

For although Basil had to admit that there was in the Book of Genesis no explicit account of this creation of time—just as there was, he acknowledged, no explicit account there of the creation of the angels—he interpreted the reference in the Septuagint translation of Genesis to "one day [hēmera mia]" rather than to "first day [hēmera prōtē]" as a way of expressing "a wish to determine the measure of day and night" and thus of indicating that "God, who made the measure of time, measured it out and determined it by intervals of days." The definition of time proposed by Eunomius, according to which time was "a certain motion of the stars," would have implied that time had not begun until the fourth day of the creation, when God made the stars; but in fact time was created together with heaven and earth and light at the beginning, before the sun and the stars. For the dramatic phrase of the Book of Job, "God suspends earth over the nothingness [kremazōn gēn epi oudenos]," implied that "the measure of time was created" when, "by the will of God," light had entered the world, making possible the division into discrete times. In sum, time was "assuredly concurrent with all created things," and it was a creature together with them. As such, it, too, had limited power and scope and could not lay claim to sovereignty over the realm of nature. Therefore, Gregory of Nyssa insisted: "It is not in the power of time to define for each one the measures of nature, but nature abides self-contained, preserving itself through suc- ceeding generations; and time has a course of its own, whether surrounding, or flowing by, this nature, which remains firm and motionless within its own limits." The sovereignty of God as the Creator over the cosmos and over time meant that "every dura- tion conceivable [pan diastēmatikon noēma]" had to be viewed as "environed by the divine nature and bounded on all sides by the infinity of the one holding the universe in his embrace [entos tēs theias physeōs perieilēptai, tēi apeiriai tou to pan peri- echontos hapantachothen emperatoumenon]."

But the sovereignty of God over time also meant that time had a positive role to play in divine providence. Time functioned constructively as "a sort of receptacle" for the natural world. Basil seems to have been quoting a proverbial saying of Classical Hellenic wisdom, something like the universal "Time heals all wounds," when he assured his correspondent, the presbyter Evagrius, "Time alone is the remedy of the ills that time has matured." Gregory of Nyssa seems likewise to have been employ- ing a standard phrase of Greek usage when, speaking in the context of natural theology, he referred to "what time has discov- ered for the service and benefit of human life." Yet he spoke about time far more profoundly when he defined change as "a perpet- ual movement toward a different state," which, he specified, could be either good or evil. But, he continued, "In the one case it is always directed toward the good; and here its progress is con- tinual, since there is no conceivable limit to the distance it can go." The technical term for this view of time in the dogmatic theology of the Cappadocians, indeed in all of Greek Christian thought, was *economy,* and it came to its most complete expres-

Gn 1:16

Bas.*Eun.*1.21
(SC 299:246)

Jb 26:7

Gr.Nyss.*Eun.*2.277
(Jaeger 1:307)

Gr.Nyss.*Eun.*3.7.30
(Jaeger 2:225)

Gr.Nyss.*Eun.*1.175
(Jaeger 1:78)

Dörrie et al. 1976,
243–60

Gr.Nyss.*Eun.*2.460
(Jaeger 1:361)

Gr.Nyss.*Eun.*1.370
(Jaeger 1:136)

Bas.*Ep.*156.1
(Courtonne 2:82)

Gr.Nyss.*Eun.*2.183
(Jaeger 1:277)

Gr.Nyss.*Or.catech.*21.3
(Méridier 102)

See pp.263–79

Zemp 1970,73–79

Gr.Nyss.*V.Mos.*2
(Jaeger 7–I:91–92)

Gr.Nyss.*Apoll.*
(Jaeger 3–I:224)

Gr.Nyss.*Hom.opif.*23
(*PG* 44:212)

Gn 1:1

Gr.Nyss.*Hom.opif.*23
(*PG* 44:209)

Gn 1:1
Arist.*Cael.*281a
Bas.*Hex.*1.3
(*SC* 26:98–100)

sion in their doctrine of the incarnation of the divine *Logos* within time and history in the life, death, and resurrection of Jesus Christ. It was, Gregory of Nyssa declared, "the mystery of our faith" that the one who was "before the times and the *aeons*" had entered time, in order to lead humanity from nonbeing to being.

Yet just as the incarnation of the *Logos* was not the only place where the materiality of the world was part of the divine order, so also that event, which, like the creation itself, took place "once and for all [hapax]," was not the only instance where time showed itself to be part of the divine order, hence also not the only instance of the divine *economy.* The materiality and temporality of the incarnation presupposed the intrinsic goodness of matter and of time as divine creations, capable of receiving the divine *Logos.* It was also on the presupposition of the divine creation of time that eschatology was based. Gregory of Nyssa summarized the connection between the doctrine of the beginning and the doctrine of the end as follows: "But if someone, beholding the present course of the cosmos, by which intervals of time are marked, going on in a certain order, should say that it is not possible that the predicted stoppage of these moving things should take place, such a person clearly also does not believe that 'in the *arche*' the heaven and the earth were made by God. For anyone who admits an *arche* of motion surely does not doubt as to its also having a *telos;* and anyone who does not allow its *telos* does not admit its *arche* either." For "the dogmas of the end, and of the renewing of the world," according to Basil, had been "announced beforehand in these short words put at the head of the inspired history: 'In the *arche* God made.'" What had begun in time would also come to an end in time. If there was a beginning, there was no reason to doubt of the end. Both of these applications of the Cappadocian philosophy of time, with their combination of Classical and Christian sources, were decisive for many other aspects of their system of thought, whether natural or revealed.

CHAPTER 8

The Image of God

Muckle 1945,55–84

Harl 1971,111–26

Macr.ap.Gr.Nyss.
Anim.res. (PG 46:44–45)

The Cappadocians recognized that in Christian theology no less than in Classical culture, no discussion of the nature of the world as a cosmos existing in space and time, whether as a scientific and philosophical construct of natural theology or as an article of faith in revealed theology, could be complete without a consideration of the nature of man. There was for all of them, as has been pointed out for Gregory of Nyssa, an identifiable correlation between cosmology and anthropology in any philosophical or theological system, Classical or Christian. But the relation ran deeper: the very capacity to formulate a cosmology and to analyze time and space—through some combination of human observation and human speculation, with perhaps the addition of divine revelation—was, as a phenomenon, evidence for the power of the human mind, despite great limitations, to trace and imitate some of the thought processes of God, and was thus no less important for anthropology than it was for cosmology. The ability of Aristotle as scientist to discover by reason the affinities

Mure 1964,124–25

Mure 1964,163–71

Arist.EN.1177a15

between the human race and other species confirmed the judgment of Aristotle as philosopher that humanity differed from other species by virtue of reason, which was "either itself divine or only the most divine element in us." Similarly, Gregory of Nyssa was speaking not only about the theology of Basil but about cosmology as such when he said, in his tribute to his brother: "The only one who has worthily considered the creation of God is someone who has truly been created in conformity with

Gr.Nyss.*Hom.opif*.pr.
(*PG* 44:125)

Bas.*Hex*.9.6
(*SC* 26:520)
Schoemann 1943,
31–53,175–200; Ladner
1958,59–94; Ladner
1959,90–107; Boer
1968,148–86

Macr.ap.Gr.Nyss.
Anim.res. (*PG* 46:57–60)

Macr.ap.Gr.Nyss.
Anim.res. (*PG* 46:28)

Gr.Naz.*Or*.38.11
(*PG* 36:321–24)
Janini Cuesta 1946,51–
52; Leys 1951,65–67

Lampe 870

Gr.Nyss.*Hom.opif*.16
(*PG* 44:177–80)

Macr.ap.Gr.Nyss.
Anim.res. (*PG* 46:44)

Pl.*Prt*.343b

[kata] God, and whose soul is fashioned in the image of the Creator—Basil, our common father and teacher, who by his own speculation made the sublime working of the universe as cosmos [tēn hypsēlēn tou pantos diakosmēsin] generally intelligible." In the course of his exposition of cosmology, therefore, a thinker like Basil found the anthropological problem constantly being raised, and he was obliged to recognize that eventually it had to receive the detailed attention it deserved. In the event, however, as the words just quoted indicate, it was his younger brother, Gregory of Nyssa, rather than Basil who went on to give it such systematic attention.

In the thought of the Cappadocians the link between cosmology and anthropology went well beyond that kind of epistemological analysis, important though this was. For in the words of Macrina, speaking in "a mere exercise in interpretation," the structure of the cosmos could be understood as having been produced "in a sort of graduated and ordered advance to the creation of humanity." Therefore, she continued a bit later, "It is said by the wise that mankind is a sort of microcosm [mikros tis kosmos]." Standing as it did on the boundary line between the "intelligible [noētos]" world and the "empirical [aisthētos]" world, mankind was created "as a sort of second world [deuteros kosmos], great in littleness, a new angel on the earth, a worshiper made up of a composite" of body and soul. But in using a concept such as "microcosm [mikros kosmos]"—always, it seems, as two words, the single Greek word "mikrokosmos" apparently occurring for the first time in John of Damascus—they were careful to lay insistent stress on this composite nature. In doing so, they repudiated any materialistic use of the concept of microcosm by Classical writers that would have posited an unbroken continuity between the material world and the human race, as though human nature were nothing more than "a representation and likeness of the world—of the transient heaven, of the changing world, and of all the things contained in them, doomed to pass away with the departure of the world surrounding them." For the human soul transcended its material existence and the transiency of this world in a way that bore at least some similarity to the transcendence of God over the cosmos; but this was a similarity defined within the confines of *apophatic* theology. The Cappadocians adapted the motto of the Delphic oracle, "Know thyself [Gnōthi sauton]," to this link between anthropology and cosmology, between the knowledge of self and the knowledge of the world, placing their characteristic emphasis on the "ineffable [arrēton]" mystery of the divine being. To those who claimed that the human mind could understand the divine essence as God understood it, they replied with the argument a minori ad maius that even the understanding of one's own essence was unattainable. Self-knowledge was the most difficult of all the sciences, Basil argued. Yet it was also, if carried out responsibly, no less a "light of theology" and no less reliable a guide to the natural knowledge of God than was the knowledge of the world; "in observing myself," he could pray, commenting on the words of the psalm about how "fearfully [phoberōs]" man had been fashioned, "I have known thy infinite wisdom." And like the knowledge of God through the knowledge of the world—about which the New Testament, quoting the Old Testament, had asked, "Who knows the mind of the Lord?"—the knowledge of one's own mind had to be interpreted *apophatically.*

In the investigation of anthropology, as well as of cosmology as a whole, the determination of answers to the questions "Whence [hothen]?" and "Wherefore [hotou]?" was fundamental to all other questions. Drawing less on Christian than on Greek sources, Nyssen made the observation that although other animals had a natural covering, such as fur or a shell, or natural weapons, such as claws or fangs, the human animal was bereft of any of these. From the same mixture of Christian and Classical sources came the identification of the erectness of the human form, "upright and extending aloft toward heaven," as evidence of a special status and dignity in comparison with that of other creatures. Thus, not only in treatises that were apologetic in intent but in those that were being written for edification or dogmatic clarification and that were addressed to church audiences, they were able to invoke the Classical sources of natural theology alongside the Christian sources of revealed theology. They felt justified in arguing this way because, on the one hand, they could take it for granted that all things had been produced by the divine essence; this was "a proposition superfluous to prove," inasmuch as it was undeniable to "anyone, with however little insight into the truth of things," and therefore it was a truth of natural theology on which everyone would have to agree. But on the other hand, they felt free to add, "We are helped in this by a word of the inspired teaching," which declared that the creation of humanity "from heterogeneous sources" had taken place subsequently to the creation of all the other things. Unlike animal life, moreover,

Gr.Nyss.*Hom.opif.*2
(*PG* 44:133)
Eun.ap.Socr.*H.e.*4.7
(Hussey 2:482)

Gr.Nyss.*Eun.*2.107–14
(Jaeger 258–59)

Ps 138:14
Bas.*Hex.*9.6
(*SC* 26:512–14)

Rom 11:34; Is 40:13
Gr.Nyss.*Hom.opif.*11
(*PG* 44:153–56)

Gr.Nyss.*Infant.*
(Jaeger 3–II:76)
Pl.*Prt.*321a–c

Gr.Nyss.*Hom.opif.*7
(*PG* 44:140–44)

Lv 26:13; Pl.*Smp.*190a

Gr.Nyss.*Hom.opif.*8
(*PG* 44:144)

Gn 2:7
Gr.Nyss.*Infant.*
(Jaeger 3–II:77)

Gr.Nyss.*Hom.opif.*3
(*PG* 44:136)

Macr.ap.Gr.Nyss.
Anim.res. (*PG* 46:60)

Gr.Nyss.*Hom.opif.*pr.
(*PG* 44:128)

Gr.Nyss.*Cant.*2
(Jaeger 6:68)

Merki 1952,138–64

Lit.Bas.
(Brightman 324)

humanity had been created on the basis of divine deliberation and out of preexistent stuff. Therefore, "every single form of life, both that of plants and that seen in brutes," could be found somewhere in the human frame; yet there was far more to human life than all of those forms put together. That made man the microcosm "second to none among the wonders of the world, perhaps even greater than any of those known to us, because no other existing thing, except the human creation" could lay claim to having been made like to God. No other existing thing— "neither the heavens nor the moon nor the sun nor the beauty of the stars nor any of the other phenomena of creation"—could lay claim to the title "image of God," which, at any rate in the authentic writings of Gregory of Nyssa, was synonymous with "likeness [homoiōsis]" to God. As the *Liturgy of Saint Basil* put it, "Having shaped humanity by taking ground from the earth, O God, thou hast honored it with thine own image."

Gr.Nyss.*Hom.opif.*16
(*PG* 44:180)

"In what then does human greatness consist, according to the doctrine of the church"—and, as has been noted, according to the doctrines of natural theology? asked Gregory of Nyssa. He immediately answered his own question: "Not in likeness to the created world, but in being in the image of the nature of the Creator." Yet the contrast between "this mortal, passible, short-lived being" and the "immortal, pure, and everlasting" divine nature made so audacious a title as "the image of God" for human nature seem altogether presumptuous. Here again, it was essential to observe the standard distinction of Cappadocian thought, as formulated by Macrina, between "the fact that

Macr.ap.Gr.Nyss.
Anim.res. (*PG* 46:121)
Gr.Nyss.*Hom.opif.*16
(*PG* 44:180)

[hoti]," which was knowable, and "the process how [pōs]," which was not. The "how" of the image of God, therefore, was known "only to the very truth itself [hē ontōs alētheia]." But the "that" of the image of God was sufficiently comprehensive as a concept for human nature to make it adequate as a designation

Gr.Naz.*Ep.*102
(*PG* 37:197)
Gr.Nyss.*Beat.*1
(*PG* 44:1200)

even for the human nature in Christ. It was sufficient as well to identify the distinctive *telos* of human life, and sufficient to serve as the basis for moral exhortations. The imperative to perform works that were morally good was specifically grounded in the

Gr.Naz.*Or.*14.2
(*PG* 35:860)

universality of the image of God in the entire human race. The universality of the image implied for someone in a position of political power, as Gregory of Nazianzus put it in addressing government officials: "You are the image of God—and you rule

Gr.Naz.*Or.*17.9
(*PG* 35:976)

over those who are the image of God!" Consequently, the failure by the rich and powerful to recognize the image of God also in the

Gr.Naz.Or.14.14
(PG 35:876)

Gr.Nyss.Or.dom.2
(PG 44:1144)

See pp.148–49

See pp.58–59

Lk 17:21

Gr.Nyss.Beat.6
(PG 44:1269)
Gr.Nyss.Cant.4
(Jaeger 6:104)

Gr.Nyss.Cant.11
(Jaeger 6:333–34)

Macr.ap.Gr.Nyss.
Anim.res. (PG 46:44)

Gr.Nyss.Cant.14
(Jaeger 6:404)

Gr.Nyss.V.Macr.
(Jaeger 8–I:382)

Gr.Nyss.Cant.9
(Jaeger 6:276–77)
Bas.Leg.lib.gent.9
(Wilson 32)
Pl.R.498b;533d

Rom.13:14; Gal.5:13

Rebecchi 1943,322–25

Macr.ap.Gr.Nyss.
Anim.res. (PG 46:124–25)

poor represented a denial of the Creator in whose image the poor, too, had been made. On that basis, God could say to a hypocrite: "If you were my child, your life would be marked by my own good qualities. I do not recognize in you the image of my nature." The doctrine of the image of God served, therefore, as a key to Cappadocian social ethics.

But the concept of the image of God likewise served as the foundation for the "Christian Socratism" of existential self-knowledge, which by transcending ordinary knowledge showed the inadequacy of any mere knowledge: "It is blessed not only to know the principle of health, but to be healthy. . . . The Lord did not say that it is blessed to know something about God, but to have God present within oneself. . . . I do not think that if the eye of one's soul has been purified, one is promised a direct vision of God. . . . 'The kingdom of God is within you.' . . . Someone whose heart has been purified from every creature and from all unruly affections will see the image of the divine nature in the *kalon* within." As the image of God, the human soul was a mirror of God, both to others and to itself. The soul stood on the boundary between two worlds, the visible and the invisible, striving for the higher reaches of the divine and seeking to find there its *arche*. There was, Macrina taught, "no sort of communion . . . on the score of substance between the simplicity and invisibility of the soul and the grossness of the body." In this she was herself an illustration of the Christian "disdain for the material life [hē tēs hylikēs zōēs hyperopsia]," and for her admiring brothers and the entire Christian community she was that in practice at least as much as in theory. Macrina and other ascetics were seen as practicing "a life on the borderline between human and noncorporeal nature," still occupying a body but already participating here and now in "the angelic and noncorporeal nature." For in a real sense, the soul belonged to human nature in a way that the body did not, because the body was that which human nature shared with the animals. On this preference for the soul over the body, according to Basil, Plato, Classical philosopher though he was, agreed with Paul the Christian apostle. Nevertheless, in opposition to theories of the preexistence of the soul, whether Classical or Christian (as in the teaching of Origen), Macrina insisted on the position, as a corollary of the doctrine of creation, that "the point of commencement of existence" had been "one and the same for the body as for the soul."

Bringing these components of the doctrine of the soul together, Macrina proposed the following definition: "The soul is an *ousia* created, and living, and intellectual [gennetē, zōsa, noera], transmitting from itself to an organized and sentient body the power of living and of grasping objects of sense, as long as a natural constitution capable of this holds together." She arrived at this definition by the now familiar method of affirmation-through-*apophasis*. Missing from the specific language of her definition here—though explicit elsewhere in this discourse of hers, and implicit throughout and especially in the list of attributes as "created, and living, and intellectual"—was any particular reference to what her brother Gregory elsewhere called "the element of our soul in the likeness of God." "It was," according to Emil Brunner, "this very concept of the *Imago Dei* which formed a synthesis between the Platonic-Aristotelian-Stoic view and the Christian view of man, which dominated the whole of the Patristic period and the Christian Middle Ages, and has been, and still is, operative." Despite this prominence of the concept of the image of God in Christian thought, neither the original use of the concept in the creation narrative of Genesis nor the subsequent references to it in the Old Testament and the New Testament, most of them in the context of ethical admonitions rather than of doctrinal formulas, provided any clear catalog of the specific attributes of the soul constituting the image. Those attributes had to be supplied, partly from the doctrine of God, some of whose attributes were reflected, to the extent that they could be reflected at all, in the human image of God, and partly from the identification of Christ as the image of God. Christ was the image of God, to which in turn the new creation in Christ was to be conformed.

In the case of Christ, though not in the case of humanity, "image [eikōn]" was a synonym for "living and active essence." As part of the "image of God," a dominion over other creatures had been vested in the human race, although only God was Lord of heaven and earth. Being made in the image of God, man was the vicegerent of the Lord of heaven and earth. God the Creator was also the only one who possessed true "blessedness [makariotēs]" in the strict sense of the word, defined as "this inexpressible beauty, very grace, wisdom, and power; this true light, the fount of all goodness, mighty above all else; the one thing lovable, always the same, rejoicing without end in infinite happiness." But through the image something of that quality could be communicated to man the creature, whom the Psalms in the Old Testament and then the Beatitudes in the New Testament could therefore properly call "blessed [makarios]." Conversely, those

Macr.ap.Gr.Nyss. *Anim.res.* (PG 46:29)

Macr.ap.Gr.Nyss. *Anim.res.* (PG 46:40)

Macr.ap.Gr.Nyss. *Anim.res.* (PG 46:57)

Gr.Nyss.*Hom.opif.*27 (PG 44:228)

Brunner 1939,92–93

Bernard 1952

Gn 1:26–27; Gn 5:1; Gn 9:6; Wis 2:23; Sir 17:3; 1 Cor 11:7; Jas 3:9

Leys 1951,123–27

Rom 8:29;1 Cor 15:49; 2 Cor 3:18;2 Cor 4:4; Col 1:15; Col 3:10 Col 1:15 Bas.*Eun.*2.17;1.18 (SC 305:66;299:234–36) Gr.Nyss.*Eun.*1.191 (Jaeger 1:82); Gr.Nyss.*Hom.opif.*4 (PG 44:136)

Ps 1:1 Mt 5:3 Gr.Nyss.*Beat.*1 (PG 44:1197)

human qualities that were reprehensible were far removed from the image of God as "the stamp indicating divinity," because they were far removed from divinity itself. Noteworthy among these were "wrath, cowardice, and greed," for by anthropopathism wrath was attributed to the justice of God because of the human association of wrath with punishment. Elsewhere, Gregory of Nyssa showed both his psychological insight and his literary power by graphically describing what happened when the dominion of the image of God was replaced by wrath: "When some word or deed or suspicion causing annoyance has roused this disease, then the blood boils around the heart, and the soul rises up for vengeance. As in pagan fables some drugged drink changes human nature into animal form, so a man is sometimes seen to be changed by wrath into a boar, or dog, or panther, or some other wild animal. His eyes become bloodshot, his hair stands on end and bristles; his voice becomes harsh and his words sharp. His tongue grows numb with passion and refuses to obey the desires of his mind. His lips grow stiff; and unable to articulate a word, they can no longer keep the spittle produced by passion inside the mouth, but dribble froth disgustingly when they try to speak. Hands and feet behave in a similar way, and such is the attitude of the whole body, every limb being affected by this passion."

According to Macrina, it was, therefore, axiomatic that there could be no excellence in the soul that was not a property as well of the divine nature. In his treatise on creation Gregory of Nyssa enumerated the following as properties of the divine nature that also belonged to the catalog of the excellences in the soul: "purity, *apatheia*, blessedness, alienation from all evil . . . , mind and word . . . and love . . . and the power of apprehending things by means of sight and hearing, and the understanding that inquires into things and searches them out." He provided a similar catalog in his *Catechetical Oration*, assigning *apatheia*, whether divine or human, a normative place. Always standing as a curb on the extravagances to which such speculations about the continuity between God the Creator and the image of God in the creature could easily lead, however, was the methodology of *apophatic* theology. This methodology insisted that it was impossible, "by means of some kind of analogy and likeness [di' analogias tinos kai homoiotētos]," to construct a doctrine of the divine essence. The method of *apophatic* theology was a necessary tool in the conflict with a heretical system that was using analogies between "the divine, simple, and nonmaterial life, and the mate-

Gr.Nyss.*Hom.opif*.18
(PG 44:192)

Gr.Naz.*Or*.31.22
(SC 250:316–18)

Hom.*Od*.20.229–40

Gr.Nyss.*Beat*.2
(PG 44:1216)

Macr.ap.Gr.Nyss.
Anim.res. (PG 46:52)

Gr.Nyss.*Hom.opif*.5
(PG 44:137)

Gr.Nyss.*Or.catech*.6.10
(Méridier 42)

See pp.40–56

Gr.Nyss.*Eun*.3.6.15
(Jaeger 2:191)

Gr.Nyss.*Eun.*3.2.4
(Jaeger 2:53)

Gr.Nyss.*Eun.*2.211–12
(Jaeger 1:286–87)

Gr.Nyss.*Hom.opif.*6
(PG 44:137–40)

Gr.Nyss.*Eun.*2.107–14
(Jaeger 1:258–59)

Gr.Nyss.*Beat.*6
(PG 44:1269–72)

Schoemann 1941,339–
40; Bálas 1966
Gr.Nyss.*Hom.opif.*16
(PG 44:184)

Gr.Nyss.*Eun.*1.191
(Jaeger 1:82)

Heb 2:5–9

Ps 8:6

Gr.Nyss.*Eun.*1.527
(Jaeger 1:178–79)

Bas.*Hex.*4.5
(SC 26:264–66)

rial existence subject to passion" as a weapon against trinitarian orthodoxy. Above all, *apophatic* theology meant that God was not separable into various faculties, such as sight, hearing, knowledge, and the like, but was "at one and the same time sight and hearing and knowledge" and whatever other divine faculties and divine attributes there might be. By contrast with the divine mind, the human mind could be divided into several distinct "faculties [dynameis]," even though it remained one mind. And so it was with all the other attributes of the divine essence that might be employed to supply the content of the image of God.

Were it left at that, the methodology of Cappadocian apophatic theology might seem to have reduced the theory of an image of God to nothing more than a grand metaphor empty of content. But Gregory of Nyssa stood the *apophatic* methodology on its head, using it as the foundation on which to construct such a theory: "When you hear that the divine majesty is exalted above the heavens, that its glory is inexpressible, its beauty ineffable, and its nature inaccessible, do not despair of ever beholding what you desire. It is indeed within your reach; you have within yourselves the standard by which to apprehend the divine . . . , the likeness of the glories of [God's] own nature, as if it were the form of a carving into wax." For because the list of individual qualities of the good conferred by the Creator was so long, the language of Scripture had expressed "participation in all good concisely in one comprehensive phrase: 'the image of God.'" Among these many qualities, three nevertheless stood out as comprising the essential content of the image: reason, free will, and immortality. Many of the other qualities, moreover, could be seen as part of one or more of these. Human reason, for example, was often the general category under which to discuss the aforementioned theme of the human dominion over the rest of creation, as celebrated in the Psalms, which declared (speaking about the human race and, according to the New Testament, about the humanity of Christ): "You have made him master over the works of your hands, putting everything in subjection under his feet." The basis for that dominion was the superiority of human nature that came from "the prerogative of rationality," which conferred "the authorization to command" and the responsibility to exercise this authority and stewardship wisely.

The other Cappadocians were unanimous in affirming with Basil the doctrine of "reason as the distinctive quality" of the human soul. "The mind is a wonderful thing," he said elsewhere,

Bas.*Ep.*233.1
(Courtonne 3:39)

Gr.Nyss.*V.Macr.*
(Jaeger 8–1:380)

Macr.ap.Gr.Nyss.
Anim.res. (PG 46:57)

Gr.Nyss.*Or.dom.*3
(PG 44:1149)

Gr.Naz.*Or.*45.18
(PG 36:648)

Gr.Naz.*Or.*32.9
(SC 318:194)

Gr.Nyss.*Apoll.*
(Jaeger 3–1:177)

Gr.Nyss.*Eun.*2.190
(Jaeger 1:279)

Macr.ap.Gr.Nyss.
Anim.res. (PG 46:52)

Lk 15:8–10

Gr.Nyss.*Virg.*12
(Jaeger 8–1:300–301)

Gr.Nyss.*V.Mos.*2
(Jaeger 7–1:62)

Pl.*Phdr.*246–47;
Pl.*R.*439d

Gn 2:7

Gr.Nyss.*Or.catech.*6.4
(Méridier 36)

"and therein we possess that which is according to the image of the Creator." His sister, Macrina, proved this position by her own behavior: at the death of their brother Naucratius, according to her brother Gregory of Nyssa, she "faced the disaster in a rational spirit [ton logismon antistēsasa]," which, the account clearly implied, was the Christian way to face it. She also articulated this position in her dialogue with Gregory when she declared: "The speculative, critical, and world-surveying faculty of the soul is its peculiar property by virtue of its very nature, and thereby the soul preserves within itself the image of the divine grace. For our reason surmises that divinity itself, whatever it may be in its inmost nature, is manifested in these very things: universal super-vision and the critical discernment between good and evil." Gregory of Nyssa himself spoke of reason as "the highest faculty" of the human mind, and the one that carried the very impress of God. Gregory of Nazianzus joined himself to these views by identifying reason as the faculty that "unreasoning animals" did not possess, as a result of which they were inferior to such ratio-nal beings as men and angels. "Order," he said, "assembled [syn-estēsato] human nature, a rational animal, out of a rational and an irrational element." It was a mistake, therefore, for Christian theologians to dismiss the noun "reason" as "a meaningless sound [phōnē asēmos]." Nor was it correct for them to take the excesses of rationalism and intellectual pride as an excuse to regard human intelligence merely as an evil in relation to God. The Cappadocians admitted quite freely that in this defense of human rationality they were, as apologists for the Christian faith, articulating a position that was shared to some extent by Classi-cal philosophy. But natural theology was in agreement here with revealed theology. The parable of the lost coin in the Gospel was an allegory of how the soul found the image of God within itself, beginning with the lighting of a candle, which was a reference to "our reason throwing light on concealed things."

They likewise acknowledged their agreement with the natural theology of Classical culture in their elevation of the rational soul over the passions and emotions. This was, as they knew, a teach-ing closely associated with the doctrines of Plato, in the figure of the charioteer and elsewhere. Human nature represented, by the design of the Creator, "the commixture of intelligence and the senses," with the Genesis account signifying the second by the earth that the Creator took and the first by the breath that the Creator infused into the earth to cause it to live. But it was like-wise the intention of the Creator that in this commixture intel-

ligence and reason should have hegemony over the senses and
emotions. For the emotions were shared by human nature with
the irrational creatures; but precisely because of the combination
of these with reason in the case of human sin it was characteristic
of "all those particular forms proceeding from the absence of
reason in brute nature to become vice by the evil use of the mind,"
whereas in the irrational beasts they were not vice. On the other
hand, "with the dominance of reason over such emotions," each
was transmuted to a form of *arete:* wrath became courage, terror
turned into caution, fear expressed itself as obedience, hatred was
transformed into aversion from vice, and the power of love was

Gr.Nyss.*Hom.opif.*18
(PG 44:193–96)

made sublime in the desire for the truly beautiful—all of these
aretai, which were inculcated also by natural theology, being
implied in the New Testament admonition to "aspire to the realm

Col 3:1

above" as well. "That laudable despotism" of the mind allied

Gr.Nyss.*Eun.*3.1.31
(Jaeger 2:14)

itself with divine wisdom to "transform the mob rule of the
passions into the monarchy of reason." When it was read in the
light of this blending of natural theology and revealed theology,
the second of the Beatitudes in the Sermon on the Mount,

Mt 5:4

"Blessed are the sorrowful; they shall find consolation," could be
paraphrased to read: "Blessed are those who are not easily turned
towards the passionate movements of the soul, but who are stead-

Gr.Nyss.*Beat.*2
(PG 44:1216)

ied by reason." Reason was, moreover, superior not only to the
passions and emotions but also to the experience of the senses,

Bas.*Hex.*6.11
(SC 26:384)

even in the observation and study of the physical universe.
Gregory of Nyssa brought the natural and the revealed together
to declare, in a polemic against all anti-intellectualism whether
Christian or non-Christian, as well as against any intellectualism
that ignored the reality of God: "Whatever discovery has been
made in human life, conducive to any useful purpose of peace or
war, came to us from no other quarter than from an intelligence
conceiving and discovering according to our several require-

Gr.Nyss.*Eun.*2.186
(Jaeger 1:278)
Phil 4:8
Gr.Nyss.*Cant.*15
(Jaeger 6:438)

ments; and that intelligence is a gift of God. It is to God, then,
that we owe all that intelligence supplies to us." This celebration
of the human intelligence as divine image paraphrased the admonition to ponder intelligence as a gift of God. In short, to be made

Gr.Nyss.*Infant.*
(Jaeger 3–II:73)

according to the image of God and therefore to be authentically
human meant to be rational. It was also because the human soul

Gr.Nyss.*Cant.*5
(Jaeger 6:169)

was "rational [logikos]" that it needed to be fed by the *Logos*
of God.

Apostolopoulos 1986,
251–71

By virtue of this rationality human nature was also endowed
with freedom, another component of the image of God. This
intimate connection between rational knowledge and free will

Lampe 317–18

Gr.Naz.Or.38.12
(PG 36:324)
Gr.Nyss.Beat.5
(PG 44:1253–56)
Gr.Naz.Or.14.25
(PG 35:892)

Gr.Nyss.Or.catech.5.9–
10 (Méridier 30)

Jn 10:18
Gr.Nyss.Ref.139
(Jaeger 2:372)

Lit.Bas.
(Brightman 327)
1 Tm 2:4

Gr.Nyss.Cant.10
(Jaeger 6:304)

Gr.Nyss.Maced.
(Jaeger 3–I:114)

Clark 1977,45–66

Gr.Nyss.Apoll.
(Jaeger 3–I:198)

Preger 1897,36–52

Gr.Nyss.Or.dom.2
(PG 44:1145)

Gr.Nyss.Hom.opif.16
(PG 44:184)

was evident in such a technical term of Greek philosophy and theology as "gnōmē," which could mean either of those qualities (as well as various others). The capacity for free choice was a gift from the Creator. God willed and intended to belong to the creature as its very own but wanted this to happen only as a result of a choice by human free will, not as a consequence of divine sovereignty and necessity. God endowed Adam and Eve with "the principles of all goodness," which had to include free will. From the beginning they possessed freedom and self-determination. The gift of free will, then, was "the most excellent and precious of all goods," being an attribute of God. The absence of free will would mean "falsifying the 'image' in that respect and so making it differ from the archetype," that is, from the divine giver. As it would have been a falsification for an image of God to be devoid of this supreme quality, so it could be argued a fortiori that it would have been an anomaly for this quality of "self-determination [autexousia]" to be absent from the humanity of the incarnate Son of God, who declared, in reference to the crucifixion, that he was laying down his life of his own free will and not by any externally imposed *ananke*. The *Liturgy of Saint Basil* described the crucifixion of Christ as "his voluntary and celebrated and life-giving death [ekousion kai aoidimon kai zōopoion autou thanaton]," a death that he freely took upon himself. From this it followed that while salvation itself was, from the divine side, the consequence of the universal salvific will of God, this did not happen without the participation, from the human side, of will and free choice, apart from which there would be no authentic salvation. The mysterious relation between grace and free will in this process was such that either could be seen as having achieved salvation, but not apart from the other.

In spite of the explicitly soteriological and Christian tenor of these statements about the doctrine of free will, the Cappadocians claimed that in espousing it they were setting forth a truth taught not only by divine revelation but by natural theology: "Who does not know that *arete* is the achievement of free choice?" Gregory of Nyssa could ask, on the assumption that this was something that everyone who had thought about virtue as *arete*, whether as pagan philosopher or as Christian theologian, could be expected to know. For if *arete* was defined as a condition or action of being set apart from evil, that had to be by the choice of a free will. Conversely, *arete* could not be "the result of compulsion and force," because *arete* was always "a voluntary thing." In what its editor has characterized as "a locus classicus

Jaeger 6:102n

Gr.Nyss.*Cant*.4
(Jaeger 6:102)

Macr.ap.Gr.Nyss.
Anim.res. (PG 46:
120–21)

Gr.Nyss.*V.Mos*.2
(Jaeger 7–I:56)

ap.Pl.*Tht*.160d

Gr.Nyss.*Cant*.9
(Jaeger 6:264–65)

See pp.154–57

Macr.ap.Gr.Nyss.
Anim.res. (PG 46:41–44)

Gr.Nyss.*Cant*.12
(Jaeger 6:343)

Gr.Nyss.*Virg*.12
(Jaeger 8–I:297–98)

Gn 1:26–27
Gr.Nyss.*Or.catech*.5.6–7
(Méridier 28)
Gr.Nyss.*V.Mos*.2
(Jaeger 7–I:143)
Sg 1:6
Gr.Nyss.*Cant*.2
(Jaeger 6:60)

of Christian philosophy" (and not merely of Christian dogmatics), Gregory of Nyssa described a "human nature capable in accordance with knowledge [dektikē kata gnōmēn] to take the direction indicated by the inclination of its free choice [hē ropē tēs proaireseōs]." That direction could be either for good or for ill; for, as Macrina pointed out, the soul could "be attracted of its own free will [tēi idiai gnōmēi] in a chosen direction, either willfully shutting its eyes to the good . . . or, conversely, preserving undimmed its vision of the truth." Or, in her brother's formula, "We human beings have here within ourselves [oikothen], in our own nature and free choice, the causes both of light and of darkness." In their apologetics, the Cappadocian theologians showed that they were Greeks as well as Christians by appropriating such philosophical themes as the familiar doctrine of Protagoras quoted by Plato, "Man is the measure of all things [pantōn chrēmatōn anthrōpon metron einai]," and adapting them to the defense of free will. At the same time, this defense served as an apologetic weapon against the determinism, both astrological and philosophical, that they perceived to be endemic to the speculations of pagan Classicism.

Just as rationality and free will were inseparable in the doctrine of the image of God, so in turn free will and immortality belonged together as components of the image. For the only path that led to eternal life was a discipline that was not coerced but voluntary. Being at one and the same time "the work and the imitation [mimēma] of the divine and imperishable mind," mankind [anthrōpos], this "reasoning and intelligent creature," was created immortal. After having listed "life, reason, wisdom, and all the good things of God" that were included in the divine image, Gregory of Nyssa turned to immortality as essential to the image: "Since eternity [aidiotēs] is also one of the good attributes of the divine nature, it is essential that the constitution of our own nature should not be deprived of this. It had to have an immortal [athanaton] element, so that it might, by this inherent faculty, recognize the transcendent and have the desire for the immortality of God. The account of creation sums all this up in a single expression when it says that mankind was created 'in the image of God.'" He described the image of God evident in Moses "the mystagogue" as "incorruption [aphtharsia]," and he interpreted the allegory of the "vineyard" in the Song of Songs as an exposition of "immortality and *apatheia* and likeness to God." He also argued that there could not be degrees of immortality: it was not

Gr.Nyss.*Eun*.2.590
(Jaeger 1:398)

Gr.Naz.*Or*.29.13
(SC 250:202)

Gr.Nyss.*V.Macr.*
(Jaeger 8–I:390)

Macr.ap.Gr.Nyss.
Anim.res. (PG 46:17)

Macr.ap.Gr.Nyss.
Anim.res. (PG 46:44–45)

Macr.ap.Gr.Nyss.
Anim.res. (PG 46:48)

Armstrong 1948,113–26

1 Thes 4:13

Macr.ap.Gr.Nyss.
Anim.res. (PG 46:12–13)

Macr.ap.Gr.Nyss.
Anim.res. (PG 46:49)
Mt 13:24–30
Macr.ap.Gr.Nyss.
Anim.res. (PG 46:64)

1 Cor 15:42

possible to be more immortal or less immortal but only to be either mortal or immortal—with the proviso, as added by Nazianzen, that although the immortality of God the Creator was without beginning as well as without end, that of men and angels as creatures did have a beginning but not an end. In 379, Nyssen devoted an entire treatise, *On the Soul and the Resurrection,* to the dialogue of Macrina on her deathbed, in which, as he reported in his biography of his sister, she had "philosophized to us about the nature of the soul and explained the reason for life in the flesh, and why the human race was made, and how it was mortal, and the origin of death and the nature of the journey from death to life again." There she identified a belief in immortality as the only valid foundation for a life of *arete,* for without it "the pleasure of the moment" would predominate; she also chided those gathered around her for fearing death. The basis of her doctrine of immortality was the distinction between soul and body, according to which the body, as a composite entity, would be dissolved and would return to its kindred physical *stoicheia* in the earth, while the soul, as a "simple and incomposite essence," would not be dissolved. But she gave this stock doctrine of the immortality of the soul a somewhat unconventional twist by asserting: "The soul exists in the actual atoms that it has once animated, and there is no force to tear it away from its cohesion with them."

The doctrine of the natural immortality of the soul, as set forth in the dialogue attributed to Macrina, strikingly illustrated the complex relation between natural theology and revealed theology, or between Christianity and Classical culture. To a casual reader the dialogue may have seemed to be presenting itself as an exercise in Christian biblical theology. In the first paragraph Macrina "quoted the apostle's words about the duty of 'not grieving for those who sleep in death,' a feeling characteristic only of the rest of mankind, 'those with no hope.'" Later in the dialogue she stated the case for the transcendence of revealed theology and biblical authority over natural theology and philosophical speculation in the strongest possible terms, quoting the parable of the wheat and the tares from the Gospels as proof that the seeds sown by God in the earth did rise to life again. Yet this biblical reference, which echoed Pauline language about "what is sown as a perishable thing [being] raised imperishable," came in response to an inquiry in which Gregory complimented her while gently chiding her: "To anyone who reflects indeed, your exposition, advancing as it does in this consecutive manner, though plain and unvarnished, bears sufficiently upon it the stamp of correctness and hits the truth. And to those who are expert only in the technical methods of proof [tas technikas ephodous], a mere syllogism suffices to convince; but as for ourselves, we were agreed that there was something more trustworthy than any of these technical conclusions, namely, that which the teachings of Holy Scripture point to. And so I deem that it is necessary to inquire, in addition to what has been said, whether this inspired teaching harmonizes with it all." For in fact what had been said up to this point had, in spite of all of her formal protestations of biblical authority, proceeded by "the technical methods of proof," employing rational argument and philosophical deduction. Early in the discourse Macrina rejected the fideism of this assertion of Gregory: "The divine utterances seemed to me like mere commands compelling us to believe that the soul lasts forever, not, however, that we were led by them to this belief by any reasoning, so that our mind within us appears to accept the enforced opinion slavishly."

As a monograph devoted entirely to this dialogue, *On the Soul and the Resurrection,* in the light of Classical philosophy, under the title *Phaedo Christianus,* has made clear, the treatise actually located its discussion of the first of those two topics in its title, the definition of the soul, within the context of various writers from the tradition of Classical Greek thought, and it proceeded largely within the framework of natural theology. It did so to a considerable extent even in its consideration of the second topic, the resurrection, which had a specifically Christian meaning. Thus it was, as a leading patrologist had already called it, "a counterpart to Plato's *Phaedo.*" When Gregory, presenting for the sake of argument the case for a theory of annihilationism, referred to "certain persons, of no small philosophical reputation among the Greeks, who held and maintained" this theory, Macrina dismissed them by snapping back: "Away with that pagan nonsense [Ea tous exōthen lērous]!" But obviously they could not be dismissed so peremptorily, for a short time later she herself felt obliged to recur to "the Epicurean and Stoic philosophers" whom the apostle Paul had encountered in Athens. Concentrating at some length on the teachings of Epicurus, she found a correlation between his doctrine of *tyche* and his view "that human life was like a bubble, existing only as long as the breath within was held in by the enveloping substance," whose death meant as well the extinction of the breath. She was likewise able to reject summarily the doctrine of Aristotle (describing him con-

Gr.Nyss.*Anim.res.*
(PG 46:64)

Gr.Nyss.*Anim.res.*
(PG 46:17)

Apostolopoulos 1986

Macr.ap.Gr.Nyss.
Anim.res. (PG 46:29)

Quasten 3:261

Gr.Nyss.*Anim.res.*
(PG 46:17)

Acts 17:18

See p.152

Macr.ap.Gr.Nyss.
Anim.res. (PG 46:21)

Arist.*An.*413b

Macr.ap.Gr.Nyss.
Anim.res. (PG 46:52)

temptuously as, by comparison with Plato, "that philosopher who came after him [ho met' ekeinon philosophos]," but not identifying him by name), "who followed out probabilities by technical rules . . . , declaring that the soul was mortal." But when she came to the teachings of Plato, she was in a more ambiguous position, for she could not reject his conclusions outright. "We must," she said, "neglect the Platonic chariot and the pair of horses of dissimilar forces yoked to it, and their charioteer, whereby the philosopher allegorizes these facts about the soul."

Pl.Phdr.246–47
Macr.ap.Gr.Nyss.
Anim.res. (PG 46:49–52)

The phrase "these facts about the soul" seemed to refer to the doctrine of immortality that she had been expounding, with the difference from Plato apparently being in the method used to arrive at the doctrine, rather than in the doctrine of immortality as such, and then also, as the title of the dialogue indicated, in the conjunction of the Greek doctrine of the immortality of the soul with the Christian doctrine of the resurrection. Elsewhere, too, Gregory of Nyssa cited with approval the speculations about the other world set forth by "the cultured heathen Plato [ho sophos en tois exō Platōn]." Yet, in spite of its long-standing relation to the doctrine of immortality, the doctrine of the philosophers about the transmigration of souls did not meet with his approval, nor with that of his brother Basil. Nor did their hypothesis that because the soul, being immortal, did not have an end it also had to be without beginning. Nevertheless, the doctrine of the immortality of the soul propounded in the natural theology of the philosophical tradition, which did not go far enough and was not really adequate and which therefore stood in need of an additional discussion informed by revelation, did have a certain validity as far as it went.

Gr.Nyss.Anim.res.
(PG 46:11–12)

Daniélou 1953,154–70

Pl.R.614b;615c
Gr.Nyss.Infant.
(Jaeger 3–II:70)
Pl.Men.81b-c
Gr.Nyss.Anim.res.
(PG 46:109)
Bas.Hex.8.2
(SC 26:436)

Gr.Naz.Or.29.13
(SC 250:202)

Macr.ap.Gr.Nyss.
Anim.res. (PG 46:49)

Bas.Leg.lib.gent.10
(Wilson 35)

Together with this doctrine of the immortality of the soul, the mortality of human nature—its tendency toward dissolution and change—also shaped the definition of the image of God, in that it emphasized the continuing metaphysical "difference between the one made 'in the image' and the archetype itself." Because of "the pitiable suffering of human nature," a phenomenon not even to be compared with the blessedness of God's life of apatheia, the term "image of God" was the right way to express both the similarity and the contrast between them. The doctrine of the image of God, therefore, could be used to prove not only that there was an affinity between God and the human mind but that they were by no means identical. However, in a prayer formulated in such a way as to substantiate the orthodox doctrine of the coequality of the Holy Spirit with the Father and the Son in

Gr.Nyss.Or.catech.21.2
(Méridier 102)

Gr.Nyss.Hom.opif.16
(PG 44:180–81)

Macr.ap.Gr.Nyss.
Anim.res. (PG 46:41)

Gr.Naz.Or.34.12
(SC 318:218)

Jaki 1978,47

See pp.280–95
2 Pt 1:4
Gr.Nyss.Beat.3
(PG 44:1225–28)

the Trinity, Gregory of Nazianzus showed how the doctrine of the image of God could also be used to illumine or to corroborate other teachings: "I dare to utter something, O Trinity, and may pardon be granted to my folly, for the risk is to my soul. I too am an image of God and of the heavenly glory, though I be placed on earth. I cannot believe that I am saved by one who is my equal. If the Holy Spirit is not God, let It first be made God, and then let It deify me to be Its equal." That closing reference to *theosis*, being "deified" by the Holy Spirit as the third *hypostasis* of the Trinity, showed what Stanley L. Jaki has called "the enormous difference which there is between Platonism and Christian Platonism." The term, therefore, was an expression both of retrospection and of anticipation. It described the human condition before the fall as one of participation in God through "the most exact likeness to the image of its prototype [tēi akribestatēi homoiōsei kata tēn eikona tou prōtotypou]," and it looked forward to the *metamorphosis* of human nature after the *apocatastasis* as the recovery, through "partaking of the divine nature," of that participation, and thus to the fulfillment of the image of God.

CHAPTER 9

The Source of All Good

Of all the titles that the Cappadocians themselves used for what we have been calling here their "natural theology," the nearest approximation to that concept may well be the term employed by Gregory of Nyssa when he spoke of "moral and natural philosophy [hē ēthikē te kai physikē philosophia]"; he identified this as the product of natural reason, which was to be "joined to the more sublime life [tōi hypsēloterōi biōi syzygos]" of supernatural revelation. Therefore he could speak, also in an address to Christians, about "not sinning against natural law [mēden eis ton tēs physeōs nomon examartanein]." Analyzing such moral and natural philosophy, Gregory of Nazianzus pointed out that "reason" (natural theology) and "theology" (revealed theology) were in agreement when it came to such a virtue as the biblical imperative, "Honor your father and your mother," though he added that the treatment of parents by their children in Classical mythology contradicted it. Arguing in a similar vein about "a natural rationality [physikos *logos*] implanted in us, telling us to identify ourselves with the good and to avoid all harmful things," Basil of Caesarea drew an embarrassing contrast between an irrational creature, such as a fish, which knew what to seek and what to avoid, and human beings, "honored with reason, instructed by law," and endowed with other benefits, who nevertheless behaved less reasonably in their own lives than the fish did. And at her death his sister, Macrina, Christian saint that she was, was celebrated also for having trained her fellow ascetics not only in

Gr.Nyss.*V.Mos.*2
(Jaeger 7–I:43)

Gr.Nyss.*Paup.*2
(Van Heck 29)

Ex 20:12; Eph 6:2

Gr.Naz.*Or.*4.121
(SC 309:286)

Bas.*Hex.*7.5
(SC 26:414–16)

Gr.Nyss.*V.Macr.*
(Jaeger 8–1:401)

Arist.*EN.*1128a.25

Gr.Nyss.*Eun.*1.169
(Jaeger 1:77)

Gr.Nyss.*Hom.opif.*12
(PG 44:161)
Gr.Nyss.*Or.dom.*4
(PG 44:1165–68)

Florovsky 7:170

Florovsky 7:83

Cesaro 1929,109–22

Reiche 1897,42

Phil 4:8
Gr.Nyss.*Cant.*15
(Jaeger 6:438)

Gr.Nyss.*Virg.*11
(Jaeger 8–I:297)

Skeat 1858,244
Gr.Naz.*Or.*30.18
(SC 250:262–64);
Gr.Nyss.*Tres dii*
(Jaeger 3–I:44)

Macr.ap.Gr.Nyss.
Anim.res. (PG 46:92)

Gr.Nyss.*V.Mos.*1
(Jaeger 7–I:3)

following the specifically Christian way of life but in "maintaining good order and decency [tetagmenon kai euschēmon]," concepts and terms familiar to students of Classical ethics at least since Aristotle. Thus, all four Cappadocians strove to articulate a "moral and natural philosophy."

It was in keeping with this emphasis on the "moral and natural" that Gregory of Nyssa also felt able to urge—in opposition to a position that it would have been "the extremest form of irrationality [alogia]" to accept and in support of a position that was confessed "even by our foes"—that "the divine and unalterable nature" of God was "absolutely unlimited in its goodness." Sometimes he spoke of God as "the most beautiful and supreme good of all, to which all things with a tendency towards the *kalon*" inclined. Elsewhere, too, he referred to "the desire for the *kalon kai agathon*." Florovsky has observed that "as a Hellenist Gregory [of Nyssa] connects love with beauty and goodness," and that Basil could speak "of the world's harmonious diversity with the enthusiastic appreciation of an aesthete"; Cesaro has spoken of Basil's aesthetic "romanticism about nature"; and Reiche has commented on "the unbroken unity between the beautiful and the good" in Nyssen's thought. Gregory also quoted from the New Testament the biblical version of the identification of the beautiful and the good with everything "honest, pure, and lovely." Therefore, it was a first principle of his natural theology, which he was sure was "intelligible, without even being said, to anyone not mentally blind," to identify "the God of the universe" as "the only absolute, and primal, and unrivalled *kalon kai agathon* and purity."

Speakers and writers of German, English, and other Germanic languages have long been fond of the etymological explanation of the name "God" on the basis of the adjective "good," but it seems clear from Indo-Germanic linguistics that this derivation was mistaken and that, as Skeat's *Etymological Dictionary of the English Language* has put it, the name God was "in no way allied to *good.*" Even without such an etymology, however, the Cappadocians, who did not agree among themselves about the etymological derivation of the word "God," identified God as "a nature surpassing every possible idea of the good," a nature "lacking in nothing good," and therefore "in itself the plenitude of every good [tōn agathōn to plērōma]." In one sense it could be said that every good, even a created good, was "by its very nature unlimited." But that principle applied in a unique way to this,

Gr.Nyss.*Virg.*10
(Jaeger 8–I:289)

"the first good, visible beyond any other good [to prōton agathon kai to epekeina pantos agathou theōreitai]." Therefore, the affirmation that "everything sublime in thought and word" was concerned with God and that "every noble thought and word" was related to God had to be prefaced by the *apophatic* qualifier:

Gr.Nyss.*Beat.*3
(PG 44:1225)

"What human thought can search out the nature of what we seek? What names or expressions can we invent to produce in us a worthy conception of the light beyond?" And the apparently affirmative statement, "The divine nature is at all times filled with all good, or rather is itself the fullness of all good," really meant that no good was adventitious to the divine nature, that it needed no addition for its perfecting, and that such negative language

Gr.Nyss.*Eun.*3.7.19–20
(Jaeger 2:221–22)
See pp.57–58
Gr.Nyss.*Beat.*6
(PG 44:1269–72)

had to be proliferated in order to do justice to the divine nature.

But just as *apophatic* theology in general, instead of disqualifying the speculative enterprise, became a justification for it, so this application of it to the question of the transcendently good and beautiful led to affirmative conclusions about immanent goodness and beauty. *Apophatic* language was the only way to speak about an "invisible and formless beauty, devoid of qualities and far removed from everything recognizable in bodies by the eye," a beauty that transcended every "beauty perceived by the senses [aisthēton *kallos*]" but that at the same time heightened

Gr.Nyss.*Virg.*10
(Jaeger 8–I:290–91)

the human appreciation of such beauty "through our power of aesthetic feeling." Ultimately, however, there would have to come that celebration of divine beauty about which Gregory of Nyssa wrote: "Admiration even of the beauty of the heavens, and of the dazzling sunbeams, and indeed of any fair phenomenon, will then cease. The beauty noticed there will be but as the hand to lead us to the love of that supernal beauty whose glory the heavens and the firmament declare and whose secret the whole

Gr.Nyss.*Virg.*11
(Jaeger 8–I:293–94)

creation sings [pasa hē ktisis anangellei tēn gnōsin]." For a "good above every good [agathon kai pantos agathou epekeina]" did

Gr.Nyss.*Beat.*8
(PG 44:1293)

not obliterate every other good, but confirmed it by the sheer fact of transcending it.

The very discovery, through an inquiry into "the nature of the transcendent good [tōn hyperkeimenōn agathōn physin]," that it was "impossible for such a thing to come within the scope of our comprehension" had the paradoxical effect that "the very fact of having been unable to perceive it" produced "an idea of the

Gr.Nyss.*Beat.*3
(PG 44:1225)

greatness of what was sought after." Because it was the nature of God to transcend all good that could be conceived or comprehended, the God who was the fullness of good, having been motivated by goodness to undertake creation, "made human

Gr.Nyss.*Hom.opif.*16
(PG 44:184)

Gr.Nyss.*Fid.*
(Jaeger 3–1:66)

Gr.Nyss.*Ref.*7–8
(Jaeger 2:315)

Phil 3:13

Gr.Nyss.*Eun.*3.6.73–74
(Jaeger 2:212)

Gr.Nyss.*Maced.*
(Jaeger 3–I:109)

Zec 9:17

Gr.Nyss.*Eun.*2.377–78
(Jaeger 1:336)

Gr.Nyss.*Beat.*5
(PG 44:1249)

Gr.Naz.*Or.*37.20
(SC 318:312)

Gr.Nyss.*Beat.*6
(PG 44:1269–72)

nature a participant in all good," which was what was meant by the doctrine of creation in the image of God. It was precisely in that way, "by participation in the transcendent good [ek tēs tou hyperkeimenou agathou metousias]," which was the Creator, that there could be any immanent good within the creation. The difference between the transcendent good, which was God, and any such immanent good, moreover, was that because "the supremely excellent always belonged to the divine and unimpaired essence," which was "incapable of change and alteration," it followed that God did not change from worse to better, much less from better to worse, both of which it would be "impiety [asebes]" to assert, apparently even on the grounds of natural theology. Instead, "everything *kalon kai agathon*" was always to be contemplated in "the source of the *kalon.*" For the created good, this participation in the uncreated good and the source of all good was an ongoing and never-ceasing process described by Paul, of "constantly being in a state of beginning to be in excellence, by a continuous advance in improvement, with each thing already acquired becoming by participation a beginning of the ascent to something greater still." To the principle recognized also by natural theology, "Whatever is *kalon* and whatever is good [agathon] comes from God," revealed trinitarian theology added that it came from God "through the Son" and that it was "perfected by the instrumentality of the Spirit." As the source of excellency and the fountain of all good, it was God, the transcendent good, from whom all good whatsoever had sprung and in whom it could be seen; for as the prophet said, nearly in the same words as these that natural theology could employ, "Whatever is good [agathon] is from God, and whatever is *kalon* is from God."

The effect of this participation in the good was likewise paradoxical. For it was possible to make the desire for the good and for participation in it an article of natural theology, as something "automatically adhering to human nature." Such an "aptitude for good," which seemed to be present in some people "by nature," was to be viewed as it was coordinated with "free will," in order to "bring the natural aptitude to effect." Yet, the natural "desire to contemplate the true good," which the image of God in human nature was intended to satisfy by providing an immanent object for such contemplation, was continually frustrated by the presence of "the evil poured all around the nature bearing the divine image," rendering the image useless unless one could "by a good life wash off the filth." As a consequence of that evil which had been poured all around human nature, most people had to

Gr.Nyss.*Virg.*11
(Jaeger 8–I:292)

"live all their lives with obtuse faculties of thinking," blinded by the desire for money and honor. Such people found it "a difficult thing to perform this feat of mental analysis and of discriminating the material vehicle from the immanent beauty," and therefore they were unable to grasp the actual nature of the *kalon* or to distinguish between the true *kalon* and its counterfeit opposite. As Gregory of Nyssa observed in regretful tones, speaking about what was natural to the human experience, "It is not easy—in fact, it is perhaps quite impossible—to prefer the invisible good [to mē phainomenon agathon] to the visible pleasant things of this life."

Gr.Nyss.*Beat.*8
(*PG* 44:1296)

Bas.*Hex.*1.1
(*SC* 26:88)
Bas.*Ep.*236.4
(Courtonne 3:52)
Keenan 1944,160–61

The counterpart of this natural inclination to the good and natural desire to contemplate the good was a "natural horror of evil," which was not only a gift of grace but was "received from nature" as well. There was observable in human nature an almost physiological repugnance at certain things that were vile and evil. The reason for this "natural aversion" was that although the natural desire for good was a desire for being and for reality, there was "no reality to the evil except the privation of the good [ho chōrismos tou beltionos]." Although this evil and nonbeing, therefore, held a fatal attraction for many because it seemed so beautiful, its beauty, like its very reality, was a matter only of appearance, not "of the *hypostasis*" of a genuine existence. And because evil was defined as nonbeing, it was also necessarily the case that evil could not come from God. God did sometimes permit evil to have a certain "scope" in human history, which might understandably seem to its anguished victims to be a confirmation of its reality. Gregory of Nyssa could even say, paradoxically, that Christ himself "voluntarily came not only to prove our good, but to prove our evil." But it was, Macrina said, the real "paradox, so to speak [ei kan paradoxon eipein]," that evil possessed "an existence in its not existing at all." At the risk of imposing an anachronistic vocabulary on her thought, her paradox might be paraphrased to say that the existential reality of evil was rooted in its very lack of metaphysical reality. Therefore, when reason asked whether darkness was created together with the world and whether it was older than light, the answer had to be that, scientifically speaking, darkness did not exist in essence but was "a condition produced in the air by the withdrawal of light," and that, morally speaking, the same was true of evil as the withdrawal and absence of good.

Gr.Nyss.*Cant.*2
(Jaeger 6:56)

Gr.Nyss.*Cant.*4
(Jaeger 6:106)

Gr.Nyss.*Or.catech.*7.4
(Méridier 48)

Gr.Nyss.*Infant.*
(Jaeger 3–II:94)

Gr.Nyss.*Eun.*2.422
(Jaeger 1:349–50)

Macr.ap.Gr.Nyss.
Anim.res. (*PG* 46:93)

See pp.79–81

Bas.*Hex.*2.5
(*SC* 26:162)

Because of this natural repugnance at evil and natural desire for good, it was in some ways as necessary—and as difficult—for Christian theology to cope with the problem of the existence of

Scholl 1881,97–100

Bas.*Hex*.5.7
(SC 26:312)

Winslow 1979,147
Gr.Nyss.*V.Mos.*2
(Jaeger 7–I:76)

Büttner 1913,14–19

Bas.*Leg.lib.gent*.5
(Wilson 24)
Konstantinou 1966,
125–51

See p.197

DTC 15:2739–99
1 Cor 13:13

Arist.*EN*.1420b20–21
Arist.*EN*.1133b33–
1134a6
Arist.*EN*.1174b24–
25;1107b4–6

Arist.*EN*.1116a10–11

Phil 4:8

Gr.Nyss.*Cant*.15
(Jaeger 6:438–42)

Bas.*Hex*.9.4
(SC 26:496–98)

natural good in the world as with the problem of the existence of evil, as for instance when Basil encountered, "outside the church, in pagan life, or in the midst of a pernicious heresy, the example of *arete* and fidelity to moral laws." Although one scholar's description of Gregory of Nazianzus as "characteristically unsystematic in his ethical views" would apply to all of them, the Cappadocians did make the doctrine of the *aretai* a recurring theme. But that very way of treating the issue suggested their dependence on Classical models. "I myself have heard a man say who was clever at understanding a poet's mind," Basil declared, perhaps quoting his pagan correspondent Libanius of Antioch, "that all of Homer's poetry is an encomium of *arete*." The familiar cardinal virtues of Classical moral philosophy, best known from Aristotle's standard treatment of them in the *Nicomachean Ethics,* were: prudence [phronēsis], justice [dikaiosynē], temperance [sōphrosynē], and fortitude [andreia]; to these four were added, in Christian ethics and specifically then in Western scholastic ethics, the three Pauline or "theological" virtues of faith [pistis], hope [elpis], and charity [agapē], for a total of seven. Aristotle defined prudence or "practical *sophia*" as "a reasoned and true state of capacity to act with regard to human goods." He interpreted justice as "a kind of mean . . . in accordance with proportion." Temperance was defined as "a mean with regard to pleasures." And fortitude was "a mean with respect to things inspiring confidence or fear." But at the hands of the Cappadocians these four qualities were no less fundamental to catalogs of the *aretai* in Christian ethics.

To justify their inclusion in such catalogs, they were followed by the formula, "and any other [*aretai*] mentioned by the apostle" when he said, in his comprehensive summary of this Classical-Christian moral ideal: "Finally, brethren, whatsoever things are true, whatsoever things are honest, whatsoever things are just, whatsoever things are pure, whatsoever things are lovely, whatsoever things are of good report; if there be any *arete,* and if there be any praise, think on these things." Such a juxtaposing of Classical and Christian virtues was legitimate because, in Basil's formula, "*Aretai* exist in us by nature, and the soul has affinity with them not by education, but by nature herself." For just as in the realm of health it was "not necessary to have lessons to hate illness," so it was in the realm of morality, where "without having need of lessons," the soul had the power to attain by itself to what was fitting and conformable to nature. The ability of Moses to appeal to that natural sense of morality in the Egyptians and not only in the Israelites now found its modern counterpart in the common ground between Classical *aretai* and Christian *aretai*, because the enlightenment of the life of *arete* was available equally to all who were enlightened. This implied that such Classical *aretai* as "good order and decency" were also Christian virtues. Conversely, when the New Testament exhorted children to love their parents, it could be seen as saying the same thing that natural morality did; for in inculcating this, according to Basil's interpretation, "Paul teaches us nothing new, but only tightens the links of nature." That was evident from the place of this very *arete* in the ethical systems of Classical philosophy. The same applied to hypocrisy, which, again according to Basil, was "the last extreme of injustice, on the basis of the words of Plato: 'to appear to be just without being so.'"

Such approval did not extend to all Classical ethical philosophers, some of whom, like the Epicureans, regarded *arete* as nothing more than a mere word and maintained that there was "nothing greater than this present life." Nevertheless, it was, as Aristotle's definitions of the cardinal *aretai* suggested, from Classical ethics, as expressed for example by his maxim in the second book of the *Nicomachean Ethics,* "Temperance and courage are destroyed by excess and defect and are preserved by the mean [between excess and defect]," that the Cappadocians learned their doctrine of the "mean [mesē]," which each of them articulated in some form. Gregory of Nyssa explicitly defined "every *arete*" as consisting of "the mean between two vices [dyo kakiōn mesē]," while one of the other Cappadocians, Gregory of Nazianzus, said about the third one, Basil of Caesarea, "He was specially devoted to the adage, 'In all things the mean is best [to pan metros ariston].'" By contrast with this consensus, they accused the enemies of orthodoxy of not understanding this fundamental principle: "All *arete* is found in moderation [mesotēs], and any declining to either side of it becomes a vice." Apart from this principle, *arete* was not genuine *arete;* in the formula of Gregory of Nyssa, "It is the union of justice with wisdom that really constitutes *arete,* for separated and taken by itself, justice is not goodness" and would not be so even in God. According to him, when justice was thus properly defined, in the light of wisdom, it was seen to be distributive justice, "the disposition to distribute equally to each, on the basis of worthiness." For this definition he quoted the authority of thinkers who had "investigated these matters," not in the first instance Christian theologians but Classical moralists and legal philosophers. Later in

Gr.Nyss.*V.Mos.*2
(Jaeger 7–I:57)
Arist.*EN.*1128a25
Gr.Nyss.*V.Macr.*
(Jaeger 8–I:401)

Eph 6:4

Bas.*Hex.*9.4
(SC 26:498)
Gr.Naz.*Or.*4.121
(SC 309:286)

Pl.*R.*361a
Bas.*Leg.lib.gent.*6
(Wilson 26)

Gr.Naz.*Or.*4.44
(SC 309:144)

Arist.*EN.*1104a25–26

Gr.Nyss.*Cant.*9
(Jaeger 6:284)

Gr.Naz.*Or.*43.60
(PG 36:573)

Gr.Nyss.*Virg.*7
(Jaeger 8–I:282)

Gr.Nyss.*Or.catech.*20.6
(Méridier 100)

Gr.Nyss.*Beat.*4
(PG 44:1233)
Pl.*R.*357–83;
Arist.*EN.*1133b33–1134a6

Gr.Nyss.Beat.5
(PG 44:1252)

Gr.Nyss.Virg.pr.
(Jaeger 8–I:247)

Gr.Nyss.Virg.7
(Jaeger 8–I:282)

Gr.Nyss.Apoll.
(Jaeger 3–I:164)

Wis 4:1;5:13;8:7
Phil 4:8;1 Pt 2:9;
2 Pt 1:3;2 Pt 1:5

See pp.129,137,141

Gr.Nyss.Beat.4
(PG 44:1244)

Gr.Nyss.Hom.opif.27
(PG 44:228)

Gr.Nyss.Virg.9
(Jaeger 8–I:286)

Gr.Nyss.Eun.2.246
(Jaeger 1:298)

Gr.Nyss.Cant.9
(Jaeger 6:271)

the same series of homilies he defined mercy as "a voluntary sorrow joining itself to the sufferings of others," though not, it would seem in the light of the foregoing, without attention also to the requirements of distributive justice. The same principle would, then, seem to have been at work when he began a treatise on virginity by stating it to be his purpose "to create in its readers a passion for the life in accordance with *arete*," regardless of whether such readers were celibate or married. For even here, the principle held: "All *arete* is found in moderation [mesotēs], and any declining to either side of it becomes a vice."

Also according to natural morality, therefore, *arete* was what was "praiseworthy [endoxon] in a human being," whereas vice was "altogether devoid of praise [pantōs to adoxon]." That was as well the implication when Gregory of Nyssa referred to "the sublime doctrine [to hypsēlon dogma]," which he had indeed learned from Christ in the Sermon on the Mount, as he said he had, but which was presumably shared by natural theology: "The only true and solidly existing thing is our zeal for *arete*." The term *arete* itself did not appear so much as once in the Sermon on the Mount. Although it was prominent in the vocabulary of the Septuagint, above all in those later books that have been designated in Christian history as "Apocrypha" or "Deuterocanonical," such as the Book of Wisdom, it appeared only four times in the entire New Testament, one of these being, significantly, the passage from Philippians that the Cappadocians were so fond of quoting. Nevertheless, Gregory concluded: "All *arete* is signified here [in the Sermon on the Mount] by the noun 'righteousness [dikaiosynē].'" But because the knowledge of natural morality, like natural theology altogether, had to some extent to be grounded in "the facts known to us through sense experience," it had to have an empirical basis, in a study of "mankind now living on the earth." Such a study of comparative anthropology revealed not only the existence of "many nations, with divergent ambitions," but even great divergences in "the standard of the *kalon* and of honor." In the case of the many languages that these many nations had developed, the awareness of their historical variety led to the recognition that there was not, and need not be, an absolute standard of language and grammar. But such relativism was unacceptable in the case of ethics and moral behavior. When Gregory of Nyssa pointed out, therefore, that "a way of life in accordance with *arete*" had shown itself to be "neither homogeneous nor uniform," he was nevertheless continuing to use the term *arete* in the singular here, as he was also

Gr.Nyss.*Cant.*14
(Jaeger 6:418)

when he spoke later in the same commentary about "the various paths from the law to *arete.*" A life in God—being, in a pale way, an imitation of the life of God the Trinity itself—revealed both an essential unity and a personal variety.

Nor was that trinitarian analogy altogether farfetched or merely rhetorical, as became clear from an analysis of the moral life on the basis of motivation: "Since we are controlled by three conditions—fear of punishment, hope for salvation and glory too, and the practice of the *aretai* that results in these last—the [divine] name that mentions retribution deals with fear, the one that mentions salvation pertains to hope, and that which refers to

Gr.Naz.*Or.*30.19
(SC 250:264–66)

Gr.Nyss.*Tres dii*
(Jaeger 3–I:331–36)

aretai disciplines us to practice them." This was not to be taken to imply in any sense that there were three gods—one of vengeance, one of salvation, and one of virtues—for God was one. But it was the expression of a recognition, psychological and also ultimately theological in its nature, that just as it was necessary to "grope

Gr.Nyss.*Eun.*2.475–78
(Jaeger 1:364–65)

after the ineffable being in diverse and many-sided ways and never to pursue the mystery in the light of one idea alone," so also the life of *arete* in adoring obedience of that ineffable being was not to be pursued by only one path or in the light of one idea alone. Such variety within unity, both in the knowledge of God and in the practice of the moral life, was in keeping with the very nature of the human soul as created in the image of God, which implied especially the three qualities of reason, freedom of the

See pp.127–35

will, and immortality. Each played a role in the motivation of the moral life. Reason was implied in the very idea of "a natural rationality implanted in us, telling us to identify ourselves with

Bas.*Hex.*7.5
(SC 26:414–16)

Gr.Nyss.*V.Mos.*2
(Jaeger 7–I:43)

the good and to avoid everything harmful." It also underlay the concept of "moral and natural philosophy" as a system of thought regulated by rationality. The second component, freedom of the will, was fundamental to morality and *arete*. Indeed, Gregory of Nyssa asked, in language suggesting that this idea of a moral and natural philosophy was accessible to anyone who

Gr.Nyss.*Apoll.*
(Jaeger 3–I:198)
Bas.*Hex.*6.7
(SC 26:362)
Macr.ap.Gr.Nyss.
Anim.res. (PG 46:117–20)
Gr.Nyss.*Or.dom.*3
(PG 44:1156)
Clark 1977,45–66;
Arist.*EN.*1109b31
Gr.Nyss.*Cant.*5
(Jaeger 6:160–61)

thought about it soundly, "Who does not know that *arete* is the achievement of free choice?" For if there were no free will, it would be useless for judges to reward *arete* and to punish vice. *Arete* would lose its value, and it would not be worthwhile to turn from vice. *Arete* was, by definition, free of the tyrannical demands of a taskmaster. Paraphrasing a definition he may have taken from Aristotle, Gregory of Nyssa described *arete* as "free of coercion, voluntary, and free of any *ananke.*" The third component of the image of God, immortality, was in many ways the most fundamental of all to morality. As Macrina put it, denying immortality was "tantamount to nothing less than abandoning *arete,* seeking the pleasure of the moment only, and despairing of the life of eternity as the only possible grounds for *arete* to claim the advantage." It was the this-worldliness of Epicureanism, its denial of immortality, that also caused it to give up on the quest for *arete.* But genuine *arete* was not limited to this world or "circumscribed by time."

In spite of their emphasis on otherworldliness, the Cappadocians insisted that it was wrong to have a greater desire for life eternal as the reward of *arete* than for the union with God that was the essential content of life eternal. The life of genuine *arete* was the path to perfection. But to attain ultimate perfection through the practice of *arete* required not only that one be elevated to live "in the sublime life [en tōi hypsēlōi biōi]," but that one attain, as far as it was possible, to the very "vision of God [pros theon blepein]." For life eternal meant "immortality," but it also meant *apatheia,* which was "likeness to God." Because it was a fundamental principle that the truly divine, unlike the gods of Olympus, was "characterized by utter *apatheia,*" it was necessary to conclude that "someone always entangled in passions" could not share in "union with God." At the same time it was also necessary to understand that the moral imperatives of the gospel, as supremely summarized in the Sermon on the Mount, did not command something that was "outside the scope of nature," as complete *apatheia* would be; for "a perfectly nonmaterial and passionless mode of life within the confines of a material existence" was impossible of attainment, and God, as "a just lawgiver, could not in fairness have commanded things not permitted by nature." Nevertheless, there was a measure of "moderation and meekness," one that was beginning to approach the divine model though it had not reached it, which was attainable within the conditions of human existence; and the attainment of that constituted the life of *arete:* "Blessed, therefore, are those who are not easily turned towards the passionate movements of the soul, but who are steadied by reason." To understand "the praise of *arete,*" consequently, it was necessary to relate it simultaneously "to the morally elegant life [kata ton euschēmona bion]" within this world and to those things that were "perceptible in the *apatheia* of the soul" beyond this world. Such was the "progress to perfection" that was both demanded and promised.

As the exposition of a system of "moral and natural philosophy," this apologetic represented, at one level, a summons to go beyond the material world to the world of ideas. The beauty that

---

Macr.ap.Gr.Nyss.
Anim.res. (PG 46:16–20)

Gr.Naz.*Or.*4.44
(SC 309:144–46)
Gr.Nyss.*Beat.*4
(PG 44:1244)

Gr.Nyss.*Cant.*1
(Jaeger 6:16)
Gr.Nyss.*Cant.*4
(Jaeger 6:117)

Gr.Nyss.*Apoll.*
(Jaeger 3–I:210)
Gr.Nyss.*Cant.*2
(Jaeger 6:60)

Gr.Nyss.*Or.dom.*1
(PG 44:1132)

Gr.Nyss.*Beat.*2
(PG 44:1216)

Gr.Nyss.*Cant.*7
(Jaeger 6:230)
Bas.*Spir.*8.18
(SC 17:310)

Gr.Nyss.*V.Mos.*
(Jaeger 7–I:43)

the eye could see was all that most people ever beheld. Yet that beauty was "only the material, waiting to be worked upon by the idea of beauty"; this "idea of beauty" was visible to anyone "with a clear mind's eye to inspect such appearances," who could therefore make use of visible beauty as "the ladder by which to climb to the prospect of that intellectual beauty [pros tēn tou noētou theōrian *kallous*], the source for the existence and name of all other beauties." Similarly, an analysis of the language of *apophasis* led to the conclusion that it was possible for the human mind to formulate "some idea of the greatness of what we have sought by the very fact of our having been unable to perceive it." The "idea of beauty" and the "idea of greatness" were thus essential elements of "moral and natural philosophy," but they were also inadequate. For it was equally necessary to insist that "any theory divorced from living examples [dicha tōn ergōn theōroumenos], however admirably dressed out," was an artificial construct, "like the unbreathing statue." This apologetic principle was directed also against the supposition of some thinkers about a "piety consisting in doctrines only." For that reason it constituted an embarrassment to those Christian believers who were mistakenly "isolated from the whole world and not ashamed of [their] solitariness," when "the Gentiles, though ignorant of God," exhibited, on the basis of their natural knowledge, a more refined social consciousness than the Christians did, forming associations with one another and seeking mutual contact. In so doing they were giving evidence of a truth about *arete* that appeared to be available both to natural theology and to revealed theology: "The distribution of *arete* is such that it is shared out to all who seek after it, and yet it is wholly present to each, without being diminished by those who share in it." In this it was like the light of the sun, in which anyone could share without depriving anyone else. Yet none of this was intended to deny the moral and religious dangers that lurked especially in social relations at highly populated places, as Gregory of Nyssa warned after having visited even the holy city of Jerusalem and as Gregory of Nazianzus also lamented on the basis of his own struggles between the contemplative life of the monk and the active life of the bishop.

Above all in systems of ethics, "theory" and "practice" had to be inseparable. The test of any such system, whether natural or revealed, was its application in the concrete situations of human life and society. Concerning family ethics, for example, there was

Gr.Nyss.*Virg.*11
(Jaeger 8–I:292)

Gr.Nyss.*Beat.*3
(PG 44:1225)

Gr.Nyss.*Virg.*23
(Jaeger 8–I:334)

ap.Gr.Nyss.*Eun.*3.9.59
(Jaeger 2:286)

Bas.*Ep.*203.3
(Courtonne 2:175)

Gr.Nyss.*Beat.*1
(PG 44:1196)
Gr.Nyss.*V.Mos.*2
(Jaeger 7–I:52)
Gr.Nyss.*Ep.*2.7–15
(Jaeger 8–II:15–18)
Gr.Naz.*Carm.*1.11.327–
429 (PG 37:1052–59)

Otis 1961,146–65
Špidlík 1976,358–64
Gr.Naz.*Or.*4.113
(SC 309:270)

Nothomb 1954,318–21

Bas.*Hex*.9.4
(*SC* 26:498)

Eph 6:4

Gr.Naz.*Or*.4.121
(*SC* 309:286–88)
Troeltsch 1960,129–32

Ettlinger 1985,368–72

Gr.Naz.*Or*.37.6
(*SC* 318:282–84)

Bas.*Hex*.9.4
(*SC* 26:498)

Bas.*Ep*.188.2
(Courtonne 2:125)

Gr.Nyss.*Maced.*
(Jaeger 3–I:101)

a considerable amount of congruence between natural and revealed norms. "Does not nature say the same?" Basil could ask,
after quoting the New Testament teaching about the family. But
the Cappadocians also took advantage of the circumstance that
in practice this norm of natural law was frequently violated or
ignored in the Classical tradition, even when "reason" affirmed
it. Christian apologists, and then Christian legislators, took
strong positions against what they took to be the all but universal
acceptance of the double standard within Classical culture. "In
respect to chastity," Gregory of Nazianzus declared, "I see that
the majority of men are ill-disposed and that their laws are un-
equal and irregular." "What was the reason," he continued,
"that they restrained the woman, and indulged the man?" If a
woman was unfaithful, she was branded as "an adulteress" and
was subjected to severe penalties by pagan law; but a husband
who violated the marriage vow did not bring a similar censure
upon himself. Gregory concluded: "I do not accept this legislation; I do not approve this custom." And although he went on to
contrast this with revealed legislation about sexual morality, it
was clear from his method of argumentation that he was rejecting
the double standard on natural no less than on revealed grounds.
Therefore, he could have asked, in the words of Basil, "Does not
nature say the same?"

The relation between natural and revealed norms was less
clear in the discussion of what was already one of the most vexing
issues in sexual ethics, the question of abortion. Basil could say
outright: "The woman who purposely destroys her unborn child
is guilty of murder"; and he could dismiss out of hand any "nice
inquiry as to the formed or unformed fetus." This judgment was
not accompanied by any reference to Scripture or Christian tradition, but it was not validated on natural grounds either, except for
the chilling observation, "In most such cases women who make
such attempts die." His brother Gregory, by contrast, almost as
though he were instituting just such a "nice inquiry as to the
formed or unformed fetus," was willing, in the course of making
a quite unrelated point in connection with the doctrine of the
Holy Spirit, to assert almost apodictically: "It would not be possible to style the unformed embryo [to antelesphorēton embryon]
a human being, but only a potential one [dynameon], assuming
that it is completed so as to come forth to human birth, while as
long as it is in this unformed state [en tōi atelei], it is something
other than a human being." And this, too, seems to have been
intended as a judgment based on reason rather than only on

authority. The relation between natural theology and revealed ethics in the area of family morality was especially striking in the Cappadocians' treatment of sexuality itself. Gregory of Nyssa appealed to a principle which, he said, he presumed "to be known to everyone," whether by natural theology or through revelation, to show that sexuality had not been part of the original divine design for human nature but had been added by the Creator in anticipation of the fall into sin. Elsewhere, however, he conceded where the burden of proof lay, because "the common instincts of mankind" were all lined up in support of sexuality on the basis of "a spontaneous bias," while his espousal of lifelong virginity seemed to "thwart this natural impulse in a way." By this he appeared to be suggesting that the case for a celibate life had to be supported by revealed authority, while the argument for a positive assessment of sexuality and marriage rested on natural as well as on revealed grounds; therefore it was, he suggested, "a superfluous task to compose an exhortation to marriage." Nevertheless, he wanted to avoid any impression that he was "depreciating the *economy* of marriage as an institution," of which he knew, apparently also on the basis of personal experience, that it was "not a stranger to God's blessing."

Nature as understood by reason was also the chief court of appeal for all three Cappadocians when they were making the case for their social and political doctrine that "those endowed by nature with equal rights" were entitled to social equality. Basil insisted, in an apparent criticism of Aristotle's teaching: "In human society no one is a slave by nature," but rather as the consequence of historical circumstances. Gregory of Nazianzus argued against Gnostic and other doctrines, which taught that the members of the human race were naturally and permanently segregated into three categories, "the earthly, the spiritual, and the mixed": "an utterly ruined nature," "a saved nature," and a nature that could turn out "either for the better or for the worse." This was mistaken, he replied, for despite differences in "aptitude [epitēdeiotēs], one more and another less," it was not this predetermination, but "reason" that produced the differences. His doctrine of the image of God required those who occupied a higher station to recognize this natural equality, by which they shared a universal human nature with those over whom they happened to have been placed in human society. For him, that principle of natural equality applied with special force to the poor, or, as Gregory of Nyssa called them, in an allusion to the parable, "those myriads of Lazaruses at your door." Gregory of

Gr.Nyss.*Hom.opif.*16
(*PG* 44:181)

Daniélou 1956,71–78
Gr.Nyss.*Virg.*7
(Jaeger 8–I:282)

Gr.Nyss.*Eun.*1.527
(Jaeger 1:178–79)
Arist.*Pol.*1254a

Bas.*Spir.*20.51
(*SC* 17:426)

Gr.Naz.*Or.*37.13
(*SC* 318:296–98)

Gr.Naz.*Or.*17.9
(*PG* 35:976)

Winslow 1965,348–59
Lk 16:20
Gr.Nyss.*Paup.*1
(Van Heck 16)

Nyssa urged someone who was "burning with anger against a servant" to remember that "not nature, but power [ou physis, alla dynasteia] divided the human race into servants and masters." Therefore, "someone subject to you by custom and law [synētheiai kai nomōi]" was nevertheless "equal to you in dignity of nature [tōi tēs physeōs axiōmati]"; for it was an ordinance of "the Lord of the universe [ho tou pantos oikonomos]" that "only the irrational nature" of animals and inanimate things should be naturally inferior to human nature, within which everyone was created equal.

Ps 8:7–9

Gr.Nyss.Or.dom.5
(PG 44:1189)

Although "the sublime laws of God" revealed in Christ did demand "something higher," the cardinal virtue of "justice [dikaiosynē]" at the level of nature, which applied both to labor and to property, was to be defined as "the disposition to distribute equally to each on the basis of worth [kat' axian]." That "natural" definition of justice, which was correct even though it was incomplete in the realm of grace, pertained, Gregory of Nyssa continued, to "the ruler of a city or the king of a nation," thus to the political order generally: "For if any of these men rules his subjects fairly, that is to say, if he does not take advantage of his power to indulge irrational impulses, he will come within the definition of those who attribute precisely such conduct to the notion of 'justice.'" From that definition he drew a cautionary tale for "human governments." The reason they had the tendency to undergo "such quickly-repeated revolutions," he warned, was that it was "impracticable for those to whom nature gave equal rights to be excluded from power." An "impulse" that was "instinct in all" by nature caused them "to make themselves equal with the dominant party, all of them being of the same blood." Political rulers who forgot that they were of the same blood as their subjects and therefore "fellow servants" with them, Gregory of Nazianzus observed, tried to govern "without taking account of the God over all and the height of that true and unapproachable kingdom." He saw patriotism and civic virtue as a moral responsibility; for if it was "a religious duty to honor one's mother," one's country was the "mother common to all." But in a lengthy oration attacking the emperor Julian, Gregory of Nazianzus joined the Christians who had lived under the emperors before Constantine in rejecting the equation of this civic virtue of patriotism with the idolatrous veneration of the Roman emperor and of his statues. The atrocities being committed against believers stood as a refutation of the claims of those who,

Geoghegan 1945,175–81

Giet 1948,56–61

Gr.Nyss.Beat.4
(PG 44:1233–36)

Gr.Nyss.Eun.1.527
(Jaeger 1:178–79)

Gr.Naz.Or.16.19
(PG 35:961)

Gr.Naz.Ep.37.1
(Gallay 1:46)

Gr.Naz.Or.4.81
(SC 309:204–6)

Gr.Naz.Or.4.91
(SC 30⸱ ⸱⸱8)

in the ironic words of Nazianzen, admired "this philosopher-king." For the Platonic doctrine of the philosopher-king, which, in the abstract if not in the concrete, Gregory seemed to be treating positively here, meant that the political decisions of a ruler were to be made in the light of rational and natural principles, not that such principles should be invoked to promote the advancement of evil rather than its repression in favor of the highest good

Gr.Naz.Or.4.45
(SC 309:146)
Gr.Naz.Or.32.2
(SC 318:86)

of society. "And what is the highest good according to our reason?" Gregory of Nazianzus asked. "Peace," he replied. Expanding on this answer, he delivered a lengthy encomium of peace and

Gr.Naz.Or.32.8–12
(SC 318:100–112)

"order [hē taxis]." It was order that had "set us apart from irrational creatures, and populated cities, and established laws,

Gr.Naz.Or.32.9
(SC 318:104)

and crowned *arete* with honor, and suppressed wickedness, and invented the arts, and achieved social harmony." Only after this celebration of order for what it had been able to achieve in the realm of natural law and natural theology, in society and in the

Gr.Naz.Or.32.10
(SC 318:106)

cosmos, did he turn to its sublime expression in the ordered society of the church. The perfection of the church as this divine society, moreover, was to be attained only in the consummation of the kingdom of God, "that true and unapproachable

Gr.Naz.Or.16.19
(PG 35:961)

kingdom."

Every good, therefore, found its consummation and its perfection in the goal of ultimate good, just as it found its origin in the source of all good; and these two, the source and the goal, were one, in the perfection that was God. To deity it belonged to have

Gr.Nyss.Eun.2.377
(Jaeger 1:336)

"justice, goodness, eternity, incapacity for evil—and infinite perfection in all conceivable goodness." That correlation of "good"

Gr.Nyss.Maced.
(Jaeger 3–I:316)

and "perfection" in God meant: "Deity exhibits perfection in every line in which the good can be found." But because anyone "endowed with reason" had to know that "terms expressing

Gr.Nyss.Eun.3.7.23
(Jaeger 2:223)

temporal interval" did not suit "the Lord who was before times and before *aeons*," perfection needed to be defined differently when it was applied to God. What made the divine nature "itself the fullness of all goods" was this very fact: "It needs no addition for its perfecting, but is, of itself and by its own nature, the

Gr.Nyss.Eun.3.7.19–20
(Jaeger 2:221–22)

perfection of all good [hē tou agathou teleiotēs]," not at the end of a process of change and development but eternally. A nature that was "simple, uniform, and noncomposite" had to involve,

Gr.Nyss.Maced.
(Jaeger 3–I:91)

"by the implication of that very name, the perfection in it of every conceivable thing befitting deity." The creation of Adam had

Gr.Nyss.Hom.opif.16
(PG 44:185)

included the creation of the entire human race, in goodness and innocence—but not, strictly speaking, in perfection. For "perfec-

Gr.Nyss.*Eun*.3.2.87
(Jaeger 2:81)

Gr.Nyss.*V.Mos*.3
(Jaeger 7–I:144–45)

tion [teleiotēs]" was, as its Greek name indicated, teleological and eschatological, and it pertained to the *telos*, not to the *arche*. To the specially chosen of God, such as Moses the mystagogue, it was granted to attain "perfection," defined as friendship with God, before the final "*apocatastasis* of all things." But for the human race as a whole, perfection pertained to the end of human history, not to its beginning, and therefore it belonged to the consideration of cosmic teleology and human destiny.

CHAPTER 10

From Tyche to Telos

Macr.ap.Gr.Nyss.
Anim.res. (PG 46:117)

The full meaning of the natural theology of the Cappadocians as a system of apologetics became evident only in their antithesis between *tyche* and *telos,* and therefore in their corresponding positive correlation between *arche* and *telos,* as they strove to draw out the ultimate implications of the purpose in creation that they believed to be discernible also to the natural mind. Addressing that antithesis and that correlation simultaneously, Macrina maintained: "If life begins in consequence of an accident of *tyche,* the whole course of it becomes at once a chapter of such accidents of *tyche* from beginning to end." The only possible conclusion from such a tyranny of fortune and chance would be to accept the prospect of "the whole of life being ruled by this accidental movement of chance and *tyche,*" and therefore to accept as well the corollary expectation that there would no longer be "any providence pervading the world." Her brother Basil also directed the attention of his readers, and with them that of all "reasonable souls" (among whom he would seem to have been including the reasonable souls who were disciples of Classicism as well as the reasonable souls who were disciples of Christianity), to the "intelligent reason presiding over the order of visible things" at the creation. From this he drew the conclusion "that the world was not conceived by *tyche* and without reason, but for a useful end and for the great advantage of all beings," which made the world "the school for reasonable souls to exercise themselves, the training ground for them to learn to know God." Without such an awareness of teleology, what would emerge, according to

Bas.Hex.1.6
(SC 26:110)

Gregory of Nazianzus, would be an explanation of the world and of history on the basis of an arbitrary "election by lot [apoklērōsis]," which would undercut "the ruling mind" and all "reasoning."

Gr.Naz.Or.37.14
(SC 318:302)

These teleological assertions from the other three Cappadocians were drawn together by Gregory of Nyssa: "That nothing happens without God we know from many sources; and, conversely, that God's *economy* has no element of *tyche* and irrationality in it, everyone will allow who realizes that God is reason, and *sophia,* and perfect *arete,* and truth." This was a succinct summary of how the natural theology of the Cappadocians interpreted the interrelated and conflicting claims of *tyche, ananke,* and *telos.* It was a natural theology that could be known not only from revelation but "from many sources" by anyone who realized that God was reason, wisdom, virtue, and truth in person, since there were so "many modes of such perception." But according to this natural theology, such a teleological perspective was grounded not only in the doctrine of beginnings through creation but in the consideration of *arete* itself. In the axiom of Gregory of Nyssa, "Human nature achieves perfection through *arete.*" Basil elaborated further on this theme of the "advance to perfection." It should be noted that in this particular passage he was speaking specifically in the context of "the blessed goal" of the Christian life as "the knowledge of God bestowed on believers by the Lord," Jesus Christ, and that therefore he was not explicitly arguing here, as he did so often elsewhere, in the context of natural theology. Nevertheless, much of what he was saying would seem to have been applicable in both contexts. For in pondering the sense in which Christ had identified himself in the New Testament as "the way" in addition to being "the truth" and "the life," he was moved to speak in quite general terms about an "advance [prokopē] to perfection, made stage by stage and in regular order." This advance proceeded "both through the works of righteousness and through the illumination of knowledge." But considered in and of themselves, knowledge and works were incomplete apart from teleology, for the advance was always "longing after future prospects and reaching forward to the remaining possibilities."

Gr.Nyss.Infant.
(Jaeger 3–II:93)

Gr.Nyss.Beat.6
(PG 44:1268)

Gr.Nyss.Cant.4
(Jaeger 6:117)

Jn 14:6

Bas.Spir.8.18
(SC 17:310)

Negatively, the correlation between *arche* and *telos* also in natural theology found corroboration in the systems of those whose lack of a proper comprehension of the *arche* led them to an inadequate understanding of the *telos.* Thus "the philosophers of Greece [hoi tōn Hellēnōn sophoi]," in their efforts to explain nature and its origins, had fallen into one error after another, from atomism to materialism, with each such error then going on to be "overturned by its successors." But for all the differences of opinion among them, it had been common to all these systems that they were "deceived by their inherent atheism," which deluded them into supposing, on the basis of a mistaken view of origins, "that there was nothing governing or ruling the universe, and that it was all given over to *tyche*." Cataloging the major alternatives among these systems, Gregory of Nazianzus put their teleology (or lack of it) into the context of their several world-views. First, in an apparent attack on the Platonists, he listed those whom he charged with "thinking up imaginary republics ['plattousi poleis,' the evident play on words between 'Platōn' and 'plattein' being untranslatable], fine-sounding in the description [logōi] but unachievable in fact [ergōi]." He went on to speak of those whom he accused of "all but worshiping august tyrannies"; although the reference was not at all clear, he may possibly have been referring here to Aristotle and his followers and pupils, who included Alexander the Great. Then there were, he continued, "the deniers of any god at all, or of a providence [ou pronoein] over events, believers in a universe borne along by luck and *tyche*." Next there were those who maintained that things were being "led along by the stars and by the configurations [schēmatismois] of *ananke;*" he added that he did not know "by whom and from where these configurations in turn" were being impelled, according to their system. And finally, there were some who taught that everything was "motivated by pleasure [eis hēdonēn], as the goal [peras] of human life," which seems to have been his way of referring to the Epicureans.

Whatever the specific identity of these several positions may have been, Gregory of Nazianzus, speaking here for the natural theology of all the Cappadocians and for Patristic thought generally, clearly saw the Classical views of a random *tyche* on the one hand, and of the deterministic *ananke* of fate and the stars on the other hand, as the principal rivals to the Christian doctrine of God and to the teleology of divine providence. The relation in his Classical sources between *moira, heimarmene,* and *ananke,* and between all three of these and *tyche*—and between all of these and divinity—had been complex from the beginning. As Peter Green has observed, "Tyche as such was simply a recognition of this random factor in human affairs, stripped of divine motivation, and thus liable to veer between the unknowable (for which

Bas.*Hex.*1.2
(SC 26:92–94)

Gr.Naz.*Or.*4.44
(SC 309:144)

Amand de Mendieta
1973,393–98,405–39

Greene 1944; Nussbaum
1986

Green 1990,400

Green 1990,586

ap.Th.1.140
Pl.*Ap*.33c

Pl.*R*.617c

Pl.*Lg*.806a

Pl.*Lg*.709b-c

Gr.Naz.*Or*.40.17
(*PG* 36:380–81)

Bidez 1938,19–21

Nock 1972,1:121

Nock 1933,100

Bas.*Ep*.1
(Courtonne 1:3)

Bas.*Ep*.236.5
(Courtonne 3:53)

Gr.Nyss.*Eun*.3.9.50
(Jaeger 2:282–83)

prayer to someone or something still seemed the only hope) and the merely inscrutable (which could, with luck, be rationalized into a pattern)." Eventually, according to Green, "against unpredictability was ranged something far worse, the other face of the same coin: a deterministic fate (*heimarmenē*) that, like most Hellenistic governments, made a macabre mockery of the principle of free will, of self-determination." Pericles had observed, commenting on the arbitrariness of the course of human history, "We usually blame *tyche* for whatever did not happen as we expected." Plato had Socrates speak about a "divine *moira*." Near the end of his *Republic* he connected fate and deterministic necessity by identifying "the fates" as "daughters of *ananke*." In the *Laws*, which also spoke about "the *tyche* of *ananke*," Plato presented one of the most incisive and comprehensive of his statements on this theme: "In all things God [theos, without the article]—and together with God, *tyche* and *kairos*—pilots all human affairs. One must, indeed, concede that these are accompanied by yet a third factor, something gentler, namely, *techne*." By the time of the Cappadocians, this combination of themes had become even more complicated—both among intellectual adherents of the Classical tradition and among the common people, including sometimes the Christian laity—through the rapid growth of astrology as an ingenious blending of the determinism represented by fate and necessity with the randomness represented by fortune and chance. "Some found satisfaction in a warm belief in the omnipotence of the stars," as Arthur Darby Nock put it; and "for the plain man," as he said elsewhere, astrology "acquired an axiomatic validity which it retained everywhere till the seventeenth century, and which for some it still has."

By describing such a blend of fate and fortune, Basil could, in the first of his letters, juxtapose the notion of *tyche* and luck with the widely held belief in "a certain *ananke* or *heimarmene*, ruling all the events of our lives both great and small, with human beings having control over nothing"; and in a letter to Amphilochius of Iconium, he dismissed as "shafts of rhetoric" the speculations about "human affairs being governed by *heimarmene*." Addressing that same combination of notions, Gregory of Nyssa attacked "the practicioners of the vain deceit" of "astrological juggling," because they espoused the doctrine that "such and such conjunctions or oppositions of the stars" were responsible for one's "lot in life" and thus for one's *heimarmene*. He rejected the hypothesis that this lot in life, whether of virtue or of vice, was "decided by *ananke*" rather than by a God who desired only an *arete* that was "free of coercion," which meant that it was also free of his

Gr.Nyss.*Cant.*5
(Jaeger 6:160–61)

own coercion. As "the one true and perfect power, above all things and governing the whole universe," God did not rule "by violence and tyrannical dictatorship [biai tini kai tyrannikēi dy-

Gr.Nyss.*Or.dom.*3
(*PG* 44:1156)
Gr.Naz.*Or.*37.14
(*SC* 318:302)

nasteiai]," nor through the overpowering force of "intimidation and *ananke.*" If this were not true and if determinism were, human effort and human thought would be useless. Useless, too, would be the very idea of the image of God, for it was impossible for "such a nature, subject to *ananke* and in servitude, to be called an image of the sovereign nature" of God, which was totally free. More outrageous still would be any suggestion that in making this world rather than some other possible world even

Gr.Nyss.*Or.catech.*5.3
(Méridier 26)

God the Creator had not acted out of a free and sovereign love but had been driven by an external "*ananke* in forming humanity," and that therefore creation was not contingent, because God was

See pp.256–59

not free and sovereign.

Such theories of deterministic necessity tried to lay claim to a scientific basis by appealing to the alleged influence of the stars;

Gaïth 1953,87–94

for it was during these centuries that, in Franz Cumont's formulation, "in place of the old methods of divination, now fallen into discredit, of deceitful portents and ambiguous oracles, astrology promised to substitute a scientific method, founded on experience of almost infinite duration." To the Cappadocians this use of

Cumont 1960,76
Courtonne 1934,99–110
Gr.Nyss.*Eun.*1.388
(Jaeger 1:140)

astronomy to validate astrology was a distortion of the fundamental scientific imperative to "investigate nature's work." In its proper expression, that imperative led to insights into the structure and motion of the heavenly bodies, and through such insights to admiration for the work of the Creator—always accompanied, of course, by the reverent admission that the "essential

Gr.Nyss.*Eun.*2.71
(Jaeger 1:247–48)

nature" of the Creator remained unknowable. Such use of astronomy could be "helpful," but this "science" could become "dangerous" when it led someone to "attribute all happenings and all

Gr.Naz.*Or.*7.7
(*PG* 35:761)

existing things to the influence of the stars." It was an "overstepping of the borders" scientifically and epistemologically, and a false interpretation of the biblical teaching that the stars had been given "for signs [eis sēmeia]," for someone to "cast horoscopes,"

Gn 1:14

on the mistaken supposition of "a dependency of our lives upon the motion of the heavenly bodies, enabling the astrologers to read our future in the planets." This astrological theorizing led to the mistaken belief, as quoted by Basil: "When the planets cross in the signs of the Zodiac, certain figures formed by their meeting

Bas.*Hex.*6.5
(SC 26:348)

give birth to certain destinies, and other [configurations] produce different destinies." Not only ultimate destinies, but individual actions, in which one had "the feeling of one's own free will ruling, that is, the practice of *arete* or of vice," were attributed to the deterministic necessity of this "influence of celestial bodies." But if it were correct "not to locate the origin of our *aretai* and of our vices in ourselves, but in the fatal consequence of our birth," all legislation and all moral judgment would become useless; for

Bas.*Hex.*6.7
(SC 26:356–62)

"merit, the first condition of all righteous judgment," would vanish "under the reign of *ananke* and of *heimarmene*." It was clear from such argumentation that this rejection of astrological determinism was not intended to be seen as a distinctively Christian theological judgment, but was of a piece with the "moral and natural philosophy [hē ēthikē te kai physikē philosophia]" of

Gr.Nyss.*V.Mos.*2
(Jaeger 7–I:43)

which Gregory of Nyssa spoke. That was also the perspective that permitted Gregory of Nazianzus to criticize the emperor Julian

Gr.Naz.*Or.*4.31
(SC 309:128)ep

for having come under the influence of theories about "astrology and beginnings and the phantasm of prognostication," and for

Gr.Naz.*Or.*5.5
(SC 309:302)

invoking the precedent of the star of Bethlehem to justify such theories. "The fault," Shakespeare had the Roman pagan Cassius say to Brutus (presumably on the basis of natural theology), "is not in our stars, but in ourselves."

In these theories of deterministic necessity, astrological or not, the Cappadocians nevertheless discerned the valid intuition that behind the changes and chances of this mortal life there was some meaning or purpose, albeit an unknowable one. Therefore those who were vexed by "the sequence of the *ananke* of events" had to learn to recognize that there was a "goal" toward which each one

Macr.ap.Gr.Nyss.
Anim.res. (PG 46:105)

of those events was tending. That goal was the "useful *telos*" that was built into creation and the natural order by the "intelligent

Bas.*Hex.*1.6
(SC 26:110)
Gr.Nyss.*V.Mos.*2
(Jaeger 7–I:141)
Gr.Nyss.*Cant.*9
(Jaeger 6:280)
Bálas 1966
Gr.Nyss.*Cant.*1
(Jaeger 6:39)

reason presiding over the order of visible things." Human life pressed on "toward a single *telos*." At any rate for "every virtuous life," that *telos* could be defined as "participation in God [hē tou theou metousia]," a concept central to Nyssen's system. And as it neared this "goal [skopos]," the soul stretched itself ever more intently. Citing the examples of navigators and archers, Basil asked: "Can it be that handicraftsmen have some end in

Bas.*Leg.lib.gent.*8
(Wilson 28)

view for their work, but that there is no goal for the life of man" as a whole? The concept of teleology stood in opposition to a theory that could be associated with astrology, "the Greek system of cycles, with the same revolutions of the stars bringing around the same events." Not only did this theory leave unsolved the problem of "the method of selection for some of the events to

Gr.Naz.Ep.101
(PG 37:192)
Or.Cels.4.67
(GCS 2:337)

occur and others to be omitted," but it also meant that the events of both sacred and secular history were to be seen as subject to cyclical repetition. In opposition to the Classical theories of cycles stood the assertion, as Charles Norris Cochrane formulated it on the basis of Latin Christian thought in his *Christianity and Classical Culture:* "Notwithstanding all appearances, human history does not consist of a series of repetitive patterns, but

Cochrane 1944,484

marks a sure, if unsteady, advance to an ultimate goal." Basil sought to show that by their organic structures and by the idiosyncracies of their anatomies, which he recounted in great scien-

Bas.Hex.9.5
(SC 26:502–10)
Bas.Hex.5.4
(SC 26:292–94)

tific detail, various animals, from elephants to scorpions, gave evidence of this teleology. "In creation," he insisted, "nothing exists without a reason." And again a little later, "Nothing

Bas.Hex.5.8
(SC 26:314)

has been done without motive, nothing by chance [apo tautomatou]."

This teleology meant that it was never permissible to regard "a blind, senseless occurrence as the work of God [to gar eikēi kai alogōs ginomenon ouk an ergon eiē theou]," but that within and behind all events, even the most cruelly baffling such as the death of an infant, there had to be, unknowable though it might be now, "some plan bearing the mark of divine wisdom and at the same time of divine providential care." For this was an axiom both of natural and of revealed theology: "Nothing in this world hap-

Gr.Nyss.Infant.
(Jaeger 3–II:72)

pens without God, but all is linked to the divine will, and the Deity is skillful and prudential." Echoing Plato's emphasis, quoted earlier, on the "third factor, something gentler, namely, *techne,*" through which, along with "*tyche* and *kairos* . . . God

Pl.Lg.709b–c

in all things pilots all human affairs," Macrina celebrated the *techne* of God, the "regularity and order in accordance with the artistic plan of the author [taxei tini kai akolouthiai kata tēn technikēn tou kathēgemonos sophian]," which was the goal for

Macr.ap.Gr.Nyss.
Anim.res. (PG 46:105)
Mt 13:39

which "intelligent beings came into existence" in the first place; and her brother Gregory, quoting the phrase in the Gospel about "the end of the *aeon,*" celebrated the *kairos* of God in similar

Gr.Nyss.Cant.5
(Jaeger 6:155–56)

language. Yet although what God did was never done "senselessly [alogōs]," that did not mean that human beings were in a position to "know the intentions of each detail of the divine

Gr.Nyss.Infant.
(Jaeger 3–II:72)
Gr.Nyss.Cant.12
(Jaeger 6:362)

economy." For God worked paradoxically, slaying in order to make alive. Hence "the reasons for events ordained by God" were beyond the grasp of the human mind, being based on "some

Bas.Ep.5.2
(Courtonne 1:17–18)

reason incomprehensible to human understanding." The plans and ways of divine providence remained "hidden before our

Gr.Naz.Or.17.4
(PG 35:969)

eyes." Here, as elsewhere, the hidden quality of those plans

See pp.57–58
Gr.Nyss.*Beat.*6
(*PG* 44:1269–72)

Gr.Nyss.*Infant.*
(Jaeger 3–II:76)

Gr.Nyss.*Infant.*
(Jaeger 3–II:90)

See pp.129–31

Gr.Nyss.*Virg.*4
(Jaeger 8–I:271)

Macr.ap.Gr.Nyss.
Anim.res. (*PG* 46:120–21)

Gr.Nyss.*V.Mos.*2
(Jaeger 7–I:56)

Gr.Nyss.*Beat.*5
(*PG* 44:1253–56)

was not to be taken to mean that the human mind was obliged to suspend all thought and speculation when confronted by the "inexpressible, ineffable, and inaccessible." Even "in the presence of unfathomable questions [epi tōn anephiktōn]" it was permissible "to exercise human judgment over everything [anakrinein panta]," and therefore to speculate about what plan and goal the providence of God might have in mind. In the case of the death of an infant, for example, some such speculation as this about divine preemptive action could apply: "This is the achievement of a perfect providence: not only to heal evils that have been committed, but also to forestall them, before they have been committed. . . . In his love to the individual, he who does all things on the basis of a plan withdraws the materials for evil."

But if theories of deterministic necessity could be said to have a valid point of sorts in speaking about a meaning or purpose, that point was negated when these theories equated teleology with the denial of free will. Just because human life was running on "to the finish with the same speed through all these opposites [dia tōn enantiōn ton tēs zōēs dromon anyesthai]," such as wealth and poverty, or comfort and distress, or other "anomalies of life [hai tou biou anōmaliai]," this did not contradict the presence in all human beings of a will that was authentically free, "the same power to choose to live a good or an evil life." The nature of the human soul and the origin of "its constitution from God" had as their direct implication the absence in the soul of "any *ananke* of being evil," but as another and corollary implication the presence in the soul of "the ability to be attracted of its own free will [tēi idiai gnōmēi] in a chosen direction," whether for evil or for good, "either willfully shutting its eyes to the good" or "preserving undimmed its sight of the truth." There was not "some sort of power of *ananke* from above" that decided the direction of human lives, but it was "up to their own nature and free choice [en tēi heautōn physei te kai proairesei] to elect light or darkness." Hence it was "dependent on us and on the power of our free will to receive the object of our desire"; and by the same token, "the inclination toward evil," when it arose, also came into existence "uncompelled by any deterministic *ananke*." This presupposition of an antithesis, in the very nature of things, between *ananke* and choice, and hence between a divine "power of *ananke*" and human "freedom of choice [proairesis]," helps to explain why the Eastern Orthodox heirs of the Cappadocian tradition have had such difficulty accepting the Augustinian theory of sin and grace, in which, as in Monophysitism, "the human is pushed into the background and, as it were, suppressed by the Divine." But underlying the attitude of the Cappadocians was this conviction: "There is in us the principle of all excellence, all *arete* and *sophia,* and every higher thing that we conceive. But preeminent among all of these is the fact that we are free from *ananke,* and not in bondage to any natural power, but have it in our own power to decide as we please. For *arete* is a voluntary thing, subject to no dominion: that which is the result of compulsion and force cannot be *arete.*"

Yet human freedom did not imply divine caprice, and it would be the worst possible misunderstanding to conclude, from this preeminence of free will among all the qualities of human personality, that Cappadocian natural theology implied the sacrifice of order to freedom as a way of avoiding fatalism. Their opposition to philosophies of *tyche* and chance was no less thoroughgoing than was their rejection of deterministic necessity. In the fundamental statement of his natural theology voicing that opposition, as quoted earlier, Gregory of Nyssa declared: "That nothing happens without God [to mēden atheei ginesthai] we know from many sources; and, conversely, that God's *economy* has no element of *tyche* and irrationality in it, everyone will allow who realizes that God is reason, and *sophia,* and perfect *arete,* and truth." Among the deities of Greek polytheism was the goddess *Tyche,* who during the Hellenistic and Roman periods had been conflated with the Roman goddess Fortuna. According to the church historian Sozomen, "The pagan temple dedicated to *Tyche,* the only one remaining in the city [of Caesarea], was overturned by the Christians after the accession [of the emperor Julian]; and on hearing of the deed, he hated the entire city intensely." But to Gregory of Nazianzus, this act of destruction sometime after Julian's accession in 361 amounted to a declaration of freedom from the tyranny of random chance and luck. For the rejection of that tyranny was a consequence of the acceptance not simply of the authority of Christian revelation but of the universally valid principle of natural theology that there was "nothing of irrationality or fortune or chance [alogon kai syntychikon kai automaton]" in God and in the actions that came from God. Belief that there was such a force as chance in the founding of the cosmos had led the natural philosophers and scientists among the Greeks astray. The very "system of the heavens" demonstrated that it was impossible for "any existing thing to have its being from chance or accident." For once the principle of chance had been introduced as an explanation for the

---

Marginal references (left column):

Florovsky 9:39

Gr.Nyss.*Hom.opif.*16
(PG 44:184)

Macr.ap.Gr.Nyss.
Anim.res. (PG 46:21)

Gr.Nyss.*Infant.*
(Jaeger 3–II:93)

OCD 1100–1101;445

Soz.*H.e.*5.4
(GCS 50:197)

Gr.Naz.*Or.*18.34
(PG 35:1029)

Gr.Nyss.*Hex.*
(PG 44:73)

Bas.*Hex.*1.2
(SC 26:92–94)

Gr.Nyss.*Eun.*2.222–23
(Jaeger 1:290)

beginning of the world, or for the beginning of an individual life, it took over as the explanation for everything. Consequently, it was fundamental to begin with the hypothesis that divine creation did not take place "by some sort of lucky accident [automatōi tini syntychiai]." From this hypothesis there followed not "randomness" or "arbitrary distribution [diaklērōsis]" but a divine teleology based on "ontological superiority." Only with the simultaneous rejection of the notion of *tyche* and of the notions of *ananke* and *heimarmene* was it possible to affirm either divine providence or human *arete*.

Whatever such doctrines as providence or fate or fortune may have meant in theory, their real test came in the specific experiences of life and of its vicissitudes. Macrina may have been able to take the death of her brother as an occasion for "lofty philosophy" that could discourse about "the divine *economy* concealed in disasters." But for souls less heroic than Macrina (which meant most souls, Christian or pagan), such a crisis as a sequence of natural calamities in an agricultural region—cattle plague, followed by drought, followed in turn by torrential rains and hail—could change these theoretical discussions into a genuine crisis of faith. "Tell us," as Gregory of Nazianzus put the challenge of his flock to himself in the aftermath of these calamities, "whence come such blows and scourges, and what account can we give of them?" The universal human experience of the weather, the subject of a thousand proverbs of folk wisdom in every language, as quoted also in the Old and the New Testament, did seem to confirm the conclusion that there was "some disordered and irregular motion or some unguided current, some unreason of the universe." From this it seemed valid to infer that there was "no ruler of the world," and therefore that the course of this world was "borne along by chance [to automaton]," with no sense or purpose. Or was it still possible to posit a teleology and to affirm, in the face of such "disturbances and changes of the universe," that all of this was being "directed by reason and order under the guidance of the reins of Providence"?

The answer of the Cappadocians to such questions took a multiplicity of forms. Ultimately, as Christian believers, they answered them with the confession of the hope of the universal *apocatastasis,* in the light of which everything that had happened in this life would finally be seen to make divine sense. Short of that, however, and in the light of reason as well as of revelation, they drew the correlation between *arche* and *telos,* between beginning and ending, which yielded a teleology that could be in-

Macr.ap.Gr.Nyss.
Anim.res. (PG 46:117)

Gr.Nyss.*Hex.*
(PG 44:72)

Gr.Nyss.*Eun.*1.526
(Jaeger 1:178)

Macr.ap.Gr.Nyss.
Anim.res. (PG 46:117)

Gr.Nyss.*Virg.*23
(Jaeger 8–I:334)

Macr.ap.Gr.Nyss.*V.Macr.*
(Jaeger 8–I:390)

Jb 37;Mt 16:2–3

Gr.Naz.*Or.*16.5
(PG 35:940)

See pp.324–26

ferred from the structure of the world as cosmos. Not only the creation narrative in the Book of Genesis but Aristotle in *De Caelo* drew such a correlation of beginning and ending when he declared: "Generated things are seen always to be destroyed." From this it followed, according to Basil, who seemed to be quoting Aristotle: "What was begun in time is condemned to come to an end in time; for if there has been a beginning, you should not doubt of the end." There was a logical connection between the two, such that a denial of the possibility of the end was also a denial of the possibility of the beginning. But in the Cappadocian system, the possibility of the beginning, in fact the certainty of a beginning, was a logical and natural, not only a theological and supernatural, certainty. Starting from that certainty, they came to the doctrine of natural theology that in the universe there was a "harmony of the whole," which involved the end no less than the beginning, teleology no less than creation. There was a system and government in the universe, from which the universe had come, toward which it tended, and by which it was sustained. All of this indicated that it had been "originally constituted, blended, bound together, and set in motion in some sort of harmony," which was still being preserved even amid calamity and disaster. Now, under the conditions of finite existence, there was evident "some sort of deficiency in our race." But from the nature of things it was possible to see "every intellectual reality fixed in a plenitude [plērōma] of its own." Since that was the general rule, Macrina could draw the conclusion: "It is reasonable to expect that humanity [to anthrōpinon] also will arrive at a goal [eis peras], for in this respect also humanity is not to be parted from the intellectual world." In the consideration of that goal, it could even be affirmed that the *economy* of divine providence had a purpose in bringing death upon human nature.

Like the teleology of which it was the most comprehensive expression, eschatology belonged in part to reason as well as to revelation, and various of its components were to be found "both in the pagan writings and in the divine writings [para te tōn exōthen kai para tēs theias graphēs]." But all such "lofty philosophy," which gave the impression of being so well informed about "the divine purpose," was qualified, as was every other theme of Cappadocian natural theology, by the limitations of human knowledge and by the requirements of *apophatic* theology. A recitation of the hope of the kingdom and of the expectation of the end concluded that the description of such transcendent

Gn 1:1

Arist.*Cael*.279b20

Bas.*Hex*.1.3
(SC 26:98–100)

Gr.Nyss.*Hom.opif*.23
(PG 44:209)

See pp.65–69

Gr.Nyss.*Infant*.
(Jaeger 3–II:71)

Gr.Nyss.*Eun*.2.222
(Jaeger 1:290)

Gr.Naz.*Or*.16.5
(PG 35:940)

Macr.ap.Gr.Nyss.
Anim.res. (PG 46:128)

Gr.Nyss.*Or.catech*.35.7
(Méridier 164)

Macr.ap.Gr.Nyss.
Anim.res. (PG 46:68)

Macr.ap.Gr.Nyss.*V.Macr*.
(Jaeger 8–I:390)

Gr.Nyss.*Hom.opif.*
(*PG* 44:204)

Gr.Naz.*Or.*16.5
(*PG* 35:940)

Macr.ap.Gr.Nyss.
Anim.res. (*PG* 46:121)

Gr.Nyss.*Hom.opif.*23
(*PG* 44:209)

Gr.Nyss.*Hom.opif.*22
(*PG* 44:208)

Gr.Nyss.*Or.dom.*1
(*PG* 44:1124–25)

Gr.Nyss.*Hom.opif.*pr.
(*PG* 44:128)
Gr.Nyss.*Infant.*
(Jaeger 3–II:76)

Bas.*Ep.*42.1
(Courtonne 1:100)

Phil 3:13–14

Gr.Nyss.*Beat.*5
(*PG* 44:1248)

things belonged "to the realm of the ineffably mysterious [en aporrētois menei]." "Harmony" there was, as well as "reason and order," built into the very structure of the cosmos, but in the strictest sense it was "a harmony known only to the one who gave it motion." This awareness of limitations, too, belonged to the correlation between *arche* and *telos*. When speaking about the beginning, the human mind was restricted to "the fact that [hoti]" the universe was created, but it had no right or ability to probe "the process how [pōs]." So also here, the confident teleological assertion that there would definitely be an end was followed immediately by the warning that "the question of the process how [to de pōs]" had to be "put beyond the reach of our meddling [polypragmosynē]."

Nevertheless, no eschatology, not even an eschatology as sublime and audacious as that of Gregory of Nyssa, could exhaust the full significance of Cappadocian teleology. For because the *telos* was not merely the end but the goal and the consummation, it comprehended the *arche* in a complete schema, which was "coextensive with the development of humanity [tēi anthrōpinēi auxēsei symparateinonta]" across all of human history. The reality of the *telos* transformed and reoriented the entire perspective. Gregory of Nyssa divided the study of mankind into three parts, corresponding to the usual divisions of time: "What we believe to have taken place previously, what we now see, and the results which are expected to appear afterwards"; each of these historical divisions was, in its own way, essential to a full understanding of the human condition. But although the question of origins and of "whence [hothen]" remained unavoidable and essential as a key to the understanding of the cosmos and of the image of God, the quest for the meaning of the whole of human life could not be contented with what had gone before. For it was characteristic of human life that it was "fed not so much on the past as on the future," as the apostle Paul had said: "Forgetting what is behind and straining towards what lies ahead, I press towards the finishing line, to win the heavenly prize to which God has called me in Christ Jesus." This pointing toward the future implied that it was impossible "to be raised to God except by always tending to the things above [ta anō]." Teleology taught the lesson of a "need for an unceasing desire for higher things [tēn tōn hypsēlōn epithymian], not a contentment to rest satisfied in past achievements." It was this unceasing desire that gave dynamism to a life and a knowledge that might otherwise, to the superficial observer, have given the impression of being something static and unchanging.

Gr.Nyss.*Cant.*2
(Jaeger 6:6:60)

See p.328

For the Cappadocians' celebration of *apatheia* as "likeness to God" did seem to substantiate such an impression of a static reality (as though *apatheia* in Patristic Greek were synonymous with "apathy" in modern English, though it definitely is not). So did the list of the qualities of God that were said to be shared by human nature as the image of God: "purity, *apatheia*, blessedness, alienation from all evil . . . , mind and word . . . and love . . . and the power of apprehending things by means of sight and hearing, and an inquisitive and searching understanding about things." But in a long and far-reaching discussion, Gregory of Nyssa sought to show that such a definition of God in absolute terms was not incompatible with dynamism: "As long as a nature is in defect as regards the good, the superior existence exerts upon this inferior one a ceaseless attraction towards itself; and this craving for more will never stop. . . . The first good is in its nature infinite, and so it follows of necessity that the participation in the enjoyment of it will be infinite also, for more will always be in the process of being grasped, and yet something beyond that which has been grasped will always be discovered, and this search will never overtake its object, because its fund is as inexhaustible as the growth of that which participates in it is ceaseless." This "ceaseless attraction" made the *telos* not only a goal but a lure, and not at all an "end" in the sense that nothing would come after it. As a lure, the transcendence of God evoked a yearning that was insatiable either in time or in eternity. For, in Macrina's words, "The life of the Supreme Being is love, seeing that the *kalon* is necessarily lovable to those who recognize it, and the Deity does recognize it, and so this recognition becomes love, that which he recognizes being essentially *kalon*. This true *kalon* the hybris of satiety cannot touch." Physical appetites for food or sex reached a "satiety [koros]" of pleasure and began to pall; but the life in God, "the possession of *arete*, once firmly established," differed fundamentally, being "neither circumscribed by time nor limited by satiety [ou chronōi metreitai, oute korōi periorizetai]."

Gr.Nyss.*Hom.opif.*5
(PG 44:137)

Gr.Nyss.*Eun.*1.290–91
(Jaeger 1:112)

Gr.Nyss.*V.Mos.*2
(Jaeger 7–I:115)

Macr.ap.Gr.Nyss.
Anim.res. (PG 46:96)

Gr.Nyss.*Beat.*4
(PG 44:1244)

That general observation about satiety and appetite came in the course of a commentary on the fourth Beatitude: "Blessed are those who hunger and thirst to see right prevail; they shall be satisfied [chortasthēsontai]," which did seem to be saying that the hunger and thirst would attain satiety / satisfaction. But the content of the observation was shaped by the sixth Beatitude, in which Christian teleology had been articulated the most fully: "Blessed are those whose hearts are pure; they shall see God." Commenting on those words of the sixth Beatitude, Gregory of

Mt 5:6

Mt 5:8

Gr.Nyss.*Beat*.6
(*PG* 44:1265)

Gr.Nyss.*V.Mos*.2
(Jaeger 7–I:116)

Gr.Nyss.*Cant*.6
(Jaeger 6:178)

Gr.Nyss.*Infant*.
(Jaeger 3–II:78–79)

Gr.Naz.*Or*.38.7
(*PG* 36:317–20)

Nyssa defined the vision of God promised there as "life without end, eternal incorruption, undying beatitude [tēn ateleutēton zōēn, tēn aïdion aphtharsian, tēn athanaton makariotēta]." In a context quite other than this *Commentary on the Beatitudes*, he set down this definition of the vision of God: "This is to see God in reality [ontōs], that the desire [for God] never finds satiety." Without retracting anything that they had said about *apophasis*, the Cappadocians thus found it possible to speak in "ontological" terms about "seeing God in reality [ontōs]." Their teleology was summed up in the vision of God, which was end and goal and ceaseless attraction. "This operation of looking upon God" was for them "the design [skopos] of all, from their very birth," and "nothing less than the life-nourishment appropriate, as like to like, to an intellectual nature." Both the comprehensive range and the fixed limitations of natural theology were expressed in this teleology of the vision of God, so much of which could be known by enlightened reason, so much more of which could be known only by grace, still more of which could be learned only gradually in an eternal quest without satiety, and infinitely more of which remained forever unfathomable in the transcendent mystery of a divine nature that was knowable only in its unknowability.

PART TWO

Natural Theology as Presupposition

Paul stood up before the Council of the Areopagus and began: "Men of Athens, I see that in everything that concerns religion you are uncommonly scrupulous. As I was going round looking at the objects of your worship, I noticed among other things an altar bearing the inscription 'To an Unknown God.' What you worship but do not know—this is what I now proclaim. The God who created the world and everything in it, and who is the Lord of heaven and earth, does not live in shrines made by human hands. It is not because he lacks anything that he accepts service at our hands, for he is himself the universal giver of life and breath—indeed of everything. He created from one stock every nation of men to inhabit the whole earth's surface. He determined their eras in history and the limits of their territory. They were to seek God in the hope that, groping after him, they might find him; though indeed he is not far from each one of us, for in him we live and move, in him we exist; as some of your own poets have said, 'We are also his offspring.'"

Acts of the Apostles 17:22–28

CHAPTER 11

Christian Theology and Classical Culture

Highet 1957,560

The fourth century has been identified by Gilbert Highet, author of *The Classical Tradition,* as preeminently "the vital period for the synthesis of Greco-Roman philosophy and Christian thought." But in the history of that century, the most overt forces determining the synthesis, through the relation between Christianity and Classical culture and through the Christian encounter with Hellenism, were not those of the three Cappadocian fathers in the Greek East, nor yet those of the corresponding (and slightly later) theological triad of Ambrose, Jerome, and Augustine in the Latin West, but, in both East and West, the forces of quite another sort of triad, the Roman-Byzantine emperors Constantine,

Armstrong 1984,1–17

Peterson 1951,45–147;
149–64

Julian, and Theodosius, through the struggles over issues that Erik Peterson has called, in the titles of two essays, "Christ as Emperor" and "Monotheism as a Political Problem."

In the formula of John Meyendorff, "it is . . . perhaps misleading to call Constantine the 'first Christian emperor,' since he did not share in the sacramental life and the liturgical celebrations of the Church until his last moments. Nevertheless . . . the Orthodox Church has recognized him as a Saint, 'equal to the Apostles.' Indeed, no single human being in history has contributed, directly or indirectly, to the conversion of so many to the Chris-

Meyendorff 1989,6–7

tian faith." In the formula of Charles Norris Cochrane, "with the entry of Julian into Constantinople (December 361), philosophy for the second time in Roman history [after Marcus Aurelius], assumed the imperial purple. . . . Unlike the movement headed by Constantine, that of Julian was one of reaction, the watchword

Cochrane 1944,261–62 of which was to be, *from Christ to Plato*." And in the formula of
Edward Gibbon, "the ruin of Paganism, in the age of Theodosius,
is perhaps the only example of the total extirpation of any ancient
and popular superstition, and may therefore deserve to be con-
Gibbon 1776,xxviii
(Bury 3:188) sidered as a singular event in the history of the human mind." The
age of the Cappadocians coincided almost exactly with this transition from the hegemony of Classical culture to the "intensely
Florovsky 8:155 ambiguous" triumph of Christianity over Classical culture.

It was no exaggeration when Reinhold Seeberg said that Basil
of Caesarea, Gregory of Nazianzus, and Gregory of Nyssa be-
Seeberg 1953,2:125 came "the creators of Greek Orthodoxy." From the writings and
correspondence of the Cappadocians, as studies of prosopogra-
phy have suggested, it would be possible to reconstruct a substantial percentage of the names of principal figures not only in the
ecclesiastical and theological affairs of the fourth-century Eastern
Mediterranean world, as might be expected, but in the whole of
Hauser-Meury 1960 its cultural, intellectual, and political life as well. Born a few years
after Constantine's conversion and his recognition of the church,
all of them therefore grew up in an atmosphere in which the
authority of the Christian church was increasingly permeating
the common life of the empire and in which the authority of
Christian theology was permeating its cultural and intellectual
Mateo-Seco–Bastero
1988,139–71 atmosphere. To them, the Council of Nicaea in 325, chaired by
Constantine, was, as Gregory of Nazianzus called it, "the holy
Synod of Nicaea, the gathering of the 318 chosen men, united by
Gr.Naz.Or.21.14
(SC 270:138) the Holy Spirit"—318 being the number not of the actual roster
of the council fathers at Nicaea but of the domestic army that
Gn 14:14
Ath.Ep.Afr.2
(PG 26:1032)
Gr.Nyss.Ep.5.1
(Jaeger 8-II:92) Abraham had mustered to rescue Lot, applied typologically al-
ready by Athanasius to the rescuers of the orthodox doctrine of
the Trinity. The council fathers were the ones who, as Gregory of
Nyssa said, "at Nicaea set forth the right and sound faith." It was
this creed that Basil called "the faith of Nicaea, to which it is
impossible for us to make even the slightest addition [pros-
Bas.Ep.258.2
(Courtonne 3:101–2) tithenai, oude to brachytaton]." To Macrina "the confession of
the lordship of Christ," surely in accordance with the creed, was a
Macr.ap.Gr.Nyss.
Anim.res. (PG 46:69–72) universal proposition. Each of the Cappadocians experienced the
challenge of the emperor Julian, not only intellectually but per-
Asmus 1910,325–67
Hauser-Meury 1960,
101–9 sonally. Both Gregory of Nazianzus and Basil addressed lengthy
apologetic treatises to Julian. These treatises (and then, even
more, the refutation written by Cyril of Alexandria, sometime
Cyr.Juln.
(PG 76:509–1064) between 433 and 441) have preserved much of what is known
today of his attacks on Christianity. "But for Cyril's quotations
[and those of Basil and Nazianzen]," the modern editor of Ju-

lian's polemic, Wilmer Cave Wright, has said, "we should have a very vague idea of Julian's treatise, and as it is we are compelled to see it through the eyes of a hostile apologist." Although he did not write a refutation of Julian, Gregory of Nyssa was well aware of what it meant, during the age of Constantine and then again during that of Theodosius the Great, for Christian theology to be taking possession of Classical culture, and to be doing so (invoking another typology) in the same way that the Israelites at the Exodus had taken possession of the riches of the Egyptians—as reparations rather than as booty.

Wright 1923,3:317

Ex 12:35–36

Gr.Nyss.V.Mos.2
(Jaeger 7–I:68)

Effectively as well as symbolically, the embodiment of this triumph of Christian theology over Classical culture, and of this possession of Classical culture by Christian theology, was Constantine's crowning achievement, the founding of New Rome, the city of Constantinople, in the year 330. The historian Sozomen, writing a century or so later, spoke of Constantinople as "this newly compacted city of Christ," and characterized it as unique among the metropolitan centers of the Mediterranean world in that it had never been "polluted by altars, Grecian temples, nor sacrifices," because it had not been transformed from a pagan to a Christian city, as Rome and Alexandria had but had been founded as a Christian capital. Except for Julian's short-lived (361–363) "introduction of idolatry," as Sozomen called it, Constantinople was and remained a Christian city, the capital of a Christian empire, and went on being that for eleven centuries, the longest uninterrupted reign in the political history of Christendom, East or West. In recognition of its special position, the ecumenical Council of Constantinople in 381 declared: "The bishop of Constantinople has the primacy of honor after the bishop of Rome, because it is the New Rome [ton mentoi Kōnstantinoupoleōs episkopon echein ta presbeia tēs timēs meta ton Rōmēs episkopon, dia to einai autēn nean Rōmēn]."

Gr.Naz.Or.42:10
(PG 36:469)

Soz.H.e.2.3
(GCS 50:51–54)

Meyendorff 1984,65–74

CCP (381) can.3
(Alberigo-Jedin 32)

The constitutional implications of this canon—and of the similar but still more controversial so-called twenty-eighth canon of the Council of Chalcedon in 451—for the jurisdictional relations between the patriarch of Constantinople as New Rome and the patriarch of Old Rome have, for understandable reasons, engaged the attention of historians of canon law. For our purposes here, these celebrations of Constantinople were important chiefly because of its cultural rather than its canonical primacy. On this score at any rate, such a primacy of Constantinople also over Rome, as a center both of Christian culture and of the Classical tradition, was never in serious question, either in the East

Grillmeier-Bacht 1951–
54,2:459–90

Holl 1928,409–17

or in the West (including Rome), throughout the Middle Ages. The rhetorical apostrophe to Constantinople by Gregory of Nazianzus therefore expressed a widely held consensus: "Established and strengthened with wholesome doctrines, a city that is the eye of the ecumene, in its exceeding strength by sea and land, a city that is, as it were, the link between the Eastern and Western shores, in which the extremities of the world from every side meet together, and from which, as the common mart of the faith, they

Gr.Naz.Or.42.10
(PG 36:469)
Gibbon 1776, xxvii
(Bury 3:150)

take their rise, a city borne hither and thither on the edifying currents of so many tongues!" It did make these words of celebration "pathetic, and almost sublime," as Gibbon put it, to recognize that they were part of the oration delivered by Gregory as his

Bernardi 1968,226–35

valedictory to the ecumenical Council of Constantinople in 381.

But it is no less important to recognize that for Gregory of Nazianzus the city of Constantinople was as well "Byzantium,

Gr.Naz.Or.7.8
(PG 35:764)

now presiding over Europe," and that at the same time it was

Gr.Naz.Or.43.14
(PG 36:513)

"Byzantium, the imperial city of the East, distinguished by the eminence of its rhetorical and philosophical teachers." Unlike other centers of Greek rhetoric and philosophy, however, Con-

Gr.Naz.Or.42.11
(PG 36:472)

stantinople was, according to Nazianzen, a city in which Classical elitism had been overcome by the Christian faith. When Gregory spoke of it as "the eye of the ecumene," it was clear from the reference that immediately followed, to "its exceeding strength by sea and land," that he was thinking of its political, indeed its military, eminence. But he followed those words with the tribute: "[Constantinople is], as it were, the link between the Eastern and Western shores." With this he obviously had in mind also its "ecumenical" significance. The "drama" of the persecu-

Gr.Naz.Or.25.13
(SC 284:186)

tions, recently concluded, had likewise been a sort of link between East and West. But now it was possible to celebrate, also from the history of the church, the more positive links between them as well. An expression of one such link was Nazianzen's

Delehaye 1921,323

"rather curious" reference to Cyprian, a saint who at the time of his death in the middle of the third century may have belonged only to Carthage and to the Latin-speaking West, but who was

Gr.Naz.Or.24.6
(SC 284:50)

"now a great name . . . of the entire ecumene [mega . . . onoma . . . nyn de tēs oikoumenēs hapasēs]." For all of their cultural and political allegiance to Constantinople, the most decisive quality that set it at its pinnacle was, according to the Cappadocians, that it was "a city established and strengthened with

Gr.Naz.Or.42.10
(PG 36:469)

wholesome doctrines." Military power and size, Gregory of Nazianzus insisted in his valedictory, were not primary: "God has not taken pleasure in numbers. . . . For nothing is so magnificent in God's sight as pure doctrine, and a soul perfect in all the dogmas of the truth."

Gr.Naz.Or.42.7–8
(PG 36:468)

Gr.Nyss.V.Mos.2
(Jaeger 7-I:68)

The triumph of theology in the fourth century, therefore, was not only its appropriation of Classical culture. It was as well the victory of this "pure doctrine" and of these "dogmas of the truth" over impure doctrine and heresy. In the eyes of the Cappadocians, these two victories were closely related, ultimately perhaps identical, for it was a characteristic of many errors that they were

Gr.Nyss.Cant.13
(Jaeger 6:376)

simultaneously "philosophical and heretical," propounded by pagans and by false Christians. When the Cappadocians were refuting such an error either in its philosophical or in its heretical formulation, consequently, they were often addressing both. This

Gr.Naz.Or.29.21
(SC 250:224)

was the obverse side of the principle of "faith as the fulfillment of our reasoning": the false theological faith of the heretic, too, was the fulfillment of his false philosophical reasoning. But the false philosophy did not of itself produce "heresy" in the strict sense of

Fedwick 1978,64–67
DTC 14:1297–98

the word; according to the distinction formulated by Basil and eventually adopted as standard in East and West, "heretics" were to be defined as "men altogether broken off and alienated in matters relating to the actual faith" on which there could be no compromise, by contrast with "schismatics," who were to be

Bas.Ep.188.1
(Courtonne 2:121)

seen as "men separated for some ecclesiastical reasons and questions capable of mutual solution" and compromise. Only in the context of the true faith, and in antithesis to it, did such heresies arise, as the sin of the people of Israel at Mount Sinai had demonstrated. They fell into the gravest worship of false gods and the

Ex 32:1–6
Gr.Nyss.V.Mos.
(Jaeger 7–I:38)

idolatry of the golden calf at the very time when they had received the revelation of the true God through his servant Moses. The Cappadocians insisted, moreover, that this emphasis on purity of doctrine was not to lead to an exclusive emphasis on doctrine at

Gr.Nyss.Eun.3.9.56–59
(Jaeger 2:285–86)

the expense of liturgy and sacraments, which was the overemphasis that they claimed to find in the heretic Eunomius. When they confronted this heretical version of the quest for pure

See pp.40–56

doctrine, they turned to the device of *apophasis*, which was so important also as a weapon in their conflict with pagan religion.

Yet, they acknowledged that even as it was being practiced among the orthodox, the quest for pure doctrine was in need of constant scrutiny. Repeatedly during the fourth century, what Gregory of Nazianzus called "the offspring of a contentious spirit [ta tēs philoneikias anaplasmata]" and "the unfailing result of contentiousness" between parties that seemed to possess equal claims to orthodoxy brought on what he also called "the danger of the whole world being torn asunder in the strife about syllables." "At the present time," he admitted, "there are some who go to war even about trivial matters and to no purpose . . . but make faith the pretext." So bitter were some of his descriptions of the quarrels among the theologians that Gibbon could point out with glee: "A suspicion may possibly arise that so unfavourable a picture of ecclesiastical synods has been drawn by the partial hand of some obstinate heretic or some malicious infidel," when it fact it had come from "one of the most pious and eloquent bishops of the age, a saint and a doctor of the church, the scourge of Arianism, and the pillar of the orthodox faith . . . in a word— Gregory Nazianzen himself." Gibbon's heavy-handed irony should not, however, be permitted to obscure the heart of Gregory's treatment of Christian theology, which was not at all his anxiety to avoid logomachy, sincere and well-placed though this was, but his overriding concern to preserve doctrinal orthodoxy. Orthodox doctrine, he relentlessly insisted, was a matter of the utmost gravity, not something "for men to make sport of, as at the horse races and the theater."

The study of theology, therefore, was to be restricted to those who were "tried and true, with a sound footing in study"; but there were some devotees of theology who were more "like the promoters of wrestling-bouts in the theaters" and whose idle chatter about the dogmas of the faith made "every square in the city buzz with their arguments." It was evident from these criticisms that a half-century after Constantine's conversion Christian theology had become sufficiently widespread in its acceptance by polite Byzantine society to be trendy. Although in Gregory's prescription the most important qualification for those who wanted to deal with theology was "purification of body and soul" through catechesis and baptism, it was, in the present context, his additional requirement of "a sound footing in study [tōn exētasmenōn kai diabebēkotōn en theōriai]" that reached the furthest with its implications. "For it is not the best order of things," Gregory warned ironically, "first to teach and only then to learn, even in matters that are trivial and of no consequence." His warning continued: "Much more is this the case in those matters that are divine and of such great importance." Theology, then, was the proper object no less of scholarly study than of devout contemplation, and the antidote to its trivialization through idle gossip was solid knowledge of it. "For is it not absurd," Gregory asked rhetorically, "that while no one,

Gr.Naz.Or.21.35
(SC 270:186)

Gr.Naz.Or.2.83
(SC 247:198)

Gibbon 1776,xxvii
(Bury 3:150)

Gr.Naz.Or.21.5
(SC 270:118–20)

Gr.Naz.Or.27.2–3
(SC 250:72–76)

Gr.Naz.Or.42.18
(PG 36:480)

however great his boorishness and lack of education [ama-thestatos], is allowed to be ignorant of the Roman law, and while there is no law in favor of sins of ignorance, the teachers of the mysteries of salvation should be ignorant of the *archai* of salvation, however simple and shallow their minds may be in regard to other subjects?"

Gr.Naz.*Or*.21.24
(*SC* 270:160)

At the same time, the Cappadocians' enthusiastic celebration of Constantinople as the political, military, and intellectual symbol of the triumph of Christian theology over Classical culture must not be permitted to obscure the mystique that continued to hover over Athens in their intellectual universe, which was in some respects analogous to the special place that Jerusalem held for them. Indeed, in paraphrase of the familiar question of Tertullian's *Prescription against Heretics*, "What has Athens to do with Jerusalem [Quid Athenae Hierosolymis]?" the Cappadocians sometimes seemed to be asking, "What has Constantinople to do with Athens?" The moving biographical memoir of Basil composed by Gregory of Nazianzus some time after Basil's death provided special documentation of this theme. Describing Basil's earliest education, Gregory spoke of the "illustrious city" of Caesarea as "the metropolis of letters," with a "distinction formed by literature." That description of Caesarea served as a foil for the next stage of Basil's schooling: "Thence to Byzantium, the imperial city of the East, for it was distinguished by the eminence of its rhetorical and philosophic teaching." But even this became a foil: "Thence he was sent by God, and by his generous craving for culture, to Athens, the very home of literature—Athens, which has been to me, if it has to anyone, a city truly of gold, and the patroness of all that is good." Returning to the matter a little later, Gregory, having criticized "the young men at Athens" for being, "in their folly, mad after rhetorical skill," nevertheless acknowledged wistfully: "There is nothing so painful to anyone as is separation from Athens and one another, for those who have been comrades there." His poetic memoir, many years later, of his student days at Athens echoed this wistful tone.

Gr.Nyss.*Ep*.2
(Jaeger 8–II:13–19);
Gr.Naz.*Or*.42.26
(*PG* 36:489)
Cochrane 1944,213–60
Tert.*Praescrip*.7.9
(*CCSL* 1:193)

Gr.Naz.*Or*.43.13
(*PG* 36:512)

Gr.Naz.*Or*.43.14
(*PG* 36:513)

Gr.Naz.*Or*.43.15;43.24
(*PG* 36:513–16;529)
Gr.Naz.*Carm*.2.211–64
(*PG* 37:1044–47)

It was important to make clear that simple Christian believers, too, were orthodox, often more so than were speculative thinkers. Yet it was equally clear that orthodox theology as a scientific discipline required a high level of education in the Classical as well as in the Christian tradition, and therefore the Cappadocians as orthodox Christian theologians repeatedly addressed themselves to the philosophy of education. Gregory of Nazianzus was speaking for all of them when, in agreement with

Gr.Naz.*Or*.42.11
(*PG* 36:472)

Giet 1941a,232–46;
Jaeger 1961,86–102

Gr.Naz.Or.43.11
(PG 36:508)

"men of sense" regardless of position, he described "the first of our advantages" as *paideusis*. Sometimes he, as well as all the other Cappadocians, could speak as though the content of this *paideusis* were predominantly, even exclusively, Christian. He contrasted the two kinds of education, Classical and Christian, in a letter of recommendation for a Christian scholar named Amazonius: "In a short time he showed proof of an extensive *paideusis*, both of the kind for which I once used to be very zealous when I was shortsighted and of that for which I am zealous in its place, now that I have been able to contemplate the summit of

Gr.Naz.Ep.39.3
(Gallay 1:48)

Hauser-Meury
1960,134–35

arete." In the same spirit he praised his mother, Nonna, who converted his father, usually called Gregory of Nazianzus the Elder, for having refused to profane "her ears and tongue, which had received and uttered divine things," with the pollutions of pagan Greek culture, "on the grounds of the incompatibility between unholy and holy things." Gregory of Nyssa also crit-

Gr.Naz.Or.18.10
(PG 35:996)

icized those who were neglecting "the faith of the fathers" in favor of a heathen learning that was inimical to Christian teach-

Gr.Nyss.V.Mos.2
(Jaeger 7–1:37)

Gr.Nyss.Eun.3.1.2
(Jaeger 2:3–4)

ing. He rejected, at least in principle, the effort to employ "weapons of argument sharpened by rhetoric" or "sharpness of dialectic" in the service of orthodoxy. In the same spirit, Gregory of Nazianzus warned against "abandoning faith to take the power of reason as our shield" and against "using philosophical inquiry to destroy the credibility of the Spirit [to tou pneumatos

Gr.Naz.Or.29.21
(SC 250:224)
Macr.ap.Gr.Nyss.
Anim.res. (PG 46:21)

Bas.Spir.17.4
(SC 17:396)

axioposton tais zētēsesi lysōmen]." Macrina joined in scorning the doctrines of Classical thought. Basil, too, blamed these doctrines for their corrupting influence on the ideas of Christian heretics. Even the emperor Julian unintentionally came to the aid of such an elevation of Christian faith over Classical "Helleniz-ing" when he confined the latter to those who worshiped the

Juln.Imp.ap.Gr.Naz.
Or.4.102 (SC 309:250)

pagan gods and assigned the former to those who equated *sophia* with an uncritical "believing."

Actually, however, the vehemence of Julian's attack was a measure of how totally alien any such fideism was to the educational thought of all the Cappadocians, as this was expressed in Nazianzen's defense of the cultivation of the Greek language as

Gr.Naz.Or.4.103
(SC 309:252–54)

the supreme expression of authentic "Hellenism." In spite of such attacks, the very concentration of Christian faith on the pursuit of eternal life implied, according to Basil, that Christians needed all the "travel supplies [ephodia]" they could find for the journey heavenward and that they were to turn to "any possible source of

Bas.Leg.lib.gent.10
(Wilson 36–37)

benefit towards that end," which included the Classical authors. As Macrina admitted, though with apparent reluctance, a train-

Macr.ap.Gr.Nyss.
Anim.res. (PG 46:52)

Gr.Naz.*Or.*36.4
(SC 318:248–50)

Gr.Nyss.*Or.dom.*5
(PG 44:1188)

Gr.Naz.*Or.*43.11
(PG 36:508–9)

Gr.Naz.*Or.*21.6
(SC 270:120)

Gr.Naz.*Or.*43.13
(PG 36:512)

Bas.*Ep.*74.3
(Courtonne 1:175)

Bas.*Leg.lib.gent.*3
(Wilson 21)

Gr.Naz.*Or.*43.11
(PG 36:508–9)

Bartelink 1960,486–92

Malingrey 1961,207–35

ing in the logical method of Classicism, which she denounced because it could "be turned to the overthrow of truth," could nevertheless be a useful tool "for the detection of falsehood." The same double-edged quality was characteristic of Classical rhetoric. Gregory of Nyssa joined himself to this attitude of Gregory of Nazianzus, Basil, and Macrina toward the "less cultivated" style of those who did not share in the culture of Hellenism. Or, as Gregory of Nazianzus put it, employing flourishes that gave unmistakable evidence of his own Classical education, "As we have compounded healthful drugs from certain of the reptiles, so from secular literature we have received principles of inquiry and speculation [exetastikon te kai theōrētikon], while we have rejected their idolatry." From time to time there were indications in the writings of the Cappadocians of their dawning suspicion that Christian thought, once it had achieved its triumph over Classical thought and learning, was in danger of neglecting it, by a kind of theological overkill, and thus of falling into the very fideism of which the emperor Julian accused it. It was, they urged, a good thing also for a Christian theologian to be trained in such subjects as Classical literature and philosophy. In Basil's youth, the Cappadocian city of Caesarea had had the reputation of being the metropolis of literature. But now in his maturity, Caesarea had deteriorated, as he himself found reason to complain: "Now we have no more meetings, no more debates, no more gatherings of wise men in the agora, nothing more of all that made our city famous. In our agora nowadays it would be stranger for someone from among the ranks of those who possess *paideia* and *logoi* to put in an appearance here than it would for men showing a brand of iniquity or unclean hands to have presented themselves in the Athens of old." Caesarea had become more Christian and more orthodox, but it had at the same time become less cultured—not, in the eyes of the Cappadocians, a healthy condition, and certainly not a necessary consequence of its Christianization. It would seem to be with this sense of cultural decline in his mind that Basil wrote his apologia for Classical education on the grounds of "some affinity [tis oikeiotēs pros allēlous] between the two bodies of teachings." It was, as Gregory of Nazianzus agreed when he spoke in memory of Basil, "poor judgment" for Christians to abhor Classical education.

In the vocabulary of the Cappadocians (as in that of other Christian thinkers) there was perhaps no more telling index of how Christian theology had taken possession of Classical culture than their usage of the Greek word "philosophia." The starting point for any consideration of the Cappadocian term "philosophia" must be its Greek and Classical provenance, that is, its original status as—in a phrase that the Cappadocians and their heretical opponents seem to have shared—"the philosophy from the outside [hē exōthen philosophia]." That phrase was conflated from several passages of the New Testament, especially from two: Paul's warning against being spoiled by "philosophy and vain deceit," and his reference to "those on the outside [hoi exōthen]." Just when each of the Three Cappadocians was in his young manhood, the intellectual standing of this Classical pagan philosophy received significant political and social reinforcement, for twenty months at any rate, through its official revival during the emperorship of Julian, the sometime Christian, whose religious syncretism found its counterpart in his encouragement of many different (and in some ways mutually contradictory) philosophical systems, with all their disquisitions about "the equality of geometry" and about "justice." It was specifically in this context that some of the most extreme aspersions upon pagan philosophy appeared in Cappadocian thought and rhetoric. Challenging Julian, "the crowned sophist," Gregory of Nazianzus drew a contrast between the "invincible syllogisms and enthymemes" of the emperor's pagan philosophers and "the fishermen and peasants" who had accepted the gospel. He was employing another stock rhetorical formula when he described himself as "someone lacking in philosophy and *paideia*"; the term "philosophy" here seems to have been used in the sense of "general culture." The so-called wise men and philosophers of Classical thought were in fact nothing of the kind, he contended. Echoing the opening lament of Solomon in the Book of Ecclesiastes about "futility, utter futility [mataitotēs mataiotētōn]," Gregory of Nyssa dismissed Classical philosophy and cosmology as "Greek futility [hē Hellēnikē mataiotēs]." Also in the course of a consideration of cosmological philosophy, Basil contrasted "the inquisitive discussions of philosophers about the heavens" with "the simple and inartificial character of the utterances of the Spirit" in the creation narrative of Genesis. In this he was carrying out the admonition he had voiced earlier in his commentary on the Hexaemeron: "At all events let us prefer the simplicity of faith to the demonstrations of reason [ei de mē, alla to ge haploun tēs pisteōs ischyroteron estō tōn logikōn apodeixeōn]."

All of these contrasts between Classical Greek philosophia and Christian doctrine were part of the Cappadocian campaign of natural theology as apologetics, but they were also an integral

Eun.ap.Gr.Nyss.*Eun.*
2.196 (Jaeger 1:282);
Gr.Nyss.*Eun.*3.6.56
(Jaeger 2:206)

Col 2:8

1 Tm 3:7

Kurmann 1988,144–46
Gr.Naz.*Or.*4.43
(*SC* 309:142–44)
Pl.*Grg.*508a;Pl.*R.*527b;
Pl.*Grg.*474b

Gr.Naz.*Or.*5.30
(*SC* 309:354)

Gr.Naz.*Ep.*101
(*PG* 37:183)

Malingrey 1961,217–21
Gr.Naz.*Or.*36.12
(*SC* 318:266)

Eccl 1:2

Gr.Nyss.*Eun.*3.2.35
(Jaeger 2:63)

Bas.*Hex.*3.8
(*SC* 26:232–34)

Bas.*Hex.*1.10
(*SC* 26:130)

element in the Cappadocian presentation and defense of Christian doctrine, natural theology as presupposition. Disavowing any suggestion of a "fellowship between the creed of Christians and a *sophia* discredited through being made foolish," Gregory of Nyssa ruled out of consideration, in the inquiry into authentic Christian teaching, the question of whether certain theories were acceptable "to some of the sages 'on the outside' "; that question was irrelevant to the determination of the meaning of "the Gospels or the rest of the teaching of the Holy Scriptures." Therefore, he urged, "Let us bid farewell to such philosophy!" A failure to do so, according to Basil, elevated "the *sophia* of this world" over "the dogmas of the fathers [ta tōn paterōn dogmata]" and "apostolic traditions." Having made that choice, the heretics had it as "their object not to teach simple souls lessons drawn from Holy Scripture, but to mar the harmony of the truth by heathen *sophia*." That "*sophia* from the outside" or "philosophy from the outside [hē exōthen philosophia]" was what Eunomius accused Basil of accepting. But Eunomius was, in turn, charged by the Cappadocians with having introduced arguments into his own theology based on the "*sophia* from the outside." Other heretics, too, such as the Macedonians or Pneumatomachoi in their doctrine of the Holy Spirit, had been "led into their error by their close study of outside writers [hē tōn exōthen paratērēsis]," specifically by philosophical doctrines of causation.

But amid all this polemic the Cappadocians never forgot that authentic "philo*sophia*," as the love of *sophia,* took its content from the content of *sophia* itself, which, for the Cappadocians, was not merely a divine attribute among other attributes but divinity itself. "God is not pain any more than he is pleasure," Gregory of Nyssa explained; but he went on to assert that God was to be identified as, among other titles, "auto*sophia*," *sophia* itself. Therefore "philo*sophia*," as the love of this "auto*sophia*," was, in some ultimate sense, the same as the love of God. To become this, however, philosophy needed to recognize that it was incomplete without "authentic religious devotion [hē alēthinē eusebeia]," as this was taught and practiced by the Christian faith. When it was combined with such devotion, as Gregory Nazianzus declared to Julian, it produced "those who are authentically lovers of wisdom and lovers of God [hoi alēthōs philosophoi kai philotheoi]." Thus, introducing a panegyric to a certain Maximus, he could employ "philosopher" simply as a synonym for "Christian." What such thinkers expounded, then, was "the authentic philosophy [hē alēthē philosophia]." The

Margin references:

1 Cor 1:20

Gr.Nyss.*Eun.*3.8.43
(Jaeger 2:255)

Bas.*Ep.*90.2
(Courtonne 1:195–96)

Bas.*Ep.*8.2
(Courtonne 1:23)
Malingrey 1961,212–13
Eun.ap.Gr.Nyss.*Eun.*
2.196 (Jaeger 1:282)

Gr.Nyss.*Eun.*3.6.56
(Jaeger 2:206)

Bas.*Spir.*2.5
(SC 17:264)

Gr.Nyss.*Virg.*16
(Jaeger 8–I:314)

Gr.Nyss.*Cant.*13
(Jaeger 6:394)

Gr.Naz.*Or.*4.60
(SC 307:166–68)

Gr.Naz.*Or.*25.1
(SC 284:156)
Gr.Nyss.*V.Mos.*2
(Jaeger 7–I:138)

Christian ethical style was a "philosophical way of life [tropos philosophos]," which meant here "the sum total of ethical values." In this sense, philosophy was identical with the knowledge of God: "philosophia te kai theognōsia." And when the authentic cosmology or "cosmogony," which was that of Moses in the Book of Genesis, was faithfully expounded, as it had been by Basil in his commentary, the result was nothing less than "the sublime philosophy [hē hypsēlē philosophia]." In the church, according to Gregory of Nyssa addressing himself to the heretic Eunomius, there were "thousands endowed with the divine gift of *sophia*" as philosophical skill. According to Gregory of Nazianzus addressing himself to the emperor Julian, these Christians, many of them common people or even monks, were philosophically superior to Plato and Aristotle. For it was characteristic of this Christian philosophy, by contrast with the antireligious or even atheistic philosophy and natural theology of Classical thinkers, that it could be accommodated to the faith and understanding of simple believers. Such believers were now capable of becoming "wise" in the fullest and truest sense of the word.

Used in this sense, "philosophia" could stand for "the full range" and scope of divine revelation. Since *sophia* could be either "theoretical" or "practical," as Aristotle had recognized, Christian philosophia could participate in the nature of *sophia* by being either practical or theoretical: it could be either a philosophy "in thoughts and words [peri logous]" or a philosophy "pertaining to morality [dia tōn ēthōn]." As theoretical philosophy, it was contemplative. Within the oeuvre of the Cappadocians, one of the masterpieces of this contemplative "philosophia" was the *Accurate Exposition of the Song of Songs* [Exēgēsis akribēs eis to Aisma tōn Aismatōn] by Gregory of Nyssa. In the preface to that commentary he took it as his assignment to make manifest "the philosophy secretly concealed in its speeches [tēn enkekrummenēn tois rētois philosophian]." He spoke almost matter-of-factly about "the philosophy of the Song of Songs [hē tou Aismatos tōn Aismatōn philosophia]." As the writer of the Song of Songs, Solomon was presenting "philosophia" also in his other books, among which the Wisdom of Solomon was a special favorite of the Cappadocians, its thirteenth chapter being a source and summary of their cosmology. The Book of Ecclesiastes was another compendium of the *sophia* of Israel's philosopher-king. Because part of the "philosophia" of Ecclesiastes was the admo-

Eccl 5:1
Gr.Nyss.*Eun.*2.93–94
(Jaeger 1:254)

Gr.Nyss.*V.Mos.*2
(Jaeger 7–I:99)

Gr.Naz.*Or.*2.78
(SC 247:192)

See pp.90–106
Serra 1955,337–74
Fox 1939,137–40;
Giet 1941a,183–216
Janini Cuesta 1947,
352–62

Gr.Nyss.*Virg.*23
(Jaeger 8–I:333)

Jb 39:5–11

Gr.Naz.*Or.*26.13
(SC 284:256)

Gr.Nyss.*V.Macr.*
(Jaeger 8–I:371)

Gr.Naz.*Or.*43.13
(PG 36:512)

Gr.Nyss.*V.Macr.*
(Jaeger 8–I:377)

nition, "God is in heaven and you are on earth, so let your words be few," the Solomonic philosophy was seen as one of *apophatic* restraint. By the time the Cappadocians had worked out their reinterpretation of "philosophia," they were also willing to reverse the polarity of the theoretical and the practical, paying special attention to "the philosophical way of life [hē philosophos diagōgē]" exemplified by Moses. When Gregory of Nazianzus wrote, "One branch of philosophy is too high for me," he explained that he was talking not about contemplation or speculation but about "the commission to guide and govern souls." "Philosophia" here referred, therefore, not to the natural philosophy of science and cosmology, nor even to metaphysics (about both of which the Cappadocians made critical comments), but to pastoral care, to which Gregory of Nazianzus was speaking in this passage, but with which Basil—both as bishop of Caesarea and as monastic founder—and Gregory of Nyssa as well all dealt in their writings and careers.

"Philosophia" in this practical sense applied above all to the practice of Christian discipline, especially the ascetic disciplines of virginity and temperance. Celebrating its heroism with alpha privatives, Gregory of Nazianzus exclaimed: "Nothing is more unassailable than philosophy, nothing more incomprehensible!" The Book of Job praised such animals as the wild ass and the unicorn for their freedom from restraint, but they were symbolic. For to the two beings that were truly "beyond being governed [dyskratēta]," namely, God and angel, there had to be added "a third, the philosopher—nonmaterial within matter, uncircumscribed within a body, heavenly while upon earth, possessing *apatheia* within passions [aÿlos en hylēi, en sōmati aperigraptos, epi gēs ouranios, en pathesin apathēs]." Macrina had managed heroically "by this kind of philosophy to raise herself to the greatest height of human *arete*." It was to this practical discipline of "philosophia" that Basil had come after passing through rhetoric. As Gregory of Nazianzus explained, "His purpose was 'philosophia,' and breaking from the world, and fellowship with God, by concerning himself, amid things below, with things above, and winning, where all is unstable and fluctuating, the things that are stable and that abide." Although he had been "puffed up beyond measure with the pride of oratory," Basil was led by Macrina "toward the mark of philosophia." Now that he was set free, therefore, Basil was in a position to characterize "philosophia" as the force that could "free our souls, as from a

prison, from association with the passions [pathē] of the body";
and he said so, moreover, specifically in his treatise commending
the study of Classical literature. It was above all the monks
among the Christians who, as "philosophers," were superior to
all Greek philosophers.

Because the traditional distinction between theoretical and
practical philosophy was in this sense transcended in Cappadocian thought, "philosophia" in both senses could become a synonym for "theology." Gregory of Nazianzus could position "philosophia" as the middle member between speculative thought
and ascetic discipline in a series of rhetorical questions attacking
the doctrines of *ananke* and deterministic necessity: "Is then the
ruling mind nothing? Nothing the labor? Nothing the reasoning?
Nothing the 'philosophia'? Nothing the fasting? Nothing the
vigils, the sleeping on the ground, the shedding of floods of
tears?" For in orthodox Christian theology, "exactness of doctrines" (theoretical "philosophia") and "the distinctive character
of customs and sacramental tokens" (practical "philosophia")
were inseparable, as the Cappadocians had to contend in opposition both to pagan critics and to Christian heretics. The message
that the Song of Songs conveyed, therefore, was "great and sublime dogmas [megala te kai hypsēla dogmata]," and this "philosophia" was "the bride's story." Thus the Song of Songs equated
"philosophia" with "dogma," and both of them with Scripture.
That use of "philosophia" explains why Gregory of Nazianzus
could claim that the inhabitants of Constantinople "whether
philosophers or simple folk," now that it had become orthodox
again after being freed from both heretical and neopagan domi-
nation, were "alike wise in divine things." That was also why he
could feel justified in speaking this way: "In the former discourse
we laid down clearly with respect to the theologian, both what
sort of character he ought to bear, and on what kind of subject he
may philosophize, and when, and to what extent." In other
words, his discourse had expounded both practical and theoretical "philosophia" as it was practiced by the Christian theologian.
And therefore, when, in that previous discourse to which he was
referring, he discussed "to peri theou philosophein," this did
mean, literally translated, "to philosophize about God"; but the
most recent translators of the oration into English were quite
right to render it as "discussion of theology."

Yet there remained the question, which was none the less demanding for being so often overlooked: Now that "philosophia"
could mean theology—theology as orthodox, dogmatic, Christian

Bas.*Leg.lib.gent*.9
(Wilson 30–31)

Gr.Naz.Or.4.73
(SC 309:188)

Špidlík 1976,358–64

See pp.155–58

Gr.Naz.Or.37.14
(SC 318:302)

Gr.Nyss.*Eun*.3.9.54
(Jaeger 2:284)

Gr.Nyss.*Cant*.6
(Jaeger 6:172–73)
Gr.Nyss.*Cant*.11;15
(Jaeger 6:333;457)

Gr.Naz.Or.42.11
(PG 36:472)

Gr.Naz.Or.28.1
(SC 250:100)

Gr.Naz.Or.27.3
(SC 250:76)

Guignet 1911,43–70

theology—what happened to "philosophia" as philosophy—philosophy as Classical, "profane," natural theology—within the systems of the theologians of the church? To address that question, the discussion that follows here in the remaining chapters of Part II under the general title "Natural Theology as Presupposition" will examine some of the central affirmations of Christian orthodoxy as these were affirmed, defended, and developed by the Cappadocians in the course of the fourth century, with a view to identifying the continuing contributions being made to that exposition of revealed theology by the natural theology that they articulated in their apologetics.

CHAPTER 12

Natural Theology as Presupposition

Whitehead 1948,49–50

"When you are criticizing the philosophy of an epoch," Alfred North Whitehead (Gifford Lecturer at Edinburgh in 1927–1928) once warned, "do not chiefly direct your attention to those intellectual positions which its exponents feel it necessary explicitly to defend. There will be some fundamental assumptions which adherents of all the variant systems within the epoch unconsciously presuppose. Such assumptions appear so obvious that people do not know what they are assuming because no other way of putting things has ever occurred to them. With these assumptions a certain limited number of types of philosophic systems are possible, and this group of systems constitutes the philosophy of the epoch." This is no less true of "the theology of the epoch" than of its philosophy, and no less true of its "natural theology" than of its "revealed theology."

Gr.Nyss.Eun.1.186
(Jaeger 1:81)
Gr.Nyss.Apoll.
(Jaeger 3–1:188)

Upon the establishment of the hegemony of Christian theology over Classical culture, the debating points of natural theology being scored by Christian apologetics against pagan thought—whether they were logical or moral or metaphysical or theological or rhetorical, or several of these at once—did not all disappear with the pagan systems against which they had been directed, but some of them continued to function as presuppositions, and often as, in Whitehead's words, "fundamental assumptions which adherents of all the variant systems within the epoch unconsciously presuppose." The several "variant systems" in this case were: the variant schools of pagan philosophy; the variant brands of Christian heresy; and the variant emphases

Gr.Naz.Or.21.34
(SC 270:184)

that, taken together, came to be defined as Christian ortho-doxy. Because of the place of these fundamental assumptions in the dogma of the fourth century and in the dogmatic theology of the Cappadocians, they assumed a position of historical domi-nance for all the subsequent centuries of the history of the church, up to and including the twentieth century. The controversy be-tween Augustine and the Pelagians, the dogmatic debates be-tween the Greek East and the Latin West, the doctrinal pluralism of the later Middle Ages, the division of Western Christendom during the age of the Reformation, the upheavals brought on by the Enlightenment and by theological liberalism, the efforts in the ecumenical movement to address these problems—through these historic changes and many others, these "fundamental assump-tions which adherents of all the variant systems within the epoch unconsciously presuppose" continued their authoritative hold.

Now if, as Part II of this book is seeking to show, the Cappado-cians transmitted, as part of their doctrinal patrimony to the inheritors of Nicene orthodoxy during the following millennium and more, some "fundamental assumptions" that were rooted in natural theology, at least two far-reaching implications appear to follow, one chiefly historiographical and the other primarily philosophical-theological. The implication for what Georges

Florovsky 2:31–65

Florovsky called "the predicament of the Christian historian" is that, to an extent that is sometimes ignored by those scholars who concentrate exclusively on one region or on one period of history, all students of the ideas and institutions of the Christian church in any period need to obtain a significant command of these early developments in order to understand their own fields of scholarly concentration. The other implication is that the Co-pernican revolution in these presuppositions, which has been precipitated in some measure by modern philosophy and modern science, confronts the Christian thought of the nineteenth and twentieth centuries, for the first time on any such scale since late antiquity, with a natural theology in which such fundamental assumptions as divine transcendence, human immortality, and cosmic teleology may no longer be taken for granted, as they were by the Cappadocians and by their successors in East and West for

Buckley 1987,337–62

more than a thousand years. The consequences of this change run through most of post-Enlightenment theology and philosophy. Thus, some such review of the Nicene orthodoxy articulated by the Cappadocians would appear to be a presupposition for re-sponsible thought in systematic or philosophical theology in the present day.

Bernardi 1968,352–61

Just as that modern change of presuppositions was associated at least in part with a transformation in the audience to which theology, especially natural theology, was being addressed, so the continuities as well as the discontinuities between Cappadocian natural theology as apologetics and Cappadocian natural theology as presupposition were rooted at least in part in the shift of audience brought about by the revolutionary political, ecclesiastical, and cultural events of the fourth century, as these have been described in the preceding chapter. Nazianzen's warning of "discussion of theology not being for everyone . . . nor for every occasion or every audience" becomes all the more relevant to this issue when it is realized that, as has already been pointed out, the Greek phrase translated here by Wickham and Williams as "discussion of theology" was in fact "to peri theou philosophein." When Basil said that he was "leaving the vanity of outsiders to those on the outside, and returning to the message of the church [epi ton ekklēsiastikon logon]," he seems to have had some such shift of audience in mind. For he explained elsewhere that in the rhetoric of the apologetic situation, "addressed to the audience of the Greeks," there was less of a "necessity to be utterly precise about phraseology [ouch chrēnai akribologeisthai peri ta rēmata]," but it was permissible "to make concessions to the character of the hearer being persuaded" in the apologetic. Nevertheless, he insisted, this did not justify the use of a similarly imprecise phraseology in such a way as to "give great support to the heretics," an audience with whom it became necessary for the orthodox Christian theologian to observe a far greater strictness and nicety of theological language. A sensitivity to the problem of audience led as well to the observation that when it was dealing with Greek polytheism Christian apologetics needed arguments that were quite divergent from those it employed in dealing with Jewish monotheism, even though the presuppositions both of Judaism and of Hellenism led to a rejection of the orthodox Christian identification of Christ, the Son of God, as "the only-begotten God."

See p.182

Gr.Naz.Or.27.3
(SC 250:76)

Bas.Hex.3.3
(SC 26:202)

Bas.Ep.210.5
(Courtonne 2:195)

Jn 1:18;see pp.224–25
Gr.Nyss.Or.catech.pr.3
(Méridier 2–4)

Gr.Naz.Or.42.16
(PG 36:476)

Gr.Nyss.Eun.3.6.26
(Jaeger 2:195)
Gr.Nyss.Cant.13
(Jaeger 6:398)

Between Hellenism and Judaism, as also between various heretical forms of Christianity, then, orthodoxy represented for the Cappadocians "the royal road between the two extremes." The intellectual enterprise in which all of them were engaged both in apologetics and in dogmatics may be interpreted as the effort to find the forms and formulas "of the orthodox mode of thought [tēs eusebous dianoias]." It was based upon a "certainty about the divine teachings [ta theia didagmata]." It was based also on the recognition that different presuppositions could lead to different dogmatic emphases, depending upon what was perceived to be the primary danger. "Are you afraid to speak of 'begetting [gennēsis]' within the Godhead, lest you attribute anything like passion to the God of *apatheia*?" Gregory of Nazianzus asked his heretical opponents, continuing with this admission: "For my part, what I am afraid of is speaking about 'creating' within the Godhead, lest I destroy [the true doctrine of] God by the insult and the untrue division, cutting the Son away from the Father or cutting the *ousia* of the Spirit away from the Son." For despite Basil's apparently clear and simple distinction between "the message of the church" and the thought of "those on the outside," the Cappadocian method of relating these two to each other, not least in his own version of what his brother Gregory called "the orthodox mode of thought," was one not of excluding the second in the name of the first but of comprehending both within the orthodox system. Gregory of Nyssa identified "two ways of joining man to God," true doctrine and clear reasoning, both of which came from God and each of which needed the other to be complete. As he urged later in the commentary, the use of reason as a path to knowledge could serve to confirm the truth of faith. In short, as Gregory of Nazianzus put it, "Some truths are knowable by faith alone [tina men tēi pistei doteon monēi], some also by reasoning [tina de kai tois logismois]." For example, Greeks on the basis of their innate ideas and Jews on the basis of their Bible would accept the doctrines of the divine *Logos* and of the Spirit of God, but both would "equally reject the *economy* by which the divine *Logos* became man," because that depended on the authority of faith alone.

Although such statements as Basil's, about "leaving the vanity of outsiders to those on the outside, and returning to the message of the church" could give the impression that the truth of the gospel made any further attention to philosophy and natural theology unnecessary, he was obliged to hear—and, in his own way, to confirm by his theological practice—the reminder that came to him in the portentous warning of a leading spokesman for Hellenism, his pagan colleague (and perhaps his teacher) Libanius of Antioch: "Keep to the books [of the Bible], which you say are inferior in style, though better in sense. No one is stopping you. But of the principles that were ever mine, and that once were yours, the roots both remain and will remain, as long as you exist. Though you water them ever so little, no length of time will ever completely destroy them." In a familiar metaphor, Gregory of

Gr.Naz.*Or*.40.42
(*PG* 36:417–20)

Bas.*Hex*.3.3
(*SC* 26:202)

Gr.Nyss.*Eun*.3.6.26
(Jaeger 2:195)

Gr.Nyss.*Cant*.13
(Jaeger 6:376)
Gr.Nyss.*Cant*.15
(Jaeger 6:460)

Gr.Naz.*Or*.22.11
(*SC* 270:242)

See pp.263–64,252–53

Gr.Nyss.*Or.catech*.5.1
(Méridier 22)

Bas.*Hex*.3.3
(*SC* 26:202)

See pp.10–11

Lib.ap.Bas.*Ep*.340
(Courtonne 3:208)

Ex 12:35–36
Gr.Nyss.V.Mos.2
(Jaeger 7–I:68)

Gr.Nyss.V.Mos.2
(Jaeger 7–I:68)

Gr.Nyss.V.Mos.2
(Jaeger 7–I:37)

Gr.Nyss.Eun.1.186
(Jaeger 1:81)

Bas.Hex.3.4
(SC 26:210)

Pl.Tim.92c

Gn 1:6–7

Gr.Naz.Or.27.3
(SC 250:76)
Gr.Nyss.Cant.13
(Jaeger 6:376)

Lenz 1925,105–19
Gr.Nyss.Apoll.
(Jaeger 3–I:188)

Gr.Nyss.Eun.2.50
(Jaeger 1:240)

Nyssa justified such a use of Hellenism on the basis of the command of God to the Israelites at the Exodus to take with them the gold of the Egyptians as reparations. In the same way, those who had received and achieved "the life of freedom through *arete*" in the church could appropriate "the riches of Classical *paideusis*" that previously had belonged to the Greeks, including "ethics, natural science, geometry, astronomy, and logic." He endorsed, therefore, the combination of profane learning and sacred learning. He coordinated—and in this order—three sources of knowledge: "those who philosophized outside the faith [tōn exō tēs pisteōs pephilosophēkontōn]"; "the inspired sayings [tais theopneustasi phōnais]" of Scripture; and "the common apprehension of mankind [tais koinais ennoiais]." In keeping with that principle of coordination, his brother Basil also linked Plato's *Timaeus* and the Book of Genesis to provide "clear proofs of the only-begotten one [monogenēs]," as this "only-begotten one [monogenēs]" had been spoken of in *Timaeus* explicitly and only implicitly in Genesis (rather than the other way around, as might have been supposed). Indeed, when Gregory of Nazianzus discussed "to peri theou philosophein," he not only laid claim to it as an activity that was permissible for believers but went so far as to insist: "It is permitted only to those who have been examined, and are past masters in meditation, and have been previously purified, or at least are in the process of being purified."

As the coupling of the two cases in their polemics suggested, the Cappadocians' consideration of the Christian case against Greek philosophy had much in common with their presentation of the orthodox case against heresy. That was particularly true of their use of natural theology as presupposition. There were also, of course, presuppositions in their arguments against heresy, for example against Apollinaris on the humanity of Christ, that were specifically and exclusively Christian. Thus Gregory of Nyssa, writing against Eunomius, declared: "The tenet which has been held in common [dogma koinon] by all who have received the word of our religion is that all hope of salvation should be placed in Christ, it being impossible for anyone to be found among the righteous unless faith in Christ supplies what is desired." Here he would seem to have been attributing this "dogma" not alone to himself and his orthodox colleagues, but even to the heretics he was attacking. The difference, he seemed to be arguing, was that the orthodox drew the correct trinitarian and christological conclusions from this shared Christian presupposition while the heretics did not. At other points in the polemic against Eunomius, however, the presuppositions with which Gregory of Nyssa dealt were based at least in part on natural theology. Thus, Eunomius and his disciples were "arguing on the grounds of the nature of the Father as having remained pure in its *apatheia*" also after the incarnation—grounds that were shared by the orthodox, the heretics, and the philosophers at their best—when they separated the Son from the Father ontologically, in order to be able to predicate of the Son that he underwent the humiliation of the cross: the one who was crucified could not be metaphysically of the same being as the God of *apatheia*. Yet, from these same grounds, Gregory insisted in his later *Refutation* against Eunomius, it was possible to argue in such a way as to validate the orthodox doctrine. His first premise seems to have come also from natural theology: "Deity by its very nature is permanently and immutably the same in all that pertains to its *ousia*, nor did it at any time fail to be anything that it now is, nor will it at any future time be anything that it now is not." The second premise came from revealed theology: "He who is the very Father is named 'Father' by the *Logos*, and in the name 'Father' the Son is implied." From the combination of these two premises Gregory of Nyssa concluded: "Since [both of] these things are so, we of necessity believe that [God], who admits no change or alteration in his nature, always was entirely what he is now"—namely, both Father and Son in the Trinity, as confessed by the orthodox faith.

See pp.202–3

Gr.Nyss.*Eun*.3.3.38
(Jaeger 2:120–21)

Gr.Nyss.*Ref*.7
(Jaeger 2:315)

The a priori doctrinal status of that major premise of divine *apatheia* and unchangeability received explicit attention from all the Cappadocians. Basil addressed and refuted a heretical position that held "that God himself was turned into flesh, that he did not assume, through Saint Mary, the nature of Adam, but, in his own proper Godhead, was changed into a material nature." Finding this to be at one and the same time "an absurd position" in relation to both natural and revealed theology and a "blasphemous" one in relation specifically to revelation, Basil refuted it with the familiar proof text from Malachi: "I am the Lord your God, and I do not change [egō kyrios ho theos hymōn, kai ouk ēlloiōmai]." Similarly, Gregory of Nazianzus, explaining what was implied by the statement, "The Son of God deigns to become and to be called Son of man," ruled out of consideration any possibility that the Son of God had changed what he was; and he took this stance on the grounds that the divine nature was unchangeable. What he taught instead was: "He assumes what he was not, for he is full of love to humanity." In contrast, Gregory of Nyssa, while setting forth the argumentation just cited on the

Graef 1963–65,1:62–68

Mal 3:6

Bas.*Ep*.262.1–2
(Courtonne 3:119–20)

Gr.Naz.*Or*.39.13
(PG 36:348–49)

Ps 76:11

basis of the premise of *apatheia* and unchangeability, had found a
text in the Bible containing this phrase: "The very change of the
right hand of the Most High [autē hē alloiōsis tēs dexias tou
hypsistou]." But he took this to be speaking about "the condescension [of the *Logos*] to the weakness of human nature, to our
pattern and image," rather than about any ontological change in
the divine nature, which would have been unthinkable either

Gr.Nyss.*V.Mos.*2
(Jaeger 7–I:41)

according to revelation or according to sound reason. The presupposition held, and it had to hold.

Gr.Nyss.*Infant.*
(Jaeger 3–II:67–79)
Schoemann 1943,178–
82; Dörrie et al. 1976,
79–82

In a short treatise that he seems to have composed late in his
life, in the 390s, entitled *On the Early Deaths of Infants*, Gregory
of Nyssa strikingly illustrated how he, and with him the other
Cappadocians, could, as theologians of the church, work on the

Malunowiczówna
1975,35–45;
Gregg 1975,219–64

basis of presuppositions, including the presuppositions of natural
theology, in providing "consolation." The issue to which he addressed the treatise was a religious crisis for his audience and a
pastoral challenge for him as a Christian bishop, and he repeatedly demonstrated his deep compassion for the numbing anguish
of parents who suddenly had to confront the questions of why
they had lost a young child and of how a loving God could have
allowed something like this to happen. Although Gregory's
brother Basil, writing in about 358 to a friend who had lost a son,

Bas.*Ep.*5
(Courtonne 1:16–18)

had likewise blended consolations from Scripture with those
from reason to comfort him, Gregory's treatise, though also topi-
cal in its immediate inspiration, approached the consolations far
more systematically. For to deal with the pastoral problem, he
first moved the entire consideration back to presuppositions and
first principles, turning it into a discourse on the nature of God,
the doctrine of angels, and the other components of his philosophical theology. Only after delivering such a discourse did he
declare: "Now that we have laid down these premises [toutōn
toinyn houtōs hēmin dieipēmenōn], it is time to examine in the

Gr.Nyss.*Infant.*
(Jaeger 3–II:81)

light of them the question proposed to us," about children who
died in infancy. Even after that, he continued to appeal, within
one paragraph, to several quite discrete sources of consolation:
the wonders of the universe, which provided "power for the enjoyment of those delights beyond"; "the studies sharpening the
mind toward moral excellence," such as geometry, astronomy,
"and every other method of furnishing a proof of the unknown
and a conviction of the known"; and finally, "before all these, the

Gr.Nyss.*Infant.*
(Jaeger 3–II:86)

'philosophia' contained in the inspired Scripture, providing a
complete purification for the initiates into the mysteries of God."

The sequence of those three sources of consolation—the first two of which belonged to natural theology, either in the sense of a theology derived from the contemplation of nature or in the sense of a perspective on natural theology derived from human science and thought, and only the third of which came strictly and exclusively from biblical revelation, with even this being identified, as

See pp.179–80

so often in Cappadocian usage, as "philosophia"—raised one question with particular acuteness: Would either the natural theology or the orthodox dogmatics of the Cappadocians have looked decisively different if "before all these [pro toutōn]," the phrase with which he introduced his reference to the third source of consolation, which was the authority of inspired Scripture, meant not only pride of place, but systematic and even chronological priority? As later chapters will suggest, when the Cappadocians interpreted God, the world, and man as topics in orthodox dogmatics, they could and did presuppose, as obvious assumptions, some views of God, the world, and man that had come to them from their heritage in Classical culture. Clearly they claimed to be ascribing authoritative priority to scriptural teaching. In the doctrine of God, they declared, the incarnation of

Gr.Nyss.*Cant.*13
(Jaeger 6:381)

the *Logos* came not to supplement but to correct all existing presuppositions about the divine nature. In the doctrine of immortality, Gregory of Nyssa acknowledged that Macrina's philosophical "exposition, advancing as it did in this consecutive manner," was convincing on purely natural grounds. But then he immediately went on to identify Scripture as "more trustworthy than any of these artificial conclusions"; and therefore he de-

Gr.Nyss.*Anim.res.*
(PG 46:64)

manded of her: "It is necessary to inquire, in addition to what has been said, whether this inspired teaching harmonizes with it all." It came as no surprise to anyone that it did harmonize; nevertheless it is appropriate to ask at this point—but to begin to answer, if at all, only after the several doctrines of Christian dogmatics have been examined in detail—not only what Macrina and Gregory would have said if it had not harmonized, but especially whether, and in what specific respects, her presentation of "this inspired teaching" on the soul showed the marks of its having presupposed the "consecutive exposition" of the natural doctrine of the rational and immortal soul. In the incarnation Christ was

Gr.Nyss.*V.Mos.*
(Jaeger 7–I:41)
Gr.Nyss.*Eun.*3.1.93
(Jaeger 2:35)

Heb 4:15

said to have conformed "to our pattern and image [pros to hēmeteron schēma te kai eidos]," so that as a result "the whole compound nature of man was in him," yet with the exception stated in the New Testament, that he remained "without sin." From this it might have seemed to follow that the most reliable index to the content of the "image" in the nature of man was the humanity of Christ, and that therefore it was possible to read off from the humanity of the incarnate *Logos* what had been meant by the original "image of God"; but that was not in fact the exclusive method that the Cappadocians followed in their anthropology, for they combined it with other presuppositions about the definition of essential humanity.

See pp.120–35

Yet, the important consideration historically is not how such presuppositions might conceivably have functioned in the dogmatics of the Cappadocians, but how in fact they did function there. All four were agreed that sound theology was impossible without careful attention to establishing first principles and moving from these to valid conclusions. "We are not entitled to the license of affirming what we please," Macrina declared; and she attacked her opponents for positing a "fundamental conception [hyponoia]" that could not "stand secure on every side." Gregory of Nazianzus denounced theological faddishness, which he described as "following the temper of the times, at one time being of one mind and of another at another time, and thinking unsoundly in the highest matters." The sound alternative to such a trend was to specify presuppositions and then to move from these to correct conclusions. Invoking the concept of *stoicheia*, which he and the other Cappadocians sometimes used as a technical scientific term for the four basic elements of earth, air, fire, and water, Basil also used it for the relation of the "elements" in the sense of the ABCs and presuppositions of a craft to the achievement of a mature faith and understanding, thus for what in English would be called "elementary" as well as for what would be called "elemental." As the most profound and speculative of them all, Gregory of Nyssa was also the most explicit about the place of presuppositions in a theological system. Criticizing Eunomius "for not using the recognized methods for establishing his views," he asserted this methodological axiom: "All such arguing must start from plain and well-known truths, to compel belief through itself in truths that are still doubtful; and none of these latter can be grasped without the guidance of what is obvious leading us towards the unknown. If, on the other hand, that which is adopted to start with for the illustration of this unknown is at variance with universal belief, it will be a long time before the unknown will receive any illumination from it." Toward the end of the treatise against Eunomius, he reaffirmed this axiom about first principles, as "demanding from one's opponents to begin by

Macr.ap.Gr.Nyss.
Anim.res. (PG 46:49)
Gr.Naz.Or.31.28
(SC 250:330–32)

See pp.174–75

Gr.Naz.Or.28.14
(SC 250:128);

Bas.Ep.8.2
(Courtonne 1:24)

Bas.Spir.1.2
(SC 17:254)

Gr.Nyss.Eun.1.217–19
(Jaeger 1:90)

establishing upon some incontrovertible basis the first principles of their argument and then to proceed to press their theory by inferences." He concluded: "So long as first principles remain unproved, it is idle to dwell on those that are secondary."

One species of "fallacy" that heretics sometimes employed in the use of presuppositions was to "lay down such premises as might naturally lead the mind of the hearers in the desired direction," and then, with these misleading presuppositions in place as an a priori, to leave it to the hearers to draw their erroneous conclusions for themselves. From a mistaken "presupposition [hypolēpsis]" heresy could proceed "by logical consequence [ek tou akolouthou]" to the conclusion of its false doctrine. For example, the pagan and heretical doctrine of metempsychosis, or the transmigration of souls, was based on the erroneous presupposition of the preexistence of souls, "with the *arche* of such a doctrine leading the argument on by logical consequence [di' akolouthou] to the next and adjacent stage." Again, there was the false presupposition: "Passion is absolutely linked with 'begetting [gennēsis].'" This was juxtaposed with the valid presupposition: "The divine nature must continue in purity beyond the reach of passion." That syllogism led to the heretical teaching: "The Son is alien to the idea of 'begetting.'" In fact, however, "admitted facts," such as the doctrine of baptismal regeneration, demonstrated that there could be a "begetting" without passion. Another such false presupposition with trinitarian implications was this seemingly self-evident proposition: "Things of one *ousia* are counted together, but those that are not *homoousios* are reckoned one by one." From this it seemed to follow that Father, Son, and Holy Spirit, being counted one by one, could not be of the same *ousia*. But the presupposition was false, Gregory of Nazianzus maintained, because it was the function of number only to "express the quantity of everything included under it, and not the nature of the things" one way or the other. Thus, it was often the case with heretical teaching that those who held to it were "compelled to it by their premises." The same was true of all teaching, including orthodox teaching; but in orthodoxy, according to the Cappadocians, the premises were valid and therefore the conclusions were valid, whereas in the systems of the heretics, sound and universally valid presuppositions were themselves being questioned. The end result of such a process was expressed by Basil in the observation: "Undeniable things have become uncertain things [amphibola gegone ta anantirrēta]!"

Gr.Nyss.*Eun*.3.2.90
(Jaeger 2:82)
Gr.Nyss.*Eun*.3.2.97
(Jaeger 2:84)

Gr.Nyss.*Eun*.2.56
(Jaeger 1:242)

Gr.Nyss.*Maced.*
(Jaeger 3–I:90)

Rebecchi 1943,322–25

Gr.Nyss.*Hom.opif*.28
(PG 44:232)

Gr.Nyss.*Eun*.3.2.58
(Jaeger 2:71–72)

Gr.Naz.*Or*.31.18
(SC 250:308–10)

Gr.Nyss.*Eun*.2.83
(Jaeger 1:251)

Bas.*Spir*.28.70
(SC 17:496)

The heretical systems also illustrated that it was possible, while holding to valid presuppositions, to draw false conclusions from them, perhaps because they had been negated or distorted by other invalid presuppositions. The confession of God as Maker was an a priori presupposition on which all of Christian thought, but also the best of Classical thought, could agree. But Gregory of Nyssa addressed the presupposition of such a confession with this argument: "If eternity was not included in this confession, and if a foolishly conceived idea curtailed and checked retrospectively our conception of the Father, true Fatherhood could no longer be predicated of him, because that preconceived idea about the Son would cancel the continuity and eternity of his Fatherhood." The presupposition, "The divine nature, whatever it is believed to be, always remains the same, being above all augmentation and being as well incapable of diminution," was a valid and universal teaching both of natural theology and of revealed theology; but it was invalid to draw from it the conclusion that when change or augmentation was predicated of the Son of God in the language of Scripture and the church, this had to make his divine nature metaphysically different from that of the Father. Natural theology could yield, as conclusions that could in turn serve as presuppositions, a doctrine of the immortality of the soul, an affirmation of the existence of God, a recognition of God as Creator, and the admission that God was good and powerful. But "philosophical and heretical" error constructed on each of these four sound presuppositions a corresponding false conclusion—namely, the transmigration of souls, the materiality of the divine nature, the coexistence and coeternity of matter, and "the *ananke* of *heimarmene*." Thus, although "the conception of the divine, by nature [automatōs] inherent in all men," was a valid presupposition of natural theology on which to build a philosophical and religious system, it was no less the case that ignorance of the true God was "responsible for the gross errors in regard to the object of worship," because the errorists, "by swerving a little from the truth, opened the door to impiety," thereby undoing their valid presupposition.

For underlying these several fallacies was a failure to recognize that the presuppositions of natural theology, even when they were valid and universal or "useful [chrēsimon]," remained inadequate for the correct knowledge of God. According to Gregory of Nyssa, the ultimate assumption and "standard of truth" underlying the use of presuppositions from philosophy and natural theology in the system of Eunomius was "the concurrence of the so-

Gr.Nyss.*Or.catech.*5.3
(Méridier 24–26)

Gr.Nyss.*Eun.*1.591
(Jaeger 1:196)

Acts 2:36

Gr.Nyss.*Eun.*3.4.62
(Jaeger 1:158)

Gr.Nyss.*Cant.*13
(Jaeger 6:376)

Gr.Nyss.*V.Mos.*2
(Jaeger 7–I:44)

Gr.Nyss.*Beat.*5
(*PG* 44:1249)

Bas.*Leg.lib.gent.*1
(Wilson 20)

Gr.Nyss.*Eun.*3.1.6
(Jaeger 2:5)

called natural order with the testimony of the knowledge given from above, confirming the natural interpretation." The answer of the Cappadocians to that Eunomian assumption was not to deny the existence of such a "natural order" and natural theology at all, but to affirm it within its proper sphere and to recognize its capacities, yet at the same time to take the position that "the knowledge given from above," as Eunomius called it, not only confirmed the natural interpretation, as he claimed, but corrected, supplemented, and transcended it. What might have been sufficient for natural theology as apologetics was insufficient for

Bas.*Ep.*210.5
(Courtonne 2:195)

natural theology as presupposition in church dogmatics. As apologetics, natural theology, relying upon the twofold testimony that came from "our very eyes" and from "the law of nature," drew the conclusion of the existence of God as "the efficient and maintaining cause of all things," a conclusion that ought to have been evident to anyone who was not "wanting in sense." But not even this argument from design, according to Gregory of

Gr.Naz.*Or.*28.6
(SC 250:110–12)

Nazianzus, provided an adequate presupposition to affirm the reality of divine transcendence. Ultimately, the only way to deal with divine transcendence was not simply to affirm, but to affirm

See pp.200–214

by means of *apophasis*. When it was pressed into service to do what it was not equipped to do—above all, to treat, in the doctrine of God, not the relation between the One and the many in an apologetic proof of monotheism, but the relation between the One and the Three in the revealed doctrine of the Trinity—nature was "not trustworthy for instruction about 'begetting' applied to the divine, not even by taking the universe itself as an illustration of the argument," because any begetting or other activity in the

Gr.Nyss.*Eun.*3.7.34
(Jaeger 2:227)

universe had to be temporal, not eternal as the divine "begetting" was.

For all four of the Cappadocians, Nicene orthodoxy presented itself as a system that was simultaneously "congruous" with the

Gr.Nyss.*Or.catech.*15
(Méridier 78–82)

presuppositions of natural theology and "consistent" with those of revealed theology—indeed, as the only system that was in a position to make that twofold claim. Macrina set forth her doctrine of demons "both on the basis of the shared presupposition and on the basis of the tradition of the Scriptures [ek te tēs koinēs

Macr.ap.Gr.Nyss.
Anim.res. (PG 46:72)

hypolēpseōs kai ek tēs tōn graphōn paradoseōs]." Her brother Basil of Caesarea, having announced his methodology as one in which "our common conceptions concerning spirit/Spirit" were correlated with "those gathered from Holy Scripture" and with

Bas.*Spir.*9.22
(SC 17:322)

"those received from the unwritten tradition of the fathers," went on to argue for what he regarded as the orthodox doctrine

Bas.*Spir.*16.4
(*SC* 17:386)

Gr.Nyss.*Eun.*1.315
(Jaeger 1:120)

Gr.Naz.*Or.*29.2
(*SC* 250:224)

Eun.ap.Bas.*Eun.*1.5
(*SC* 299:170)
Eun.ap.Gr.Nyss.*Eun.*
3.7.26 (Jaeger 2:224)

Gr.Naz.*Or.*29.16–17
(*SC* 250:212)

Gr.Nyss.*Eun.*1.530
(Jaeger 1:179)

Bas.*Ep.*235.1
(Courtonne 3:44 [var.])

See pp.263–79

Gr.Nyss.*Or.catech.*20.1
(Méridier 98)

Asmus 1894,325
See pp.136–51

Gr.Nyss.*V.Mos.*2
(Jaeger 7–I:43)

Jaeger 1948,117–18

Gr.Nyss.*Apoll.*
(Jaeger 3–I:198)

of the Holy Spirit in the Trinity by appealing to "any careful user of reason [tis akribōs logizomenos]." Her other brother Gregory of Nyssa also spoke about "our reason, under the guidance of the Scripture" as the instrument for theological thinking. The other Gregory, too, argued for "faith as the fulfillment of our reasoning." On the other hand, although Eunomius claimed to be teaching "in accordance with natural knowledge and in accordance with the doctrine of the fathers [kata te physikēn ennoian kai kata tēn tōn paterōn didaskalian]," and to be deriving his views "from nature itself and also from the divine laws," Cappadocian polemic against him and against other heretics found them in fact to be delinquent on both scores.

Thus, according to Gregory of Nyssa, "Anyone who keeps steadfast to the sound doctrine and believes that the Son is of the nature which is divine without admixture, will find everything in harmony with the other truths of his religion." Conclusion logically and necessarily followed from presupposition. Within the circle of "disciples [mathētōn]" faith could be said to precede knowledge; but in another way it was also permissible to "assert knowledge as coming before faith," on the condition that knowledge was to be "understood within the bounds of the possibilities of human comprehension." The orthodox interpretation of the divine *economy* could not be permitted to violate "the universal confession [homologeitai para pasi] about the nature of the divine." As interpreted by the Cappadocians, then, Christian theology was able to presuppose that it shared with the best of Classical culture a definition of "the divine [to theion]" and of "the divine nature [hē theia physis]," as well as a host of other a priori assumptions, whose "consistency" and "congruity" with orthodoxy it was obliged to defend both against the Greek systems and against other Christian systems. Although the relation between these presuppositions and orthodox doctrine is the subject of subsequent chapters, the several categories of presuppositions do at least merit identification and classification here.

Of these categories, moral presuppositions were in many respects the least ambiguous and the most "natural." The terms "ethical philosophia [hē ēthikē philosophia]" and "natural philosophy [hē physikē philosophia]" were closely related, if not interchangeable. Celebrated by Plato and Aristotle, *arete* represented a distinctive Greek principle. Therefore, it was possible for the Cappadocians to take the Greek understanding of *arete* for granted as a presupposition in dealing with either pagans or Christians. Even when introducing a theological treatise about the Trinity, they could appeal, directly and unequivocally, to "the presupposition of the law of nature" about human behavior, assuming that any reader regardless of background would affirm it. What was identifiable as "the common law of all human beings [koinos pantōn anthrōpōn nomos]" was affirmed, if intensified and expanded, by "the special peculiar law of us Christians [hēmeteros tōn christianōn idios]." Discussed at length in the *Nicomachean Ethics* of Aristotle, the traditional *aretai* of Greek ethical thought applied to Christian ethics, too. Gregory of Nyssa appealed for so problematical a notion as his theory of the double creation, first of human nature as such and only then of male and female, not only to the authority of Scripture and "the doctrine of the church," but to the general and universally accessible description of God as "being in his own nature everything conceivable as good, or rather, transcending all conceivable or imaginable good."

As that form of argumentation indicated, a related set of presuppositions could be identified as principally logical and epistemological. As Raoul Mortley has said, "the *via negativa* . . . is the most remarkable feature of the philosophical life of late antiquity, Greek and Christian," so that when the Cappadocians propounded their version of it, they were able to take for granted that much of their language would be intelligible to both Greeks and Christians. Eunomius appears to have drawn an antithesis between what was "natural" and what was "paradoxical," an antithesis the Cappadocians did not accept. At the same time, they did draw a similar antithesis between "nature" and "contradiction," asserting against Apollinarism the logical axiom of "the natural inadmissibility of two mutually contradictory doctrines on the same subject both being true." Against what they took to be the Macedonian doctrine that the Holy Spirit was both created and uncreated, they insisted that this was "impossible by the nature of things," and that on the basis of revelation it was up to "logic to discover the answer [eurisketai ek tēs akolouthias tou *logou*]." The resolution of the apparent contradiction between this acceptance of paradoxical negation and this rejection of logical contradiction—both of these on the grounds of "nature," and not only of revelation—appeared to lie in the function of *apophasis* as the language of transcendence. Given this function, however, the Cappadocians could argue that because truly rational Greeks, no less than truly rational Christians, were obliged to accept "the absolute certainty of the immutability of the divine counsel [hē men theia boulē pantē te kai pantos to ametatheton

Gr.Nyss.*Tres dii*
(Jaeger 3–I:37)

Bas.*Ep.*276
(Courtonne 3:148)
Arist.*EN.*1115a-1119b;
1129a-1138b
See p.141

See pp.292–93

Gr.Nyss.*Hom.opif.*16
(PG 44:181)

See pp.18–19

Mortley 1986,2:15

Eun.ap.Gr.Nyss.*Eun.*
1.606 (Jaeger 1:201)

Gr.Naz.*Ep.*202
(PG 37:333)

Gr.Nyss.*Maced.*
(Jaeger 3–I:104)

See pp.200–214

echei]," they also had to accept the principle that evil, which was
mutable, was less powerful than good, which participated in the
very immutability of God.

Gr.Nyss.*Hom.opif.*21
(*PG* 44:201)

That presupposition about good and evil was not only epistemological, however, but primarily ontological, as were others
that the Cappadocians invoked in their specifically dogmatic and
polemical writings; for whether pagan or heretical or orthodox,
everyone accepted the presupposition of "a universe linked to one
first cause, with nothing in it owing its existence to itself." In the
confession of the divine nature of the Holy Spirit, Gregory of
Nyssa declared, it was impossible to "recognize any distinctions
suggested either by scriptural teachings or by common sense
[oute ek tēs tōn graphōn didaskalias oute ek tōn koinōn en-
noiōn]," because it was the consensus of both that the divine
nature was simple and undivided. Therefore he could assert the
proposition, as something that everyone knew: "To be exact,
simplicity in the case of the Holy Trinity admits of no degree."
Similarly, in a letter to him his brother Basil could recommend,
for the understanding of the trinitarian terms *ousia* as referring to
what was shared and *hypostasis* as referring to what was particular in the Godhead, that he "transfer to the divine dogmas [epi
tōn theiōn dogmatōn] the same standard of difference recognized
in the case both of *ousia* and of *hypostasis* in human affairs."
Both from Scripture and "from its own reasonings [dia te tēs
theias graphēs kai tōn oikeiōn logismōn]," the human mind
could learn that the divine nature, whatever it may have been in
itself, was "absolute goodness, holiness, and joy, power, glory,
and purity, an eternity always absolutely the same." Hence, no
one would regard the being of God as something "heterogeneous
and composite." Nor was it solely with regard to the divine
nature, but also with regard to human nature, that the Cappadocians felt entitled to invoke such presuppositions. Not only orthodox Christians but "everyone with a spark of sense" were
obliged to acknowledge "the flesh as less precious than the soul,"
according to Gregory of Nazianzus. The ground for such an
assertion was formulated in the introduction to the treatise *On
the Making of Man* by Gregory of Nyssa, when he identified not
only Scripture but also reason as a valid source for understanding
human nature.

Gr.Nyss.*Infant.*
(Jaeger 3–II:76–77)

Gr.Nyss.*Maced.*
(Jaeger 3–I:90–91[cj])

Gr.Nyss.*Eun.*1.231–32
(Jaeger 1:94–95)

Bas.*Ep.*38.3
(Courtonne 1:83)

Gr.Nyss.*Or.dom.*2
(*PG* 44:1140)

Gr.Nyss.*Eun.*1.208
(Jaeger 1:87)

Gr.Naz.*Ep.*101
(*PG* 37:189)

Gr.Nyss.*Hom.opif.*pr.
(*PG* 44:128)

It was, then, with such presuppositions, and with such presuppositions about presuppositions, that the Cappadocians faced
not only the task of apologetics toward Classical culture but the
task of dogmatics toward the church, as that task was described

See pp.22–39

at the opening of that treatise by Gregory of Nyssa: "We must fit together, according to the explanation of Scripture and to that derived from reasoning, statements that seem, by a kind of necessary sequence, to be opposed, so that our whole subject may be consistent in train of thought and in order." In doing this during the half-century or so following the Council of Nicaea, they were still obliged to deal directly with Classical culture as an intellectual and spiritual (and, indeed, political) reality in their world; but they were already obliged to deal as well with a Christianity that had become, through the work of the emperor Constantine, not only the established church politically but a creedal church doctrinally. Because the generation of the Cappadocians was at the same time the period during which Christian orthodoxy achieved its most definitive and abiding creedal formulation, in the Niceno-Constantinopolitan Creed promulgated by the Council of Constantinople of 381, every article and phrase of that creed bore marks of this two-front war. Much of what follows in subsequent chapters will consist basically of an exposition of the Niceno-Constantinopolitan Creed in the light of this dual task.

Gr.Nyss.*Hom.opif*.pr.
(PG 44:128)

CHAPTER 13

The Lexicon of Transcendence

Bas.*Spir.*18.46
(SC 17:408)

Bas.*Hex.*2.2
(SC 26:148)

See pp.41–42,50

Bas.*Hex.*9.3
(SC 26:494)

The most fundamental of the presuppositions of natural theology to come out of the Cappadocian enterprise of apologetics and into the Cappadocian enterprise of dogmatics was *apophasis*, the language of negation, which underlay and permeated all the other themes of the Cappadocian system. There is much to be said in favor of the historical thesis that, coming at the point where they did in the history of thought, the Cappadocians made even more extensive use of *apophasis* in their dogmatics than they did in their apologetics. Hence, a principle that functioned as a defense of all Christian teaching, whether heretical or orthodox, against all pagan teaching, whether mythological or philosophical, now also became a means for vindicating Christian orthodoxy against Christian heresy, by simultaneously affirming, in the words of Basil of Caesarea, "the close relation" between Father, Son, and Holy Spirit, as confessed by the dogma of the Trinity, and qualifying it through a continued emphasis on the "ineffable existence" of the divine. Thus Basil, whose polemical formula about a mystery of the divine nature that was "at one and the same time incomprehensible to human reason and inexpressible by the human voice" could serve as an epitome of the apologetic case for a negative theology, went on, in a later section of the same exposition of the creation narrative from Genesis, to apply this negative theology to Christian thought no less than to pagan thought, and to orthodox dogmatics no less than to heretical dogmatics. "What language can attain to the marvels of the Creator?" he asked, "What ear could understand them?" And by a reductio ad absurdum the same negative theology could serve his brother Gregory of Nyssa as a means of refuting the accusations of heretics, who were so "keen to see unsubstantial entities" that they found the church's teaching of the Trinity unacceptable.

At times the Cappadocians, and most other orthodox Christian theologians, could appear to be giving the impression that negative theology applied with particular force to the pagan philosophers and to their accomplices among Christian heretics, but not in the same way to the church's teaching. Gregory of Nazianzus, for example, was able to speak, in a passage of rhetorical power, about God as a transcendent object of thought that nevertheless seemed somehow attainable: "[The light], which bestows on the things that see and that are seen both the power of seeing and the power of being seen, is itself the most beautiful of visible things. So it is also with the God who created both the power of thinking and the power of being thought of. For those who think and for that which is thought of, God is the highest of the objects of thought, in whom every desire finds its goal and beyond whom it cannot go any further. For not even the most philosophical, the most piercing, or the most curious intellect has a more exalted object than this, nor can it ever have one. This, then, is the utmost of things desirable, and those who arrive at it find a total rest from speculation." The promise extended here to the speculative intellect did identify God as the point "beyond" which it was impossible for human understanding to go, but not as the point "to" which it was impossible for human understanding to go. Similarly, when Basil, referring to God as "the very truth [hē autoalētheia]," defined "knowing our God" as "the primary function of our mind," he seemed to be making the same promise. But by adding the stipulation that this was qualified by "the knowability of the infinitely great to the very small," he made it clear that there were definite limits to such knowledge, though he did not here specify those limits more precisely.

It does seem that such statements as those attributed to the heterodox Eunomius, "To you it is given to be perfect in knowledge," and again, "Nothing is incomprehensible," helped to compel the specification of these limits by orthodox theologians. Almost as though he were seeking to clarify Basil's reference to God as "the very truth," Gregory of Nyssa reminded his audience that if even Paul, after having been caught up to the third heaven in ecstasy, had to acknowledge, "I do not know—God knows," those to whom a similar ecstasy had never been granted were

Gr.Nyss.*Eun*.1.426–29
(Jaeger 1:150–51)

Gr.Naz.*Or*.21.1
(*SC* 270:112)

Bas.*Ep*.233.2
(Courtonne 3:40)

ap.Gr.Nyss.*Eun*.2.64
(Jaeger 1:244)
ap.Gr.Nyss.*Eun*.3.2.8
(Jaeger 2:54)

Bas.*Ep*.233.2
(Courtonne 3:40)

Lewy 1929,132–37
2 Cor 12:1–10

Gr.Nyss.*Cant.*5
(Jaeger 6:138)

Gr.Nyss.*Eun.*2.142–44
(Jaeger 1:266–67)

Mühlenberg 1966,142–47
Gr.Nyss.*Virg.*10
(Jaeger 8–I:291)

Gr.Nyss.*V.Mos.*2
(Jaeger 7–I:86–87)

Gr.Nyss.*Cant.*13
(Jaeger 6:381)

Plantinga 1986,352

Bas.*Spir.*9.22
(SC 17:322)

See pp.24–25,241

under a still greater obligation to make such an acknowledgment of their inability to see this "very truth" itself. He warned Eunomius that regardless of whether it employed an alpha privative, human language about God did not give "a positive account" of that to which it was applied, but only a catalog of the evil qualities from which God was exempt. In putting forth these warnings, he did foresee the danger that the theology of negation could impose a chill on the entire philosophical and intellectual enterprise, in fact on the religious and mystical enterprise itself, by describing the height and mystery of the transcendent *kalon* that was God as so unknowable and so unattainable that there was no point in trying to attain it. Therefore, he urged on his audience the necessity of striving for it with all the greater effort. Such striving did achieve a genuine increase in knowledge about God, but that knowledge consisted of an ever-growing recognition of the transcendence of the divine nature over any contemplation of it. Initially it was ignorance that had to admit that it did not know; but eventually it was knowledge, as enlightened by divine revelation, that had to declare: "That which is uncreated and which precedes all the *aeons* and which is eternal remains incomprehensible." Clearly, then, it would have been a dangerous oversimplification to maintain, as the rhetoric of the Cappadocians sometimes seemed to imply, that *apophatic* theology applied to Classical philosophies of religion but not to Christian theology, or that within Christian theology it applied to heterodox doctrine but not to orthodox doctrine. If anything, at least within Christian theology, the situation was the reverse of that, for they made the claim that *apophatic* theology was consistently serving as an explicit presupposition for the orthodox, but not for the heretics (although it should have done so). As Cornelius Plantinga has put it, Nyssa's definition of divine transcendence was shaped by the ideas of "the infinity and sheer ineffability of the divine nature and the unthinkable unity of the divine work."

The effort to clarify this presupposition and others did play a significant part in the thought of the Cappadocians. For example, as the basis for a debate about doctrinal differences concerning the legitimacy of calling the Holy Spirit "God," the starting point was to be the investigation of the common conceptions concerning the Spirit shared by the two sides. As previous chapters have suggested, many of these common conceptions actually belonged also to the realm of natural theology, for they were based not only on the explicit statements of divine revelation but on what was taken to be generally knowable through sense experience and

Gr.Nyss.*Maced.*
(Jaeger 3–I:96)

Gr.Nyss.*Apoll.*
(Jaeger 3–I:228–29)

Gr.Nyss.*Eun.*1.169
(Jaeger 1:77)

Gr.Nyss.*Eun.*1.418
(Jaeger 1:148)

Gr.Nyss.*Eun.*1.59
(Jaeger 1:42)

Eun.ap.Gr.Nyss.*Eun.*
3.7.1 (Jaeger 2:215)

Gr.Nyss.*Eun.*2.596
(Jaeger 1:400)

Gr.Nyss.*Maced.*
(Jaeger 3–I:91)

See pp.259–62

reason. They were seen to be in agreement with both revelation and reason, since a contrary position would have been at one and the same time "ridiculous and blasphemous," violating both criteria. It was axiomatic for all theological positions and parties that no one was to entertain any thoughts about the divine that were "degraded and abject [chamairiphē kai chamaizēla]," even as judged by the criteria of reason. Because it was utterly unreasonable to suppose that there could be either excess or defect in the infinite one, it was a fundamental principle of *apophatic* theology, which all sides in the controversy were prepared to grant, that the divine and unalterable nature of God was incapable of degeneracy and therefore that it was absolutely unlimited in its goodness, which by definition could never be excessive. The *apatheia* of the divine nature, its transcendence over all passions, such as envy, was a logical conclusion at which any right-thinking person would arrive even without the aid of revelation. Heretics were often portrayed as manifesting a general inability to think correctly, both in their intellectual outlook as a whole and in their theological doctrine. But since certain principles were accepted by all sides, the acceptance of one of these by a heretic had to be met with approval, as when Eunomius confessed: "God is the most highly exalted of all goods, and the mightiest of all, and free from all *ananke*." It was, the orthodox theologians said, deplorable that from these general presuppositions of negative theology, which Eunomius appeared to share with them and with others, he frequently drew conclusions, for example about the relation of the Son to the Father or about the relation of Creator to creature, that were not consistent with them but contradictory to them. The correct method, correct in the light both of natural theology and of church doctrine, was to proceed, by necessary and logical implication, from such principles to various doctrinal corollaries.

As became evident in their ambiguity about the status of angelic "higher natures and purer intelligences" that were nevertheless "created natures," the effort of the Cappadocians to ground the necessity for *apophasis* not only in sin and ignorance but in creaturehood and finiteness confronted major problems, both conceptually and exegetically. The fundamental Christian tenet of the revelation of the eternal God through the incarnation, death, and resurrection of the eternal *Logos* in the person of Jesus Christ had to be refined so to mean that such propositions about Christ as "That about him which is uncreated and precedes the *aeons* and is eternal remains incomprehensible" were to be assigned to *theology*, whereas such propositions as "That which

Gr.Nyss.*Cant.*13
(Jaeger 6:381)

has been disclosed to us through his flesh can in some measure
enter into our knowledge" belonged to *economy.* The no less
fundamental Christian ethical metaphor of holiness as a "dwell-

Eph 2:21–22
Gr.Nyss.*Cant.*15
(Jaeger 6:438)

See pp.316–17

ing place" of God in the hearts and lives of the faithful stood in
need of a similar refinement. So did the Christian concept of the
vision of God as the goal and the promise of life everlasting,
which was magnified, in the Cappadocian system, into the promise of a genuine *metamorphosis* of human nature that would

See pp.295,317–18

grant it nothing less than *theosis.* But the vision of "the boundless
and incomprehensible beauty [to amēchanon kai aperinoēton

Gr.Nyss.*Virg.*10
(Jaeger 8–1:290)

kallos]" in the mystical experience of the saints stood as a cautionary tale against any presumptions about all of this. To the
question, "What then is the *ousia* of God?" the answer had to be:
"It is for your infatuation to define this. . . . But to us it will be a
very great thing if ever we learn this, even in the future when this
darkness and dullness is done away for us, as has been promised
by the one who cannot lie. Such, then, may be the thought and
hope of those who are purifying themselves with a view to this."

Gr.Naz.*Or.*29.11
(*SC* 250:200)

The closing statement of the Gospel of John, that the world itself
would not be able to contain the books that could be written
about God and Christ, was taken as a warning against any in-

Jn 21:25
Gr.Nyss.*Eun.*2.119–24
(Jaeger 1:260–62)

quiry into the mystery of the divine *ousia.*

As that reference to the Gospel indicated, the consistent and
rigorous application of *apophatic* theology had to deal exegetically with those many passages in Scripture (for example, the
experiences of the Old Testament prophets, especially Elijah,
Isaiah, and Ezekiel) that did seem to promise the knowledge of
God or the vision of God to believers without explicitly hedging

Gr.Naz.*Or.*28.19
(*SC* 250:138–40)

the promise in by means of any *apophatic* qualifiers. Thus Psalm
8 appeared to make a simple equation of the divine "praise as

Ps 8:2–3

high as the heavens" with the glory that was chanted "from the

Gr.Naz.*Or.*28.3
(*SC* 250:106)

mouths of babes and infants at the breast" and "throughout the
world." The problem in interpreting such passages was how to

Gr.Nyss.*Cant.*8
(Jaeger 6:247)

speak about the vision of God in a way that would preserve the
transcendence of God unimpaired. Perhaps the most sublime and
unqualified of all such passages anywhere in the Scriptures was
the promise of the sixth Beatitude at the beginning of the Sermon
on the Mount, in which Christ pronounced: "Blessed are those

Mt 5:8

whose hearts are pure; they shall see God." "This promise,"

Gr.Nyss.*Beat.*6
(*PG* 44:1265)

Jn 1:18

1 Tm 6:16

Gregory of Nyssa recognized, was "so great as to transcend the
utmost limits of blessedness." But after quoting the words of
John, "No one has ever seen God," and the words of Paul, "Him
no one has ever seen or can ever see," he explained: "This is the

slippery, steep rock that affords no basis for our thoughts, which the teaching of Moses, too, declares to be so inaccessible that our mind can nowhere approach God. For this explicit denial takes away all possibility of apprehending God, 'No mortal man may see me and live.'" Both the exegetical and the conceptual difficulties demonstrated that *apophatic* theology, far from being merely an apologetic or heuristic or rhetorical device or even only a presupposition of natural theology among other such presuppositions, had to provide the lexicon for a distinctive and comprehensive theological method, above all in church dogmatics: "Following the theologies that have been handed down to us by the Holy Spirit" meant to acknowledge, by means of alpha privatives, that the ways of God were "characterized by *apatheia*, indivisibility, inseparability, and timelessness."

Macrina, who is being dubbed here the Fourth Cappadocian, described this general method as follows: "In the very act of saying that a thing is 'not so and so,' we by implication interpret the very nature of the thing in question." Elaborating on this method, her brother Gregory spoke of a "duty to expel the low, human way of thinking, by means of the more transcendent ideas [tais hypsēloterais tōn ennoiōn], and to make a calculation more worthy of the transcendence [tou hypsous] of the objects in question." Elsewhere, too, he identified it as "a sacred duty to use concerning God names privative of the things abhorrent to the divine nature." It was characteristic of these privative titles that "the meaning inherent in each" was intended "to inform us only of the privation of the obvious data of our sense experience, but not to interpret the actual nature" of what had been "removed from these abhorrent conditions." The titles answered the question, "What is the Deity not?" while leaving undisclosed the answer to the next question, "What is that further thing, which is not these things, in its own *ousia*?" And even those titles that were positive in form and language, "indicating some position or some state," had to be interpreted in such a way as "not to afford an indication of the divine nature itself, but only the results of our reverent speculations about it," which had to be *apophatic*.

The fundamental problem was: How to name the invisible, or describe the nonmaterial, or show what could not be seen, or comprehend what had neither size nor quantity, neither quality nor form, what was neither in space nor in time, eluding all limitation and every form of definition? And the lexicon for handling the problem still consisted of such apparently *cataphatic* terms, since they were the only ones available, but it required

Ex 33:20

Gr.Nyss.*Beat*.6
(*PG* 44:1263)

Bas.*Eun*.2.16
(*SC* 305:64)

Macr.ap.Gr.Nyss.
Anim.res. (*PG* 46:40)

Gr.Nyss.*Maced.*
(Jaeger 3–I:99)

Gr.Nyss.*Eun*.2.581–82
(Jaeger 1:396)

Gr.Nyss.*Beat*.3
(*PG* 44:1225)

Gr.Naz.*Or*.37.4
(*SC* 318:278)

Gr.Nyss.*Eun*.1.630
(Jaeger 1:107–8)
Dix 1953,79
Gr.Naz.*Or*.30.4
(*SC* 250:230–32)
Mt 22:44; Mk 12:36;
Lk 20:42; Acts 2:34;
Heb 1:13

Ps 109:1

Bas.*Spir*.6.15
(*SC* 17:292)

Bar 3:3
Gr.Nyss.*V.Mos*.2
(Jaeger 7–I:111)
Gr.Naz.*Or*.28.18–19
(*SC* 250:136–40)

Ex 13:21

Gr.Nyss.*V.Mos*.1
(Jaeger 7–I:14)

putting them through the process of "taking away [exairethentos] these and all suchlike ideas" of *cataphasis* from them. When the words of Psalm 109—interpreted christologically on the basis of the Septuagint, as that Psalm consistently was by the Cappadocians and as it had been interpreted already in the New Testament—represented the Father as saying to the Son, "Sit at my right hand," it was necessary to remove all physical and finite connotations and to interpret these words as a reference to "the immutability and immobility of the divine mode of existence"; for Scripture said of God, "Thou sittest for the *aeon* [sy kathēmenos ton aiōna]." Applied to such passages of the Old Testament, a literalistic method of exegesis would lead to the irrational blasphemy of making God changeable. But the Old Testament itself insisted that the nature of God remained incomprehensible. The cloud that led the people of Israel in the desert, therefore, was not a natural cloud but one that "transcended human comprehension."

As has been indicated, the sacred duty of applying this method of *apophasis* to the lexicon of transcendence was nowhere more urgent than in the interpretation of the central trinitarian metaphor of the Bible and of the church's tradition, the relation between the Father and the Son in the Godhead, and of the various terms employed both in biblical and in dogmatic language about

See pp.87–89
Gr.Naz.*Or*.23.11
(*SC* 270:302)

it. Orthodox trinitarian language, too, was an *apophatic* language. At the heart of the difficulty was, as everyone has to recognize, the "ambiguity" of the terms "generation or begetting [gennēsis]" and "begotten [gennētos]." (With their double "nu" in Greek, these terms should be distinguished from "beginning [genēsis]" and "originated [genētos]," which have a single "nu"

Prestige 1933,260

in Greek, even though neither the church fathers nor the copyists of their manuscripts seem to have observed that distinction with

Lampe 310–11

any precision or consistency.) In its human and physical sense, "begetting" was used, also in Scripture, "concerning a material existence subject to passion"; but in its transcendent sense, it was

Gr.Nyss.*Eun*.3.2.4
(Jaeger 2:53)

used "concerning that divine, simple, and noncorporeal life." Therefore, when Scripture or the church spoke about the Father and the Son, it left out of sight "all the other things visible to human nature in earthly generation." Then, after all such connotations had been eliminated by the *apophatic* method of exclusion, "the word 'Son' is employed concerning the only-begotten one to indicate the close and true character of his manifestation

Gr.Nyss.*Eun*.3.6.36–37
(Jaeger 2:198–99)

from the Father." For once these other connotations had been

Gr.Nyss.*Eun*.3.1.78–79
(Jaeger 2:31)

Gr.Nyss.*Virg*.2
(Jaeger 8–1:253)

Gr.Nyss.*Eun*.3.6.15
(Jaeger 2:191)

Gr.Naz.*Or*.38.7
(PG 36:317)

Gr.Nyss.*Eun*.2.197
(Jaeger 1:282)

Gr.Nyss.*Eun*.2.234–35
(Jaeger 1:294)
Gr.Nyss.*Or.catech*.3.1
(Méridier 18)

Gr.Nyss.*Cant*.13
(Jaeger 6:383)

Gr.Nyss.*Eun*.1.541
(Jaeger 1:183)

Bas.*Spir*.1.2
(SC 17:252)

Gr.Nyss.*Eun*.1.620–23
(Jaeger 1:205–6)

Gr.Nyss.*Eun*.1.300–301
(Jaeger 1:115)

Lenz 1925,51–55

"purged away," it was possible for "the transcendent begetting" to be clear—but only by the method of negation. It was that recourse to *apophatic* theology that lay behind the meaning of such biblical paradoxes as "incorrupt Father" and "passionless begetting."

Resorting to *apophasis*, which was in a special sense the only proper language of transcendence, was necessary for theology because there could not be a perfect analogy for God. Being of a simple and uncomposite nature, God had to be "either wholly incomprehensible or perfectly comprehensible": obviously the latter was out of the question, and therefore the human lexicon about God was obliged to reflect the true state of affairs, which meant that it had to be *apophatic*. Like the invention of language itself, the compilation of this lexicon was a work of the rational faculty, which God had implanted in human nature, rather than a direct divine creation. God had gifted humanity with speech, "so that we might be able thereby to signify the thoughts of our minds"; but when those thoughts were thoughts about God, that implied the immense difference between any and all human notions about the divine nature and the "inherent majesty and deity" of that nature itself. For it always remained "impossible to express the ineffable depth of the mystery in words." It was not to be expected "for the ineffable to be made manifest by the power of words." This was not to deny in any way that the right attitude of the soul toward God was more important than any of the language it used. That very situation, however, made it all the more crucial to pay careful attention to getting the language exactly right, which meant above all coming to terms with its never being exactly right or precise in a *cataphatic* sense. Underneath the superficial similarity between human language about creatures and human language about the Creator was the great gulf of "a wide difference of meanings." When it was used in such a context and carefully controlled by *apophatic* theology, the language of this lexicon of transcendence had, "at one and the same time, a human sound but not a human meaning." Only then could such language become a "symbol" for transcendent reality, containing a deeper meaning than the literal one.

If, then, it was impossible either to grasp or to express the divine nature "in and of itself" because it transcended all understanding, where was the human mind to turn for specific evidence about this incomprehensible reality? To this question the Cappadocian answer was: "It is absolutely necessary for us to be

guided to the investigation of the divine nature by its actions
[energeiai]"; taken together, these "actions" constituted the divine *economy*. It was characteristic of these divine actions that
while the divine *ousia* was by definition "simple [haplous]" and
remained unknowable, the actions were various and knowable.
They were also paradoxical—an attribute no less central to pastoral care than to speculative theology—as the actions of a God
who, as Scripture said, killed, but did so in order to make alive.
They were, moreover, not only various and paradoxical but num-
berless, as *apophatic* theology probed the mysteries of all the
ways in which the divine being was set apart from all created
beings. All divine actions were "of like rank with one another
[isodynamei allēlois]" and could not be distinguished as to the
signification of their subject. Otherwise God would have been
separable into individual faculties, as the human mind was; but
that would have been the violation of a nature that was "at one
and the same time sight and hearing and knowledge"—and yet
none of these in the human sense. It was unthinkable, also according to natural theology, that God should be a composite of
several attributes. No one, not even a heretic or a heathen, would
affirm, Gregory of Nyssa declared, such a proposition as this:
"We should consider the being of God to be a thing of some sort
that is heterogeneous and composite [poikilon ti chrēma kai
syntheton]."

It was indeed possible for finite mortals to know, as attributes
of God and actions of God, the greatness, the power, the wisdom,
the goodness, the providence, and the justice of God, but it was
not possible for them to know the very *ousia* of God. For that
ousia was too transcendent to be possessed of any distinctive
attributes. Even when all such divine actions, attributes, and
predicates had been set forth in all their *apophatic* force, they did
not, even put together, present the *ousia* of God. Those who did
not accept *apophatic* theology as constituting the lexicon of transcendence failed to acknowledge the mystery of the ineffable being of God, because they presumed that whatever could not be set
forth in human language would nevertheless "either be accessible
to them alone or else have no existence," because they had not
comprehended it. To say concerning the relation of *ousia* and
existence in God, as Eunomius did in the interests of rejecting the
Nicene doctrine, that God was "not separated in regard to the
unifying *ousia*," was, according to Gregory of Nyssa, meaningless: "For how does any being remain in existence when it is
separated from its own *ousia*?" It was "absurd as well as impious

Gr.Nyss.*Trin.*
(Jaeger 3–I:10–11)
See pp.263–79

Bas.*Ep.*234.1
(Courtonne 3:42)
Bas.*Ep.*5.2
(Courtonne 1:17–18)
Dt 32:39
Gr.Nyss.*Cant.*12
(Jaeger 6:362)
Gr.Nyss.*Eun.*2.515
(Jaeger 1:377)

Balás 1966,121–40

Gr.Nyss.*Trin.*
(Jaeger 3–1:8)

Gr.Nyss.*Eun.*2.211–12
(Jaeger 1:286–87)

Gr.Nyss.*Eun.*1.597
(Jaeger 1:198)

Gr.Nyss.*Eun.*1.208
(Jaeger 1:87)

Bas.*Ep.*234.1
(Courtonne 3:42)

Gr.Nyss.*Eun.*1.373–75
(Jaeger 1:137)

Gr.Naz.*Or.*28.9
(SC 250:116–20)

Gr.Naz.*Or.*42.18
(PG 36:480)

Gr.Nyss.*Ref.*34–35
(Jaeger 2:325–26)

[atopon kai dyssebes]," a violation both of natural theology and of divine revelation, to implicate the divine *ousia* in any nonexistence, either a nonexistence out of which it had come or a nonexistence into which it would pass through corruption and transiency. For in some ways the most fundamental metaphysical presupposition of all about God was this: "God always is that which the God now existing is; God does not become worse or better by any addition; God does not become altered by taking something from another source; God always maintains self-identity."

For the Cappadocians, what G. Christopher Stead, speaking about Gregory of Nyssa, has called "logic and the application of names to God" became—as it had been earlier in Jewish-Christian theology, and as it was to become a century or so later for Pseudo-Dionysius the Areopagite in his treatise *On the Divine Names,* who "follows the Cappadocians," and then, later still, for the theologians of Islam—a device for building a fence around the language of religion and worship. Their characterization of the names of God as being "all names of denial" may therefore serve as a summary of their *apophatic* theology. It might have appeared at first glance that the use of names for God, and especially the use of those names for God that were warranted by Scripture's use of them, was an exception to the rules of *apophaticism* and that such names did have a *cataphatic* content. Going beneath the surface of these names, however, showed how mistaken such an impression would be. It was the explicit teaching of Scripture that the nature of God was "unnameable and ineffable [akatonomaston te kai arraston]." This led to the necessary conclusion: "Every name, whether invented by human custom or handed down by the Scriptures, is indicative of our conceptions of the divine nature, but it does not signify what that nature is in itself." Mentioning names "invented by human custom" that way right alongside those "handed down by the Scriptures," and putting both sets of divine names on the same level, was a reference to the ability and inherent right of the human mind to invent names and words in the course of the development of a language, and thus also to the divine practice of using such names and words for communicating a revelation. But regardless of which of these two sources had produced them, none of the names for the divine nature itself conveyed its essence, which remained "unsignified [asēmantos]." No name was worthy to express the nature of God. Moreover, there was no one name for the complete divine nature. Nevertheless, there remained no alternative to using some

Gr.Nyss.*Eun.*3.7.51
(Jaeger 2:233)

Gr.Nyss.*Eun.*1.592
(Jaeger 1:196–97)

Mateo-Seco–Bastero
1988,303–20

Daniélou 1964,147–63

Florovsky 10:211

Burrell 1991,20–34

Bas.*Eun.*1.10
(SC 299:206)

Gr.Nyss.*Tres dii*
(Jaeger 3–I:42–43)

Gr.Nyss.*Eun.*2.246
(Jaeger 1:298)

Gr.Nyss.*Trin.*
(Jaeger 3–I:14)
Gr.Nyss.*V.Mos.*2
(Jaeger 7–I:92)
Bas.*Eun.*1.10
(SC 299:204)

Gr.Nyss.*Eun*.3.5.42–43
(Jaeger 2:175–76);
Gr.Naz.*Or*.28.11
(*SC* 250:122)

Gr.Nyss.*Beat*.4
(*PG* 44:1241)

Gr.Nyss.*Eun*.2.144–45
(Jaeger 1:267)
Gr.Nyss.*Eun*.2.352–53
(Jaeger 1:329)
Lenz 1925,51–55
Bas.*Ep*.5.2
(Courtonne 1:17–18);

Gr.Nyss.*Cant*.12
(Jaeger 6:362)

Balás 1966,108–15

Gr.Nyss.*Eun*.2.149
(Jaeger 1:268)
Gr.Nyss.*Eun*.2.298
(Jaeger 1:314)

Gr.Nyss.*Tres dii*
(Jaeger 3–1:52–53)

Gr.Nyss.*Eun*.2.131
(Jaeger 1:263–64)
Gr.Nyss.*Virg*.10
(Jaeger 8–1:291)

Bas.*Spir*.1.2
(*SC* 17:252)

Iren.*Haer*.4.10.1
(Harvey 2:172–73)

Jgs 13:18

Gr.Nyss.*Eun*.3.6.4
(Jaeger 2:187)

Gr.Nyss.*Cant*.1
(Jaeger 6:37)

Gr.Naz.*Or*.2.86
(*SC* 247:202)

names for God; but it was essential that these names be appropriate, which meant above all that they point beyond themselves to the mystery of the incomprehensible nature of God.

Precisely because no one name could be adequate, there turned out to be "innumerable" names for God, each with some special but *apophatic* implication. Each of these diverse appellations "by some distinctive touch" added something of its own, so as to make it possible "by a variety of nomenclature to gain some glimmerings" of the divine mystery. The source of this diversity of divine names was traced by Gregory of Nyssa, speaking in defense of Basil, to the diverse "actions [energeiai]" of God, each of which found expression in some distinctive title. So diverse were these actions that to the limited human perspective they seemed utterly contradictory. Therefore, Gregory formulated the lexicographical rule: "God is not an expression, neither does the *ousia* of God consist in voice or utterance, but the divine nature is of itself what also it is believed to be. Nevertheless it is named, by those who call upon God, not what it is essentially (for the nature of God, who alone is being, is ineffable), but it receives its appellations from what are believed to be its operations in regard to our life." All such terms had their special fitness, because each variety of the divine beneficence took shape "in the mould of a name." Yet none of these diverse appellations could be thought of as limiting God in any way. Nor instead was the lack of *cataphatic* signification in such names to be taken as leading to a counsel of despair that would conclude that because they all meant nothing they all meant the same thing. For this sort of conclusion could produce indifference and inattention. But the lexicon of transcendence implied the very opposite, the obligation to look in detail at every name for God in order to discover what it contributed, not indeed to a knowledge of the divine *ousia* as such, but to the knowledge of these multifarious operations. When, therefore, the "angel of the Lord" in the Old Testament (whom Christian exegesis had long taken as a theophany of the preexistent and preincarnate *Logos*), in response to the question, "What is your name?" replied, "Wonderful [thaumaston]," this was not the name of God in essence, but a reference to "the wonder arising unspeakably in our hearts concerning it." From this sense of wonder arose the "theological names" for God, such adjectives as "wise, powerful, good, holy, blessed, and eternal," and such nouns as "Judge and Savior."

The same was true of the other revelations of "the power of the name" of God or of Christ in the Scriptures. Each exegetical

Mt 6:9
Gr.Nyss.*Or.dom.*3
(*PG* 44:1153–56)
Gr.Naz.*Or.*30.17
(*SC* 250:260–62);
Bas.*Spir.*18.44
(*SC* 17:404)

See pp.221–24

encounter with the very term "name," for example in the first petition of the Lord's Prayer, became an occasion for repeating these warnings. Quite apart from the pious Jewish practice of treating the unutterable Hebrew divine name in a special way, for example by pronouncing it as "Lord," a practice with which the Cappadocians seem to have had at least some acquaintance despite their acknowledged ignorance of the Hebrew tongue, their Bible contained nearly a thousand references, one hundred or so in the Book of Psalms alone, to the term "name" (the Greek "onoma" and cognates), as well as several thousand references to the term "Lord [kyrios]," whether as a rendering of the tetragrammaton or in its own right as a divine name in the Septuagint, then also in the New Testament for Jesus Christ as Lord. Among these thousands of passages, at least three, two in the New Testament and one in the Old Testament, certainly appeared to be revelations of the divine *ousia* through a divine name if anything was, but these instead became, at the hands of the Cappadocians, proof texts for the principle of *apophasis* as the language of transcendence: "the formula of the Father and the Son and the Holy

Bas.*Spir.*18.44
(*SC* 17:402)
Pelikan 1971–89,
1:256–66

Murray 1964,5

Spirit" in Matthew 28:19–20, as "delivered by the Lord himself"; the key statement of "preexistence, kenosis, and exaltation" in Philippians 2:6–11; and the "towering text" of the theophany of the divine name to Moses in Exodus 3:14. These were three biblical oracles of such massive importance as to merit special attention.

Together with the Pauline benediction, "The grace of the Lord Jesus Christ, and the love of God, and the fellowship of the Holy

2 Cor 13:14

Spirit, be with you all," which was written down earlier but presumably spoken later, the baptismal formula from the Gospel of Matthew, "in the name of the Father and the Son and the Holy

Luislampe 1981,35–49

Bas.*Spir.*25.59
(*SC* 17:458–60)

Bas.*Spir.*29.75
(*SC* 17:516)

Spirit," constituted the most explicit biblical identification of all three *hypostases* of the Trinity; and the two passages were therefore seen to be closely related. As such an identification, the baptismal formula was a keystone of trinitarian orthodoxy, so that Basil, for example, gave it priority in his list of proofs for the Nicene doctrine of the Trinity. It had the additional advantage of containing an explicit reference to the concept of "the name." Closer inspection of the formula, however, showed it to be a particularly striking piece of evidence for the "unnameability of the name" of God; for after seeming to promise a disclosure of the name, Christ in fact "did not add the actual term of signification that 'the name' indicates." Because the uncreated nature of God transcended "all signification of names," this baptismal formula became instead an authorization for Christian believers to apply equally to Father, Son, and Holy Spirit "whatever name our intelligence by pious effort" had managed to find "to indicate the transcendent nature," such names as the good or the incorruptible. These three names of Father, Son, and Holy Spirit were, then, not names of *ousia*, which, because they pointed to "the transcendent power," would have had to be *apophatic* in form or at any rate in content. They were, rather, names of "relationship," of the relationship of God to humanity and of the relationship of the divine *hypostases* to one another. Christ had deliberately passed over "all those names employed to indicate the surpassing transcendence [hyperkeimenē] of the divine nature," since in fact there were no *cataphatic* names that could do this, in favor of "the title of 'Father' as better suited to indicate the truth." Such names of relationship could connote a variety of meanings, but they did not and could not denote the *ousia* of the one being named. The baptismal formula in Matthew 28:19–20, far from conveying an essential divine name, had rather laid down the rule that the divine *ousia* remained "ineffable and incomprehensible." For if it had been either possible or necessary for salvation to know about the divine *ousia*, then God would have made it known. But by his silence about the name of the divine *ousia*, an *ousia* "beyond our power to know," Christ delivered in his great commission to the disciples and to the church the knowledge of what was sufficient for salvation, a knowledge and a set of names that were within human grasp.

The same *apophatic* method was applicable to another New Testament text about a "name," the climax of the christological hymn in the second chapter of the Epistle to the Philippians: "Therefore God raised him to the heights and bestowed on him the name above all names, that at the name of Jesus every knee should bow—in heaven, on earth, and in the depths—and every tongue acclaim, 'Jesus Christ is Lord,' to the glory of God the Father." Again, first impressions could be deceiving; for this text appeared to be saying that the name "Jesus" as bestowed by God was "some one name preferred above all others, though still comparable with them," one in a series of names, when in fact it identified him "as having no name that could possibly give a knowledge of his *ousia*, but transcending all the power of names to express." Everyone would agree that the transcendence expressed in the phrase "the name above all names" applied to all such names as had obviously been derived from the physical world. But the text applied, as it itself stated quite unam-

Gr.Nyss.*Ref.*14–15
(Jaeger 2:318)

Gr.Nyss.*Ref.*124
(Jaeger 2:365)

Gr.Nyss.*Eun.*1.568–71
(Jaeger 1:190–91)

Gr.Nyss.*Ref.*10
(Jaeger 2:316)
Gr.Nyss.*Eun.*1.554
(Jaeger 1:186)

Gr.Nyss.*Ref.*16–17
(Jaeger 2:318–19)

Phil 2:9–11

Gr.Nyss.*Eun.*3.9.41
(Jaeger 2:279)

Gr.Naz.*Or.*37.4
(SC 318:276–80)

biguously, to "all names" whatever, including spiritual and metaphysical ones "in heaven, on earth, and in the depths," no less
than it did to such physical names. There was, then, "only one
name for representing the proper nature [of God], the single
'name of being above all names [to onoma to hyper pan onoma].'"
That led to the oxymoron: "The one who is above all names has
for us many names." Each of these names for one who was also
"beyond all signification [hyper pasan sēmasian]" pointed to the
true God, but it did so "analogically." Proof for this came from
the statement of the Book of Wisdom: "The greatness and beauty
of created things analogically [analogōs] give us an idea of their
Creator." And "the name above all names," which was therefore
unnameable, was not to be regarded as one name among others,
not even as the highest of these, but as an *apophatic* reference to
the confession, "The one who verily 'is' is above all names."

That reference to "the one who verily 'is'" was, at least in part,
an echo of the most profound and sublime of all biblical references to a "name" for God. It came, as did the identification of
the name of God as "Wonderful [thaumaston]," in response to an
inquiry, this time from Moses before the burning bush, about
what the divine name was: "God said to Moses, 'I am the one
who is [Egō eimi ho ōn].'" On the basis of this text, Gregory of
Nazianzus, having identified "God [theos]" and "the one who is
[ho ōn]" as the two "special names of God's essence," then went
on to show that even "theos" was still in fact a name of relationship rather than a name of essence. As for "the one who is,"
however, this not only carried the authority of the encounter of
Moses with the divine but was "the more strictly appropriate" on
its own merits. For this title made it the identifiable mark of "the
truly divine" to possess "eternity and infinity in respect to being,
making everything contemplated therein always the same, neither growing nor being consumed," a divine quality symbolized
by the burning bush, which was "on fire but was not being burnt
up." Throughout the Bible, the use of the verb "to be" for God—
as in such passages from Isaiah as "I God, the first and to all
futurity, I am [egō theos prōtos, kai eis ta eperchomena egō
eimi]," and "I am: before me there was no other god, and after
me there shall be none [egō eimi, emprosthen mou ouk egeneto
allos theos, kai met' eme ouk estai]"—ascribed being in the fullest sense to God, and to God alone. The word "is," therefore, was
to be supplied with every divine attribute and "with every name
used concerning the divine nature." It followed that "'being' in

Gr.Nyss.*Apoll.*
(Jaeger 3–I:161)

Gr.Nyss.*Eun.*1.683
(Jaeger 1:222)
Gr.Nyss.*Eun.*3.8.10–11
(Jaeger 2:242)

Gr.Nyss.*Eun.*3.6.32
(Jaeger 2:197)

Wis 13:5

Gr.Nyss.*Eun.*2.154
(Jaeger 1:270)

Gr.Nyss.*Eun.*3.9.41
(Jaeger 2:279)

Jgs 13:18
Gr.Nyss.*Eun.*3.6.4
(Jaeger 2:187)

Ex 3:14

Gottwald 1906,22–23

Gr.Naz.*Or.*30.18
(SC 250:264)

Ex 3:2
Gr.Nyss.*Eun.*3.6.3
(Jaeger 2:186)

Is 41:4

Is 43:10
Gr.Naz.*Or.*31.23
(SC 250:318–20)

Gr.Nyss.*Eun.*3.5.57–60
(Jaeger 2:180–82)

Gr.Nyss.*Eun.*3.8.32
(Jaeger 2:250–51)

the true sense of that word [to alēthōs einai]" was "the special distinction of Godhead."

But in the Cappadocian lexicon of transcendence this equation of God with being, like every other divine name, could be rescued from grave misunderstanding only by invoking *apophatic* theology. For if the word from the burning bush meant,

Gr.Nyss.*Eun.*3.6.8
(Jaeger 2:188)

"We know nothing else of God but this one thing, that God is," the "we know" in that declaration had to be qualified by the warning: "We do not by this negative predication understand the

Gr.Nyss.*Eun.*3.5.59–60
(Jaeger 2:181–82)

subject, but are guided as to what we must not think concerning the subject." Thus the self-revelation of God did not in fact an-

Bas.*Eun.*1.13
(SC 299:218)

swer the request of Moses for a name, nor did it provide a disclosure of the transcendent *ousia* of God. That kind of exegetical argumentation by the Cappadocians inevitably raised the question of whether this left any room for faith in a reliable divine revelation, together with the question of how a divine being defined in such negative terms could at the same time serve as the foundation for the Cappadocian doctrine of the relation between the one divine *ousia* and the three divine *hypostases* in the Trinity.

CHAPTER 14

Faith as the Fulfillment of Reason

Bas.*Ep*.125.1
(Courtonne 2:130)

Symb.Nic.
(Alberigo-Jedin 5)

Gr.Naz.*Or*.28.9
(*SC* 250:118)

Although the lexicon of divine transcendence according to the Cappadocians was based on *apophasis,* the language of negation, it may be surprising to discover that the Nicene Creed—the most authoritative and ecumenical of all statements of the orthodox Christian faith in the transcendent God and the document that Basil of Caesarea called "the doctrine of truth, the faith written down by the blessed fathers in the council that met at Nicaea"— was in fact almost completely devoid of such language. In its articles of faith, the only alpha privative came in the coordination of "visible and invisible [oratōn te kai aoratōn]" creatures, and the only other negative appeared in its explanation of the origin of the Son of God as "begotten, not made [gennēthenta ou poiēthenta]." There were negatives in its condemnatory clauses, but all of these were part of the heretical doctrines anathematized by "the catholic and apostolic church," not of the orthodox teachings that the catholic and apostolic church itself was here confessing. At least at one level, then, it was not only permitted but required by the orthodox faith, according to Gregory of Nazianzus, to declare: "An inquirer into the nature of a real being cannot stop short at saying what it is not but must add to these denials a positive affirmation [dei pros tōi eipein ha mē esti, kai ho estin eipein]—and how much easier it is to take in a single thing than to run the full gamut of particular negations!" Gregory of Nyssa, too, asking, "Do you mention what the Holy Spirit has, or do you honor It by what It does not have?" argued: "If you mention what It has, such and such a quality pertains to

2 Tm 2:13
Gr.Nyss.*Maced.*
(Jaeger 3–I:97)

Heb 11:1

Macr.ap.Gr.Nyss.
Anim.res. (PG 46:96)

Acts 17:23

Bas.*Ep.*52.3
(Courtonne 1:136)

Eun.ap.Gr.Nyss.*Ref.*
116–17 (Jaeger 2:361–62)

Gr.Nyss.*V.Mos.*1
(Jaeger 7–I:22)

Gr.Nyss.*Beat.*6
(PG 44:1264)

Gr.Nyss.*Hex.*
(PG 44:73)

Bas.*Mor.*8.3
(PG 31:713–16)

the nature, whether or not it is confessed to be there"; and in support, he cited the statement of the apostle Paul, "God remains the object of faith even if we do not have the faith." Macrina also cited a passage from the apostle, one that followed both methods, defining faith *cataphatically* as "the substance of things hoped for," and then *apophatically* as "the evidence of things not seen." On the Areopagus the apostle Paul, citing the inscription on an Athenian altar, "To an Unknown God," had declared: "What you worship but do not know—this is what I now proclaim."

When it came to the faith and to statements of the faith, therefore, all four Cappadocians seemed to counterbalance the extremes of their *apophatic* insistence on "taking the starting point of arguments for religion from negative opposition [ek tōn enantiōn lambanein tas aphormas pros tēn eusebeian]," by resorting repeatedly to *cataphatic* assertion. Certain negations—and alpha privatives—were unacceptable to orthodox faith, for example, the idea of Eunomius, expressed in an alpha privative, that the glory of God the Father was "incommunicable [ametadotos]" even to the Son of God. The basic ground for this further refinement of *apophasis* in the Cappadocian system was that the God who was beyond thought was nevertheless not beyond faith. "For faith," rather, "the divine has its being precisely there where thought does not reach [ekei pisteuein einai to theion eph' hōn ouk aphikneitai hē katanoēsis]." And in that sense it was permissible to speak about actually being able to "look into the ineffable depths of the thoughts of God [eis to adiexitēton tōn noēmatōn bathos]." The God who was the object of faith was one in whom there was "neither the absence of *logos* nor the presence of *tyche* nor any deterministic necessity [automaton]." From this the conclusion that followed had to be that as (in relation to the latter two of those three divine qualities, freedom from *tyche* and from deterministic necessity) there could not be a fundamental opposition between divine providence and human free will, so also (in relation to the first of these three divine qualities, that of *logos* and of freedom from irrationality) there could not be a permanent contradiction between sound reason and correct faith. Nevertheless, such a recognition came only after both the difference between faith and reason and the supremacy of faith had been acknowledged. Gregory of Nazianzus made that version of the relation between reason and faith clear in two successive orations.

"You philosopher, you thunder from the ground!" he exclaimed. "You lack even the shine a few sparks of truth might give you." The path to truth was to admit: "Faith rather than reason shall lead us, if that is, you have learned the feebleness of reason . . . and have acquired enough knowledge of reason to recognize things that surpass reason." Only then, he concluded, would the philosopher "not be a wholly earthbound thinker, ignorant of your very ignorance." But once he had put reason in its place, Nazianzen could almost immediately go on in the very next oration to portray "faith as the fulfillment of our reasoning [hē gar pistis tou kath' hēmas logou plērōsis]." This possibility for reason was, however, defeated if someone abandoned "faith, to take the power of reason as our shield." For when that happened, reason would "give way in the face of the vastness of the realities," as indeed it had to, because "the organ of human understanding" was so "frail." Paradoxically, therefore, the abandonment of "smartness of argument" was the only trustworthy path to the deliverance of reason. The doctrine of resurrection, for example, was demonstrated by faith and by the authority of Scripture; nevertheless Gregory of Nyssa urged, in requesting Macrina to push her philosophical speculations further: "Since the weakness of the human understanding is strengthened still further by any arguments [logismois] that are intelligible to us, it would be well not to leave this part of the subject without philosophical examination." Basil, too, cited the authority of "our faith" as "the universal answer" to the question, "Whence is it that we are Christians?" But if it was correct to confess, "Salvation is established through the Father and the Son and the Holy Spirit," then it was folly to "fling away that received 'pattern of teaching [typos didachēs]'" as the content of the trinitarian faith, which identified Christians as Christians and which saved them. For by authoritatively defining faith as "the substance of things hoped for, the evidence of things not seen," the New Testament put an entirely new interpretation on the relation between God and the ways of knowing, by interposing "the mediation of faith." Thus, when Abraham was summoned by God into an unknown country, he "left behind him the curiosity arising from knowledge" and relied instead on faith in God. This faith it was, according to both the Old Testament and the New Testament, that was "counted to him as righteousness"—not knowledge but faith. For knowledge acted like a merchant, dealing only with the known, Gregory of Nyssa explained, whereas the faith of Christians acted otherwise. It was characteristic of such a faith to "make the invisible our own, assuring us of the imperceptible by its own certainty about it."

Gr.Naz.Or.28.28
(SC 250:164)

Gr.Naz.Or.29.21
(SC 250:224)

Gr.Nyss.Anim.res.
(PG 46:108)

Rom 6:17
Bas.Spir.10.26
(SC 17:336)

Heb 11:1

Macr.ap.Gr.Nyss.
Anim.res. (PG 46:96)

Gn 15:6;Rom 4:3

Gr.Nyss.Eun.2.91–93
(Jaeger 1:253–54)

Prv 7:4
Gr.Naz.Or.6.5
(PG 35:728)

Florovsky 4:131–35

Ath.Ar.2.18–22
(PG 26:184–93)

Although the identification of the second *hypostasis* of the
Trinity as *Logos,* the personal Word and Reason of God, was the
most familiar and the most comprehensive expression in the language of the Bible for this positive understanding of *logos* and
therefore also for faith as the fulfillment of reason, a somewhat
less familiar title for Christ carried, especially in the Greek Christian East, much of the same meaning, but with some important
and far-reaching connotations of its own: Christ as *Sophia,* the
personified Wisdom of God. The greatest churches in the Greek
Christian East bore the name Hagia Sophia, not Hagios Logos.
The doctrinal counterpart to that architectural preeminence of
the title *Sophia* was its prominence in the Arian controversies. A
major focus of these controversies was the statement of *Sophia*
(taken to be speaking as the preexistent and preincarnate second
hypostasis of the Trinity) in the eighth chapter of the Book of
Proverbs: "The Lord created me as the *arche* of his ways for his

Prv 8:22

works [Kyrios ektise me archēn hodōn autou eis erga autou]."
The Cappadocians and their opponents were agreed on the applicability of "this expression to our Savior himself as the true

Gr.Naz.Or.30.2
(SC 250:228)
Gr.Nyss.Apoll.
(Jaeger 3–I:188)
Gr.Nyss.Cant.7
(Jaeger 6:202–3)

Sophia." Indeed, that affirmation could be regarded the common
property of all who shared the Christian faith, including Arian
and Eunomian heretics. King Solomon had great *sophia,* but
Jesus Christ was *Sophia* in person. Thus the title "*Sophia* of God"
took its place among the standard titles for him, alongside the
Pauline title "power [dynamis] of God," the Johannine title

Gr.Nyss.Apoll.
(Jaeger 3–I:219)
Jn 1:1
Portmann 1954,109–24
Gr.Nyss.Cant.8
(Jaeger 6:945)

"light" (including the Nicene "God out of God, light out of light,
true God out of true God"), and the Johannine title "life"—and
of course the Johannine title "*Logos* of God."

In part, *Sophia* connoted the special implication that the divine *Logos* was a "pedagogue." Like *Logos* itself, moreover,
Sophia was at one and the same time an epistemological and a
cosmological concept, but it was its cosmological status that gave
such an ultimate authority to its epistemological significance; for
"the creation of all beings," which Moses in the opening verses of

Gn 1:3

his cosmogony attributed to "the voice of God," thus to the
Logos as the personal Word of God, David then went on to

Ps 103:24
Gr.Nyss.Hex.
(PG 44:73)

attribute to the personal *Sophia* of God when he declared, "Thou
hast made all things by *Sophia.*" But when the heretics went on to
deduce from the words of *Sophia* in the Book of Proverbs, "The
Lord created me as the *arche* of his ways for his works," that

Prv 8:22

therefore the Son of God was a creature, though the first among
creatures, Gregory of Nyssa objected vehemently. He argued in

opposition that by applying the titles "Power of God and *Sophia* of God" to Christ, Paul had intended to assert that this was the "uncreated [acheiropoiētos] *Sophia* in its very nature," therefore Creator not creature. On that basis Nyssen could even identify *Sophia* as the very "being [to einai]" of Christ, along with "truth." And that combination of truth and *Sophia* lent special emphasis to the saying of Macrina that truth was "stored up in the hidden treasure-rooms of *Sophia*," apparently a reference to *Sophia* as the second *hypostasis* of the Trinity. As divine *Sophia* in person and divine truth in person, the Christ of the Gospels was also the revealer of timeless truths, the precepts of which Basil said: "They do not share in the changes and chances of human seasons and circumstances, but abide forever the same."

Therefore, "truth and objectivity [alētheia te kai bebaiotēs]" could be identified as "the basis of faith." There was, in the perspective of Cappadocian thought, no contradiction or disjunction at all between such a seemingly intellectualistic formula as that and the seemingly more personalistic thesis, "God remains the object of faith." For in spite of his radically *apophatic* emphasis, especially in the polemics against Eunomius, on the unattainability of any positive knowledge about the divine *ousia*, Gregory of Nyssa also insisted, specifically in opposition to Eunomius, that the two formulas, "What God is" and "What God is also believed to be," had to be identical. To anyone who might have supposed the opposite—namely, that what God was said to be was not really what God was by nature—he retorted, later in the same polemical treatise: "When we say that God is just, and almighty, and Father, and imperishable, we are not saying this merely by contrast with the *aeons* of time, nor on the basis of any relation to any other thing that exists." Rather, he continued, "Even supposing that neither the *aeons* of time nor any other created thing had been made, God would be no less what we believe God to be, there being no need for the *aeons* of time to constitute God as God" or to make God just, almighty, imperishable, and the Father of the Son. Divine revelation, therefore, neither abolished nor compromised divine transcendence, but the divine nature transcended "every way of knowledge purporting to comprehend it [pasēs hyperkeitai katalēptikēs dianoias]."

The resolution of this apparent contradiction lay in the dual doctrines of grace and of faith. On the divine side, it lay in God's accommodation to the human predicament: because it was "impossible for the naturally finite to rise above its prescribed limits,

1 Cor 1:24
Gr.Nyss.*V.Mos.*2
(Jaeger 7–I:91)

Gr.Nyss.*Cant.*1
(Jaeger 6:17)

Macr.ap.Gr.Nyss.
Anim.res. (PG 46:145)

Bas.*Ep.*254.8
(Courtonne 3:82)

Gr.Nyss.*Cant.*14
(Jaeger 6:417)

Gr.Nyss.*Maced.*
(Jaeger 3–I:97)

Gr.Nyss.*Eun.*2.89
(Jaeger 1:252–53)

Gr.Nyss.*Eun.*2.149
(Jaeger 1:268)

Gr.Nyss.*Eun.*2.534–35
(Jaeger 1:382)

Gr.Nyss.*Cant.*3
(Jaeger 6:86)

or to lay hold of the superior nature of the Most High," what was needed was for "the divine power" to endow human nature with what it was capable of receiving, by condescending to it in the incarnation; in short, God "bestowed on us this helpful gift of grace." And on the human side, the resolution of the contradiction lay in faith, which put the human reason in touch with "things celestial" by teaching it "to recognize things that surpass reason." That was what was meant by Nazianzen's axiomatic definition of faith as "the fulfillment of our reasoning." Faith, then, was not simply one in a series of the several ways of knowing, but it was the most radically *apophatic* of such ways, which granted "certainty about nonapparent reality" by recognizing the enormous limitations under which all human knowledge was obliged to labor. That was also what Nyssen meant by his statement quoted earlier, that for faith, the divine had its being precisely there where thought did not reach. In that way faith accomplished what reason and knowledge purported to accomplish and could not, but it did so by its reverent acceptance both of divine transcendence and of human finitude.

Those radically *apophatic* definitions of faith, truth, and the grace of revelation also determined the place occupied in the Cappadocian system by the doctrine of Scripture. As orthodox Christian theologians, Basil and the two Gregorys were all unambiguously certain of its divine inspiration and of its authority, quoting and affirming the language of the apostle Paul about "divinely inspired [theopneustos] Scripture," and applying it to the New Testament no less than to the Old Testament, about which it had been specifically spoken. Macrina was speaking in the name also of the other three when she said: "We make the Holy Scriptures the rule and the measure of every tenet; we necessarily fix our eyes upon that, and approve only that which may be made to harmonize with the intention of those writings." The historical descriptions and prophecies of the Old Testament, therefore, even such seemingly trivial ones as those that prescribed the vestments of the Levitical priesthood, were to be read as speaking authoritatively "concerning the things happening now, in our own time." All of this was important as a part of their exposition of the church's revealed teachings, and it would bulk large as prolegomenon in any attempt to construct their system of church dogmatics. But there was also a role for natural theology and for the understanding of faith as the fulfillment of reason within their doctrine of Scripture, and it became the most explicit and the most distinctive at several crucial points: in prescribing

Gr.Nyss.*Eun.*2.417–19
(Jaeger 1:348)

Gr.Naz.*Or.*28.28
(SC 250:164)
Gr.Naz.*Or.*29.21
(SC 250:224)

Gr.Nyss.*Eun.*2.91–93
(Jaeger 1:253–54)

Gr.Nyss.*V.Mos.*1
(Jaeger 7–I:22)

Bas.*Spir.*21.52
(SC 17:438);
Gr.Naz.*Or.*28.9
(SC 250:116);
Gr.Nyss.*Cant.*15
(Jaeger 6:436)

2 Tm 3:16

Macr.ap.Gr.Nyss.
Anim.res. (PG 46:49)

Gr.Nyss.*V.Mos.*2
(Jaeger 7–I:103)

the technical methodology for their philological scholarship
when they handled the sacred text as text; in setting the metaphysical context for their allegorical and typological exegesis of
the Bible; and in providing the framework for their correlation of
Scripture and tradition through what we are calling here the
metamorphosis of natural theology.

Trained as the Cappadocians were in the literary, rhetorical,
and grammatical methodologies of the post-Hellenistic Classical
schools, they were functioning as Greek philologists whether the
text before them happened to come from Homer or from the
Holy Spirit. Many of the principles and procedures of a sound
philology, originally developed for the textual criticism of Homer
by pagan Classical scholars, were now adapted by Christian
scholars for the textual criticism of Scripture. For example, Basil
found that the "obelos," a mark developed by Classical textual
critics to indicate a spurious passage in a manuscript, was no less
useful for the textual criticism of the Septuagint Pentateuch. In
that sense these philological principles and procedures must be
said to have belonged no less to natural theology when they were
being applied to the text of the Bible. Nevertheless, the biblical
text, even seen purely as text, presented unique problems and
special opportunities to these Christian practitioners of "sacred
philology." The most obvious problem for the Cappadocians as
products of a Classical education, accustomed as they were to
being able to read Homer or Plato in Greek with ease, was that in
confronting the Septuagint version of the Old Testament they
were obliged to deal with a translation, not the original. To be
sure, they could propound a special theory about linguistic history: "The Hebrew tongue is not ancient like the others, but
along with other miracles this miracle was wrought on behalf of
the Israelites, and after the Exodus from Egypt the language was
hastily improvised for the use of the [Israelite] nation." But that
did not mitigate the undeniable linguistic reality that this miracle
had determined the original language of the Old Testament Scriptures to be Hebrew, which they were unable to read. And so,
although they may have been, as Basil said, dedicated to the
principle of taking the meaning "in every phrase and in every
syllable" of Sacred Scripture with the utmost seriousness, these
phrases and syllables had to be Greek, not alone in the New
Testament, whose original was written in Greek, but also in the
Old, where the Greek version was only a later translation.

Gregory of Nyssa, for example, responded to a challenge from
Eunomius concerning the interpretation of the Book of Exodus

Metzger 1975,340–49

Harl 1971,127–43
Amand de Mendieta
1965

Field 1875,1:lii-lvii

Bas.*Hex*.4.5
(*SC* 26:264)

Kristeller 1961,79

Gr.Nyss.*Or.dom*.5
(*PG* 44:1188)

Gr.Nyss.*Eun*.2.256
(Jaeger 1:301)

Bas.*Spir*.1.2
(*SC* 17:252)

by declaring: "If he says that this is the sense of what is written, we must examine the original language of Scripture [ho prōto-typos tēs graphēs logos]." Yet he was in fact still compelled to be appealing, despite what he seemed to be saying, only to the Greek of the Septuagint, not to the genuine Hebrew "original language of Scripture" for a passage from Exodus. That became obvious when in this very context he quoted the title for Christ from Isaiah as "angel of mighty counsel [megalēs boulēs angelos]," which appeared in the Greek version but not in the original Hebrew text. Similarly, when Basil wrote about his biblical studies to the pagan master of Greek rhetoric, Libanius, he said, with evident embarrassment at having to admit this to another Hellenic purist, that he was "now spending [his] time with Moses and Elijah, and saints like them, telling me their stories in a barbarous tongue [ek tēs barbarou phōnēs]." Nevertheless, this did not mean, in his case either, that he was studying the Old Testament in the "barbarous tongue" of the original Hebrew, as a casual reader of his words might surmise, but rather that even in the Greek of the Septuagint the sayings of Moses and Elijah were "rude in phrase," in comparison with those of the Attic masters whom both he and Libanius so revered. A theory was attributed to Eunomius, on the basis of the statement of Psalm 146, "God numbers the stars one by one and calls each by name [ho arithmōn plēthē astrōn, kai pasin autois onomata kalōn]," that the names of the individual stars had come directly from God at creation. In response, Gregory of Nyssa argued: "If there were other names of stars [that is, divinely given ones], Holy Scripture would not have cited those that are in common use among the Greeks, as when Isaiah says, 'Who makes the Pleiades, and Hesperus, and Arcturus' . . . or when Job names 'Orion' and 'Asteroth' "—almost as though he not only had reversed Isaiah and Job but had been under the impression that these Greek names used for the stars by the Septuagint were actually the original words of Hebrew Scripture.

Nevertheless, as the general usage of Nyssen and of the other Cappadocians showed, they remained quite aware that the ultimate authority of the biblical text did repose in "the precise meaning of the Hebrew phrases [akribeia tōn Hebraikōn lexeōn]," even though they themselves were not technically equipped to handle such phrases in Hebrew. Thus, despite the homiletical and edifying attractiveness of such an etymology, it was the Hebrew original "pesach," not the similar-sounding Greek verb "paschein [to suffer]," that constituted the ety-

Is 9:5

Gr.Nyss.*Eun.*3.9.33
(Jaeger 2:276)

See pp.20–21

Bas.*Ep.*339
(Courtonne 3:207)

Ps 146:4

Eun.ap.Gr.Nyss.*Eun.*
2.437 (Jaeger 1:354)

Jb 9:9

Is 13:10

Gr.Nyss.*Eun.*2.437
(Jaeger 1:354)

Gr.Nyss.*Cant.*14
(Jaeger 6:410)

mological origin of "pascha," the name for Passover in the Septuagint, as in the passage, "It is a Passover to the Lord [pascha estin kuriōi]," which then went on to become the Greek Christian name for Easter. The name Jacob meant "supplanter," as Esau indicated when he said that Jacob "supplanted me" ("epterniken me," as the Septuagint had it); Gregory of Nyssa explained the Hebrew etymology of the name, being careful, however, to avoid the impression that this information came from his own linguistic erudition, but making clear that he got this from "the learned in such matters." Therefore, the Cappadocians could occasionally take it upon themselves to criticize the Septuagint translation as an unsatisfactory rendering of the Hebrew original. One method they could sometimes invoke to cope with this quandary, of knowing that the Greek version was wrong but being unable to correct it themselves on the basis of the original Hebrew, was to have recourse to other Greek translations from the second century of the Christian era, those of Symmachus (who was probably a Jewish proselyte), of Theodotion, and of Aquila (who was said to have been a convert from paganism to Christianity, and subsequently from Christianity to Judaism), as a way of amplifying or correcting the Septuagint version. But for some Hebrew terms there simply was no adequate Greek word in any of these translations. Thus "ouranos" was the Greek word for "heaven," no less in the Greek Christian Scriptures—for example, in the very first verse of the Bible—than in Classical usage; but it was important to be reminded that this was not what "the [original] Hebrew called it." "Darkness [skotos]," too, had in Hebrew a name different from that Greek word. This display of a borrowed linguistic erudition or (as the Latin West would call it) "Hebraica veritas" served the purpose of presenting the exegete's credentials as a qualified philologist, credentials that were necessary no less for Christian scholarship than for Classical.

But sometimes a critical awareness of the differences between the Hebrew original and the Greek translation could also become a matter of great theological as well as philological import. Above all, that issue was repeatedly brought home to Christians in their encounters with Judaism, with which they shared "the divinely inspired Scriptures" but not the christological interpretation of those Scriptures; thus, the prophecy of Isaiah that read in the Septuagint, and then in the New Testament, "Behold, the virgin will conceive [idou, hē parthenos en gastri exei]," which was being applied to the Virgin Mary by Christians, did not, according to Jewish philology and Jewish exegesis of the original

Ex 12:11
Gr.Naz.Or.45.10
(PG 36:636–37)

Gn 27:36

Gr.Nyss.Eun.2.286
(Jaeger 1:310)
Sg 1:6
Gr.Nyss.Cant.2
(Jaeger 6:53–54)

Gr.Nyss.Hex.
(PG 44:80)

Gr.Nyss.Cant.13
(Jaeger 6:390)

Gn 1:1
Gr.Nyss.Eun.2.406
(Jaeger 1:344)
Gr.Nyss.Virg.4
(Jaeger 8–1:271)

Smalley 1964,329–55

Gr.Nyss.Or.catech.4.1
(Méridier 20)

Is 7:14

Mt 1:23

ap.Ath.*Ar.*1.54
(PG 26:125)

Prv 8:22

Bas.*Eun.*2.20
(SC 305:84)

Ath.*Ar.*2.18–22
(PG 26:184–93)
Gr.Nyss.*Ref.*110
(Jaeger 2:358)
Bas.*Eun.*2.2
(SC 305:84)
Gr.Nyss.*Eun.*2.286
(Jaeger 1:310)

Field 1875,1:7;13

Brooks 1991,108–9

Hebrew, refer to the Virgin at all, neither to the Virgin Mary nor to any other virgin, but simply to "a young woman of marriageable age." But perhaps the most crucial passage where the theological import of the relation between the Hebrew and the Greek manifested itself in the intramural Christian disputes of the fourth century was the saying quoted earlier from personified *Sophia* in the Book of Proverbs: "The Lord created me [ektise me] as the *arche* of his ways for all his works." Basil insisted that this was the only passage in all of Scripture that seemed to say something like this, and he explained as well that Solomon in the Book of Proverbs, though undoubtedly inspired by God, had made it a practice to speak obscurely and in parables. But then he went on, in his refutation of the theory of Eunomius according to which this passage made Christ as *Sophia-Logos* the creature through whom God had made all the other creatures, to cite the authority of "other translators" who had rendered the Hebrew more faithfully with "The Lord possessed me [ektēsato me] as the *arche* of his ways for all his works" rather than "The Lord created me [ektisen me] as the *arche* of his ways for all his works." This was a theological point that had appeared before Basil, in the response of Athanasius to the Arian exegesis of the passage, and that then appeared again, in the defense of Basil against Eunomius by Gregory of Nyssa. Although the Cappadocians often spoke vaguely of "other translators" or sometimes of "the learned in such matters" in identifying the source for all this information about the Hebrew text and about the differences between the Septuagint and the versions of Aquila, Symmachus, Theodotion, and other Greek translators, there is every reason to believe that it had come to them in considerable measure from that massive six-thousand-page compilation of sacred philology known as the *Hexapla*. Prepared by Origen of Alexandria between 228 and 245, the *Hexapla* is now largely lost except for fragments, some of which have been preserved in the writings of the Cappadocians.

Even when the original was in Greek, moreover, as with the New Testament, it was the task of Christian sacred philology, in some sort of dialectical dependence upon the natural philological methodology of the Classical schools, to become involved in determining of the correct text of Scripture. Without attempting here to reconstruct all the principles of textual criticism as practiced by the Cappadocians, in comparison or contrast with those of Origen, we may briefly cite two instances of their way of reading textual variants. In John 1:18 there was a choice to be made between calling Christ "the only-begotten God [monogenēs theos]" and the title "the only-begotten Son [ho monogenēs huios]," with significant evidence from manuscripts and ancient versions supporting each reading. Although he sometimes employed it elsewhere, the variant did not figure in Nazianzen's five *Theological Orations,* where "the only-begotten God" would have been useful to make the theological point. But Nyssen in his *Refutation of the Confession of Eunomius* consistently followed the reading "the only-begotten God," and Eunomius does not seem to have countered with the less explicit-sounding version; Basil, too, made use of the reading "the only-begotten God." Similarly, there was a choice in 1 Timothy 3:16 between "he was manifested in flesh [hos ephanerōthē en sarki]" and "God was manifested in flesh [theos ephanerōthē en sarki]." Once again, it was the reading more favorable to Nicene orthodoxy that Gregory of Nyssa adopted in writing against Eunomius.

Faith in the transcendent reality of God, which was known both to faith and to natural theology, could act as "the fulfillment of reasoning" in another fundamental way, by providing both the rationale and the method for the spiritual interpretation of Scripture. The basic assumption was the *apophatic* one, that the operations of God took place "in a hidden way [en apokryphōi]," from which it followed not only that the believer in the exercise of the apologetic task was obliged to "search out some reasonable solution of the question posed," but also that the words of God describing such operations were to be understood in a special way. A knowledge dealing with "a truth outside our nature" necessarily had to be a knowledge that was, as the apostle Paul warned, "imperfect [ek merous]"; therefore, it had to come to terms with the special qualities of biblical language and be ready to interpret it allegorically. Gregory of Nyssa often warned that the literal meaning of the text could be dangerously misleading. He spoke of "a supreme necessity for exegesis not to stick to the letter [pasan anankēn einai mē parameinai tōi grammati tēn exēgēsin]." The reason he gave for this commendation of a non-literal, spiritual exegesis was "the divine intention lying hidden under the body of the Scripture, as it were under a veil, because some legislative enactment or historical narrative was cast over the truths being contemplated by the mind." So it came about that "often the obvious interpretation, when not taken according to the proper sense," would have "an effect contrary to that life indicated by the Spirit," and therefore it could not be the correct interpretation. Spiritual interpretation, consequently, had to be

Fennema 1985,124–35
McReynolds 1981,105–18
Gr.Naz.*Ep.*202
(*PG* 37:333)

Norris 1991,173;203

Gr.Nyss.*Ref.*8;61;162
(Jaeger 2:315;336;380)

Bas.*Spir.*8.19
(*SC* 17:312)

Sanders 1971,15–17

Brooks 1991,235
Gr.Nyss.*Ref.*2
(Jaeger 2:312–13)

Fedwick 1981, 1:337–60

Ps 30:20

Gr.Nyss.*Or.catech.*17.3
(Méridier 92)

1 Cor 13:12
Gr.Nyss.*Cant.*11
(*PG* 44:1001)
Gr.Nyss.*V.Mos.*2
(Jaeger 7-I:110–11)

Gr.Nyss.*Cant.*6
(Jaeger 6:190)

2 Cor 3:15

Gr.Nyss.*Eun.*3.5.9–10
(Jaeger 2:163)

Gr.Nyss.*Cant*.pr.
(Jaeger 6:4–5)

applicable also to "historical narratives [ta historika diēgēmata]" in the Bible, not only to biblical poetry and prophecy. The proper technique was to "take the words allegorically, and so penetrate to the inner sense of the history, yet without losing sight of the truth of its facts"—and neither of these without the other: biblical history and biblical allegory were interdependent. Sometimes he, too, avoided the spiritual interpretation even when it might have seemed to be applicable.

Gr.Nyss.*Eun*.2.85
(Jaeger 1:251)

Gr.Nyss.*Hex*.
(PG 44:121)

Evidently, that exegetical method did not apply equally to all parts of Scripture; nor, for that matter, did all the Cappadocians apply it equally. It was at least in part the dangers in the allegorical interpretation of the Old Testament that seem to have prompted Basil's recommendation that the New Testament receive a preferred position in the believer's reading. And in one of the most vigorous criticisms of allegorical exegesis to come from any orthodox Christian theologian in the fourth (or any other) century, Basil declared: "I know the laws of allegory, though less by myself than from the works of others. There are those truly, who do not admit the common meaning of the Scriptures, for whom water is no water, but some other nature, who see in a plant, in a fish, what their fancy wishes, who change the nature of reptiles and of wild beasts to suit their allegories, like the interpreters of dreams who explain visions in sleep to make them serve their own ends. For me grass is grass; plant, fish, wild beast, domestic animal—I take them all in the literal sense." Yet none of that prevented him from taking even New Testament passages in the spiritual sense when it suited. The authority of the New Testament permitted him to acknowledge that Old Testament events were "intended as a shadow and type [eis skian kai typon]." Holy Scripture, he asserted, taught "through mysteries [di' aporrētōn]" and "as it were in shadows and reflections [hōsper en skiais tisi kai katoptrois]." Precisely because of divine transcendence, divine realities were "very frequently represented by the shadow paintings [skiagraphiai] of the types."

Bas.*Ep*.42.3
(Courtonne 1:103)

Bas.*Hex*.9.1
(SC 26:478–80)
Acts 1:6–7
Bas.*Ep*.8.7
(Courtonne 1:31)

Bas.*Leg.lib.gent*.2
(Wilson 21)

Bas.*Spir*.14.31
(SC 17:354)

That reference to "shadow paintings" was reminiscent of Plato's use of this term, and of the allegory of the cave in Book VII of the *Republic*. But the New Testament itself had invoked the term "shadow [skia]" in its interpretation of the ceremonial laws of the Old Testament: "These are no more than a shadow of what was to come; the body is Christ's [ha estin skia tōn mellontōn, to de sōma tou Christou]." Such New Testament usage enabled Gregory of Nazianzus to speak of how God had showed Moses

Pl.*Cri*.107c-d

Pl.*R*.514–17

Col 2:16–17

Ex 25:40;Heb 10:1

Gr.Naz.*Or*.45.11
(PG 36:637)

See pp.222–23

Gr.Naz.*Or*.1.3
(SC 247:74–76)

Gr.Naz.*Or*.4.118
(SC 309:282)

Gr.Naz.*Or*.45.16
(PG 36:645)

Gr.Nyss.*Or.catech*.4.1
(Méridier 20)

See p.43

Gr.Naz.*Or*.21.22
(SC 270:156)
Gr.Naz.*Or*.28.28
(SC 250:164)

"the visible things as an adumbration of and design for the invisible things." He made productive use of the typological method to spiritualize the history of the Jewish Exodus into an allegory for the resurrection of Christ ("pascha" being the Greek name both for the Jewish Passover and for the Christian Easter): "Yesterday the lamb was slain and the door posts were anointed, and Egypt bewailed her firstborn, and the destroyer passed us over. . . . To-day we have completely escaped from Egypt and from Pharaoh; and there is none to hinder us from keeping a feast to the Lord our God, the feast of our own exodus [heortēn tēn exodion]." Yet this method, also as it was carried on by Nazianzen, manifested its ties with the Classical heritage, and not only with the Christian heritage. Some Christian exegetes practiced allegory without being aware that pagans were also doing so; some condemned pagan allegory but did not resort to it themselves; and some avoided it but did not condemn the pagans for using it. But Gregory, while criticizing the pagan allegory of Classical poems and myths as unwarranted, admitted at the same time—to the emperor Julian, who was well aware of it—that a similar allegory was also being practiced "within our own circle." Because it was within the circle, he also warned his Christian hearers, after an extensive typological interpretation of Old Testament sacrifices, not to "carry any of this abroad." He added the explanation: "Most of our mysteries may not be carried out to those who are on the outside."

It was thus an advantage to share with one's opponents an acceptance of the same biblical authority. Nevertheless, the realities of theological polemics made it clear that such an acceptance of authority was not sufficient of itself to guarantee agreement on doctrine. At the Synod of Seleucia in 359, Gregory of Nazianzus reported, "the ancient and pious doctrine that defended the Trinity was abolished, by setting up a palisade and battering down the *homoousion*," on the grounds that this Nicene term did not appear in Scripture (any more, he might have added, than "Trinity [trias]" itself did). Yet this argument from Scripture, he charged, was a pretext for "really introducing unscriptural Arianism." That heresy in turn was, according to Nazianzen, the result of refusing to let "faith rather than reason lead us." In opposition to it, he joined Basil and Nyssen in trying to argue dialectically, but then he turned to biblical authority. "Now that we know just how invincible you are in logical twists," he asserted sarcastically to Eunomius, "let us see what strength you

Gr.Naz.Or.29.16–17
(SC 250:212)

Gr.Naz.Or.43.69
(PG 36:589)

Florovsky 1:85–89

Bas.Leg.lib.gent.7
(Wilson 27)

See pp.252–53
See pp.304–5

1 Cor 2:7

Amand de Mendieta
1965,21–39

Bas.Spir.27.66
(SC 17:478–80)

Pelikan 1971–89,4:121
Pelikan 1971–89,
4:276–77

can muster from Holy Scripture!" The reason for citing Scripture as the ultimate authority, he declared, was this: "We, after all, understand and preach the divinity of the Son on the basis of its grand and sublime language." At the same time, the biblical case for orthodox doctrine did not imply that there was any uniformity in that "grand and sublime language"; for among the evangelists, there were "some more occupied with the human side of Christ, and others paying attention to his deity." The reason for this was: "Some [the Synoptic Gospels] commenced their history with what is within our experience, others [the Gospel of John] with what is above us." But if heretics, too, could quote Scripture, the standard of orthodoxy, in order to be faithful to Scripture, had to involve something more than Scripture, namely, the traditions of the church. For the Cappadocians said that it was characteristic of the truth of revelation, as they knew it had also been of Classical paganism, that "the virtuous deeds of the men of old were preserved for us, either through an unbroken oral tradition or through being preserved in the words of poets or writers of prose."

The most critical example of this problem of Scripture and tradition in Cappadocian theology was the doctrine of the Holy Spirit, because of the ambiguities of scriptural usage and the undeveloped state of biblical and ecclesiastical doctrine. To deal with the paucity in the Scriptures of explicit instances of the identification of the Spirit as "God," Basil invoked the authority of nonbiblical traditions: "Of the beliefs and practices, whether generally accepted or publicly enjoined, which are preserved in the church, some we possess derived from written teaching [tōn en tēi ekklēsiai pephylagmenōn dogmatōn kai kērygmatōn ta men ek tēs eggraphou didaskalias]; others we have received delivered to us 'in a mystery' by the tradition of the apostles [ek tēs tōn apostolōn paradoseōs]; and both of these in relation to true religion have the same force. And these no one will gainsay—no one, at all events, who is even moderately versed in the institutions of the church. For were we to attempt to reject such customs as have no written authority [ta agrapha tōn ethōn], on the ground that the importance they possess is small, we should unintentionally injure the gospel in its very vitals; or, rather, we should make our public definition a mere phrase and nothing more." This passage continued to be quoted for many centuries also in the Latin West, being incorporated into Gratian's collection of canon law and then figuring in the controversies of the Reformation. But the most intriguing aspect of it here is its relation to the *meta-morphosis* of natural theology; for as has been suggested earlier, in the thought of the Cappadocians natural theology and religious tradition were not seen as antithetical—as they were in the Classical period, and would be again during the Enlightenment—but as complementary and mutually supportive.

Basil took one of his arguments for nonwritten tradition as an authority from a deft combination of Mosaic precedent and natural law, posing the question: "What was the meaning of the mighty Moses in not making all the parts of the tabernacle open to everyone?" The answer was: "Moses was wise enough to know that contempt attaches to the trite and the obvious, while a keen interest is naturally associated with the unusual and the unfamiliar." For the Cappadocians, Moses was the supreme example in Scripture of how "pagan learning" and wisdom could be exploited to impart *sophia* also to the believer. It was, Basil seems to have been arguing, from that knowledge and *sophia* that Moses became "wise enough" to keep the inner sanctum of the tabernacle secret. Again, one of the Christian practices that Basil cited as possessing traditionary authority without being set down in Scripture was orientation, prayer facing the rising sun in the East; orientation was shared by Christians and pagans. "What writing has taught us," he demanded, "to turn to the East at prayer [to pros anatolas tetraphthai]?" Orientation was a practice explicitly endorsed also by his brother Gregory of Nyssa, in his words, and by their sister, Macrina, in her religious actions. Natural theology, therefore, had the function not of undermining unwritten tradition but of supporting it, and of doing so in conjunction with the authority of Scripture. Similarly, Gregory of Nazianzus could invoke the natural processes of growth and development as a key metaphor for the gradual "additions, advances and progressions" of Christian history to the divine revelation of what the New Testament had described as "that faith which God entrusted to his people once for all."

In their celebration of the uniqueness of faith, therefore, the Cappadocians could emphasize that no amount of philological learning was sufficient for the correct understanding of Scripture, which was accessible only "through spiritual contemplation [dia tēs pneumatikēs theōrias]" and true faith. Yet that did not keep them from exploiting a natural knowledge of philology to the fullest; for there was no opposition between that exclusionary emphasis on faith and their celebration of reason's worship of a

Nm 4:20;Ex 30:10;Lv 16

Bas.*Spir.*27.66 (SC 17:482)

Gr.Nyss.*V.Mos.*1;2 (Jaeger 7–I:7–8;139)

See p.112

Gr.Nyss.*Or.dom.*5 (PG 44:1184) Macr.ap.Gr.Nyss. *V.Macr.* (Jaeger 8–I:396)

Gr.Naz.*Or.*31.25–26 (SC 250:324–26)

Jude 3

Gr.Nyss.*Cant.*15 (Jaeger 6:436)

Bas.*Hex*.1.2
(*SC* 26:96)

Gr.Naz.*Or*.29.21
(*SC* 250:224)

Bas.*Eun*.2.22
(*SC* 305:88)

God who was "a worthy object of love for all beings endowed with reason, the *kalon* most to be desired, the *arche* of all existing things, the source of life, intellectual light." For other ways of knowing, including the way of reason, were simultaneously refuted and yet fulfilled by following the way of faith. And nowhere did that paradox manifest itself more dramatically for them than in the "chief dogma" of revealed religion, the doctrine of God as Trinity.

CHAPTER 15

The One and the Three

Bas.*Eun.*2.22
(SC 305:88)

When the doctrine of God as one, articulated in the context of natural theology as the center of the apologetic case of the Cappadocians against Classical polytheism, became in turn the presupposition for the center of all revealed teaching, the orthodox dogma of the Trinity articulated in the confession of the Council of Nicaea as, in Basil's words, the "chief dogma," its critics interpreted this as some kind of relapse into polytheism. Such allegations had arisen already in response to the theology of Athanasius, in which the interrelation between apologetics and presupposition set up many of same the tensions between "synthesis" and "antithesis" that again became discernible in Cappadocian thought. But now that the opposition to orthodox trinitarianism was coming no longer from Arius but from Aetius and Eunomius, with their much more sophisticated dialectics and metaphysics, the result was an even greater potential for tension when, having moved from the many to the One, the doctrine of God moved on to the One and the Three. Coping with that tension was in many ways the gravest of all the challenges not alone to the dogmatics of the Cappadocians but to their natural theology as well; for they could not simply consign natural theology to apologetics but were obliged to prove that they were speaking about the relation of the One and the Three in a manner that was consistent in both thought and language with the way they spoke about the relation of the many and the One. Judaism, Hellenism at its best as represented by those whom Gregory of Nazianzus called its "more advanced philosophers," and Chris-

Meijering 1968

Vandenbussche 1944,
47–72

Hanson 1988,676–737

Gr.Nyss.*Maced.*
(Jaeger 3–I:101)

Gr.Naz.*Or.*31.15
(SC 250:304)

Gr.Naz.Or.38.15
(PG 36:328–29)
Gr.Nyss.Eun.3.2.94
(Jaeger 2:83)

tianity of every stripe—all three claimed to be repudiating what Gregory of Nyssa labeled "the superstition of polytheism." To borrow the phraseology of the familiar antithesis from Blaise Pascal, the God of Abraham, Isaac, and Jacob was one God; and the God of the philosophers, rightly understood, was one God. But was the God confessed as Father, Son, and Holy Spirit by Christians, both orthodox and heretical, still one God, and one in the same sense? It was the fundamental argument of the Cappadocian case for Nicene trinitarianism that authentic monotheism was the rejection of the many for the sake of the One, but not of the Three for the sake of the One. The ground of that argument was formulated by Basil: "The terms 'one' and 'only' are predi-

Bas.Ep.8.3
(Courtonne 1:26)
Stephan 1938,25–38;
Prestige 1956,242–64

cated of God not to mark a distinction from the Son and the Holy Spirit, but to exclude the unreal gods falsely so called." Given the complexity of Cappadocian trinitarianism in its own right, what was its relation to Cappadocian natural theology?

Casting the *apophatic* theology of the Cappadocians back at

Eun.ap.Bas.Eun.1.17
(SC 299:232)

them, Eunomius affirmed a truly divine "transcending all understanding." But Eunomius was making this concession to the language of transcendence, Basil replied, only in order to demon-

Bas.Eun.1.27
(SC 299:266)

strate that the Son of God was on the same level with the created world, rather than on the same level with God the Father. In a similar use of such language, the formal statement of faith by Eunomius contained this confession concerning the relation be-tween the Father and the Son: "There is the supreme and absolute

Eun.ap.Gr.Nyss.Eun.
1.151 (Jaeger 1:72)

being, and then there is another being existing by reason of the first, but after it though before all others." This, too, Gregory of Nyssa charged, was an attempt to distort the orthodox doctrine of divine transcendence and absoluteness in such a way as to

Gr.Nyss.Eun.1.156
(Jaeger 1:74)

prove that it was contradicted by the orthodox doctrine of the Trinity. But, as he said later in the same treatise, "If the majesty of the divine nature transcends all height, and if it excels every

Gr.Nyss.Eun.3.1.136
(Jaeger 2:49)

power that calls forth our wonder, what idea remains that can carry the meaning of the name 'Son' to something greater still?" When Eunomius was speaking clearly and consistently, according to the Cappadocians, his chief presupposition was not *apophasis* or the proper language of transcendence at all, but his claim to "a knowledge without anything being incomprehensible

Gr.Nyss.Eun.3.2.8
(Jaeger 2:54)

to it" and therefore also to a capacity to explain "the ineffable begetting [gennēsis] of the Son."

Apophasis remained in force, however, to supply the proper

Gr.Nyss.Eun.1.377–79
(Jaeger 1:137–38)

lexicon of transcendence, also in the church's confession of the doctrine of the Trinity. On the basis of the statement of the Gospel

See pp.224–25

Jn 1:18

Gr.Nyss.*Eun*.2.12
(Jaeger 1:230)

Gr.Nyss.*Eun*.3.6.63
(Jaeger 2:208)

Bas.*Spir*.8.20
(*SC* 17:316–18)

Gr.Nyss.*Ref*.127–28
(Jaeger 2:367)

Pelikan 1971–89,
1:211–25

Bas.*Spir*.19.49
(*SC* 17:418–22)

Gr.Nyss.*Fid*.
(Jaeger 3–1:66)
Ps 142:10

Gr.Naz.*Or*.31.8
(*SC* 250:290)

Bas.*Ep*.38.4
(Courtonne 1:85)
Gr.Naz.*Or*.6.12
(*PG* 35:737)

Gr.Nyss.*Comm.not*.
(Jaeger 3–1:21–22)

of John (and with the textual variant of which he was fond), "No one has ever seen God; but the only-begotten God, who is nearest to the Father's heart, has made him known," Gregory of Nyssa affirmed: "The main point of Christian orthodoxy is to believe that the only-begotten God, who is the truth and the true light, is truly all that he is said to be . . . , who never at any time was not, nor ever will cease to be, whose being, such as it essentially is, is beyond the reach of the curiosity that would try to comprehend it." Thus, the Son shared fully in the transcendence of the Father; as Nyssen declared later in the treatise, "There is no kinship between the created world and all the things which the orthodox doctrine assumes that we assert concerning God the only Son." The alternative was to deny the Son a participation in the eternal and transcendent being of the Godhead. His divine nature, too, had to be described in *apophatic* language and in alpha privatives, as remaining "incapable of evil, unchangeable, unalterable." In taking upon themselves, for the first time in Christian history, an extended and thorough exploration of the doctrine of the Holy Spirit, as it fell to the generation of the Cappadocians to do, it was likewise necessary to acknowledge the Spirit as a fully transcendent being, beyond anything conceivable by the human mind. The creation could be called good "because of its participation in the transcendent good"; but by contrast with this participation by the creation, the participation of the Holy Spirit in the transcendent good of the divine nature was eternal and without beginning, essential and not derivative, by nature and not by grace, as the biblical title "your good Spirit" showed. Both the "begetting of the Son" and the "procession of the Spirit" within the Godhead, consequently, remained ineffable and transcendent.

A fundamental component of the trinitarian dogma, therefore, was the confession that all three of the divine *hypostases* in the Trinity shared in the *apophatic* qualities of the divine nature: "the communion and the distinction" within the Trinity remained "ineffable and inconceivable." So did the harmony and freedom from conflict that the *hypostases* shared. The Nicene dogma did not abolish the need for *apophasis*, as a shallow interpretation of orthodox doctrine might have led someone to suppose. If anything, orthodox trinitarianism intensified that need, for any increase in knowledge about God (above all, the revelation of the knowledge of God as Father, Son, and Holy Spirit) ultimately consisted in an increase in the knowledge that God was and remained incomprehensible and transcendent. The mys-

Gr.Nyss.*Cant.*3
(Jaeger 6:85)

2 Cor 12:3–4

tery of divine being transcended not only the rational and philosophical constructs of Classical natural theology but the revealed
and orthodox truth of the church's dogmatic theology itself. For
"every doctrine concerning the ineffable nature," no matter how
sublime, divinely inspired, and orthodox it was, was still "only a
copy of the gold, not the gold itself," involving as it did "words so
secret as to be unrepeatable by human lips." So profound and
transcendent was that mystery, also for Christian revelation and
for orthodox theology, that Gregory of Nyssa was constrained to
explain: "Whoever searches the whole of revelation will find
there no doctrine of the divine nature at all, nor indeed a doctrine
of anything else that has a substantial existence, so that we pass
our lives in ignorance of much, being ignorant first of all of
ourselves as human beings, and then of all other things besides,"

Gr.Nyss.*Eun.*2.106
(Jaeger 1:257–58)

including the soul and its relation to the body. He was moved to
this explanation in part by his shock at the declaration of Eunomius that the specific content of "the mystery of our religion"

1 Tm 3:16

was "exactness of doctrines" rather than "the distinctive charac-

Eun.ap.Gr.Nyss.*Eun.*
3.9.54 (Jaeger 2:284)

ter of customs and sacramental tokens." In opposition to this

Gr.Nyss.*Eun.*3.9.56;59
(Jaeger 2:285–86)

Gregory insisted that it was a characteristic of paganism, but not
of Christianity, "to think of a piety consisting in doctrines only."
And the doctrine of the Trinity, being a doctrine about why Father, Son, and Holy Spirit must (as the Nicene Creed required)

Symb.Nic.-CP
(Alberigo-Jedin 24)

"be worshiped and glorified together," was no exception to this
rule.

As the Cappadocians found it consistent with the *apophatic*
definition of transcendence in their natural theology to predicate
such a transcendence of the Son and the Holy Spirit in the revealed doctrine of the Trinity, so they also drew a line from their
apologetic definition of creation as a creatio ex nihilo to the
trinitarian dogma. That definition of creation was drawn in opposition to the Classical teaching that creation had a "double
arche," with matter coming to the Creator "from without" and

Bas.*Hex.*2.2
(SC 26:146)

therefore having an eternal existence of its own. But when Eunomius tried to apply the same schematism to the doctrine of the
Trinity by teaching "the transition of the only-begotten one from
nothing into being," which Gregory of Nyssa described as "the
doctrine that he who made us and all creation out of nothing is
himself out of nothing," Gregory rejected that as a "horrible and

Gr.Nyss.*Eun.*3.6.1–2
(Jaeger 2:185)

godless doctrine, more to be shunned than all impiety." And yet,
for a rather curious reason, the Cappadocians found that the
Classical idea of creation as involving "two eternal and unbegot-

Gr.Nyss.*Hom.opif.*23
(PG 44:212)

ten existences, having their being concurrently with each other" did represent an intuition that was valid in Christian thought: that the one God who was the Creator had always stood in a relationship, but nevertheless did not have need of the world to know the meaning of authentic relationship, because this authentic relationship was the one between the Father, the Son, and the Holy Spirit in the eternal Trinity before the *aeons,* rather than with any creature. Therefore, in Basil's words, "God has not only wished to create the world, but to create it with the help of a cooperator." That made the Son of God and *Logos* "the Creator of the universe [ho dēmiourgos tōn holōn]," fellow Creator with the Father and not fellow creature with the universe. And therefore, as Gregory of Nyssa conceded, "In all other cases it is true that the word 'one' carries with it the significance of not being coupled with anything else, but in the case of the Father and the Son, 'one' does not imply isolation." The Greeks put creation into eternity, and the heretics put the Trinity into time. But the true situation was the opposite, and on both counts: "The begetting of the Son does not fall within time, any more than the creation was before time." It was the failure to make this distinction that prompted Eunomius to insist, "If you allow that God the *Logos* is to be believed to be eternal, you must allow the same of the things that have been created." But the kingdom of God was "a kingdom of all the *aeons,*" as the Psalm said, not because the world was eternal but because God the Trinity was eternal. The Trinity, therefore, was "beyond the sphere of time," despite the limitations of the language that had to be used about it, language that always had to be understood *apophatically* in order to be rescued from distortion. With that *apophatic* proviso placed upon it, it was valid to use a temporal preposition such as "before" in confessing "the Father and the Son and the Holy Spirit eternally with one another in the perfect Trinity also 'before' all creation and 'before' the *aeons.*"

Another concept of natural theology that pertained, though in radically divergent ways, both to the revealed doctrine of creation and to the revealed doctrine of the Trinity, was "causality [aitia]." Gregory of Nyssa went so far as to declare: "The only way by which we distinguish [one *hypostasis* of the Trinity] from the other is by believing that one [the Father] is the cause and that the other [the Son] depends on the cause." When he classified various kinds of cause and effect—the combination of art and matter as in building, the combination of matter and nature as in procreation, and the combination of a nonmaterial cause with corporeal means as in the issuance of word from mind—he showed

Bas.*Hex.*3.2
(SC 26:192–94)

Bas.*Spir.*2.4
(SC 17:262)

Gr.Nyss.*Eun.*3.9.21
(Jaeger 2:271)

Gr.Nyss.*Eun.*1.381
(Jaeger 1:138–39)

Eun.ap.Gr.Nyss.*Eun.*
3.6.60 (Jaeger 2:207)
Ps 144:13
Gr.Nyss.*Maced.*
(Jaeger 3–I:101)

Gr.Naz.*Or.*29.3
(SC 250:182)

Gr.Nyss.*Maced.*
(Jaeger 3–I:98)

Gr.Nyss.*Tres dii*
(Jaeger 3–I:56)

Gr.Nyss.*Eun*.3.6.28–29
(Jaeger 2:196)

Gr.Nyss.*Ref*.89–94
(Jaeger 2:348–50)

Gr.Nyss.*Eun*.1.686
(Jaeger 1:223)

Gr.Nyss.*Tres dii*
(Jaeger 3–1:57)
DTC 10:2201–8

Gr.Nyss.*Eun*.1.397
(Jaeger 1:142)

See pp.103–4

Wis 7:26;Heb 1:3
Symb.Nic.
(Alberigo-Jedin 6);
Symb.Nic.CP
(Alberigo-Jedin 20)

Bas.*Eun*.2.25
(SC 305:104–6)

how each of these meanings of "cause" could legitimately be employed, *apophatically* and only in this sense metaphorically and "analogically," to describe transcendent reality. In its use of each of these senses of the word "cause" for "the ineffable power of God" and for the begetting of the Son of God, therefore, Scripture excluded "the physical senses attaching to the words," leaving only "the commonality of nature in the Trinity." The potential dangers in such language and thought were evident: "If, in conceiving of the Father 'before' the Son on the single score of causation, we inserted any mark of time before the subsistence of the only-begotten one, the belief we have in the Son's eternity might with reason be said to be in jeopardy." But it was this "acknowledgment of such a distinction in the Holy Trinity, namely, our belief in [the Father] as the cause and in [the Son] as depending on him," that was taken to protect orthodoxy against "the charge of dissolving the distinction of the *hypostases* in the commonality of the nature," which was taken to be the heresy of Sabellianism, or "modalistic Monarchianism." When Eunomius, in formulating his own theory of causality, stated the principle, apparently intended as a principle that was valid already in the realm of natural theology, "The same divine actions [energeiai] produce a sameness of works," this could be quoted against him to prove that there was "no gulf whatever between the being of the Son and the being of the Spirit." Thus, the insights of natural theology could be placed into the service of revealed truth; or, to put it the other way around, as some historians of Christian thought would prefer to state it, the implications of natural theology as apologetics were permitted to shape revealed theology as its presupposition.

Each of the principal clusters of imagery and terminology for the concept of causality that were invoked by the Cappadocians in their defense of the dogma of the Trinity also participated in their natural theology: the metaphysics of light; the relation of Father and Son; and the concept of *arche*. The vision of the eternal and primal light, elaborated by them in their scientific speculations, was the underpinning for the interpretation of the trinitarian metaphor from the Nicene Creed, and before it from both the Old Testament and the New Testament, according to which the Son of God was "light out of light [phōs ek phōtos]," the "radiance [apaugasma]" that came from the Father as the light. In his attack on Eunomius, Basil drew upon the metaphysics of light and its biblical ground to vindicate trinitarian orthodoxy. Gregory of Nyssa also, in each of the three books of his own massive polemic against Eunomius, made use of this fundamental metaphor. In the first book he spoke of having been "taught by *Sophia* to contemplate the radiance of the everlasting light in, and together with, the very everlastingness of that primal light, joining in one idea the radiance and its cause and admitting no priority." Although he referred to it more briefly in the second book, he went on in the third book to make it a key part of his case against Eunomius. There he summarized Eunomius's case as follows: "He says that our God, too, is composite, in that while we suppose the light to be common, we yet separate the one light from the other by certain special attributes and various differences. For that is none the less composite which, while united by one common nature, is yet separated by certain differences and conjunctions of peculiarities." It was by an even more refined application of the metaphysics of light that Gregory strove to reaffirm the Nicene definition. That is why it was specifically in this polemic against Eunomius that Gregory spoke with such theological precision—which was at the same time also a scientific precision and a philosophical precision—about both the usefulness and the limitations of the Nicene metaphor of "light out of light."

Gr.Nyss.*Eun*.1.358
(Jaeger 1:132–33)
Gr.Nyss.*Eun*.2.6.51
(Jaeger 2:203–4)

Gr.Nyss.*Eun*.3.10.46
(Jaeger 2:307)

Gr.Nyss.*Eun*.1.533
(Jaeger 1:180)

Bas.*Spir*.10.26
(SC 17:336)
Rom 6:17
Gr.Nyss.*Ref*.10
(Jaeger 2:316)
See pp.87–89

Gr.Nyss.*Eun*.1.548
(Jaeger 1:184–85)

Gr.Nyss.*Ref*.10
(Jaeger 2:316)

Speaking about "Father" and "Son" in the Trinity was hallowed by biblical and liturgical usage, throughout the New Testament and, within the New Testament, in such cherished monuments of Christian worship as the Lord's Prayer and the baptismal formula; Basil identified the latter as "the pattern of teaching," and Gregory of Nyssa called it the "profession of faith." As part of their apologetic analysis of such terminology, the Cappadocians rejected the notion that since everyone knew what "fatherhood" meant in a natural sense, the use of it for God was simply a symbolic projection of that natural sense. Out of "all the names employed to indicate the surpassing excellence of the divine nature," Christ had passed over all the others and had delivered "as part of our profession of faith the title of 'Father' as better suited to indicate the truth," together with the title "Holy Spirit," as well as the title "Son." Having established, as natural theology, the validity and indispensability of the *apophatic* language of transcendence when applied to God as Father, they found this language to be just as valid and indispensable when applied, as revealed theology, to God as Son; for it was not as though the Father were transcendent and the Son were not. The name "Son" in everyday usage referred, Gregory of Nyssa pointed out, to the combination of matter and nature in procrea-

See pp.235–36

tion, which was one of the kinds of causality he discussed in his classification of causes. When Scripture used "our language here by calling him by the name 'Son,'" it did so because, in speaking about "that ineffable and transcendent existence received by the only-begotten one from the Father," the transcendence of the Son, no less than the transcendence of the Father, represented a "truth too high for speech or thought." For if God was Father, that fatherhood must be eternal, not dependent on any creature to which God was Father. But if it was from eternity and by nature that God was Father, as it was from eternity and by nature that God was "imperishable and immortal," there was no other possible conclusion than that from eternity and by nature the Father was Father to the Son, who therefore also had to be eternal, imperishable, and immortal.

Gr.Nyss.*Eun*.3.6.36
(Jaeger 2:198)

Gr.Nyss.*Eun*.2.558
(Jaeger 1:389)

Another connection between the apologetic discussion of the many and the One and the dogmatic discussion of the One and the Three was concentrated in the clarification of the Greek term *arche*. The case developed by Cappadocian apologetics against Greek polytheism had as one of its central arguments the charge that the Greeks were also able to recognize, even without revelation, the untenability of the belief that there could be many supreme *archai*; for if there were many *archai*, as by definition the term "polyarchy" maintained, the necessary outcome of such a belief would be "disorder" and "dissolution" within the divine nature itself. Expositors of the One and the Three in Christian dogmatics, therefore, were in turn precluded from building their case on the explanation that the reason why the Three were equal in deity was that each of the Three was an *arche* on its own. "We do not teach three *archai*," Gregory of Nazianzus declared in defending the Trinity, "because we want to avoid being Greek or polytheistic." In another oration he warned Christian theologians against depriving the Father of the Son, but at the same time against denying that in the mysterious relationship within the Trinity it was God the Father who alone remained the "cause" and the *arche*; for, he continued, only this version of the doctrine of the Trinity preserved the monotheism for which, in so many other places, he and his colleagues were doing battle so fiercely against the Greeks. Gregory of Nyssa devoted an entire treatise, brief but closely reasoned, to a rejection of the superficially attractive interpretation of the dogma of the Trinity as a doctrine of "three gods," and he ruled out any such locution as that. Basil, too, came out in favor of the doctrine of only one *arche*, on the basis of the biblical assertion that the Holy Spirit

Bas.*Hex*.1.5–6
(*SC* 26:108–10)

Gr.Naz.*Or*.29.2
(*SC* 250:178)

Gr.Naz.*Or*.25.16
(*SC* 284:194)

Gr.Naz.*Or*.20.6–7
(*SC* 270:68–72)

Gr.Nyss.*Tres dii*
(Jaeger 3–1:37–57)
Bas.*Ep*.125.3
(Courtonne 2:34)

proceeded from the Father. At the same time it was the unanimous assertion of this orthodox trinitarianism that in speaking about the Trinity the fundamental ontological terms, such as *ousia,* were not to be restricted to the Father but had to include the Son and the Holy Spirit, and yet that they had to be used only in the singular.

In this context it should not be construed as an unwarranted anachronism, but as a legitimate question a posteriori, to inquire about the position of the Cappadocians on the notorious issue of the Filioque, the medieval Western doctrine of the eternal procession of the Holy Spirit, not from the Father only, but "from the Father and the Son [ex Patre Filioque]," which has for so long been a matter of dogmatic dispute between the Eastern and the Western churches. For the acknowledgment of the orthodoxy and authority of the Cappadocian fathers by both East and West has made their answer to this question, as well as their careful attention to the need for theological precision about only one "cause [aitia]" and only one *arche* in the Trinity as essential to monotheism, an important issue not only for historical research but for theological inquiry and ecumenical discussion. All of the Cappadocians, where to a Western ear a reference to the Filioque would have seemed to be in place, repeatedly avoided it. Gregory of Nazianzus, on the basis of the words of Christ, "The Spirit of truth that proceeds from the Father," explicitly spoke in such a way as to attribute the source of the proceeding of the Spirit to the Father, not to the Son. Quoting those same words of Christ elsewhere, he warned: "Let us confine ourselves within our limits, and speak of the unbegotten [the Father] and the begotten [the Son] and that which proceeds from the Father [the Holy Spirit]." Thus he could describe "the Father as 'parent' of the offspring [the Son] and originator of the 'emanation' [the Spirit]," but in a manner characterized *apophatically* by "*apatheia,* nontemporality, and noncorporeality." For the Godhead was "common to the Father and the Son and the Holy Spirit," but what was common to the Son and the Holy Spirit in turn was "their being from the Father." In response to the canard of Eunomius of "preaching two causeless beings," Gregory of Nyssa labeled it "a misrepresentation of our faith" to charge it with "preaching two first causes." In a brief essay explaining the meaning of technical terminology in the doctrine of God, he acknowledged that it was true of human life that one human being proceeded from one while another proceeded from another. But, he went on, "It is not so in the case of the Holy Trinity, but there is one person [pros-

Jn 15:26

Gr.Nyss.*Eun.*1.161–62
(Jaeger 1:75)

DTC 5:2309–43

Gr.Naz.*Or.*20.6–7
(*SC* 270:68–72)

Jn 15:26

Gr.Naz.*Or.*31.8
(*SC* 250:290)

Gr.Naz.*Or.*29.2
(*SC* 250:180)

Gr.Naz.*Or.*25.16
(*SC* 284:198)

Gr.Nyss.*Eun.*1.483–86
(Jaeger 1:166–67)

Gr.Nyss.*Comm.not.*
(Jaeger 3–I:224–25)

Bas.*Eun.*2.34
(SC 305:142)

ōpon], and that the person of the Father, from which the Son is begotten and from which the Holy Spirit proceeds." Basil, too, spoke axiomatically about the Holy Spirit as "proceeding from the Father." That consistency would seem, though admittedly at least somewhat on the basis of an argument from silence, to line up all three of the Cappadocian fathers against the Filioque.

Jn 15:26

Gr.Nyss.*Eun.*1.413–14
(Jaeger 1:147)

ap.Dräseke 1907,
390–400
Lohn 1929,354–64
Gomes de Castro
1938,114–17

But such language was in part the reflection of the usage of the New Testament when it spoke about the "proceeding" of the Holy Spirit, and in part the observance of what they themselves called the "natural order" in speaking about the three *hypostases*. For alongside the explicit identification of the Father, and the Father only, as "cause" and *arche,* other kinds of language also appeared in the writings of the Cappadocians; and such language has often been taken by Western theologians as favoring the doctrine of the Filioque, albeit sometimes on the basis of texts that are rather problematical. For example, arguing for the doctrine that the Holy Spirit had "an exact identity" with the Father and with the Son, Gregory of Nyssa declared, consciously speaking "in accordance with Scripture," that the Spirit was "from God [the Father] and of Christ," with the English "from" repre-

Gr.Nyss.*Maced.*
(Jaeger 3–I:89–90)

Rom 8:9;2 Cor 3:17;Gal
4:6;Phil 1:19;1 Pt 2:11

senting the Greek preposition "ek" and the English "of" representing the Greek genitive case. And that was indeed "in accordance with Scripture," which repeatedly employed the genitive to identify the Holy Spirit as "the Spirit of" Christ or of the Son or of the Lord. In addition, the Cappadocians sometimes made use of a formula that more than a millennium later, at the Council of Florence in 1439, became a point of discussion as a possible compromise between East and West: "The Holy Spirit proceeds from the Father through the Son [ek patros di' hyiou, ex Patre per Filium]." Much of the time, it seems, the Cappadocians were·invoking such language in dealing not with the eternal relations of the *hypostases* to one another within the Trinity according to *theology* (which was the specific point at issue in the Filioque dispute), but with the historical dispensations of the Trinity toward the world and the church according to *economy.* Thus, Gregory of Nyssa was speaking *economically* when he said: "Whatever is *kalon,* whatever is good [agathon], coming from God as it does through the Son, is completed by the instrumentality of the Spirit." And elsewhere he asserted: "Every operation that extends from God to creation and that is designated according to our differing conceptions of it has its origin in the Father, proceeds through the Son, and reaches its completion by the Holy Spirit." But a few sentences later it does seem that he was

CFlor.(1438–45) *Def.*
(Alberigo-Jedin 525)

González 1938,280–301

Gr.Nyss.*Maced.*
(Jaeger 3–I:109)

Gr.Nyss.*Tres dii*
(Jaeger 3–I:47–48)

speaking not only according to *economy* but according to *theology* when he declared: "There is one motion and disposition of the good will that is communicated from the Father through the Son to the Spirit." From the perspective of the Cappadocians, at least some of the polemical literature on the Filioque in subsequent centuries would also seem to have crossed the boundaries of reverent and *apophatic* propriety by claiming to be better informed than it had any right to be about the mysterious inner life of the Trinity and the eternal *theological* relations of the divine *hypostases* to one another. Thus it would appear to have merited the rhetorical outburst of Gregory of Nazianzus: "What, then, is 'proceeding'? You explain the ingeneracy of the Father and I will give you a biological account of the Son's begetting and the Spirit's proceeding—and let us go mad the pair of us for prying into God's secrets!"

Probably the most obvious contribution of the natural theology of the Cappadocians to their dogmatic theology came in their use of arguments for this dogmatic theology that were based on what was seen as "fitting to say about God [theoprepon]" in the light of their natural theology (which they treated as common property with their heretical as well as with their philosophical opponents). Eunomius objected to Basil's doctrine on the grounds, "The very nature of things is repugnant to this." But Gregory of Nyssa, when comparing the theology of Eunomius with that of Basil and himself, did seem to be proceeding in a similar fashion when he issued the challenge: "Let the intelligent reader . . . judge which better preserves in the text those conceptions that are befitting the divine." He felt able to aver with confidence: "The most boorish and simpleminded would not deny that the divine nature, blessed and transcendent as it is, is 'single.' That which is viewless, formless, and sizeless cannot be conceived of as multiform and composite." From this he concluded: "Who does not know that, to be exact, simplicity [haplotēs] in the case of the Holy Trinity admits of no degrees?" He seemed to be explicitly invoking a somewhat similar argument from the generalities of natural theology to the particularities of revealed theology when, in his treatise on the Holy Spirit, he proceeded "on the basis of the common conceptions" concerning the divine nature—at least possibly meaning conceptions that were common to all, not only to believers—to show that the Holy Spirit, as spoken of in inspired Scripture, was fully entitled to the name "God." Gregory of Nazianzus, dealing with the same problem, asked the general question, "What is deity if it is incom-

Gr.Nyss.*Tres dii*
(Jaeger 3–1:48–49)

Gr.Naz.*Or.*31.8
(*SC* 250:290)

Gr.Nyss.*Or.catech.*9.1
(Méridier 64)
ap.Gr.Nyss.*Eun.*3.3.19
(Jaeger 2:114)

Gr.Nyss.*Eun.*3.1.54
(Jaeger 2:22)

Gr.Nyss.*Eun.*1.231–32
(Jaeger 1:94–95)

Gr.Nyss.*Maced.*
(Jaeger 3–1:90)

Gr.Naz.Or.31.4
(SC 250:282)

Schermann 1901

Gr.Nyss.Or.catech.pr.6
(Méridier 6)

Gr.Nyss.Eun.3.1.75
(Jaeger 2:30)

Rasneur 1903,189–
206,411–31

Bas.Ep.8.3
(Courtonne 1:25–27)

Bas.Eun.2.4
(SC 305:18)

Heb 1:3

plete?" and then proceeded to the specific declaration: "Something is missing if it does not have holiness, and how could it have holiness without having the Holy Spirit?" It is noteworthy that it should so often have been in the process of proving their doctrine of the Holy Spirit that the Cappadocians had recourse to such argumentation. For the presupposition of their case was a doctrine of God and of the divine nature that they had established as both rational and scriptural primarily in the course of their ongoing controversy about the relation of the Father and the Son. That presupposition now went on to become a fundamental part of their theological methodology, and they could now employ it on the doctrine of the Holy Spirit with the rise of the new challenge that their generation was the first to confront.

At the center of the most celebrated (and most controverted) formula of the trinitarian confession, as affirmed by the declaration of the Council of Nicaea that the Son was "homoousios with the Father," was a concept that also belonged to Cappadocian natural theology, the concept of ousia. Gregory of Nyssa, therefore, was able to argue on the basis of the principle, evident to anyone who was "reasonable," that although Adam was unbegotten and his son Seth was begotten, nevertheless they had an "essential nature marked by the same characteristics," and that therefore there was "one ousia in both." Having made that point in natural theology, he felt entitled to continue: "What, then, we learn in the case of human nature by means of the inferential guidance afforded to us by the definition, this I think we ought to take for our guidance also to the pure apprehension of the divine doctrines. For when we have shaken off from the divine and exalted doctrines all carnal and material notions, we shall be most surely led by the remaining conception, once it is purged of such ideas, to the lofty and unapproachable heights." When the natural concept of ousia was applied to the revealed doctrine of the Trinity, it led to the homoousios. Dealing as it did with "the Father as God in ousia, who generated the Son as God in ousia," the doctrine of the Trinity could not be rendered adequately by the compromise term, "similar in ousia [homoiousios]." The reason, according to Basil, was this: "Similarity and dissimilarity are predicated in relation to quality, and the divine is free of quality. . . . From this the homoousia is proved." For it was not only a revealed principle but a natural and rational one that a diversity of name did not imply a diversity of ousia. To this nonbiblical vocabulary it was appropriate to adapt the vocabulary of biblical usage. Thus the Epistle to the Hebrews spoke of Christ as

Gr.Nyss.*Eun*.3.2.147
(Jaeger 2:100)
Phil 2:6
Bas.*Eun*.1.18
(SC 299:236)

"the stamp of God's very being [charaktēr tēs hypostaseōs autou]." And the biblical term "morphē" in the phrase of the Epistle to the Philippians, "He was in the form of God [en morphēi theou hyparchōn]," meant the same as the term *ousia*.

But the passage from Hebrews also documented a vexing problem of trinitarian terminology, for it did seem to be using *hypostasis* in the sense of *ousia*. The two terms appeared as synonyms also in the original text of the creed adopted at Nicaea in 325 when it condemned "those who say that [the Son] is of

Symb.Nic.
(Alberigo-Jedin 5)

another *hypostasis* or *ousia* than the Father." As G. L. Prestige has pointed out, "the Cappadocian Settlement finally fixed the statement of Trinitarian orthodoxy in the formula of one *ousia* and three *hypostaseis*. It was worked out largely by Basil . . . , preached by the inspired populariser, Gregory of Nazianzus, and elaborated by the acute and speculative mind of Gregory of

Prestige 1956,233–34

Nyssa." That "Cappadocian Settlement" became even more complicated because of the differences between East and West, differences of language that in this period as in all periods also seemed to become differences of thought and belief. As Gregory

Gr.Naz.*Or*.21.35
(SC 270:184–86)

of Nazianzus noted, "We use in an orthodox sense the terms 'one *ousia*' and 'three *hypostases*,' the one to denote the nature of the Godhead, the other the properties of the three. The Italians mean the same; but, owing to the scantiness of their vocabulary and its poverty of terms, they are unable to distinguish between *ousia* and *hypostasis*, and therefore introduce the term 'persons [prosōpa],' to avoid being understood as asserting three *ousiai*. The result, were it not piteous, would be laughable. This slight differ-

Grandsire 1923,130–52

ence of sound was taken to indicate a difference of faith." Basil observed that some Western writers had, "from a suspicion of the inadequacy of their own [Latin] language, taken over the word

Bas.*Ep*.214.4
(Courtonne 2:205)
Strong 1901,224–35;
1902,22–40; 1903,
28–45

ousia from Greek." Part of the difficulty for the Latins lay in the linguistic tradition of translating the Greek word *hypostasis* with the Latin word "substantia," of which it was the literal rendering, as the Latin "essentia" was the literal rendering of the Greek *ousia*. When, as in the passage from the creed of Nicaea just quoted, *hypostasis* and *ousia* were more or less synonymous, it created little difficulty to speak indiscriminately of one "substantia" or of one "essentia" in the Godhead. Augustine, whose treatise *De Trinitate* was by common consent one of the most profound ever written in Latin on the subject, acknowledged, a full

Martland 1965,252–63;
Altaner 1950,17–24;
Altaner 1951,57–58

two generations after the Cappadocians and perhaps on the basis of a reading of them in Latin translation, "The Greeks intend to posit a difference, though I do not know what it is, between *ousia*

Aug.*Trin*.5.8.10
(CCSL 50:216–17)

and *hypostasis*"; as a result, he said, "Most of ourselves who treat these things in the Greek language are accustomed to say, 'mian ousian treis hypostaseis,' or in Latin, 'una essentia tres substantiae.'" Later in the treatise he returned to the topic of the differences between Greek and Latin trinitarian usage, explaining that although the Greeks did refer to the Three as "prosōpa" (which he rendered into Latin as "personae"), they preferred to use the more precise technical term for the Three and to speak of them as *hypostases*.

Aug.*Trin*.7.6.11
(CCSL 50:261)

For our purposes here, the important question is not Augustine's misunderstanding of Greek trinitarianism but the role played by the natural theology of the Cappadocians in fixing the terms for the eventual settlement. In dealing with the assertion of Eunomius, "There are three *ousiai*," which was tantamount to saying, "The actual substantial being of each [of the Three] is different from those of the others," Gregory of Nyssa argued for the case that there was, and must be both by reason and by revelation, a singleness of the divine *ousia*. From this it followed, he insisted, that the term *homoousios* was appropriate for the relation of each of the Three to each of the others—because *ousia*, and only in the singular, was the appropriate term for the One, shared by Father, Son, and Holy Spirit. The term *ousia*, therefore, was to be used, even when it was being applied to the divine being, in its "natural" philosophical sense. Although Gregory of Nyssa was invoking a biblical illustration, he was making a point philosophically and was not claiming to be proving his point exegetically when he declared: "We cannot properly say that Adam begat [in Abel] another *ousia* besides himself, but rather that of himself he begat another self, with whom was produced the whole definition of the *ousia* of the one who begat him." Although Basil may, similarly, have been citing the names of Paul, Silvanus, and Timothy as characters from biblical narrative, he was making a "natural" point that derived from Gregory's: "The same words that have been employed in setting forth the *ousia* of Paul will apply to the others also. Therefore those who are described by the same definition of *ousia* are *homoousios* to one another when the inquirer has learned what is common" to all three, namely, one *ousia*.

Gr.Nyss.*Eun*.1.235
(Jaeger 1:95)

González 1939,193

Gr.Nyss.*Eun*.3.1.75
(Jaeger 2:30)

Bas.*Ep*.38.2
(Courtonne 1:82)

Bas.*Eun*.2.22
(SC 305:88)

The congruence of Cappadocian trinitarianism, this "chief dogma," with Cappadocian apologetics, was summarized in their repeated claim that the orthodox doctrine of the Trinity was located "between the two conceptions" of Hellenism and Judaism, by "invalidating both ways of thinking, while accepting the useful components of each." Gregory of Nyssa put this claim boldly: "The Jewish dogma is destroyed by the acceptance of the *Logos* and by belief in the Spirit, while the polytheistic error of the Greek school is made to vanish by the unity of the [divine] nature abrogating this imagination of plurality." In sum, therefore, "Of the Jewish conception, let the unity of the nature stand; and of the Hellenic, only the distinction as to the *hypostases*, the remedy against a profane view being thus applied, as required, on either side." This apologetic symmetry permitted him to assert:

Gr.Nyss.*Or.catech.*3.3 (Méridier 20)

"It is as if the number of the Three were a remedy in the case of those who are in error as to the One, and the assertion of the unity for those whose beliefs are dispersed among a number of divinities." To the heretics who asserted that the Son of God was a creature but who nevertheless worshiped him as God, he posed the alternative of committing idolatry by "worshiping someone

Gr.Nyss.*Fid.*3 (Jaeger 3–I:62)

alien from the true God," or of falling into Judaism by "denying the worship of Christ." He summarized the same polemical point by accusing this heretical view of simultaneously "advocating the

Gr.Nyss.*Eun.*2.14–15 (Jaeger 1:231)

errors of Judaism and partaking to a certain extent in the impiety of the Greeks," accepting the worst of both while orthodoxy accepted the best of both. His brother Basil pitted the orthodox doctrine of the Trinity against twin errors of "maintaining many

Bas.*Ep.*189.3–4 (Courtonne 2:134–35)

godheads or maintaining none." That was shown in the creation narrative as Basil interpreted it, in which the plural phrases "Let us make [poiēsōmen]" and "in our image [kat' eikona hēme-

Gn 1:26
Gn 1:27

teran]" were followed by the singular verb: "So God created [epoiēsen]." Thus he concluded: "Scripture, after having enlightened the Jew, dissipates the error of Hellenism by putting itself under the shelter of unity, to make you understand that the Son is

Bas.*Hex.*9.6 (SC 26:520)

with the Father, and by guarding you from the danger of polytheism." The third of the Cappadocian fathers, Gregory of Nazianzus, likewise saw the Trinity as such a remedy against

Gr.Naz.*Or.*38.8 (PG 35:320)

Gr.Naz.*Or.*20.6 (SC 270:70)

"either Judaizing to save monotheism or Hellenizing by the multitude of our gods." Elsewhere he denounced a purportedly monotheistic "trivialization [smikrologia]" that impoverished the deity of God by lapsing back into Judaism. "The worshipers of the Father and the Son and the Holy Spirit," therefore, managed "simultaneously to avoid going too far and to avoid not going far enough in their worship [mēde hypersebontes mēde

Gr.Naz.*Or.*22.12 (SC 270:244)

hyposebontes]."

Nevertheless, in a fashion that did not come through as explicitly in their apologetics, the dogmatics of the Cappadocians was engaged not only in affirming the trineness of the Godhead but in

Koperski 1936,45–65
Gr.Nyss.*Tres dii*
(Jaeger 3–1:39)
Gr.Nyss.*Comm.not.*
(Jaeger 3–1:19)

Gr.Nyss.*Ref.*
(Jaeger 2:328)

Gr.Nyss.*Eun.*1.235
(Jaeger 1:95)

Gr.Naz.*Or.*40.43
(PG 35:420)

Gr.Naz.*Or.*31.12
(SC 250:300)

Arnou 1934,242–54

Gr.Naz.*Or.*6.13
(PG 35:740)
Jn 10:30

Gr.Nyss.*Ref.*20–21
(Jaeger 2:320–21)

González 1939,25–39

See pp.104–5
Bas.*Ep.*8.2
(Courtonne 1:24)

redefining its oneness. The Cappadocians did indeed consistently strive "to avoid the appearance of any similarity with Greek polytheism." They rejected any implication that in saying "three persons" they were necessarily saying "three gods." What they were positing as the relation between Father, Son, and Holy Spirit, they insisted, was "not partnership but unity [oute koinō-nian . . . all' henotēta]." It was to set themselves apart from heresy as well as from Hellenism, both of which talked about "divine beings" in the plural, that they spoke of God as "a being really single and absolutely one, identical with goodness rather than merely possessing it." And yet, although he was in the first instance making a rhetorical rather than a theological point, Gregory of Nazianzus could ask: "But are you afraid of being reproached with tritheism?" Elsewhere, he could even suggest that—if one had to make such a choice, although one definitely did not—it would be "better to take a meager view of the unity than to venture on total blasphemy" by degrading the Son and the Holy Spirit into mere creatures. He did not intend to "take a meager view of unity" at all, but he was pointing to a view of unity that he took to be richer and more complex than such a phrase as "a being really single and absolutely one" seemed to suggest. "To be one," he said, making a point "on the basis of the laudable and holy Trinity," referred no less to a oneness of harmony than to a oneness of *ousia*. For when Christ said that he and the Father were "one," Gregory of Nyssa argued, this showed: "The word 'one' does not indicate the Father alone, but comprehends in its significance the Son with the Father"; and the same was true of the word "God" itself. Speaking in response to the accusations of "tritheism," Basil could go so far as to answer: "We confess a God who is one not in number but in nature." Drawing here upon natural theology, Basil posited the ontological distinction between a "God universally confessed to be simple and not composite," and, in contrast, "everything called one in number as not one absolutely, nor yet simple in nature." Therefore, he concluded, "God is not one in number," and added: "What I mean is this. We say that the world is one in number, but not one by nature, nor yet simple; for we divide it into its constituent *stoicheia*, fire, water, air, and earth." The oneness of God was just the opposite, a oneness in nature but not in number. And in his treatise on the Holy Spirit he made the same point: "Count, if you must, but you must not by counting do damage to the faith!" It was best to "let the ineffable be honored by silence," or at any rate to "let holy things be counted consistently with true religion." When Christian orthodoxy confessed "each of the *hy-postases* singly," it did not "let an ignorant arithmetic carry us away to the idea of a plurality of gods." Trinitarian monotheism, consequently, was seen as a distinctive view of oneness, "a monotheism not limited to one prosōpon," in which there was numerical distinction but no severance of *ousia*. "Therefore," Gregory of Nazianzus concluded, "unity having from all eternity arrived by motion [within itself] at duality, found its rest in trinity." "This," he added, "is what we mean by Father and Son and Holy Spirit." And it was in the name of what was "philosophical," by which he seems to have meant here what was "theological," that he pitted the dogma of the Trinity against polytheism. In the Cappadocian system, trinitarian orthodoxy was seen as the overcoming of polytheism by drawing the primary distinction not between spiritual and material reality, or between the visible and the invisible realm (although both these distinctions were present and prominent in the system), but ultimately between Creator and creature, as the opening words of the Nicene Creed declared, and then by putting the *Logos* and the Holy Spirit on God's side of that metaphysical boundary. Replacing polytheism with this kind of trinitarian monotheism did not imply a diminution of deity. On the contrary, it redefined the very meaning both of deity and of oneness, and thus it implied an infinite maximizing of Godhead. And that was the sense in which the Cappadocians could posit a consistency between their apologetics and their dogmatics, by presenting their doctrine of the One as simultaneously a rejection of the many and an affirmation of the Three.

Bas.*Spir.*18.44
(SC 17:402–4)

Gr.Naz.*Or.*29.2
(SC 250:180)

Gr.Naz.*Or.*25.15
(SC 284:192)

Mateo-Seco–Bastero
1988,353–79
Symb.Nic.
(Alberigo-Jedin 5)

Gr.Nyss.*Eun.*3.2.94
(Jaeger 2:83)

CHAPTER 16

Cosmos as Contingent Creation

Symb.Nic.(325)
(Alberigo-Jedin 5)

The definitive affirmation of the orthodox Christian faith in the One and the Three, formulated at the Council of Nicaea in 325, opened with the declaration: "We believe in one God, Father, all-sovereign Maker of all things, both of those that are visible and of those that are invisible [pantōn horatōn te kai aoratōn poiētēn]." That affirmation is still authoritative and binding upon most of Christendom, albeit in the slightly different formulation that was adopted at the First Council of Constantinople in 381: "We believe in one God, Father, all-sovereign Maker of heaven and earth, of all things, both of those that are visible and of those that are invisible [pantōn horatōn te kai aoratōn poiētēn]." It is essential to recognize that both of these statements of trinitarian doctrine opened with an unequivocal confession of the monotheistic faith, in keeping with the unanimous insistence of orthodox theologians that the dogma of the Trinity was not only compatible with monotheism but essential to it (given the universal Christian practice of treating Christ as divine). No less noteworthy in the creeds is their use of cosmology as the point of reference for the trinitarian doctrine. The trinitarian doctrine and the cosmological doctrine of the Cappadocians were based upon Nicaea and then contributed to Constantinople, and each of these two doctrines was used to clarify the other. Trinity and cosmology were therefore intimately related, and in some sense correlative, doctrines. The four constituent terms in the opening formulation both of Nicaea and of Constantinople may be taken as a succinct statement of the fundamental cosmological and trinitarian prin-

Symb.Nic.-CP
(Alberigo-Jedin 24)

See p.245

Gr.Nyss.Eun.1.383
(Jaeger 1:139)

ciple of the Cappadocians, not only that the world was a cosmos but that this cosmos in turn was a contingent creation: "one God" as Trinity; this one trinitarian God as the "all-sovereign Maker of all things"; the "visible things" as creatures; and the "invisible things" as creatures.

The Cappadocians repeatedly made it clear that by their doctrine of creation they were not in the first instance contending for a particular philosophical theory of cosmology or a scientific worldview. For example, when, in the dialogue between Macrina and Gregory of Nyssa about the soul and the resurrection, Gregory had quoted various Classical or Christian theories about where within the cosmos Hades might be physically located, Macrina could be quite cavalier in her response, because, she said with confidence, the Christian doctrine would "in no wise be injured by such speculation." She gave this as her reason: "As long as this objection does not shake our central doctrine of the [continued] existence of those souls after the life in the flesh, there need be, to our mind, no controversy about the whereabouts" of Hades in the cosmos. In this sense the Cappadocians may be said to have shared their opponents' interest in determining "the nature of things" not only on the basis of biblical authority but, when appropriate, also on the basis of empirical evidence and of scientific study. They brought natural theology as developed by such evidence and study to their consideration of the biblical testimony concerning the creation, as this was set down above all in "the cosmogonic narrative" in the Book of Genesis. At the same time, as Basil's commentary on that cosmogonic narrative—for which Basil was praised by his fellow Cappadocians, both by his brother Gregory of Nyssa and by Gregory of Nazianzus—made clear in great detail, they were acutely aware of the severe limitations under which the empirical and scientific consideration of the universe had to labor, and above all of its inability, on the basis even of careful investigation, to construct a valid and consistent teleology, something to which scientists and philosophers "did not know how to raise themselves," and this despite the insistence of the Cappadocians elsewhere that teleology was valid also as part of natural theology.

What both Gregorys had frequent occasion to praise above all in Basil's exposition of Genesis, as well as frequent opportunity to practice themselves, was the consistent identification of the God who, according to the part of the Bible that Christians shared with Jews, "created the heavens and the earth" with the God who, according to the part of the Bible that was exclusively Chris-

Prestige 1923,476–85

Macr.ap.Gr.Nyss.
Anim.res. (PG 46:68–69)

Eun.ap.Gr.Nyss.*Eun.*
3.3.19 (Jaeger 2:114)

Gr.Nyss.*Beat.*3
(PG 44:1228)

Gr.Nyss.*Hom.opif.*pr.
(PG 44:125)
Gr.Naz.Or.43.67
(PG 36:585)

Bas.*Hex.*1.4
(SC 26:102)

See pp.152–54

Gr.Nyss.Or.catech.18.4–4
(Méridier 94–96)
Gn 1:1

Mt 28:19;2 Cor 13:14

Gr.Nyss.*Ref*.20–21
(Jaeger 2:320–21)

Gr.Nyss.*Cant*.8
(Jaeger 6:257–58)

Macr.ap.Gr.Nyss.
Anim.res. (PG 46:57–60)

See p.117

Gr.Nyss.*Maced.*
(Jaeger 3–1:98)

Gr.Nyss.*Eun.*3.3.3–4
(Jaeger 2:108)

Bas.*Spir.*2.4
(SC 17:262)

Eun.ap.Gr.Nyss.*Ref.*
68–69 (Jaeger 2:340–41)

ap.Gr.Nyss.*Eun.*3.6.1–2
(Jaeger 2:185)

tian, was Father, Son, and Holy Spirit. For neither the name "God" there in Genesis nor the term "one" in the creed was to be taken "as indicating the Father alone, but as comprehending in its significance the Son with the Father," together with the Holy Spirit. Whenever he referred to "the one God," Gregory of Nyssa explained, he meant "the one apprehended in the unchangeable and eternal nature, the true Father and the only-begotten Son and the Holy Spirit." On the basis of the narrative in Genesis and even on the basis of natural theology, the *economy* of creation itself could be seen as having taken place in a series of divine actions, each set of creatures superior to its predecessors, ascending from inanimate objects to plants to animals to humanity. (The angels were, in some sense, superior to all of these, but for some reason their creation had not been specifically mentioned in the cosmogonic narrative.) But God the Creator was to be affirmed as the Holy Trinity, "the Father and the Son and the Holy Spirit eternally with one another in the perfect Trinity, before all creation and before all the *aeons* and before every sublime thought [epinoia]." A failure to make that distinction between Creator and creature with the utmost precision led to "a total transformation of the doctrines of religion into a kind of anarchy and democratic independence," in which the sovereignty of the Creator was compromised and eventually dissolved into a plurality of divine beings scattered throughout the cosmos. It was against such "pluralism," which was only a euphemism for polytheism, that the Cappadocian doctrine of the Trinity as Creator was directed.

In the Cappadocian system as in other systems in the history of Christian thought, both earlier and later, the principal weight for the defense of that doctrine, even when the issue was the doctrine of the Holy Spirit, fell on the identification of the *Logos* and Son of God as "the Creator of the universe" rather than a mere "instrument" of creation. It was an axiom, derived presumably from the doctrine of God in natural theology and apparently shared by the Cappadocians and their opponents, that God did not "stand in need, in the act of creation, of matter or parts or natural instruments." But from this axiomatic presupposition of natural theology the two sides drew diametrically opposite trinitarian conclusions with respect to the doctrine of creation: on the one side, "the doctrine that [the *Logos*], who made us and all creation out of nothing, was himself out of nothing," and therefore the corollary notion of "the transition of the only-begotten one from nothing into being"; and, in opposition to what the Cappa-

Gr.Nyss.*Eun*.3.6.25
(Jaeger 2:195)

Gr.Nyss.*Eun*.3.6.59
(Jaeger 2:207)

Eun.ap.Gr.Nyss.*Eun*.
3.6.60 (Jaeger 2:207)

Gr.Nyss.*Eun*.1.381
(Jaeger 1:138–39)

Jn 1:1

Jn 1:3

Gn 1:1

Gn 1:3

Gr.Nyss.*Apoll*.
(Jaeger 3–I:191)

See pp.238–40
Bas.*Ep*.125.3
(Courtonne 2:34)

González 1938,280–301
DTC 13:646–47
Jn 1:3;Gn 1:3

Jn 1:3

docians characterized as this "horrible and blasphemous utterance," the affirmation of a fundamental metaphysical "difference between [the Logos as] the Lord of creation and the general body of creation." In support of the first of these conclusion, Eunomius was represented as arguing: "If you allow that God the *Logos* is to be believed to be eternal, then you must allow the same of the things that have been created." But in response to such an argument, the orthodox conclusion, by sharply distinguishing the metaphysical status of "God the *Logos*" from that of "the things that have been created," asserted: "The begetting [gennēsis] of the Son does not fall within time, any more than the creation was before time, so that it can in no way be right to partition the indivisible, and, by declaring that there was a time when the author of all existence did not exist, to insert this false idea of time into the creative source of the universe."

By linking its opening affirmation that the *Logos* had existed already at the *arche* with the affirmation that followed almost immediately, "Through him all things came to be," the Gospel of John was evidently writing a gloss on the opening affirmation of the Book of Genesis, "In the *arche* God created the heavens and the earth," which was followed almost immediately by "God said," speaking through his Word. Picking up on that use of *arche*, Gregory of Nyssa declared: "God the *Logos* not only is the one who is in the *arche*, but he is also himself the *arche*." This Cappadocian usage of *arche* for the *Logos*, it should be stipulated immediately, pertained not to the relations between the divine *hypostases* within the Trinity, in which according to Cappadocian trinitarianism only the Father was the one *arche*, but specifically to the creation, which was the topic about which both the Book of Genesis and the Gospel of John were speaking—thus, employing the technical trinitarian terminology of the Latin West, to the "opera ad extra" rather than to the "opera ad intra" of the Trinity. Drawing from the words of the Gospel of John and of the Book of Genesis what he took to be the only possible orthodox conceptualization of the relation between Trinity and creation, and identifying the common ground between himself and his opponents, Gregory of Nyssa reasoned as follows: "Since, then, all things are of God, and the Son is God, the creation is properly seen as the opposite of the Godhead, while, since the only-begotten one is something other than the nature of the universe (seeing that not even those who fight against the truth contradict this), it follows of necessity that the Son also is equally the opposite of the creation, unless the words of the saints are untrue which testify that 'through him all things came to be.'" Earlier in the same treatise he also felt able to base his argumentation on something he could call "the tenet that has been held in common by all who have received the word of our religion." As the Creator *Logos*, then, the Son of God was "related to the Father as word to mind," and was "existing inherently in real things," because everything was held together in the *Logos*. In God, therefore, word and deed, *Logos* as word and *Logos* as reason, coincided. For it was "conformable with true religion" to insist on the *apophatic* principle that, in speaking at the creation, God did not speak in human fashion and that the *Logos*, as the Word and Reason of God in person, was ontologically the opposite of all creatures.

When, in the 360s and 370s, this long-standing controversy about whether the Son of God was Creator or creature turned to the closely related but by no means identical question of the relation between the Holy Spirit and the creation, the writings of the three Cappadocian fathers occupied a central position in that development: Gregory of Nyssa's *Sermon on the Deity of the Son and Holy Spirit;* the fifth and last of the *Theological Orations* of Gregory of Nazianzus; and the treatise *On the Holy Spirit* by Basil of Caesarea. The statement of the cosmogony of Genesis, "The Spirit of God moved over the water," provided Basil, as the author both of a word-by-word exposition of the Hexaemeron and of the most celebrated of all fourth-century Greek works on the Holy Spirit, with the need and the opportunity to find an *apophatic* clarification of the relation between the doctrines of Spirit and of creation. For the Spirit was "of God [theou]," but not in the same sense that creatures were "of God"; the Spirit was the "breath" and the "mouth" of God, but not as the words "breath" and "mouth" applied to creatures. And so, he assured his readers, "The close relation is made plain, while the mode of the ineffable existence is safeguarded." The title "Spirit of God," therefore, was "the special name, the favorite name above all others for Scripture to give to the Holy Spirit," from which Basil concluded: "Always by 'pneuma theou' the Holy Spirit is meant, the Spirit that completes the divine and blessed Trinity."

Like the Father and the Son, the Holy Spirit, too, was transcendent over all creatures. Nevertheless, also like the Father and the Son, the Holy Spirit could in some degree be known by the natural theology of the Greeks, with their intuitions about "the mind of the universe" and the like—according to the Cappadocians, known better by them without the aid of specific revelation

Gr.Nyss.*Eun*.2.50
(Jaeger 1:240)

Gr.Naz.*Or*.30.20
(SC 250:266–68)
Gr.Nyss.*Hex*.
(PG 44:73)

Bas.*Hex*.3.2
(SC 26:192–94)

Hanson 1988,676–737
Gr.Nyss.*Deit*.
(PG 46:553–76)
Gr.Naz.*Or*.31
(SC 250:276–342)
Bas.*Spir*.
(SC 17:250–530)

Gn 1:2

Bas.*Spir*.18.46
(SC 17:408)

Gn 1:2

Bas.*Hex*.2.6
(SC 26:166–68)

Bas.*Spir*.22.53
(SC 17:440)

Pl.*Phd*.97c-d

Gr.Naz.Or.31.5
(SC 250:282–84)

than by the Sadducees, heretics among the Jews, who rejected the doctrine of the Holy Spirit despite the testimony of their own Scriptures. Perhaps even more than in the case of the second *hypostasis* of the Trinity, the status of the third *hypostasis* did depend on the definition of the doctrine of creation and thus also on some clarification of natural theology. The system of numbering, "devised as a symbol indicative of the quantity of object," could, by a fallacious application to the doctrine of the Holy Spirit, lead to speaking about the Holy Spirit as "third" and therefore as somehow inferior, even though the principle, "Nothing undergoes any [substantive] change in consequence of the addition of number," was true even in natural philosophy. The best-known celebration of the intimate connection of the Holy Spirit with the cosmos as contingent creation was by a Latin Christian poet rather than by a Greek, and came from the ninth century rather than from the fourth, in the "Veni Creator Spiritus." But it was the Greek rather than the Latin liturgy, and specifically the Greek liturgy bearing the name of Basil of Caesarea, that extended the concept of the "Creator Spiritus" from the cosmos to the Eucharist, by the invocation, in the epiclesis: "Send now thy Spirit, the all-holy one, to descend upon us and upon these gifts here set forth, so that this bread might be blessed and sanctified and made manifest as the worshipful body of our Lord and God and Savior Jesus Christ. Amen." As one commentary on the liturgy has summarized it, "The consecration . . . is the work of the Holy Spirit, who transforms both the congregation and the gifts." That assignment of the eucharistic transformation to the invocation of the Holy Spirit, rather than to the recitation of the words of institution "This is my body" and "This is my blood," also became a point of controversy between East and West.

Bas.*Spir.*18.44
(SC 17:402–4)

See p.304

Lit.Bas.
(Brightman 329–30)

Kallis 1989,132

LTK 3:935–37

To the affirmation of the oneness of God, both the Creed of Nicaea in 325 and the Niceno-Constantinopolitan Creed of 381 added, in apposition, the title "all-sovereign Maker of all things," employing the Greek term "pantokratōr," which could be used either as an adjective or as a substantive; either way, the title was predominantly, though not exclusively, Jewish and Christian, there being "abundant authority for its use in the Septuagint" (with well over a hundred occurrences) but relatively little documentation for it from Classical sources. Applying also to this title the categories worked out for the doctrine of God in their *apophatic* theology, the Cappadocians were careful to specify that it was a "relational" title, not an "absolute" one: "Accordingly,

Lampe 1005

Kelly 1950,136

See pp.42,49

when we hear the name 'pantokratōr,' our conception is this, that God sustains in being all intelligible things as well as things of a material nature, . . . so that all things may remain in existence, controlled by that encompassing power." It is likewise necessary to keep their *apophatic* theology in mind when reading such statements as that of Basil: "We propose to study the world as a whole, and to consider the universe, not by the light of the *sophia* of this world, but by that with which God wills to enlighten someone by speaking in person and without enigmas." This pejorative reference to "the *sophia* of this world" was in no wise intended to remove from consideration the vast amount of scientific information that Basil himself brought to his exposition of the Genesis cosmogony, for which also Gregory of Nyssa commended him. On the other hand, Basil's reference to God's "speaking in person and without enigmas" was also not intended to make the language of the Christian doctrine of creation about the "all-sovereign Maker of all things" somehow an exception to the universal rule of *apophasis,* that the intention of all language about God was to describe not the essence of God, but the conditions under which God could be thought of as existing; for "pantokratōr" was not an "absolute" title, but a "relational" one.

This reference to the "speaking" of God was, however, intended to provide justification for the critical intelligence, both in its speculation and in its biblical exegesis, as Basil put it in his treatise on the Holy Spirit, "to count the terms used in theology as of primary importance, and to endeavor to trace out the hidden meaning in every phrase and in every syllable," which was just what the Cappadocians were constantly doing in their commentaries on the Hexaemeron and elsewhere. Forced as they were to rely on Greek translations, they considered the implications, for example, of alternate renderings of the Hebrew text of Genesis by the Septuagint and by the translations of Aquila and of Symmachus. Such scriptural terms as "begetting" were probed for their bearing on the doctrine of creation as well as on the doctrine of the Trinity. The same was done with predominantly extrascriptural terms for these doctrines, such as "causality [aitia]." The purpose of such linguistic investigation was, nevertheless, not chiefly philological at all, but philosophical and theological. As Gregory of Nyssa put it, "The true power, and authority, and dominion, and sovereignty of God do not, we think, consist in syllables, because if that were so, any and every inventor of words might claim equal honor with God." Whatever the human usage of words may have been, therefore, a sound theology, natural or

Gr.Nyss.*Ref.*126
(Jaeger 2:366)

Bas.*Hex.*6.1
(SC 26:326)

See pp.99–104
Gr.Nyss.*Hom.opif.*pr.
(PG 44:125)

Gr.Nyss.*Eun.*2.142–44
(Jaeger 1:266–67)

Bas.*Spir.*1.2
(SC 17:252)

See pp.220–30

Gr.Nyss.*Hex.*
(PG 44:69)
Gr.Nyss.*Hex.*
(PG 44:80)

Gr.Nyss.*Ref.*89–94
(Jaeger 2:348–50)
Gr.Nyss.*Eun.*3.6.28–29
(Jaeger 2:196)

Gr.Nyss.*Eun.*2.291
(Jaeger 1:312)

Gr.Nyss.*Eun*.3.2.154
(Jaeger 2:102)

Bas.*Hex*.8.7
(SC 26:470)

Gr.Nyss.*Hom.opif*.29
(PG 44:233)

Gr.Naz.*Or*.16.16
(PG 35:956)

revealed, required that the term "to be" when applied to creatures be understood as meaning "to be created"—that is, not possessing an independent reality. The God who was "pantokratōr" and "Maker of all things," consequently, had "created nothing unnecessarily and omitted nothing necessary." For the ultimate ground of all created realities was "in the power of God's foreknowledge." This was the God who, as the "all-sovereign Maker of all things," also filled the universe, yet without being identified with it.

Gr.Nyss.*Hex.*
(PG 44:68)

But the Nicene and Niceno-Constantinopolitan creeds, and the Cappadocians as expositors of the Nicene faith and of "the cosmogonic narrative," were concerned with the implications not only of the words "all-sovereign Maker," but also of the words that followed: "of all things, whether visible or invisible." This concern manifested itself not alone in their meticulous attention to scientific data but in both their natural theology and

See pp.99–104

their dogmatic theology. Although Macrina was determined to assign primary authority to "the Holy Scriptures [as] the rule and

Macr.ap.Gr.Nyss.
Anim.res. (PG 46:49)
Gr.Nyss.*Anim.res.*
(PG 46:64)

the measure" of every teaching, whether theological or philosophical, that does not seem to have prevented her at all from invoking philosophical methods of proof and demonstration. Such were the methods at work in her picture of the cosmos: "We see all this with the piercing eyes of mind, nor can we fail to be taught through such a spectacle that a divine power, working with *techne* and *sophia,* is manifesting itself in this actual world and, penetrating each portion, combines these portions with the whole and completes the whole by the portions and encompasses the universe with a single all-controlling force, self-possessed and

Macr.ap.Gr.Nyss.
Anim.res. (PG 46:25–28)

self-contained, never ceasing from its motion, yet never altering the position that it holds." Thus it was in accordance with both natural and revealed authority that she formulated her doctrine of creation on the basis of all things, whether visible or invisible.

Macrina's vision of "all things" as a whole and in constituent portions—which seemed to be accessible, by her interpretation, within the confines also of natural theology—was basic as well to revealed theology, for which the statements of the Scriptures

Jer 23:6;1 Cor 1:30

identifying Christ as "the righteousness of God" became the ground for the affirmation: "Whether you look at the cosmos as a

Gr.Nyss.*Eun*.3.4.34
(Jaeger 2:147)

whole or at the parts of the world that make up that complete whole, all these are works of the Father." And because it was impossible for "all created nature . . . to hold together without the care and providence of God," it was Christ, "the Creator *Logos,* the only-begotten God," who distributed his "mercies

Bas.*Spir.*8.19
(SC 17:312)

varied and manifold on account of the many kinds and characters of the recipients of his bounty, but appropriate to the necessities of their individual requirements." Yet the presupposition of such christocentric affirmations remained an insight that came from natural theology and "from philosophy"—which in this instance does seem to have referred to philosophy as such, rather than, as it sometimes did, to Christian dogmatic theology or even to asceticism—to anyone "with the soul-insight and the acquired enlightenment to comprehend the phenomena of the heavens." Such a person had learned to "look at the harmony of the whole." It was on the basis of such observations that in spite of "the dissimilarity among the *stoicheia*," one could perceive "in each thing making up the framework of the whole, an adherence to its natural opposite." Basil was speaking as an expositor of the revelation of the origins of creation in the Book of Genesis, but he was also drawing from the Platonic doctrine of forms, when he said that God had "created matter in harmony with the form that it was the will of God to give it," and that God had "finally welded all the diverse parts of the universe by a link of indissoluble attachment, and established between them so perfect a fellowship and harmony, that the most distant, in spite of their distance, would appear united in one universal sympathy." This harmony and kinship among "all created things" was the direct consequence of "their having equally proceeded from nonbeing into being."

See pp.177–82

Gr.Nyss.*Infant.*
(Jaeger 3–II:71)

Gr.Nyss.*Eun.*1.402
(Jaeger 1:143–44)

Bas.*Hex.*2.2
(SC 26:148)

Gr.Nyss.*Or.catech.*39.6
(Méridier 188)

But all of this celebration of the symmetry, harmony, and affinity between the component parts of the cosmos, in which nothing had been created unnecessarily and nothing necessary had been omitted, should not be permitted to obscure a central point of the Cappadocian doctrine of creation: the contingency of the created world. Their polemics simultaneously against *ananke* and against *tyche* not only protected them against a theory of randomness that would have changed the notion of cosmos back into chaos, but against the opposite extreme as well, a theory of cosmic necessity as an iron law over which even the all-sovereign Creator was powerless, what Stanley L. Jaki in his Gifford Lectures called "Aristotelian necessitarianism" (which, as he explained, was not only Aristotelian). For, as Jaki pointed out, summarizing the *apophatic* methodology shared by the Cappadocians though without referring to them explicitly, "The theist also knows that the universe must be queerer than he can imagine, because he knows he can never be privy to the Creator's

Bas.*Hex.*8.7
(SC 26:470)

Unterstein 1903,45–47
See pp.152–65

Gr.Nyss.*Or.catech.*5.3
(Méridier 26)

Jaki 1978,39

Jaki 1978,278

Grant 1952,210–11

Gr.Naz.Or.8.16–
18;18.36
(PG 35:808–12;1033)

Gr.Naz.Or.43.35
(PG 36:544)

Gr.Nyss.V.Macr.
(Jaeger 8–I:413–14)

Gr.Nyss.Or.catech.13.2
(Méridier 74)

Gr.Nyss.Eun.2.228–32
(Jaeger 1:292–93)

Gr.Nyss.Or.catech.24.2
(Méridier 112)

Bas.Hex.8.1
(SC 26:428–30)

Gn 1:5
Bas.Hex.4.2
(SC 26:250)

Gr.Nyss.Eun.2.549
(Jaeger 1:386)

Gr.Nyss.Hom.opif.1
(PG 44:128)

sovereign choice in creating a world of which man is an equally contingent constituent." Support for the doctrine of contingency came in Cappadocian thought from what might seem an unlikely quarter, the concept of miracle. In their hagiography the Cappadocians followed the standard Christian pattern of celebrating not only the piety but the miracles of the saints, even when these saints happened to have been members of their own families. At the same time they were sensitive to the apologetic embarrassment that was created by the contrast between the many miracles said to have occurred during biblical times and the (relative) dearth of such occurrences during postbiblical times. Therefore, they explained that such gifts as the performance of miracles were given according to the measure of the individual's faith, "little to those of little faith, much to those with plenty of free space in their faith." They also sought to turn that very awkwardness to constructive use, by interpreting miracles, past or present, as signs of the sovereignty of the divine nature and the contingency of the created nature. "Do you fail to believe the miracle?" Gregory of Nyssa asked. "I welcome your incredulity. For by your very recognition that what we have said transcends belief, you acknowledge that the miracles transcend nature." In God there was no difference between will and action; and because "God made all things by an act of will," the will of God remained sovereign over them and they in turn remained contingent. And within the total scheme of the divine *economy*, the incarnation of the *Logos* was a clearer evidence of divine sovereignty than any miracle.

In the axiomatic formulation of Basil, therefore, "The divine *Logos* is the nature of the things that have been created." Or, earlier in the same commentary, "A spoken word [phōnē] of God makes the nature [of a thing], and this order is for the creature a direction for its future course. There was only one creation of day and night, and since that moment they have been incessantly succeeding each other and dividing time into equal parts." Or, in the formulation of his brother Gregory, "All that now grows upon the earth continues always, owing to a transmission of its seed from the first creation." This was because "the divine *techne* and power was implanted in the very nature of all existing things." Yet such formulations were anything but pantheistic; for by the sharpest possible metaphysical contrast with the eternity of God the Trinity, there was "nothing to prevent the creation, being in its own nature something other than its Creator and in

Gr.Nyss.*Eun*.1.383
(Jaeger 1:139)

Heb 11:3

Gr.Nyss.*Eun*.3.7.5
(Jaeger 2:216–17)

Gr.Nyss.*Eun*.2.435
(Jaeger 1:353–54)
Gr.Nyss.*Eun*.3.2.123–24
(Jaeger 2:92–93)
Gr.Nyss.*Hex.*
(PG 44:104)

Macr.ap.Gr.Nyss.
Anim.res. (PG 46:124)

Col 1:17

Gr.Nyss.*Or.catech*.6.4
(Méridier 36)

Gr.Nyss.*Or.catech*.32.6–8
(Méridier 146–48)

Eph 3:18
Ladner 1955,88–95
Gr.Nyss.*Eun*.3.3.40
(Jaeger 2:121–22)

Aug.*Trin*.1.6.12
(CCSL 50:41)

Rom 11:36

Edsmann 1939,11–44

no point trenching on that pure pretemporal world, from having, in our belief, an *arche* of its own," since it was, in the *apophatic* words of the New Testament, made "from the invisible things [mē ek phainomenōn]." It was, moreover, made "at the time when the only-begotten God willed it," and not at any other time: "Vegetation, fruits, the generation of animals, the formation of humanity—these all appeared at the time when each of these things seemed expedient to the *sophia* of the Creator." Thus, the knowledge and the sovereignty of God extended not only to the contingency of the cosmos as a whole but to the contingency of each of the myriads of particulars within it. Every one of these particulars was, by the will of the Creator, a unique individual. Also by the will and power of the Creator, each of the *stoicheia* was likewise "circumscribed within limits." As Macrina put it, "The movement of God's will becomes a fact at any moment that God pleases, and the intention becomes at once realized in nature."

This contingency of the creation was seen as christocentric, rooted in the metaphysical reality of the one of whom the New Testament said: "In him all things are held together as a system [ta panta en autōi synestēken]." According to Gregory of Nyssa, the original creation of Adam, shaped from the dust of the earth but animated by the very breath of God, had communicated "a single grace extending equally through all creation." Now after the fall and the redemption, as he said later in the same treatise, Christ the crucified was "binding all things to himself and making them one, and through himself bringing the diverse natures of existing things into one accord and harmony." The metaphysical ground of this state of things was: "The eyes of all creation are set on him and he is its center, and it finds its harmony in him." This implied that by speaking about "grasping the breadth and length and height and depth of Christ's love, and knowing it, though it is beyond knowledge," Paul was "describing by the figure of the cross the power controlling the universe and holding it together." Applying to Christ as *Logos* and Son of God—rather than, as Augustine did, to the three *hypostases* of the Trinity—another saying of Paul, "For from him and through him and to him are all things," Basil could formulate that christocentric principle to mean: "For it is 'from him' that the cause of their being comes to all things that exist, according to the will of God the Father. 'Through him' all things have their continuance and constitution; for he created all things, and distributes to each severally what is necessary for its health and preservation. Therefore 'to

Bas.*Spir*.5.7
(SC 17:274–76)

Bas.*Spir*.8.19
(SC 17:312)

him' all things are turned, looking with irresistible and ineffable affection to the author and maintainer of their life." Created nature could not hold together without the Creator *Logos,* who distributed his mercies to all creatures. And "all creatures" meant nothing less than all creatures: "The earth is stable without being immutable, while the heaven, on the contrary, as it has no mutability, so it has no stability either. Thus the divine power, by interweaving change in the stable nature and interweaving motion with that which is not subject to change, can, by the interchange of attributes, at once join them both closely to each

Gr.Nyss.*Hom.opif*.1
(PG 44:129)

other—and at the same time make both of them alien from the conception of deity." It was this distinction between "earth" as the visible creation and "heaven" as the invisible creation, but much more importantly the ontological distinction between both of them and "deity," that the creed expressed in its opening

Symb.Nic.-CP
(Alberigo-Jedin 24)

words: "We believe in one God, Father, all-sovereign Maker of heaven and earth, of all things, whether visible or invisible."

By making it explicit that the Maker of heaven and earth was the Creator of "all things," a phrase that included "the invisible things" and not only "the visible things," the orthodox creed, and all the Cappadocians as its defenders, addressed the decisive instance of their teaching that the cosmos was a contingent cre-

Daniélou 1944,152–82

Eun.ap.Gr.Nyss.*Eun*.
3.9.54 (Jaeger 2:284)

ation: the doctrine of angels. In keeping with their rejection of any suggestion that precise formulations were to be regarded as more important in the Christian religion than worship, the Cappadocians constantly emphasized, even in their most polemical and their most speculative works, the specifically religious con-

Peterson 1964

Mt 18:10
Bas.*Eun*.3.1
(SC 305:148)

tent also of this doctrine. Thus it was in a polemical writing against Eunomius that Basil issued a reminder of the idea of the guardian angel, that there was "an angel accompanying each individual among the faithful." There was a close association between the angels and the Holy Spirit. A bishop was to look

Gr.Naz.*Or*.13.4
(PG 35:856)
Gr.Nyss.*Trin*.7
(Jaeger 3–I:12)

Bas.*Spir*.16.38
(SC 17:384)

upon his congregation as "handed over to you by the Holy Spirit and presented to you by the angels." The holiness of the angels, too, was a gift from the Holy Spirit. It was the Holy Spirit who conferred on them "the grace flowing for the completion and perfection of their *hypostasis.*" For human morality, therefore, the doctrine of angels furnished a model and guide for ascetic discipline, a discipline defined as "the *techne* in the science of the

Mt 22:30
Gr.Nyss.*Virg*.4
(Jaeger 8–I:277)
Gr.Nyss.*V.Macr.*
(Jaeger 8–I:382)

more divine life, teaching those still living in the body to achieve an approximation of that noncorporeal life." That ascetic way of life served as an "imitation of the angelic life," as Macrina lived it. The angels were a reminder of the religious imperative to obey the

limitations that this physical existence placed on human speech,
even on the speech of prayer and adoration, and therefore of the
imperative of *apophasis*. For the exclusionary principle in the
Gospel of John, "No one has ever seen God," applied to them in
their nonmaterial existence no less than it did to humanity. The
inner mysteries of the divine being transcended their comprehension, too. They also proved that it was not physical existence as
such, but creatureliness, that produced the desire for God; for the
angels also were obliged to find "the fountain, the *arche*, the
uncreated supply of every good in the world, the object of yearning for the whole creation [including the angels], with a contact
and share in supreme being coming to it only by virtue of its part
in the first good."

An important proof text for the doctrine of angels in Cappadocian thought was a passage from the epistle of Paul to the
Colossians, distinguishing between "things visible" and "the invisible orders." When Macrina spoke of "the unembodied angel-
world 'in heaven,'" she was dealing directly with a passage from
Philippians, but also echoing this one. Gregory of Nazianzus
invoked it explicitly in support of going beyond "matter and
objects of sight" to "the whole world, namely, the world of things
'visible and invisible.'" Basil took it to be saying: "The virtues or
hosts of angels or the dignities of archangels fill the essence of this
invisible world, as Paul teaches us." It taught him to "glorify the
Maker by whom all things were made, visible and invisible, prin-
cipalities and powers, authorities, thrones, and dominions, and
all other unnameable rational natures." Gregory of Nyssa was
sometimes capable of citing the passage as proof for the thesis:
"The ultimate division of all being is into the intelligible [and
invisible] reality and the empirical [and visible] reality. . . . Reason again divides the invisible into the uncreated and the created,
inferentially comprehending it, with the uncreated as that which
effects the creation, and the created as that which owes its origin
and its force to the uncreated." Thus, God and the angels were on
one side of this "ultimate division of all being," whereas man and
the brutes and the inanimate world were on the other side. But a
little later in the same treatise Gregory invoked the same passage
to draw the distinction between God the Trinity on one side, and
on the other all the invisible realities cataloged in that very passage: "Whether thrones or dominions or rulers or powers—all
things have been created through [Christ] and for [Christ]."

The confession that the angels, too, invisible though they
were, belonged to the "all things" that had been created through

---

Gr.Nyss.*Eun.*2.391
(Jaeger 1:340)
Jn 1:18
Gr.Nyss.*V.Mos.*2
(Jaeger 7–I:87)

Gr.Naz.*Or.*29.8
(SC 250:192)

Gr.Nyss.*Eun.*1.272–74
(Jaeger 1:106)

Col 1:16
Phil 2:10
Macr.ap.Gr.Nyss.
Anim.res. (PG 46:69)

Gr.Naz.*Or.*28.31
(SC 250:170)

Bas.*Hex.*2.3
(SC 26:148)

Bas.*Spir.*16.38
(SC 17:376)

Gr.Nyss.*Eun.*1.270–71
(Jaeger 1:105–6)

Gr.Nyss.*Eun.*1.306–7
(Jaeger 1:117)

Werner 1941,302–49

Is 9:5

See pp.267–69
Gr.Nyss.Eun.3.9.39
(Jaeger 2:278)

Gr.Nyss.Eun.1.270–71
(Jaeger 1:105–6)

Gr.Nyss.Eun.2.67–69
(Jaeger 1:245–46)

Lovejoy 1936,24–66

Gr.Naz.Or.38.10
(PG 36:321)

Bas.Ep.189.7
(Courtonne 2:139)
Mateo-Seco–Bastero
1988,353–79

Christ and in Christ and that therefore the angels were part of the contingent creation rather than of the divine reality had it as one of its trinitarian points to refute the effort of an Arian "angel christology" to classify Christ as an angel. When Isaiah, in his prophecy of the incarnation and nativity of Christ, gave him the title of "angel of mighty counsel [megalēs boulēs angelos]," this term was "an indication, in clear and uncontrovertible terms, of the *economy* of his humanity," rather than of the divine nature that he shared with the Father and the Holy Spirit in the Trinity. But although that distinction between *economy* and *theology* may have been the primary, or certainly the most crucial, implication of this confession, the Cappadocians were likewise concerned, and ultimately for the same reason, to get the metaphysics straight. Later in the same work in whose first book he postulated the thesis of "the ultimate division of all being into the intelligible realities" (including both God and the angels) and the "empirical realities," Gregory of Nyssa was prepared to refine that thesis in a fundamental way by declaring, even concerning the angels with their "pure naked intelligence": "If we weigh even their comprehension with the majesty of the one who really is, it may be that if anyone should venture to say that even their power of understanding is not far superior to our own weakness, that conjecture would fall within the limits of probability. For wide and insurmountable is the intervening barrier that divides and fences off the uncreated nature from the created *ousia*." There he was going far beyond what he had called "the ultimate division" of reality, to that division of reality which truly was ultimate, the division between "the uncreated nature" and "the created *ousia*"; and the doctrine of angels, by unequivocally locating them in the latter category and thereby defining their being as part of the contingent creation, made a major contribution to that clarification of the issue.

The natural theology of the Cappadocians could sometimes lead them to a doctrine of the great chain of being: "Akin to deity are those natures that are intellectual and only to be comprehended by mind; but all those of which the senses can take cognizance are utterly alien to deity, and of these the furthest removed are all those that are entirely destitute of soul and of power of motion." Not only divine revelation, but "the plain testimony of the evidence in human life," supported the thesis that "the divine *economy* beyond us," the world of angels and of the Platonic forms, was "governed by the Spirit." But a deeper contemplation of the world of angels, as such contemplation was informed by

Gr.Naz.Or.6.13
(PG 35:740)

Gr.Nyss.Maced.
(Jaeger 3–I:109)

I Cor 12:6

Gr.Nyss.Hex.
(PG 44:92)
Bas.Hex.1.7
(SC 26:114)
Bas.Hex.4.6
(SC 26:270)

Bas.Hex.3.10
(SC 26:238–40)

Gr.Naz.Or.29.21
(SC 250:224)

revelation, led to the recognition that their existence and their unity were "derived from the praiseworthy and holy Trinity." That recognition, moreover, had to be generalized into a universal ontological principle: The Trinity was the source of "everything *kalon kai agathon*," for it was God the Trinity who, in the language of the New Testament, "works all in all." Not only the angels and humanity, which shared a rational nature, but the irrational creation as well—indeed every creature—could be called *kalon* and could be said "to be fulfilled in the *kalon* in its own manner." Thus, the cosmos, as a whole and in each of its parts, was, as the created world, "a work of *techne,* displayed for the beholding of all people." But its *kalon* was grounded in its divine purpose as a "creation." Hence, it would have been a mistake to conclude, on the basis of natural theology, that there was some way of moving by direct analogy from human criteria of the *kalon* in the cosmos to the divine criterion of the *kalon;* for what God, as "the supreme artist," regarded as the *kalon* had the quality of "presenting in its perfection all the fitness of *techne,* and of tending toward the usefulness of its *telos.*" Once again, therefore, it was the transcendent that preserved the immanent, the Creator that perfected the creation, and faith that gave fullness to reasoning.

CHAPTER 17

The Economy of Salvation

Eph 4:15–16
Gr.Nyss.*Cant*.7
(Jaeger 6:234)

An essential component of the Cappadocians' definition of the cosmos as contingent creation was their affirmation, based on that of the New Testament, that the Christ who became incarnate in time and history was "the true head of the universe." Even as they presented their doctrine of the creation, they were pointing toward their presentation of the doctrine of the incarnation: "That the omnipotent nature was capable of descending to man's lowly position is a clearer evidence of power than are great and supernatural miracles. For it somehow accords with God's nature, and is consistent with it, to do great and sublime things by divine power. It does not startle us to hear it said that the whole creation, including the invisible world, exists by God's power, and is the realization of God's will. But descent to man's lowly

Gr.Nyss.*Or.catech*.24.2
(Méridier 112)

position is a supreme example of power—of a power that is not bounded by circumstances that are contrary to its nature." In their doctrine of the Trinity, similarly, they were conscious of being able to assume that Judaism on the basis of its revealed knowledge in the Scriptures, together with Hellenism on the basis of its natural knowledge in "innate ideas," would both assent, in some sense and to some measure, to the thesis that God had both a *Logos* and a "Spirit"; where that assent broke off for both Hellenism and Judaism was at the point of "the *economy* by

Gr.Nyss.*Or.catech*.5.1
(Méridier 22)

which the *Logos* of God became man, as something unbelievable and unbefitting to say of God." It was the specific message of the Christian gospel that the *Logos* as Creator, known to natural reason or at any rate knowable by it, was also the Savior, who

Gr.Nyss.*Eun.*3.3.51
(Jaeger 2:125–26)

See pp.259–62
Rousse 1965,147–52

became incarnate by "taking to himself humanity in its completeness," a truth that was knowable by divine revelation alone. Similarly, the doctrine of angels was a component not only of their cosmology but of their doctrine of economy.

Within the schema of the Cappadocian system as within the sequence of the Nicene Creed, therefore, the doctrine of the incarnation occupied a special dialectical position in relation to all that had preceded it. By opening with the declaration, "We believe [pisteuomen]," the creed as quoted by the Cappadocians can be said to have identified everything that followed, including that which was knowable also to natural theology, as the object of faith. The New Testament's most specific definition of faith described it as "the evidence of things not seen." Therefore, according to Basil, "The mind is led by the sight of things that are visible and empirically perceptible to the contemplation of things that are invisible." Yet what followed now in the Nicene Creed would seem to be the very opposite; for by the incarnation the mind was actually led from the contemplation of invisible things back to the utterly visible and empirically perceptible, from spirit back to flesh, and from the timelessly transcendent back to the historically immanent. A mind that was quite willing to speak *apophatically* about God as "that incomprehensible, inconceivable, and ineffable reality, transcending all glory of greatness," now found itself "staggered" by the incarnation; and it balked at the very idea. It had been characteristic of God already under the Old Testament *economy* to work paradoxically. Although the incarnation was the supreme instance of "that with which God wills to enlighten someone by speaking in person and without enigmas," the paradox was in fact heightened, not resolved, in the New Testament revelation. Its title "Christ," in accordance with that paradox, did not "pertain to the eternity of the Godhead, but to the human being who received God [pros ton theodochon anthrōpon], the one who was seen here on earth and who [as the Old Testament said] 'associated with human beings'"; and it was about this "man who received God" that the New Testament in turn affirmed, "It is in Christ that the Godhead in all its fullness dwells embodied"—as though, in the striking phrase of Gregory of Nyssa, a flame were to be pointing downward rather than upward.

To cope with this paradox reverently without attempting to resolve it rationalistically, the tradition of Greek Christian thought, which also used the word in its more general, usual

Bas.*Ep.*125.2
(Courtonne 2:32)
Heb 11:1
Macr.ap.Gr.Nyss.
Anim.res. (PG 46:96)

Rom 1:20

Bas.*Hex.*1.6
(SC 26:110)

Gr.Naz.*Or.*29.19
(SC 250:216)

Gr.Nyss.*Or.catech.*14
(Méridier 76)
Gr.Nyss.*Cant.*12
(Jaeger 6:362)

Bas.*Hex.*6.1
(SC 26:326)

Bar 3:38

Col 2:9

Gr.Nyss.*Cant.*13
(Jaeger 6:390–91)

Gr.Nyss.*Or.catech.*24.3
(Méridier 112–14)

Lampe 627–28
Lampe 940–43

Symb.Nic.
(Alberigo-Jedin 5);
Symb.Nic.-CP
(Alberigo-Jedin 24)
Is 22:19,21;Lk 16:2,3,4;
1 Cor 9:17;Eph 1:10,3:2,
3:9;Col 1:25;1 Tm 1:4

Gr.Presb.V.Gr.Naz.
(PG 35:288)

See pp.209–14

Gottwald 1906,22–23

Gr.Naz.Or.30.18–19
(SC 250:262–66)

Gr.Nyss.V.Macr.
(Jaeger 8–I:390)

Macr.ap.Gr.Nyss.
Anim.res. (PG 46:105)

sense (as we have been doing here, too), distinguished *theology*, as the doctrine of the Godhead as God, from *economy*, the doctrine of the historical dispensations of God in dealing with the human race and the world, through the creation, through the history of Israel, and above all through the incarnation of the Son of God. In speaking about the Son of God, *theology* pertained to the language of the creed describing him as "God out of God, light out of light"; *economy* pertained to its language about the events that took place "for our salvation [dia tēn hēmeteran sōtērian]," beginning with his incarnation. Only the second of these terms, *economy*, appeared in the Bible, and fewer than a dozen times as a noun. In a few manuscripts of the heading of the Book of Revelation, however, Saint John was called "ho theologos" (with the definite article), "Saint John the Divine," as the one who had dealt preeminently, especially in the prologue of his Gospel, with *theology* as the trinitarian mystery of the Godhead; it was an epithet shared with him by Gregory of Nazianzus and, at any rate in Eastern Christendom, by no one else. Gregory himself invoked the distinction between *theology* and *economy* in his analysis of the names for God. He identified "the one who is [ho ōn]" and "God [ho theos]" as the two technical terms distinctively pertaining to *theology*, with the first, "ho ōn," being technically "superior" as a precise ontological title. These titles he contrasted with those belonging to *economy* (as, for example, "Creator" and "Savior" did), an *economy* that was, as these two titles indicated, "twofold, involving, and not involving, incarnation [dittēs, tēs men hyper to sōma, tēs de en sōmati]." The concept of the divine *economy* seems to have occupied a special position in the thought of Macrina. Gregory of Nyssa reported that when their brother Basil died, she "treated the mention of the saint as an occasion for yet loftier philosophy, discussing various subjects, inquiring into human affairs, and revealing in her conversation the divine *economy* concealed in disasters." And when facing her own death, she addressed "those with hearts failing over these calamities" with the comfort of the divine *economy:* "It is foolish, good people, for you to fret and complain of the chain of *ananke* in the fixed sequence of life's realities. You do not know the goal towards which each single *economy* of the universe is moving."

In his exposition of the distinction between *theology* and *economy*, Gregory of Nyssa applied it to the classification of theological terms: "It is possible to make a twofold division of the signification of the divine names, as it were by a scientific rule; for

Gr.Nyss.*Eun.*3.1.131–32
(Jaeger 2:48)

to one class [that is, to *theology*] belongs the indication of the lofty and ineffable glory of God, whereas the other class indicates the variety of the *economy*." This was, moreover, a distinction held in common by the orthodox Nicene party and by its heretical opponents, such as Eunomius. "There is," Nyssen explained,

Gr.Nyss.*Eun.*3.3.61–62
(Jaeger 2:129)

"no mutual conflict between what is said by us and what is said by him, for we both consider the *economy* in the flesh apart, and regard the divine power in itself." But when it came to the application of the distinction to the dogma of the Trinity, the divergence between the two parties was profound and far-reaching. It was epitomized in their debate over the interpretation of the words of Peter at Pentecost, as recorded by Luke in the Acts of the Apostles: "God has made this same Jesus, whom you crucified,

Acts 2:36

both Lord and Christ." From that verb "made [epoiēsen]," which appeared to imply a change or promotion to the status of "Lord" and "Christ" for a man who had not had that status previously, it did seem possible to draw the conclusion, attributed already by Athanasius to his Arian opponents, "that the Savior was not Lord and King even before he became man and endured

ap.Ath.*Ar.*2.13
(PG 26:173)

the cross, but only then began to be Lord." In opposition to such

Ath.*Ar.*2.12
(PG 26:172)

an exegesis of the passage, Athanasius had invoked the principle of "the human *economy*, which he undertook for our sake." Both the exegesis of the passage against the *homoousion* by the heretics and the application of the hermeneutical principle of *economy* to it by the orthodox continued in the age of the Cappadocians. Writing against the exegesis of it by Eunomius, Basil addressed himself "to the intention of this apostolic phrase," concluding: "By no means does it hand down to us a relationship according to *theology*, but it intimates the terms of the divine

Bas.*Eun.*2.3
(SC 305:16)

economy." In *theology* the divine nature always was Lord, the human nature became Lord in *economy*. Defending Basil on this point against Eunomius, Gregory of Nyssa combined that controverted saying of Peter with a familiar saying of Paul, to argue

Phil 2:7

that the verb "made" here was being predicated only of "'the form of a slave,' which he assumed for the sake of the divine

Gr.Nyss.*Eun.*3.3.12
(Jaeger 2:111)

economy."

Gr.Nyss.*Eun.*1.637
(Jaeger 1:209)

As "the one who is [ōn]," the Son of God was eternal, superior to all marks of time. But expounding "the mystery of our faith" in the course of his *Life of Moses*, Gregory of Nyssa formulated the meaning of the incarnation this way: "He is, alone among all, the only one who both had being before all the *aeons* and who began to be in this final *aeon*. . . . He whose being extends back before all times and before all the *aeons* entered this world of temporal

Gr.Nyss.V.Mos.2
(Jaeger 7–I:91–92)

Gr.Nyss.Apoll.
(Jaeger 3–I:224)

Bas.Hex.6.2
(SC 26:332)

Gr.Nyss.Or.catech.24.3
(Méridier 114)

Gr.Nyss.Hom.opif.22
(PG 44:205–8)

Gr.Nyss.Eun.3.7.30
(Jaeger 2:225)

Gr.Nyss.Or.dom.1
(PG 44:1124–25)

Rom 5:17
Bas.Spir.14.31
(SC 17:356)
1 Cor 15:22
Gr.Nyss.Hom.opif.23
(PG 44:209)

Gr.Nyss.Or.catech.27.2
(Méridier 126)

Gr.Nyss.Or.catech.9.1
(Méridier 64)

Gr.Nyss.Cant.13
(Jaeger 6:380)
Daniélou 1951,85

Gr.Naz.Or.1.1
(SC 247:72)
Gr.Naz.Or.45
(PG 36:645–64)
Gr.Naz.Or.38
(PG 36:312–33)

becoming for our sakes, in order to lead that which existed outside the realm of being back into being." A characteristic common to the *economy* of creation and to the *economy* of salvation was that they both took place "not before all the aeons, but just once [hapax]," within time and history. It was the pattern of the divine *economy*, as was evident already from the *economy* of creation, that it was the way for God to have "planted into history everywhere, in mystic language, the dogma of *theology*." That became true above all in the case of the *economy* of salvation. As Nyssen said in his *Catechical Oration*, "God's transcendent power is not so much displayed in the vastness of the heavens or in the luster of the stars or in the orderly arrangement of the universe or in the perpetual supervision of it, as it is rather to be seen in the condescension of God to our weak nature." This *economy* of salvation, too, took place within time, which extended between precise and fixed limits, a beginning and an end. Because time was concurrent with all things that were produced in creation, it was necessary that the eternal Son of God, who was its Creator, himself be outside time. Yet, his incarnation had to take place within time, which was divided into past, present, and future.

In the first Adam, who was the product of the *economy* of creation, "death established its reign," being "transmitted until the end in a sequence of succession"; thus, all died in Adam, as Paul had also said. The beginning of time necessarily implied the end of time as well. The *economy* of salvation in Christ, the second Adam, had to reach both of those points, by "touching the *arche* and extending to the *telos* and covering everything between" the *arche* and the *telos* of human life. What lay between his human *arche* and his human *telos* was "the human birth, the advance from infancy to manhood, the eating and drinking, the weariness, the sleep, the grief, the tears, the false accusations, the trial, the cross, the death, and the burial in the tomb" of Jesus Christ, as these events of the *economy* were narrated in the Gospels. At each of these stages, "in accordance with the *economy* he underwent on our behalf, he was conformed to the body of our low estate." As each of these events in the life of Christ came up on the calendar of the church year, it could become the subject of homilies and exhortations. For example, the first of the orations of Gregory of Nazianzus opened with the words, "It is Easter Day [Anastaseōs hēmera]!"; and the last was likewise delivered on Easter Day. Moreover, his "Oration on the Theophany," delivered in 380 or 381, seems to be the earliest

Usener 1911,260–73

Bas.*Ep.*99
(Courtonne 1:214–18)
Gr.Naz.Or.21
(*SC* 270:110–92);
Gr.Naz.Or.43
(*PG* 36:493–605)

List 1928,24–31
Musurillo 1957,370–75
Gr.Nyss.*V.Macr.*
(Jaeger 8–I:370–414)
Gr.Nyss.*V.Mos.*
(Jaeger 7–I:1–145)

Lk 2:52

Gr.Nyss.*Cant.*15
(Jaeger 6:467)

Gr.Nyss.*Hom.opif.*22
(*PG* 44:205)

Gr.Nyss.*V.Mos.*2
(Jaeger 7–I:82)

Gr.Nyss.*Cant.*3
(Jaeger 6:96)

Jn 20:17

surviving Christmas sermon from the East. There was nothing resembling a biography of Christ either by him or by any of the other Cappadocians, although all were familiar with biography as a literary genre. Some of Basil's letters were autobiographical and biographical. Even more, several of Nazianzen's panegyric orations, notably those on Athanasius and on Basil, were in effect miniature biographies or hagiographies, the difference between panegyric and history being important to him. More than either of the other two, Gregory of Nyssa wrote a brief and touching *Life of Macrina* about his sister soon after her death in 379, and a much more extended *Life of Moses* a decade or so later. What Gregory of Nyssa did do, instead of writing a biography of Christ, was to engage in bold speculation about the implications of the single lapidary sentence in which the Gospel of Luke summarized most of what could be known of that biography: "And Jesus increased in wisdom, in stature, and in grace [chariti] with God and with people."

Christ's growing up from childhood to complete maturity became for Gregory of Nyssa a paradigm for the movement of human life through the *economy* of time. Within the temporal *economy*, he said, "God is the one who governs all things in a certain order and sequence." Yet it was through that very "sequence in accordance with the historical order [di' akolothou kata tēn tēs historias taxin]" that the ineffable knowledge about God was revealed. This emphasis on the human growth of Christ, in turn, enabled Gregory to pay attention, in the light of the divine *economy*, to the diversity that characterized the response of believers to the life of Christ: "Jesus, the child who is born in us, develops differently in wisdom and in stature and in grace among those who have received him. He is not the same in all of them, but according to the measure of the one in whom he is born and to the degree that the one who comprehends him has the capacity, he appears as one who is still a child, or as one who is growing up, or as one who has achieved full and perfect maturity." That diversity was reflected also in the variety of names for Christ in scriptural usage. When Christ said to his disciples, "I am ascending to my Father and your Father, to my God and your God," the distinction between *theology* and *economy* helped in making sense of these titles: "God is not called the 'God' of the *Logos*—for how could God, in the strict [trinitarian] sense of the term, have a 'God'?—but God of the one who was visible, in the same way as God was 'Father,' not of the one who was visible but of the *Logos*. In fact there was a duality about him, with the result that in both cases the reverse of what does or does not properly apply to us holds good of him. In the strict [trinitarian] sense of the term, God is our 'God' but not our 'Father.' What leads heretics astray is the coupling together of titles, titles which, because of the intermingling, overlap. This means that when the natures are distinguished, the titles are differentiated along with the ideas." The Christ who, within *economy*, had "appeared in these last days in the flesh" was the one, within *theology*, to whom such titles as "the power and wisdom of God, the light and the life" all applied. The incarnate one also had, within *economy*, other titles, such as "door, stone, axe," and the like. But Gregory of Nyssa explained: "None of these names represents the nature of the only-begotten one or his deity or the peculiar character of his essence. Nevertheless he is called by these names, and each appellation has its own special appropriateness." He continued: "As our Lord provided for human life in various forms, each variety of his beneficence is suitably distinguished by his several names."

Likewise, in a passage that J. N. D. Kelly has described as "a highly original theory of doctrinal development," Gregory of Nazianzus explicitly invoked the distinction between *economy* and *theology* to speculate no less boldly, by applying these christological principles—growth [auxēsis], progress [prokopē], sequence [akolouthia], and historical order [taxis]—to the history of Christian doctrine itself, in fact, to the very history of what Basil identified as the "chief dogma," the dogma of the Trinity, the unchangeable doctrine about the unchangeable divine nature. Basil spoke of a doctrinal "development [prokopē]" in himself from childhood to manhood, preserving continuity and identity and "not changing in kind though gradually being perfected in growth." But Nazianzen projected the development from the individual to the history of salvation: "[Under the Old Testament *economy*, development came through the subtraction of legal regulations, one by one.] But in the case of *theology* . . . maturity is reached by additions. For the matter stands thus. The Old Testament proclaimed the Father openly, and the Son more obscurely. The New [Testament] manifested the Son, and suggested the deity of the Spirit. Now [that is, after the New Testament] the Spirit Itself dwells among us, and supplies us with a clearer demonstration of Itself. For it was not safe, when the deity of the Father was not yet acknowledged, plainly to proclaim the Son; nor, when that of the Son was not yet received, to burden us further (if I may use so bold an expression) with the Holy Spirit.

Gr.Naz.*Or.*30.8
(*SC* 250:240–42)

1 Cor 1:24;Jn 1:4
Gr.Nyss.*Apoll.*
(Jaeger 3-I:219)
Jn 10:7;Ps 117:22;
Mt 3:10

Gr.Nyss.*Eun.*2.298
(Jaeger 1:314)

Kelly 1958,261

Bas.*Eun.*2.22
(*SC* 305:88)

Bas.*Ep.*223.3
(Courtonne 3:12–13)

2 Cor 3:18
Gr.Naz.Or.31.25–26
(SC 250:324–26)

Gr.Naz.Or.4.110
(SC 309:264)

Florovsky 7:136

Gr.Nyss.Eun.1.341
(Jaeger 1:128)
Gr.Nyss.Apoll.
(Jaeger 3–I:134)

. . . But [the revelation has moved in such a way through time] that by gradual additions . . . and advances and progressions 'with ever-increasing glory' the light of the Trinity might shine upon the more illuminated." It was this same contrast that underlay his declaration to the emperor Julian, in defending Christian doctrine, that it was "ancient and yet new." Thus, as Georges Florovsky has summarized Gregory's position, "The spiritual experience of the Church is also a form of revelation." It was on the basis of the *economy* of salvation in the incarnation and life of Christ that the Cappadocians in their dogmatics, having argued in their natural theology for a divine reality and "a prime nature transcending all ideas of time and surpassing all reach of thought," now directed the attention of their audience not to eternity but to time. That repolarization was a radical reversal of what, without having thought about it as profoundly as they did, a superficial common sense might take to be the proper relation between natural theology as apologetics and natural theology as presupposition, as well as, even more basically, a reversal of how it might define the difference between natural theology and the theology of revelation. It was, in short, a fundamental *metamorphosis* of natural theology.

For in Cappadocian thought the most profound difference between natural theology and the theology of revelation was this: natural theology as *theology* could deal with eternity (as, of course, the theology of revelation as *theology* could also, and much more faithfully), but the theology of revelation as *economy* had to deal with time. Natural theology as *theology* could consider "the vast variety in the order of the cosmos," but it was for the theology of revelation as *economy* to address the paradox: "[Nothing] so well sets forth the excellence of his might as this, that God, being incomprehensible, should have been able, with *apatheia* but through flesh, to have come into close conflict with death, to the end that by his own suffering he might give us the boon of *apatheia*." In relation to such a consideration of the *economy* of salvation, it was not the responsibility of "natural theology" to prove the truth of the gospel. Sometimes the Cappadocians did seem to be saying that such was its responsibility (and even its capacity), and that natural reason should lead the honest inquirer to the knowledge and acceptance of that truth. In somewhat the same way, they sometimes also spoke as though revelation permitted the believer to go beyond negation to making unambiguously positive assertions. Particularly in his *Cate-*

Bas.Spir.8.18
(SC 17:308)

Gr.Naz.Or.28.9
(SC 250:118)

chetical Oration (despite a title that seemed to be aimed at cate-
chumens within the Christian community, whatever their age),
Gregory of Nyssa was in fact presenting apologetics at least as
much as dogmatics, as he made clear at the outset when he cataloged what he saw as his potential audience: the adherent of the
Jewish faith, the one reared in Hellenism, the Anomoean, the

Gr.Nyss.*Or.catech*.pr.2
(Méridier 2)

Manichean, the followers of Marcion, Valentinus, and Basilides,
"and the rest on the list of those astray in heresy." Even there,
however, he drew the line sharply and unequivocally between his
presentation of creation and the fall, which had preceded and in
which he had stated his case also according to the criteria of
natural theology, and his presentation of the incarnation and its
implications, which followed and which relied almost exclusively
on the authority of revelation: "Up to this point, perhaps, one
who has followed the course of our argument will agree with it,
inasmuch as we do not appear to have said anything unbefitting a
proper conception of deity [exō ti tēs theoprepous ennoias]. But

Gr.Nyss.*Or.catech*.9.1
(Méridier 64)

towards what follows and constitutes the strongest part of this
revelation of truth, he will not take a similar view." Although he
was quite willing to go on to refer to the relation between body

Gr.Nyss.*Or.catech*.10.3
(Méridier 68)

and soul as an "understandable example, in order to form some
sort of proper conception of the divine *economy*," he was definitely not "proving" the doctrine of the *economy* of salvation and
the incarnation by this. Rather, what he and the other Cappadocians were arguing was that a properly formulated natural theology about divine transcendence, far from leading necessarily to

ap.Bas.*Eun*.1.27
(*SC* 299:266)
Gr.Nyss.*Or.catech*.25.1
(Méridier 118)

the heterodox doctrine of the Trinity, as Eunomius and his adherents were alleging, was at any rate compatible with Nicene orthodoxy, including its doctrine of the divine *economy* of salvation.

Because, therefore, there could not be a contradiction between
a sound natural theology and the revealed *theology* and *economy*, the perennial Christian question "Cur deus homo?" formu-

Florovsky 3:163–70
Gr.Nyss.*Apoll.*
(Jaeger 3-I:217)

lated by Anselm of Canterbury in his treatise of 1097–98, could
receive a special answer in Cappadocian dogmatics. As was so
often the case, it took the challenges of heresy to evoke a summary statement of that answer: "He appeared on earth and 'asso-

Bar 3:38

ciated with human beings,' so that human beings might no longer
have opinions according to their own notions about the self-
existent one, formulating into a doctrine the hints that had come
to them from vain conjectures; but so that we might rather be

1 Tm 3:16

convinced that truly 'God has been manifested in flesh' . . . and
that we might receive the teaching concerning the transcendent

1 Cor 13:12
Gr.Nyss.*Ref*.2
(Jaeger 2:312–13)
Gr.Naz.*Or*.4.66
(SC 309:174)
Ladner 1955,88–95
Gr.Naz.*Or*.30.6
(SC 250:236)

Aulén 1969; Dunstone
1964

Gr.Nyss.*Cant*.8
(Jaeger 6:252)

Rom 9:3
Gr.Nyss.*Cant*.15
(Jaeger 6:443)

Aulén 1969,51–55

Gr.Nyss.*Or.catech*.24.4
(Méridier 114)

Florovsky 7:143

Gr.Naz.*Or*.1.5
(SC 247:78)

Mt 20:28;16:26

Gr.Naz.*Or*.45.22
(PG 36:653)

nature of the Deity that is given to us, as it were, 'in a mirror' from the older Scriptures . . . as an evidence of the truth fully revealed to us." At the center of this *economy* of salvation was "the banner of the cross." In the course of their treatment of the *economy* of the cross—this "marvelously constructed drama dealing with us"—the Cappadocians could invoke many of the metaphors for the atonement from the great variety in the history of Christian thought. Sometimes they spoke, as Gregory of Nyssa did in his exposition of the Song of Songs, as though the purpose of the incarnation and atonement were to instruct humanity. Again, as Gregory spoke elsewhere in the same commentary, the atonement had it as its purpose to evoke from believers an imitation of Christ's offering of himself, as for example in Paul's willingness to become "an outcast" for the sake of his people just as Christ had been.

The long-standing Patristic imagery of the cross as a giant "fishhook" on which the devil was impaled after being deceived by the bait of the humanity of Christ also found an echo in Cappadocian thought. "In order to secure that the ransom on our behalf might be easily accepted by him who required it," Gregory of Nyssa wrote, "the deity was hidden under the veil of our nature, that so, as with ravenous fish, the hook of the deity might be gulped down along with the bait of flesh." But for Gregory of Nazianzus, by contrast, "The full significance of the Crucifixion is not expressed by the concepts of sacrifice and retribution alone." In his first Easter oration he, too, said that Christ "gave himself a ransom and a reconciliation for us [lytron hyper hēmōn kai antallagma]," both "lytron" and "antallagma" being terms employed by Christ himself, as reported in the Greek of the Gospel of Matthew. But in a later and more mature Easter oration, which was also the final oration of the forty-five, he rejected as an "outrage [hybris]" any suggestion that the ransom of the death of Christ had been offered to the devil. He explained that the situation was quite the opposite: "The Father accepts him, but neither asked for him nor demanded him; but it was on account of the incarnation, and because humanity must be sanctified by the humanity of God, that he might deliver us himself, and overcome the tyrant." It would appear that here Gregory of Nazianzus was invoking a presupposition about the doctrine of God that he shared with Gregory of Nyssa, but that he was drawing from it a divergent conclusion about the atonement; for, again drawing on Florovsky's discussion of Nyssen, "This doctrine [of ransom to the devil] is incompatible with the rest of

Florovsky 7:195

Florovsky 3:99–103

Heb 7:25

Gr.Naz.Or.30.14
(SC 250:256)

Gr.Nyss.Or.catech.15
(Méridier 78–82)

Bas.Spir.8.18
(SC 17:308)

Gr.Naz.Or.6.12
(PG 35:737)
Mt 27:46;Ps 21:2
Gr.Nyss.Apoll.24
(Jaeger 3-I:168)

Bas.Ep.261.3
(Courtonne 3:117)

Gr.Nyss.Eun.3.3.31
(Jaeger 2:118–19)

Eun.ap.Gr.Nyss.Eun.
3.4.5 (Jaeger 2:135)

Eun.ap.Gr.Nyss.Eun.
3.3.38 (Jaeger 1:120–21)

Gregory's system of theology and is also self-contradictory." There were two theories of the atonement, therefore, that seem to have been fundamentally alien to the Cappadocian interpretation of the *economy* of salvation. One was the familiar Western and Anselmic theory of "legal satisfaction [ekdikēsis]." For, quoting the New Testament description of Christ as "always alive to plead on their behalf," Gregory of Nazianzus insisted: "'Pleading' does not imply here, as it does in popular parlance, a desire [on the part of God the Father] for legal satisfaction—there is something humiliating in the very idea." The other explanation, which Gregory of Nyssa, too, rejected out of hand, was the suggestion that Christ as the only-begotten God did not have to undergo the *economy* of the cross at all but could have achieved salvation by the mere fiat of a universal amnesty.

In this exposition of the *economy* of salvation, a fundamental presupposition of the doctrine of God in natural theology, the doctrine of the *apatheia* of the divine nature, appeared to stand in contradiction with a no less fundamental affirmation of revealed theology, the suffering of Christ on the cross. As the Cappadocians insisted in their critique of polytheism, it was utterly inconceivable that there could be any "discord [lysis] in the Godhead." What, then, was to be made of the cry of dereliction on the cross, "My God, my God, why have you forsaken me!"? Only those "with no order in their thinking," Basil said, could speak about "human feelings being transmitted to the actual Godhead" in the incarnation and passion of Christ. Arguing against Eunomius, whom he often accused of having no order in his thinking, Gregory of Nyssa stated: "It is clear that the reason why he sets the Father above the Son and exalts him with supreme honor is this: that the shame of the cross is not seen in the Father. And the reason why he asserts that the nature of the Son varies in the sense of inferiority is this: that the reproach of the cross is referred to him alone, and does not touch the Father." By the reasoning of Eunomius, "The deity of the Son suffers, while that of the Father is preserved in absolute *apatheia*. [Therefore] the nature that is characterized by *apatheia* is essentially different from [the nature] that admits suffering." According to Eunomius and his party, "The Father's nature remained pure in *apatheia* and could not in any way admit of an association that tended toward suffering, while the Son, by reason of the divergence of his nature by way of humiliation, was not incapable of being brought to experience the flesh and death"; this was, to them, "proof of the Son's otherness in nature from the Father."

These same presuppositions and arguments, however, could also be invoked in support of the orthodox interpretation. Gregory of Nyssa summarized these undisputed presuppositions about the *economy* of salvation: "The tenet that has been held in common by all who have received the word of our religion is that all hope of salvation should be placed in Christ, it being impossible for anyone to be found among the righteous unless faith in Christ supplies what is desired." Everyone acknowledged that God had from eternity been "not devoid of reason [alogos]"; therefore, the *Logos* of God had to be eternal. Also in the begetting of the Son, the divine nature was marked by *apatheia,* and it remained so eternally. "The divine nature, whatever it is believed to be, always remains the same, being above all augmentation and also being incapable of diminution"—this assumption, shared by natural and revealed theology, as well as by orthodox and heretical theology, meant to the Cappadocians that any predication of "changing" or "becoming" or "being made" affecting the Son had to apply to his humanity rather than to his divinity. Another assumption likewise shared by all of these parties— "Deity is by its very nature permanently and immutably the same in all that pertains to its essence, nor did it at any time fail to be anything that it now is, nor will it at any future time be anything that it is now is not"—meant that because God "assuredly always was Father," this carried "the implication of the name 'Son' in the name 'Father,'" an implication that had been in force eternally. Indispensable as all of these considerations were for the articulation and defense of the orthodox doctrine of the Trinity, they were no less fundamental to the doctrine of the person of Christ and specifically to the doctrine of the two natures in Christ. This was a doctrine whose full-scale development in the fifth and sixth centuries went well beyond the problematics of Cappadocian Christology, but, as Aloys Grillmeier has said, not without "positive contribution towards the solution of the outstanding questions" from Cappadocian thought.

For even after the debates of the nineteenth and twentieth centuries over the connections between the development of trinitarian or christological dogma and the Hellenization of Christianity, it remains an issue for historical speculation to ask whether the orthodox christological doctrine of the two natures in Christ, as formulated above all by the Council of Chalcedon in 451, would exist in its present form if it had not been for presuppositions about the Godhead that the orthodox Cappadocians, together with their predecessors and successors, shared not only

Gr.Nyss.*Eun.*2.50
(Jaeger 1:240)

Gr.Nyss.*Or.catech.*1.1
(Méridier 8)

Gr.Naz.*Or.*25.17
(SC 284:198)

Acts 2:36
Gr.Nyss.*Eun.*3.4.62
(Jaeger 2:158)

Gr.Nyss.*Ref.*7
(Jaeger 2:315)

Grillmeier 1965,278

Grillmeier 1958,
21–55,528–58

See p.21

Gr.Nyss.*Eun*.2.50
(Jaeger 1:240)

Mal 3:6

Bas.*Ep*.262.2
(Courtonne 2:120)

Gr.Naz.*Or*.39.13
(*PG*36:349)
Ps 76:11
Gr.Nyss.*V.Mos*.2
(Jaeger 7–I:41)

2 Cor 5:19

Gr.Nyss.*Or.catech*.9.1
(Méridier 64)

See pp.224–25

Gr.Naz.*Ep*.202
(*PG* 37:333)

Gr.Nyss.*Eun*.3.4.5
(Jaeger 2:135)

Gr.Nyss.*Apoll*.
(Jaeger 3–I:223)

ap.Bas.*Ep*.261.3
(Courtonne 3:117)

Gr.Nyss.*Eun*.3.3.31
(Jaeger 2:118–19)

with one another within the circle of Nicene orthodoxy—indeed, not only with "all those who have received the word of our religion," including heretical Christians—but also with the natural theology of the Greeks. What they invoked over and over as beyond all controversy was the axiom concerning the divine nature set down in the Old Testament: "I am, and I do not change [Egō eimi, kai ouk ēlloiōmai]"; any alternative to that ontology was both "blasphemy [blasphēmia]" in relation to revealed truth and "absurdity [atopia]" in relation to natural theology. Applied to the incarnation, that axiom produced the declaration: "The Son of God deigns to become and to be called Son of Man, not changing what he was (for it is unchangeable) but assuming what he was not." A biblical passage that appeared to be attributing "change" to "the Most High" had actually been "accommodated to our pattern [pros to hēmeteron schēma]." Because the *apatheia* and unchangeability of the divine nature was a non-negotiable presupposition, the meaning of the second passage had to be conformed to that of the first, and not vice versa; and the interpretation of what was meant by the New Testament text, "God was in Christ reconciling the world to himself," had to be squared with the prior view of what God was—and of what God was also apart from the *economy* of Christ.

Among all the kinds of change, none of which could be predicated of the divine nature, there was one that was most of all "unbefitting a right conception of God," namely, suffering and death, especially in the case of Christ. To "declare that the only-begotten God . . . was mortal and underwent the passion in his proper Godhead" was "the most serious" implication of an inadequate doctrine of two natures, and a "monstrous absurdity [atopia]." It was equally absurd to argue on the basis of the suffering and death of Christ that his divine nature was in its essence different from and inferior to the full and proper deity of God the Father. For both of those absurdities the Cappadocians proposed what they took to be the only acceptable orthodox alternative: "We confess that the Godhead is present in the one who suffers, but not that the nature that was *apathes* became passible." That confession precluded, as both logically and theologically unacceptable, any suggestion of "the transmission of the human feelings [pathē] to the actual Godhead" in Christ. Although the Cappadocians did not label it error when Eunomius reached for the formulation, "The reproach of the cross . . . does not touch the Father," they found his solution to be at least as threatening as the problem. What was necessary instead was a

Gr.Nyss.*Fid.*
(Jaeger 3-I:63)
Grillmeier-Bacht 1951–
54, I:389–418

CChalc.*Def.*
(Alberigo-Jedin 86–87)

Jn 11:1–44

Gr.Nyss.*Eun.*3.3.65
(Jaeger 2:130–31)

Jn 20:17

Gr.Nyss.*Eun.*3.10.17
(Jaeger 2:295–96)

Stephan 1938

Gr.Nyss.*Ref.*143
(Jaeger 2:374)

1 Tm 2:5

Gr.Nyss.*Apoll.*
(Jaeger 3–I:133)

Gr.Nyss.*Apoll.*
(Jaeger 3–I:136)

Gr.Nyss.*Cant.*13
(Jaeger 6:381)

methodology that would sort out the "attributes belonging to his fleshly begottenness" and those pertaining to "his divine nature." In an anticipation of the phraseology of the *Tome* of Pope Leo I three-fourths of a century later, in 449, which became the most important source for the decree of the Council of Chalcedon in 451, Gregory of Nyssa carried out such an enterprise of sorting out attributes in an exegesis of one event in the life of Christ, the death and raising of Lazarus: "It is not the human nature that raises up Lazarus; nor, on the other hand, is it the power that is *apathes* that weeps for him when he is lying in the grave. But the tear proceeds from the man, the life from the true [divine] life." The same was true of a later incident at the end of the same Gospel, the command of the risen Christ to Mary Magdalen to tell Peter and the disciples about the resurrection: "It was not the intangible, immutable, and invisible God, but the moving, visible, and tangible nature that is proper to humanity."

All of this christological specification of natures and of attributes had as its ultimate purpose not simply to avoid heresy and to preserve true doctrine as ends in themselves—supremely important though orthodoxy was, also for its own sake—but to safeguard the *economy* of salvation. The answer to the question, "Cur deus homo?" lay in "the revolt of humanity against God, its bondage to sin, and its alienation from the true life." In response to this predicament, the Lord of the creature called the creature back and became man while still remaining God, "being both God and man in the entirety of two distinct natures." In this way the incarnation of the *Logos* accomplished "the indissoluble link of humanity with God," because in that linking of the two it was not the divine nature of the *Logos* but "the man who was in Christ" who carried out the work of mediation about which Paul spoke. The immutability of the divine nature had to remain intact in the incarnation, and the *apatheia* of the divine *Logos* had to be preserved in the crucifixion, for the sake of the soteriological "purpose that [hina]" by his unchangeability he might deliver changeable human nature from the evil that so easily beset it. That purpose was not served, but was ultimately undermined, by the device of interpreting the nature that was *apathes* as though it were not *apathes*. Not only did the divine nature in Christ remain *apathes* and unchangeable, also after the incarnation; above all, the axiom had to hold: "That which is uncreated and pretemporal and eternal remains incomprehensible [alēpton]." Gregory of Nyssa went on to say that the incarnation did not negate or abolish divine transcendence ontologically, and therefore it did not do away with the necessity for *apophatic* language *theologically*: there could be no authentic *economy* without authentic *theology*, and an authentic *theology* was *apophatic*.

The basic presupposition of the *economy* of salvation at work in the doctrine of the two natures in Christ was succinctly formulated by Gregory of Nazianzus but common to all the Cappadocians: "He remained what he was; what he was not, he assumed." From this presupposition followed another of his succinct axioms: "What has not been assumed in incarnation has not been cured in salvation [to aproslēpton atherapeuton]." The full implications of this axiom, particularly as it affected the human nature, were not worked out by the Cappadocians, in part because they were facing only the beginnings of the controversy over the question. Yet they did touch on many of the salient points, especially in confronting what they, justly or not, took to be the teaching of Apollinarianism, that in the incarnation the divine *Logos* had taken the place of the human mind in Jesus Christ. The threefold content of the doctrine of the creation of humanity in the image of God also summarized for the Cappadocians what the *Logos* had assumed in incarnation, and therefore likewise what the *Logos* had healed in salvation: rationality, free will, and immortality. One consequence of the Apollinarist negation of a human mind in the incarnate *Logos,* as the Cappadocians interpreted it, would have been a denial of free will in him, and consequently a denial that of all things, the human will, which needed it most, had found a cure and restoration through him. For that restoration depended on the human free will of the incarnate *Logos,* who said of himself that he was laying down his life of his own free will. The third component of the image of God, immortality, likewise had to be part of the human nature of Christ, which was "transformed by the commixture [with the *Logos*] into that which it was not by nature." Thus, in a passage of the New Testament to which Macrina alluded, "We shall be changed, for this perishable body must be clothed with the imperishable, and what is mortal with immortality." For this to happen, it was necessary that the *Logos,* who "by his own agency drew the human nature up once more to immortal life," must have "taken to himself humanity in completeness" through the incarnation.

But because the Greek word *logos* was the technical term both for "rationality" and for "the Word of God," as the Cappadocians argued in their play on words with the term, the definition of the image of God as rationality was at one and the same time

Gr.Naz.Or.29.19
(SC 250:216)
Wiles 1968,47–56
Gr.Naz.Ep.101
(PG 37:181)

Dräseke 1892b,473–512;
Lietzmann 1904,33–36,
67–75;Hübner 1974,
129–42;Grillmeier
1965,220–33

See pp.127–35

Gr.Nyss.Apoll.
(Jaeger 3–I:207)
Gr.Nyss.Ref.139
(Jaeger 2:372)

Jn 10:18

Gr.Nyss.Eun.3.4.43
(Jaeger 2:150)
Macr.ap.Gr.Nyss.
Anim.res. (PG 46:136)

1 Cor 15:52–53

Gr.Nyss.Eun.3.3.51
(Jaeger 2:125–26)

Gr.Nyss.Or.catech.1.2
(Méridier 8)

Ps 39:6
Gr.Nyss.*Eun*.2.235
(Jaeger 1:294–95)
Jn 1:1
Gr.Nyss.*Eun*.3.6.40
(Jaeger 2:200)

Gr.Nyss.*Ref*.58
(Jaeger 2:335)

Jn 1:14

Heb 4:15
Srawley 1906,434–41
Gr.Nyss.*Ref*.172–81
(Jaeger 2:384–89)

Gr.Naz.*Ep*.101
(PG 37:181)

Gr.Nyss.*Apoll*.
(Jaeger 3-I:145)

Gr.Nyss.*Or.catech*.9.1
(Méridier 64)
Jo.D.*Trans*.
(PG 96:545–76)
Mt 17:1–9;Mk 9:2–10;
Lk 9:28–36;2 Pt 1:16–18
Gr.Nyss.*Eun*.2.247
(Jaeger 1:298)

1 Tm 2:4

Mt 17:2

Gr.Naz.*Or*.29.19
(SC 250:218)

the most obvious and most problematical of the three components of the image in relation to the doctrine of the incarnation of
the *Logos* or Word of God, and it set the basis for the other two.
The Cappadocians insisted that the human *logos* was "as nothing
in comparison" with the divine *Logos*. Therefore, the evangelist
John took special pains to dissociate his language about the divine *Logos* from "the common understanding of *logos*." Yet in
some respects there was nevertheless an analogy between them;
"the generation of the human *logos* from the human mind without division" corresponded in some respects to the generation of
the divine *Logos*. The central text for the doctrine of the incarnation, "The Word became flesh [ho logos sarx egeneto]," all too
easily provided the basis for a confusion between these two
meanings of *logos*. It was a confusion that Gregory of Nyssa
claimed to find implied in the thought of Eunomius, and against
it he championed the teaching: "The man of God is complete,
united to the deity in body and in soul, so that he 'who has been
tested in every way, only without sinning' left no part of our
nature that he did not take upon himself. The soul is not sin."
When Apollinaris, justly or unjustly, was charged with a similar
confusion, that was what evoked from Gregory of Nazianzus the
axiom quoted earlier about the incarnation, whose full formulation read, in opposition to Apollinarism: "Anyone who trusts in
him as a man without a human mind is really bereft of mind and
quite unworthy of salvation. For that which he has not assumed
he has not cured, but that which is united to his deity is also
saved." By a corollary, therefore, just as "no one bereft of mind"
was capable of grasping the faith in the incarnate one, so the
incarnate one could not be bereft of mind.

This dimension of the *economy* of salvation was visible
throughout the earthly life of Jesus Christ, at each step of the way
in the Gospel narrative. But for the Cappadocians, as for the
Greek Christian tradition generally, the event that had comprehended it in a special way was the transfiguration or *metamorphosis* of the human nature of Christ on Mount Tabor. At the
transfiguration, as Gregory of Nyssa expounded it, "there came a
voice from heaven," from the God of whom the apostle Paul said,
"It is his will that all should find salvation and come to know the
truth." And it was there, on the mount, that he shone forth,
"becoming more luminous than the sun," to act, in the words of
Gregory of Nazianzus, "as our mystagogical guide to the future
[epi tou orous astraptei, kai hēliou phōtoeidesteros ginetai, to
mellon mystagogōn]." That future, which was the content of his

Tyciak 1961,93–97

"mystagogy" and the outcome of the entire *economy* of salvation, was nothing less than the very transfiguration or *metamorphosis* of human nature. The image of God as rationality, the image of God as free will, and the image of God as immortality—each was, for the Cappadocians, a necessary and inescapable corollary of natural theology; and denying any of these was not only a contradiction of the explicit teaching of divine revelation but a contravention of human reason or *logos*. At the same time, however, when they took up the *metamorphosis* of human nature as the gift and blessing of the incarnation of the divine *Logos,* the Cappadocians celebrated the restoration of these qualities through the incarnation and through the *economy* of salvation, as a miracle transcending not merely human achievement but human comprehension.

CHAPTER 18

The Metamorphosis of Human Nature

Symb.Nic.-CP
(Alberigo-Jedin 24)

Daniélou 1953,154–70

See pp.131–34

Janini Cuesta 1946,51–52

Gr.Naz.Or.38.11
(PG 36:321–24)

Macr.ap.Gr.Nyss.
Anim. res. (PG 46:28)

Gr.Nyss.Hom.opif.16
(PG 44:177–80)

When the Niceno-Constantinopolitan Creed articulated the eschatological hope of the church in the sentence, "We await the resurrection of the dead [prosdokōmen anastasin nekrōn]," the relation between this expectation and the doctrine of the immortality of the soul in the theology of the Cappadocians was a documentation of the complexity of the relations between the various Classical and Christian definitions of the image of God. The complexity made itself no less evident when they took it upon themselves, without embarrassment or even without ascription, to appropriate the Classical definition of human nature as a microcosm, which at least sometimes they seem to have felt able to present as though it were nothing more nor less than a doctrine of the orthodox church. And yet, when they did ascribe that definition to some source, either they could praise it as a doctrine maintained "among the wise [para tōn sophōn]," apparently intending this principally as a reference to the "wise" among Classical philosophers, or, they could attack it as a doctrine that was "mean and unworthy of the majesty of human nature" and as a "fancy of pagan writers who magnified human nature, as they supposed, by a comparison of it to the world."

Their doctrine of the *metamorphosis* of humanity in Christ likewise illustrated the complexity of the relation between natural theology and revealed theology in their systems. For in their judgment whatever validity natural theology may have been able to claim for its doctrine of the image of God was fatally flawed by

Gr.Nyss.*Anim.res.*
(PG 46:116)

Winslow 1979

Gr.Naz.*Or.*40.34;32
(PG 36:408;404)

Gr.Nyss.*Cant.*2
(Jaeger 6:53)

McClear 1948,175–212

Gr.Nyss.*Or.dom.*5
(PG 44:1181)

See pp.42–49

Gr.Nyss.*Virg.*10
(Jaeger 8–I:288)

Gr.Nyss.*V.Mos.*2
(Jaeger 7–I:126)

Gr.Nyss.*Or.dom.*2
(PG 44:1145)

Gross 1938,219–50

its inability to encompass at one and the same time the several contradictions of the human condition, what has been called "the grandeur and the misery of man," neither of which could be adequately discussed without the other, the misery as present reality in human sin and the grandeur as future reality in the prospect of *theosis,* a sharing in the very being and nature of God. A person who was originally created in the image of God now had to undergo baptism, in order to "scrape off the evil matter and receive again the image whole." That *metamorphosis* was called for because an honest assessment of the present human state had to describe it as "disfigurement [metapoiēsis]." So disfigured had human nature become and so appalling was its misery that the Cappadocians found it necessary, amid all their celebration of the grandeur of the image of God, to speak soberly about nothing less than "the defacing of that image and the destruction of that divine impress [ho tēs eikonos aphanismos kai hē lymē tou theiou charaktēros] which had been formed in us when we were first created." The transcendence of the divine nature was so elevated that it defied expression in human words; but "the greatness of that loss in falling away from the possession of real goodness" was a tragedy that was also inexpressible, in this case not because it was so glorious but because it was so abject. Human nature, though destined for the heights of participation in the divine nature through *theosis,* had instead proven itself capable of finding innumerable pathways downward. There was, therefore, a demonic image corresponding to the divine image and caricaturing it. "As there are obvious characteristics of resemblance to God through which one may become a child of God," Gregory of Nyssa explained, "so also there are certain signs belonging to the evil character [tou ponērou charaktēros sēmeia], the bearer of which cannot be the child of God, because of being stamped with the image of the contrary nature." The features of this evil character were: "envy and hate, slander, conceit, cupidity, passionate lust, and mad ambition." As a consequence of the fall of man into sin, each of the three principal components of the image of God enumerated earlier—reason, free will, and immortality—now had its demonic counterpart in this "image of the contrary nature."

Conversely, as a consequence of what had been accomplished in the economy of salvation in the life, death, and resurrection of Christ, each of those three components was also raised to an infinitely higher power. For the language of all the Cappadocians made it clear that so grand a definition of the creation of human nature in the image of God as the one they propounded now had to be exalted, in Florovsky's phrase, to "something greater than a 'natural' immortality"—or than a natural rationality or a natural freedom of the will, to itemize all three components of the image. Florovsky went on to correct current misinterpretations: "There is nothing 'naturalistic' or pantheistic about the term. Theosis means no more than an intimate communion of human persons with the Living God. To be with God means to dwell in Him and to share His perfection."

Florovsky 3:240

The relation between the two images came through in Basil's encomium on the powers of the mind: "The mind is a wonderful thing, and therein we possess that which is after the image of the Creator. And the operation of the mind is wonderful, too, in that in its perpetual motion it frequently forms imaginations about things that do not exist as though they did exist, and it is frequently carried straight to the truth." But that consideration of the operation of the mind carried Basil himself straight to this truth: "There are in [the mind] two faculties, according to the view of those of us who believe in God: the evil and demonic, which draws us on to the apostasy of the demons; and the divine and good, which brings us to the likeness of God." This contrast between the human mind as created and the human mind as fallen made its presence known and especially palpable in the status of the natural knowledge of the divine law. Before the fall of humanity into sin, the mind was "adorned with the unwritten imprints of the law [tois agraphois tou nomou kekallōpismenē charagmasi]," as a consequence of the "will in accordance with the law, which had been naturally [physikōs] implanted in us"; but then sin came, twisting that will and distorting that knowledge. Sometimes this emphasis on the effect of sin upon the mind could lead to the identification of "ignorance [agnoia]" as the source of evil in human life. This was in agreement with the teaching of Socrates and Plato, who also sometimes equated knowledge with *arete* and therefore sometimes implied that *arete* could be taught. But Cappadocian thought went beyond the identification of sin with ignorance, and thus also beyond the identification of *arete* with knowledge, in a number of decisive ways. The most fundamental to their system as a whole was the recognition that the inability of the human mind to grasp any ultimate truth about the divine *ousia* was a consequence not only of sin but of the qualitative difference between a transcendent God and a finite creation, even a creation that had not fallen;

Bas.*Ep.*233.1
(Courtonne 3:39)

Gr.Nyss.*V.Mos.*2
(Jaeger 7–I:108)
Gr.Nyss.*Infant.*
(Jaeger 3–II:80)

Gronau 1922,96–109

Pl.*Prt.*361a

Gr.Nyss.*Eun*.2.138–40
(Jaeger 1:265–66)

hence the oxymoron, "It is a sort of knowledge to know that what is being sought transcends knowledge." But a rather surprising corollary of this recognition of the limitations of finite thought was the conclusion that such ignorance, far from putting a quietus on reflective thinking, provided the human mind with a justification for speculating. As Gregory of Nyssa formulated that rationale, "Because our reason in this matter must grope in the dark, clearly no one can complain if its conjecturing [stochasmos] leads our mind to a variety of conclusions."

Gr.Nyss.*Infant.*
(Jaeger 3–II:93)

There was, according to Cappadocian anthropology, a similar interaction at work between "the twofold directions of the movement of free choice [diplē tēs hekastou proaireseōs hē kinēsis] . . . , towards temperance on the one hand, or towards license on the other." As was the case with natural reason and with natural immortality, some sort of natural free will had to be predicated also of fallen humanity, to avoid any evasion of responsibility. "Do not look for the guiding cause beyond yourself," Basil warned the sinner, "but recognize that evil, rightly so called, has no other origin than our voluntary falls." There was "no such thing in the world as evil irrespective of a will, and discoverable in a substance apart from that; 'for everything that God created was good' and nothing belonging to God was 'to be rejected,' since all that God made was 'very good.'" This meant that when the theme was moral responsibility and accountability, "the power of becoming bad" could be said to "reside in the will." Human nature, having originally "come into being through change," was now constantly subject to change. But change was not necessarily bad. "If it acts according to its true nature," Nyssen explained, "this continual change is for the better; but if it is diverted from the straight path, there follows a movement in the opposite direction"—still a change, though not an improvement but a deterioration. But when, on the other hand, the emphasis was on the contrast between the original creation and the fall, humanity could be said to have "exchanged for the liberty of the free will the wicked slavery of sin, by preferring the tyranny of the power of darkness to the companionship of God." Therefore, it was proper to "pray for the choice of the good things [tēn agathēn proairesin] to come to us from God," for there was this fundamental moral and psychological distinction between the two directions of free will: "If we feel an impulse to do evil we need no help, because evil accomplishes itself in our will. But if there is an inclination towards something good, we need God to carry the desire into effect."

Gr.Nyss.*Beat*.2
(*PG* 44:1213)

Bas.*Hex*.2.5
(*SC* 26:160)

Gn 1:31;1 Tm 4:4
Gr.Nyss.*Virg*.12
(Jaeger 8–I:299)

Gr.Nyss.*Eun*.1.92
(Jaeger 1:53)

Gr.Nyss.*Or.catech*.8.18
(Méridier 62)

Gr.Nyss.*Or.dom*.5
(*PG* 44:1181)

Gr.Nyss.*Or.dom*.4
(*PG* 44:1164–65)

Gr.Nyss.*Virg.*12
(Jaeger 8–I:297–98)

Gr.Nyss.*Beat.*3;5
(PG 44:1228;1257)

Gr.Nyss.*V.Mos.*2
(Jaeger 7–I:59)

Gr.Nyss.*Anim.res.*
(PG 46:68)

Gr.Nyss.*Eun.*3.6.77
(Jaeger 2:213)

Gr.Nyss.*Anim.res.*
(PG 46:13)
Janini Cuesta 1946,73–75

2 Cor 4:16
Gr.Nyss.*Virg.*20
(Jaeger 8–I:324–25)

Mossay 1966,271–79

See pp.79–81
Gr.Nyss.*Cant.*12
(Jaeger 6:350)

Gr.Nyss.*Eun.*2.203–4
(Jaeger 1:284)

As free will and immortality were closely tied to each other in the definition of the image of God, so the loss of the first through the fall implied the loss of the second: "What had been meant to rule was enslaved, and what had been created for immortality was destroyed by death." Together with other evils, even the ultimate evil of the darkness and eternal death of hell was a matter of the free choice of the human will. Although Christian eschatology was chiefly a doctrine of revelation, the awareness of this ultimate evil, as summarized in the very term "hell [haidēs]" with its various possible meanings, was widespread not only in Christian but also in Classical thought. There were also various possible meanings for the basic terms "life" and "death," both in revealed theology and in natural theology. Thus, whatever may have been the status of human immortality as a doctrine of natural theology, human mortality was undeniably "natural [physikos]," both as an objective and as a subjective reality; so was human anxiety over death. Here again the word "twofold [diplous]" was applicable, for it was necessary to distinguish within human nature between "the outwardly visible nature, with its natural fate to decay," and that nature which was "perceptible only in the secret of the heart, yet capable of renewal." Despite "the absence of a systematic thanatology," therefore, the Cappadocians made it clear that metaphysically speaking, death, like every other evil, could not be said to possess a positive existence of its own but was only the privation of the positive quality of life. Because all bodies were composite in their nature, Gregory of Nyssa insisted, in opposition to Eunomius: "Where you see composition, you see also dissolution; and dissolution, as the notion implies, is the same thing as destruction [and death]."

The interaction between change and continuity in the Cappadocian doctrine of the *metamorphosis* of human nature was a striking instance of the interweaving of continuity and change throughout their conceptions of reason and revelation, nature and grace, creation and new creation, the first Adam and Christ as the second Adam. It was an explicit description of the change, but an implicit affirmation also of the continuity, to declare: "The first time, [God the *Logos*] took dust from the earth and formed humanity; this time, he took dust from the Virgin and did not merely form humanity, but formed humanity around himself. The first time, he created; this time, he was created. The first time, the *Logos* made the flesh; this time, the *Logos* was made flesh, so that he might change our flesh to spirit, by being made

Gr.Nyss.*Eun*.3.2.54
(Jaeger 2:70)

Pelikan 1990,71–72

partaker with us in flesh and blood. Of this new order in Christ, therefore, which he himself began, he is called the firstborn." This interpretation of the incarnation had an important bearing upon the eventual development of Byzantine aesthetic theory, but its dialectic between the two creations had implications no less far-reaching for the idea of the *metamorphosis* of natural theology.

That dialectic between the two images of God, and the *metamorphosis* of the first creation into the second, was formulated with characteristic trenchancy, and with his special blending of subjective and objective language, by Gregory of Nazianzus: "I had a share in the image, but I did not keep it. [Christ] shares in my flesh that he may both save the image and make the flesh immortal. He communicates a second fellowship [with God] far more marvelous than the first had been. For then he imparted the better nature [to humanity], whereas this time he himself participates in the worse nature [of humanity]. This is more Godlike than the former action, this is more sublime in the eyes of all who understand." This process spoken of by the two Gregorys could be described by the third of the Cappadocians, Basil of Caesarea, as "coming back to natural beauty" and as "restoring the ancient form of the royal image." So complete had been humanity's original "sharing in this good surpassing every power of perception" that "the human being seemed to be another one of the same [that is, of God], since it was fashioned to the most exact likeness according to the image of its prototype [tēi akribestatēi homoiōsei kata tēn eikona tou prōtotypou]"; it was endowed with "all those attributes of God" that could now be the subject only of "speculation and conjecture." Therefore, the *metamorphosis* of human nature through the restoration of this image of God had to be a divine gift, coming from none other than the Creator who had originally conferred the original image. In the parable in the Gospel, the ring with its carved stone, which the father placed on the finger of the prodigal son, represented "the regaining of the image [tēn tēs eikonos epanalēpsin]" by the gift of the heavenly Father. A related sculptural metaphor for the restoration could refer to it as "modeling us anew from the evil mould of sin once more to God's own image."

Yet "restoration" was far too bland a term for a *metamorphosis* that had not simply gone back to the original but had, in the words of Gregory of Nazianzus quoted earlier, "communicated a second fellowship vastly more marvelous than the first had been," the fellowship of *theosis*. The process had moved

Gr.Naz.*Or*.38.13
(*PG* 36:325)

Bas.*Spir*.9.23
(*SC* 17:326–28)

Gr.Nyss.*Beat*.3
(*PG* 44:1225–28)

Gr.Nyss.*Virg*.12
(Jaeger 8–1:300)

Lk 15:22

Gr.Nyss.*Or.dom*.2
(*PG* 44:1144–45)

Gr.Nyss.*Ref*.112
(Jaeger 2:359)

Lovejoy 1955,277–95

Gr.Naz.*Or*.38.13
(*PG* 36:325)

Gr.Nyss.*Cant.*15
(Jaeger 6:458)

"according to a certain sequence and order [dia tinos akolouthias kai taxeōs]," indeed, according to a definite progression. It had progressed from the lesser to the greater, that is to say, from human nature in Adam to human nature in Christ. The reason it was possible nonetheless to be accurate in characterizing this progression as a "restoration" was a corollary of the Cappadocian doctrine of creation: the model of the original image, too, was Christ the creating *Logos*. When, according to the Genesis account, God the Creator said, using the plural pronouns and

Gn 1:26

verbs, "Let us make man in our image, after our likeness," that was taken to be a trinitarian reference to the "living image," to the one who was "the radiance of God's splendor, the stamp of

Heb 1:3; Wis 7:26
Col 1:15
Bas.*Hex.*9.6
(SC 26:518)
Gr.Nyss.*Cant.*15
(Jaeger 6:458)
Gr.Nyss.*Beat.*8
(PG 44:1301)

Phil 3:10

God's very being," the one who was in the most complete, metaphysical, and personal sense "the image of the invisible God," Christ as the image of God in person. Christ himself was, then, the goal and the prize toward which this "certain sequence and order" and this progression had been moving all along and from the very beginning. Therefore "being 'co-*metamorphosed*' with [symmemorphōsthai] Christ" meant taking on "his own beauty [*kallos*], the primal beatitude of our nature, being adorned ac-

Gr.Nyss.*Cant.*15
(Jaeger 6:439)

cording to the image and likeness of the primal and only and authentic beauty," that beauty which had been the preexistent and creating *Logos* before the incarnation and which had become the redeeming and renewing *Logos* since the incarnation. But in the Cappadocian understanding of the *kalon,* the ethical and the aesthetic were closely connected, though not quite identi-

Courtonne 1934,131–36

fied.

For despite the connection between them that has just been described, in the identification of the preexistent *Logos* as the image according to which the primal creation took place and the incarnate *Logos* as the image according to which the second creation was fashioned, there remained a problematic tension between two distinct paradigms, and a tension that permeated the entire subject matter of the discussion. Both paradigms were well stated in the language of Basil of Caesarea. On the one hand, Basil could apply to the *Logos* spoken of in the Gospel of John the words of the Wisdom of Solomon echoed by the Epistle to the Hebrews about personified *Sophia*: "She is the radiance that

Wis 7:26; Heb 1:3

Bas.*Ep.*38.8
(Courtonne 1:92)

streams from everlasting light, the flawless mirror of the active power of God, and the image of his goodness." As has already been suggested earlier, that seemed to require a doctrine of the image of God derived from the study of the person of the incarnate *Logos* in Jesus Christ, by reading off from his life and attri-

See pp.277–79

Bas.*Spir*.9.23
(SC 17:326–28)

butes those qualities that belonged to the divine image and that could be seen in the new humanity, but only after its *metamorphosis* through him. But on the other hand, Basil could also speak of "coming back again to natural beauty, cleansing the royal image, and restoring its ancient form." That reference to "natural beauty [to ek physeōs *kallos*]" would appear to provide justification for filling the concept "image of God" after the *metamorphosis* of humanity through the incarnate *Logos* with those qualities that could be discerned, also by the limited resources of natural theology, as belonging to human nature as such. These latter qualities have been summarized earlier under

See pp.127–35

the three headings: reason, free will, and immortality. Therefore, it seems appropriate to examine the place of natural theology in the definition of the image of God—and in the definition of the *metamorphosis* of human nature as image through *theosis*—by reviewing these three qualities, considered in reverse order and now defined more amply as: immortality wrought through resurrection; *apatheia* as freedom from sin and liberation from passion; and the illumination of the human *logos* by the divine *Logos*.

The tension between the two paradigms was already discernible, at least according to many interpreters of the Pauline epistles, in the New Testament's treatment of the resurrection of Christ. Sometimes the New Testament appeared to be presenting the Easter event as one instance, the supreme instance but still one instance, of the general and universal teaching of resurrection: "If there is no resurrection," the apostle Paul could reason

1 Cor 15:13

in writing to the Corinthians, "then Christ was not raised." This might seem to imply, as its logical converse, that because there was a resurrection in general, the resurrection of Christ was also a possibility. But sometimes, by contrast, the raising of Christ was seen as the source and the cause for the general and universal teaching of resurrection: "We believe that Jesus died and rose again," the same apostle Paul could write, this time to the Thessalonians; "so [houtōs] too will God bring those who died

1 Thes 4:14

as Christians to be with Jesus." And the message of the Epistles to Timothy was: "[God] alone possesses immortality"; and again, "Our Savior Jesus Christ has broken the power of death and

1 Tm 6:16;2 Tm 1:10

brought life and immortality to light through the gospel." The Cappadocians seem to have read the passage from 1 Corinthians

Gr.Nyss.*Hom.opif*.25–26
(PG 44:224)

to support this thesis: "The resurrection is not beyond probability." Thus Gregory of Nyssa could interpret the assertion later in the same chapter of 1 Corinthians, "But the truth is, Christ was

1 Cor 15:20

Gr.Nyss.*Ref.*79
(Jaeger 2:344–45)

Macr.ap.Gr.Nyss.
Anim.res. (PG 46:148)

See pp.324–26

Pl.*Smp.*193d

Malingrey 1961,212–13

Macr.ap.Gr.Nyss.
Anim.res. (PG 46:108-9)

Gr.Nyss.*Anim.res.*
(PG 46:76)

raised to life—the first fruits of the harvest of the dead," to mean: "He first by his own act loosed the pains of death, so that his new birth from the dead is made a way for us also." But when it came to specifying the content of the resurrection, he was able (quoting his sister Macrina) to formulate the definition in the words: "Resurrection is the *apocatastasis* of our nature in its original form," that word *apocatastasis* carrying portentous meaning in his eschatology. Commentators on this definition have noted its derivation from a passage in Plato's *Symposium*: "[The god Eros] is our greatest benefactor, both leading us in this life back to our own nature, and giving us high hopes for the future, for he promises that if we are pious, he will restore us to our original nature [katastēsas hēmas eis tēn archaian physin], and heal us and make us happy and blessed."

That parallel with the *Symposium* was in keeping with Macrina's (and her brother Gregory's) treatment of "the thinkers outside our system of philosophy [hoi exō tēs kath' hēmas philosophias]," or at any rate of some of them. "They have," she said, "with all their diverse ways of looking at things, approached and touched the doctrine of the resurrection [merei tini tou kata tēn anastasin ephēpsanto dogmatos], one in one point, another in another." This review of philosophical opinions permitted her to conclude: "While none of them exactly coincides with us, they have in no case abandoned such an expectation [as the resurrection]. . . . It is not contrary to probability that the soul should again inhabit a body [oukoun to men mē exō tou eikotos einai to palin tēn psychēn en sōmati genesthai]." Such a combination of philosophical arguments, scientific parallels, and artistic analogies as hers constituted, in Gregory's judgment, "an excellent defense of the faith in the resurrection." The purpose was, he concluded, "gradually to lead the opponents of this doctrine to consider it as a thing not absolutely impossible that the atoms should again coalesce and form the same human being as before." It was, he said elsewhere, "the hope of the resurrection" that constituted the only difference, "except for the difference of terminology," between "the state of 'nonbeing' of that which has never been generated in the first place and the 'nonbeing' of that which has died." The explanation was: "In speaking of living creatures [including human beings], while we use different words to denote the dissolution into a state of 'nonbeing' of that which has been, and the condition of nonexistence of that which has never had an entrance into being, and say either that a thing has never come into being at all, or that that which was generated

Gr.Nyss.*Eun*.3.7.48–50
(Jaeger 2:231–32)

Gr.Nyss.*Apoll*.
(Jaeger 3–I:178)

Macr.ap.Gr.Nyss.
Anim.res. (PG 46:108–9)

Gr.Nyss.*Hom.opif*.27
(PG 44:225)

Gr.Nyss.*Anim.res.*
(PG 46:141)

Gr.Nyss.*Eun*.3.10.36
(Jaeger 2:303)

Gr.Nyss.*Apoll*.
(Jaeger 3–I:161)

has died, yet employing either form of speech we equally represent by our terminology 'nonexistence.'"

In one sense, the doctrine of the resurrection also constituted
the difference distinguishing this hope from the general doctrine
of the immortality of the soul. Not only was the soul immortal
(as the best of the philosophers had recognized), but the body,
too, would, by its resurrection, participate in that immortality.
Macrina had another way to state this "divergence": "Our view,
which maintains that the body, both now and in the future, is
composed of the *stoicheia* of the cosmos, was held equally by
these pagans. . . . The divergence lies in this: we assert that the
same body again as before, composed of the same *stoicheia,* is
compacted around the soul." But even this formulation of the
divergence needed to be significantly qualified. For the Cappadocians took it to be demonstrable on purely naturalistic and scientific grounds, to "anyone examining our nature with careful attention," that human existence did "not consist altogether in flux
and change," since a nature without any continuity at all would
be "altogether incomprehensible," and that therefore it was
"more accurate" to assert: "Some one of our constitutent parts is
stationary, while the rest go through a process of alteration." On
the basis of this combination of stability and flux it was possible
to present a rational argument for the resurrection, which was
rendered more plausible by the recognition that no particular
human being was "the same today as yesterday, but different,
through the transmutation" that was taking place all along.

The connection between immortality and resurrection in the
metamorphosis of human nature was a documentation of the tension of paradigms described earlier. On the one hand, Gregory of
Nyssa could assert: "To all those who are in their right minds
[tois eu phronousi], the crowning blessing among the goods that
pertain to us as human beings is held to be the return to life." This
apparently made the *metamorphosis,* at any rate as the object of
hope if not also as a matter of fact or as the content of faith, part
of the deposit of natural theology. Yet his very next words were an
explicit appeal to the authority of revealed theology: "[This return to life] is secured by the *economy* carried out by the Lord
[Jesus Christ] in his human nature." It was primarily that *economy* carried out by the resurrection of Jesus Christ to which he
was referring when he declared: "The resurrection of this one
human being from death [hē ek thanatou tou anthrōpou an-
astasis] is the destruction of death." For "the mystery of God's
economy with regard to death, and of the resurrection from the

dead" was that Christ, instead of "preventing the soul's separation from the body by death in accordance with the inevitable course of nature," as he might have done in the exercise of his sovereign and divine power, chose to die first himself and then to bring soul and body together through his resurrection, thus becoming "the meeting point of both, of death and of life," indeed, "restoring in himself the nature disrupted by death and becoming himself the principle for the reuniting of the separated parts." Through the calamity of "death-dealing sin [hē thanatopoios hamartia]," mortality and death had been mingled with human nature itself and had been propagated by a deadly "succession [diadochē]" throughout human history. And so, although Macrina's argumentation for the doctrine of the resurrection was an attempt to find common ground with the philosophical doctrine of immortality, her own behavior in the face of death was a negation of that common ground. Her brother Gregory reported, with a note of awe: "That she did not even in her last breath find anything strange in the hope of the resurrection, nor even shrink at the departure from this life—all this seemed to me more than human." For, as Gregory of Nazianzus put it, the death of the Christian was not really to be called a "departure" at all but rather "a fulfillment, a loosing of bonds, or a relief from a great burden."

Calamitous and destructive though it certainly was, death also had a constructive purpose in the workings of divine providence. In Nyssen's formulation, "It was this: to refashion human nature once more by means of the resurrection into a sound creature, *apathes,* pure, and with no admixture of evil, after this has been eliminated by the dissolution of body and soul." In the death of the body, passion died with it; but when the body was raised, passion remained dead and life was free of it. As a constituent of the *metamorphosis* of humanity, such an *apatheia* was the counterpart to the freedom of the will as a constituent of the image of God, and was in fact the means through which the will could regain its freedom after sin. When God the Creator made human nature, as Gregory of Nazianzus said in one of his orations, "from the beginning free and self-determining [ap' archēs . . . eleutheron . . . kai autexousion]," that freedom and self-determination could be threatened by the conflict he described in a later oration between "pleasure" and "the gift of reason," namely, of the reason by which it was possible to conquer pleasure and passion. When it remained unconquered and "unre-

Gr.Nyss.*Or.catech.*16.9
(Méridier 90)

Gr.Nyss.*Cant.*12
(Jaeger 6:350–51)

Macr.ap.Gr.Nyss.
Anim.res. (PG 46:108)

Gr.Nyss.*V.Macr.*
(Jaeger 8–I:395)

Gr.Naz.*Or.*24.17
(SC 284:76)

Mossay 1966

Gr.Nyss.*Or.catech.*35.7
(Méridier 164)

Schoemann 1943,42–46
Dirking 1954,206

Gr.Naz.*Or.*14.25
(PG 35:892)

Gr.Naz.*Or.*45.18
(PG 36:648)

Gr.Nyss.*Eun*.3.1.31
(Jaeger 2:14)

Gr.Nyss.*Or.dom*.4
(*PG* 44:1161)

Macr.ap.Gr.Nyss.
Anim. res. (*PG* 46:148)

Rom 6:11

Gal 2:20

Gr.Nyss.*Cant*.15
(Jaeger 6:440)
OED 7–II:533–34
Gr.Naz.*Or*.20.9;23.10
(*SC* 270:74;300)
Gr.Nyss.*Apoll*.
(Jaeger 3–I:136;224)
Lit.Bas.
(Brightman 328)

Dirking 1954,202–12

strained," passion spawned "carnal and earthly thoughts," which could alienate human nature from its Creator. The balance that belonged to the original creation was upset "when the concupiscent element gained the upper hand" over rational *arete*. An essential component in the *metamorphosis* of human nature and in the "restoration" of the divine image, therefore, had to be the achievement of this "freedom from passion," or, as Macrina called it, "restoration to the state of an *apathes* blessedness." Paul's language about being "dead to sin and alive to God, in union with Christ Jesus" and his affirmation, "The life I now live is not my life, but the life which Christ lives in me," described a life that had, already in this present world, transcended "passions [pathēmata]." In the Greek of the Cappadocians as well as in English usage, "passion [pathos, pathēma]" could often connote sexuality—although not necessarily so in either language, as was evident from its use by the Cappadocians (and in English) for the sufferings of Christ on the cross; it was used for Christ's sufferings also in the *Liturgy of Saint Basil*. But its sexual connotations meant that the concept of *apatheia* as freedom from passion did raise the question of the place (if any) of sexuality in the Cappadocian doctrines of the image of God and the *metamorphosis* of human nature, including the question of whether its place was the same for the image as it was for the *metamorphosis*.

Gal 3:28
Gr.Nyss.*Hom.opif*.16
(*PG* 44:181)

This latter question was complicated by the testimonies of Scripture. "As the apostle says," Gregory of Nyssa could aver on the basis of the New Testament, "in Christ Jesus there is no such thing as male and female." And in the confrontation between Christ and the Sadducees—one of the relatively few references in the Gospels to the general resurrection from the dead at the end of the present *aeon* of history—Christ said: "The men and women of this world marry; but those who have been judged worthy of a place in the other world, and of the resurrection from the dead, do not marry, for they are no longer subject to death. They are like angels; they are children of God, because they share in the resurrection." On the strength of that saying, it was clear to Gregory of Nyssa that after the *metamorphosis* of human nature, the resurrection life, like the angelic life, would be a life free of the constraints of sexuality and, moreover, that "the blessing of this promise" could become a reality now for someone who was living the "life equal to that of the angels [isangelos hē zōē]," the life of virginity, in the present *aeon*. By transcending these constraints, therefore, the asceticism of virgins such as Macrina had

Lk 20:34–36

Gr.Nyss.*Virg*.14
(Jaeger 8–I:309)

Gr.Nyss.V.Macr.
(Jaeger 8–I:382)

Gr.Nyss.Or.catech.13.3
(Méridier 74–76)

Gr.Naz.Or.8.8
(PG 35:797)

Gr.Nyss.V.Macr.
(Jaeger 8–I:375)

Armstrong 1948,121

Gr.Nyss.Virg.12
(Jaeger 8–I:297–98)

Gn 1:27

Gr.Naz.Or.38.13
(PG 36:325)

Gaïth 1953,54–58

Hübner 1974,67–74

Gr.Nyss.Or.catech.6.10
(Méridier 42)
Gr.Nyss.Hom.opif.5
(PG 44:137)

Gr.Nyss.Virg.12
(Jaeger 8–I:297–98)

already approximated "the angelic and immaterial nature" in the here and now, except insofar as they still appeared in bodily form. That capacity to rise above physical constraints, including sexuality, had been true in a preeminent and unique sense of Christ, whose virgin birth and resurrection "transcended our nature both in the manner of his birth and in not being subject to the change of corruption" at his death. On the other hand, so long as "mind [nous]" and *logos* had the upper hand, *arete* was possible in marriage as well as in virginity. "Neither of them," Nazianzen added, referring to virginity and marriage, "absolutely binds us to, or separates us from, God or the world." The doctrine of the resurrection from the dead did imply, moreover, that here in this life only one marriage could be permitted.

But what did this expectation of the "angelic life" without sexuality after the *metamorphosis* of humanity imply for the connection between sexuality and the original image of God? The first chapter of the Book of Genesis, the divine "cosmogony," was the authoritative source for the doctrine of creation in the image of God. But the full text of its testimony to that doctrine read: "God created man in his own image; in the image of God he created him; male and female he created them." On the face of it, that would appear to be saying that the distinction between male and female had belonged to the original creation of human nature as intended in the purpose of God, and that human nature as both male and female had been created in the divine image. Yet, even with the explanation, as formulated by Gregory of Nazianzus, that the *metamorphosis* of human nature in the resurrection implied a condition "far more marvelous [paradoxoteran] than the first had been," it seemed troubling to Gregory of Nyssa that sexuality should have belonged to the image of God originally if it was destined not to belong to the resurrection eventually.

That appeared to him to call for a closer reading of the Genesis cosmogony, and thus for more audacious speculation about it. The doctrine of the image of God necessarily implied that "humanity by nature was free from passion, for it was a copy of the one who was without passion." *Apatheia* was, therefore, part of the content of the original image, as was freedom from death. This made it clear that "this creature did not, in the course of its original production [para tēn prōtēn genesin], have united to the very essence of its nature [ou kata physin oude synousiōmenon] either the liability to passion or the liability to death," but did possess free will. And this, it seemed to Gregory, made it clear "that the creation of our nature was in a sense twofold [diplē]: one made like God, the other divided according to this distinction" between male and female. For "the divine, the rational and intelligent element did not admit the distinction between male and female," while "the division into male and female" pertained only to "the irrational, our bodily form and structure." There was, therefore, a kind of caesura in the cosmogony of the first chapter of Genesis. After the words about creation in the image of God, as Gregory read the text, "There was an end [telos echei] of the creation of that which was made 'in the image.'" Following the caesura, there came in the narrative of the Book of Genesis "a resumption of the account of creation, saying, 'Male and female [God] created them.'" In proof of this quite idiosyncratic reading of Genesis, Gregory appealed to a universally accepted principle, which was "presumably known to everyone [panti gar oimai gnōrimon einai]," namely, that the division into male and female was "a departure from the prototype [exō tou prōtotypou]." If this was indeed "presumably known to everyone," it, too, would appear to be an axiom of natural theology, knowable also apart from revelation, for example to the Greek philosophers who had rejected the myths of the pagan gods, with their amorous adventures; for the superiority of the rational soul to all passion was also "the paideusis of those on the outside," that is, of the pagan philosophers. And both of these helped to define the terms for the formulation of revealed theology on the basis of Scripture and tradition.

Gr.Nyss.Hom.opif.16
(PG 44:181)

See pp.77–78

Gr.Nyss.V.Mos.2
(Jaeger 7–I:62)

To achieve this boon of *apatheia,* believers were to "defeat passion by reasonings [tois logismois to pathos apōsasthai]" and to be "steadied by reason." For because the third component of the image of God in human nature, alongside immortality and free will, was human reason, the third component of the *metamorphosis* of human nature, alongside resurrection and freedom from passion, had to be the transformation of reason and knowledge through the knowledge of the divine reason in person, Christ the *Logos.* "The distinguishing characteristic of human nature [to idion tēs anthrōpinēs physeōs]," which set it apart from the rest of the visible world, though not from the angelic world, was, according to Gregory of Nyssa, the human reason as *logos.* He acknowledged, moreover, that in this doctrine of the rationality of human nature, which he was equating with the biblical doctrine of the image of God, he was also echoing the teachings of pagan philosophy, which affirmed, according to

Gr.Nyss.Beat.2
(PG 44:1216)

See pp.259–62

Gr.Nyss.Cant.2
(Jaeger 6:66)

Macr.ap.Gr.Nyss.
Anim. res. (PG 46:52)
Macrina, "the fact of the reasoning animal, man, being capable of understanding and knowing." As Vladimir Lossky has observed,
· "Whenever Gregory tries to locate the 'image of God' only in the higher faculties of humanity, identifying it with the *nous*, he seems to want to make the human spirit the seat of grace by
Lossky 1974,138–39
reason of a certain proximity it has with the divine nature." Gregory's tendency, already in his doctrine of creation, to assign the normative position in the image of God to "the higher faculties of humanity" as identified with the "nous" exhibited profound affinities with the natural theology of the Greeks. Such affinities became, if anything, more prominent in his language, and in that of all the Cappadocians, when they came to speak
See pp.219–20
about the place of mind and reason in the Christian life. This, too, exhibited the power of their natural theology as the presupposition for their ecclesiastical theology, together with the correlative, and often more explicit, dependence of their apologetics on the doctrines of Scripture and the dogmas of the Christian tradition.

For example, Basil began the epistle quoted earlier about the place of the mind in "the constitution of humanity,"—that is, the creation—by describing it as "according to the image of the Creator," and he praised its wondrous operation and powers. Then
Holl 1904
he proceeded to warn his colleague Amphilochius of Iconium about the dangers of unaided human reason as it functioned now, when the fall could "nullify its proper judgment and cause it to be concerned with monstrous fancies" and to fall into idolatry. After these initial discussions, first of the mind as created and secondly of the mind as fallen, Basil turned to address his third point, the power of sanctified reason; this was in keeping with his
Bas.Spir.9.23
(SC 17:326–28)
language about "coming back again to natural beauty, cleansing the royal image, and restoring its ancient form." "The mind that is impregnated with the divinity of the Spirit," he asserted, "is at once capable of viewing great objects. . . . It beholds the divine beauty—though only to the extent that grace imparts and that its
Bas.Ep.233.1
(Courtonne 3:40)
nature is capable of receiving." That concluding specification, "only to the extent that its nature is capable of receiving," stood as a reminder of the limitations that the *apophatic* theology of the Cappadocians tended to place on any claims about "knowing God," not solely on the claims of pagans nor on the claims of heretics such as Eunomius, but also on the claims that could be
See pp.200–202
put forward in the name of the orthodox faith of the church. The important point to be noted here, however, is that despite the force with which they urged the obligation to employ the lan-

guage of negation, it sometimes seemed to become less prominent when they came to their descriptions of the expanded capacity that the human *logos* and spirit would eventually acquire, and could in some measure acquire now, through union by grace with the divine *Logos* and the divine Spirit.

As has been noted, the technical term of Cappadocian theology—indeed, of Greek Patristic theology in general—by which that promise was most comprehensively and most sublimely articulated was *theosis,* for which "deification" and "divinization" are the usual, though not completely satisfactory, English equivalents. It was a direct corollary of the doctrine of the incarnation, passion, and resurrection of Christ. "Even the body in which he underwent his passion," Gregory of Nyssa declared against Eunomius, "by being mingled with the divine nature, was made by that commixture [anakrasis] to be that which the assuming nature was." From this it was only a short distance to the claim, as a matter of "belief," that in Christ—and not only in Christ, but in all humanity as a result of Christ—"if anything belonging to our lowly nature was assumed in his *economy* of love for men, even this was transformed [metapoiēsthai] by becoming divine and incorruptible." As a consequence, all three of the constituent elements of the *metamorphosis* of humanity—immortality wrought through resurrection, *apatheia* as freedom from sin and liberation from passion, and the illumination of the human *logos* by the divine *Logos*—were a manifestation of the deification that was the outcome and fulfillment of the image of God, "of the likeness with God [tēs pros ton theon homoiōseōs]," through which the bearer of the new image of God would "pass automatically and without effort from this earthly life to the life of heaven."

Aubineau 1956,25–52

Lampe 643–44;649–50

Gr.Nyss.*Eun.*3.3.34
(Jaeger 2:119)

Gr.Nyss.*Or.dom.*2
(*PG* 44:114)

CHAPTER 19

The Worship Offered by Rational Creatures

Otis 1961,146–65

Gr.Naz.Carm.1.11.327–
429 (PG 37:1052–59)

In 362, Gregory of Nazianzus, who had always preferred the "mountain" of asceticism to the "throne" of the episcopacy, attempted to return to monastic seclusion. This brought upon him the accusation of having disgraced the priesthood of the church by desertion. In the peroration of his defense against that charge

Fleury 1930,131–33

in the second of his orations, after having summarized the requirement of ritual purity that had been imposed on Levitical worship in the Old Testament, he proceeded to characterize the distinctive requirements of Christian worship in a periodic sentence that employed a catena of passages from Scripture to clothe

Gr.Naz.Or.2.95
(SC 247:212–14)

Christian liturgical spirituality in the style of Classical rhetoric:

"I knew that no one is worthy of the greatness of God and of the sacrifice and of the high priesthood who has not first presented himself to God as a living and holy sacrifice, who has not

Rom 12:1

adored God with the well-pleasing worship which we, as rational creatures, should offer, and who has not rendered to God the

Ps 49:14

sacrifice of praise and of a contrite spirit, which is the only sacrifice required of us by the giver of all. How then could I dare to offer to God the external sacrifice, the antitype of the great mysteries, or to clothe myself with the garb and name of priest, before my hands had been made perfect by holy works, before my eyes had been accustomed to gaze safely upon created things and without injury to the creature, before my ear had been sufficiently

Is 50:4

opened to the instruction of the Lord . . . , before my tongue had been filled with exultation and become an instrument of divine

Ps 56:9

melody, awaking with glory?" But it was a characteristic of the

metamorphosis of natural theology in the thought of Gregory
and the other Cappadocians—and a characteristic of their view
of its compatibility with the orthodoxy of the church—that he
did not follow the example of the natural theologians of Classical
philosophy in seeing this "worship which we, as rational crea-

Rom 12:1

tures, should offer [logikē latreia]," of which the apostle Paul
spoke to the Romans, as standing in opposition to "the external
sacrifice, the antitype of the great mysteries," which the Christian
"high priest [archiereus]" offered up in the liturgy of the Eucharist; rather, he saw the rational worship as expressed most fully of
all, at any rate here below, in the liturgical mysteries. It was the
very consideration of the sacrifice of the temple in the cultic

Gr.Nyss.*Or.dom.*3
(*PG* 44:1149)

worship of Israel that evoked an emphasis on the rational and
"living sacrifice" to which Paul referred in these words.

As part of the Anaphora of the *Liturgy of Saint Basil,* therefore, the priest, in the name of the congregation, also drew on
both Classical and Christian vocabularies to intone: "It is righteous and proper to praise thee, to hymn thee, to bless thee, to
worship thee, to give thanks to thee, and to glorify thee, the God
who alone has real being [ton monon ontōs onta theon], and to
present to thee in a contrite heart and a spirit of humility this

Rom 12:1
Lit.Bas.
(Brightman 322)

worship which we as rational creatures should offer [tēn logikēn
tautēn latreian hēmōn]." In the course of this second oration
(which, judging from its length and complexity, was apparently
not intended for oral delivery as an oration or sermon, but for
reading and study as a treatise), Gregory managed to expound
the central issues of the Christian understanding of the priesthood, both doctrinal and practical, in formulations that shaped
much of subsequent theological literature on the subject, including the best-known work of John Chrysostom, the treatise *On*

Volk 1893,56–63

the Priesthood, which, according to the ecclesiastical historian
Socrates Scholasticus, was written while Chrysostom was a dea-

Socr.*H.e.*6.3
(Hussey 2:661–62)

con, thus between 381 and 386. But Nazianzen also touched on
three fundamental questions: in his own words, "the external
sacrifice, the antitype of the great mysteries [tēn exōthen thysian,
tēn tōn megalōn mystēriōn antitypon]," that is, the celebration of
the sacramental mysteries in Christian worship, and above all the

Maier 1915

celebration of the Eucharist; "the spirit of speaking mysteries and
dogmas [to pneuma laloumenōn mystēriōn te kai dogmatōn],"
that is, the relation between mysteries as "the rule of prayer [lex
orandi]" and dogmas as "the rule of faith [lex credendi]" in the
definition of Christian orthodoxy; and the requirement that the
priest's "hands be made perfect by holy works [hosiois ergois

teleiōsai tas cheiras]," that is, the principle that moral virtue was the appropriate vehicle for divine service. These three questions within Christian liturgical theology are of the most direct significance for an understanding of the role of natural theology in the Cappadocian system of church dogmatics, because in their treatment of each question the Cappadocians did presuppose and draw upon insights and principles that they formulated in their reasonings about "moral and natural philosophy," which was joined to "the more sublime life [of Christian worship]."

Gr.Nyss.V.Mos.2
(Jaeger 7–1:43)

Gr.Naz.Or.2.95
(SC 247:212–14)

By describing the eucharistic mystery as "the external sacrifice, the antitype of the great mysteries," Gregory of Nazianzus affirmed, as did Nyssen, the indissoluble tie between the sacraments of the church and the historical *economy* of salvation in the events of the incarnation, life, death, and resurrection of Jesus Christ. For it was in the first instance these events of the divine *economy* that he was identifying as "the great mysteries [megala mystēria]," indeed the greatest of all the mysteries, from which the sacramental mysteries such as the Eucharist, baptism, and other "external" liturgical actions, being "antitypes," derived their efficacy and to which they were in that sense subordinated. He invoked the same term "antitype" elsewhere in speaking about the miraculous eucharistic cure once experienced by his sister, Gorgonia. After human medicines had failed her in a grave illness, she "applied her medicine to her whole body, that is, such a portion of the antitypes of the precious body and blood [of Christ] as she treasured in her hand [ti tōn antitypōn tou timiou sōmatos ē tou haimatos hē cheir ethēsaurisen]," and she was healed miraculously by divine power. It remains a matter of controversy among scholars whether this statement provides early documentary evidence for the practice of reserving the elements of the Eucharist. But there can be no doubt that the liturgical rites of "celebrating the mysteries," even in truncated form, did carry a special and miraculous power for Gregory, as was evident from the oration that he delivered on the death of his father in 374. The very formulas of the liturgy were identified there as "mystical," and the eye of the worshiper was "mystically sealed," as Gregory said in speaking about the liturgical piety of his mother, Nonna. Because the Eucharist was properly identified as a "mystery [mystērion]," it called forth the language appropriate to religious mysteries (including the language of non-Christian religious mysteries). What Christ transmitted to his disciples when he said in instituting the Eucharist, "Take, eat," and "Drink from it,"

Gr.Nyss.Or.catech.9.1
(Méridier 64)

Daniélou 1951,76–93

Gr.Naz.Or.8.18
(PG 35:809)

Mt 9:22

Thurston 1909–10,
275–79

Gr.Naz.Or.18.29
(PG 35:1020)

Gr.Naz.Or.18.9–10
(PG 35:996–97)
Hauser-Meury
1960,134–35

See pp.22–23

Mt 26:26–27

Gr.Nyss.*Cant.*10
(Jaeger 6:308)

Lenz 1925,117–18

Gr.Nyss.*Or.catech.*37.12
(Méridier 182)

See pp.104–5

OED 11–II:256

Mt 17:2

Gr.Naz.*Or.*29.19
(*SC* 250:218)

Gr.Nyss.*Or.catech.*18.2
(Méridier 92)

Gr.Naz.*Or.*39.3
(*PG* 36:336–37)

DTC 15:1396–1406

Gr.Naz.*Or.*8.20
(*PG* 35:812–13)

Fleury 1930,25–27

was, according to Gregory of Nyssa, properly called a "mystagogy [mystagōgia]."

More problematical is the precise meaning of Nyssen's term "transelementation [metastoicheiōsis]" in speaking of what happened to the elements in the Eucharist. He explicitly declared: "[In the Eucharist, Christ], by virtue of the benediction [eulogiai], transelements [metastoicheiōsas] the natural quality of these visible things to that immortal thing," his own body. On the basis of the extensive use of the scientific concept of *stoicheia* as a technical term in the theological vocabulary of the Cappadocians, it does seem justifiable, in translating this Greek verb, to resort to the somewhat rare but well attested English verb "to transelement." *Metamorphosis* was a change of "morphē" or "form" in the *metamorphosis* or transfiguration of Christ, when Christ acted "as our mystagogical guide to the future" but did not change what he himself was essentially and eternally; and then the same word identified the *metamorphosis* of human nature through him. But here the *stoicheia* of bread and wine themselves were changed into the body of Christ. Thus, in spite of their hostility to the Greek religious mysteries as an "idol mania [eidōlomania]," as "nonsense and a dark invention of demons and a figment of an unhappy mind, aided by time and hidden by fable," the Cappadocians do seem to have been willing to invoke the vocabulary of Greek science and philosophy when they came to specify the content of the Christian mysteries. At the very least—whatever may have been its analogies to the much later Latin eucharistic term "transsubstantiatio," for which the (apparently still later) Greek eucharistic equivalent was "metousiōsis"—this term of Nyssen's did legitimate the domestication within Christian eucharistic theology of the Classical concept of *stoicheia*.

The history of Gorgonia, the sister of Gregory of Nazianzus, with its tribute to the power of the eucharistic mystery, referred also to the sacramental mystery of baptism, but in the context of the end of Gorgonia's earthly life. For, Gregory explained, "Only recently had she obtained [in baptism] the blessing of cleansing and perfection [katharsis kai teleiōsis]. . . . In her case almost alone, I will venture to say, the mystery was a seal rather than a gift of grace"; and before she died, her husband joined her in being baptized. The circumstances and timing of Gregory's own baptism are not entirely clear. But in his fortieth oration, which seems to have been the most extensive discussion of baptism in his writings (probably in the Cappadocian corpus as a whole), he did urge: "Those who are still children, and conscious neither of the loss nor of the grace, [should be baptized early], especially if any danger presses. For it is better that they should be unconsciously sanctified than that they should depart this life unsealed and uninitiated." In any case it was to come by the end of the third year, more or less. His definition of the effects of baptism was in keeping with his standard definition of the duality of human nature, a presupposition that was for him, and for Cappadocian thought as a whole, not only a doctrine of divine revelation but a demonstrable fact available also to the natural reason. Therefore, his doctrine of baptism, which was a doctrine of revelation, saw the sacrament as dealing with both "soul and body, one part visible and the other invisible." The Cappadocian metaphysics of light, another presupposition in which the insights of philosophy and natural science and the teachings of revelation both had a part, was echoed in their use of the patristic metaphor for baptism as "the grace of illumination [tou phōtismatos charis]." But even while formulating their doctrine of baptism, and of the sacramental mysteries in general, they continued to be acutely conscious of the primacy of the transcendent reality of baptism over any "doctrine" about baptism.

For the Cappadocians, baptism was in many ways the most cogent example of what Nazianzen called "the spirit of speaking mysteries and dogmas"—which meant both mysteries and dogmas, and ultimately neither dogmas without mysteries nor mysteries without dogmas. This can, then, be taken as an enunciation of the principle, "The rule of prayer determines the rule of faith [lex orandi lex credendi]," which in that Latin formulation was a Western principle, but which in its content was universal throughout patristic thought and was probably applied even more fully and more frequently in the Christian East than in the Christian West. "As we were baptized," Basil summarized the orthodox axiom, "so we profess our faith; and as we profess our faith, so also we offer our praise [hōs baptizometha, houtō kai pisteuomen; hōs pisteuomen, houtō kai doxologoumen]. As then baptism has been given us by the Savior in the name of the Father and of the Son and of the Holy Spirit, so we make our confession of the creed in accordance with our baptism, and our doxology in turn in accordance with our creed." The most nearly appropriate language for rational creatures to use in acknowledging divine transcendence was not the language of doctrine at all, not even that of the orthodox Nicene doctrine, but the language of doxology and worship, and of silent worship at that, which was how

Gr.Naz.Or.40.28
(PG 36:400)

Gr.Naz.Or.38.11
(PG 36:321–24)

Gr.Naz.Or.40.8
(PG 36:368)
See pp.103–4,236–37

Lampe 1509–10
Gr.Nyss.Cant.2
(Jaeger 6:52–53)

Gr.Nyss.Or.catech.35.1
(Méridier 160)

LTK 6:1001–2

Florovsky 13:86–94
Luislampe 1981,35–49

Mt 28:19

Bas.Ep.159.2
(Courtonne 2:86)

Scazzoso 1975,171–81

2 Cor 12:4
Gr.Nyss.*Eun*.1.314
(Jaeger 1:120)

Gr.Nyss.*Eun*.3.1.16
(Jaeger 2:9)
Gr.Naz.*Or*.28.20
(SC 250:140)
Gr.Naz.*Or*.32.14
(SC 318:114)

Rom 11:33
Gr.Nyss.*Eun*.3.1.104–6
(Jaeger 2:39)
Gr.Naz.*Or*.14.30
(PG 35:900)

Gr.Nyss.*Or.dom*.1
(PG 44:1120)
Humbertclaude 1932,
293–309

Gr.Nyss.*Or.catech*.34.4
(Méridier 158)

Sophocles 946
Gr.Nyss.*Maced*.
(Jaeger 3–I:110–13)

Gr.Nyss.*Eun*.2.265
(Jaeger 1:303–4)

Gr.Naz.*Or*.29.8
(SC 250:192)

the orthodox Nicene doctrine of the Trinity was intended to be read.

That implication of negative theology was based on the experience of Paul when he was taken up to the third heaven "and heard words so secret as to be unrepeatable by human lips." It could be formulated in the paradoxical theory of language cited earlier: "Unspoken meditation becomes the word of instruction, because it teaches to the purified heart, by means of the silent illumination of the thoughts, those truths which transcend speech." The experience of Paul's "progress, ascent, or assumption" required that the mystery should "have the tribute of our silence." "How great a gift from God silence is!" Gregory of Nazianzus could exclaim; and Gregory of Nyssa took the *apophatic* doxology and the alpha privatives with which Paul concluded his speculations about the mystery of divine predestination—"How deep are the wealth and the wisdom and the knowledge of God! How inscrutable [anexereunēta] his judgments, how unsearchable [anexichniastoi] his ways!"—to be a way of using words to put the divine nature beyond all words, as the mystery that was to be "honored in silence." The mystery remained adorable in worship, even though it was inaccessible to language or thought. A rigorous application of the principle "lex orandi lex credendi" to "the science of prayer" itself, as Gregory of Nyssa called it and as Basil elaborated it, might have seemed to raise questions about the presupposition of divine *apatheia*; for a doctrine of God defined by the "lex orandi" of prayer could be taken to imply that the Christian God and Father of the Lord Jesus Christ was the kind of God who could be affected by prayer. But Gregory himself seems to have anticipated such an objection elsewhere, when he explained: "Those who pray God that the sun may shine on them in no way blunt the promptitude of that which is actually going to take place, yet no one will say that the zeal of those who pray this way is useless on the ground that they are praying God for what must happen."

"Worship [proskynēsis]" was a concept that was not without ambiguity, being addressed not only to God but also to earthly rulers. What was not ambiguous about it when it was addressed to God was its consistently *apophatic* character. For as divine worship, it was addressed to one whom Nyssen called the "God whose praise the whole world and all the wonders that are therein are incompetent to celebrate." The inner mysteries of the Holy Trinity had to be honored by "the tribute of our reverent silence." Hence, the divine nature was and had to remain inscru-

Gr.Nyss.*Cant.*1
(Jaeger 6:27)

Bas.*Ep.*234.2
(Courtonne 3:43);
Gr.Nyss.*Eun.*3.1.109
(Jaeger 2:40)

1 Tm 3:16

Eun.ap.Gr.Nyss.*Eun.*
3.9.54 (Jaeger 2:284)

Pelikan 1971–89,
5:140–41

Jas 2:19

1 Cor 13:13

Aug.*Enchir.*2.8
(CCSL 46:52)

Newman 1901,445–68

Gr.Nyss.*Trin.*
(Jaeger 3–I:6)

Bas.*Spir.*7.16
(SC 17:300)

table, but in worship it became possible to speak in silence about the ineffable, and in adoration to love the inaccessible. In short, "Knowledge of the divine essence involves perception of its incomprehensibility, and the object of our worship is not that of which we comprehend the essence, but that of which we comprehend only that the essence exists." It was therefore a fundamental misunderstanding of the nature of Christianity when Eunomius's credo confessed: "We, in agreement with holy and blessed men, affirm that 'the mystery of our religion' does not consist in venerable names, nor in the distinctive character of customs and sacramental tokens, but in exactness of doctrines." This represented the elevation of theology over worship. For it was undeniable that there could be a "theologia irregenitorum" (as later centuries would call it), and even an accurate one, that is, a system of theology put together from Scripture and tradition by thinkers who were curious about Christian doctrine as an intellectual construct without having any personal share at all in the divine mysteries. Thus, as Augustine suggested, it could even be presumed that the demons—of whom the New Testament said, "You have faith and believe that there is one God. Excellent! Even demons have faith like that, and it makes them tremble"—were capable of formulating an orthodox doctrine of God. But of the three virtues identified by Paul as "abiding," namely, "faith, hope, and love," the demons were not capable either of "love" or of "hope," and were consequently also incapable of the worship which they, as rational creatures, ought to offer, of which not only faith as intellectual assent, but hope and love, were necessary components.

When John Henry Newman spoke of "the orthodoxy of the faithful during the supremacy of Arianism," he was, on the basis of such passages as these from the Greek church fathers, positing the existence of an orthodox consensus about the oneness of God the Father and God the Son, implicit all along in church liturgy and in popular devotion, which then eventually became explicit in creed and dogma. Actually, both sides in the trinitarian controversy felt able to cite their "custom [synētheia]" as authority, and in such a case it was necessary to appeal to a higher court: "Let the inspired Scripture, then, be our umpire, so that the vote of truth will surely be given to those whose dogmas are found to agree with the divine words." Underlying the "tradition of the fathers," therefore, was "the express intent of Scripture [to boulēma tēs graphēs]." Nevertheless, the congruence between "lex orandi" and "lex credendi" was expressed in Nazianzen's

coordination of "the orthodox party" with "the devout senti-
ment of the laity [tōn laōn to philotheon]," as twin bulwarks of
Nicene doctrine and as sources of pressure on those who hesi-
tated to take a stand. Elsewhere he contrasted this congruence
between "lex orandi" and "lex credendi" with the relation between truth and fable according to "the mysteries" of Greek
paganism: "For what they worship as true, they veil as mythical.
But if these things are true, they ought not to be called 'myths' but
to be proved not to be shameful; and if they are false, they ought
not to be the objects of worship [thaumazesthai]." He also
charged that Judaism had similarly restricted itself to the externals of cultic observance, but without "attaining to the spiritual
law."

Perhaps the most vigorous affirmation of this congruence and
continuity between "lex orandi" and "lex credendi" anywhere in
the writings of the Cappadocians appeared in an autobiographical letter of Basil, amounting to an "apologia pro vita sua" and
written perhaps four years before his death, thus in about 375:
"The teaching about God that I had received as a boy from my
blessed mother and my grandmother Macrina ['the Elder'], I have
ever held with increasing conviction [auxētheisan]. On my coming to the mature years of reason, I did not shift my opinions from
one to another, but carried out the principles handed on to me as
tradition [paradotheisas] by my parents. Just as the seed when it
grows is tiny at first and then grows bigger but always preserves
its identity [tauto estin heautōi], not changed in kind though
gradually perfected in growth, so I consider that the same doctrine has in my case grown through a development [dia tēs pro-
kopēs]. What I hold now has not replaced what I held at the
beginning." This came in response to such accusations as those of
Eunomius, that Basil was "substituting his own mind for the
intention of the apostles" and was "referring his own nonsense to
the memory of the saints." For Basil consistently presented himself as being (in a phrase he used to describe one of his departed
colleagues) "a guardian of the principles of the fathers, an enemy
of novelty-mongering [phylax patrōiōn thesmōn, neōteropoiias
echthros], exhibiting in himself the ancient pattern [schēma] of
the church and making the state of the church placed under him
conform to the ancient constitution." Doctrinal novelty was so
dangerous, according to Basil's brother Gregory, because "the
dogmas of religious devotion [ta tēs eusebeias dogmata]" had
been clearly and decisively, if *apophatically,* revealed.

Gr.Naz.Or.21.34
(SC 270:184)

Gr.Naz.Or.39.3
(PG 36:337)

Gr.Naz.Or.41.1
(PG 36:429)

Bas.Ep.223.3
(Courtonne 3:12–13)

Eun.ap.Gr.Nyss.Eun.
3.3.17 (Jaeger 2:113)

Bas.Ep.28.1
(Courtonne 1:66)

Gr.Nyss.Eun.1.70
(Jaeger 1:46)

For Basil personally as theologian and churchman, but also for the other Cappadocians and for their entire generation in the decade preceding the First Council of Constantinople in 381, the crucial test case for such assertions of continuity in general, but specifically also for this claim of continuity between worship and

Fedwick 1981,1:337–60

doctrine, was the doctrine of the Holy Spirit. A sharing in Christian "experience [paschein]," according to Gregory of Nazianzus, involved a sharing in Christian "faith," and both involved a

Gr.Naz.Or.26.1
(SC 284:224)

"sharing in the Spirit." But if, in another of his formulas, the church was obliged "to avoid either going too far or not going

Gr.Naz.Or.22.12
(SC 270:244)

far enough in its worship [mēde hypersebontes mēde hyposebontes]," the doctrinal implications of such a sharing in the Holy Spirit through both experience and faith demanded careful theological attention in the light of the principle of "lex orandi lex credendi." When they were applying that principle to the doctrine of Christ as the Son of God, the Cappadocians were able to repeat the long-standing logic of Nicene trinitarian orthodoxy,

Jn 20:28;Acts 7:59;
Phil 2:9–11
ap.Ath.Ar.1.8
(PG 26:28)

according to which the worship of Christ and prayer to Christ, which had precedents in the New Testament and in which the Arians also engaged, led by logical consistency to the Nicene doctrine of the *homoousion,* the alternative being idolatry and

Gr.Nyss.Fid.3
(Jaeger 3–I:62)

polytheism, as the worship of a being as God who was not God in the full sense of the word. But if that logic were applied strictly to the doctrine of the Holy Spirit, it would produce the challenge, as quoted by Nazianzen: "But who worships the Spirit? Is there any ancient or modern example? Who prays to the Spirit? Where is the scriptural authority for worshiping or praying to the Spirit?

ap.Gr.Naz.Or.31.12
(SC 250:296)

Where did you get the idea from?" There were in the New Testament no unambiguous indications of prayer or other worship being addressed to the Holy Spirit, and the two medieval Latin hymns to the Holy Spirit, the "Veni Creator Spiritus" (perhaps

LTK 10:665–66

by Rabanus Maurus in the ninth century) and the "Veni Sancte

LTK 10:666

Spiritus" (probably by Stephen Langton, who died in 1228), arose long after the determination of the dogmatic status of the deity of the Holy Spirit and therefore could not be invoked as proof for it. If anything, the fixing of the dogma was a presupposition for the hymns, not the other way around.

Rather, the process of making sense out of the practice of Christian worship in order to reason through to a doctrine was obliged, in the case of the doctrine of the Holy Spirit, to concen-

Mt 28:19–20

trate most of its attention on the baptismal formula, and on

Dörries 1956,132–
34,148–56

liturgical formulas such as the Gloria Patri that were presumed to be derived from the formula for baptism. Basil's exploration of

Florovsky 9:21

Bas.*Spir*.1.3
(SC 17:257)

Bas.*Spir*.10.24
(SC 17:332)

Gr.Nyss.*Maced.*
(Jaeger 3–I:105)
Symb.Nic-CP
(Alberigo-Jedin 24)

Gr.Naz.*Or*.29.21
(SC 250:224)

Gr.Naz.*Or*.2.95
(SC 247:214)

Gr.Naz.*Or*.2.95
(SC 247:214)

Mt 7:24–27

Gr.Naz.*Or*.4.11
(SC 309:102)
Mt 7:20

that process of making sense of worship was evoked by the "innovation" he had introduced into the Gloria Patri, when he pronounced it "in both forms, at one time 'with [meta] the Son together with [syn] the Holy Spirit,' and at another, 'through [dia] the Son in [en] the Holy Spirit.'" But the issue of liturgical form was clearly, both for his opponents and for him, not only an end in itself but even more importantly a way of discussing trinitarian doctrine. By its "coordination [syntaxis]" of the Spirit with the Father and the Son, whom it linked together by means of the simple copula "and [kai]," the fundamental liturgical form derived from the great commission of Christ required, Basil urged, that the church's doctrine accordingly affirm an ontological "fellowship and conjunction [koinōnia kai synapheia]" and hence an equality among all three. Arguing similarly, but from the effects of baptism rather than from the baptismal formula as such, Gregory of Nyssa asserted that because baptism conferred "a participation in a life no longer subject to death [to zōēs metechein ouketi thanatōi hypokeimenēs]," the Spirit who effected such a participation in immortality had to be not only immortal but capable of conferring immortality—as the Niceno-Constantinopolitan Creed declared, "life-giving [zōopoion]." The importance of this method of argumentation as part of the process leading up to the codification of the orthodox dogma of the Trinity properly belongs to the history of the development of Christian doctrine, but it carries special interest also here; for the method was a particularly intriguing documentation of the process by which faith could give fullness to reasoning, but also of the process by which reasoning gave fuller expression to faith, the faith represented by Nazianzen's "spirit of speaking mysteries and dogmas [to pneuma laloumenōn mystēriōn te kai dogmatōn]."

Even while they were speaking both about the sacramental mysteries and about the orthodox dogmas, however, the Cappadocians did not lose sight of the moral categorical imperative that the priest's "hands must be made perfect by holy works," and that therefore not only the clergy but also the laity had to go beyond the externals of liturgical observance to authentic holiness. The words with which the Sermon on the Mount concluded, contrasting the man who built his house on a rock with the man who built his house on sand, were for Gregory of Nazianzus a warning to those casual converts who did not take faith and its imperatives seriously. Just before those words stood the warning of Christ, "You will recognize them by their fruit," which for Gregory of Nyssa provided a norm of "every doctrine [pasēs didaskalias]," meaning also every orthodox doctrine, by which to measure whether anyone who held to it belonged to "the recipients of salvation according to the standards of the church [tōn kata tēn ekklēsian sōzomenōn]." Basil of Caesarea, too, "deeply concerned with the problem of social reconstruction" as he was and therefore carrying out here the responsibilities of a canon lawyer as well as those of a theologian, linked his legislation about church discipline and about the punishment of "someone guilty of denying Christ and of sinning against the mystery of salvation [to tēs sōtērias mystērion]" with specific prescriptions for dealing with penances after other kinds of immorality, including sorcery, murder, adultery, and incest, grave issues in the ongoing life and discipline of the fourth-century church and therefore also in its legislation. By contrast with the sins of heresy and of apostasy from the mystery of salvation, of which only members of the community could be guilty, and by contrast with those aspects of the Christian ethic that involved going beyond what people felt instinctively and "by nature [physikōs]" to distinctively Christian forms of behavior, these immoral acts were counted to be immoral also on the basis of "moral and natural philosophy" and not only on the basis of "the more sublime life" revealed and commanded by Christ. Hence, this component of "the worship which we as rational creatures should offer" provides a fruitful perspective from which to explore the place of natural theology in the specifically Christian thought of the Cappadocians about "proper conduct in God's household," thus about worship and ethics as acts of service to God.

As worship and as ethics, or as "faith" and as "conscience," therefore, love to God and love to neighbor were, also according to the explicit teaching of Christ, coordinates in the service of God. A favorite schematism of Gregory of Nazianzus for expressing the coordination was the Aristotelian—and generally Classical—distinction between "the active and the contemplative life [bios praktikos, bios theōrētikos]." Dividing "all philosophy" into "contemplation [theōria]" and "action [praxis]," Nazianzen praised and laid claim to both of them as characteristic of the Christian life, the first "being the more sublime [hypsēloteras ousēs]" but also harder to attain, the second "being the more humble but the more useful in a practical sense [tapeinoteras, chrēsimōteras de]." Thus, in his panegyric in memory of Basil, he contrasted him with those who were "either exclusively

Gr.Nyss.*Apoll.*
(Jaeger 3–1:131)

Florovsky 2:133
Janini Cuesta 1947,
348–52

See pp.146–50

Gr.Nyss.*V.Mos.*
(Jaeger 7–1:38)

Gr.Nyss.*Paup.*2
(Van Heck 35)

Gr.Nyss.*V.Mos.*2
(Jaeger 7–1:43)

Rom 12:1

1 Tm 3:15

Gr.Nyss.*Cant.*14
(Jaeger 6:419)

Mt 22:37–40
Bas.*Mor.*3.1
(PG 31:705)

Arist.*EN.*1098a;1095b

Špidlík 1976,358–64

Gr.Naz.*Or.*4.113
(SC 309:270)

men of affairs or exclusively men of ideas and books, while being deficient in the other"; he compared these to "one-eyed men, suffering from a great loss but an even greater deformity, both in their own view of themselves and in that of others." On the other hand, there were those who, like Basil, successfully combined the life of thought and the life of action, "attaining eminence in both alike, being ambidextrous, achieving perfection and passing their lives with the blessedness of heaven." Another such ambidextrous exemplar whom Gregory of Nazianzus celebrated was Athanasius, who had "combined the two [amphotera synērmosato]." For that reason among others, Athanasius was, as Nazianzen said in the introduction to his memorial oration, the very paragon of the complete Christian life: "In praising Athanasius," he opened the oration, "I shall be praising *arete*." Even in this celebration of the great champion of Nicene orthodoxy and the vindicator of trinitarian worship, therefore, Nazianzen held worship and ethics together; as he reminded his hearers elsewhere, of all the *aretai,* none was more pleasing to God precisely as worship than the *arete* of showing mercy to others. And the *aretai,* as Gregory of Nyssa reminded his readers in turn, were the highest treasure to which human ambition could aspire.

In the *Nicomachean Ethics* of Aristotle, the immediate counterpart to "the contemplative life [bios theōrētikos]" was not "the active life [bios praktikos]" (to which he did turn some pages later), but "the political life [bios politikos]." As they expounded the *aretai* of the Christian life and of the contemplative life, the Cappadocians were never unaware of the claims of the political life, being as deeply involved as they were, both personally and officially, in the upheavals of the Roman Empire in the East during the turbulent half-century following the conversion of Constantine. Nor did they, churchmen though they were, merely introduce the state as a foil in order to celebrate the superiority of the church. Sometimes, indeed, they seemed to be doing quite the reverse, as when Gregory of Nazianzus rather gloomily acknowledged: "I am almost inclined to believe that the civil government is more orderly [eutakōteras] than ours, to which divine grace is attributed." This emphasis on "order [taxis]" carried special force for him, because he saw it as a universal characteristic, under the sovereignty of a God of reason and order, that was present, or that at any rate should have been present, not only throughout the cosmos but throughout civil society and the church. In the repeated dogmatic crises of the church between the Councils of Nicaea in 325 and of Constantinople in 381,

Gr.Naz.Or.43.12
(PG 36:509)

Gr.Naz.Or.21.19–20
(SC 270:148–50)

Gr.Naz.Or.21.1
(SC 270:110)

Gr.Naz.Or.14.5
(PG 35:864)

Gr.Nyss.Virg.4
(Jaeger 8–I:266–68)

Arist.EN.1139a
Arist.EN.1095b

Nikolaou 1981,24–31

Van Dam 1986,53–76;
Dvornik 1955,71–80

Gr.Naz.Or.18.35
(PG 35:1032)

Gr.Naz.Or.32.10
(SC 318:104–6)

however, order had given way to a situation where, as at the Battle of Adrianople in 378, the members of the same body were consuming, and being consumed by, one another, in the grim irony of their being divided not only by politics but by disputes about the unity of the indivisible Trinity. This came from a community that prayed in its liturgy: "May all of us who participate in one bread and cup be united with others into the fellowship of the one Holy Spirit, with all the saints who from eternity have been well-pleasing to thee." Therefore, it was part of the responsibility of the Christian emperor to abjure the worship of Caesar and to work for the goal for which Christ had prayed, "'that all may be one' and may be of one mind [hōste pantas hen einai kai symphronein]."

The Cappadocians brought together many of these motifs in the familiar New Testament metaphor, in which the apostle Paul spoke of the church as "the body of Christ." So radically did the members of the church transcend the barriers of ordinary society that not only slavery but even the difference between man and woman was relativized: "O nature of woman," in the apostrophe of Gregory of Nazianzus to his sister, "overcoming that of man in the common struggle for salvation, and demonstrating that the distinction between male and female is one of body, not of soul!" Or, as he might well have put it, the distinction between male and female was in their physical bodies, but not in the body of Christ. Elaborating the metaphor further on the basis of the Song of Songs, Gregory of Nyssa described how "those who had been united to [Christ] in accordance with the fellowship of the mystery" became "his own body, the church." The result was an identification: "Someone who looks at the church is looking directly [antikrys] at Christ." But because of who Christ was, as the *Logos* who gave order to the cosmos and in whom all things were "held together as a system [synestēken]," it was not only Christ who was visible through the church, but the universe and the very nature of being were made known through the church as well. It was not always clear precisely how this knowledge of the universe through Christ and the church was correlated in the thought of the Cappadocians with the natural knowledge of the universe as cosmos, a natural knowledge that had the assignment, according to Gregory of Nyssa, of investigating its origin and its destiny. But Gregory of Nazianzus did express the antithesis between the church and natural religion in a discourse about the Christian "philosopher and wise man," in which he contrasted the spectacle of a Greek player in the theater acting out a

Gr.Naz.Or.33.2
(SC 318:158–60)

Lit.Bas.
(Brightman 330)
Reilly 1945,21–24
Jn 17:21
Gr.Naz.Or.4.37
(SC 309:136)
Rom 12:5;1 Cor 12:27;
Eph 1:23;Eph 4:12;
Col 1:24;2:19
Gr.Naz.Or.14.8
(PG 35:868)

See pp.148–49

Gr.Naz.Or.8.14
(PG 35:805)

Welsserheimb 1948,
423–33
Malevez 1935,260–80;
Nothomb 1954,318–21
Gr.Nyss.Cant.13
(Jaeger 6:383)
Gr.Naz.Or.30.20
(SC 250:266–68)
Col 1:17
Eph 3:10–12
Gr.Nyss.Cant.8
(Jaeger 6:255)

Gr.Nyss.Eun.2.222
(Jaeger 1:290)

Gr.Naz.Or.25.2
(SC 284:158–60)

See pp.177–83

Callahan 1958b,29–57

Gr.Nyss.Cant.7
(Jaeger 6:222–23)

Gr.Nyss.V.Macr.
(Jaeger 8–I:385)

Gr.Naz.Or.18.35
(PG 35:1032)

Batiffol 1922,9–30

Bas.Ep.203.3
(Courtonne 2:170–71)

Gr.Nyss.Beat.1
(PG 44:1196)
Giet 1944,95–128;
Winslow 1965,348–59

Mt 25:40
Gr.Nyss.Paup.1–2
(Van Heck 3–37)

Gr.Naz.Or.14
(PG 35:858–909)
Gr.Naz.Or.2.95
(SC 247:214)

Gr.Naz.Or.40.25
(PG 36:393)

See pp.136–51

Wilken 1970,437–58

Is 52:5

Rom 2:24

"myth" and a Christian martyr who carried out his action "before the face of God and of the angels and of all the fullness of the church." It may therefore have been more than simply a play on the Greek word "philosophia," which referred both to "philosophy" and to "monasticism," and on the Greek word "kosmos," which meant both "universe" and "ornament," when Gregory of Nyssa used "philosophia" to identify monasticism as "kosmos ekklēsias," or when he spoke of an ordination as "philosophy enriched by priesthood [tēi hierōsynēi tēs philosophias epauxētheisēs]."

Nazianzen's rhetorical praise for the "order" in the civil community as superior to that in the church had a counterpart in Basil's ecclesiology. Basil criticized the social indifference of Christians, which was "neither decorous before men nor pleasing to God." They were being shamed by the social consciousness of "those who do not know God." He continued: "Yet we, the sons of fathers who have laid down the law that by brief notes the proofs of communion should be carried about from one end of the earth to the other, and that all should be citizens and family members with all [kai pantas pasi politas kai oikeious einai], now cut ourselves off from the whole world." But "the distribution of arete" was such that it was both individual and collective. Above all, the members of the church were not to cut themselves off from the poor. The words of Christ at the last judgment, "Anything you did for one of my brothers here, however insignificant, you did for me," provided Gregory of Nyssa with his text for two powerful sermons of advocacy on behalf of the poor. Gregory of Nazianzus also devoted an entire oration to the plight of the poor and to the responsibility of individual believers and of the church for their care. His insistence that the priest had to have "hands made perfect by holy works" rather than by mere ritual purity applied as well to the laity, who were not to excuse themselves from their social responsibility for the poor on the grounds that they wanted to be able to make financial contributions to the church. Because so much of this moral content of Christian arete was available to, and present in, the natural order of those who did not share in the grace of Christ, admonitions to Christians to lead a moral life within Greco-Roman society had an apologetic significance as well as a hortatory and liturgical one, as the apostle Paul had indicated when he warned the Romans, quoting Isaiah, "Because of you the name of God is profaned among the Gentiles." Gregory of Nyssa was paraphrasing that apostolic warning when he admonished: "Those who have not yet believed the word of truth closely examine the lives of those who have received the mystery of the faith. If, therefore, people are 'faithful' only in name, but contradict this name by their life . . . then the pagans immediately attribute this not to the free choice of these evil-living men, but to the mystery that is supposed to teach these things. For, they say, such and such a man who has been initiated into the divine mysteries would not be such a slanderer, or so avaricious and grasping, or anything equally evil, unless sinning were lawful for them." Thus, Christian worship by those who had been "initiated into the divine mysteries" had to be, also in this sense, "the well-pleasing worship which we, as rational creatures, should offer" and which other rational creatures, including those people who were not believers, or not yet believers, could recognize as valid, as Christ had warned his disciples in the Sermon on the Mount. But when Basil objected that Christians, whose duty it was to "be citizens and family members with all" were instead "cutting [themselves] off from the whole world"; or when Gregory of Nazianzus, describing the final judgment, spoke of it as "bringing together in a moment all mankind, to stand before its Creator"; or when Gregory of Nyssa exhorted his hearers to their duties toward the downcast of society by invoking the coming of the Son of man at the end of human history to judge the sheep and the goats—they were all raising, in the context of both "eschatology and ethics," the question of the contribution of natural theology as well as of revealed theology to the universality of the human hope and of the Christian hope for "the life of the *aeon* to come."

Gr.Nyss.*Or.dom.*3
(PG 44:1153)

Mt 5:23–24
Bas.*Mor.*5.4
(PG 31:709)

Bas.*Ep.*203.3
(Courtonne 2:170–71)

Gr.Naz.*Or.*40.2
(PG 36:361)

Gr.Nyss.*Paup.*1
(Van Heck 9)

Mt 25:32–33

Wilder 1939

CHAPTER 20

The Life of the Aeon to Come

Symb.Nic.-CP
(Alberigo-Jedin 24)

See pp.131–34

See pp.287–90

Gr.Nyss.Hom.opif.25–26
(PG 44:224)

Gr.Naz.Or.29.19
(SC 250:218)

Coulie 1985,195–201
Gr.Nyss.Hom.opif.pr.
(PG 44:128)
Bas.Ep.42.1
(Courtonne 1:100)

Gr.Nyss.Cant.1
(Jaeger 6:17)

The conclusion and climax of the Niceno-Constantinopolitan Creed affirmed: "We await . . . the life of the *aeon* to come." The human condition in the life to come was specified in Cappadocian thought by the doctrine of the immortality of the soul in combination with the doctrine of the resurrection of the body. They found that the first of these doctrines was common to natural theology and to revealed theology, but that the second was principally the domain of revealed theology. But Gregory of Nyssa did claim to be able to show, by means of natural theology, that the resurrection was not beyond probability, though he could not demonstrate it beyond reasonable doubt. Speaking about the transfiguration or *metamorphosis* of Christ, Gregory of Nazianzus described it as "a mystagogy into the future," and in that sense it is fair to contrast the earthly and the heavenly world in his thought. For Gregory of Nyssa, too, the past and present of the human race were to be interpreted in the light of the ultimate future. Or, in the axiom of Basil, "The whole of human life is fed not so much on the past as on the future."

In the thought of each of the Cappadocians, the interpretation of the life of the *aeon* to come was thus an epitome of the entire relation between natural and revealed theology. Such a movement toward the perfection of the coming *aeon* was represented, for example, in the progression of three of the books attributed to Solomon, beginning with Proverbs, continuing with Ecclesiastes, and climaxing with the sublime "philosophy of the Song of Songs." It was a movement or an "advance [prokopē] to perfection, made stage by stage, and in regular order, through the works of righteousness and the illumination of knowledge, ever longing after future prospects and reaching forward to the remaining possibilities." For the system of the Cappadocians, all of this was set into explicit opposition to pagan theories both of *tyche* and of *ananke*. This consideration of their eschatology will follow the lead of that eschatology and take the form of a rehearsal, "stage by stage and in regular order [heirmōi kai taxei]," of the several issues in the Cappadocian system with which this book has been dealing throughout. For each issue was, in some ultimate sense, defined by eschatology, and each was "fed not so much on the past as on the future." Cappadocian eschatology was the fulfillment of Cappadocian teleology, as that was summarized in the comprehensive formula of Gregory of Nyssa cited earlier: "That nothing happens without God [to mēden atheei ginesthai] we know from many sources; and, conversely, that God's *economies* have no element of *tyche* and irrationality in them everyone will allow who realizes that God is *logos,* and *sophia,* and perfect *arete,* and truth."

It was by identifying the eschatological goal toward which that "advance to perfection" was moving that the Cappadocians could articulate a universalism that permitted them to comprehend not only Christianity but Classical culture within a single system. "Universalism" has been defined as meaning either "the fact or scope of being universal in character or scope," as when it is said that Christ "belongs to humanity, not to Israel," or "the doctrine of universal salvation or redemption." The relation between these two meanings was crucial to Cappadocian eschatology. As Gregory of Nyssa formulated it in the summary conclusion of his exposition of the Song of Songs, this universalism (in the first sense) implied "the unification of all mankind, joined in looking toward the same goal of their yearning [heōs an pantōn hen genomenōn tōn pros ton auton skopon tēs epithymias blepontōn]." Gregory of Nazianzus proved the unity of the human race by referring to "one heaven" and to the "equal share [isomoiria]" of night and day, as well as to the universality of sun and rain, as described in the Gospels. But invoking for his description of the universal goal the New Testament's imagery of the heavenly Jerusalem, he also located the unity of mankind there: "Everyone that is of high mind has one country, the heavenly Jerusalem, in which we store up our citizenship. All have one family—if you look at what is here below the dust—or if you look higher, that inbreathing of which we are partakers [the Holy

Bas.*Spir.*8.18
(SC 17:310)

Gr.Naz.*Or.*4.44
(SC 309:144)

Bas.*Spir.*8.18
(SC 17:310)

Bas.*Ep.*42.1
(Courtonne 1:100)

Gr.Nyss.*Infant.*
(Jaeger 3–II:93)

Bas.*Spir.*8.18
(SC 17:310)

OED 11–III:243

Gr.Nyss.*Cant.*15
(Jaeger 6:469)
Gr.Naz.*Or.*33.9
(SC 318:174–76)
Gr.Naz.*Or.*14.25
(PG 35:889)

Mt 5:45

Gal 4:26;Phil 3:20

Spirit], and which we are bidden to keep, and with which I have to stand before my Judge to give an account of my heavenly nobility, and of the divine image. Everyone, then, is noble who has guarded this through *arete* and through consent to the archetype." The unity of mankind was, in such a context, to be found in its standing before Christ as the one judge of heaven and earth; and it was thus a corollary of the monotheism for which Cappadocian apologetics contended and which it claimed to find expressed, though ever so faintly, in Greek thought, especially in the philosophical theology of Plato.

The God in whom Jew believed was, according to Gregory of Nyssa, "our God, too." Yet despite this privileged position that the Cappadocians acknowledged for the historical revelation of God to Israel, both their view of the beginning and their vision of the end required them to affirm that God had not been only "known in Judea [gnōstos en tēi Ioudaiai]" through revealed theology, but by natural theology known also to the Chaldeans, Egyptians, and Babylonians. The Greeks occupied a special place among those Gentiles whose salvation with "the nature of humanity as a whole [pasan tēn anthrōpinēn physin]" was part of Paul's eschatological vision in Romans. To that ultimate goal of salvation, "the totality of mankind, without exception" were "equally called without respect to rank, age, or nationality," as the miracle of the apostles' speaking in all the tongues of the world at Pentecost had showed. At the same time, this eschatological equality of all mankind did not preclude variations and degrees of glory in a heavenly "Father's house" that was not uniform but had "many dwelling-places." Both for the positive recognition of natural theology and for the polemic against its inadequacies, eschatology provided Cappadocian thought with ammunition. Although they were by no means undiscriminating in their willingness to invoke linguistic parallels from Classical Greek for the vocabulary of the New Testament, they were often willing to do so. Specifically, Macrina and her brother Gregory did cite such parallels between what was found "in the writings of those on the outside and the divine Scripture [para de tōn exōthen kai para tēs theias graphēs]" for its eschatological vocabulary, which was "in frequent circulation both in the relationships of daily life and in the writings of those on the outside and in our own." Conversely, one of the major criticisms directed by all the Cappadocians—by Basil, by Macrina according to the report of her brother Gregory of Nyssa, as well as by Gregory of Nazianzus in an oration delivered in 373—against the natural

Gr.Naz.Or.33.12
(SC 318:182)

Gr.Nyss.Ref.48
(Jaeger 2:332)
Gr.Naz.Or.4.117
(SC 309:280)
Pl.Tim.39e-41a

Gr.Nyss.Maced.
(Jaeger 3-I:101)

Ps 75:1
Gr.Nyss.V.Mos.1
(Jaeger 7–I:6)

Gr.Nyss.Cant.14
(Jaeger 6:427-28)
Rom 11:16
Stephan 1938,9-23
Gr.Nyss.Or.catech.30.3
(Méridier 138)

Acts 2:4

Jn 14:2
Gr.Nyss.Cant.15
(Jaeger 6:459-60)

Gr.Naz.Or.45.10
(PG 36:636)

Gr.Nyss.Anim.res.
(PG 46:68)
Bas.Hex.1.2
(SC 26:92-94)
Macr.ap.Gr.Nyss.
Anim.res. (PG 46:21)
Gr.Naz.Or.16.5
(PG 35:940-41)

theology propounded by "the Greek philosophers [hoi tōn Hellēnōn sophoi]" was their lack of a satisfactory doctrine about the
direction in which nature and history were headed under the
guidance of divine providence.

It was, however, particularly in the exposition of their doctrine
of divine providence that the Cappadocians emphasized its hid-
denness, and it was likewise in their very celebration of divine
revelation about the end of life and the end of the world that they
insisted upon the language of negation as constituting the proper
lexicon of transcendence. There was, as Gregory of Nyssa
pointed out, an insatiable human curiosity to know about the
"intentions of each detail of the divine *economy*," especially as it
pertained to the end of life. Faith did make the affirmation: "If
nothing in the cosmos happens without God [atheei], but all is
linked to the divine will; and if the Deity is skillful and prudential, then it follows necessarily that there is some plan in these
things bearing the mark of his *sophia,* and at the same time of his
providential care. A blind unmeaning occurrence can never be the
work of God [to gar eikēi ti kai alogōs ginomenon ouk an ergon

Gr.Nyss.Infant.
(Jaeger 3–II:72)

eiē theou]." On this score any natural theology that led to doctrines either of *tyche* or of *ananke* would have to be a deception.
Nevertheless it was, according to Gregory of Nazianzus, "a divine decree, ancient and firm [dogma theou palaion te kai pag-

*Gr.Naz.Or.*17.4
(PG 35:969)

ion]," that the future plans of the providence of God were to
"remain hidden from our eyes." Drawing on the riches of biblical
imagery, Nyssen could recount a catalog of names about the
eternal honor and glory that were in store for the saved, which, at
first glance, could give the impression of providing explicit and
cataphatic information about the minutiae of the life of the *aeon*

*Gr.Nyss.V.Mos.*2
(Jaeger 7–I:119)

to come. Not so, he warned elsewhere: "The promised blessings,
held out to those who have lived a good life, defy description. For

1 Cor 2:9
*Gr.Nyss.Or.catech.*40.7
(Méridier 194–96)

how can we describe 'things beyond our seeing, things beyond
our hearing, things beyond our imagining'?" Any effort to penetrate this veil and to ferret out *cataphatic* information he labeled

*Gr.Nyss.Hom.opif.*23
(PG 44:209)

"the inquisitiveness of busybodies [polypragmosynē]." The
promise of Paradise regained and of the image of God restored
could be expressed only in "a description confined to inef-

*Gr.Nyss.Hom.opif.*21
(PG 44:204)

fabilities [hēs ho logos en aporrētois menei]." For the divine
nature, even when it was holding out to humanity the prospect of
a future and final participation in itself, retained a transcendence
of which it was finally permissible to speak only in *apophatic*
language, with a generous sprinkling of alpha privatives: "a
simple and pure and constant and undeviating and unchang-

ing nature [haplē kai kathara kai monoeidēs kai atreptos kai analloiōtos physis]."

It was typical of Cappadocian thought to declare that this way of knowing could be achieved only "by that well-known inexpressible knowledge of the divine [tēi aporrētōi ekeinēi theognōsiai]." Thus, the apostle Paul, after being "caught up as far as the third heaven," was "filled with what he had tasted"—and yet the eschatological fruits of Paradise that he tasted were "ineffable." The difficulty of achieving some sort of harmony between the language of negative theology and the expectation of a *metamorphosis* of knowledge in the life to come was well represented in a passage from the orations of Gregory of Nazianzus, which deserves to be quoted in full: "What God is in nature and essence, no one has ever yet discovered or can discover. Whether it will ever be discovered is a question that someone who wishes to do so may examine and decide. In my opinion it will be discovered when that within us which is Godlike and divine, I mean our mind and *logos*, will have mingled with its like [the divine *Logos*], and the image will have ascended to the archetype, of which it now has the desire. And this, I think, is the solution of that vexed problem as to the meaning of the words: 'Our knowledge then will be whole, like God's knowledge of us.' But in our present life all that comes to us is but a little effluence, and as it were a small effulgence from a great light." The quotation, "Our knowledge then will be whole, like God's knowledge of us," was a reference, not quite verbatim, to the familiar passage from the apostle Paul: "At present we see only puzzling reflections in a mirror, but one day we shall see face to face. My knowledge now is imperfect; then it will be whole, like God's knowledge of me." Basil used this passage to assert that because the kingdom of the heavens consisted in contemplation, the present life consisted in "beholding the shadows [of the heavens] as in a mirror [hōs en katoptrōi]," but that the future life, "set free from this earthly body and clad in the incorruptible and the immortal," would consist in "beholding their archetypes." Yet, Gregory of Nazianzus elsewhere quoted the first half of that same passage, Paul's statement about seeing "puzzling reflections in a mirror [en ainigmati]," as a warning against intellectual presumption. The experience of mystical rapture that Paul described in 2 Corinthians could likewise be read in both directions. It served as a primary instance of a state described in the words of Gregory of Nyssa: "Every voice that conveys meaning by verbal utterance is stilled, and unspoken meditation becomes the word of instruc-

Gr.Nyss.*Cant.*5
(Jaeger 6:158)

Gr.Nyss.*V.Mos.*2
(Jaeger 7–I:82)
2 Cor 12:1–5
See pp.47–48

Gr.Nyss.*Beat.*4
(PG 44:1248)

Gr.Naz.*Or.*28.17
(SC 250:134–36)

1 Cor 13:12

Wis 7:26

1 Cor 13:12

Bas.*Ep.*8.12
(Courtonne 1:36)

Gr.Naz.*Or.*20.12
(SC 270:82)

Gr.Nyss.*Eun*.3.1.16
(Jaeger 2:9)

Gr.Nyss.*Virg*.13
(Jaeger 8–I:304)

Koch 1898,397–420;
Horn 1927,113–31
Gr.Nyss.*Infant*.
(Jaeger 3–II:78–79)
Gr.Nyss.*Cant*.6
(Jaeger 6:178)

Mt 5:8

Ex 33:20;Jn 1:18;
1 Tm 6:16
Gr.Nyss.*Beat*.6
(PG 44:1273)

Gr.Nyss.*Cant*.8
(Jaeger 6:247)

Gr.Nyss.*V.Mos*.2
(Jaeger 7–I:116–18)

Pl.*Phdr*.240c

Gr.Nyss.*Beat*.4
(PG 44:1244)

Macr.ap.Gr.Nyss.
Anim.res. (PG 46:96)

tion, teaching to the purified heart by means of the silent illu-mination of the thoughts those truths which transcend speech." Yet it could also be taken as a promise that by being cleansed and having the image of God restored, the believer could be "taken up again into Paradise, in which Paul, too, heard and saw unspoken and unseen things, not repeatable by human lips."

As their constant reiteration of the language of seeing and contemplating suggested, a central figure in the language of the Cappadocians about the knowledge of God in the life of the *aeon* to come was the biblical concept of the vision of God, which was "the design [skopos] of everything being born." This was the goal of the soul's advance toward heavenly bliss. Expounding the promise of the vision of God in the Beatitudes of the Sermon on the Mount, "Blessed are those whose hearts are pure; they shall see God," Gregory of Nyssa distinguished two definitions of how the term could be understood: "[It can mean], on the one hand, knowing the nature that transcends the universe [tēn tou pantos hyperkeimenēn physin], and on the other hand, being united to him through purity of life." Only the second of these was being promised in the words of Christ, because the authority of Scrip-ture ruled out a knowledge of the divine nature in itself as "im-possible." No notion of the vision of God was acceptable if it appeared to compromise the impenetrable transcendence of God. Above all, the emphasis on the vision of God enabled Cap-padocian eschatology to articulate "the ultimate paradox of be-ing static and dynamic at the same time [to pantōn paradox-otaton, pōs to auto kai statis esti kai kinēsis]," by its insistence that the essence of the vision of God consisted in "never reaching the point of satiety in yearning [touto estin ontōs to idein ton theon, to mēdepote tēs epithymias koron heurein]." Physical pleasures and human relationships, according to Plato in the *Phaedrus*, reached the point where "you may have more than enough of this [homōs koron ge kai hē toutōn synousia echei]." Echoing those words of the *Phaedrus*, Gregory of Nyssa pointed out: "The possession of *arete*, on the other hand, where it is once firmly established, is neither circumscribed by time nor limited by satiety [ou chronōi metreitai, oute korōi periorizetai]," but eternal, like its divine object. For, in Macrina's words, "The life of [God as] supreme being is love, seeing that the *kalon* is neces-sarily lovable to those who recognize it. . . . This true *kalon* the insolence of satiety cannot touch [tou de alēthōs kalou hē hybritēs ou prosaptetai koros]." Such a freedom from cloying satiety was true already here and now of "the soul with the vision of God." But it was chiefly in speaking about life eternal after the resurrection that deliverance from any surfeit of the vision of God was central. For it was not only the case that there was "a ceaseless attraction" exerted upon lesser goods by the supremely good; but being "in its nature infinite," this first good granted to those who participated in the enjoyment of it an infinite sharing, with "more always in the process of being grasped, and yet something even beyond that always waiting to be discovered." In the ascent to God, already here in time but especially also hereafter in eternity, there was no stopping and no satiety.

Yet even such language about the knowledge of God and the vision of God was not an adequate vehicle for Cappadocian eschatology, which embraced nothing less than the combination of all of the following graces: "Foreknowledge of the future [mellontōn prognōsis], understanding of mysteries, apprehension of hidden reality, distribution of good gifts, the heavenly citizenship, a place in the chorus of angels, joy without end, abiding in God, being made like to God—and, highest of all, being made God [theon genesthai]!" The life of the *aeon* to come, of which the creed spoke, was not merely the vision of God but *theosis*. An eschatology of *theosis* called for careful defining and precise distinguishing, in the dual context of Cappadocian apologetics and Cappadocian dogmatics. Sometimes, therefore, in describing this process, the Cappadocians could also employ terminology that was rather less audacious than *theosis* was. Appropriating the concept of the "imitation [mimēsis]" of the divine model, which had roots in both the Classical and Christian traditions, Macrina spoke of "the real assimilation [homoiōsis] to the divine" as consisting "in making our own life in some degree an imitation [en tōi mimeisthai pōs] of the transcendent being." As he looked for an expression of the new reality, Gregory of Nyssa had recourse to similar language. Basil, too, described Paul as "the imitator of Christ [ho mimētēs tou Christou]." It was a more vivid description when Gregory of Nyssa referred to it as a "union [symphyïa] with the only good." He also spoke rather unspecifically about "some sort of transformation of human nature into something more divine [metabalōn tropon tina tēn anthrōpinēn physin pros to theioteron]."

Then, however, he immediately asserted: "He is legislating that those who approach God should themselves become gods." *Theosis* was "the very *telos* of the life of *arete*." But it was as well the complement of the orthodox doctrine of the Trinity of Father,

Gr.Nyss.*Cant.*12
(Jaeger 6:366)

Gr.Nyss.*Cant.*1
(Jaeger 6:32)

Gr.Nyss.*Eun.*1.290–91
(Jaeger 1:112)
Gr.Nyss.*Cant.*5
(Jaeger 6:159);
Gr.Nyss.*V.Mos.*2
(Jaeger 7–I:113)

Bas.*Spir.*9.23
(SC 17:328)
Gr.Nyss.*Or.dom.*2
(PG 44:1137)

Merki 1952

Pl.*Tim.*48e
1 Cor 11:1

Macr.ap.Gr.Nyss.
Anim.res. (PG 46:89–92)
Gr.Nyss.*Or.dom.*5
(PG 44:1177)
Bas.*Spir.*15.35
(SC 17:366)

Gr.Nyss.*Cant.*15
(Jaeger 6:466)

Gr.Nyss.*Or.dom.*5
(PG 44:1177–80)
Mt 6:12
Gr.Nyss.*Or.dom.*5
(PG 44:1177–80)
Gr.Nyss.*Cant.*9
(Jaeger 6:280)

Gr.Nyss.*Eun.*3.3.67
(Jaeger 2:131)

Gr.Naz.*Or.*29.19
(SC 250:218)

Bas.*Spir.*9.23
(SC 17:328)

Gr.Naz.*Or.*39.17
(PG 36:353–56)

Gr.Nyss.*Beat.*7
(PG 44:1280)

Gr.Nyss.*Maced.*
(Jaeger 3–I:91)

Gr.Nyss.*Virg.*11
(Jaeger 8–I:296)

Gr.Nyss.*Cant.*1
(Jaeger 6:28–29)

Gr.Nyss.*Eun.*3.2.94
(Jaeger 2:83)
Gr.Naz.*Or.*39.7
(PG 36:341)

Faller 1925,405–35
Gr.Naz.*Ep.*101
(PG 37:180)

Son, and Holy Spirit. It was the necessary corollary of the incarnation, for through the incarnation "the human nature [of the Son of God] was renewed by becoming divine through its commixture with the divine [dia tēs pros to theion anakraseōs]." In the person of the incarnate Son "man and God . . . became a single whole . . . , in order to make me God to the same extent that he was made man [hina genōmai tosouton theos, hoson ekeinos anthrōpos]." The doctrine of *theosis* and the doctrine of the deity of the Holy Spirit were also mutually supportive corollaries, for example in Basil's argument that the Holy Spirit had to be divine. "How could [the Holy Spirit] not be God," in the statement of the same case by Gregory of Nazianzus, "by whom you, too, were made God?" It does seem that in presenting this eschatology of *theosis,* the Cappadocians were thinking of a fundamental ontological change, as in the apostrophe of Gregory of Nyssa: "With what words, what thoughts that move our mind can we praise this abundance of grace [tēn tēs charitos hyperbolēn]? Man transcends [ekbainei] his own nature, he who was subject to corruption in his mortality becomes immune from it in his immortality, becomes eternal instead of being stuck in time— in a word, from a man he becomes God [theos ex anthrōpou ginomenos]."

The content of the term "God," however, even when used in such a context, came at least in part from a process of natural theology: "When once our minds have grasped the idea of a divine nature, we accept by the implication of that very name the perfection in it of every conceivable thing that befits deity." That divine perfection expressed itself in the "incorruptibility [aphtharsia]" of the nature of God, and it was by attaining, "through 'aphtharsia,' the utmost purity possible" that the soul reached *theosis.* The perfection of God expressed itself as well in the divine *apatheia,* which was likewise communicated through *theosis* to a deified humanity. Yet all of this Christian language about a humanity made divine was part of a total Cappadocian system in which the Classical religion of deified men and women and of anthropomorphic gods and goddesses was described as "the superstition of polytheism" and as the error of those mere mortals who had "turned aside the honor of God to themselves." Therefore, the Cappadocians insisted that it was as essential for *theosis* as it was for the incarnation itself not to be viewed as analogous to Classical Greek theories about the promotion of human beings to divine rank, and in that sense not to be defined by natural theology at all; on such errors they pronounced their "Anathema!"

The doctrine of creation was, in the conventional meaning of the word also for the Cappadocians, a doctrine of beginnings, an answer to the quest for "a cause of the system and government of the universe." It was, therefore, primarily for his explanation of the beginnings of creation that Gregory of Nyssa celebrated his brother Basil. On closer and more profound inspection, however, they were impelled to interpret also the doctrine of creation eschatologically. There was, Gregory of Nyssa insisted, an inescapable correlation for any thinker between the concept of the beginning and the concept of the end: "[Anyone who denies eschatology] clearly also does not believe that in the *arche* the heaven and the earth were made by God; for anyone who admits an *arche* of motion surely does not doubt as to its also having an end, and anyone who does not allow its end does not admit its *arche* either," this principle apparently being derived also from natural theology. This was a direct and necessary corollary of the teaching that the created world was not the product of *tyche* and accident. In the world of nature as in the *economy* of the life and work of Christ, therefore, the *arche* and *telos* had to be seen together. And at any rate "according to the teaching of Scripture," as well as perhaps according to natural reason, this universe, which "took being from nothing," was also destined to "be transformed into some other state." That, according to Macrina's teleology, was "the goal [skopos] of each single *economy* of the universe." This was to happen, she continued, "in a certain regularity and order [taxei tini kai akolouthiai], in accordance with the *sophia* at work in the *techne* of their author."

The subject of this predicate of "regularity and order" of which Macrina was speaking was "all things [ta panta]." That inclusive view was decisive for the eschatology of the Cappadocians, by whose definition salvation embraced not merely the human soul or the entire human person or the entire human race, but nothing less than "ta panta" or "to pan," the cosmos, the world of angels and of material things as well as of man. Gregory of Nyssa could even suggest that the specific reason why "the power above both the heavenly and the earthly universe" had created man was so that the earth, too, would be inhabited, as the heavens were by the angels, and so that "all parts of the creation" could participate in the divine goal of the vision of God. God the Creator was not content with a universe made up only of angelic beings, but explicitly for his eschatological purposes he created man, as the link that would, through its union of body and soul, eventually unite the entire cosmos: "The other nature [of human-

Gr.Nyss.*Eun.*2.222
(Jaeger 1:290)

Gr.Nyss.*Hom.opif.*pr.
(PG 44:125)

Gn 1:1

Gr.Nyss.*Hom.opif.*23
(PG 44:209)

Gr.Nyss.*Hex.*
(PG 44:72)

Gr.Nyss.*Or.catech.*27.2
(Méridier 126)

Gr.Nyss.*Hom.opif.*24
(PG 44:213)

Macr.ap.Gr.Nyss.
Anim.res. (PG 46:105)

Gillet 1962,62–83

Gr.Nyss.*Infant.*
(Jaeger 3–II:78–79)

ity] has necessarily been allotted to the earthly life because of the kinship of our body, which is, as it were, a sediment of mud, with what is earthly. Now I do not know what the purpose of the divine will was in so ordering it. Perhaps it was to bring the whole creation into relationship with itself. . . . Thus the creation of man would effect in each of the *stoicheia* a participation in the things belonging to the other; for the spiritual nature of the soul, which seems to be decidedly akin to the heavenly powers, dwells in earthly bodies, and in 'the *apocatastasis* of all things' this earthly flesh will be translated into the heavenly places together with the soul." These words implied that it was the entire cosmos, "our world and everything in it," that participated in "the system and government of the universe [hē tou pantos systasis kai dioikēsis]," as directed from beginning to end by God as its "origin and cause," as its end and goal, and as the principle of its continuity. The movement from the "origin and cause" of all things to their end under God's system and government meant that because of "the variegated [polyoikilos] *sophia* of God, through the *economy* among the human race in Christ," not only human nature but the universe beyond humanity had come to participate in the grace of the divine mysteries, by means of which it was receiving a divine *paideia*.

Viewed eschatologically, therefore, the divine *economy* was a process of *paideia*. Through it, "by a sequence according to the order of history [di' akolothou kata tēn tēs historias taxin]," the *Logos* was "leading our thought, as if by the hand, to the more sublime heights of *arete*." All the events of human history and of sacred history were divine instruments by which God was instructing and chastening the human race. Thus, the world was "really the school for rational souls to exercise themselves, the training ground for them to learn to know God." But the eschatological perspective led to the conclusion that at least as far as "the most vital of all questions relating to our faith" were concerned, this educational process would in many respects become more intelligible a posteriori than it had been while it was going on. For this was the message of Scripture: "That when our race has completed the ordered chain of its existence as the *aeons* lapse through their complete circle [pote taxei tini kai heirmōi tēs physeōs hēmōn kata tēn parodikēn tou chronou kinēsin diexiousēs], this current streaming onward as generation succeeds generation will cease altogether; but also that then, when the completed universe [tēs tou pantos symplērōseōs] no longer admits of further increase, all the souls in their entire number will

Acts 3:21

Gr.Nyss.*Or.dom*.4
(*PG* 44:1165)

Gr.Nyss.*Eun*.2.222
(Jaeger 1:290)

Gr.Nyss.*Cant*.8
(Jaeger 6:254)

Portmann 1954,20–21

Gr.Nyss.*V.Mos*.2
(Jaeger 7–1:82)

Gr.Naz.*Or*.38.13
(*PG* 36:325)

Bas.*Hex*.1.6
(*SC* 26:110)

come back." The resurrection would follow, and only in the light of this final eventuality would "the ordered chain of its existence, the lapsing of the *aeons* through their complete circle" of human history and of cosmic history make ultimate sense. It was, similarly, the final eventuality of the death of her brother Basil that evoked from Macrina "still loftier philosophy" and reflection on "the divine *economy*."

The expectation articulated by the apostle Paul, of being "caught up in clouds to meet the Lord in the air" at the second coming of Christ, therefore led to the conclusion that human history was to be be viewed as "the time necessarily coextensive with the development of humanity [oukoun anameinatō ton chronon ton anankaiōs tēi anthrōpinēi auxēsei symparateinonta]." The Christ who had entered time and who had provided the key to its mysteries was himself one who transcended it. The eschatological understanding of the divine *economy* and of time located human death itself within the sweep of divine providence, but it did so in the light of the death of Christ. Such christocentrism defined the content of the orthodox and creedal doctrine of "the life of the *aeon* to come." For, in Nyssen's formula, "The genuine life made manifest in us is none other than Christ himself [tēn alēthinēn en hēmin phanerōthēnai zōēn, hētis estin ho Christos]." It was specifically in the light of the events of the life, suffering, death, and resurrection of Christ that Gregory of Nazianzus attacked the astrological and cyclical interpretation of history; for if that interpretation was correct, he asked, "What hinders Christ also from being born a second time . . . and being betrayed again by Judas and being crucified and buried and rising again?" On the basis of these events of the life of Christ it was possible as well "to describe the gospel as a foretaste of the life following on the resurrection." It was also possible, in the light of the rewards prepared for the life of the *aeon* to come, to identify rewards granted by God here in time. The expectation of the life of the *aeon* to come made the experiences of the present life a "foretaste" of eternity. As Christ was already the center of time and history but had not yet returned to be its consummation, so the transformation that he both promised and figured forth was here already and not yet here. For he was, from eternity with the Father and in time and history through the incarnation, "the stamp of God's very being," "the image of the invisible God," and "the image of his goodness."

As such, Christ was the one who effected "the transformation of our nature from mortality to immortality." The Cappadocian

Gr.Nyss.*Anim.res.*
(PG 46:129)

Gr.Nyss.*V.Macr.*
(PG 46:978)

1 Thes 4:17

Gr.Nyss.*Hom.opif.*22
(PG 44:208)
Gr.Nyss.*Eun.*3.7.30
(Jaeger 2:225)

Gr.Nyss.*Or.catech.*35
(Méridier 160–70)

Symb.Nic.-CP
(Alberigo-Jedin 24)

Col 3:1–4

Gr.Nyss.*Cant.*9
(Jaeger 6:262)

Gr.Naz.*Ep.*101
(PG 37:192)

Bas.*Spir.*15.35
(SC 17:370)

Bas.*Hex.*3.1
(SC 26:190)

Gr.Naz.*Or.*8.19
(PG 35:812)

Gr.Nyss.*Cant.*9
(Jaeger 6:262)
Bas.*Ep.*38.8
(Courtonne 1:92)
Heb 1:3;Col 1:15;
Wis 7:26

Gr.Nyss.*Ref.*4
(Jaeger 2:314)

See pp.127–35

doctrine of the image of God described it as reason, free will, and immortality. But that formulation should not be permitted to obscure—as it sometimes was in danger of doing also in their own discussions of it—the profoundly eschatological cast of their doctrine about the resurrection and about what Macrina in her dying prayer called "the *metamorphosis,* through immortality and grace, of our mortal and unsightly remains." Therefore, it was an eschatological *theosis* that finally provided the justification for declaring: "I too am an image of God and of the heavenly glory." It likewise provided insight into the qualities conferred by the image, "such as incorruptibility and beatitude, the power to govern onself without a master and to lead a life devoid of grief and labor," which were now the subject only of "speculation and conjecture" rather than of empirical observation; for the image of God was conferred on man in the original creation, and "we did once share in this good that surpasses every power of perception." But except for the glimpses that natural theology could provide, all of that was knowable now only on the basis of "the restoration of its ancient form," which had to be read back into any depiction of the state of integrity from which man had since fallen through sin. Only through death, which was a sharing in the death of Christ, did this participation in God come. Therefore, Gregory of Nyssa's *Accurate Exposition of the Song of Songs,* which closed with the vision of "the unification of all mankind, joined in looking toward the same goal of their yearning," opened with the vision of a mankind that would, through the *metamorphosis* of Christ be "co-*metamorphosed*" with him by being "conformed to his *apatheia.*" The gift of *apatheia* was brought by the eschatological kingdom of God, whose coming was the subject of the plea of the second petition of the Lord's Prayer.

Macr.ap.Gr.Nyss. *V.Macr.*
(Jaeger 8–I:397)

Gr.Naz.*Or.*34.12
(*SC* 318:218)

Gr.Nyss.*Beat.*3
(*PG* 44:1225–28)

Bas.*Spir.*9.23
(*SC* 17:326–28)
Gr.Nyss.*Cant.*9
(Jaeger 6:290)

Gr.Nyss.*Cant.*15
(Jaeger 6:469)
Gr.Nyss.*Cant.*1
(Jaeger 6:14–15)
Gr.Nyss.*Or.dom.*3
(*PG* 44:1157)

Mt 6:10

Such "blessedness and *apatheia* and union with God and estrangement from evil and assimilation to the *kalokagathon* in its very being" constituted the form that humanity would receive when it had attained its *telos.* The vindication of *arete,* the fulfillment of hope, and the annihilation of evil were thus the component elements of the eschatological triumph of the good. "The *telos* of a life lived in accordance with *arete,*" in the formula of Gregory of Nyssa, was "assimilation to God," which, as has been noted earlier, was tantamount to *theosis.* But "*arete* as freedom from the fear of a taskmaster, the ability to choose the good by a voluntary act" was axiomatic, because God, as "the one true and

Gr.Nyss.*Cant.*1
(Jaeger 6:28–29)

Zemp 1970,177–96

Gr.Nyss.*Beat.*1
(*PG* 44:1200)

Gr.Nyss.*Or.dom.*3
(*PG* 44:1156)

Gr.Nyss.*Cant.*5
(Jaeger 6:160–61)

Gr.Nyss.*Or.dom.*5
(*PG* 44:1177)

Mt 6:12

Gr.Nyss.*Cant.*6
(Jaeger 6:186)

See pp.152–53,161–65

Gr.Nyss.*Cant.*4
(Jaeger 6:117)
Gr.Nyss.*V.Mos.*2
(Jaeger 7–I:143)

Gr.Naz.*Or.*17.2
(*PG* 35:968)

Bas.*Leg.lib.gent.*2
(Wilson 20)

Gr.Nyss.*V.Macr.*
(Jaeger 8–I:395)

Gr.Nyss.*Beat.*8
(*PG* 44:1301)

Gr.Nyss.*Beat.*7
(*PG* 44:1289)

Gr.Nyss.*V.Mos.*2
(Jaeger 7–I:59)

perfect power above all things and governing the whole universe," did "not rule by violence and tyrannical dictatorship." The life of *arete,* therefore, could reach its *telos* only if it was free of external constraint. Exercising itself by free will in this *arete,* it could attain to its goal. "It comes," according to Gregory of Nyssa, "to the very peak of *arete,* for the words of the [Lord's] Prayer outline what sort of a man one should be if one would approach God. Such a man is almost no longer shown in terms of human nature, but, through *arete,* is likened to God himself, so that he seems to be another God, in that he does the things that God alone can do," as, for example, to forgive sins. Human nature would not attain to this *telos* immediately, but gradually and by stages. For the very reason that a life of *arete* was by definition teleological, it involved a "progress [prokopē]" toward this *telos* and a "growth [epauxēsis]" that made it dynamic. "Teleology," which was the doctrine of the *telos,* was fulfilled in the achievement and gift of "teleiōsis," perfection. And "*telos,*" Nyssen explained in defining it, "I call that for the sake of which everything happens."

As "teleiōsis," perfection was, then, the *telos* and object of the eschatological hope. Gregory of Nazianzus called up all his rhetorical powers to describe in graphic terms what it meant to live without hope. For as Basil said in the very process of commending the study of Classical Greek literature, "Our hopes lead us forward to a more distant time, and everything we do is by way of preparation for the other life [pros heterou biou paraskeuēn]." It was this "hope of the resurrection [hē elpis tēs metastaseōs]" that sustained his sister, Macrina, on her deathbed. What were the "prize" and "crown" toward which this teleology moved? asked Gregory of Nyssa. And he answered: "It seems to me that what we hope for is nothing else than the Lord himself." The obverse side of this hope for the triumph of good was the annihilation of evil, or, as he called it earlier in the same commentary, "the annihilation of anything foreign to the good and devoid of affinity with the good." With his characteristic and consistent emphasis on the freedom of the will, Gregory insisted that the "darkness" and "fire" of "hell [geenna]," too, had to be the result of human "choice [proairesis]," not of divine necessity. That emphasis was not easy to square with his articulation of the hope for the eventual divine annihilation of evil: free will seemed to mean that a human being had to be able to choose evil, not only provisionally but permanently; and the annihilation of evil

Aufhauser 1910,205–7

2 Cor 5:10
Gr.Nyss.*Beat.*5
(*PG* 44:1260)

Gr.Nyss.*Or.catech.*8.10
(Méridier 56)

Macr.ap.Gr.Nyss.
Anim. res. (*PG* 46:72)

Macr.ap.Gr.Nyss.*Anim.
res.* (*PG* 46:100–101)

Phil 2:10–11
1 Cor 15:28

Zemp 1970,242–44

Capéran 1934

OED 11–III:243

Michaud 1902,37–52;
Daniélou 1940,328–47
Daniélou 1970,205–26

seemed to mean that God would finally exercise his sovereign authority over the powers of darkness. Gregory affirmed his agreement with the faith of the church "that all mankind will be presented before 'the tribunal of Christ,' so that each may receive what is due to him for his conduct in the body." But he did not want this to be interpreted as a "future judgment" that acted as "a threat and a harsh means of correction," which was how "the thoughtless" spoke of it. Rather, it was "a healing remedy provided by God, to restore his own creation to its original grace," which was how "the more thoughtful" saw it. Or, in the version of this hope that he attributed (whether accurately or not) to his sister, Macrina, "When evil shall have been someday annihilated in the long revolutions of the *aeons,* nothing will be left outside the world of the good, but even from those evil spirits shall rise in harmony [homophōnōs] the confession of Christ's divinity." Thus, she went on to say, evil would be annihilated through purgation. That was the promise of the New Testament: "That at the name of Jesus every knee shall bow—in heaven, on earth, and in the depths—and every tongue acclaim, 'Jesus Christ is Lord,' to the glory of God the Father." And again: "When all things are subject to him, then the Son himself will also be made subject to God who made all things subject to him, and thus God will be all in all."

In propounding that comprehensive and cosmic version of the Christian eschatological hope and of Christian teleology, Gregory of Nyssa (and, by his account, also his sister, Macrina) had to face the perennial question of the eventual salvation of all. The question was well summarized in the two distinct meanings of the English word "universalism" quoted earlier: "the fact or scope of being universal in character or scope," as when it is said that Christ "belongs to humanity, not to Israel"; and "the doctrine of universal salvation or redemption." As has been noted, universalism in the first sense was, for all the Cappadocians, a necessary implication of their entire theology, including their eschatology, and was indeed the ground for all of their natural theology. But what bearing did that have for universalism in the second sense? Gregory's special word for it was *apocatastasis,* which carried heavily Origenist connotations but was not simply identical with Origen's view. In the thought of Gregory of Nyssa it came as a corollary of his teleology, a teleology whose essentials he did share with the other Cappadocians. Gregory of Nazianzus identified a purpose in the creation of humanity: "We were cre-

Gr.Naz.*Or*.45.28
(*PG* 36:661)
Bas.*Hex*.5.4
(*SC* 26:292–94)

Macr.ap.Gr.Nyss.
Anim.res. (*PG* 46:105)
Macr.ap.Gr.Nyss.
Anim.res. (*PG* 46:152)

Gr.Nyss.*Cant*.10
(Jaeger 6:303–4);
Gr.Nyss.*Beat*.4
(*PG* 44:1240)

Jn 4:34
1 Tm 2:4
Gr.Nyss.*Ref*.16–17
(Jaeger 2:318–19)

Florovsky 7:211–19

Gr.Nyss.*Cant*.4
(Jaeger 6:131)

Gr.Nyss.*V.Mos*.2
(Jaeger 7–1:57)

Gr.Nyss.*Anim.res*.
(*PG* 46:160)

Otis 1958,97

Girardi 1978,183–90
Bas.*Mor*.1.1
(*PG* 31:700)

Bas.*Mor*.pr.1.8
(*PG* 31:672)

Ellversen 1981,82

Daley 1991,84
1 Cor 15:28
Althaus 1972,144–45

ated that we might be made happy. We were made happy when we were created." Again, Basil declared, "In creation nothing exists without a reason." There was, in Macrina's words, a "goal [skopos] towards which each single *economy* in the universe is moving." That goal she defined as "the transcendent good of the universe [to tou pantos hypereimenon]."

Specifying the biblical authority for his version of *apocatastasis* more precisely on the basis of this teleology, Gregory of Nyssa combined two passages from the New Testament: the words of Jesus, "For me it is meat and drink to do the will of him who sent me until I have finished his work"; and the words of Paul addressed to Timothy about "God our Savior, whose will it is that all should find salvation and come to know the truth." And he found the goal of human and cosmic history, the promise of eschatology and the fulfillment of teleology, in the final and total accomplishment of that universal salvific will, which Christ had come to carry out as his "meat and drink." To Gregory, this could mean nothing short of "*apocatastasis* after all these things in the kingdom of heaven." Or, in the words of Gregory and Macrina at the end of their dialogue, "Finally, when [evil] has been purged from it and utterly removed by the healing processes worked out by the fire, then every one of the things that make up our conception of the good will come to take its proper place: incorruption, that is, and life, and honor, and grace, and glory, and everything else that we conjecture was seen in God, and in his image, man as he was made."

In spite of what we have called, quoting Brooks Otis, "the agreement of thought among the three great Cappadocians" and "the real coherence of their doctrinal system," the Cappadocians did not treat the question of *apocatastasis* uniformly. At one end of the spectrum, Gregory's brother Basil left no room for so audacious a vision, warning: "In the *aeon* to come there will be a just judgment of retribution [antapodosis]." He could, he said, "see no forgiveness left at all, in connection with any of [God's] commands, for those who have not been converted from their infidelity, unless one dares to think that some other position— one that contradicts such bare, clear, and absolute statements— accords with the meaning [of Scripture]." Gregory of Nazianzus, in contrast, took the middle road between Basil and Gregory of Nyssa; as Brian E. Daley has put it, he offered "a cautious, undogmatic support of the Origenist position" on the hope for universal salvation. Quoting the words of Paul that "thus God will be all in all," he spoke of this as not only *theosis* but *apocatastasis*,

Gr.Naz.Or.30.6
(SC 250:238)

Macr.ap.Gr.Nyss.
Anim.res.(PG 46:160)

"when we are no longer what we are now, a multiplicity of impulses and emotions, with little or nothing of God in us, but are
fully like God, with room for God and God alone." And at the
other end of the spectrum (depending on how one reads the
treatise On the Soul and the Resurrection), Macrina shared her
brother Gregory's doctrine unequivocally, and dared to "take
some other position" from that of her brother Basil. Nevertheless, whatever the implicit and explicit differences among the
three (or four) of them may or may not have been, Gregory of
Nyssa did seem to be propounding apocatastasis as the only
possible expression for the eschatological hope that they all
shared, and indeed for the entire system of Cappadocian theology, both for the apologetics of their natural theology and for the
presuppositions and implications of their revealed theology.

GLOSSARY OF GREEK TECHNICAL TERMS

FROM SOURCES ANCIENT & MODERN

These words, italicized throughout the book, are here arranged according to the English alphabet. Most of them, either on their own or in compounds, have been domesticated as English words and have appeared in one or another English dictionary (although often with meanings quite different from these, as the word "economy" dramatically illustrates); and they are being spelled accordingly here—for example, "apocatastasis" rather than "apokatastasis"—and without diacritical marks. Geoffrey Lampe's *A Lexicon of Patristic Greek* is the standard authority to which to turn for all such terms, and I have relied on it throughout. But these additional quotations and definitions have been selected, and put into the form of a précis, from various other reference books or works of scholarship— Classical, Patristic, and modern. In such works, the various meanings of a term are often separated by quotations from primary sources and by similar material, but it seemed preferable in such précis as these to dispense with most of those quotations as well as with ellipsis points, and to adapt the punctuation.

Aeon   Age, era; "saeculum" in Latin, usually "world" in older English transla-
[αἰών]   tions. Bauer 17–28: "1. very long time, eternity—a. of time gone by, the earliest times, then eternity; b. of time to come which, if it has no end, is also known as eternity. 2. a segment of time, age—a. the present age (nearing its end); b. the age to come, the Messianic period. 3. the world as a spatial concept." Florovsky 7:209: "Gregory [of Nyssa] maintains a clear distinction between the terms *aeōnios* (from *aeon*) and 'aïdios' (from 'aei'). He never applies the second term to the torments [of hell] and he never applies the first term to bliss or the Deity. 'Aei' designates that which is superior to time or outside of time. It cannot be measured by the ages and it does not move within time. This is the sphere of the Divinity. Creation, however, abides within time and 'can be measured by the passing of the centuries.' *Aeon* designates temporality, that which occurs within time."

327

Ananke
[ἀνάγκη]

Necessity, determination. Arist.*Met.*1015a20–35: "We call *anankaion* (1) (a) that without which, as a condition, a thing cannot live; (b) the conditions without which the good cannot be or come to be, or without which we cannot get rid or be freed of evil. (2) The compulsory and compulsion, i.e. that which impedes and tends to hinder, contrary to impulse and purpose. For the compulsory is called *anankaion,* and compulsion is a form of *ananke.* And *ananke* is held to be something that cannot be persuaded— and rightly, for it is contrary to the movement which accords with purpose and with reasoning. (3) We say that that which cannot be otherwise is as it is by *ananke.* And from this sense of *anankaion* all the others are somehow derived."

Apatheia, apathes
[ἀπάθεια, ἀπαθής]

Impassibility, impassible; but despite the obvious etymological connection, not "apathy, apathetic," in the sense in which these terms are employed in modern English. Florovsky 3:88: "The *apatheia* of the Greeks is in general poorly understood and interpreted. It is not an indifference, not a cold insensibility of the heart. On the contrary, it is an active state, a state of spiritual activity, which is acquired only after struggles and ordeals. It is rather an independence from passions. Each person's own 'I' is finally regained, freeing oneself from fatal bondage. But one can regain onself only in God. True 'impassibility' is achieved only in an encounter with the Living God."

Apocatastasis
[ἀποκατάστασις]

Restoration, restitution. Bultmann 1957, 26 (Gifford Lectures): "Another modification of the myth [of the world-year] . . . abandons the idea of the eternal cyclical movement of world-years but retains the idea of the periodicity of the course of time. . . . A sign of this was the usage of the Greek word, *apokatastasis* (restoration). In astrological literature it refers to the periodical return of a star to its starting-point, and consequently the Stoic philosophers use the word for the return of the Cosmos at the end of a world-year to the origin from which a new world-year starts. But in the Acts of the Apostles (iii.21) and in later Christian language, following Origen, *apokatastasis* became a technical term of eschatology."

Apophasis
[ἀπόφασις];
Cataphasis
[κατάφασις]

Negation, negative; affirmation, affirmative. Meyendorff 11–12: "The whole of Byzantine theology—and particularly its 'experiential' character—would be completely misunderstood if one forgets its other pole of reference: *apophatic,* or negative, theology. Usually associated with the name of the mysterious sixth-century author of the *Areopagitica,* the form of *apophaticism* which will dominate Byzantine thought is, in fact, already fully developed in the fourth century in the writings of the Cappadocian fathers against Eunomios. Rejecting the Eunomian view that the human mind can reach the very essence of God, they affirm the absolute transcendence of God and exclude any possibility of identifying Him with any human concept. By saying what God is not, the theologian is really speaking the truth, for no human word or thought is capable of comprehending what God is. The Greek fathers affirm in their *apophatic* theology not only that God is above human language and reason because of man's fallen inadequacy, but that he is inaccessible in himself."

Arche
[ἀρχή]

Principle, beginning, ground of being; "principium" in Latin. Müller 153– 55: "I. Beginning, 1. of universal time; 2. of creation; 3. of the coming of

Christ and of the gospel; 4. any beginning at all. II. specifically, the beginning of existence: 1. as something that is a property of things that have been created; 2. attributed to the *Logos*-Son by the heretics, denied by the orthodox. III. Concretely, the first part of a thing, specifically the beginning of a book or of a passage taken from Scripture, etc. IV. The principal causes of things: 1. the elements of bodies; 2. by metonymy, God himself: a) the divine *Sophia*; b) the Father; c) the *Logos*; 3. in the trinitarian controversies, the *ousia* of the Father. V. In the political sense, rule: 1. the province of someone who rules; 2. the power of someone who rules; 3. public office; 4. by metonymy, in the plural, the celestial hierarchs."

Arete [ἀϱετή]	Excellence, valor; virtue. Jaeger 1939, 1:5: "We can find a natural clue to the history of Greek culture in the history of the idea of *arete*, which goes back to the earliest times. There is no complete equivalent for the word *arete* in modern English: its oldest meaning is a combination of proud and courtly morality with warlike valor. But the idea of *arete* is the quintessence of early Greek aristocratic education. In Homer, as elsewhere, the word *arete* is frequently used in a wide sense, to describe not only human merit but the excellence of non-human things—the power of the gods, the spirit and speed of noble horses. But ordinary men have no *arete*; and whenever slavery lays hold of the son of a noble race, Zeus takes away half of his *arete*—he is no longer the same man as he was. *Arete* is the real attribute of the nobleman. The root of the word is the same as that of 'aristos,' the word which shows superlative ability and superiority; and 'aristos' was constantly used in the plural to denote the nobility. It was natural for the Greeks, who ranked every man according to his ability, to use the same standard for the world in general. That is why they could apply the word *arete* to things and beings which were not human, and that is why the content of the word grew richer in later times."
Cataphasis [κατάφασις]	Affirmation. *See* Apophasis.
Economy [οἰκονομία]	*OED* 4–II:35: "The method of the divine government of the world, or of a specific department of portion of that government, especially: A 'dispensation,' a method or system of the divine government suited to the needs of a particular nation or period of time, as the Mosaic, Jewish, Christian economy." *See* Theology.
Heimarmene [εἰμαϱμένη]	Fate. *See* Tyche.
Homoousios [ὁμοούσιος]	One in being, of one substance. Prestige 1939, 197–219: "The original signification of *homoousios*, apart from all theological technicality, is simply 'made of the same stuff.' 'Stuff' here bears a generic sense, necessarily, since no objects of physical experience are composed of identical portions of matter; it really means 'kind of stuff.' The Nicene creed reaffirmed *homoousios* in the following terms: 'begotten of the Father, only-begotten, that is out of the *ousia* of the Father, God out of God . . . *homoousios* with the Father.' This word [the emperor Constantine] interpreted, stating that *homoousios* was not intended in the sense attaching to the conditions

of physical objects, nor as if the Son subsisted out of the Father by way of division or any sort of severance. The two sides are seen perfectly balanced in Athanasius' own mind; *homoousios* implies 'of one stuff' as against Arius, and 'of one content' as against the retort that thereby was implied the existence of two gods. The employment of *homoousios* by Athanasius to express substantial identity was a new development in the Greek language. Philologically, it was a pure accident, arising from the peculiar circumstances of the object to which the term was on other grounds applied; the special sense which it acquired was derived simply from theological associations, which belonged to the realm of thought rather than to that of language."

Hypostasis [ὑπόστασις]	*ODCC* 685: "The Greek word has had a variety of meanings. In popular language it was used originally for 'objective reality' as opposed to illusion. In the New Testament this seems to be roughly its meaning at Heb 1:3. It often came to be almost identical with *ousia,* i.e., to denote 'being' or 'substantial reality.' But side by side with this usage the term also came to mean 'individual reality' and, from the middle of the fourth cemtury onwards especially in Christological contexts, a 'person.' It was mainly under the influence of the Cappadocian Fathers that the terminology was clarified and standardized, and the theological ambiguities removed. From the Council of Constantinople of 381 onwards the formula 'three *hypostases* in one *ousia*' came to be everywhere accepted as an epitome of the orthodox doctrine of the Holy Trinity."
Kairos [καιρός]	Bauer 394–95: "Time, i.e., point of time as well as period of time: 1. generally, 'kairos dektos,' a welcome time; 'kairoi karpophoroi,' in which the tree bears fruit, in contrast to late autumn, when there is none. 2. the right, proper, favorable time. 3. one of the chief eschatological terms: 'ho kairos,' the time of crisis, the last times."
Kalos, to kalon, kalokagathia [καλός, τὸ καλόν, καλοκαγαθία]	Nussbaum 1990, xiii: "*Kalon* is a word that signifies at once beauty and nobility. It can be either aesthetic or ethical and is usually both at once, showing how hard it is to distinguish these spheres in Greek thought."
Logos [λόγος]	Word, reason: as qualities of the human mind, but originally and eternally as the personal Word and Reason of God, the second *hypostasis* of the Trinity. Jn 1:1–14: "In the beginning the *Logos* already was. The *Logos* was in God's presence, and what God was, the *Logos* was. He was with God at the beginning, and through him all things came to be; without him no created thing came into being. In him was life, and that life was the light of mankind. The light shines in the darkness, and the darkness has never mastered it. The true light was in being, which gives light to everyone entering the world. So the *Logos* became flesh; he made his home among us, and we saw his glory, such glory as befits the Father's only Son, full of grace and truth."
Metamorphosis [μεταμόρφωσις]	Transformation; the transfiguration of Christ, as event (Mt 17:1–9; Mk 9:2–10; Lk 9:28–36; 2 Pet 1:16–18), and then as paradigm for the transformation of human nature through *theosis.* Jo.D.*Trans.* (*PG* 96:545–76):

"Continuing in the majesty of his own deity, he takes the meaner nature upon himself, granting *theosis* to humanity. We do not glory in the *sophia* of Hellenism, [but in him who declared]: 'My heavenly Father has revealed to you this divine and ineffable *theology*.' What divine and ineffable realities! He became flesh, the almighty *sophia* and power of God. On Mount Tabor, taking with him those who were preeminent in *arete,* he underwent transfiguration-*metamorphosis* in their presence. Thus in the *aeon* to come we shall be forever with the Lord, receiving transfiguration-*metamorphosis* from glory to glory [from] the Lord of the living and the dead, who has been transfigured."

Ousia
[οὐσία]

Essence, being, as a concept in metaphysics, but, preeminently here, as a designation of the One in the divine Trinity. Prestige 1939, 188: "To sum up briefly the relations of *hypostasis* and *ousia,* it may be said first that they are often, for practical purposes, equivalent. Nevertheless, they are probably never strictly identical in meaning, except in the Western instances in which *hypostasis* may be regarded as a literal representation of the Latin 'substantia.' Both *hypostasis* and *ousia* describe positive, substantial existence, that is, that which subsists: 'to on, to hyphestēkos.' But *ousia* tends to regard internal characteristics and relations, or metaphysical reality, while *hypostasis* regularly emphasizes the externally concrete character of the substance, or empirical objectivity. Hence, with regard to the Trinity, it never sounded unnatural to assert three *hypostases,* but it was always unnatural to proclaim three *ousiai.*"

Paideia, Paideusis
[παιδεία, παίδευσις]

Education, culture. Jaeger 1939, 1:303: "The meaning of education ('paideuein') was extended beyond the training of children 'paides') to the education of young men in particular, so as to encourage the belief that education might extend throughout the whole of life. Suddenly the Greeks realized that grown men too could have *paideia*. Originally the concept *paideia* had applied only to the process of education. Now its significance grew to include the objective side, the content of *paideia*—just as our word 'culture' or the Latin 'cultura,' having once meant the process of education, came to mean the state of being educated; and then the content of education, and finally the whole intellectual and spiritual world revealed by education, into which any individual, according to his nationality or social position, is born. The historical process by which the world of culture is built up culminates when the ideal of culture is consciously formulated. Accordingly it was perfectly natural for the Greeks in and after the fourth century [B.C.], when the concept finally crystallized, to use the word *paideia*—in English, 'culture'—to describe all the artistic forms and the intellectual and aesthetic achievements of their race, in fact the whole content of their tradition."

Sophia
[σοφία]

Wisdom, often personified as divine Wisdom and identified with *Logos*. Wis 7:22–30: "I was taught by *Sophia,* by her whose skill made all things. In *Sophia* there is a spirit intelligent and holy. She is the radiance that streams from everlasting light, the flawless mirror of the active power of God, and the image of his goodness. She is but one, yet can do all things; herself unchanging, she makes all things new; age after age she enters into holy souls, and makes them friends of God and prophets, for nothing is acceptable to God but the person who makes his home with *Sophia*."

Stoicheia   Elements, alphabet; thus, what is "elemental," as well as what is "elemen-
[στοιχεῖα]   tary." Pl.*Tim.* 48b: "We must consider in itself the nature of fire and water, air and earth, before the generation of the heaven, and their condition [pathē] before the heaven was. For to this day no one has explained their generation, but we speak as if men knew what fire and each of the others is, positing them as *archai, stoicheia* (as it were, letters) of the universe, whereas one who has ever so little intelligence should not rank them in this analogy even so low as syllables."

Techne   Skill, art, craft, discipline. Arist.*EN*.1140a7–17: "Since architecture is a
[τέχνη]   *techne* and is essentially a reasoned state of capacity to make, there is neither any *techne* that is not such a state nor any such state that is not a *techne*. Therefore *techne* is identical with a state of capacity to make, involving a true course of reasoning. All *techne* is concerned with coming into being, i.e., with contriving and considering how something may come into being which is capable of either being or not being, and whose origin is in the maker and not in the thing made; for *techne* is concerned neither with things that are, or come into being, by *ananke,* nor with things that do so in accordance with nature (since these have their origin in themselves). Making and acting being different, *techne* must be a matter of making, not of acting."

Telos   End, goal, achievement, final cause; and, as "teleiōsis," perfection in the
[τέλος]   attainment of the goal. Arist.*Met*.994b9–13: "The final cause is a *telos,* and that sort of *telos* which is not for the sake of something else, but for whose sake everything else is; so that if there is to be a last term of this sort, the process will not be infinite; but if there is no such term, there will be no final cause, but those who maintain the infinite series eliminate the good without knowing it." Arist.*EN*.1094a18–22: "If there is some *telos* of the things we do, which we desire for its own sake (everything else being desired for the sake of this), and if we do not choose everything for the sake of something else, clearly this must be the good and the chief good."

Theology   As distinct from *economy* (in addition to its more general use [indicated
[θεολογία]   here by the absence of italics] to designate any orderly reflection about divine things, whether natural or revealed). *OED* 11-I:275: "Greek 'theologia' meant 'an account of the gods, or of God (whether legendary or philosophical).' In Christian Greek, the verb 'theologein' was used [as equivalent to] 'to speak of as God, to attribute deity to,' whence *theologia* had the specific sense of 'the ascription of a divine nature to Christ,' in contrast to *oikonomia,* the doctrine of his incarnation and human nature."

Theosis   Deification, divinization. Meyendorff 163–64: "Christ's humanity is pene-
[θέωσις]   trated with divine 'energy.' It is, therefore, a *deified* humanity, which, however, does not in any way lose its human characteristics. Quite to the contrary. These characteristics become even more real and authentic by contact with the divine model according to which they were created. In this deified humanity of Christ's, man is called to participate, and to share

in its deification. This is the meaning of sacramental life and the basis of Christian spirituality." Florovsky 3:240: "Christians, as Christians, aspire to something greater than a 'natural' immortality. They aspire to an everlasting communion with God, or, to use the startling phrase of the early Fathers, to a *theosis.*"

Tyche [τύχη]
Chance, luck; "fortuna" in Latin. Jo.D.*F.o.*2.25 (*PG* 94:957): "Of all the things that happen, the cause is said to be either God, or *ananke,* or *heimarmene,* or nature [physis], or *tyche,* or accident [to automaton]. But God's function has to do with *ousia* and providence; *ananke* deals with the movement of things that ever keep to the same course; *heimarmene* with the necessary accomplishment of the things it brings to pass (for *heimarmene* itself implies *ananke*); nature with birth, growth, destruction, plants and animals; *tyche* with what is rare and unexpected. For *tyche* is defined as the meeting and concurrence of two causes, originating in choice but bringing to pass something other than what is natural."

BIBLIOGRAPHY

Ackermann, Walter. 1903. *Die dikaktische Poesie des Gregorius von Nazianz*. Leipzig: Gustav Fock.

Adam, James. 1908. *The Religious Teachers of Greece*. Gifford Lectures at Aberdeen 1904/06. Aberdeen: University of Aberdeen.

Albertz, Martin. 1908. *Untersuchungen über die Schriften des Eunomius*. Wittenberg: Herrosé und Ziemsen.

———. 1909. "Zur Geschichte der jung-arianischen Kirchengemeinschaft." *Theologische Studien und Kritiken* 82:205–78.

Alexander, Samuel. 1920. *Space, Time, and Deity*. Gifford Lectures at Glasgow 1916/18. 2 vols. London: Macmillan.

Allard, Paul. *Saint Basile*. 1903. 8th ed. Paris: J. Gabalda.

Altaner, Berthold. 1950. "Augustinus und Basilius der Grosse: Eine quellenkritische Untersuchung." *Revue Bénédictine* 60:17–24.

———. 1951. "Augustinus, Gregor von Nazianz und Gregor von Nyssa: Quellenkritische Untersuchungen." *Revue Bénédictine* 61:54–62.

Althaus, Heinz. 1972. *Die Heilslehre des heiligen Gregor von Nazianz*. Münster: Aschendorff.

Amand de Mendieta, Emmanuel. 1949. *L'ascèse monastique de saint Basile de Césarée: Essai historique*. Maredsous: Editions de Maredsous.

———. 1965. *The "Unwritten" and "Secret" Apostolic Traditions in the Theological Thought of St. Basil of Caesarea*. Edinburgh: Oliver and Boyd.

———. 1973. *Fatalisme et liberté dans l'antiquité grecque: Recherches sur la survivance de l'argumentation morale antifataliste de Carnéade chez les philosophes grecs et les théologiens chrétiens des quatre premiers siècles*. Amsterdam: A. M. Hakkert.

Ameringer, Thomas Edward. 1921. *The Stylistic Influence of the Second Sophistic on the Panegyrical Sermons of St. John Chrysostom: A Study in Greek Rhetoric.* Washington, D.C.: Catholic University of America Press.

Antoniadis, Sophie. 1939. *Place de la liturgie dans la tradition des lettres grecques.* Leiden: A. W. Sijthoff.

Apostolopoulos, Charalambos. 1986. *Phaedo Christianus: Studien zur Verbindung und Abwägung des Verhältnisses zwischen dem platonischen "Phaidon" und dem Dialog Gregors von Nyssa "Über die Seele und die Auferstehung."* Frankfurt: Lang.

Armstrong, A. Hilary. 1948. "Platonic Elements in St. Gregory of Nyssa's Doctrine of Man." *Dominican Studies* 1:113–26.

———. 1984. "The Way and the Ways: Religious Tolerance and Intolerance in the Fourth Century A.D." *Vigiliae Christianae* 38:1–17.

———. 1985. "The Escape of the One: An Investigation of Some Possibilities of Apophatic Theology Imperfectly Realised in the West." *Studia Patristica* 13–II:77–89.

Arnou, René. 1934. "Unité numérique et unité de nature chez les pères après le Concile de Nicée." *Gregorianum* 15:242–54.

Asmus, Johann Rudolf. 1894. "Gregor von Nazianz und sein Verhältnis zum Kynismus: Eine patristisch-philosophische Studie." *Theologische Studien und Kritiken* 67: 314–38.

———. 1904. *Julians Galiläerschrift im Zusammenhang mit seinen übrigen Werken: Ein Beitrag zur Erklärung und Kritik der julianischen Schriften.* Freiburg im Breisgau: U. Hochreuther.

———. 1910. "Die Invektiven des Gregorius von Nazianz im Lichte der Werke des Kaisers Julian." *Zeitschrift für Kirchengeschichte* 31:325–67.

Athanassiadi-Fowden, Polymnia. 1981. *Julian and Hellenism: An Intellectual Biography.* Oxford: Clarendon Press.

Aubineau, Michel. 1956. "Incorruptibilité et divinisation selon Irénée." *Recherches de science religieuse* 44:25–52.

Aufhauser, Johannes Baptist. 1910. *Die Heilslehre des hl. Gregor von Nyssa.* Munich: J. J. Lentner (E. Stahl).

Aulén, Gustaf. 1969. *Christus Victor: An Historical Study of the Three Main Types of the Idea of Atonement.* Translated by A. G. Hebert. Reprinted with an introduction by Jaroslav Pelikan. New York: Macmillan.

Backus, Irénée. 1990. *Lectures humanistes de Basile de Césarée: Traductions latines (1439–1619).* Paris: Etudes Augustiniennes.

Balás, David L. 1966. *Metousia theou: Man's Participation in God's Perfections according to St. Gregory of Nyssa.* Rome: Studia Anselmiana.

Balthasar, Hans Urs von. 1942. *Présence et pensée: Essai sur la philosophie religieuse de Grégoire de Nysse.* Paris: G. Beauchesne.

Barbel, Joseph, ed. 1963. *Gregor von Nazianz: Die fünf theologischen Reden. Text und Übersetzung mit Einleitung und Kommentar.* Düsseldorf: Patmos-Verlag.

———. 1971. *Die grosse katechetische Rede: Oratio catechetica magna von Gregor von Nyssa.* Stuttgart: A. Hiersemann.

Barrois, Georges A., ed. 1986. *The Fathers Speak: St Basil the Great, St Gregory of Nazianzus, St Gregory of Nyssa.* Foreword by John Meyendorff. Crestwood, NY: St. Vladimir's Seminary Press.

Bartelink, Gerhardus Johannes Marinus. 1960. " 'Philosophie' et 'philosophe' dans quelque oeuvres de Jean Chrysostome." *Revue d'ascétique et de mystique* 36:486–92.

Barth, Karl. 1938. *The Knowledge of God and the Service of God according to the Teaching of the Reformation: Recalling the Scottish Confession of 1560.* Gifford Lectures at Aberdeen 1937/38. Translated by J. L. M. Haire and Ian Henderson. London: Hodder and Stoughton.

Batiffol, Pierre-Henri. 1922. "L'ecclésiologie de saint Basile." *Echos d'Orient* 21:9–30.

Bauer, Johannes. 1892. *Die Trostreden des Gregorios von Nyssa in ihrem Verhältnis zur antiken Rhetorik.* Marburg: J. A. Koch.

Bayer, Johannes. 1935. *Gregors v. Nyssa Gottesbegriff.* Giessen: R. Glagow.

Beck, Hans-Georg. 1959. *Kirche und theologische Literatur im byzantinischen Reich.* Munich: C. H. Beck'sche Verlagsbuchhandlung.

Bernard, Régis. 1952. *L'image de Dieu d'après saint Athanase.* Paris: Aubier.

Bernardi, Jean. 1968. *La prédication des pères cappadociens: Le prédicateur et son auditoire.* Montpellier: Presses universitaires de France.

Bethune-Baker, James Franklin. 1901. *The Meaning of Homoousios in the "Constantinopolitan" Creed.* Cambridge: Cambridge University Press.

Bevan, Edwyn Robert. 1940. *Holy Images: An Inquiry into Idolatry and Image-Worship in Ancient Paganism and in Christianity.* Gifford Lectures at Edinburgh 1934. London: George Allen and Unwin.

Bidez, Joseph. 1938. "Le traité d'astrologie cité par saint Basile dans son Hexaéméron." *Antiquité classique* 7:19–21.

———. 1945. *Eos; ou, Platon et l'Orient.* Gifford Lectures at St. Andrews 1938/39. Brussels: M. Hayez.

Bjerge-Aspergen, Kerstin. 1977. *Bräutigam, Sonne und Mutter: Studien zu einigen Gottesmetaphern bei Gregor von Nyssa.* Lund: n.p.

Blond, Georges. 1944. "L' 'hérésie' encratite vers la fin du quatrième siècle (chez Basile)." *Recherches de science religieuse* 32:157–210.

Boer, S. de. 1968. *De anthropologie van Gregorius van Nyssa.* Assen: Van Gorcum.

Braun, René. 1978. "Julien et le christianisme." In *L'empereur Julien: De l'histoire à la légende (331–1715),* 159–88. Edited by René Braun and Jean Richer. Paris: Société d'édition "Les Belles Lettres."

Bréhier, Emile. 1958. *The Philosophy of Plotinus.* Translated by Joseph Thomas. Chicago: University of Chicago Press.

Bring, Ragnar. 1929. *Dualismen hos Luther.* Lund: H. Ohlsson.

Brooks, James A. 1991. *The New Testament Text of Gregory of Nyssa.* Atlanta: Scholars Press.

Brown, Peter Robert Lamont. 1978. *The Making of Late Antiquity.* Cambridge, Mass.: Harvard University Press.

———. 1988. *The Body and Society: Men, Women, and Sexual Renunciation in Early Christianity.* New York: Columbia University Press.

Browning, Robert. 1975. "Homer in Byzantium." *Viator* 6:15–33.

Bruce, Alexander Balmain. 1899. *The Moral Order of the World in Ancient and Modern Thought.* Gifford Lectures at Glasgow 1898. New York: Charles Scribner's Sons.

Brunner, Emil. 1939. *Man in Revolt: A Christian Anthropology.* Translated by Olive Wyon. London: Lutterworth Press.

Buckley, Michael J. 1987. *At the Origins of Modern Atheism.* New Haven: Yale University Press.

Bultmann, Rudolf. 1948. "Zur Geschichte der Lichtsymbolik im Altertum." *Philologus* 97:1–36.

———. 1953. *Theologie des Neuen Testaments.* Tübingen: J. C. B. Mohr (Paul Siebeck).

———. 1957. *History and Eschatology.* Gifford Lectures at Edinburgh 1954/55. Edinburgh: University Press.

Burrell, David. 1973. *Analogy and Philosophical Language.* New Haven: Yale University Press.

———. 1991. "Naming God among Jews, Christians, and Muslims." *James I. McCord Memorial Lectures Fall 1990,* 20–34. Princeton: Center of Theological Inquiry.

Bury, John Bagnell. 1958. *History of the Later Roman Empire.* 2 vols. Reprint edition. New York: Dover.

Büttner, Georg. 1908. *Basileios des Grossen Mahnworte an die Jugend über den nützlichen Gebrauch der heidnischen Literatur: Eine Quellenuntersuchung.* Munich: H. Kutzner.

———. 1912–13. *Beiträge zur Ethik Basileios' des Groszen.* Landshut: Humanistisches Gymnasium.

Caird, Edward. 1904. *The Evolution of Theology in the Greek Philosophers.* Gifford Lec-

tures at Glasgow 1900/1902. 2 vols.
Glasgow: James MacLehose and Sons.

Callahan, John F. 1948. *Four Views of Time in Ancient Philosophy.* Cambridge, MA: Harvard University Press.

———. 1958a. "Basil of Caesarea: A New Source for St. Augustine's Theory of Time." *Harvard Studies in Classical Philology* 63:437–54.

———. 1958b. "Greek Philosophy and the Cappadocian Cosmology." *Dumbarton Oaks Papers* 12:29–57.

Camelot, Thomas, ed. 1947. *Athanase: Contre les païens et Sur l'incarnation du Verbe.* Paris: Editions du Cerf.

———. 1966. "Amour des lettres et désir de Dieu chez saint Grégoire de Nazianze: Les *logoi* au service du *Logos*." *Littérature et religion,* supplement to *Mélanges de science religieuse* 22:22–30.

Campbell, James Marshall. 1922. *The Influence of the Second Sophistic on the Style of the Sermons of St. Basil the Great.* Washington, D.C.: Catholic University of America Press.

Campbell, Lewis. 1898. *Religion in Greek Literature: A Sketch in Outline.* Gifford Lectures at St. Andrews 1894/96. New York: Longmans, Green.

Capéran, Louis. 1934. *Le problème du salut des infidèles.* 2d ed. 2 vols. Toulouse: Grand séminaire.

Carol, Juniper B., ed. 1954–61. *Mariology.* 3 vols. Milwaukee: Bruce Publishing.

Cavallin, Anders. 1944. *Studien zu den Briefen des hl. Basilius.* Lund: C. W. K. Gleerup.

Cavarnos, John P. 1955. "Gregory of Nyssa on the Nature of the Soul." *Greek Orthodox Theological Review* 1:133–41.

Cazeaux, Jacques. 1980. *Les échos de la sophistique authour de Libanios; ou, Le style "simple" dans un traité de Basile de Césarée.* Paris: Société d'édition "Les Belles Lettres."

Cesaro, Maria. 1929. "Natura e cristianesimo negli 'Exameron' di san Basilio e di sant' Ambrogio." *Didaskaleion: Studi di letteratura e storia cristiana antica,* n.s., 7–I:53–123.

Chadwick, Henry. 1966. *Early Christian Thought and the Classical Tradition: Studies in Justin, Clement, and Origen.* New York: Oxford University Press.

Cherniss, Harold Fredrik. 1930. *The Platonism of Gregory of Nyssa.* Berkeley: University of California Publications in Classical Philology.

Clark, Elizabeth A. 1977. *Clement's Use of Aristotle: The Aristotelian Contribution to Clement of Alexandria's Refutation of Gnosticism.* New York: Edwin Mellen Press.

Clark, Stephen R. L. 1984. *From Athens to Jerusalem: The Love of Wisdom and the Love of God.* Gifford Lectures at Glasgow 1981/82. Oxford: Clarendon Press.

Clarke, W. K. Lowther. 1913. *St. Basil the Great: A Study in Monasticism.* Cambridge: Cambridge University Press.

Cochrane, Charles Norris. 1944. *Christianity and Classical Culture: A Study of Thought and Action from Augustus to Augustine.* London: Oxford University Press.

Cooke, John Daniel. 1927. "Euhemerism: A Mediaeval Interpretation of Classical Paganism." *Speculum* 2:396–410.

Copleston, Frederick Charles. 1982. *Religion and the One: Philosophies East and West.* Gifford Lectures at Aberdeen 1979/81. London: Search Press.

Cornford, Francis MacDonald. 1957. *Plato's Cosmology: The "Timaeus" of Plato Translated with a Running Commentary.* Reprint edition. New York: Liberal Arts Press.

Coulie, Bernard. 1983. "Méthode d'amplification par citation d'auteurs dans les Discours IV et V de Grégoire de Nazianze." In *Symposium Nazianzenum,* 42–46. Edited by Justin Mossay. Paderborn: Ferdinand Schöningh.

———. 1985. *Les richesses dans l'oeuvre de Saint Grégoire de Nazianze: Etude littéraire et historique.* Louvain: Université catholique.

Courcelle, Pierre. 1967. "Grégoire de Nysse, lecteur de Porphyre." *Revue des études grecques* 80:402–6.

Courtonne, Yves. 1934. *Saint Basile et l'hellénisme: Etude sur la rencontre de la pensée chrétienne avec la sagesse antique dans l'Hexaméron de Basile le Grand.* Paris: Typographie Firmin-Didot.

Cross, Frank Leslie. 1945. *The Study of Athanasius.* Oxford: Clarendon Press.

Crouzel, Henri. 1955. *Théologie de l'image chez Origène.* Paris: Aubier.

———. 1957. "Grégoire de Nysse est-il le fondateur de la théologie mystique? Une controverse récente." *Revue d'ascétique et de mystique* 33:189–202.

Cumont, Franz. 1960. *Astrology and Religion among the Greeks and Romans.* 1912. Reprint edition. New York: Dover.

Cushman, Robert E. 1981. *Faith Seeking Understanding: Essays Theological and Critical.* Durham: Duke University Press.

Daley, Brian E. 1991. *The Hope of the Early Church: A Handbook of Patristic Eschatology.* Cambridge: Cambridge University Press.

Daniélou, Jean. 1940. "L'apocatastase chez Grégoire de Nysse." *Recherches de science religieuse* 30:328–47.

———. 1944. *Platonisme et théologie mystique: Essai sur la doctrine spirituelle de saint Grégoire de Nysse.* Paris: Aubier.

———. 1951. "Le mystère du culte dans les sermons de saint Grégoire de Nysse." *Vom christlichen Mysterium: Festschrift Odo Casel,* 76–93. Edited by Anton Mayer, Johannes Quasten, and Burkhard Neunheuser. Düsseldorf: Patmos-Verlag.

———. 1953a. "Akolouthia chez Grégoire de Nysse." *Recherches de science religieuse* 27:219–49.

———. 1953b. "La résurrection des corps chez Grégoire de Nysse." *Vigiliae Christianae* 7:154–70.

———. 1955. "Moïse exemple et figure chez Grégoire de Nysse." *Cahiers sioniens* 2–4:386–400.

———. 1956. "Le mariage de Grégoire de Nysse et la chronologie de sa vie." *Revue des études Augustiniennes* 2:71–78.

———. 1957. *God and the Ways of Knowing.* Translated by Walter Roberts. New York: Meridian Books.

———. 1960. *From Shadows to Reality: Studies in the Biblical Typology of the Fathers.* Translated by Dom Wulstan Hibberd. Westminster, Md.: Newman Press.

———. 1964. *The Theology of Jewish Christianity.* Translated by John A. Baker. London: Darton, Longman and Todd.

———. 1970. *L'être et le temps chez Grégoire de Nysse.* Leiden: E. J. Brill.

Delehaye, Hippolyte. 1921. "Cyprien d'Antioche et Cyprien de Carthage." *Analecta Bollandiana* 39:314–32.

Dehnhard, Hans. 1964. *Das Problem der Abhängigkeit des Basilius von Plotin: Quellenuntersuchungen zu seinen Schriften "De Spiritu Sancto."* Berlin: W. de Gruyter.

Des Places, Edouard. 1964. *Syngeneia: La parenté de l'homme avec Dieu d'Homère à la patristique.* Paris: Librairie C. Klincksieck.

Diekamp, Franz. 1896. *Die Gotteslehre des heiligen Gregor von Nyssa: Ein Beitrag zur Dogmengeschichte der patristischen Zeit.* Münster: Aschendorff.

———. 1899. *Die origenistischen Streitigkeiten im sechsten Jahrhundert und das fünfte allgemeine Concil.* Münster: Aschendorff.

———. 1909. "Literaturgeschichtliches zur Eunomianischen Kontroverse." *Byzantinische Zeitschrift* 18:1–13, 190–94.

Dirking, Augustinus. 1911. *S. Basilli Magni de divitiis et paupertate sententiae quam habeant rationem cum veterum philosophorum doctrina: Commentatio philosophica.* Münster: Aschendorff.

———. 1954. "Die Bedeutung des Wortes Apathie beim hl. Basilius dem Grossen." *Theologische Quartalschrift* 134:202–12.

Dix, Gregory. 1953. *Jew and Greek: A Study in the Primitive Church.* London: Dacre Press.

Dölger, Franz. 1932. "Das Anhängekreuzchen der hl. Makrina und ihr Ring mit der Kreuzpartikel: Ein Beitrag zur religiösen Volkskunde des 4. Jahrhunderts nach der *Vita Macrinae* des Gregor von Nyssa." *Antike und Christentum* 3:81–116.

———. 1936. "Lumen Christi." *Antike und Christentum* 5-I:1–43.

Donders, Adolf. 1909. *Der hl. Kirchenlehrer Gregor von Nazianz als Homilet.* Münster: Druck der Westfälischen Vereinsdruckerei.

Dörrie, Heinrich, Margarete Altenburger, and Uta Schramm, eds. 1976. *Gregor von Nyssa und die Philosophie.* Leiden: E. J. Brill.

Dörries, Hermann. 1954. "Christlicher Humanismus und mönchische Geist-Ethik." *Theologische Literaturzeitung* 79:643–56.

———. 1956. *De Spiritu Sancto: Der Beitrag des Basilius zum Abschluss des trinitarischen Dogmas.* Göttingen: Vandenhoeck und Ruprecht.

Downey, Glanville. 1957. "Themistius and the Defense of Hellenism in the Fourth Century." *Harvard Theological Review* 50:259–74.

———. 1957–58. "Julian and the Schools." *Classical Journal* 53:97–103.

Dräseke, Johannes. 1892a. *Apollinaris von Laodicea.* Leipzig: J. C. Hinrichs, 1892.

———. 1892b. "Gregorios von Nazianz und sein Verhältnis zum Apollinarismus." *Theologische Studien und Kritiken* 65:473–512.

———. 1906. "Neuplatonisches in des Gregorios von Nazianz Trinitätslehre." *Byzantinische Zeitschrift* 15:141–60.

———. 1907. "Zu Gregorios von Nyssa." *Zeitschrift für Kirchengeschichte* 28:387–400.

Dubedout, Ernestus. 1901. *De D. Gregorii Nazianzeni carminibus.* Paris: Apud Ch. Poussielgue.

Dunstone, Alan Sidney. 1964. *The Atonement in Gregory of Nyssa.* London: Tyndale Press.

Dvornik, Francis. 1955. "The Emperor Julian's 'Reactionary' Ideas on Kingship." In *Late Classical and Mediaeval Studies in Honor of Albert Matthias Friend, Jr.,* 71–80. Edited by Kurt Weitzmann. Princeton: Princeton University Press.

Edsmann, Carl-Martin. 1939. "Schöpferwille und Geburt Jac 1,18: Eine Studie zur altchristlichen Kosmologie." *Zeitschrift für die neutestamentliche Wissenschaft und die Kunde der alten Kirche* 38:11–44.

Ellverson, Anna-Stina. 1981. *The Dual Nature of Man: A Study in the Theological Anthropology of Gregory of Nazianzus.* Uppsala: Almkvist and Wiksell.

Elert, Werner. 1957. *Der Ausgang der altkirchlichen Christologie: Eine Untersuchung über Theodor von Pharan und seine Zeit als Einführung in die alte Dogmengeschichte.* Edited by Wilhelm Maurer and Elisabeth Bergsträszer. Berlin: Lutherisches Verlagshaus.

Eriau, Jean-Baptiste. 1914. *Pourquoi les pères de l'église ont condamné le théâtre de leur temps.* Paris: H. Champion.

Ernst, Viktor. 1896. "Basilius' des Grossen Verkehr mit den Occidentalen." *Zeitschrift für Kirchengeschichte* 16:626–64.

Ettlinger, Gerard H. 1985. "'Theos de ouch houtōs' (Gregory of Nazianzus, *Oratio* xxxvii): The Dignity of the Human Person according to the Greek Fathers." *Studia Patristica* 16-II:368–72.

Eynde, Damien van den. 1933. *Les normes de l'enseignement chrétien dans la littérature patristique des trois premiers siècles.* Paris: Gabalds et fils.

Fabricius, Caius. 1962. *Zu den Jugendschriften des Johannes Chrysostomos: Untersuchungen zum Klassizismus des vierten Jahrhunderts.* Lund: C. W. K. Gleerup.

Fairbairn, Andrew Martin. 1902. *The Philosophy of the Christian Religion.* Gifford Lectures at Aberdeen 1891/93. New York: Macmillan.

Faller, Otto. 1925. "Griechische Vergottung und christliche Vergöttlichung." *Gregorianum* 6:405–35.

Farnell, Lewis Richard. 1921. *Greek Hero Cults and Ideas of Immortality.* Gifford Lectures at St. Andrews 1919. Oxford: Clarendon Press.

Fedwick, Paul Jonathan. 1978. *The Church and the Charisma of Leadership in Basil of Caesarea.* Toronto: Pontifical Institute of Mediaeval Studies.

Fedwick, Paul Jonathan, ed. 1981. *Basil of Caesarea: Christian, Humanist, Ascetic.* 2 vols. Toronto: Pontifical Institute of Mediaeval Studies.

Fennema, D. A. 1985. "John 1:18: 'God the Only Son.'" *New Testament Studies* 31:124–35.

Field, Frederick, ed. 1875. *Origenis Hexaplorum quae supersunt.* 2 vols. Oxford: Clarendon Press.

Flesseman-Van Leer, Ellen. 1953. *Tradition and Scripture in the Early Church.* Assen: Van Gorum.

Fleury, Eugène. 1930. *Hellénisme et christianisme: Saint Grégoire de Nazianze et son temps.* 2d ed. Paris: G. Beauschesne.

Floeri, F. 1953. "Le sens de la division des sexes chez Grégoire de Nysse." *Recherches de science religieuse* 27:105–11.

Fox, Margaret Mary. 1939. *The Life and Times of St. Basil the Great as Revealed in His Works.* Washington, D.C.: Catholic University of America Press.

Freeland, John. 1902. "St. Gregory Nazianzen, from His Letters." *Dublin Review* 130:333–54.

Gaïth, Jérôme. 1953. *La conception de la liberté chez Grégoire de Nysse.* Paris: J. Vrin.

Gallay, Paul. 1933. *Langue et style de Saint Grégoire de Nazianze dans sa correspondance.* Paris: J. Monnier.

Galtier, Paul. 1946. *Le Saint-Esprit en nous d'après les pères grecs.* Rome: Analecta Gregoriana.

Geffcken, Johannes. 1907. *Zwei griechische Apologeten.* Leipzig and Berlin: B. G. Teubner.

———. 1908. *Sokrates und das alte Christentum.* Heidelberg: C. Winter.

———. 1909. *Kynika und Verwandtes.* Heidelberg: C. Winter.

Geoghegan, Arthur T. 1945. *The Attitude towards Labor in Early Christianity and Ancient Culture.* Washington, D.C.: Catholic University of America Press.

Geyer, Bernhard. 1960. *Die patristische und scholastische Philosophie.* 11th ed. 1927. Reprint edition. Basel: Benno Schwabe.

Ghellinck, Joseph de. 1930. "Quelques appréciations de la dialectique et d'Aristote durant les conflits trinitaires du IVe siècle." *Revue d'histoire ecclésiastique* 26:5–42.

Gibbon, Edward. 1776–88. *The History of the Decline and Fall of the Roman Empire.* Edited by J. B. Bury. 7 vols. London: Methuen, 1896–1900.

Giet, Stanislas. 1941a. *Les idées et l'action sociales de saint Basile.* Paris: Lecoffre, J. Gabalda.

———. 1941b. *Sasimes: Une méprise de Saint Basile.* Paris: Lecoffre, J. Gabalda.

———. 1944. "De saint Basil à saint Ambroise: La condemnation du prêt à intérêt au IVe siècle." *Recherches de science religieuse* 32:95–128.

———. 1948. "La doctrine de l'appropriation des biens chez quelques-uns des pères." *Recherches de science religieuse* 35:55–91.

Gillet, R. 1962. "L'homme divinisateur cosmique dans la pensée de saint Grégoire de Nysse." *Studia Patristica* 6–IV:62–83.

Gilson, Etienne. 1944. *L'esprit de la philosophie médiévale.* Gifford Lectures at Aberdeen 1930/32. 2d ed. Paris: Libraire philosophique J. Vrin.

———. 1964. *The Spirit of Thomism.* Reprint edition. New York: Harper Torchbooks.

Girardi, Mario. 1978. "Il giudizio finale nella omiletica di Basilio di Cesarea." *Augustinianum* 18:183–90.

Glawe, Walther Karl Erich. 1912. *Die Hellenisierung des Christentums in der Geschichte der Theologie von Luther bis auf die Gegenwart.* Berlin: Trowitzsch.

Goemans, Monald. 1945. *Het tractaat van Basilius den Groote over de klassieke studie.* Nijmegen: Dekker and Van de Vegt.

Goggin, Sister Thomas Aquinas. 1947. *The Times of St. Gregory of Nyssa as Reflected in His Letters and the "Contra Eunomium."* Washington, D.C.: Catholic University of America Press.

Gomes de Castro, Michael. 1938. *Die Trinitätslehre des hl. Gregor von Nyssa.* Freiburg im Breisgau: Herder.

González, Severino. 1938. "La identidad de operación en las obras exteriores y la unidad de la naturaleza divina en la teologia trinitaria de S. Gregorio de Nisa." *Gregorianum* 19:280–301.

————. 1939. *La fórmula "mia ousia treis hypostaseis" en San Gregorio de Nisa*. Rome: Universitas Gregoriana.

Gottwald, Richard. 1906. *De Gregorio Nazianzeno Platonico*. Breslau: H. Fleischmann.

Graef, Hilda. 1963–65. *Mary: A History of Doctrine and Devotion*. 2 vols. New York: Sheed and Ward.

Grandsire, A. 1923. "Nature et hypostases divines dans saint Basile." *Recherches de science religieuse* 13:130–52.

Grant, Robert M. 1952. *Miracle and Natural Law in Graeco-Roman and Early Christian Thought*. Amsterdam: North Holland Publishing.

Green, Peter. 1990. *Alexander to Actium: The Historical Evolution of the Hellenistic Age*. Berkeley: University of California Press.

Greene, William C. 1944. *Moira: Fate, Good, and Evil in Greek Thought*. Cambridge, Mass.: Harvard University Press.

Gregg, Robert C. 1975. *Consolation Philosophy: Greek and Christian Paideia in Basil and the Two Gregories*. Cambridge, Mass.: Philadelphia Patristic Foundation.

Gribomont, Jean. 1952. "Obéissance et Evangile selon saint Basile le Grand." *La vie spirituelle*: supplement 21:195–215.

————. 1953. *Histoire du texte des Ascétiques de S. Basile*. Louvain: Publications Universitaires.

————. 1957. "Les règles morales de saint Basile et le Nouveau Testament." *Studia Patristica* 2-II:416–26.

Grillmeier, Aloys. 1958. "Hellenisierung-Judaisierung des Christentums als Deuteprinzipien der Geschichte des kirchlichen Dogmas." *Scholastik* 33:321–55, 528–58.

————. 1965. *Christ in Christian Tradition from the Apostolic Age to Chalcedon (451)*. Translated by J. S. Bowden. New York: Sheed and Ward.

Grillmeier, Aloys, and Heinrich Bacht, eds. 1951–54. *Das Konzil von Chalkedon: Geschichte und Gegenwart*. 3 vols. Würzburg: Echter-Verlag.

Gronau, Karl. 1922. *Das Theodizeeproblem in der altchristlichen Auffassung*. Tübingen: J. C. B. Mohr (Paul Siebeck).

Gross, Jules. 1938. *La divinisation du chrétien d'après les pères grecs: Contribution historique à la doctrine de la grâce*. Paris: Lecoffre, J. Gabalda.

Grote, George. 1865. *Plato and the Other Companions of Sokrates*. 3 vols. London: John Murray.

Grumel, Venance. 1922. "Saint Basile et le siège apostolique." *Echos d'Orient* 21:280–92.

Guignet, Marcel. 1911. *Saint Grégoire de Nazianze et la rhétorique*. Paris: Alphonse Picard et fils.

Gwatkin, Henry Melvill. 1898. *The Arian Controversy*. London: Longmans, Green.

————. 1906. *The Knowledge of God and Its Historical Development*. Gifford Lectures at Edinburgh 1903/05. 2 vols. Edinburgh: T. and T. Clark.

Hahn, Ferdinand. 1963. *Christologische Hoheitstitel: Ihre Geschichte im frühen Christentum*. Göttingen: Vandenhoeck und Ruprecht.

Hanson, Richard Patrick Crosland. 1968. "Basil's Doctrine of Tradition in Relation to the Holy Spirit." *Vigiliae Christianae* 22:241–55.

————. 1988. *The Search for the Christian Doctrine of God: The Arian Controversy 318–381*. Edinburgh: T. and T. Clark.

Harl, Marguerite, ed. 1971. *Ecriture et culture philosophique dans la pensée de Grégoire de Nysse*. Leiden: E. J. Brill.

Harnack, Adolf von. 1905. *[Grundrisz der] Dogmengeschichte*. 4th ed. Tübingen: J. C. B. Mohr (Paul Siebeck).

————. 1906. "Sokrates und die alte Kirche." In *Reden und Aufsätze*, 1:27–48. 2d ed. Giessen: Alfred Töpelmann.

————. 1931. *Lehrbuch der Dogmengeschichte*. 5th ed. 3 vols. Tübingen: J. C. B. Mohr (Paul Siebeck).

Hatch, Edwin. 1957. *The Influence of Greek Ideas on Christianity*. 1890. Reprinted with an introduction by Frederick C. Grant. New York: Harper Torchbooks.

Hauser-Meury, Marie-Madeleine. 1960. *Prosopographie zu den Schriften Gregors von Nazianz*. Bonn: Peter Hanstein Verlag.

Hefele, Carl Joseph. 1855–60. *Conciliengeschichte*. 4 vols. Freiburg im Breisgau: Herder'sche Verlagsbuchhandlung.

Heine, Ronald E. 1975. *Perfection in the Virtuous Life: A Study in the Relationship between Edification and Polemical Theology in Gregory of Nyssa's "De Vita Moysis."* Cambridge, Mass.: Philadelphia Patristic Foundation.

Henry, Paul. 1934. *Plotin et l'Occident*. Louvain: Spicilegium Sacrum Lovaniense.

Henry, Rose de Lima. 1943. *The Late Greek Optative and Its Use in the Writings of Gregory Nazianzen*. Washington, D.C.: Catholic University of America Press.

Highet, Gilbert. 1957. *The Classical Tradition: Greek and Roman Influences on Western Literature*. Galaxy edition. New York: Oxford University Press.

Hoey, George William Patrick. 1930. *The Use of the Optative Mood in the Works of St. Gregory of Nyssa*. Washington, D.C.: Catholic University of America Press.

Holl, Karl. 1904. *Amphilochius von Ikonium in seinem Verhältnis zu den grossen Kappadoziern*. Tübingen: J. C. B. Mohr.

———. 1928. *Der Osten*. Volume 2 of *Gesammelte Aufsätze zur Kirchengeschichte*. Tübingen: J. C. B. Mohr (Paul Siebeck).

Horn, Gabriel. 1925. "L'amour divin: Note sur le mot 'Eros' dans S. Grégoire de Nysse." *Revue d'ascétique et de mystique* 6:378–89.

———. 1927. "Le 'miroir,' la 'nuée,' deux manières de voir Dieu d'après S. Grégoire de Nysse." *Revue d'ascétique et de mystique* 8:113–31.

Hübner, Reinhard M. 1974. *Die Einheit des Leibes Christi bei Gregor von Nyssa: Untersuchungen zum Ursprung der "physischen" Erlösungslehre*. Leiden: E. J. Brill.

Humbertclaude, Pierre. 1932. *La doctrine ascétique de saint Basile de Césarée*. Paris: G. Beauschesne et ses fils.

Inge, William Ralph. 1918. *The Philosophy of Plotinus*. Gifford Lectures at St. Andrews 1917/19. 2 vols. London: Longmans, Green.

Isaye, Gaston. 1937. "L'unité de l'opération divine dans les écrits trinitaires de Saint Grégoire de Nysse." *Recherches de science religieuse* 27:422–39.

Ivánka, Endre von. 1936. "Vom Platonismus zur Theorie der Mystik: Zur Erkenntnislehre Gregors von Nyssa." *Scholastik* 11:163–95.

———. 1948. *Hellenisches und Christliches im frühbyzantinischen Geistesleben*. Vienna: Herder.

———. 1951. "Zur geistesgeschichtlichen Einordnung des Origenismus." *Byzantinische Zeitschrift* 44:291–303.

———. 1964. *Plato Christianus: Übernahme und Umgestaltung des Platonismus durch die Väter*. Einsiedeln: Johannes.

Jacks, Leo V. 1922. *St. Basil and Greek Literature*. Washington, D.C.: Catholic University of America Press.

Jaeger, Werner. 1939–44. *Paideia: The Ideals of Greek Culture*. Translated by Gilbert Highet. 3 vols. New York: Oxford University Press.

———. 1947. *The Theology of the Early Greek Philosophers*. Gifford Lectures at St. Andrews 1936/37. Oxford: Clarendon Press.

———. 1948. *Aristotle: Fundamentals of the History of His Development*. Translated by Richard Robinson. 2d ed. Oxford: Clarendon Press.

———. 1954. *Two Rediscovered Works of Ancient Christian Literature*. Leiden: E. J. Brill.

———. 1961. *Early Christianity and Greek Paideia*. Cambridge, Mass.: Harvard University Press.

———. 1966. *Gregor von Nyssa's Lehre vom Heiligen Geist*. Edited by Hermann Dörries. Leiden: E. J. Brill.

Jaki, Stanley L. 1978. *The Road of Science and the Ways to God*. Gifford Lectures at·Edinburgh 1974/76. Chicago: University of Chicago Press.

———. 1986. *Lord Gifford and His Lectures: A Centenary Retrospect*. Edinburgh: Scottish Academic Press.

Janini Cuesta, José. 1946. *La antropologia y la medicina pastoral de San Gregorio de Nisa.* Madrid: Consejo superior de investigaciones científicas.

———. 1947. "La penitencia medicinal desde la Didascalia Apostolorum a S. Gregorio de Nisa." *Revista española de teologia* 7:337–62.

Joosen, Jos. [Pater Calasanctius]. 1941. *Beeldspraak bij den heiligen Basilius den Grote, met een inleiding over de opvattingen van de griekse en romeinse auteurs aangaande beeldspraak.* Nijmegen-Utrecht: Dekker en van de Vegt.

Kallis, Anastasios, ed. 1989. *Die Göttliche Liturgie der Orthodoxen Kirche: Deutsch— Griechisch—Kirchenslawisch.* Mainz: Matthias-Grünewald-Verlag.

Kannengiesser, Charles. 1967. "L'infinité divine chez Grégoire de Nysse." *Recherches de science religieuse* 55:55–65.

Keenan, Mary Emily. 1941. "St. Gregory of Nazianzus and Early Byzantine Medicine." *Bulletin of the History of Medicine* 9:8–30.

———. 1944. "St. Gregory of Nyssa and the Medical Profession." *Bulletin of the History of Medicine* 15:150–61.

———. 1950. "*De Professione Christiana* and *De Perfectione*: A Study of the Ascetical Doctrine of Saint Gregory of Nyssa." *Dumbarton Oaks Papers* 5:167–207.

Kelly, John Norman Davidson. 1950. *Early Christian Creeds.* London: Longmans, Green.

———. 1958. *Early Christian Doctrines.* New York: Harper and Row.

Kennedy, George A. 1983. *Greek Rhetoric under Christian Emperors.* Princeton: Princeton University Press.

Kertsch, Manfred. 1978. *Bildersprache bei Gregor von Nazianz: Ein Beitrag zur spätantiken Rhetorik und Popularphilosophie.* Graz: Grazer Theologische Studien.

Keydell, Rudolf. 1951. "Ein dogmatisches Lehrgedicht Gregors von Nazianz." *Byzantinische Zeitschrift* 44:315–21.

Koch, Hal. 1932. *Pronoia und Paideusis.* Berlin: Walter de Gruyter.

Koch, Hugo. 1898. "Das mystische Schauen beim hl. Gregor von Nyssa." *Theologische Quartalschrift* 80:397–420.

Konstantinou, Evangelos G. 1966. *Die Tugendlehre Gregors von Nyssa im Verhältnis zu der antik-philosophischen und jüdisch-christlichen Tradition.* Würzburg: Augustinus-Verlag.

Kopecek, Thomas A. 1973. "The Social Class of the Cappadocian Fathers." *Church History* 42:453–66.

———. 1979. *A History of Neo-Arianism.* 2 vols. Cambridge, Mass.: Philadelphia Patristic Foundation.

Koperski, Victor. 1936. *Doctrina S. Gregorii Nysseni de processione Filii Dei.* Rome: Pontificia Universitas Gregoriana.

Kötting, Bernhard. 1950. *Peregrinatio religiosa: Wallfahrten in der Antike und das Pilgerwesen in der alten Kirche.* Münster: Regensbergsche Verlagsbuchhandlung.

Krampf, Adam. 1889. *Der Urzustand des Menschen nach der Lehre des hl. Gregor von Nyssa.* Würzburg: F. X. Bucher.

Kristeller, Paul Oskar. 1961. *Renaissance Thought: The Classic, Scholastic, and Humanist Strains.* New York: Harper Torchbooks.

Kurmann, Alois. 1988. *Gregor von Nazianz Oratio 4 gegen Julian: Ein Kommentar.* Basel: Friedrich Reinhardt.

Labriolle, Pierre-Henri-Marie Champagne de. 1942. *La réaction païenne: Etude sur la polémique antichrétienne du Ier au VIe siècle.* 2d ed. Paris: Artisan du livre.

Ladner, Gerhart B. 1953. "The Concept of the Image in the Greek Fathers and the Byzantine Iconoclastic Controversy." *Dumbarton Oaks Papers* 7:1–34.

———. 1955. "St. Gregory of Nyssa and St. Augustine on the Symbolism of the Cross." In *Late Classical and Mediaeval Studies in Honor of Albert Matthias Friend, Jr.,* 88–95. Edited by Kurt Weitzmann. Princeton: Princeton University Press.

———. 1958. "The Philosophical Anthropology of St. Gregory of Nyssa." *Dumbarton Oaks Papers* 12:59–94.

———. 1959. *The Idea of Reform: Its Impact on Christian Thought and Action in the Age of the Fathers*. Cambridge, Mass.: Harvard University Press.

———. 1971. "Aspects of Patristic Anti-Judaism." *Viator* 2:355–63.

Laistner, Max Ludwig Wolfram. 1951. *Christianity and Pagan Culture in the Later Roman Empire*. Ithaca: Cornell University Press.

Langerbeck, H. 1957. "Zur Interpretation Gregors von Nyssa." *Theologische Literaturzeitung* 82:81–90.

Laun, Ferdinand. 1925. "Die beiden Regeln des Basilius, ihre Echtheit und ihre Entstehung." *Zeitschrift für Kirchengeschichte* 44:1–61.

Lazzati, Giuseppe. 1938. *L'Aristotele perduto e gli scrittori cristiani*. Milan: Società editrice "Vita e pensiero."

Lebon, Joseph. 1938. "Le Pseudo-Basile (*Adv. Eunom.* IV-V) est bien Didyme d'Alexandrie." *Le Muséon* 50:61–83.

———. 1953. "Le sort du consubstantiel nicéen: Saint Basile et le 'consubstantiel' nicéen." *Revue d'histoire ecclésiastique* 48:632–82.

Lefherz, Friedhelm. 1958. *Studien zu Gregor von Nazianz: Mythologie, Überlieferung, Scholiasten*. Bonn: Rheinische Friedrich Wilhelms-Universität.

Lenz, Johann. 1925. *Jesus Christus nach der Lehre des hl. Gregor von Nyssa: Eine dogmengeschichtliche Studie*. Trier: Paulinus-Druckerei.

Levie, J. 1920. "Les sources de la septième et huitième Homélie de St. Basile sur l'Hexaméron." *Musée belge*:113–49.

Lewy, Hans. 1929. *Sobria ebrietas: Untersuchungen zur Geschichte der antiken Mystik*. Giessen: Alfred Töpelmann.

Leys, Roger. 1951. *L'image de Dieu chez Grégoire de Nysse: Esquisse d'une doctrine*. Brussels: Edition universelle.

Lieske, Aloisius. 1938. *Die Theologie der Christusmystik Gregors von Nyssa*. Münster: Aschendorff.

Lietzmann, Hans. 1904. *Apollinaris von Laodicea und seine Schule: Texte und Untersuchungen*. Tübingen: J. C. B. Mohr (Paul Siebeck).

List, Johann. 1928. "Zwei Zeugnisse für die Lobrede bei Gregor von Nazianz." *Byzantinisch-neugriechische Jahrbücher* 6:24–31.

Lohn, Ladislaus. 1929. "Doctrina sancti Basilii Magni de processionibus divinarum personarum." *Gregorianum* 10:329–64, 461–500.

Loofs, Friedrich. 1898. *Eustathius von Sebaste und die Chronologie der Basiliusbriefe: Eine patristische Studie*. Halle: Max Niemeyer.

Lossky, Vladimir. 1974. *In the Image and Likeness of God*. Edited by John H. Erickson and Thomas E. Bird. Introduction by John Meyendorff. Crestwood, N.Y.: St. Vladimir's Seminary Press.

———. 1976. *The Mystical Theology of the Eastern Church*. Reprint edition. Crestwood, N.Y.: St. Vladimir's Seminary Press.

Lovejoy, Arthur O. 1936. *The Great Chain of Being: A Study of the History of an Idea*. Cambridge, Mass.: Harvard University Press.
———. 1955. *Essays in the History of Ideas*. New York: George Brazilier.

Luislampe, Pia. 1981. *Spiritus vivificans: Grundzüge einer Theologie des Heiligen Geistes nach Basilius von Caesarea*. Münster: Aschendorff.

Luneau, Auguste. 1964. *L'histoire de salut chez les pères de l'église: La doctrine des âges du monde*. Paris: Beauchesne.

McClear, Ernest V. 1948. "The Fall of Man and Original Sin in the Theology of Gregory of Nyssa." *Theological Studies* 9:175–212.

McKeon, Richard Peter. 1939. "Aristotelianism in Western Christianity." In *Environmental Factors in Christian History*, 206–31. Edited by John Thomas McNeill et al. Chicago: University of Chicago Press.

MacMullen, Ramsay. 1969. *Constantine*. New York: Dial Press.

McReynolds, Paul R. 1981. "John 1:18 in Textual Variation and Translation." In *New Testament Textual Criticism: Its Significance for*

Exegesis. Essays in Honor of Bruce M. Metzger, 105–18. Edited by Eldon J. Epp and Gordon D. Fee. Oxford: Clarendon Press.

Maier, Johannes. 1915. *Die Eucharistielehre der drei grossen Kappadozier, des hl. Basilius, Gregor von Nazianz und Gregor von Nyssa*. Freiburg im Breisgau: Herder.

Malevez, Léopold. 1935. "L'église dans le Christ." *Recherches de science religieuse* 25:257–91.

Malingrey, Anne-Marie. 1961. *"Philosophia": Etude d'un groupe de mots dans la littérature grecque, des Présocratiques au IVe siècle après J.-C.* Paris: Libraire C. Klincksieck.

Malunowiczówna, Leokadia. 1975. "Les éléments stoïciens dans la consolation grecque chretiénne." *Studia Patristica* 13–II:35–45.

———. 1985. "Le problème de l'amité chez Basile, Grégoire de Nazianze et Jean Chrysostome." *Studia Patristica* 16–II:412–27.

Marcel, Gabriel. 1950–51. *The Mystery of Being*. Gifford Lectures at Aberdeen 1948/50. Translated by G. S. Fraser and R. Hague. 2 vols. London: Harvill Press.

Marrou, Henri I. 1956. *A History of Education in Antiquity*. Translated by George Lamb. New York: New American Library.

Martland, Thomas Rodolphe. 1965. "A Study of Cappadocian and Augustinian Trinitarian Methodology." *Anglican Theological Review* 47:252–63.

Mason, Arthur James, ed. 1899. *The Five Theological Orations of Gregory of Nazianzus*. Cambridge: Cambridge University Press.

Mateo-Seco, Lucas F., and Juan L. Bastero, eds. 1988. *El "Contra Eunomium I" en la producciòn literaria de Gregorio de Nisa*. Pamplona: Ediciones Universidad de Navarra.

Matter, E. Ann. 1990. *The Voice of My Beloved: The Song of Songs in Western Medieval Christianity*. Philadelphia: University of Pennsylvania Press.

Meeks, Wayne A. 1986. *The Moral World of the First Christians*. Philadelphia: Westminster Press.

Meijering, Eginhard Peter. 1968. *Orthodoxy and Platonism in Athanasius: Synthesis or Antithesis?* Leiden: E. J. Brill.

———. 1985. *Die Hellenisierung des Christentums im Urteil Adolf von Harnacks*. Amsterdam: North-Holland Publishing.

Merki, Hubert. 1952. *Homoiōsis Theōi: Von der platonischen Angleichung an Gott zur Gottähnlichkeit bei Gregor von Nyssa*. Fribourg: Paulusverlag.

Merlan, Philip. 1960. *From Platonism to Neoplatonism*. 2d ed. The Hague: M. Nijhoff.

Metzger, Bruce M. 1975. "The Practice of Textual Criticism among the Church Fathers." *Studia Patristica* 12–I:340–49.

Meyendorff, John. 1969. *Christ in Eastern Christian Thought*. Washington, D.C.: Corpus Books.

———. 1974. *Byzantine Theology: Historical Trends and Doctrinal Themes*. New York: Fordham University Press.

———. 1984. "Byzantium as Center of Theological Thought in the Christian East." In Patrick Henry, ed. *Schools of Thought in the Christian Tradition*, 65–74. Philadelphia: Fortress Press.

———. 1989. *Imperial Unity and Christian Divisions: The Church, 450–680 A.D.* Crestwood, N.Y.: St. Vladimir's Seminary Press.

Meyer, Wilhelm. 1894. *Die Gotteslehre des Gregor von Nyssa: Eine philosophische Studie aus der Zeit der Patristik*. Halle: E. Karras.

Michaud, Eugène. 1902. "St. Grégoire de Nysse et l'apocatastase." *Revue internationale de théologie* 10:37–52.

Momigliano, Arnaldo, ed. 1963. *The Conflict between Paganism and Christianity in the Fourth Century*. Oxford: Oxford University Press.

———. 1987. *On Pagans, Jews, and Christians*. Middletown, Conn.: Wesleyan University Press.

Morison, Ernest Frederick. 1912. *St. Basil and His Rule*. London: Henry Frowde, Oxford University Press.

Mortley, Raoul. 1986. *From Word to Silence.* 2 vols. Bonn: Peter Hanstein Verlag.

Mossay, Justin. 1964. "Perspectives eschatologiques de saint Grégoire de Nazianze." *Questions liturgiques et paroissiales* 4:320–39.

———. 1966. *La mort et l'au-delà dans saint Grégoire de Nazianze.* Louvain: Bibliothèque de l'université.

Moulton, James Hope. 1908. *Prolegomena.* Volume 1 of *A Grammar of New Testament Greek.* 3d ed. Edinburgh: T. and T. Clark.

Muckle, Joseph Thomas. 1945. "The Doctrine of Gregory of Nyssa on Man as the Image of God." *Mediaeval Studies* 7:55–84.

Mühlenberg, Ekkehard. 1966. *Die Unendlichkeit Gottes bei Gregor von Nyssa: Gregors Kritik am Gottesbegriff der klassischen Metaphysik.* Göttingen: Vandenhoeck und Ruprecht.

Mure, Geoffrey Reginald Gilchrist. 1964. *Aristotle.* Galaxy ed. New York: Oxford University Press.

Murphy, Margaret Gertrude. 1930. *Saint Basil and Monasticism.* Washington, D.C.: Catholic University of America Press.

Murray, John Courtney. 1964. *The Problem of God Yesterday and Today.* New Haven: Yale University Press.

Musurillo, Herbert. 1957. "History and Symbol: A Study of Form in Early Christian Literature." *Theological Studies* 18:357–86.

Nager, Franz. 1912. *Die Triniätslehre des hl. Basilius des Grossen: Eine dogmengeschichtliche Studie.* Paderborn: F. Schöningh.

Newman, John Henry. 1901. *The Arians of the Fourth Century.* 4th ed. London: Longmans, Green.

———. 1852. *The Idea of a University.* Edited byIan T. Ker. Oxford: Clarendon Press, 1976.

Nikolaou, Th. 1981. "Der Mensch als politisches Lebewesen bei Basilios dem Grossen." *Vigiliae Christianae* 35:24–31.

Nock, Arthur Darby. 1933. *Conversion: The Old and the New in Religion from Alex-* *ander the Great to Augustine of Hippo.* London: Oxford University Press.

———. 1972. *Essays on Religion and the Ancient World.* Edited by Zeph Stewart. 2 vols. Oxford: Clarendon Press.

Norris, Frederick W., ed. 1991. *Faith Gives Fullness to Reasoning: The Five Theological Orations of Gregory Nazianzen.* Translated by Lionel Wickham and Frederick Williams. Leiden: E. J. Brill.

Nothomb, Dominique Marie. 1954. "Charité et unité: Doctrine de saint Basile le Grand sur la charité envers le prochain." *Proche-Orient chrétien* 4:309–21.

Nussbaum, Martha. 1986. *The Fragility of Goodness: Luck and Ethics in Greek Tragedy and Philosophy.* Cambridge: Cambridge University Press.

———. 1990. "Introduction" to *The Bacchae of Euripides.* Translation by C. K. Williams. New York: Farrar Straus Giroux.

O'Meara, Dominic J., ed. 1982. *Neoplatonism and Christian Thought.* Albany, N.Y.: State University of New York Press.

Otis, Brooks. 1958. "Cappadocian Thought as a Coherent System." *Dumbarton Oaks Papers* 12:95–124.

———. 1961. "The Throne and the Mountain: An Essay on St. Gregory Nazianzus." *Classical Journal* 56:146–65.

———. 1976. "Gregory of Nyssa and the Cappadocian Conception of Time." *Studia Patristica* 14–III:327–57.

Owen, Edward Charles Everard. 1925. "St. Gregory of Nyssa: (1) Grammar; (2) Vocabulary and Style." *Journal of Theological Studies* 26:64–71.

Pasquali, Giorgio. 1923. "Le lettere di Grigorio di Nissa." *Studi italiani di filologia classica* 3:75–136.

Pease, Arthur Stanley. 1941. "Caeli enarrant." *Harvard Theological Review* 34:163–200.

Pelikan, Jaroslav. 1962. *The Light of the World: A Basic Image in Early Christian Thought.* New York: Harper and Brothers.

———. 1971–89. *The Christian Tradition: A History of the Development of Doctrine.* 5 vols. Chicago: University of Chicago Press.

———. 1990. *Imago Dei: The Byzantine Apologia for Icons.* A. W. Mellon Lectures at the National Gallery of Art for 1987. Princeton: Princeton University Press.

Pellegrino, Michele. 1932. *La poesia di S. Gregorio Nazianzeno.* Milan: Società editrice "Vita e pensiero."

———. 1938. "Il Platonismo di San Grigorio Nisseno nel Dialogo intorno all' anima e alla risurrezione." *Rivista di filosofia neoscolastica* 30:437–74.

Pépin, Jean. 1982. "Grégoire de Nazianze, lecteur de la littérature hermétique." *Vigiliae Christianae* 36:251–60.

Petit, Paul. 1956. *Les étudiants de Libanius.* Paris: Nouvelles éditions latines.

Peterson, Erik. 1951. *Theologische Traktate.* Munich: Kösel-Verlag.

———. 1964. *The Angels and the Liturgy.* Translated by Ronald Walls. New York: Herder and Herder.

Philippou, Angelos James. 1966. "The Doctrine of Evil in St. Gregory of Nyssa." *Studia Patristica* 9–III:251–56.

Pichler, Theodorich. 1955. *Das Fasten bei Basilius dem Grossen und im antiken Heidentum.* Innsbruck: Universitätsverlag Wagner.

Pinault, Henri. 1925. *Le Platonisme de saint Grégoire de Nazianze: essai sur les relations du Christianisme et de l'Hellenisme dans son oeuvre théologique.* La Roche-sur-Yon: Libraire G. Romain.

Plagnieux, Jean. 1952. *Saint Grégoire de Nazianze théologien.* Paris: Editions franciscaines.

Plantinga, Cornelius, Jr. 1986. "Gregory of Nyssa and the Social Analogy of the Trinity." *The Thomist* 50:325–52.

Portmann, Franz Xaver. 1954. *Die göttliche Paidagogia bei Gregor von Nazianz: Eine dogmengeschichtliche Studie.* Sankt Ottilien: Eos Verlag.

Preger, Franz Christoph. 1897. *Die Grundlagen der Ethik bei Gregor von Nyssa.* Würzburg: H. Stürtz.

Prestige, George Leonard. 1923a. "'Agen(n)ētos'and 'Gen(n)ētos' and Kindred Words, in Eusebius and the Early Arians." *Journal of Theological Studies* 24:486–96.

———. 1923b. "Hades in the Greek Fathers." *Journal of Theological Studies* 24:476–85.

———. 1933. "'Agen(n)ētos' and Cognate Words in Athanasius." *Journal of Theological Studies* 34:258–65.

———. 1948. *Fathers and Heretics: Six Studies in Dogmatic Faith with Prologue and Epilogue.* London: SPCK.

———. 1956. *God in Patristic Thought.* London: SPCK.

Ramsay, William Mitchell. 1927. *Asianic Elements in Greek Civilization.* Gifford Lectures at Edinburgh 1915/16. London: John Murray.

Rasneur, G. 1903. "L'homoiousianisme dans ses rapports avec l'orthodoxie." *Revue d'histoire ecclésiastique* 4:189–206, 411–31.

Raven, Charles Earle. 1923. *Apollinarianism.* Cambridge: Cambridge University Press.

———. 1953. *Natural Religion and Christian Theology.* Gifford Lectures at Edinburgh 1950/52. 2 vols. Cambridge: Cambridge University Press.

Rebecchi, Luigi. 1943. "L'antropologia naturale di San Gregorio Nisseno." *Divus Thomas* 46:176–95, 309–41.

Reiche, Armin. 1897. *Die künstlerischen Elemente in der Welt- und Lebensanschauung des Gregor von Nyssa.* Jena: Ant. Kämpfe, 1897.

Reilly, Gerald F. 1945. *Imperium and Sacerdotium according to St. Basil the Great.* Washington, D.C.: Catholic University of America Press.

Richardson, Cyril C. 1937. "The Condemnation of Origen." *Church History* 6:50–64.

Riedel, Wilhelm. 1898. *Die Auslegung des Hohen Liedes in der jüdischen Gemeinde und der griechischen Kirche.* Leipzig: A. Deichert.

Rougier, R. 1916–17. "Le sens des termes 'ousia,' 'hypostasis' et 'prosôpon' dans les controverses trinitaires postnicéennes." *Revue de l'histoire des religions* 73:48–63; 74:133–89.

Rousse, Jacques. 1965. "Les anges et leur ministère selon Saint Grégoire de Nazianze." *Mélanges de science religieuse* 22:133–52.

Ruether, Rosemary Radford. 1969. *Gregory of Nazianzus: Rhetor and Philosopher.* Oxford: Clarendon Press.

Sajdak, Jan. 1917. *De Gregorio Nazianzeno poetarum christianorum fonte.* Cracow: Sumptibus Akademiae Litterarum.

Sanders, Jack T. 1971. *The New Testament Christological Hymns.* Cambridge: Cambridge University Press.

Scazzoso, Piero. 1975. *Introduzione alla ecclesiologia di san Basilio.* Milan: Società editrice "Vita e pensiero."

Schatkin, Margaret, and Paul Harkins, eds. 1985. *St. John Chrysostom, Apologist.* Washington, D.C.: Catholic University of America Press.

Schermann, Theodor. 1901. *Die Gottheit des Heiligen Geistes nach den grieschischen Vätern des vierten Jahrhunderts: Eine dogmengeschichtliche Studie.* Freiburg im Breisgau: Herder.

Scheve, Basilius. 1943. *Basilius der Grosse als Theologe: Ein Beitrag zur Frage nach der theologischen Arbeitsweise zur Zeit der Väter.* Nijmegen: Centrale Drukkerij.

Schippers, Jacobus Wilhelmus. 1952. *De Ontwikkeling der Euhemeristische Godencritiek in de Christelijke Latijnse Literatuur.* Groningen: J. B. Wolters.

Schoemann, Johann Baptist. 1941. " 'Eikon' in den Schriften des hl. Athanasius." *Scholastik* 16:335–50.

———. 1943. "Gregors von Nyssa theologische Anthropologie als Bildtheologie." *Scholastik* 18:31–53, 175–200.

Scholl, Eugen. 1881. *Die Lehre des heiligen Basilius von der Gnade.* Freiburg im Breisgau: Herder.

Schönborn, Christoph von. 1972. *Sophrone de Jérusalem: Vie monastique et confession dogmatique.* Paris: Beauchesne.

———. 1976. *L'icône du Christ: Fondements théologiques élaborés entre le Ier et le IIe Concile de Nicée (325–787).* 2d ed. Fribourg: Editions universitaires.

Schucan, Luzi. 1973. *Das Nachleben von Basilius Magnus ad adolescentes: Ein Beitrag zur Geschichte des christlichen Humanismus.* Geneva: Droz.

Seeberg, Reinhold. 1953. *Lehrbuch der Dogmengeschichte.* 4th ed. 5 vols. Basel: Benno Schwabe.

Seeck, Otto. 1906. *Die Briefe des Libanius zeitlich geordnet.* Leipzig: J. C. Hinrichs.

Serra, M. 1955. "La carità pastorale in S. Gregorio Nazianzeno." *Orientalia Christiana Periodica* 21:337–74.

Sherrard, Philip. 1959. *The Greek East and the Latin West: A Study in the Christian Tradition.* London: Oxford University Press.

Shook, Laurence K. 1984. *Etienne Gilson.* Toronto: Pontifical Institute of Mediaeval Studies.

Sinko, Tadeusz. 1917. *De traditione orationum Gregorii Nazianzeni.* Cracow: Sumptibus Akademiae Litterarum.

Skeat, Walter W. 1958. *An Etymological Dictionary of the English Language.* 4th ed. Oxford: Clarendon Press.

Sleeman, J. H., and Gilbert Pollet, eds. 1980. *Lexicon Plotinianum.* Leiden: E. J. Brill.

Smalley, Beryl. 1964. *The Study of the Bible in the Middle Ages.* 2d ed. Notre Dame: University of Notre Dame Press.

Söderblom, Nathan. 1933. *The Living God: Basal Forms of Personal Religion.* Gifford Lectures at Edinburgh 1930/31. London: Oxford University Press.

Söll, Georg. 1951. "Die Mariologie der Kappadozier im Lichte der Dogmengeschichte." *Theologische Quartalschrift* 131:163–88, 288–319, 426–57.

Špidlík, Thomas. 1961. *La sophiologie de S. Basile.* Rome: Institutum Studiorum Orientalium.

———. 1971. *Gregoire de Nazianze: Introduction à l'étude de sa doctrine spirituelle.* Rome: Institutum Studiorum Orientalium.

———. 1976. "La *theoria* et la *praxis* chez Grégoire de Nazianze." *Studia Patristica* 14–III:358–64.

———. 1985. "Y a-t-il un pluralisme théologique en Grégoire de Nazianze? La théologie est-elle une poésie ou une science?" *Studia Patristica* 16–II:428–32.

Srawley, James Herbert. 1906. "St. Gregory of Nyssa on the Sinlessness of Christ." *Journal of Theological Studies* 7:434–41.

Stephan, Leo. 1938. *Die Soteriologie des hl. Gregor von Nazianz.* Vienna: Missionsdruckerei St. Gabriel.

Stephanu, E. 1932. "La coexistence initiale du corps et de l'âme d'après saint Grégoire de Nysse et saint Maxime l'Apologète." *Echos d'Orient* 31:304–15.

Stoppel, Paul. 1881. *Quaestiones de Gregorii Nazianzeni poetarum scaenicorum imitatione et arte metrica.* Rostock: Typis Academicis Adleriani.

Stritzky, Maria-Barbara von. 1973. *Zum Problem der Erkenntnis bei Gregor von Nyssa.* Münster: Aschendorff.

Strong, Thomas Banks. 1901–3. "The History of the Theological Term 'Substance.'" *Journal of Theological Studies* 2(1901):224–35; 3(1902):22–40; 4(1903):28–45.

Sutcliffe, E. F. 1931. "St. Gregory of Nyssa and Paradise: Was It Terrestrial?" *American Ecclesiastical Review* 84:337–50.

Sykes, D. A. 1985. "Gregory Nazianzen as Didactic Poet." *Studia Patristica* 16–II:433–37.

Thurston, Herbert. 1909–10. "The Early Cultus of the Reserved Eucharist." *Journal of Theological Studies* 11:275–79.

Troeltsch, Ernst. 1960. *The Social Teachings of the Christian Churches.* Translated by Olive Wyon. Reprinted with an introduction by H. Richard Niebuhr. New York: Harper Torchbooks.

Trunk, J. 1911. *De Basilio Magno sermonis Attici imitatore.* Stuttgart: J. B. Metzler.

Tumarkin, Anna. 1943. "Der Begriff des Apeiron in der griechischen Philosophie." *Jahrbuch der Schweizerischen Philosophischen Gesellschaft* 3:55–71.

Tyciak, Julius. 1961. *Das Herrenmysterium im byzantinischen Kirchenjahr.* Freiburg im Breisgau: Lambertusverlag.

Ullmann, Karl. 1867. *Gregorius von Nazianz der Theologe: Ein Beitrag zur Kirchen- und Dogmengeschichte des vierten Jahrhunderts.* 2d ed. Gotha: F. A. Perthes.

Unterstein, Karl. 1903. *Die natürliche Gotteserkenntnis nach der Lehre der kappadocischen Kirchenväter Basilius, Gregor von Nazianz und Gregor von Nyssa.* Straubing: Cl. Attenkofer.

Usener, Hermann Karl. 1911. *Das Weihnachtsfest.* 2d ed. Foreword by Hans Lietzmann. Bonn: Friedrich Cohen.

Van Dam, Raymond. 1986. "Emperor, Bishops, and Friends in Late Antique Cappadocia." *Journal of Theological Studies,* n.s., 37:53–76.

Vandenbussche, E. 1944–45. "La part de la dialectique dans la théologie d'Eunomius 'le technologue.'" *Revue d'histoire ecclésiastique* 40:47–72.

Viller, Marcel, and Karl Rahner. 1990. *Aszese und Mystik in der Väterzeit: Ein Abrisz der frühchristlichen Spiritualität.* 2d ed. Foreword by Karl Heinz Neufeld. Freiburg im Breisgau: Herder.

Volk, J. 1895. "Die Schutzrede des Gregor von Nazianz und die Schrift über das Priestertum von Johannes Chrysostomus." *Zeitschrift für praktische Theologie* 17:56–63.

Völker, Walther. 1952. "Die Ontologie Gregors von Nyssa in ihren Grundzügen." *Festschrift G. Biundo,* 9–16. Grünstadt: Verein für Pfälzische Kirchengeschichte.

———. 1955a. *Gregor von Nyssa als Mystiker.* Wiesbaden: F. Steiner.

———. 1955b. "Zur Gotteslehre Gregors von Nyssa." *Vigiliae Christianae* 9:103–28.

Vollert, Wilhelm. 1897. *Die Lehre Gregors von Nyssa, vom Guten und Bösen und von der schliesslichen Überwindung des Bösen.* Leipzig: A. Deichert.

———. 1935. "Hat Gregor von Nyssa die paulinische Eschatologie verändert?" *Theologische Blätter* 14:106–12.

Vööbus, Arthur. 1987. *Studies in the History of the Gospel Text in Syriac: New Contributions to the Sources Elucidating the History of the Traditions.* Louvain: E. Peeters.

Wagner, M. M. 1948. "A Chapter in Byzantine Epistolography." *Dumbarton Oaks Papers* 4:129–40.

Walther, Georg. 1914. *Untersuchungen zur Geschichte der griechischen Vaterunserexegese.* Leipzig: J. C. Hinrichs.

Ware, Timothy [Kallistos]. 1969. *The Orthodox Church.* Revised edition. Harmondsworth: Penguin Books.

Way, Agnes Clare. 1927. *The Language and Style of the Letters of St. Basil.* Washington, D.C.: Catholic University of America Press.

Weigl, Eduard. 1925. *Christologie vom Tode des Athanasius bis zum Ausbruch des nestorianischen Streites (373–429).* Munich: J. Kösel und F. Pustet.

Weiss, Hugo. 1872. *Die grossen Kappadozier: Basilius, Gregor von Nazianz und Gregor von Nyssa als Exegeten. Ein Beitrag zur Geschichte der Exegese.* Braunsberg: A. Martens.

Weiswurm, Alcuin A. 1952. *The Nature of Human Knowledge according to Saint Gregory of Nyssa.* Washington, D.C.: Catholic University of America Press.

Welssersheimb, L. 1948. "Das Kirchenbild der griechischen Väterkommentare zum Hohenlied." *Zeitschrift für katholische Theologie* 70:423–33.

Werner, Martin. 1941. *Die Entstehung des christlichen Dogmas problemgeschichtlich dargestellt.* Bern and Leipzig: Paul Haupt.

Whitehead, Alfred North. 1929. *Process and Reality: An Essay in Cosmology.* Gifford Lectures at Edinburgh 1927/28. Cambridge: Cambridge University Press.

———. 1948. *Science and the Modern World.* Reprint edition. New York: Mentor Books.

Whittaker, John. 1979. "Christianity and Morality in the Roman Empire." *Vigiliae Christianae* 33:209–25.

Wilder, Amos Niven. 1939. *Eschatology and Ethics in the Teaching of Jesus.* New York: Harper and Brothers.

Wiles, Maurice F. 1966. "Soteriological Arguments in the Fathers." *Studia Patristica* 9–III:321–25.

———. 1968. "'The Unassumed Is the Unhealed.'" *Religious Studies* 4:47–56.

Wilken, Robert L. 1970. "Toward a Social Interpretation of Early Christian Apologetics." *Church History* 39:437–58.

———. 1983. *John Chrysostom and the Jews: Rhetoric and Reality in the Late Fourth Century.* Berkeley: University of California Press.

Winslow, Donald F. 1965. "Gregory of Nazianzus and Love for the Poor." *Anglican Theological Review* 47:348–59.

———. 1979. *The Dynamics of Salvation: A Study in Gregory of Nazianzus.* Cambridge, Mass.: Philadelphia Patristic Foundation.

Wolfson, Harry A. 1947. *Philo of Alexandria.* 2 vols. Cambridge, Mass.: Harvard University Press.

———. 1956. *The Philosophy of the Church Fathers.* Cambridge, Mass.: Harvard University Press.

Wright, Wilmer Cave, ed. 1923. *The Works of the Emperor Julian.* 3 vols. London and New York: Loeb Classical Library.

Young, Frances M. 1989. "The Rhetorical Schools and Their Influence on Patristic Exegesis." In *The Making of Orthodoxy: Essays in Honour of Henry Chadwick,* 182–99. Edited by Rowan Williams. Cambridge: Cambridge University Press.

Zemp, Paul. 1970. *Die Grundlagen heilsgeschichtlichen Denkens bei Gregor von Nyssa.* Munich: M. Hueber.

INDEX

Classical and Biblical

Passages from the Greek Classics are arranged alphabetically by author, and within the alphabet by works under the author, employing the abbreviations and sequence in the list of Abbreviations. In the text of the book and in the marginal notes, I have followed the Septuagint's system of numbering chapters and verses in the Psalms and elsewhere, on the grounds that this was the Bible of the Cappadocians; for that reason, I have observed its distinctive order of biblical books here.

General

The names of Basil of Caesarea, Gregory of Nazianzus, Gregory of Nyssa, and Macrina appear on almost every page of the book, as do such concepts as philosophy and transcendence, and therefore they are not listed separately in the Index. Similarly, because the names of Classical and biblical authors appear also in the Classical and Biblical Index, under the specific passages from their writings that are cited in the book, references to them in this index focus primarily on their life and thought rather than on their works as such.

ALBANIA

Vardar R.   *Struma R.*   *Marica (Maritsa) R.*

B

• Hadrianople
(Adrianople)

MACEDONIA

THRACE

EPIRUS   • Thessalonica

THESSALY

*AEGEAN
SEA*

PHRY•

BOEOTIA
• Delphi   EUBOEA

ARCADIA   • Athens

• Ephesus
Maean

MOREA

CARIA

CRETE

(CANDIA)

MEDITERR

THE WORLD OF THE CAPPADOCIANS